Balancing Agile and Disciplined Engineering and Management Approaches for IT Services and Software Products

Manuel Mora
Autonomous University of Aguascalientes, Mexico

Jorge Marx Gómez
University of Oldenburg, Germany

Rory V. O'Connor
Dublin City University, Ireland

Alena Buchalcevová
University of Economics, Prague, Czech Republic

A volume in the Advances in Systems Analysis, Software Engineering, and High Performance Computing (ASASEHPC) Book Series

Published in the United States of America by
  IGI Global
  Engineering Science Reference (an imprint of IGI Global)
  701 E. Chocolate Avenue
  Hershey PA, USA 17033
  Tel: 717-533-8845
  Fax: 717-533-8661
  E-mail: cust@igi-global.com
  Web site: http://www.igi-global.com

Library of Congress Cataloging-in-Publication Data

Names: Mora, Manuel, 1961- editor. | Gómez, Jorge Marx, 1959- editor. |
  O'Connor, Rory V., 1977-2019 editor. | Buchalcevová, Alena, 1958- editor.
Title: Balancing agile and disciplined engineering and management
  approaches for IT services and software products / Manuel Mora, Jorge
  Marx Gómez, Rory V. O'Connor, and Alena Buchalcevová, editors.
Description: Hershey, PA : Engineering Science Reference, an imprint of IGI
  Global, [2021] | Includes bibliographical references and index. |
  Summary: "This book explores the theoretical foundations of balanced
  design methods for software and IT service"-- Provided by publisher.
Identifiers: LCCN 2020002824 (print) | LCCN 2020002825 (ebook) | ISBN
  9781799841654 (hardcover) | ISBN 9781799853794 (paperback) | ISBN
  9781799841661 (ebook)
Subjects: LCSH: Information technology--Management. | Agile software
  development. | Project management.
Classification: LCC HD30.2 .B349 2021 (print) | LCC HD30.2 (ebook) | DDC
  004.068/4--dc23
LC record available at https://lccn.loc.gov/2020002824
LC ebook record available at https://lccn.loc.gov/2020002825

This book is published in the IGI Global book series Advances in Systems Analysis, Software Engineering, and High Performance Computing (ASASEHPC) (ISSN: 2327-3453; eISSN: 2327-3461)

British Cataloguing in Publication Data
A Cataloguing in Publication record for this book is available from the British Library.

All work contributed to this book is new, previously-unpublished material. The views expressed in this book are those of the authors, but not necessarily of the publisher.

For electronic access to this publication, please contact: eresources@igi-global.com.

Advances in Systems Analysis, Software Engineering, and High Performance Computing (ASASEHPC) Book Series

Vijayan Sugumaran
Oakland University, USA

ISSN:2327-3453
EISSN:2327-3461

MISSION

The theory and practice of computing applications and distributed systems has emerged as one of the key areas of research driving innovations in business, engineering, and science. The fields of software engineering, systems analysis, and high performance computing offer a wide range of applications and solutions in solving computational problems for any modern organization.

The **Advances in Systems Analysis, Software Engineering, and High Performance Computing (ASASEHPC) Book Series** brings together research in the areas of distributed computing, systems and software engineering, high performance computing, and service science. This collection of publications is useful for academics, researchers, and practitioners seeking the latest practices and knowledge in this field.

COVERAGE

- Network Management
- Enterprise Information Systems
- Metadata and Semantic Web
- Human-Computer Interaction
- Performance Modelling
- Engineering Environments
- Distributed Cloud Computing
- Computer System Analysis
- Software Engineering
- Storage Systems

IGI Global is currently accepting manuscripts for publication within this series. To submit a proposal for a volume in this series, please contact our Acquisition Editors at Acquisitions@igi-global.com or visit: http://www.igi-global.com/publish/.

Titles in this Series

For a list of additional titles in this series, please visit:
http://www.igi-global.com/book-series/advances-systems-analysis-software-engineering/73689

Advancements in Model-Driven Architecture in Software Engineering
Yassine Rhazali (Moulay Ismail University of Meknes, Morocco)
Engineering Science Reference • © 2020 • 300pp • H/C (ISBN: 9781799836612) • US $215.00

Urban Spatial Data Handling and Computing
Mainak Bandyopadhyay (DIT University-Dehradun, India) and Varun Singh (MNNIT-Allahabad, India)
Engineering Science Reference • © 2020 • 300pp • H/C (ISBN: 9781799801221) • US $245.00

Formal and Adaptive Methods for Automation of Parallel Programs Construction Emerging Research and Opportunities
Anatoliy Doroshenko (National Academy of Sciences of Ukraine, Ukraine) and Olena Yatsenko (National Academy of Sciences of Ukraine, Ukraine)
Engineering Science Reference • © 2020 • 195pp • H/C (ISBN: 9781522593843) • US $195.00

Cloud-Based Big Data Analytics in Vehicular Ad-Hoc Networks
Ram Shringar Rao (Ambedkar Institute of Advanced Communication Technologies and Research, India) Nanhay Singh (Ambedkar Institute of Advanced Communication Technologies and Research, India) Omprakash Kaiwartya (School of Science and Technology, Nottingham Trent University, UK) and Sanjoy Das (Indira Gandhi National Tribal University, India)
Engineering Science Reference • © 2020 • 300pp • H/C (ISBN: 9781799827641) • US $245.00

FPGA Algorithms and Applications for the Internet of Things
Preeti Sharma (Bansal College of Engineering, Mandideep, India) and Rajit Nair (Jagran Lakecity University, Bhopal, India)
Engineering Science Reference • © 2020 • 257pp • H/C (ISBN: 9781522598060) • US $215.00

Advancements in Instrumentation and Control in Applied System Applications
Srijan Bhattacharya (RCC Institute of Information Technology, India)
Engineering Science Reference • © 2020 • 298pp • H/C (ISBN: 9781799825845) • US $225.00

Cloud Computing Applications and Techniques for E-Commerce
Saikat Gochhait (Symbiosis Institute of Digital and Telecom Management, Symbiosis International University, India) David Tawei Shou (University of Taipei, Taiwan) and Sabiha Fazalbhoy (Symbiosis Centre for Management Studies, Symbiosis International University, India)
Engineering Science Reference • © 2020 • 185pp • H/C (ISBN: 9781799812944) • US $215.00

701 East Chocolate Avenue, Hershey, PA 17033, USA
Tel: 717-533-8845 x100 • Fax: 717-533-8661
E-Mail: cust@igi-global.com • www.igi-global.com

Table of Contents

Detailed Table of Contents

Chapter 1

    Eduardo Miranda, Carnegie Mellon University, USA

This chapter introduces a hybrid software development framework, called Milestone-Driven Agile Execution, in which the empirical process control and the just-in-time planning of tasks of agile development are retained but the prioritization of the backlog is done according to a macro or strategic plan that drives the execution of the project. Selecting work items from the product backlog according to a plan instead of following the immediate concerns of a product owner adds visibility, predictability, and structure to the work of the team while preserving the adaptive advantages of agile development.

Chapter 2

    Mirna Muñoz, Centro de Investigación en Matemáticas A.C., Mexico
    Jezreel Mejía, Centro de Investigación en Matemáticas A.C., Mexico
    Claude Y. Laporte, École de Technologie Supérieure, Canada

Most very small entities (VSEs) develop software for medium and large companies and organizations. This situation creates an opportunity for them to become key players in the production chain by providing quality software within schedule and budget. A feature of most VSEs is that they do not have experience in the implementation of engineering standards due to specific features such as lack of support, lack of resources, time-consuming, and the use of agile approaches. This chapter presents an analysis of a set of eight VSEs that used agile approaches to develop software and that have implemented the software Basic profile of the ISO/IEC 29110 to reinforce their agile approach. The results show that ISO/IEC 29110 were easily implemented and helped VSEs to improve their agile approaches while helping them to understand the importance of formalizing some key artifacts produced during the development of a software product.

Chapter 3

Software architecture design, when performed in context of agile software development (ASD), sometimes referred to as "agile architecting," promotes the emerging and incremental design of the architectural artifact in a sense of avoiding "big design upfront" (BDUF). This chapter presents the Agile Modeling Process for Logical Architectures (AMPLA) method, an approach for supporting the emergence of a candidate (logical) architecture, rather than BDUF, the architecture in an early phase. The architecture then emerges throughout agile iterations, where AMPLA plays a key contribution for providing traceability between models, from the business need to service specifications, ranging from design stages to deployment, hence covering a software development life cycle (SDLC).

Chapter 4

Software development methodologies (SDMs) have had an accepted evolution (i.e., the replacement of SDMs of one era to the next) through the pre-methodology and early-methodology eras to the methodology era. But in the last 20 years, the transition of the methodology era (rigor-oriented) to the post-methodology era (agile-oriented) has led a debate on benefits and drawbacks of rigor vs. agile orientation. Regarding the general software-engineering evolution, the service-oriented software engineering (SOSE) that studies service-oriented computing (SOC) development approaches, which are widely used to develop software-oriented computing applications (SOCA), has emerged. SOSE developers then face the problem of selecting and adapting a SOCA SDM. This chapter compares 11 SOCA SDM on agility-rigor balance by a framework of Boehm and Turner addressing the rigor-agility conflicts by defining three factors and their methodological characteristics. Each characteristic is evaluated for each SDM with a novel agility-rigor 45-point scale. Results suggest three of such SDMs are agility-rigor balanced.

Increasingly, agile approaches are being followed in a distributed setup to develop software. An agile approach is characterised by the need to regularly welcome change requests and update the software artefact accordingly whereas distributed teams prefer to work towards following a plan to fulfil project objectives defined upfront. This results in contradictory tensions when agile is practised with teams operating in a globally distributed format. This chapter focuses on exploring the central conflict and discuss approaches to manage the conflicting forces in an agile distributed development setup. Furthermore, it presents an industry case study to provide more clarity on conflict management in such settings.

Agile Software Development (ASD) can be considered the mainstream development method of choice worldwide. ASD are used due to features such as easy management and embrace of changes, where change in requirements should be taken as a positive feature. However, some domain verticals, such as medical-healthcare, are classified as critical-safety system, which usually requires traditional methods. This chapter presents a practical use case describing the evolution of a software product that was conceived as a wellness software for end-users in mobile platforms to a medical-healthcare product restricted to regulatory standard recommendations. It presents the challenges and how the ASD is compatible to standards such as ISO/IEC 82304-1.

Software requirements changes become necessary due to changes in customer requirements and changes in business rules and operating environments; hence, requirements development, which includes requirements changes, is a part of a software process. Previous studies have shown that failing to manage software requirements changes well is a main contributor to project failure. Given the importance of the subject, there is a plethora of efforts in academia and industry that discuss the management of requirements change in various directions, ways, and means. This chapter provided information about the current state-of-the-art approaches (i.e., Disciplined or Agile) for RCM and the research gaps in existing work. Benefits, risks, and difficulties associated with RCM are also made available to software practitioners who will be in a position of making better decisions on activities related to RCM. Better decisions can lead to better planning, which will increase the chance of project success.

Software development has been considered a socio-technical activity over the past decades. Particularly, in the case of software engineering, the necessity to communicate effectively with stakeholders and team members has been progressively emphasized. Human resources play a critical role in the success of software projects. Many techniques, methods, tools, models, and methodologies have been proposed, applied, and improved in order to help and ease the management of the software development process. Regardless of the software development methodology adopted, delivering a quality product in a predictable, efficient, and responsive manner is the objective for every team. Disciplined and Agile teams have different characteristics, but also share common aspects when working to accomplish their goals. The main motivation of this chapter is to present the differences and similarities of both teams in the context of software development.

Chapter 9

Improving software security in software development teams is an enduring challenge for software companies. In this chapter, the authors present one strategy for addressing this pursuit of improvement. The approach is ambidextrous in the sense that it focuses on approaching software security activities both from a top-down and a bottom-up perspective, combining elements usually found separately in software security initiatives. The approach combines (1) top-down formal regulatory mechanisms deterring breaches of protocol and enacting penalties where they occur and (2) bottom-up capacity building and persuasive encouragement of adherence to guidance by professional self-determination, implementation, and improvement support (e.g., training, stimulating, interventions). The ambidextrous governance framework illustrates distinct, yet complementary, global and local roles: (1) ensuring the adoption and implementation of software security practices, (2) enabling and (3) empowering software development teams to adapt and add to overall mandates, and (4) embedding cultures of improvement.

Rapidly increasing of requirements of business pushed researchers to define new approaches and methodologies to meet marketing needs. Agile methodology has been created and replaced the traditional-driven development methods that focus on soliciting, documenting a complete set of requirements, and take a long time comparing to market change. On the other hand, customers need to be closer to the development process and collaborate with team development. Despite agile advantages, introducing new tools, coordination, and collaboration concepts, some challenges still need to be discussed and improved. These challenges relate to achieve balanced IT service development process in the organization. As a result, new trends have been created to facilitate new changes in software development. This chapter will study agile methodologies and different challenges with suggested solutions generated from agile philosophy itself.

Chapter 11

Michal Dolezel, University of Economics, Prague, Czech Republic
Alena Buchalcevova, University of Economics, Prague, Czech Republic

People rely on structures to make their worlds orderly. This chapter conceptually probes into the problem of the differences between organizational structures deployed in traditional and agile environments. The authors develop an argument that all common forms of organizational entities can be classified by involving a two-dimensional classification scheme. Specifically, they constructed a typology to examine the issues of formal vs. informal authority, and disciplinarity vs. cross-functionality in terms of their significance for traditional and agile software development workplaces. Some examples of concrete organizational forms—including traditional project team, independent test team, self-organizing agile team and developers' community of practice—are discussed. In sum, they argue that by employing this classification scheme, they can theorize the nature of the on-going structural shift observed in conjunction with deploying agile software development methods. They acknowledge that the structures have fundamentally changed, terming the move "democratization" in the software development workplace.

Chapter 12

Konstantinos Tsilionis, Katholieke Universiteit Leuven, Belgium
Yves Wautelet, Katholieke Universiteit Leuven, Belgium

Large organizations often describe IT needs in terms of services. IT governance mechanisms ensure investments lead to systems aligned with the long-term objectives. This business and IT alignment is often evaluated at the early stages when a service development decision needs to be taken. Evaluating such an alignment nevertheless requires knowledge and details on the tasks, activities, and requirements that the service is supposed to support. This is incompatible with agile development principles that prescribe to focus on an ad-hoc design built during a sprint. The latter indeed uses an operational approach where value delivered to stakeholders is the driver. This chapter advocates that investment decisions based on (coarse-grained) services is reconcilable with their agile development. It proposes Agile-MoDrIGo, a model-driven IT governance framework using services as scope elements and relying on agile to determine run-time behavior. To this end, the framework uses parallel top-down and bottom-up approaches based on conceptual models where integration is ensured by a middle layer.

The current and most used IT Service Management (ITSM) frameworks (ITIL v2011, CMMI-SVC, and ISO/IEC 20000) correspond to a rigor-oriented paradigm. However, the high dynamism in business requirements for IT services has fostered the emergence of agile-assumed ITSM frameworks. In contrast with the Software Engineering field where the rigorous and agile development paradigms co-exist because both paradigms are well-known and well-accepted, in the ITSM field, agile ITSM frameworks are practically unknown. This chapter, thus, reviews the main emergent proffered agile ITSM frameworks (Lean IT, FitSM, IT4IT, and VeriSM) focusing on the IT service design process category. This process category is relevant because an IT service is designed after its business strategic authorization and the IT service design determines the future warranty and utility metrics for the IT service. The main findings suggest the need for clear and effortless agile ITSM frameworks with agile design practices to guide potential ITSM practitioners to cope with the new digital business environment.

Chapter 14

This contribution describes two different types of requirements engineering analysis of the necessary dimensions of a possible maturity model for Smart Grids to be implemented for utilities. For the first case study, the requirements engineering for necessary dimensions for a Smart Grid maturity model was elicited using a systematic literature research. On the contrary a more agile approach is used for the second requirements engineering. For this more agile approach, interviews with energy suppliers were conducted, taking into account the analysis of the literature research. Various energy suppliers from Germany took part in the survey. The results were used to develop the basic framework for a maturity model for Smart Grids, which can still be tailored if necessary. Finally, future research activities for the application and further development of maturity models for Smart Grids in the energy industry are explained as well as the different procedural variants in the requirements analysis.

Chapter 15

In today's fast-changing environment, many organizations are applying the DevOps (Development and Operations) concept to transform their IT functions and establish cross-functional IT teams to deliver software services quickly, reliably, and safely with end-to-end responsibility. The results of an empirical study on which this chapter is based presents platform-oriented, application-oriented, and mobile-oriented DevOps setups, outlining areas of potential collaboration between these DevOps setups and the importance of aligning the aims of development (process agility) and operations (process rigor). Based on the study, six indicators of successful DevOps integration formulated as recommendations for successful IT function transformation were identified.

Foreword

Agile methodologies are now well accepted by both practitioners in the industry and the researchers in the academia. Although there is not an absolute definition for Agile process, it is known as a family of methodologies and techniques to develop software in small, incremental iterations. Some of the defining characteristics include the following:

- Multiple, short and fast releases to the customers
- User involvement in defining the software and in providing constant feedbacks
- Incremental design and development
- Constant, informal communications and less formal documentation
- High expectation of and readiness for changes in business, requirements, and environment

Incremental and evolutionary development with continuous integration was studied and practiced by some practitioners even in the early days of software engineering. But Agile methodologies were a serious departure from the traditional processes which involved large organizations, long development cycle, formal and complex steps, heavy documentation, well-defined but rigid requirements, and much fewer user interactions. It has been approximately twenty years since Ken Beck first wrote about one of the earliest Agile methods, Extreme Programming or XP. From the start, Agile process was not just a technical development process, but it also included many management and people-oriented aspects. Today, SCRUM is one of the most commonly practiced Agile methodologies. Practitioners are also modifying, improving and adapting the Agile methodologies to their specific environments.

However, this field still is far from maturing. It is continuously evolving, and there is more to learn and understand. This book entitled *Balancing Agile and Disciplined Engineering and Management Approaches for IT Services and Software Products*, to the credit of the editorial efforts of Dr. M. Mora, Dr. J. Marx-Gomez, Dr. A. Buchalcevova and Dr. R. O'Connor (in Memorial), brings together many relevant topics associated with Agile methodologies and approaches. It provides an extensive study of this growing area of software engineering. The assembled articles in this book cover the following areas:

- In-depth analysis of Agile approaches, the many challenges encountered and several suggested solutions.
- Comparison of merits of Agile approaches against the various aspects of traditional approaches.
- Case studies of utilizing and adapting Agile practices in real, commercial application development settings.

- Introduction and description of various new enhancements and modifications made to Agile approaches.
- Evaluations of Agile approaches for differing architectural structures.
- Extension of Agile practices to include IT operational services and management, covering the goals of business and deployment.

This book covers software development and operational (DevOps) issues, both separately and jointly. It is very comprehensive in its scope and quite timely in its publication. I believe the book is applicable for serving the multiple audiences listed below:

- Researchers, teachers, and graduate students of software engineering, computer science, information technology and services, and business information management.
- Professional and commercial practitioners of software engineering, computer science, information technology and business services.
- Designers, auditors and regulators of information and engineering standards, of industry and service standards, of governmental and international standards.

My formal education is in computer science. I have been involved with the software industry and software engineering for nearly forty-five years. The first thirty years of my professional life were spent in developing software and managing software organizations for commercial, business organizations of both large and small sizes. The last fifteen years or so were spent in the academic environment, teaching and researching software engineering topics in a university. I feel qualified to make an equitable assessment of this book, and I believe that you will find it to be extremely beneficial and useful. Thus, I would highly recommend the book to all of you who are involved in software, information technology and computing-related professions.

Frank Tsui
Kennesaw State University, USA

Frank Tsui has more than 30 years of software development, project management, and vice-presidential level executive experiences with companies such as IBM, BlueCrossBlueShield and PSINet/Metamor before joining Kennesaw State University's (formerly Southern Poly) Software Engineering Program. Several well-known IBM products were developed/enhanced under his guidance: IBM MVS-JES3 operating system, IBM CMAS software, IBM MAPICS software, IBM EDI software, etc. Frank has been an adjunct faculty at Georgia Tech, an adjunct and fulltime faculty at Southern Poly and a fulltime associate professor and interim CS Department Chair in the College of Computing and Software Engineering at Kennesaw State University. (He has retired on August 1, 2016 and has been elected as an emeritus faculty.) Dr. Tsui has also authored and co-authored three books: Essentials of Software Engineering (with O. Karam & B. Bernal) (4th ed., 2017), Managing Systems and IT Projects (2011), Managing Software Projects (2004).

Preface

While several Agile Software-System Development methods (such as Scrum, XP) have permeated in the Software Engineering academic and professional communities in the last 10 years (Hoda et al., 2018), they have been also criticized for trying of using them in all kind of software engineering projects (Boehm, 2002; Meyer, 2018) and by their large learning curve to be mastered (Ganesh & Thangasamy, 2012).

Even inventors of the main agile methodologies have indicated subtly that agile methods do not imply easiness of utilization. For instance, Beck (1999; chapter 24) reported "XP is simple in its details, but it is hard to execute". Similarly, Schwaber and Jeff Sutherland (2017; p. 3) "SCRUM is: lightweight, simple to understand, (but) difficult to master". Additionally, while some studies (Schwaber & Beedle, 2002; Holvitie et al., 2018) have reported that agile software-system development methods help to reduce the negative effects of technical debts, other studies have also reported (Schwanke et al., 2013; Guo et al., 2016) that agile software-system development methods are prone to introduce technical debts by "an emphasis on quick delivery and architecture and design issues" (Behutiye et al. 2017; p. 154).

Consequently, balanced discipline-agility methods and approaches have been proposed by researchers (Boehm & Turner, 2004; Rodriguez-Martinez et al., 2012) and some particular adaptations (maturity models, scalation models, enhancement models) to agile methods have been also explored (Boehm & Turner, 2005; Campanelli & Parreiras, 2015; Galvan-Cruz et al., 2017; Dingselyr et al., 2018; 2019; Ozcan-Top & Demirors, 2019). Furthermore, new ISO/IEC standards like the ISO/IEC 29110 standard, pursue similar aims (O'Connor, 2019).

Similarly, in the domain of IT service management (TSO, 2012) it has been an extensive utilization of disciplined best practices and process frameworks such as ITIL v3.2011 (TSO, 2012), the ISO/IEC 20000 (ISO/IEC 2010), CMMI-SVC (SEI, 2010), and the proprietary ones ITUP (IBM, 2010) and MOF 4.0. (Microsoft, 2008). However, in the last 5 years, the agile paradigm has also permeated to the IT Service Management field and at present days there are several available agile IT service management best practices and process frameworks such as VeriSM (Mann, 2018), IT4IT (Open Group, 2017), FitSM (FitSM, 2016a; 2016b) and Lean IT (LeanIT, 2015).

Furthermore, with the current high interest in business and governmental organizations for making Digital Transformations (World Bank, 2018; Open Group, 2018) providing innovative services, the need for agile effective and efficient IT service design methods arises in this modern worldwide context. Thus, despite the classic IT Service Management best practices and process frameworks have caused beneficial economic and positive performance impacts in the recent past, however, the current highly dynamic world pushes strong pressures on the IT area for delivering quickly and correctly IT services. New claimed agile (and flexible integrative) IT Service Management best practices and process frameworks (i.e. LeanIT, IT4IT, FitSM, and VeriSM) have already emerged in this last 5-year period, but scarce scientific evidence of their effectiveness is available.

Both disciplined and agile approaches rely on very separate assumptions, and consequently, their straight integration of balanced methods is not a trivial task (Siau et al., 2015). The high dynamic context of the software-system and IT services customer demands and the emergence of highly related information technology and innovations such as cloud computing (Younas et al., 2018), Internet of things (Jacobson et al., 2017), microservices architecture (Pautasso et al., 2017), and DevOps approach (Dingsoyr, T., & Lassenius, 2016) claim for a reconsideration of the adequate utilization of disciplined vs agile vs balanced IT services and software development methods. Nevertheless, these concerns have been few explored.

Consequently, this book asked high-quality research-oriented chapters related to the following topics - but not limited to -

- Agile, disciplined and balanced values, principles and assumptions for software or IT services development
- Agile, disciplined and balanced software or IT services development methods
- Agile, disciplined and balanced software or IT services process frameworks and standards
- Successful/failed case studies on agile, disciplined and balanced software or IT services development process
- Surveys on the utilization of agile, disciplined and balanced software or IT services development process
- Teaching cases on agile, disciplined and balanced software or IT services development process
- Open source tools for agile, disciplined and balanced software or IT services development process
- Impact of emergent technologies (cloud, microservices, IoT) on agile, disciplined and balanced software or IT services development process
- Impact of business trends (digitalization, industry 4.0, analytics, big data) on agile, disciplined and balanced software or IT services development process
- Challenges and trends of agile, disciplined and balanced software or IT services development process

This book is useful for a target audience composed of:

- International research centers on software engineering
- International research centers on IT service management
- Graduate programs (Master and Doctoral level) on software engineering
- Graduate programs (Master and Doctoral level) on IT services management
- Software industries using agile methods
- Organizations using IT service management process frameworks.

This book was elaborated from an open and international call for chapters, and after a careful editorial process with a blind-mode review procedure applied in two or three rounds for each chapter that lasted 10 months, we selected finally 15 high-quality ones. Chapters 1 to 9 can be grouped as chapters devoted to balanced engineering and operational management methods and techniques to develop software or IT services. The remainder chapters 10 to 15 can be grouped in chapters focused on challenges and trends on achieving balanced development approaches for software or IT services.

Chapter 1, entitled "Milestone-Driven Agile Execution," is authored by Dr. Eduardo Miranda from Carnegie-Mellon University, USA. This chapter reports an innovative balanced rigor-agility software development methodology that while keeps many agile operational tasks, also introduces a product backlog driven from a business strategy perspective. This balanced methodology provides better project predictability and structure to agile developers than the alone agile version. Chapter 2, entitled "Analysis of the Evolution of Eight VSEs Using the ISO/IEC 29110 to Reinforce Their Agile Approaches," is authored by Dr. Mirna Muñoz, Dr. Jezreel Mejia, and Dr. Claude Laporte, from CIMAT, Mexico (first and second authors), and École de technologie supérieure, Canada (third author). The authors report a case study on eight very small entities (VSEs) that use agile software development methods but with the interest and need to fit market regulatory demands imposed by medium and large customers. To fit these demands, the studied VSEs implemented a Basic profile of the ISO/IEC 29110 standard, and all of them found benefits particularly on having a disciplined control of key software artifacts. Chapter 3, entitled "AMPLA: An Agile Process for Modeling Logical Architectures," is authored by Nuno Santos, Nuno Ferreira, and Ricardo Machado from CCG\ZGDV Institute, in Portugal (first and third authors) and i2S Insurance Knowledge company, in Portugal (second author). Authors report the Agile Modeling Process for Logical Architectures (AMPLA), that privileges the relevance of a software architecture artifact (a first-class artifact in the disciplined arena) but that introduces an agile technique to guide developers to jointly emerge an agreed software architecture. Chapter 4, entitled "Service-Oriented Computing Applications (SOCA) Development Methodologies: A Review of Agility-Rigor Balance," is authored by Laura C. Rodriguez-Martinez, Hector Duran-Limon, and Manuel Mora from Technology Institute of Aguascalientes, Mexico (first author), CUCEA University of Guadalajara, Mexico (second author), and Autonomous University of Aguascalientes, Mexico (third author). The authors report an analysis of eleven SOCA software development methodologies to evaluate their rigor-agility level. For this aim, the authors use a framework derived from Bohem and Turner and identify three of them as balanced methodologies. The remaining eight are still classified as rigor-oriented ones and none is found as agile. Chapter 5, entitled "Managing Contradictory Tensions in Agile Distributed Development: An Ambi-dextrous Approach," is authored by Ashay Saxena, Shankar Venkatagiri, and Rajendra K. Bandi, from Indian Institute of Management Bangalore, India. Authors report an analysis of the conflicts that arise in distributed software development settings that are pushed to use agile approaches when they usually prefer disciplined ones. The authors propose potential solutions and report as these were implemented in the case study.

Chapter 6, entitled "Adapting Agile Practices During the Evolution of a Healthcare Software Product," is authored by Danilo Santos, André Rodrigues, Walter Guerra, and Marcos Pereira, all of them in the Federal University of Campina Grande, Brazil. Authors report a case study on the transition from a mobile wellness application to a regulated healthcare software, where the agile system development approach fitted the ISO/IEC 82304-1:2016 standard referring to requirements for health software products. Chapter 7, entitled "Disciplined or Agile? Two Approaches for Handling Requirement Change Management," is authored by Danyllo Albuquerque, Everton Tavares-Guimarães, Felipe Barbosa, Antonio Moura, Alexandre Gomes, Emanuel Dantas, Mirko Perkusich, Hyggo Almeida, in the Federal University of Campina Grande, Brazil (first, third, fifth, sixth, and eight authors), the Pennsylvania State University, USA (second author), the Federal Institute of Paraiba, Brazil (fourth author), and VIRTUS company, Brazil (seventh author). Authors review the state of the art on Requirement Change Management including both disciplined and agile approaches, reporting benefits, risks, and challenges. Chapter 8, entitled "Disciplined Teams Versus Agile Teams: Differences and Similarities in Software Development," is authored by Antonio Moura, Felipe Barbosa, Dalton Gomes, Danyllo Albuquerque, Emanuel Dantas, Alexandre Braga, Mirko Perkusich, and Hyggo Almeida, in Federal Institute of Paraiba, Brazil (first author), Federal University of Campina Grande, Brazil (second, fourth, fifth, sixth, and eighth authors), Federal Institute of Pernambuco, Brazil (third author), and VIRTUS company, Brazil (seventh author). Authors analyze the similar and different socio-technical characteristics of software development teams using disciplined and agile approaches. Chapter 9, entitled "Building an Ambidextrous Software Security Initiative," is authored by Daniela Soares, and Espen Agnalt, in SINTEF Digital and VISMA companies, Norway, respectively. Authors report findings from an Action Research approach conducted in their companies to implement an ambidextrous (disciplined top-down and agile alike bottom-up) strategy to include security practices in the development of software.

Chapter 10, entitled "Challenges and Trends of Agile," is authored by Fayez Salma, and Jorge Marx-Gomez, both in the Carl von Ossietzky University of Oldenburg, Germany. Authors review the agile software development approaches and identify challenges and hidden problems, as well as provide potential solutions to them. Chapter 11, entitled "A Framework for Analyzing Structural Mechanisms Deployed to Support Traditional and Agile Methods: Making Sense of 'Democratization' in the Software Development Workplace," is authored by Michal Dolezel, and Alena Buchalcevova, both in University of Economics Prague, Czech Republic. Authors elaborate a conceptual framework to classify the organizational structures of software development organizations and teams, contrasting the formal vs informal authority, and disciplinary vs cross-functionality characteristics. Chapter 12, entitled "Aligning Strategic-Driven Governance of Business IT Services With Their Agile Development: A Conceptual Modeling-Based Approach," is authored by Konstantinos Tsilionis, and Yves Wautelet, both in Catholic University Leuven, Belgium. Authors address the problem of defining IT services aligned to business strategies using an agile approach and solving it through a proposed IT Governance framework that combines disciplined coarse-grained IT services and agile operational issues. Chapter 13, entitled "A Review of the IT Service Design Process in Agile ITSM Frameworks," is authored by Manuel Mora, Fen Wang, Jorge Marx-Gomez, and Oswaldo Diaz, in Autonomous University of Aguascalientes, Mexico (first author), Central Washington University, USA (second author), Carl von Ossietzky University of Oldenburg, Germany (third author), and INEGI, Mexico (fourth author). Authors review the IT service design process reported in three rigor-oriented IT service management (ITSM) frameworks, and four emergent proffered agile ITSM ones, and conclude that just one of them can be qualified as agile one. Chapter 14, entitled "Requirements on Dimensions for a Maturity Model for Smart Grids Based on Two Case Studies: Disciplined vs. Agile Approach," is authored by Agnetha Flore, and Jorge Marx-Gomez, in OFFIS - Institute for Information Technology, Germany, and Carl von Ossietzky University of Oldenburg, Germany respectively. Authors review the state of the art on dimensions included in maturity models for Smart Grids, which are software-intensive cyber-physical systems to deliver electric power to organizations, from a disciplined and agile perspective. Finally, Chapter 15, entitled "Transforming Disciplined IT Functions: Guidelines for DevOps Integration," is authored by Anna Wiedemann, Manuel Wiesche, Heiko Gewald, and Helmut Krcmar, in Neu-Ulm University of Applied Sciences, Germany (first and third authors), Technical University of Dortmund, Germany (second author), and Technical University of Munich, Germany (fourth author). Authors report an empirical study based on platform-oriented, application-oriented, and mobile-oriented Development and Operations (DevOps) setups, and formulate six indicators of successful DevOps integration.

Hence, this book pursued the objective to collect and disseminate high-quality theoretical and applied research on a very relevant topic in the software engineering and IT service management domains. We consider that these 15 selected high-quality contribute to paving the path toward better development methods for software and IT services based on the convergence of disciplined and agile approaches. These topics are causing at present relevant academic and professional debates demanding efficient and effective solutions. This book contributes to innovative studies and potential solutions to this relevant and contemporaneous research problem.

Manuel Mora
Autonomous University of Aguascalientes, Mexico

Jorge Marx Gómez
University of Oldenburg, Germany

Rory V. O'Connor
Dublin City University, Ireland

Alena Buchalcevová
University of Economics, Prague, Czech Republic

REFERENCES

Beck, K. (1999). *Extreme Programming Explained.* Addison-Wesley.

Behutiye, W. N., Rodriguez, P., Oivo, M., & Tosun, A. (2017). Analyzing the concept of technical debt in the context of agile software development: A systematic literature review. *Information and Software Technology, 82,* 139–158. doi:10.1016/j.infsof.2016.10.004

Boehm, B. (2002). Get ready for agile methods, with care. *Computer, 35*(1), 64–69. doi:10.1109/2.976920

Boehm, B., & Turner, R. (2004, May). Balancing agility and discipline: Evaluating and integrating agile and plan-driven methods. In *Software Engineering, 2004. ICSE 2004. Proceedings. 26th International Conference on* (pp. 718-719). IEEE.

Boehm, B., & Turner, R. (2005). Management challenges to implementing agile processes in traditional development organizations. *IEEE Software, 22*(5), 30–39. doi:10.1109/MS.2005.129

Campanelli, A. S., & Parreiras, F. S. (2015). Agile methods tailoring-A systematic literature review. *Journal of Systems and Software, 110,* 85–100. doi:10.1016/j.jss.2015.08.035

Dingselyr, T., & Lassenius, C. (2016). Emerging themes in agile software development: Introduction to the special section on continuous value delivery. *Information and Software Technology, 77,* 56–60. doi:10.1016/j.infsof.2016.04.018

Dingselyr, T., & Moe, N. B. (2018). Exploring software development at the very large-scale: A revelatory case study and research agenda for agile method adaptation. *Empirical Software Engineering, 23*(1), 490–520. doi:10.100710664-017-9524-2

Fit, S. M. (2016a). *FitSM - standards lightweight for IT service management - part 0 overview and vocabulary*. FitSM.

Fit, S. M. (2016b). *FitSM - standards for lightweight service management in IT federated infrastructures- introducing FitSM*. FitSM.

Galvan-Cruz, S., Mora, M., & O'Connor, R. (2017, October). A Means-Ends Design of SCRUM+: an agile-disciplined balanced SCRUM enhanced with the ISO/IEC 29110 Standard. In *International Conference on Software Process Improvement* (pp. 13-23). Springer.

Ganesh, N., & Thangasamy, S. (2012). Lessons learned in transforming from traditional to agile development. *Journal of Computational Science*, *8*(3), 389–392. doi:10.3844/jcssp.2012.389.392

Guo, Y., Spinola, R. O., & Seaman, C. (2016). Exploring the costs of technical debt management-a case study. *Empirical Software Engineering*, *21*(1), 159–182. doi:10.100710664-014-9351-7

Hoda, R., Salleh, N., & Grundy, J. (2018). The rise and evolution of agile software development. *IEEE Software*, *35*(5), 58–63. doi:10.1109/MS.2018.290111318

Holvitie, J., Licorish, S. A., Spinola, R. O., Hyrynsalmi, S., MacDonell, S. G., Mendes, T. S., Buchan, J., & Leppanen, V. (2018). Technical debt and agile software development practices and processes: An industry practitioner survey. *Information and Software Technology*, *96*, 141–160. doi:10.1016/j.infsof.2017.11.015

IBM. (2010). *ITUP Electronic Process Guidelines Tool*. IBM.

ISO/IEC. (2010). *ISO/IEC 20000-4 Information Technology - Service Management Part 4 Process Reference Model*. ISO.

Jacobson, I., Spence, I., & Ng, P. W. (2017). Is there a single method for the Internet of Things? *Communications of the ACM*, *60*(11), 46–53. doi:10.1145/3106637

Lean, I. T. (2015). *Lean IT Foundation Increasing the Value of IT*. The Lean IT Foundation.

Mann, S. (2018). *Protect Your ITIL Investment with VeriSMm*. VeriSM.

Meyer, B. (2018). Making Sense of Agile Methods. *IEEE Software*, *35*(2), 91–94. doi:10.1109/MS.2018.1661325

Microsoft. (2008). *MOF Executive Overview version 4.0*. www.microsoft.com/mof4

O'Connor, R. V. (2019). Software Development Process Standards for Very Small Companies. In *Advanced Methodologies and Technologies in Digital Marketing and Entrepreneurship* (pp. 681-694). IGI Global. doi:10.4018/978-1-5225-7766-9.ch053

Open Group. (2017). *The IT4ITm Reference Architecture, version 2.1 - a pocket guide*. Van Haren Publishing.

Open Group. (2018). *Enabling Organizations in the Digital Age - How to Achieve Business Outcomes using The Open Group IT4ITTM Standard and the IFDC VeriSMTh Approach Together*. The Open Group and the IFDC.

Ozcan-Top, O., & Demirors, O. (2019). Application of a software agility assessment model-AgilityMod in the field. *Computer Standards & Interfaces, 62*, 1–16. doi:10.1016/j.csi.2018.07.002

Pautasso, C., Zimmermann, O., Amundsen, M., Lewis, J., & Josuttis, N. M. (2017). Microservices in Practice, Part 1: Reality Check and Service Design. *IEEE Software, 34*(1), 91–98. doi:10.1109/MS.2017.24

Rodriguez-Martinez, L., Mora, M., Alvarez, F., Garza, L., Duran, H., & Munoz, J. (2012). Review of Relevant System Development Life Cycles (SDLCs) in Service-Oriented Software Engineering (SoSE). *Journal of Applied Research and Technology, 10*(2), 94–113. doi:10.22201/icat.16656423.2012.10.2.396

Schwaber, K., & Beedle, M. (2002). *Agile software development with Scrum* (Vol. 1). Prentice Hall.

Schwaber, K., & Sutherland, J. (2017). *The Scrum Guide- The Definitive Guide to Scrum: The Rules of the Game*. https://www.scrumguides.org

Chapter 1
Milestone–Driven
Agile Execution

Eduardo Miranda

https://orcid.org/0000-0001-8195-7506

Carnegie Mellon University, USA

ABSTRACT

This chapter introduces a hybrid software development framework, called Milestone-Driven Agile Execution, in which the empirical process control and the just-in-time planning of tasks of agile development are retained but the prioritization of the backlog is done according to a macro or strategic plan that drives the execution of the project. Selecting work items from the product backlog according to a plan instead of following the immediate concerns of a product owner adds visibility, predictability, and structure to the work of the team while preserving the adaptive advantages of agile development.

INTRODUCTION

Whether traditional or agile, any project of any size or consequence needs a high-level plan that allows everyone to contribute towards the desired outcome. According to Brechner (2015), this plan can take many forms but will typically include a vision for what the end product will look like, a technical strategy, and a schedule with the dates of key events (conferences, press announcements, or launch), expected dates for when major product capabilities must come together and target metrics (such as performance, scale, or participation) must be reached.

Without such a plan, project members struggle with what to do next and stakeholders with what to expect when. Cohn (2010), for example, suggests the use of a release plan, without which *teams move endlessly from one iteration to the next* and Cockburn (2004), *a coarse-grained project plan, possibly created from a project map or a set of stories and releases to make sure the project is delivering suitable business value for suitable expense in a suitable time period.*

The Milestone Driven Agile Execution (MDAX), see Figure 1, is a hybrid software management framework (Kneuper, 2018; Kuhrmann, et al., 2017) where the empirical process control and the just-in-time planning of tasks advocated by agile methods are retained, but the prioritization of the backlog

DOI: 10.4018/978-1-7998-4165-4.ch001

is done according to a macro or strategic plan instead of being driven by the immediate concerns or impulses of the product owner. Selecting work items from the backlog according to a plan adds visibility, predictability, and structure to the work of the team while preserving the adaptive advantages of agile development. MDAX is method agnostic in the sense that the development approach, much like an app running in a Java Virtual Machine, is not encoded in its mechanics, but rather in the plan that drives it. This allows organizations using MDAX to choose the development approach that suits them best.

The technique proposed to create the macro or strategic plan that will drive the project work is called *milestone planning* (Andersen, 1996; Andersen, Grude, & Haug, 2009). In this planning approach, a plan for a project is formulated not in terms of the tasks that make it up, but in terms of the relevant states or sub-objectives the project must go through on its way to achieving its objective, such as the website information architecture is approved, a basic version of the app is released, a necessary piece of hardware is made available to the project, and so forth. In other words, the plan outlines the chosen strategy but does not dictate the tasks that ought to be executed to realize it, which will be decided as work progresses. As relevant states synthetize the results of the (usually) many tasks necessary to reach them, there will be fewer of them than the corresponding tasks, making milestone plans more robust and easier to produce and communicate.

Figure 1. Milestone driven agile execution

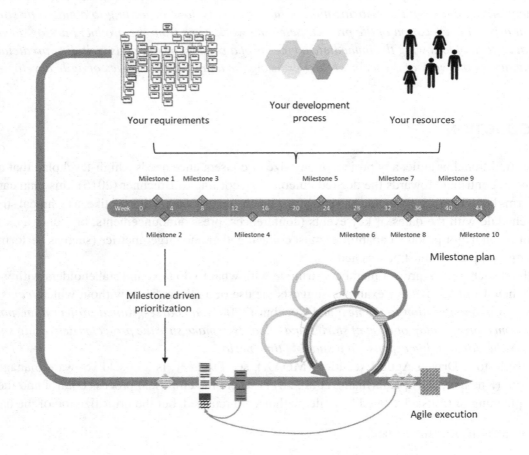

For space reasons, it is not possible to provide a complete and equally detailed description of all aspects of the method, so in what follows, we will focus on what is novel or unique about the approach and assume the reader has a basic understanding of Scrum, which will allow him or her to fill in the blanks in the cases where we have borrowed a established practice or concept from another method. In the Background section, we will introduce the Milestone Plan and the Work Package Schedule constructs. In the MDAX Framework section, we will provide a detailed description of MDAX in terms of its roles, activities, meetings, and artifacts. In the section Planning and Knowledge Sharing as Motivational Tools, we will discuss what makes MDAX work and the visual milestone planning technique at the core of the approach. In the Milestone Planning Example, we will walk the reader through the entire planning process, and in the last section, Conclusion, we will provide a summary of the framework and its advantages.

BACKGROUND

Andersen (1996) defines a milestone not *as the completion of an activity, usually an especially important one,* but as *a result to be achieved, a description of a condition or a state that the project should reach by a certain point in time. A milestone describes what is to be fulfilled, not the method to fulfil it.* This is what makes milestone plans suitable to act as guide posts while preserving the just-in-time task planning nature of agile methods.

Figure 2 shows a typical milestone plan. As can be observed, a milestone plan is short, typically confined to a size that will allow it to be grasped at once and written using a vocabulary a project sponsor can understand. The plan comprises the sequence of states the project will go through, from its inception to its successful conclusion, and not the activities the team needs to perform to achieve those states. For example, the "Design concept approved" milestone defines a state where the project team has presented an idea that satisfies the needs of the sponsor and he or she has acquiesced to it. The plan does not stipulate how the team will get there. Will they build wireframe diagrams, develop high-fidelity prototypes, make a PowerPoint presentation, perform user testing, or employ focus groups? At some point, these issues will certainly have to be addressed by the team, but they have no place in a milestone plan. This focus on states is what makes the plan robust, since independent of what tasks are performed to get there, when, and by whom, the project sponsor would like to approve the design concept before it is implemented, and that is unlikely to change.

The dependencies between milestones are "Finish to Finish" relations, meaning that if "Milestone B" depends on "Milestone A", "Milestone B" cannot be completed until "Milestone A" has been completed. Finish to Finish relations are easy to spot and provide great freedom as to when the activities leading to the realization of the milestone could start.

Milestones can be hard or soft. Hard milestones are milestones that, if not accomplished by a set date, lose all or most of their value or result in severe penalties. For example, the date a government resolution that the system under development is supposed to address goes into effect, and the start of the holiday shopping season, would be hard milestones a project might need to satisfy. Soft milestones, on the other hand, have completion dates that result from the planning process. They might be associated with penalties or other liabilities after a statement of work is agreed upon, but in principle they are discretionary.

Associated with the milestone plan will be a work packages schedule (see Figure 3), which defines when the work associated with a given milestone, called its work package, will have to be executed. Within the constraints imposed by the milestones' hard dates and the dependencies identified in the plan,

Figure 2. A typical milestone plan showing due dates, responsibilities, and milestones' descriptions

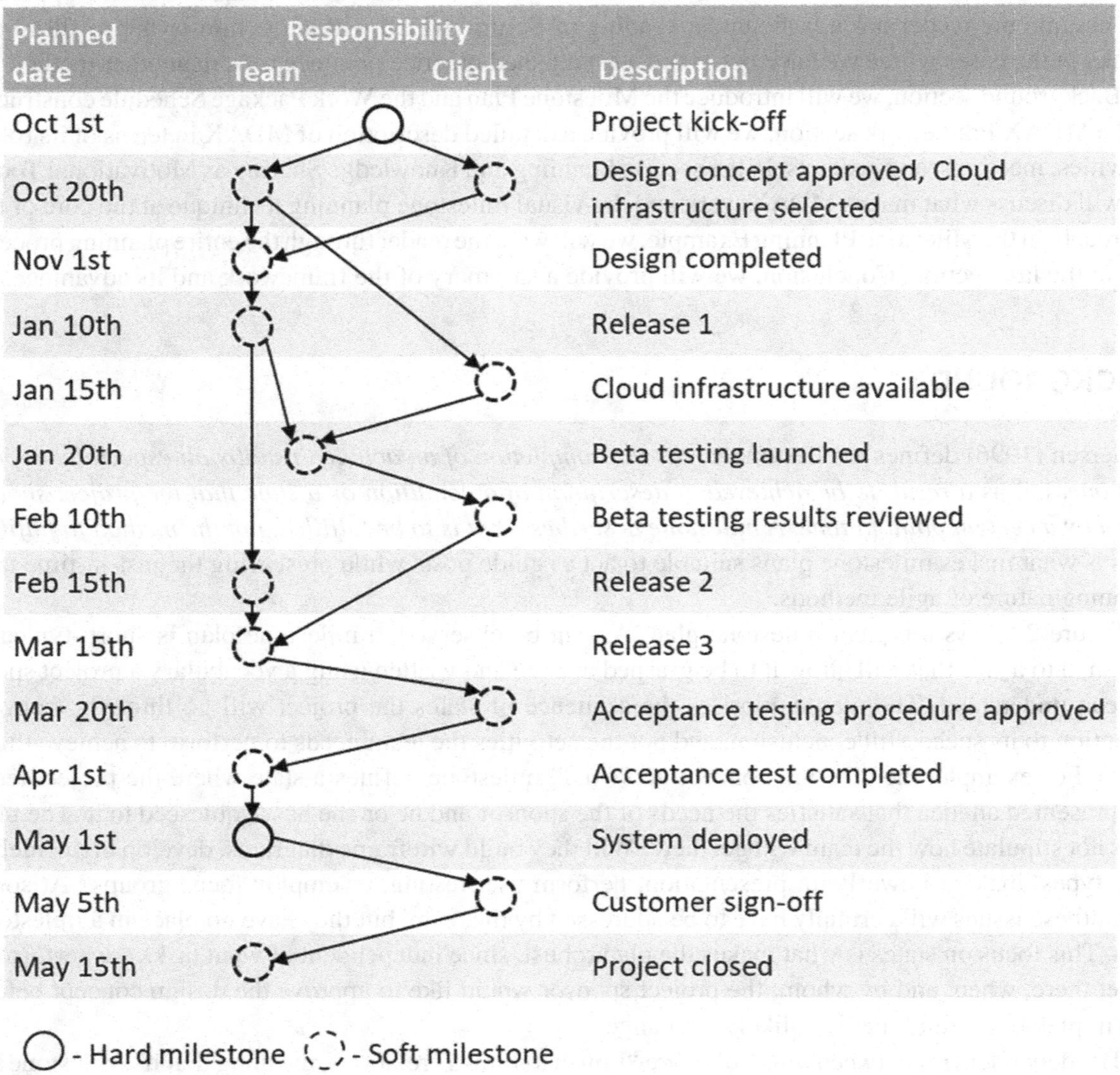

Planned date	Responsibility		Description
	Team	Client	
Oct 1st			Project kick-off
Oct 20th			Design concept approved, Cloud infrastructure selected
Nov 1st			Design completed
Jan 10th			Release 1
Jan 15th			Cloud infrastructure available
Jan 20th			Beta testing launched
Feb 10th			Beta testing results reviewed
Feb 15th			Release 2
Mar 15th			Release 3
Mar 20th			Acceptance testing procedure approved
Apr 1st			Acceptance test completed
May 1st			System deployed
May 5th			Customer sign-off
May 15th			Project closed

◯ - Hard milestone   ⟨ ⟩ - Soft milestone

the work packages schedule will be constructed according to the team and business timing and staffing strategies, such as we need to do this before that, do as much work as possible at the earliest, start slow to minimize risk and then aggressively ramp up, maintain a constant workforce, do not exceed six months, do not use more than five people, and so on.

To execute the milestone plan, the project team progressively refines the elements of the work package into the tasks necessary to realize them within the time and resource frame established by the work packages schedule. The work to be taken on in a given iteration is thus dictated by the work packages schedule derived from the milestone plan the product owner helped to create and not by whimsical biweekly or monthly decisions. As work progresses, the plan is updated to reflect new circumstances

Figure 3. Work packages schedule

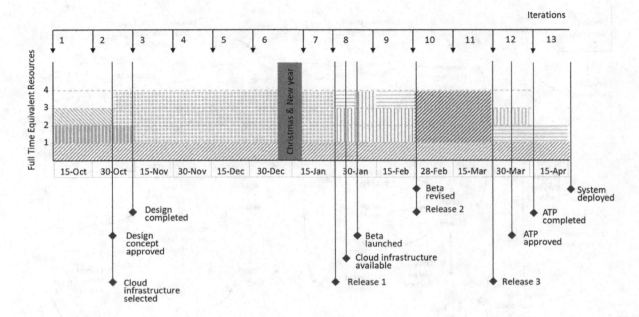

arising from the work completed or from changes in the project context, but since milestones are basically states or goals to be attained, and the plan does not specify when tasks must begin, how long they should take, nor who should perform them, it tends to be pretty stable.

This represents one possible arrangement of work packages corresponding to the milestone plan in Figure 2. Each shaded area corresponds to the work associated with the milestone immediately to its right. The resource-time frame enclosing the work package is its time box. During iteration 1 and part of iteration 2, two members of the team will work on UX Design and the selection of infrastructure. From iteration 2 to 6, the team will mainly work on the items included in the first release; from iteration 7 to 9, the team will work on the features included in the second release and in Beta testing.

THE MDAX FRAMEWORK

In this section, we describe and explain the MDAX framework (see Figure 4) in terms of its roles, artifacts, activities, meetings, and workflow. Activities are tasks performed once at the start of the project or as new knowledge or circumstances require it, while meetings are recurring tasks that must be carried out at every iteration.

Roles

In MDAX, there are four fundamental roles to consider: stakeholders, product owner, project leader, and team member.

Figure 4. Detailed MDAX workflow

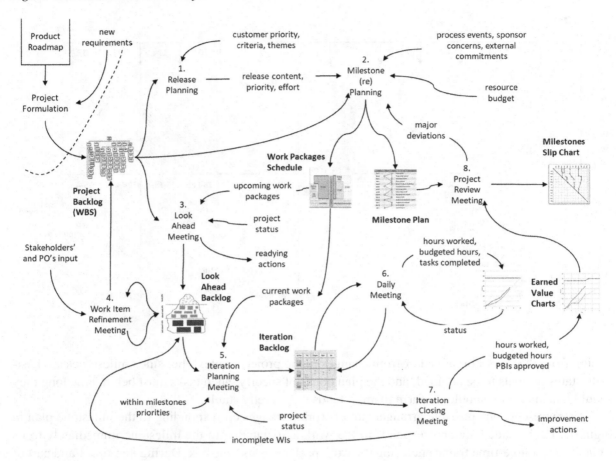

A stakeholder is anyone who does not work for the project but could be affected by its outcome and must be consulted regarding one or more project decisions. Stakeholders include the project sponsors, users, operators, regulators, and support personnel, among others.

The product owner is the person accountable for building the right thing. Specifically, he or she defines, prioritizes, and accepts the work performed.

Project leader is a generic term used to encompass the project manager and the Scrum master roles, as some organizations prefer to have an induvial with overall responsibility for the project, while others resort to self-organizing teams. MDAX accepts both styles of governance so long as the project leader works collobaratively with and empowers the team. As will be discussed in more depth in the Planning and Knowledge Sharing as Motivational Tool section, autocratic behaviors are discouraged. Basic responsibilities of the project leader include serving as point of contact between management and the team, enacting the MDAX framework, coordinating with external actors, following up on action items, ensuring the team is fully functional and productive, and shielding the team from external interferences.

A team member is any person working on the project on a regular basis who is directly involved in the creation, maintenance, or disposition of the project's deliverables. Collectively, team members are referred to as the development team. This definition aims to include all the people that need to have a shared understanding of the project goals and how to realize them; in that sense, it excludes people such as experts or others whose participation might be ephemeral.

The contribution of each of the roles to the activities and meetings in the MDAX framework is outlined in Table 1.

Table 1. Responsibility assignment in MDAX

Role	Release Planning	Milestone (re) Planning	Look Ahead Meeting	Work Item Refinement	Iteration Planning Meeting	Daily Meeting	Iteration Closing Meeting	Project Review Meeting
Stakeholders	Influence, inform priorities			Inform			Provide feedback (optional)	
Product Owner	Prioritizes, has final word	Concurs	Selects next work items within plan scope	Clarifies	Selects work items for next iteration within plan scope		Approves work, reviews performance	Re-prioritizes work
Project Leader	Concurs	Has final word, works with team	Drives and follows up on issues	Facilitates	Facilitates	Facilitates	Facilitates, reports progress	Drives, has final say
Team Member	Challenges, makes suggestion	Builds the plan		Raise issues, makes suggestions	Designs, breaks down into tasks, estimates	Reports progress, selects new tasks	Runs demonstrations, Assesses group performance	Raises issues, makes suggestions

Artifacts

Besides the Milestone Plan and the Work Packages Schedule described above, MDAX defines six other artifacts that support its execution: the Project Backlog, the Look Ahead Backlog, the Iteration Backlog, the Iteration and Project Earned Value Charts, and the Milestone Slip Chart.

In MDAX, the Project Backlog is implemented by means of a Work Breakdown Structure (see Figure 5), which is a hierarchical enumeration of all the outputs, including functionality, documentation, infrastructure, gadgets, services, and so forth, to be delivered to the customer to meet the project objectives, and the work necessary to produce them.[1] These items, whether outputs or work, are generically called work items (WIs). The hierarchical nature of the Work Breakdown Structure is mandated by the need to facilitate the comprehension of the project's scope and to support both the progressive refinement of the identified items and their estimation and the collective assignment of WIs to milestones.

Unlike the Product Backlog used in Scrum and in other agile development methods, the MDAX Project Backlog does not define the order in which the different items will be tackled, a responsibility that in MDAX is assigned to the Milestone Plan. The need to separate scope comprehension and sequence of realization is clearly illustrated by the example below, borrowed from Radigan (2019), which shows the different usages of the two views.

Since the Teams in Space website is the first initiative in the roadmap, we'll want to break down that initiative into epics (see Figure 6) and user stories for each of those epics.

The product owner then organizes each of the user stories into a single list for the development team. The product owner may choose to deliver a complete epic first (Figure 7, left). Or, it may be more

Figure 5. A Work Breakdown Structure and its relation to the project's outputs and the work necessary to realize them

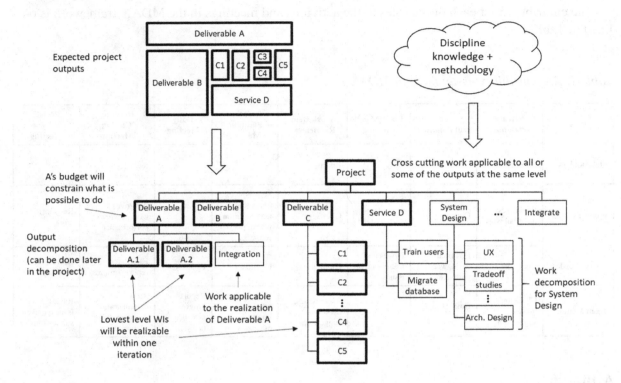

Figure 6. A hierarchical decomposition of the work to be delivered

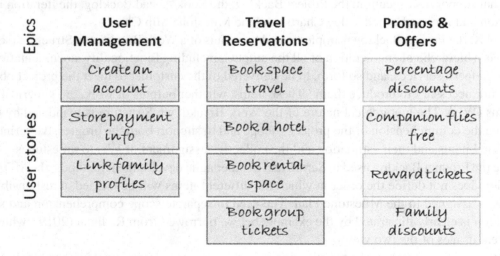

important to the program to test booking a discounted flight, which requires stories from several epics (Figure 7, right). See both examples below.

Figure 7. Two different orders of realization of the work stipulated in Figure 6

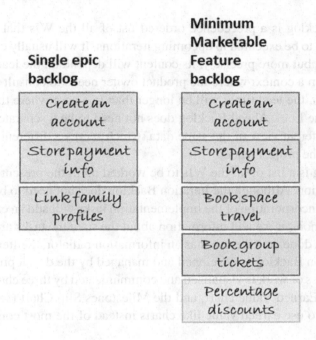

Also, in contrast with the traditional Product Backlog, the Project Backlog is not open ended, but bounded. This means that although its items do not need to be completely specified at the beginning of the project, for the purpose of planning, we will make a budgetary allowance for them, in the understanding that when the time comes and they are refined, either we will circumscribe our level of ambition to the available budget, or the plan will need to be revisited.

The first level of the hierarchy in the Project Backlog will define a set of outcomes and activities that collectively and exclusively represent the entirety of the project scope. Each descending level in the hierarchy represents an increasingly detailed definition of the project work. The WIs can be defined from the bottom up, for example, aggregating the results of a brainstorming or requirements elicitation session, or through a process of decomposition, starting from the top and working downward. Outputs can contain

lower-level outputs and work elements as descendants, but work elements can only have other work elements as descendants. This convention assures consistency in the determination of which work applies to which outputs. The decomposition will stop as soon as we reach iteration-sized WIs, that is, outputs or work elements that could be realized by the team in the course of an iteration.

Notice that, as defined, WIs at different levels of the Work Breakdown Structure definition map nicely to agile concepts such as epics, features, user stories, enablers, and technical stories, and although these terms might be favored by agile practitioners, we will limit their use to the Milestone Planning Example section of the chapter to minimize the need to enumerate them all the time.

The Project Backlog is jointly controlled by the product owner and the development team. The former needs to consult with the team to determine what is feasible within the confines established by a project's budget and time frame, and the latter cannot change the committed scope without the approval of the product owner.

The Look Ahead Backlog is a precedence ordered list of all the WIs that are ready, or are in the process of being readied, to be executed in upcoming iterations. It will usually contain from one to three iterations worth of work, but more precisely, its content will depend on the lead time required to ready the items. For example, in a context where the product owner needs to consult with many stakeholders before making a decision, the lead times will be longer than in a case where the product owner makes the decision by itself. The Look Ahead Backlog does not need to be a separate entity from the Project Backlog, but rather a different view of the same data, which serves a different need. The Look Ahead Backlog is managed by the project leader.

The Iteration Backlog is a list of all the WIs to be worked on in the present iteration, plus the tasks required for their realization. Although the Iteration Backlog does not need to be a different entity from the Project Backlog, the incorporation of the implementation tasks will add an extra dimension not present in the latter. Furthermore, if we add information about the state the tasks are in, such as to be done, in progress, blocked, and done, and we use it as an information radiator, the Iteration Backlog becomes a task board. The Iteration Backlog is developed and managed by the development team.

In MDAX, the progress of work is visualized and communicated by three charts: the Iteration Earned Value chart, the Project Earned Value chart, and the Milestones Slip Chart (see Figures 8, 9, and 10). There are three reasons to use earned value like charts instead of the most common burndown charts.

Figure 8. Iteration earned value chart

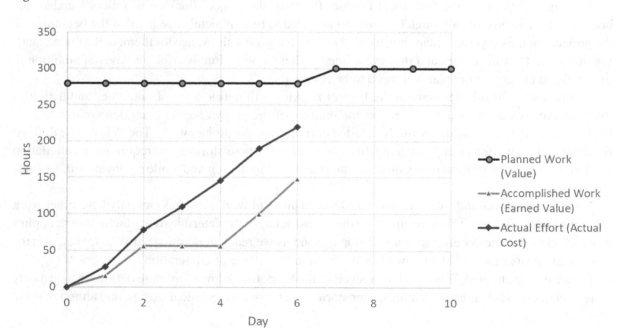

Figure 9. Project earned value chart

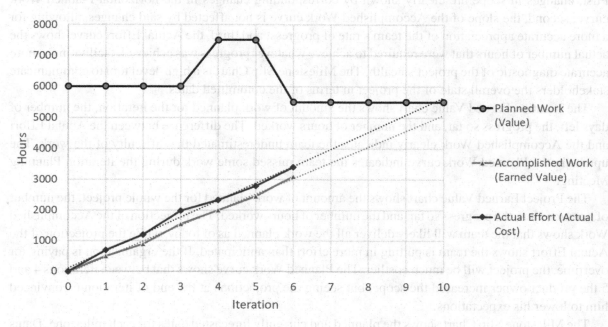

Figure 10. Milestone slip chart

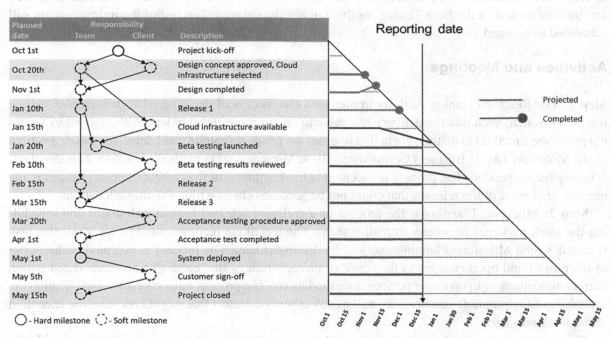

First, changes in scope are clearly shown by corresponding changes in the horizontal Planned Work curve; second, the slope of the Accomplished Work curve is not affected by said changes, allowing for a more accurate appreciation of the team's rate of progress; and third, the Actual Effort curve shows the actual number of hours that were required to achieve whatever progress was achieved, facilitating a more accurate diagnostic of the project's health. The Milestone Slip Chart is a high-level tool to communicate stakeholders the overall state of the project in terms of the committed dates.

The Iteration Earned Value chart shows the amount of work planned for the iteration, the number of days left, the progress so far, and the number of hours worked. The difference between the Actual Effort and the Accomplished Work clearly indicates the team underestimated the difficulty of the work. The uptake in the Planned Work curve indicates the team missed some work during the Iteration Planning Meeting.

The Project Earned Value chart shows the amount of work planned for the whole project, the number of iterations left, the progress so far, and the number of hours worked. The projection of the Accomplished Work shows that the team will likely deliver all the work planned as of today, while the projection of the Actual Effort shows the team is putting in more effort than anticipated. If the organization is paying for overtime, the project will be much costlier. The Planned Work curve shows that between iterations 4 and 5 the product owner increased the scope, but seeing the projections at the end of iteration 6 convinced him to lower his expectations.

The Milestone Slip Chart shows the planned and currently forecasted dates for each milestone. Dates with a round ending have been completed. The first three milestones were completed on time or ahead of schedule. Currently, we are anticipating that the cloud infrastructure will not be available on time and that the review of the Beta Testing results will also be delayed. The rest of the milestones are still scheduled as planned.

Activities and Meetings

Step 1: The Release Planning Activity implements the process of deciding what deliverables will be released together, such that the delivery has value to one or more stakeholders. Although MDAX does not prescribe a method to do this, given that releases are prime milestone candidates, the use of a variant of the MoSCoW (Agile Business Consortium, 2019; Miranda, 2011) method to protect their due dates is highly recommended. The process is executed at the beginning of the project or upon changes in the number or content of the releases that could not be accommodated within existing allocations.

Step 2: Milestone Planning is the process of identifying relevant project milestones and scheduling the work packages necessary to realize them. The technique recommended to carry out this task is called Visual Milestone Planning and will be discussed later. The process is executed at the outset of the project and upon changes to the scope or project strategy that cannot be accommodated within current allocations or upon major performance deviations. The process must take into consideration the availability of appropriate resources as well as any other constraints that might condition the execution of the work packages.

The milestone plan, instead of the immediate concerns of the product owner, will then guide the selection of which WIs to work on.

Steps 3 & 4: As WIs exist at different levels of specificity and readiness, they need to be readied before they can be selected for execution. This readying process involves: 1) breaking down those WIs whose realization efforts do not fit comfortably within the confines of an iteration into smaller WIs that do, 2) completing any details that might be needed to implement the WIs, 3) addressing external dependencies and preconditions that left unsettled could disrupt the work on the WI once this is started, and 4) "moving"[2] the resulting WIs into the Look Ahead Backlog.

The readying function is accomplished through the Look Ahead Meeting, also called the Rolling Lookahead (Cohn, 2010) in other processes, and the Work Item Refinement Meeting. Both meetings are part of the work routinely performed in every iteration besides the work on the WIs scheduled for that iteration. At the Look Ahead Meeting, the product owner and the project leader select the WIs that will need to be executed two or three iterations down the road, raising any issues that will need to be addressed prior to their execution; the product owner and project leader also follow up on previously open ones. The purpose of this is to make sure there is enough time to make ready the upcoming WIs. The decision as to which WIs to consider is informed by the Work Packages Schedule and the project status, but as the Schedule only specifies order at the work package level, there is considerable latitude regarding which WIs to select. During the Work Item Refinement Meeting, the team addresses the issues raised during the Look Ahead Meeting. The rationale for unfolding the readying function over two distinct meetings is efficiency, as there might not be readily available answers when the issues are raised, and so it makes no sense to have the whole team involved at this time.

Step 5: The Iteration Planning Meeting is the first activity of each iteration. Its purpose is to select the WIs to be worked on in accordance with the Work Packages Schedule and prepare a task plan for the iteration that is about to start. The meeting starts by selecting candidate WIs from the Look Ahead Backlog, based on what the Work Packages Schedule mandates, the WIs' readiness state, and what was accomplished during previous iterations. Once the candidate WIs have been selected, they are broken down into the tasks required for their realization, and these are estimated. The estimates are then aggregated and its total compared with the team availability to determine a feasible set of WIs. The decomposition of WIs into tasks is documented in the Iteration Backlog.

Step 6: The Daily Meeting serves two purposes: coordination and control. At this meeting, which, as it names implies, takes place every day of the iteration, members of the team discuss the work done, the obstacles faced, and the tasks to be undertaken next by whoever becomes available. From the control perspective, the fact that each team member has to report his or her progress to the group on a daily base serves to mitigate the social loafing effects that might otherwise arise because of the self-paced rhythm of the pool mechanism employed for task assignment and perhaps the lack of a strict supervisory role proper of the agile methods.

Step 7: Every iteration concludes with an Iteration Closing Meeting, which consists of three distinct activities: the deliverables demonstration, the performance review, and the work practices reflection. The goal of the deliverables demonstration activity is twofold: to get approval and feedback on the work done and to maintain stakeholders' engagement through their continued involvement. The goal of the performance review is to assess what was done and how much it took to accomplish it, so that this information could be used to decide whether it is necessary to update the plan or not. Finally, the goal of the work practices reflection activity is to identify what worked well, what did not work, and to give team members the chance to change it. Having a say over its way of working gives team members a sense of ownership, out of which grows a greater commitment to the project and a lesser need for an overt control system.

Step 8: The purpose of the Project Review Meeting is to go over the progress of the team against the plan, keeping all interested parties abreast of any change in the milestones' due dates and triggering a replanning in case of major deviations. The meeting will usually have the same periodicity as the Iteration Closing Meeting since it is there that all project-level indicators are updated.

PLANNING AND KNOWLEDGE SHARING AS MOTIVATIONAL TOOLS

While most of the activities and meetings described above are pretty straightforward, or have a counterpart in Scrum and other agile methods that one could use as reference, milestone planning, a cornerstone of MDAX, is not, and for that reason we will dedicate the rest of the space available in the chapter to deepen the discussion on it. In this and the following sections we will use interchangeably the generic term WI and its more concrete agile counterparts: epics, features, user stories, enablers, and technical stories to make the examples more tangible. The process steps are numerated 2.x since this is a decomposition of Activity 2 in Figure 4.

Agile processes are largely based on tacit knowledge and consensus decision making, so participation in the planning process, as a means to develop a shared understanding and the willingness to embrace it by those who will be executing the plan, is indispensable. Lewis (2008) expresses this forcefully: *When a few people work on a vision and then try to communicate it to others, it just never has the same impact. People to whom the vision is communicated either (1) don't get it, (2) don't agree with it, or (3) don't buy into it, because 'it is their vision, not ours'.* When the people responsible for doing the work are included in its planning, they develop better and more comprehensive plans as a consequence of the involvement of a mixture of people, which brings different perspectives to the process. They also develop a better appreciation of what to do and become more committed to it because they had the opportunity to be heard and understand how their efforts fit in into the larger picture. Successful examples of participative planning in industry are numerous: the pull planning process in the "Last Planner System" used in the construction industry (Ballard, 2000), visual planning (Jurado, 2012), Blitz Planning (Cockburn, 2004), and Cards on the Wall (Forsberg, Mooz, & H., 2005; Phillips, 2001).

The process presented here, called the Visual Milestone Planning (VMP) Method (Miranda, 2019) (see Figure 11), uses a large physical and visual canvas to promote the participation of team members (Whittaker & Schwarz, 1999) who collectively build the plan by manipulating milestones and work packages, reified through sticky notes, which must be accommodated, much like pieces in a puzzle or in a Tetris game, on a resource and time-scaled work packages scheduling canvas. The process creates a playful environment, which entices the willing, yet exposes loafing behaviors, nudging the reluctant.

We assume here that all WIs to be considered for inclusion in the milestone plan have an estimate of the effort required for its realization and that releases' content has been defined by the release planning process but not yet scheduled.

Step 2.1: The team starts by defining the milestones the plan will be based on. Milestones are chosen for its relevance to the sponsor and the team, to signal, for example, the making of a major decision, the completion of a release, or the achievement of an important process step, or to mark a commitment made to the team, such as a customer makes proprietary equipment or technology required by the project available to it. The name of each identified milestone is written on a separate sticky note, using color or some other marker to distinguish between hard and soft milestones.

Notice that in the diagram there are arrows back and forth between the definition of milestones and the product backlog. This is so because sometimes the definition of a milestone might result in the creation of a new WI that must be accounted for.

Correctly identifying the set of milestones to include in the plan is essential to its acceptance, as these milestones will become the vocabulary that will be utilized to explain the work logic to stakeholders as well as to gauge its progress. A good milestone set will include, as a minimum, the things the sponsors care about. For example, if the project sponsor wanted to have a review of the user interface before moving forward with the rest of the of the software, it would make sense that the milestone set included a "UI Approved" milestone.

Figure 11. The visual milestone planning process

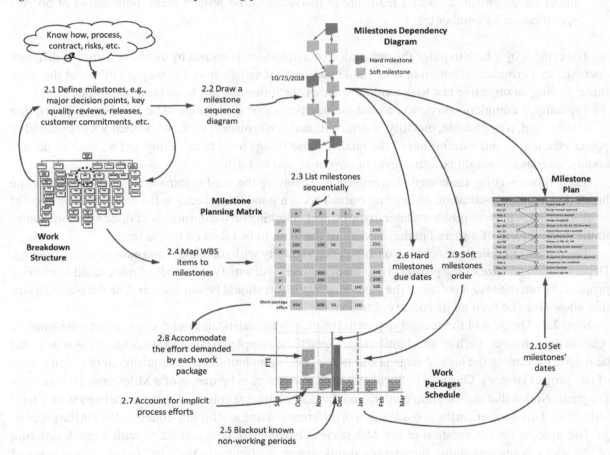

Typical sources of milestones are the project contract, the team's know how, the chosen process, risks, seasonal sales, trade shows, external commitments, and so on. Milestones tend to fall in one of three categories: the realization of an output, the attainment of a relevant project state, or the satisfaction of a commitment made to the project team by an external party. The first two types of milestones are achieved upon the completion of all work items included in the milestone's work package. In the case of a commitment to the team, the milestone is achieved when the party responsible for it fulfils its obligation. Milestones corresponding to external commitments tend not to have a work package associated with them and are an excellent instrument to synchronize work across multiple teams, each working according to its own plans.

The following are examples of the different types of milestones:

- **Outputs:** A document, a partial or total system capability, a prototype, the results of a survey
- **Desired States:** A major decision; an approval; an attainment of some kind, such as number of transactions per second or number of users trained
- **Satisfaction of Commitment:** Delivery of proprietary equipment necessary to test the software under development, a special hardware is delivered to the project team, publication of an API specification by another team

The criteria by which to judge the realization of a milestone is known by different names in different contexts: exit criteria, definition of done, and conditions of satisfaction, but they are all about the same thing: having an objective test to determine whether the milestone has been reached or not.

Typically, a completion criterion would include the list of work items to be finished; a description of its state, and, if applicable, quantity; a demonstrated performance, such as transactions per second or power efficiency; and a definition of the quality those things need to be completed at, such as defects counts, tolerances, weight budgets, level of coverage, and so forth.

Many times, writing the completion criteria will bring up the need to introduce new WIs or force the break down and re-estimation of existing ones. This is a good thing because the early identification of work gaps helps prevent problems later in the project. Working on the definition of done also contributes to the development of a shared understanding of the work to be taken on by the team.

The number of milestones chosen must balance visibility with robustness and ease of understanding. Depending on the size of the project, 10 to 50 milestones will satisfy the needs of most small to midsize projects. Given the visual nature of the method, every effort should be made to confine the plan to a size that allows it to be seen on its entirety at a glance.

Step 2.2: The goal of the second step of the process is to understand and document the milestones in relation to each other, such as which milestones need to be completed before a successor milestone could be reached. Defining the logical sequence of milestones' completion is a prerequisite for the formulation of any project strategy. One way to document such a sequence is by means of a Milestones Dependency Diagram. Notice that the diagram contains no dates, with the exception of those associated with a hard milestone. This is to permit the consideration of different staffing and timing strategies later in the process.

The process for the creation of the Milestones Dependency Diagram starts with a quick ordering of the sticky notes containing the identified milestones, according to their most obvious sequence of completion, and follows with the discussion of specific dependencies, the connecting of the corresponding milestones, and, if necessary, the reordering of the original sequence. The initial ordering of milestones according to their most obvious sequence saves the team from drawing dependencies that are implied by the transitivity of the "depends on" relationship. It is worth repeating here that the dependencies between milestones are finish to finish and not the most common start-to-finish dependencies, so the question the team needs to answer for each milestone is what milestones should be completed to be able to reach this one. A simple example of a finish-to-finish dependency is that between coding and testing. One could start writing test cases even before coding begins, but one cannot finish until the coding is done.

Two alternatives to the Milestone Dependency Diagram that the author has used to capture the pair-wise dependencies between milestones are: the use of a tilted matrix similar to the "roof of a house on quality" on top of the Milestone Planning Matrix and the use of a design structure matrix (Eppinger & Browning, 2012), followed by a partition operation to obtain a dependency rank order. The first approach is very good at quickly capturing the pairwise dependencies but does not provide visibility into the overall structure of the problem; the second, which is also good, requires the introduction of knowledge and a tool, which some practitioners might deem as foreign to an agile approach.

Step 2.3: In this step, the header of the Milestone Planning Matrix is populated with the name of the milestones. Although not strictly required by the process, listing them chronologically from left to right greatly contributes to the matrix readability and ease of work.

Step 2.4: In this step, WIs are associated with the milestones they help realize via the body of the Milestone Planning Matrix. The association is informed by the milestone definition, for example, a "Vendor Selected" milestone would be associated with all exploration enablers or technical stories leading to the selection of said vendor. The association is done by labeling a row in the planning matrix with the name of the top-most WI element whose descendants all contribute to the same milestone and recording the effort required by it at the intersection of the row with the column corresponding to the milestone with which the element is being associated. A milestone can have multiple WIs associated with it, that is, several WIs must be completed to realize the milestone. In most cases, a WI would be associated with a single milestone; there are, however, a few instances, which will be discussed later, in which it is convenient to allocate fractions of the total effort required by the WI to multiple milestones. As said before, the set of WIs associated with a milestone is called its work package.

The Milestone Planning Matrix (MPM) (see Figure 12) is a multiple domain matrix (Eppinger & Browning, 2012) that maps WIs to the milestones they help realize.

The mapping of WIs to milestones should be done at the highest possible level, that is, if all user stories within an epic contribute to a single milestone, we will map the epic, not each of the single stories, to it, but if some of the user stories contributed to one milestone, such as a release, and others to another, such as a second release, as was the illustrated by the Radigan example above, the highest level will be the user story level.

Most of the time, WIs will map naturally and entirely to a single milestone, but this will not always be the case. Assume, for example, that at the beginning of the project we define an epic to which a number of hours is allocated, but we don't know yet the user stories to be implemented and, because of our commercial strategy, we plan to develop half of those in one release and the other half in another. In this case, one solution could be to split the epic into two dummy features, assigning half the effort to one feature and the other half to the other and to map each feature to its corresponding milestone. While this would solve the problem, to create dummy features just to satisfy the choice of notation seems artificial and unnecessarily complicates the Project Backlog. Similarly, the team might introduce a refactoring epic to account for work that presumably will be required over the life of the project but is not known yet. To address these types of situations without creating dummy WIs, the proposed approach, as illustrated by row r in Figure 12, is to allocate a fraction of the total effort to each milestone to which the WI contributes.

Another special case is when we have a milestone that corresponds to a commitment made to the team by other parties, for example, the provision of a special hardware or software, the approval of a document, delivery of training, and so on. In this case, there is no work package associated with the milestone, so, as illustrated by column λ in Figure 12, the column will be empty.

The beauty of the MPM approach is that it provides a straightforward mechanism to make visible the relationship between WIs and milestones to everybody involved in the planning process, which is

Figure 12. The milestone planning matrix

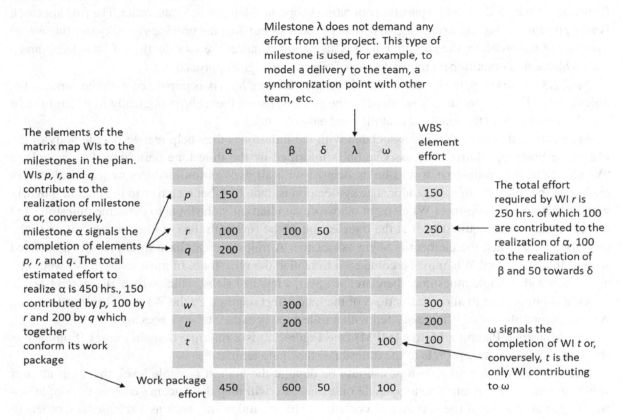

Milestone λ does not demand any effort from the project. This type of milestone is used, for example, to model a delivery to the team, a synchronization point with other team, etc.

The elements of the matrix map WIs to the milestones in the plan. WIs *p, r,* and *q* contribute to the realization of milestone α or, conversely, milestone α signals the completion of elements *p, r,* and *q*. The total estimated effort to realize α is 450 hrs., 150 contributed by *p,* 100 by *r* and 200 by *q* which together conform its work package

The total effort required by WI *r* is 250 hrs. of which 100 are contributed to the realization of α, 100 to the realization of β and 50 towards δ

ω signals the completion of WI *t* or, conversely, *t* is the only WI contributing to ω

	α	β	δ	λ	ω	WBS element effort
p	150					150
r	100	100	50			250
q	200					
w		300				300
u		200				200
t					100	100
Work package effort	450	600	50		100	

key in preventing gaps and overlaps in the plan and in the achievement of its shared understanding by stakeholders.

Step 2.5: In this step, the team will black out known non-working periods such as the holidays, training, and mandatory vacations, since in principle, there would be no work carried out during that time.

Step 2.6: In this step, the team marks hard milestones in the work package scheduling canvas. Hard milestones will act as anchor points for the plan.

Steps 2.7, 2.8, & 2.9: In these steps, the team iteratively builds the Work Packages Schedule by posting sticky notes on an empty space in the work package scheduling canvas, according to its timing and staffing strategies, such as do as much work as possible at the earliest, start slow to minimize risk and then aggressively ramp up, maintain a constant workforce, do not exceed six months, do not use more than five people, and so on; its domain and its technical and process knowledge.

Figure 13 below shows a typical Work Packages Schedule. The Work Packages Schedule is a key piece of the process since it is there that the plan materializes. As the planning involves the physical positioning of sticky notes representing the effort required by a work package on a scheduling canvas, there has to be a correspondence between the work hours represented by each note and the canvas' physical dimensions. If, for example, we choose each 3"x 3" sticky note to represent 40 hours of work, each three-inch span on the date axis of the canvas will correspond to a week, and three inches on the resources axis will correspond to a full-time equivalent (FTE) resource. Had we chosen the sticky note to represent 150 hours of work, for example, for a larger project, each three inches on the time axis would correspond to a month instead of a week. If necessary, sticky notes might be ripped off to express fractions of effort or time.

In constructing the Work Packages Schedule, we will assume the distribution of competencies in the plan matches the tasks' needs. This is a sensible assumption in an agile context that assumes either generalists or balanced, cross-functional, teams. In cases where this assumption does not hold, it would be possible to break the work into competency lanes and assign the corresponding effort to each lane. The same approach could be used to scale up the method to be used in projects with multiple teams.

First, the team must account for all the effort required by process meetings and background work, which, although not explicitly listed as WIs, will consume between 10 and 20% of the hours available.[3] The team does this by laying the corresponding amount of sticky notes at the bottom of the scheduling canvas, along the makespan of the project. After doing this, the team lays on sticky notes that correspond to the effort required by the milestones' work packages, starting with those corresponding to the hard milestones followed by those corresponding to the soft ones. All the effort required by a milestone's work package should be fitted in a time box to the left of it while respecting the milestones' order. The shape of a time box does not need to be regular. As much as possible, its contour should reflect the nature of the work performed, such as front loaded, back loaded, flat, early peaked, late peaked, and so forth. In any case, the time box's height cannot surpass at any point the amount of resources available that could reasonably be applied to the execution of the work package, nor can the cumulative height of any stacked time boxes go above the total number of resources available for the project. The time box's length would be such that the area enclosed by it is equal to the work package's effort. Time boxes cannot overlap, as this would imply that somebody is actually performing, not switching, between two tasks at the same time.

The leftmost side of the time box will indicate the time at which work on the milestone is planned to start, and the rightmost will mark the date by which they should be reached at risk of delaying other milestones or the whole project. If somehow the plan is not feasible, for example, if there are not enough resources or the hard milestone dates cannot be met, the project scope should be renegotiated, the work approach should be reformulated, or the constraints should be lifted.

Step 2.10: In this step, the plan is completed by sprucing the milestone sequence diagram, assigning due dates to the soft milestones, adding responsibility information, and integrating all of them in a common document. The approximate due date for each soft milestone is found by looking in the Work Packages Schedule for the date aligned with the right edge of the time box associated with the milestone. Hard milestones have, by definition, a set date.

MILESTONE PLANNING EXAMPLE

The example presented here corresponds to the development of a milestone plan for a fictitious online book publisher called AmazonLight and is organized around the method's steps shown in Figure 11. In illustrating the steps, we will use tables and stylized diagrams, when in practice we will use sticky notes and large-sized papers, which will be physically manipulated and drawn upon.

AmazonLight has asked your company to develop an ecommerce site to support the sale of the books it publishes and, after some conversations with its top brass, you sketched the following notes:

Figure 13. Work packages schedule

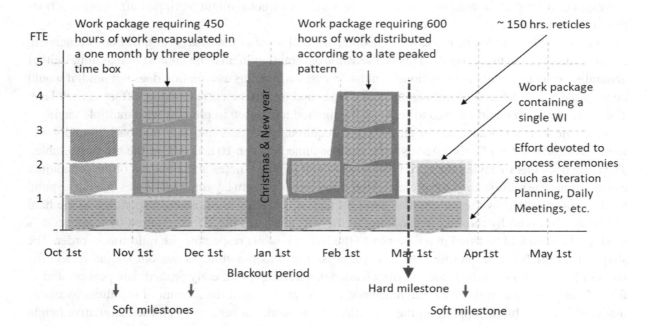

- The system shall provide the functionality described in Table 2.
- The project must include a beta testing period to validate the site design.
- AmazonLight will not accept deployment until a system-wide acceptance test is satisfactorily completed.
- Sign-off will follow satisfactory deployment of the system.
- Would like to have at least three software releases: one to collect users' feedback via beta testing, another one to confirm the progress of the system towards the launch date, and the final one to complete the system with minimum risk to the launch date.
- The customer is preparing to launch its business in May of next year, so he would like the system to be ready at least one month before that.

For its part, your company:

- Cannot start the project until the end of September.
- Will assign four developers to work on the project.

Based on the requirements above and its professional knowledge, the development team produced the Work Breakdown Structure shown in Figure 14, describing its understanding of the project's scope and the estimated effort required for its execution. Although not shown here, the customer and the team conducted a release-planning session where they agreed on the content of each of three releases. Release 1 will include browsing by product category, looking inside the book, adding books to a cart, checkout functionality, and the design and implementation of the system data base. Release 2 will include the

Table 2. Required functionality for AmazonLight project

Id	User Story
1	As a customer I would like to browse the product catalog according to categories to find items I know what they are but not their names
2	As a customer I would like to browse the book catalog according to genre in order to find a book in a specific category
3	As a customer I would like to browse through the book's chapters to see if I like it before purchasing
4	As a customer I would like to add a book to a purchase cart so I can buy several products in a single visit to the store
5	As a customer I would like to remove a book from my purchase cart if I change my mind about purchasing it
6	As a customer I would like to choose between different shipping methods to minimize speed of delivery, cost and packaging options
7	As a user I would like to check out my purchase so I can receive the goods purchased
8	As a user I would like to pay for the purchase with my credit card so I can receive the goods
9	As a user I would like to pay for the purchase with PayPal so I can receive the goods
10	As the seller I would like to submit the transaction to the corresponding financial partner so I can receive the proceeds from a purchase

following user stories: browsing by book genre, removing books from a cart, and selecting shipping method. Finally, Release 3 will include entering payment details and processing payments.

Step 2.1: After considering what was important to communicate to the customer about the advance of the project, the team chose the milestones listed in Table 3. Beware that the solution is not unequivocal. While there are self-evident milestones like project kick-off, software releases, and the client request for a beta test, others are created by the team, based on its best judgment as to what is important and what is not. The completion criteria associated with each milestone define its meaning and help identify which WIs should be mapped to them.

Steps 2.2: To construct the Milestone Dependency Diagram, we start by organizing the milestones identified in the previous step in what seems like the most logical sequence, and then we identify and connect them using finish-to-finish dependencies. Figure 15 shows one possible Milestone Dependency Diagram for the project. The way to read the diagram is as follows: milestone x cannot be completed until all its direct predecessors have been completed. For example, the cloud infrastructure cannot be made available until the cloud infrastructure is selected, and the Beta testing cannot be launched until the infrastructure is made available and Release 1 is completed. Notice that the dependency chart says nothing about when the preparation work for it ought to start.

Step 2.3: In this step, we just list the milestones from left to right as headers of the MPM.

Step 2.4: In this step, we assign WIs to their corresponding milestones. Although this tends to be a pretty mechanical process whose value resides on the transparency it brings to the planning process, there are a number of points worth highlighting (see Table 4). The first is that the milestone "Cloud Infrastructure Available" has no WI associated with it. This is so because, although the work to select the infrastructure is part of the scope of the project, the effort to provision it is not. The reason to include it as a milestone is that it represents a commitment made to the project team by the customer, so they can beta test the system, and to signal that a delay in fulfilling this promise could affect the completion date of such a test. The second is the case of the "Refactoring & Feedback" WI, in which a certain number

Figure 14. Work breakdown structure for the amazonlight development

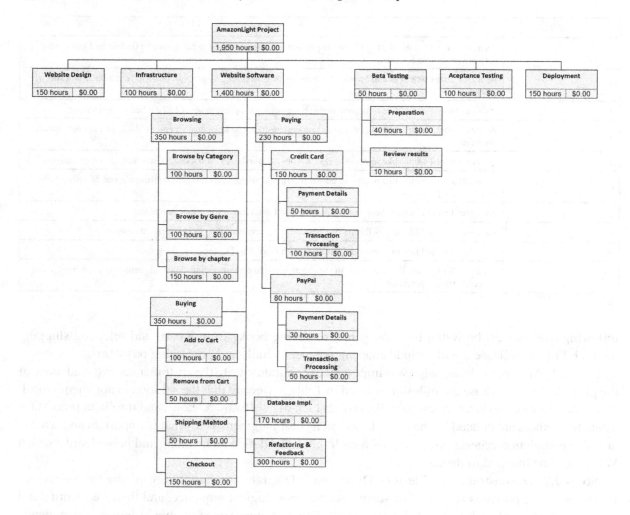

of hours were allocated to Release 2 and others to Release 3. We did not allocate any effort to Release 1, because it was assumed the refactoring would be the result of introducing new functionality and feedback from beta testing in the later releases. There are multiple criteria on how to allocate effort to each milestone. In this case, we thought it would be best to allocate more hours to Release 3 because in it we will remove all technical debt, and we will have to accommodate any changes resulting from beta testing. The third point of interest is the "Paying" WI. In this case, we could have listed individual WIs as we did for Release 1 and 2. We did not do that because all WIs subordinated to "Paying" contributed to the same milestone, and so the resulting matrix is simpler. That being said, if one wanted greater visibility of the allocations, listing all individual WIs would be perfectly acceptable as well.

Step 2.5: In this step, we black out any known non-working periods involving the whole team, such as holidays, closings, and special vacation periods.

Step 2.6: By definition, to be successful, a plan must satisfy its hard milestones, so they tend to act as anchoring points for the whole project. The accommodation of the work elements in the scheduling canvas starts by marking on it any hard milestones the project might have.

Table 3. Potential project milestones

Milestone	Hard date	Completion criteria
Project kick-off	October of this year	Development team assembled, meeting with project sponsor concluded
Design concept approved		Information architecture and UI designed and approved by sponsor
Infrastructure selected		Cloud provider selected. Consider AWS, Azure, Google Cloud, and at least one other
Design completed		Feedback from sponsor incorporated into design
Cloud infrastructure available		Cloud production environment available. AmazonLight must provide
Release 1		Functionality is ready and tested at 90% coverage and working in production configuration. No broken menus or links. Includes: browsing by product category, looking inside the book, adding books to a cart, checkout functionality, and the design and implementation of the system data base
Beta testing launched		Release 1 software made available to beta users. User behavior hypotheses defined. Website instrumentation working
Release 2		Functionality is ready and tested at 90% coverage and working in production configuration. Includes: browsing by book genre, removing books from a cart, and selecting shipping method
Beta testing results reviewed		All insights arising from the beta testing disposed
Release 3		Functionality is ready and tested at 90% coverage and working in production configuration. Changes resulting from beta testing implemented. Technical debt removed. Includes: entering payments details and processing payments
Acceptance testing procedure approved		Acceptance test suite approved by sponsor. Includes at least one positive, one negative, and one invalid test case for each functionality
Acceptance test completed		All acceptance tests passed, with no objection from sponsor
System deployed	Beginning of May next year	All functionality running in production environment, operators trained. System must run for at least 15 consecutive days without a fault attributable to software
Customer sign-off		Customer accepts ownership of the software
Project closed		Project postmortem executed, all records archived

Steps 2.7, 2.8 & 2.9: The goal of these steps is to establish a time frame in which the work represented by each work package could be executed. To do this, the team labels a number of sticky notes proportional to the effort required by the work package and accommodates them in an appropriate empty space on the work packages scheduling canvas. The team starts by accommodating the effort corresponding to MDAX recurring activities, followed by the work packages connected to hard milestones, and finally those corresponding to the soft milestones, in the order dictated by the milestone dependency chart, and using the team's best judgment. If necessary, the team might intersperse buffers to protect critical milestones.

Figure 3 above showed a possible Work Packages Schedule for the AmazonLight project that was constructed following this process. Notice that due to the holiday period extending from late December to early January the effort for the Release 1 work package was spread over two months by splitting the sticky notes. Since there is no work associated with "Cloud Infrastructure Available," the team might choose where best to put it within the order constraints. Should the plan have not been feasible, such as not meeting its hard deadline (in this case, the deployment in early April), the team could ask for addi-

Figure 15. Milestone dependency diagram for the Amazonlight project

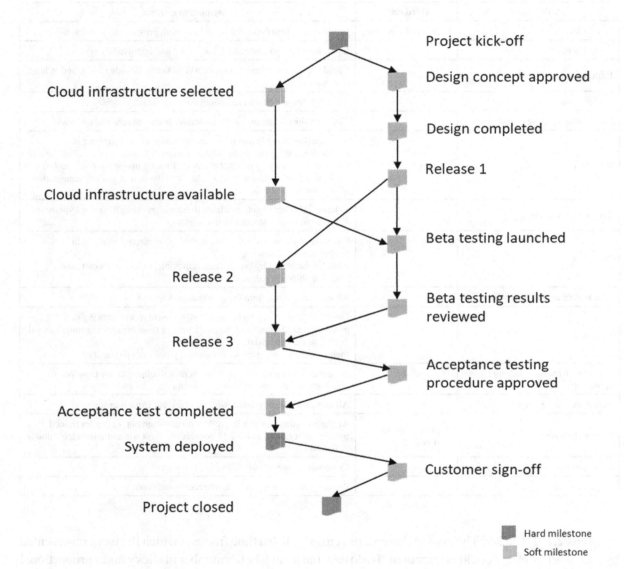

tional resources; reorganize the work, for example, relax the condition of not doing development work before the design concept has been approved; negotiate the scope; change the completion deadline; or just take its chances.

Step 2.10: In this step, the milestone plan is completed by reading the approximate date the work associated with each milestone will be completed from the Work Packages Schedule and assigning it as the due date for the milestone. The resulting plan is shown in Figure 2 above.

Table 4. Milestone planning matrix for the AmazonLight project

Id	WI	Project kickoff	Design concept approved	Infrastructure selected	Design completed	Release 1	Infrastructure available	Beta testing launched	Release 2	Beta testing results reviewed	Release 3	Acceptance testing procedure approved	Acceptance test completed	System deployed	Customer sign-off	Project closed	WI effort
1	Website design		140		10												150
2	Infrastructure selection			100													100
3	Browse by category					100											100
4	Browse by genre								100								100
5	Browse by chapters					150											150
6	Add to cart					100											100
7	Remove a book from purchase basket								50								50
8	Choose shipping method								50								50
9	Check out purchase					150											150
10	Paying										230						230
11	Database Impl.					170											170
12	Beta testing - Preparation							40									50
13	Beta testing - Review									10							
14	Refactoring & Feedback								100		200						300
15	Acceptance testing											50	50				100
16	System Deployment													150			150
	Work package effort	0	140	100	10	670	0	40	300	10	430	50	50	150	0	0	1950

CONCLUSION

Developing a complete activity plan at the outset of a project has been demonstrated to be ineffective. This does not mean however, we should not plan, but rather, we need to find a balance between the structure needed to organize and guide the work, with the need to adjust it as we progress. This is the essence of hybrid approaches. The MDAX framework described in this chapter does that by combining milestone planning with a Scrum-like execution approach in a seamless way.

MDAX has been taught, and successfuly applied, by over two years at the Master of Software Engineering Program at Carnegie Mellon University by students working in groups of four or five, on year-long, real-world projects.

ACKNOWLEDGMENT

The authors offer a special thank you to Raul Martinez, Gaetano Lombardi, and Diego Fontdevila for their advice, contributions of knowledge, and investments of time to discuss earlier versions of this manuscript.

REFERENCES

Agile Business Consortium. (2019). *Chapter 10: MoSCoW Prioritisation*. Retrieved from https://www. agilebusiness.org/page/ProjectFramework_10_MoSCoWPrioritisation

Andersen, E. (1996). Warning: Activity planning is hazardous to your project's health! *International Journal of Project Management, 14*(2), 89–94. doi:10.1016/0263-7863(95)00056-9

Andersen, E., Grude, K., & Haug, T. (2009). *Goal directed project management* (4th ed.). Kogan Page.

Ballard, H. (2000). *The last planner system of production control* (Dissertation). Birmingham: University of Birmingham.

Brechner, E. (2015). *Agile project management with Kanban*. Microsoft Press.

Cockburn, A. (2004). *Crystal clear: A human-powered methodology for small teams*. Addison Wesley.

Cohn, M. (2010). *Succeeding with Agile*. Addison Wesley.

Eppinger, S., & Browning, T. (2012). *Design structure matrix methods and applications*. MIT Press. doi:10.7551/mitpress/8896.001.0001

Forsberg, K., Mooz, H., & H., C. (2005). *Visualizing project management: Models and frameworks for mastering complex systems* (3rd ed.). Hoboken, NJ: Wiley.

Haugan, D. (2008). *Work reakdown Structures for Projects, Programs, and Enterprises*. Management Concepts.

Jurado, M. (2012). *Visual Planning in Lean Product Development*. KTH Royal Institute of Technology.

Kneuper, R. (2018). *Software Processes and Life Cycle Models*. Springer. doi:10.1007/978-3-319-98845-0

Kuhrmann, M., Diebold, P., Münch, J., Tell, P., Garousi, V., & Felderer, M. (2017). Hybrid Software and System Development in Practice: Waterfall, Scrum, and Beyond. *Proceedings of the 2017 International Conference on Software and System Process*. 10.1145/3084100.3084104

Lewis, J. (2008). *Mastering Project Management* (2nd ed.). McGraw-Hill.

Miranda, E. (2011). Time Boxing Planning: Buffered Moscow Rules. *Software Engineering Notes, 36*(6), 1–5. doi:10.1145/2047414.2047428

Miranda, E. (2019). Milestone Planning: A Participatory and Visual Approach. *Journal of Modern Project Management, 7*(2).

Phillips, D. (2001). *Cards-on-the-Wall Sessions*. Retrieved from Dr. Dobbs: https://www.drdobbs.com/cards-on-the-wall-sessions/184414750

Radigan, D. (2019). *The Product Backlog: Your Ultimate To Do List*. Retrieved from https://www.atlassian.com/agile/scrum/backlogs

Whittaker, S., & Schwarz, H. (1999). Meetings of the Board: The Impact of Scheduling Medium on Long Term Group Coordination in Software Development. *Computer Supported Cooperative Work, 8*(3), 175–205. doi:10.1023/A:1008603001894

KEY TERMS AND DEFINITIONS

Hard Milestones: Milestones that, if not accomplished by a set date, usually externally imposed, lose all or most of their value or result in severe penalties.

Iteration Backlog: A list of all the WIs to be worked on in the present iteration plus the tasks required for their realization.

Look-Ahead Backlog: A precedence-ordered list of all the WIs ready, or in the process of being readied, to be executed in upcoming iterations.

Milestone: An event that marks the realization of an outcome, the attainment of a verifiable and relevant project state, or the fulfillment of a commitment made to the team.

Milestone Plan: A plan for a project formulated in terms of the relevant states or sub-objectives the project must go through on its way to achieve its objective, not the the tasks that must be executed to achieve them.

Project Backlog: A hierarchical enumeration of all the outputs: functionality, documentation, infrastructure, gadgets, services, and so on, to be delivered to the customer to meet the project objectives, and the work necessary to produce them. Each descending level represents an increasingly detailed definition of the project work.

Soft Milestones: Milestones whose completion dates result from the planning process. They might be associated with penalties or other liabilities after a statement of work is agreed upon, but, in principle, they are discretionary.

Work Item: Any element in the project backlog.

Work Package: The set of work items associated with a milestone.

ENDNOTES

[1] Traditionally, this type of Work Breakdown Structure has been called a product-oriented Work Breakdown Structure. For an excellent description on the process for creating them, refer to the work of Haugan (2008).

[2] "moving" is just a metaphor for showing the WI in the Look Ahead Backlog, it only implies the physical movement in the case of a physical implementation. In the case of a digital implementation, it will suffice with the change of a state variable indicating the WI must now be included in the Look Ahead Backlog view.

[3] $\sim \dfrac{\begin{matrix} DurationIterationPlanningMeeting + DurationDailyMeeting \times NumberMeetings \\ + DurationIterationClosingMeeting + DurationWorkItemRefinementMeeting \end{matrix}}{HoursPerPersonPerIteration} \times 100$

Chapter 2
Analysis of the Evolution of Eight VSEs Using the ISO/ IEC 29110 to Reinforce Their Agile Approaches

Mirna Muñoz
 https://orcid.org/0000-0001-8537-2695
Centro de Investigación en Matemáticas A.C., Mexico

Jezreel Mejía
 https://orcid.org/0000-0003-0292-9318
Centro de Investigación en Matemáticas A.C., Mexico

Claude Y. Laporte
 https://orcid.org/0000-0002-3453-740X
École de Technologie Supérieure, Canada

ABSTRACT

Most very small entities (VSEs) develop software for medium and large companies and organizations. This situation creates an opportunity for them to become key players in the production chain by providing quality software within schedule and budget. A feature of most VSEs is that they do not have experience in the implementation of engineering standards due to specific features such as lack of support, lack of resources, time-consuming, and the use of agile approaches. This chapter presents an analysis of a set of eight VSEs that used agile approaches to develop software and that have implemented the software Basic profile of the ISO/IEC 29110 to reinforce their agile approach. The results show that ISO/IEC 29110 were easily implemented and helped VSEs to improve their agile approaches while helping them to understand the importance of formalizing some key artifacts produced during the development of a software product.

DOI: 10.4018/978-1-7998-4165-4.ch002

INTRODUCTION

Nowadays Very Small Entities (VSEs), which can be an enterprise, an organization (e.g. public or non-profit organization), a project or a department having up to 25 people (ISO/IEC, 2011), are a key element in the software development chain since they develop software for most medium and large companies and organizations such as government agencies.

This fact motivates VSEs to develop quality software products to keep its competitiveness in the software industry. However, most of the time they do not have experience in the implementation of models and/or engineering standards due to their specific features such as lack of support, lack of resources and time-consuming (Muñoz, et al., 2019).

Besides, most VSEs prefer the use agile approaches to develop software (Muñoz, et al., 2017) because they believe that the use of proven software engineering practices is not appropriate for their environments, this fact contributes to inefficiencies in the development of software such as quality, cost and time.

Moreover, the implementation of proven practices of software quality models and standards in real environments of software development organizations, especially in VSEs represent an actual challenge (Sánchez-Gordon, de Amescua, O'Connor, & Larrucea, 2017) (Larrucea, O'Connor, Colomo-Palacios, & Laporte, 2016) (Muñoz, et al., 2019b).

As a solution, the ISO Working Group 24 developed the ISO/IEC 29110 series of standards and guides, which aims to help VSEs in the implementation of proven practices related to the Project Management Process and Systems or Software Implementation Process (Laporte & O'Connor, 2017).

However, the lack of knowledge and experience in the implementation and use of proven practices provided by quality models and standards becomes a common barrier in VSEs.

One of the main features of the ISO/IEC 29110 standard is that it can be adapted to the development cycle of most VSEs. Therefore, this chapter aims to present an analysis of a set of trials in eight VSEs that used agile approaches to develop software and that implemented the software Basic profile of the ISO/IEC 29110 to reinforce their agile approach.

After the introduction, this chapter is structured as follows: section 2 presents the background of this research composed of key concepts as well as related research works; section 3 shows the evolution of the eight VSEs that reinforced their agile approaches using the software Basic profile of the ISO/IEC 29110; section 4 presents the benefits obtained and difficulties that the VSEs encountered during the reinforcement of their agile approaches; section 5 provides the next steps of this research, including the development of an ISO/IEC 29110 agile guide; finally, section 6 presents the conclusions.

Background

This section covers 2 concepts in which this research work is based, i.e., the ISO/IEC 29110 series and agile approaches. Besides, the section provides a set of related works in which the benefits of the implementation of ISO/IEC 29110 are provided.

Key Concepts

ISO/IEC 29110 Series

The ISO/IEC 29110 series of systems and software engineering standards and guides were developed to help VSEs to implement proven practices to get advantages such as increasing their product quality, reducing their development time and help them develop their product within budget and schedule.

The main features of the ISO/IEC 29110 series for VSEs developing non-critical software are:

1. It has 4 software profiles that VSEs can use according to their goals (ISO/IEC, 2011):

    a. *Entry profile* to be selected if the VSE works on small projects such as six person-month effort or VSEs are start-ups;

    b. *Basic profile* to be selected if the VSE develops a single project by a work team at a time;

    c. *Intermediate profile* to be selected if the VSE develops more than one project in parallel with more than one work team; and

    d. *Advanced profile* to be selected if the VSE wants to grow and maintain as an independent competitive development business.

    The software Basic profile is the only profile, at the moment, in which a VSE can be certified.

2. It has, as a foundation for the 4 profiles, two main processes (ISO/IEC, 2011):

    a. The *Project Management process* aims to establish and carry out all activities related to the project management that are needed to complete a project in a systematic way. It provides 4 activities: project planning, project plan execution, project assessment and control, and project closure.

    b. The *Software Implementation process* aims to execute the activities related to software development in a systematic way and according to the specified or new requirements. It contains six activities: software implementation initiation, software requirements analysis, software architecture and design, software construction, software integration, and test and product delivery.

3. It can be used to establish processes in VSEs using any development approach or methodology.

4. It has been developed using a set of process elements such as objective, activities, tasks, roles and work products.

Figure 1 shows an overview of the 2 processes and 10 activities of the software Basic Profile of the ISO/IEC 29110.

To get a certification to this standard, a VSE must demonstrate that is achieved the 7 objectives of Project Management process and the 7 objectives of the Software Implementation process (ISO/IEC, 2011):

*   **Project Management Process Objectives:** (1) to develop a project plan for the execution of the project according to the statement of work. This plan should contain the identification and estimation of the task and resources necessary to complete the project; (2) to monitor the project progress versus the project plan and recording the project progress and performing corrective

Figure 1. Overview of the software Basic profile of ISO/IEC 29110.
Source: (Laporte & O'Connor, 2016) and (Laporte & O'Connor, 2017)

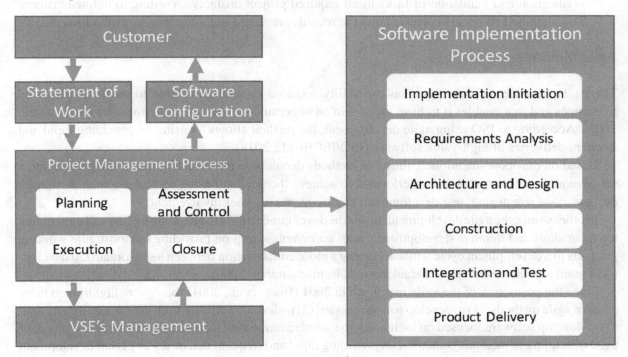

actions if need to correct detected deviations. Besides, at the end of the project there should be documented customer acceptance; (3) to address change requests when a change arises. Besides, it should be evaluated regarding cost, schedule and technical impact; (4) to carry out meetings with both customers and the work team and registering and tracking agreements; (5) to identify risk at the beginning and during the project execution; (6) to develop a version control strategy, to control project artifacts and that allows managing software configuration and; (7) to perform software quality assurance to assure that products and the processes comply with the project plan and the requirements specification.

- **Software Implementation Process Objectives:** (1) to perform tasks of the activities according to the current project plan; (2) to define software requirements analyzing their correctness and testability. Besides, they should be approved by the customer, included in the baseline and communicated; (3) to develop software architecture and detailed design, which describes software components and internal and external interfaces of them and located them in the baseline. Besides, their consistency and traceability with software requirements are established; (4) to produce software components defined in the design. Besides, unit tests are defined and executed to verify their consistency with the requirements and design and establish their traceability records among them; (5) to produce the software by integrating software components and verify it using test cases and test procedures. The results should be recorded in the test report. Besides, the founded defects are corrected and its consistency and traceability with the design are established; (6) to integrate the requirements specification agreed with the customer, including user, operation and maintenance documentation. Besides, it should be baselined and stored in the project repository and the changes to software configuration are needed change requests should be initiated; and (7) To perform verification and validation of tasks to all required project artifacts according to defined criteria. The identified errors are corrected and the records are stored in the verification/validation results.

Agile Methods

The Agile Alliance defines "Agile" as the ability acquired by an organization to create and respond to changes and that enables it to have success in an uncertain and turbulent environment (Beck, et al., 2001). According to ISO using agile development, the method allows focusing on providing rapid and frequent deliveries of high-value software (ISO/IEC/IEEE, 2018).

Based on the above-mentioned, the agile methods decompose the overall scope of the project into a set of requirements or work to be performed to achieve the goal and using techniques such as simpler designs, code refactoring, test-development, and frequent customer involvement.

In other words, the agile development means the development of software performed by self-organizing teams in short and iterative development cycles and emphasizing on providing demonstrable working products in a development cycle while achieving a close collaboration between a self-organized development team and the customers (Chetankumar & Ramachandran, 2009).

Since the promotion of the agile manifesto in 2001 (Beck, et al., 2001) there were highlighted three goals of agile methods: (1) to develop software faster; (2) to develop software in an incrementally way and; (3) to develop software focused on increasing the satisfaction of the customer. Nowadays, the concept of agile development methods is focused on providing rapid and frequent deliveries by giving development teams the ability to have a rapid and flexible response to requirement change (ISO/IEC/IEEE, 2018).

To achieve these goals, the agile manifesto provides a conceptual framework of practices and principles (Beck, et al., 2001). However, this manifesto is not well understood by organizations, besides they do not get the adequate knowledge regarding the correct implementation of agile methods, neither in the use of software engineering proven practices, this fact contributes to inefficiencies in their development software such as quality, cost and time (Muñoz, et al., 2019b).

Since 2001, several agile methods have been developed, the most popular methods are Rapid Application Development (RAD); eXtreme Programming (XP), Scrum and Feature-Driven Development (FDD) (Harleen, et al., 2014).

Related Works

Authors around the world have published success cases in the implementation of ISO/IEC 29110, all of the next reported implementations have demonstrated very good results, such as reduce rework, access to new customers, increase quality, improve their processes among others next a set of successful implementations are briefly mentioned:

Laporte and O'Connor (2016) reported a set of three success cases of the implementation of ISO/IEC 29110 in different countries: one from IT start-up from Peru and six from Canadian (two IT start-ups, one of them with location in Canada and Tunisia; one software team in a large Canadian financial institution's IT division; one software development team in a Large Canadian Automotive domain; one IT Division of a Large Canadian transportation enterprise and one division of a large American engineering company). The paper focuses on demonstrating the benefits of implementing practices provided by

ISO/IEC 29110, such as properly plan and execute or conduct projects and the development of products without interfering with the creativity of developers.

O'Connor and Laporte (2012) reported pilot projects one from Canada conducted with an IT department; one from Belgium in a VSE; one in France that builds and sells counting systems about the frequenting of natural spaces and public sites. It also mentions some projects executed by graduates and undergraduates' students of the École de technologie supérieure (ÉTS), one in the software development department of an engineering firm and another one from a website developed by a VSE. The paper focuses on the benefits of using ISO/IEC 29110, then the main benefits discussed in this paper are the reinforcement in the definition of new processes, the start point toward the implementation of improvements in the organizations, the use of deployment packages to implement the ISO/IEC 29110.

Díaz, de Jesús, Melendez and Davila (Díaz, et al., 2016) reported the implementation of ISO/IEC 29110 in two very small software development companies in Perú, both with eight employees. The paper list the activities performed to implement the ISO/IEC 29110. Besides, it presents in more detail the way the VSEs were assessed and a list of experiences that could help to start other improvement initiatives. The paper highlights as the main benefit of the implementation of ISO/IEC 29110 for the VSEs are providing the templates to be used as well as the definition of the processes to be used in new projects.

Laporte, Muñoz, Mejía and O'Connor (Laporte, et al., 2018) a previous work of the authors of this chapter, reported the implementation of ISO/IEC 29110 in eleven VSEs: one IT start-up; one IT start-up with locations in Canada and Tunisia, one development team at a Canadian IT start-up; four VSEs in México; one software developers at a power train manufacturer; one project teams in a large engineering company's Transmission & Distribution of Electricity division; one software team at a large public utility and a software team in a large financial institution's IT division. The paper is focused on providing an overview of the as-it situation of VSEs and the results of implementing the ISO/IEC 29110. Besides, this paper highlights the importance to reduce the gap between academia and industry by producing the transfer instruments from researchers to practitioners.

Castillo-Salinas, et al (Castillo-Salinas, et al., 2020) reported the results of the implementation of a subset of the Software implementation process of the Basic profile of ISO/IEC 29110 in four teams of students of Ecuador. They concluded that teams using the ISO/IEC TR 29110–5–1–2 guide had a better performance and quality software than those not using it. They also mentioned that VSEs could be more competitive and it could open new niches in national or international markets. The paper provides the instruments used to get the data for the quality evaluation of the software process and the analysis of the results. Besides, it provides the difficulties encountered in teams following the ISO/IEC 29110 and a set of recommendations for improving the quality of the implementation of the SI process.

It is important to mention that all of the related works have demonstrated excellent benefits in the implementation of the Basic profile of the ISO/IEC 29110. However, only one of them (Díaz, et al., 2016) focuses on listing the activities to implement ISO/IEC 29110, but none of them present or focus on the method description and execution. Most of them highlight the detected problems and their evolution toward the reinforcement of their agile environment, this becomes relevant since most of the VSEs certified are from Mexico (46 of a total of 53 VSEs), especially from the state of Zacatecas where are located 20 VSEs (NYCE, 2020).

The contribution of this paper regarding the current state of the art is that it provides: (1) the method developed to implement ISO/IEC 29110 that could be used as transfer instrument to reduce the gap among academic and industry; (2) the analysis of common problems that VSEs using agile environments could have; (3) the analysis of how the implementation of practices from ISO/IEC 29110 helped the reinforcement of their agile environment in a pace supported by them and the most important allowing them to continue using their agile practices and (5) Finally, this paper highlights the benefits and difficulties that the VSEs understudy had regarding the implementation of ISO/IEC 29110.

EVOLUTION OF THE EIGHT VSES BY USING THE BASIC PROFILE OF ISO/IEC 29110 TO REINFORCE THEIR AGILE APPROACH

This section shows the analysis performed to the evolution that the VSEs under study had with the implementation of the ISO/IEC 29110 series to reinforce their agile approaches. This section starts with a brief description of the method used to implement the ISO/IEC 29110 in the VSEs. After, the VSEs participating in this project are described. Finally, the analysis of their evolution is presented.

Method Used to Implement the ISO/IEC 29110 in the Eight VSEs

To perform the adoption and implementation of the software Basic profile of ISO/IEC 29110 in the VSEs, a six-step method was used (Muñoz, et al., 2019), (Muñoz, Mejía & Laporte, 2019). Figure 2 shows the six-step method and then each step is described. As Figure 2 shows, to implement the method, a set of meetings and work sessions with VSEs were held.

Figure 2. Six-step method adapted from (Muñoz, et al., 2019) and (Muñoz, Mejía & Laporte, 2019).

1. **Train the team in Software Basic profile of ISO/IEC 29110 and Process Definition:** This step aims to perform, on the one hand, a set of workshops and seminars focused on the training of ISO/IEC 29110 in which the concepts, the structure, the processes of the software Basic profile of ISO/IEC 29110 and some examples of its implementation are presented and discussed. On the other hand, two sessions focused on process definition were performed, in which the process elements, identification of best practices of their processes and the formalization of their processes.

2. **Identify and Formalize the VSE's Practices in their Current Processes:** This step aims to formalize the current organizational practices regarding the Project Management process and the Software Implementation process.

3. **Identify the Actual Problems and Gaps that the VSEs Have:** This step aims to identify problems each VSE has with their actual way of developing software, regarding the Project Management and Software Implementation processes.

4. **Map the VSE's Current Processes to the ISO/IEC 29110 Processes:** This step aims to perform the mapping between the VSE's current processes and the processes of the software Basic profile of ISO/IEC 29110.

5. **Select and Adapt the Practices Provided by the ISO/IEC 29110 to Improve the VSE's Processes:** This step aims to help VSEs to implement practices that help them to improve their development processes according to the previously identified problems and gaps.

6. **Review the VSE's Improved Processes as well as Their Implementation in a Project:** This step aims to evaluate how the VSE is using its improved processes in a project so that it allows identifying the non-conformities respect to the standard.

Description of the Eight VSEs

In this section, the results of 8 VSEs under study are reported to analyze their evolution in the reinforcement of their agile environments by using the software Basic profile of the ISO/IEC 29110. Table 1 provides a brief description of the VSEs that participated to this research providing the next data: VSE identification number (VSE ID, column 1 on the left side); the type of agile approach used to develop software (column 2); the software product used in the certification process of the Basic profile of ISO/IEC 29110 (column 3); their detected problems (column 4); and the number of employees that the VSE has (column 5).

It is important to mention that the problems presented in column 4 were detected in step 3 of the performed method, by having a work-session meeting in which the VSE provides an overview of their current software development process and we applied as instrument an Excel spreadsheet based on ISO/IEC 29110 (activities, tasks, and work products).

Evolution Analysis

It is important to mention that the implementation of the method, which was presented in the subsection *method used to implement the Software Basic profile of the ISO/IEC 29110 in the VSEs*, was carried out in four months' period and by performing a set of workshops as well as a set of 2 to 6 meetings depending on the experience of the VSE regarding the use of models and standards: VSE-1 had 5 meetings; VSE-2 had 6 meetings; VSE-3 had 5 meetings; VSE-4 had 5 meetings; VSE-5 had 5 meetings; VSE-6 had 5 meetings; VSE-7 had 2 meetings and; finally, VSE-8 had 4 meetings.

Table 1. Description of the eight VSEs

VSE-ID	Agile approach	Developed product	Detected problems	# of employees
VSE-1	None, but using some agile practices	Embedded software	• Definition of delivery instructions. • Carry out planned activities. • Project efforts and costs. • Integration of a project plan. • Control of some work products produced by the project. • Outdated project information. • Record Project reviews. • Traceability records. • Adequate risk management is not performed. • Design or update and perform unit cases. • Management of change requests is not performed. • Management of corrective actions is not performed. • Project artifacts verification. • Project artifacts validation. • Use of test cases and test procedures. • Results of test are not registered. • Perform repository backups. • User, operation and maintenance documentation are not developed. • Formalization of project closure.	2
VSE-2	Hybrid using TSP-Scrum	Automation of the quality management system	• Definition of delivery instructions. • Carry out planned activities. • Record the project reviews. • Project efforts and costs. • Control of some work products produced by the project. • Outdated project information. • Adequate risk management is not performed. • Management of change requests is not performed. • Version control strategy. • Record the project reviews. • Traceability records. • Design or update and perform unit cases. • Project artifacts verification. • Project artifacts validation. • Perform repository backups. • User, operation and maintenance documentation are not developed. • Formalization of project closure.	5
VSE-3	Scrum	System of inventory control	• Definition of delivery instructions. • Adequate risk management is not performed. • Project efforts and costs. • Version control strategy. • Control of some work products produced by the project. • Record the project reviews. • Traceability records. • Management of change requests is not performed. • Outdated project information. • Management of corrective actions is not performed. • Design or update and perform unit cases. • Results of tests are not registered. • Project artifacts verification. • Project artifacts validation. • Perform repository backups. • User, operation and maintenance documentation are not developed. • Formalization of project closure.	5
VSE-4	Scrum	Medical consultation management	• Statement of work. • Definition of delivery instructions. • An adequate risk management is not performed. • Control of some work products produced by the project. • Outdated project information. • Version control strategy. • Traceability records. • Implementation environment. • Management of change requests are not performed. • Management of corrective actions is not performed. • Record the project reviews. • Design or update and perform unit cases. • Results of test are not registered. • Project artifacts verification. • Project artifacts validation. • User, operation and maintenance documentation are not developed. • Perform repository backups. • Formalization of project closure.	4

continued on following page

Table 1. Continued

VSE-ID	Agile approach	Developed product	Detected problems	# of employees
VSE-5	Scrum	System for a fitness center management	• Definition of delivery instructions. • Identify and document project resources. • Team composition. • Adequate risk management is not performed. • Control of some work products produced by the project. • Outdated project information. • Version control strategy. • Integration of a project plan. • Record the project reviews. • Traceability records. • Implementation environment. • Management of change requests is not performed. • Management of corrective actions is not performed. • Design or update and perform unit cases. • Results of test are not registered. • Project artifacts verification. • Project artifacts validation. • User, operation and maintenance documentation are not developed. • Perform repository backups. • Formalization of project closure.	5
VSE-6	Scrum	Insurance management	• Statement of work. • Definition of delivery instructions. • Adequate risk management is not performed. • An adequate description of project goals. • Outdated project information. • Record the project reviews. • Meetings with teamwork are not registered. • Version control strategy. • Integration of a project plan. • Design or update and perform unit cases. • Results of test are not registered. • Traceability records. • Management of change requests is not performed. • Management of corrective actions is not performed. • Project artifacts verification. • Project artifacts validation. • User, operation and maintenance documentation are not developed. • Perform repository backups. • Formalization of project closure.	5
VSE-7	Hybrid using CMMI®-Scrum	Transport management system	• Control of some work products produced by the project. • Project efforts and costs. • Version control strategy. • Integration of a project plan. • Alignment of project elements with those defined by the standard. • Refine project documentation to avoid multiple understandings. • Project artifacts verification. • Project artifacts validation. • Record the project reviews. • Design or update and perform unit cases. • Results of test are not registered. • User and operation documentation are not developed. • Formalization of project closure.	5
VSE-8	Hybrid using CMMI®-Scrum	Livestock system	• Statement of work. • Definition of delivery instructions. • Adequate risk management is not performed. • Integration of a project plan. • Control of some work products produced by the project. • Version control strategy. • Traceability records. • Outdated project information. • Refine project documentation to avoid multiple understandings. • Design or update and perform unit cases. • Management of change requests is not performed. • Management of corrective actions is not performed. • Project artifacts verification. • Project artifacts validation. • Conducting revision meetings with the customer. • Results of test are not registered. • User, operation and maintenance documentation are not developed. • Perform repository backups. • Formalization of project closure.	4

To perform the analysis of the evolution of the VSEs, three milestones meeting were established as follows:

- *The first milestone* was set after the execution of the first four steps of the method because at that time the VSEs had defined their development processes.
- *The second milestone* was set after the execution of the step fifth of the method because at that time the VSEs started the execution of the ISO/IEC 29110 processes to develop software.
- *The third milestone* was set after the execution of the sixth step of the method because at that stage, VSEs were ready to start a formal audit process to be certified to the software Basic profile of the ISO/IEC 29110.

Figure 3. Steps carried out to analyze each of the 8 VSEs.

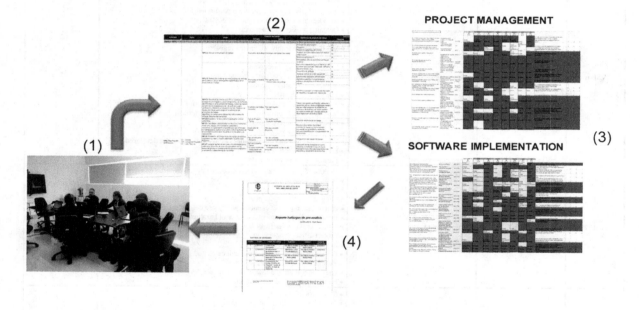

Figure 3 shows the 4 steps carried out to analyze each of the 8 VSEs, as the figure shows we use as technique the performance of a set of work-session meetings, as next described: (1) we request each VSE to provide information about how they were using their processes to develop software; (2) to achieve this activity we develop an instrument in an Excel spreadsheet that allows us to registered data regarding the activities followed by the VSE. The instrument is based on ISO/IEC 29110 processes, activities, tasks and work products, then it allows registering data regarding the activity and work products performed by the VSE; (3) after reviewing the notes gotten from the VSEs, we evaluate their level of coverage regarding the ISO/IEC 29110, to achieve it, we used as an instrument a second Excel spreadsheet, which allows registering the level of coverage of VSEs according to a six-scale of values (covered, high coverage, partially coverage, low coverage, very low and no covered) Besides, we could use colors to highlight the low coverage values. It is important to mention that the coverage level was analyzed for both the Project Management and Software Implementation processes and; (4) the last step was to provide a report in

Table 2. VSEs problems at the first milestone

VSE-ID	Agile approach	Analysis of the evolution regarding the eliminated errors	Current problems at milestone one
VSE-1	None, but using some agile practices	Number of Initial Detected problems were 19 and problems detected at milestone 1 are 8, this means that at this moment they have eliminated 58% of their problems. The VSE still has problems with quality activities, project assessment and control and, project closure.	• Project artifacts verification. • Project artifacts validation. • Record Project reviews. • Traceability records. • Use test cases and test procedures. • Results of test are not registered. • User, operation and maintenance documentation are not developed. • Formalization of project closure.
VSE-2	Hybrid using TSP-Scrum	Number of Initial Detected problems were 17 and problems detected at milestone 1 are 9, this means that at this moment they have eliminated 48% of their problems. The VSE still has problems with the implementation of control version strategy, quality activities and project closure.	• Version control strategy. • Performing repository backups. • Project artifacts verification. • Project artifacts validation. • Record the project reviews. • Traceability records. • Design or update and perform unit cases. • Results of tests are not registered. • Formalization of project closure.
VSE-3	Scrum	Number of Initial Detected problems were 17 and problems detected at milestone 1 are 8, this means that at this moment they have eliminated 53% of their problems. The VSE still has problems with the implementation of delivery instructions, control version strategy, project assessment and control, and project closure.	• Definition of delivery instructions. • Record the project reviews. • Management of change requests is not performed. • Version control strategy. • Management of corrective actions is not performed. • Design or update and perform unit cases. • Results of test are not registered. • Formalization of project closure.
VSE-4	Scrum	Number of Initial Detected problems were 18 and problems detected at milestone 1 are 10, this means that at this moment they have eliminated 45% of their problems. The VSE still has problems with project start, quality activities, execution of control version, assessment and control, and project closure.	• Statement of work. • Project artifacts verification. • Project artifacts validation. • Perform repository backups. • Record the project reviews. • Management of corrective actions is not performed. • Implementation environment. • Traceability records. • Design or update and perform unit cases. • Results of test are not registered.
VSE-5	Scrum	Number of Initial Detected problems were 20 and problems detected at milestone 1 are 13, this means that at this moment they have eliminated 35% of their problems. The VSE still has problems with project planning, quality activities, execution of control version, project assessment and control, and project closure.	• Version control strategy. • Identify and document project resources. • Team composition. • Integration of a project plan. • Perform repository backups. • Project artifacts verification. • Project artifacts validation. • Record the project reviews. • Implementation environment. • Traceability records. • Design or update and perform unit cases. • Results of test are not registered. • Formalization of project closure.
VSE-6	Scrum	Number of Initial Detected problems were 19 and problems detected at milestone 1 are 13, this means that at this moment they have eliminated 32% of their problems. The VSE still has problems with project start, control version, quality activities, project assessment and control, and project closure.	• Statement of work. • Definition of delivery instructions. • Version control strategy. • Integration of a project plan. • Project artifacts verification. • Project artifacts validation. • Management of change requests is not performed. • Management of corrective actions is not performed. • Meetings with teamwork are not registered. • Design or update and perform unit cases. • Results of tests are not registered. • Traceability records. • Formalization of the project closure is not performed.
VSE-7	Hybrid using CMMI®-Scrum	Number of Initial Detected problems were 13 and problems detected at milestone 1 are 9, this means that at this moment they have eliminated 31% of their problems. The VSE still has problems with project planning, control version, quality activities, and project monitoring.	• Control of some work products produced by the project. • Project efforts and costs. • Version control strategy. • Integration of a project plan. • Project artifacts verification. • Project artifacts validation. • Record the project reviews. • Design or update and perform unit cases. • Results of tests are not registered.
VSE-8	Hybrid using CMMI®-Scrum	Number of Initial Detected problems were 19 and problems detected at milestone 1 are 10, this means that at this moment they have eliminated 48% of their problems. The VSE still has problems with project start, project planning, quality activities, and project assessment and control.	• Statement of work. • Team composition. • Integration of a project plan. • Management of corrective actions is not performed. • Project artifacts verification. • Project artifacts validation. • Conducting revision meetings with the customer. • Design or update and perform unit cases. • Results of test are not registered. • Traceability records.

which the non-conformances detected were listed, this non-conformances were based on the low level of coverage detected in the analysis of the activities and work products provided by the VSEs. The instrument used was a Word template, which allows us to provide a list of identified gaps regarding their works products or the adoption of an ISO/IEC 29110 practice, toward being able to start a certification process.

First Milestone Results

After the implementation of the first four steps of the method, seven of the eight VSEs had achieved an important improvement by formalizing their current practices and by identifying those practices and tools that helped them to achieve better coverage of the practices provided by the Software Basic profile of the ISO/IEC 29110.

At this time, the practices that had less coverage are those practices related to project monitoring and control, quality, testing, version control and the formalization of project initiation and closure.

- The activities provided by ISO/IEC 29110 regarding the project monitoring and control are those related to analyzing the project progress respect to the estimation values as well as the management of change requests and the corrective actions.
- The activities provided by ISO/IEC 29110 regarding quality are focused on the verification and validation of artifacts.
- The activities provided by ISO/IEC 29110 regarding testing are focused on performing unit tests and integration tests as well as registering the test results.
- The activities provided by ISO/IEC 29110 regarding the formalization of project initiation and closure are focused, on one hand by ensuring that the project's goal, description, deliverables as well as delivery instructions are clear for both the team and the customer and accepted by the customer. On the other hand, by ensuring that the project's artifacts are delivered according to the delivery instructions and the requirements and are accepted by the customer.

Table 2 summarizes the problems detected by the VSEs in the first milestone. As Table 2 shows, VSE-6 is the one that had more problems at this stage.

Second Milestone Results

After the implementation of the fifth steps of the method, all VSEs had an important coverage of the proven practices provided by the Software Basic profile of the ISO/IEC 29110. At that time, the VSEs had adopted the practices of the ISO/IEC 29110 as the way they develop and manage their software projects.

At that time, one VSE had covered 100% of practices provided by the ISO/IEC 29110. The rest of the VSEs had between 1 to 5 not covered practices that mean they have coverage above 88%. The practices that have less coverage are the practices related to project quality and the management of corrective actions. However, some VSEs still had problems with testing and monitoring and control.

Table 3 summarizes the problems detected by the VSEs in the second milestone. As Table 3 shows, VSEs 6 and 8 had more problems at this stage. Besides, VSE-5 had not implemented the practice related to verification in any artifact.

Table 3. VSEs problems at the second milestone

VSE-ID	Agile approach	Analysis of the evolution regarding the eliminated errors	Current problems at the second milestone
VSE-1	None, but using some agile practices	Number of Initial Detected problems were 19 and problems detected at the second milestone are 1, this means that at this moment they have eliminated 95% of their problems. The VSE still has problems with quality activities, specifically validations.	• Project artifacts validation.
VSE-2	Hybrid using TSP-Scrum	Number of Initial Detected problems were 17 and problems detected at the second milestone are 9, this means that at this moment they have eliminated 94% of their problems. The VSE still has problems with the implementation of the control version strategy.	• Traceability records.
VSE-3	Scrum	Number of Initial Detected problems were 17 and problems detected at the second milestone are 2, this means that at this moment they have eliminated 88% of their problems. The VSE still has problems with project assessment and control.	• Record the project reviews. • Management of corrective actions is not performed.
VSE-4	Scrum	Number of Initial Detected problems were 18 and problems detected at the second milestone are 1, this means that at this moment they have eliminated 94% of their problems. The VSE still has problems with project assessment and control.	• Management of corrective actions is not performed.
VSE-5	Scrum	Number of Initial Detected problems were 20 and problems detected at the second milestone are 1, this means that at this moment they have eliminated 95% of their problems. The VSE still have problems with quality activities, specifically verification.	• Project artifacts verification.
VSE-6	Scrum	Number of Initial Detected problems were 19 and problems detected at the second milestone are 3, this means that at this moment they have eliminated 84% of their problems. The VSE still has problems with project start, quality activities, and project closure.	• Definition of delivery instructions. • Project artifacts verification. • Formalization of the project closure is not performed.
VSE-7	Hybrid using CMMI®-Scrum	Number of Initial Detected problems were 13 and problems detected at the second milestone are 0, this means that at this moment they have eliminated 100% of their problems. The VSE was able to eliminate 100% of their problems.	• No problems detected
VSE-8	Hybrid using CMMI®-Scrum	Number of Initial Detected problems were 19 and problems detected at the second milestone are 10, this means that at this moment they have eliminated 74% of their problems. The VSE still has problems with quality activities and assessment and control.	• Management of corrective actions is not performed. • Project artifacts verification. • Conducting revision meetings with the customer. • Design or update and perform unit cases. • Results of tests are not registered.

Third Milestone Results

After the implementation of the sixth step of the method, all the VSEs had 100% coverage of the practices provided by the software Basic profile of the ISO/IEC 29110 and they were ready to start a formal audit. At that time, all VSEs had defined and improved processes that helped them to achieve the objectives of the ISO/IEC 29110. Table 4 summarizes the problems detected by the VSEs in the third milestone. As Table 4 shows, all VSEs have 100% of errors eliminated.

Table 4. VSEs problems at the third milestone

VSE-ID	Agile approach	Analysis of the evolution regarding the eliminated errors	Current problems at the third milestone
VSE-1	None, but using some agile practices	Number of Initial Detected problems were 19 and problems detected at the third milestone are 0, this means that at this moment they have eliminated 100% of their problems. The VSE was able to eliminate the 100% of their problems.	• No problems detected.
VSE-2	Hybrid using TSP-Scrum	Number of Initial Detected problems were 17 and problems detected at the third milestone are 0, this means that at this moment they have eliminated 100% of their problems. The VSE was able to eliminate 100% of their problems.	• No problems detected.
VSE-3	Scrum	Number of Initial Detected problems were 17 and problems detected at the third milestone are 0, this means that at this moment they have eliminated 100% of their problems. The VSE was able to eliminate 100% of their problems.	• No problems detected.
VSE-4	Scrum	Number of Initial Detected problems were 18 and problems detected at the third milestone are 0, this means that at this moment they have eliminated 100% of their problems. The VSE was able to eliminate 100% of their problems.	• No problems detected.
VSE-5	Scrum	Number of Initial Detected problems were 20 and problems detected at the third milestone are 0, this means that at this moment they have eliminated 100% of their problems. The VSE was able to eliminate 100% of their problems.	• No problems detected.
VSE-6	Scrum	Number of Initial Detected problems were 19 and problems detected at the third milestone are 0, this means that at this moment they have eliminated 100% of their problems. The VSE was able to eliminate 100% of their problems.	• No problems detected.
VSE-7	Hybrid using CMMI®-Scrum	Number of Initial Detected problems were 13 and problems detected at the third milestone are 0, this means that at this moment they have eliminated 100% of their problems. The VSE was able to eliminate 100% of their problems.	• No problems detected
VSE-8	Hybrid using CMMI®-Scrum	Number of Initial Detected problems were 19 and problems detected at the third milestone are 0, this means that at this moment they have eliminated 100% of their problems. The VSE was able to eliminate 100% of their problems.	• No problems detected.

It is important to mention that the 8 VSEs have been formally audited and all of them obtained a certification of the Software Basic Profile of ISO/IEC 29110.

Discussion

With the implementation of the six-step method, it was possible to coach the 8 VSEs to reinforce their agile environment. Figure 4 provides a summary of the evolution of the 8 VSEs. As figure 4 shows, at the second milestone, all VSEs had an important improvement in the practices covered of both processes compared with the first milestone.

Figure 4. The evolution of the 8 VSEs.

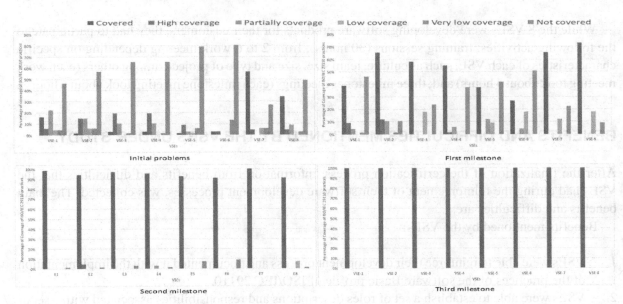

At the third milestone, all VSEs had a high level of coverage of the practices of the software Basic profile of ISO/IEC 29110 for both processes.

The practices implemented by processes are next listed:

- **Project Management Process:** (1) Validation and verification, (2) risk management, (3) project monitoring and control, (4) change requests, (5) configuration management, (6) delivery instructions and (7) formalization of project beginning and closure.
- **Software Implementation Process:** (1) Requirements definition, (2) design, (3) test and test results, (4) traceability records and (5) validation and verification.

Regarding the viability of the six-step method used the following 5 findings have been identified:

- For the execution of the steps 1 to 4, it is possible to obtain the commitment of the VSEs because they understood the needs for improving their processes.
- The six-step method can be used in agile environments by VSEs to improve and reinforce their software development processes by allowing them to continue working as they used to work.

- The six-step method helped the VSEs to identify and formalize their current practices regarding the project management and software implementation processes. It enabled the VSEs to become aware of the importance of using documented processes. It also enabled VSEs to become aware of the use of a standard that provides proven practices that could cover their current needs.
- The support gave to VSEs by implementing the six-step method, from the beginning until they got the certification, allowed the clarification of their needs and doubts regarding the implementation and adoption of software engineering practices within their environment.
- The feedback meetings held throughout all steps reduced the resistance to change of VSEs regarding the implementation of proven practices provided by the ISO/IEC 29110.

While the 8 VSEs were developing software products for their customers, they had to participate to the following activities: training sessions (30 hours); from 2 to 6 work meeting depending on specific characteristics of each VSE, such as culture, team size, size and type of project, among others (each work meeting took about 4 hours) and; three milestones meetings (each milestone meeting took about 6 hours).

BENEFITS AND DIFFICULTIES MENTIONED BY THE VSES UNDER STUDY

After the finalization of the certification process, information from benefits and difficulties that the VSEs had during the reinforcement of their software development processes, was collected. The main benefits and difficulties are:

Benefits mentioned by the VSEs:

1. VSEs were able to reinforce their development process and documented it with the implementation of the practices of the software Basic profile of ISO/IEC 29110.
2. VSEs were able to establish a set of roles descriptions and responsibilities associated with a set of tasks that help to reinforce a self-organized team.
3. VSEs have adopted practices related to monitoring and control that facilitated better control and visibility of projects.
4. VSEs improved its project closure by adopting the establishment of the delivery instructions.
5. VSEs improved the commitments between their development teams and their customers by including the registration of meeting agreements.
6. VSEs formalized and improved the management of risks throughout the project.
7. VSEs were able to make documentation that provides value to them and their customers.
8. VSEs reinforced their knowledge related to getting the approval of the stakeholders without assuming "things" in which there should be an agreement.
9. VSEs improved the changes during a project by implementing the use of change requests.
10. VSEs improved the verification of the project artifacts.
11. VSEs improved the validation and approval of the project artefacts by their customers.
12. VSEs improved their test procedures, test cases, and test results documentation.

Difficulties mentioned by the VSEs:

1. VSEs using agile methods have a lack of experience in the use of processes as well as proven practices from standards.
2. VSEs have a misunderstanding regarding the use of the necessary documentation in agile environments.
3. VSEs have difficulties to understand the ISO/IEC 29110 within the Mexican context mainly because of the terms' translation. There is not a Basics profile of ISO/IEC 20110 translated using Mexican terminology.
4. VSEs have difficulties in using the documentation templates of the ISO/IEC 29110 guide (it was necessary to provide completed examples of documents).
5. VSEs have problems with the correct interpretation of the ISO/IEC 29110 by all members of a team.
6. VSEs have a lack of software tools available to support the implementation of ISO/IEC 29110.
7. VSEs have not the commitment of VSE's owners for their improvement implementation.

FUTURE RESEARCH DIRECTIONS

This chapter presented one research project regarding the implementation of the software Basic profile of the ISO/IEC 29110 series. However, derived from this research, other research projects are being carried out: (1) the development of a software quality ecosystem in one state of Mexico; (2) the development of a guide to facilitate the implementation of ISO/IEC 29110 using agile approaches; (3) the development of software tools to facilitate the implementation of the ISO/IEC 29110 and (4) the dissemination of the project for improving the competitiveness of VSEs by implementing the ISO/IEC 29110.

Development of a Software Quality Ecosystem in the State of Zacatecas

This research is focused on building a software quality ecosystem in the state of Zacatecas, which aims to provide human resources, information, and communication technology infrastructure and a legal framework, so that it enables government, software producers such as VSEs and software users to develop and share a national vision and a national strategy. The main elements to be developed are briefly described (adapted from UNCTAD 2012):

- **Human Resources:** Universities play an important role in the education and training of high-quality human resources to be integrated into VSEs or to create start-ups. As part of this element, the method presented in this chapter has been implemented at Software Development Centers (SDC) of 10 Universities of Zacatecas. SDCs aim to provide an environment in which students apply their knowledge in software projects with real customers. Besides, SDCs reinforce their software engineering knowledge by having students participate as a team to software development projects. One feature that makes it relevant to have an SDC in a university is that students get the experience of working in real projects.
- **Information and Communication Technology Infrastructure:** A set of activities are being performed by the process management and software assurance research group of the Mathematics Research Centre (CIMAT): (a) the development of software tools to facilitate the implementation

and use of ISO/IEC 29110 by VSEs; (b) training VSEs in software tools that could help them implement and adopt proven practices provided by the ISO/IEC 29110; (c) the definition of software development processes to help VSEs; (d) the selection of adequate technology to be implemented by VSEs; and (e) the Spanish translation of the Entry profile ISO/IEC 29110 for Mexican VSEs.

• **Legal Framework:** There are Mexican' programs that aim to create the conditions to help VSEs to be competitive at the international level and to provide conditions to ensure the long-term growth of software enterprises such as the PROSOFT program. This program has two strategies focused on reinforcing Mexican organizations to make them more competitive: (a) increasing the quality and quantity of talent in software development and it services that focus on providing a better human capital to take advantage of the great growth of the software industry sector in both at a local level and to access to international markets; and (b) achieving an international level in process capacity of the IT services sector so that Mexican industry can be more competitive internationally through the adoption of proven practices of models and standards that could help to increase the productivity and quality of organizations.

An ISO/IEC 29110 Agile Guide

Since a large number of VSEs around the world are using agile approaches in an effort to produce software that meets the time requested by their customers, and their lack of knowledge about how to correctly apply agile methodologies, the authors of this paper are developing an ISO guide to help VSEs in the implementation of ISO/IEC 29110 in agile environments.

This ISO guide aims to provide VSEs acquainted with SCRUM and XP methodologies with the practices needed to perform a project under an agile environment, such that they can plan, monitor and evaluate projects, conduct lessons learned to improve the VSEs by reinforcing their development process with practices provided by the ISO/IEC 29110. The ISO guide is also targeted at VSEs that have already implemented the software Basic profile of the ISO/IEC 29110 and want to implement agile practices to their software development cycle.

The ISO/IEC 29110 software agile guide aims to achieve two goals (ISO/IEC, in press):

1. To help VSEs, working in an agile environment, to understand how they can implement ISO/IEC 29110 while performing their agile practices and;
2. To provide practices that can reinforce their development process used to develop software products.

Figure 5 illustrates, on the left side, the project management process using a 'Waterfall' notation and, on the right side an 'agile' approach for the same process. An agile profile specification document will be developed to meet the needs of VSEs that want to obtain an ISO/IEC 29110 certification using an agile approach.

Software Development Tools to Facilitate the Implementation of the ISO/IEC 29110

The authors of this chapter are also leading the development of a set of master degree thesis which aims to provide software tools and knowledge to facilitate the implementation of the ISO/IEC 29110 by VSEs. Some of the research works that are being developed are:

Figure 5. The 'Waterfall' notation on the left side and the 'Agile' approach on the right side.

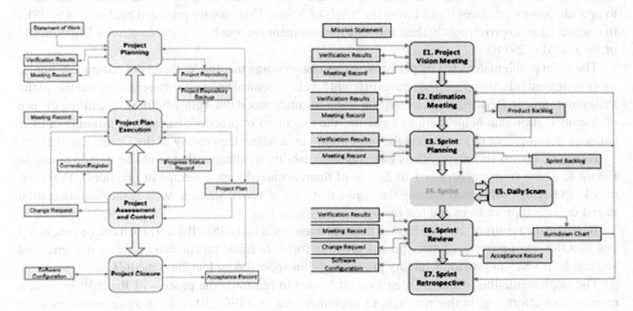

- The development of a guide to help VSEs to implement the ISO/IEC 29110 in DevOps environments.
- The development of a software tool that aims to facilitate the implementation of ISO/IEC 29110 in VSEs. This software tool will help the VSEs to create and manage their control of versions of work products (e.g. documents, code, test cases).
- The establishment of a body of knowledge of software tools that aims to help VSEs in the adoption and usage of proven practices provided by the ISO/IEC 29110.
- The gamification of the training of the Basic profile of the ISO/IEC 29110.

Dissemination of Improving the Competitiveness of VSEs by Implementing the ISO/IEC 29110

Due to the excellent results obtained at the Zacatecas region, the head office of CIMAT requested the CIMAT Centre of Zacatecas to coach VSEs in other states of México, which have demonstrated interest in the project. Therefore, the software engineering group is talking with people from other states to replicate this project.

CONCLUSION

Very Small Entities have increased their importance around the world because they create valuable products and services for medium and large organizations, this fact provides an opportunity for them to grow up. However, it brings the responsibility to improve their development processes. In this context, these types of organizations find it difficult regarding the use of standards.

As a solution, the ISO/IEC developed the ISO/IEC 29110 series of standards and guides, which aims to provide proven practices that address the needs of VSEs. This chapter provided evidence of 8 VSEs that achieved an improvement in their software development process by using the software Basic profile of the ISO/IEC 29110.

The main problem detected by performing this research was that the VSEs do not adequately implement agile methods, therefore, they have different levels of control and maturity regarding the use of the agile environment. Besides, we detected that VSEs misunderstood the Agile Manifesto regarding the use of documentation that helps them to formalize the execution of practices carried out throughout their software development processes and the most important a misunderstanding of the Definition of Done.

However, due to its nature, VSEs have high availability to change (that could be demonstrated in Figure 4, which from milestones 1 to 2 most of them achieved high coverage of practices). However, they keep having problems regarding the implementation of verifications as well as the documentation of test cases and procedures and test results.

Based on the results of the 8 VSEs with the implementation of the ISO/IEC 29110, it can be concluded that that the set of proven practices provided by the software Basic profile can be easily implemented and can help VSEs in providing quality products within approved budget and schedule.

The implementation of our six-step method helped to reinforce the process of the 8 VSEs with a minimum of effort, e.g. in this research, to implement the ISO/IEC 29110 in an agile environment, it took no longer than 4 months while the VSEs also had to meet their business commitments by developing software products for their customers. Besides, they reinforced their development processes without changing the way they work and solved their software development problems.

Finally, we considered important to list a set of lessons learned observed by implementing the method at the 8 VSEs:

- The time invested by VSEs took no longer than 4 months distributed as follows: training sessions (30 hours), the work meetings (each work meeting took 4 hours) and the milestone meetings (each milestone meeting took 6 hours) that represent a very minimum effort. Besides, the effort required by each team to implement the ISO/IEC 29110 varied due to the specific characteristics of each VSE, such as culture, team size, size and type of project, among others.
- Start with training in the software Basic profile of the ISO/IEC 29110 and the use of processes allows them to perceive the implementation of ISO/IEC 29110 as easily adapted to their development cycle.
- The involvement of the VSEs members since the beginning allows them to understand the need for improving their processes, then, this fact facilitated to get their commitment to the improvement.
- Each team had a different level of control and maturity regarding the methodology used to develop software, that is the reason why they are implementing practices as their pace of change. However, all of them were able to reinforce their agile environments is no more than 4 months.
- Many VSEs using agile methods have resistance with practices related to software quality, specifically the validation and verification of produced artifact. Many VSEs also have problems with registered data related to error and the unit and integration test to be performed to software components.
- The most difficult work product to be implemented by the 8 VSEs was the traceability records.
- Most of them understand quickly the benefits to formalize the project start and closure.

REFERENCES

Beck, K., Beedle, M., van Bennekum, A., Cockburn, A., Cunningham, W., Fowler, M., . . . Thomas, D. (2001). Manifesto for agile software development. Retrieved from: www.agilemanifesto.org/

Castillo Salinas L., Sanchez-Gordón S., Villarroel-Ramos J. & Sánchez-Gordón M. (2020) Evaluation of the implementation of a subset of ISO/IEC 29110 Software Implementation process in four teams of undergraduate students of Ecuador. An empirical software engineering experiment. Journal of Computer Standards & Interfaces, 70.

Chetankumar, P., & Ramachandran, M. (2009). Agile maturity model (AMM). (2009). A software process improvement framework for agile software development practices. *International Journal of Software Engineering*, 2(1), 3–28.

Díaz, A., De Jesús, C., Melendez, K., & Dávila, A. (2016). ISO/IEC 29110 Implementation on two Very Small Software Development Companies in Lima. Lessons Learned. IEEE Latin America Transactions Journal, VOL., 14(5), 2504–2510. doi:10.1109/TLA.2016.7530452

Flora, H. K., & Chande, S. V. (2014). A Systematic Study on Agile Software Development Methodologies and Practices. *International Journal of Computer Science and Information Technologies*, 5(3), 3626–3637.

ISO/IEC. (2011). Software engineering- Lifecycle profiles for Very Small Entities (VSEs) - Part 5-1-2: Management and engineering guide: Generic profile group: Basic profile. ISO/IEC TR 29110-5-1-2:2011. Available at no cost from ISO: http://standards.iso.org/ittf/PubliclyAvailableStandards/index.html

ISO/IEC. (in press). ISO/IEC TR 29110-5-4 - Systems and software engineering — Lifecycle profiles for Very Small Entities (VSEs) — Part 5-4: Agile software development guidelines.

ISO/IEC/IEEE. (2018). International Standard ISO/IEC/IEEE 26515. Systems and software engineering — Developing information for users in an agile environment. Second Edition. 2018-12.

Laporte, C., Muñoz, M., Mejía, J., & O'Connor, R. (2018). Applying Software Engineering Standards in Very Small Entities - From Startups to Grownups. *IEEE Software Journal*, 35(1), 99–103.

Laporte, C. Y., & O'Connor, R. (2016). A Multi-Case Study Analysis of Software Process Improvement in Very Small Companies using ISO/IEC 29110. In 23rd European Software Process Improvement Conference (Euro SPI2 2016). Springer-Verlag.

Laporte, C. Y., & O'Connor, R. (2017, May/June). Software Process Improvement Standards and Guides for Very Small Organizations - An Overview of Eight Implementation. *Crosstalk*, 30(3), 23–27.

Larrucea, X., O'Connor, R. V., Colomo-Palacios & R., Laporte, C.Y. (2016). Software Process Improvement in Very Small Organizations. IEEE Software Journal, 33(2), 85-89. Advance online publication. doi:10.1109/MS.2016.42

Muñoz, M., Mejia, J., Calvo-Manzano, J. A., San Feliu, T., Corona, B., & Miramontes, J. (2017). Diagnostic Assessment Tools for Assessing the Implementation and/or Use of Agile Methodologies in SMEs: An Analysis of Covered Aspects. *Software Quality Professional Journal*, 19(2), 16–27.

Muñoz, M., Mejia, J., & Laporte, C. Y. (2019). Reinforcing Very Small Entities Using Agile Methodologies with the ISO/IEC 29110. In J. Mejia, M. Muñoz, Á. Rocha, A. Peña, & M. Pérez-Cisneros (Eds.), *Trends and Applications in Software Engineering. CIMPS 2018. Advances in Intelligent Systems and Computing* (Vol. 865). Springer.

Muñoz, M., Mejia, J., & Laporte, C. Y. (2019b). *Implementing ISO/IEC 29110 to reinforce four very small entities of Mexico under an agile approach.* IET Software Journal; doi:10.1049/iet-sen.2019.0040

Muñoz M., Mejia J., Peña A., Lara G. & Laporte, C. Y. (2019). Transitioning international software engineering standards to academia: analyzing the results of the adoption of ISO/IEC 29110 in four Mexican universities. Journal of Computer Standards & Interfaces. Doi:10.1016/j.csi.2019.03.008

Muñoz, M., Peña, A., Mejia, J., Gasca-Hurtado, G. P., Gómez-Alvarez, M. C., & Laporte, C. (2019). A Comparative Analysis of the Implementation of the Software Basic Profile of ISO/IEC 29110 in Thirteen Teams That Used Predictive Versus Adaptive Life Cycles. In A. Walker, R. O'Connor, & R. Messnarz (Eds.), *Systems, Software and Services Process Improvement. EuroSPI 2019. Communications in Computer and Information Science* (Vol. 1060). Springer.

NYCE. (2020). Companies certified to the ISO/IEC 29110-4-1:2011 standard. Retrieved https://www.nyce.org.mx/wp-content/uploads/2020/01/PADRON-DE-EMPRESAS-CERTIFICADAS-EN-LA-NORMA-ISO-IEC-29110-4-1-16-01-2020.pdf

O'Connor, R. V., & Laporte, C. Y. (2012). Software Project Management in Very Small Entities with ISO/IEC 29110. In D. Winkler, R. V. O'Connor, & R. Messnarz (Eds.), *EuroSPI 2012, CCIS 301* (pp. 330–341). Springer-Verlag.

Sánchez-Gordon, M.-L., de Amescua, A., O'Connor, R. V., & Larrucea, X. (2017, November). A standard-based framework to integrate software work in small settings. *Journal of Computer Standards & Interfaces*, *54*(Part 3), 162–175. doi:10.1016/j.csi.2016.11.009

UNCTAD. (2012). *Information Economy Report 2012 - The Software Industry and Developing Countries*. United Nations Publication.

KEY TERMS AND DEFINITIONS

Activity: A set of cohesive tasks. A task is a requirement, recommendation, or permissible action, intended to contribute to the achievement of one or more objectives of a process.

Agile Manifesto: A document developed by the Agile Alliance to guide agile software development. It contains 4 values and 12 principles.

Agile Method: Known as lightweight methods, these types of methods are characterized by short, iterative development cycles, performed by self-organizing teams, to achieve frequent customer involvement.

Capability Maturity Model® Integration: CMMI® models provide a set of proven practices to guide organizations to improve their processes. CMMI® for Development aims to help improve processes for developing better products and services.

Definition of Done: A list in which the team agrees on and that must be met before a product increment. It is normally associated with a user story. Then, a failure in meeting these criteria at the end of a sprint implies that the work should not be counted in that sprint velocity.

Quality Ecosystem: Enabling environment to position the state of Zacatecas as a software producer for medium and large international software organizations. It is composed by a set of VSEs which have implemented the Basic profile of ISO/IEC 29110 and have been certified in the standard.

SCRUM: A process framework used to manage product development by a self-organized team.

Small and Medium Enterprise (SME): An enterprise which employs fewer than 250 person employees.

Team Software Process[SM] **(TSP**[SM]**):** A performance framework that guides engineering teams that are developing software-intensive products.

Very Small Entity (VSE): An enterprise, an organization (e.g. public or non-profit organization), a project or a department having up to 25 people.

Chapter 3
AMPLA:
An Agile Process for Modeling Logical Architectures

Nuno António Santos
https://orcid.org/0000-0002-8247-7253
CCG, Universidade do Minho, Portugal & ZGDV Institute, Portugal

Nuno Ferreira
https://orcid.org/0000-0003-3561-331X
i2S Insurance Knowledge, S.A., Portugal

Ricardo J. Machado
CCG, Universidade do Minho, Portugal & ZGDV Institute, Portugal

ABSTRACT

Software architecture design, when performed in context of agile software development (ASD), sometimes referred to as "agile architecting," promotes the emerging and incremental design of the architectural artifact in a sense of avoiding "big design upfront" (BDUF). This chapter presents the Agile Modeling Process for Logical Architectures (AMPLA) method, an approach for supporting the emergence of a candidate (logical) architecture, rather than BDUF, the architecture in an early phase. The architecture then emerges throughout agile iterations, where AMPLA plays a key contribution for providing traceability between models, from the business need to service specifications, ranging from design stages to deployment, hence covering a software development life cycle (SDLC).

INTRODUCTION

At the time that the 'Agile Manifesto' (Agile Alliance, 2001) was proposed, there was a big shift on focusing in delivering software and less in technical documentation and specifications. Based in one of the values of the Manifesto, '*Working software over comprehensive documentation*', specification of requirements have been reducing to as minimum as possible. Thus, the use of software models was also

DOI: 10.4018/978-1-7998-4165-4.ch003

reduced, both in requirements and in design tasks, where only models that actually help teams develop software are used (Schwaber & Beedle, 2001).

In plan-driven approaches (e.g., Waterfall), tasks related to Requirements Engineering (RE) discipline are traditionally managed in a phase separated in time from design and development. In change-driven approaches, like ASD, RE discipline – also called "*Agile RE*" – activities remain the same but are executed continuously (Grau & Lauenroth, 2014), and takes an iterative discovery approach (Cao & Ramesh, 2008). Additionally, requirements modeling require an agile approach in order to prevent unnecessary efforts in "*You Aren't Gonna Need It*" (YAGNI) features.

In ASD frameworks, the requirements are included in a product backlog, typically in form of use User Stories (IIBA, 2017) as items in the backlog for "reminders of a conversation" about a functionality. However, using only User Stories, without attached requirements specifications or models, may be insufficient to assure a common understanding or, in case of multi-teams, to clearly define inter-systems interaction.

Typically, a first release on a new product encompasses a product's subset able to address priority scenarios, previously identified in order to respond to market needs. In fact, many of these product releases are market-driven, where the release is deployed into the market so it is possible to get feedback from it, *i.e.*, a minimum viable product (MVP). Alongside with these requirements concerns, projects struggle to design candidate architectures for the MVP, endangering development when they conclude that the architecture requires modifications and updates. In an era where software development is more and more agile-oriented, the upfront effort is replaced by the emergence of the design throughout iterative cycles. Such efforts are in opposition to "*Big Design Upfront*" (BDUF). In ASD contexts, BDUF approaches often result in features that are disregarded after some time (YAGNI features).

This chapter introduces an Agile Modeling Process for Logical Architectures (AMPLA), an approach for supporting the emergence of a candidate (logical) architecture, rather than BDUF the architecture in an early phase. AMPLA includes the core known features within the initial phase and designs a logical architecture using a stepwise method, without refining information. The emerging characteristics of AMPLA are supported in four stages, two performed before development cycles or Sprints and two in parallel with ASD cycles: (1) eliciting a small set of high-level requirements; (2) deriving a candidate logical architecture; (3) define subsystems for refinement; and (4) refine requirements and the architecture regarding the subsystem in small cycles or Sprints. As the name implies, AMPLA is guided by the Agile Modeling (AM) (S Ambler, 2002) philosophy. AM is about modeling practices, aiming to deliver small portions of models and collecting feedbacks, within ASD processes. AMPLA is driven to be "lean", because it aims to minimize waste within modeling, since the emerging modeling of the features enables leaving out YAGNI features. AMPLA is based in UML models, namely Use Cases diagrams for requirements, and Components diagrams for the logical architecture design. A logical architecture is a view that primarily supports the functional requirements, taken mainly from the problem domain (Kruchten, 1995). For the architecture derivation, AMPLA uses the *Four-Step-Rule-Set* (4SRS) method (Ferreira, Santos, Machado, Fernandes, & Gasevic, 2014) in order to assure the logical components are aligned with the functional requirements. AMPLA is demonstrated in this chapter within a research project called Unified Hub for Smart Plants (UH4SP).

Background

The requirements discipline is no longer performed only in the early phase of the project, but rather in a continuous way (Grau & Lauenroth, 2014; IIBA, 2017). In ASD contexts, where widely known frameworks, such as Scrum, XP, Kanban, Crystal, etc. don't promote extensive use of requirements models (*e.g.*, UML), modeling tasks are able to be included if performed continuously and incrementally (S Ambler, 2002). The agile model-driven development (AMDD) (SW Ambler, 2007) point out that a project can start with "just-enough" requirements and "just-enough" architecture and then continuously specify requirements and update this so-called candidate architecture design alongside implementation efforts (e.g., Scrum Sprint cycles). In these contexts, the architecture design must assure that at least the organization of high-level software components is included. These components do not have to be refined for implementation purposes, but rather to provide a first insight on the structure of the aimed solution. AMPLA is aligned with AMDD, with the enhancement of providing a method for assuring the alignment of the architecture with the elicited needs.

In this agile era, even the project's early phase is intended to be as short as possible. The inception, like the pregame phase or Sprint zero in Scrum, aims providing a shared understanding of the project and the required information for the development phase. The lean inception (Caroli, 2019) relates to lean startup (and MVPs) contexts, where the product scope is characterized as quickly as possible. In AMPLA this reasoning is also applicable, since actors, features and architecture are defined as soon as possible.

Minimize the waste is a universal concern in every project, regardless its nature. Specifically, within software architecture, some approaches aiming agility and lean architecting intend to leave out YAGNI features in the minimal time possible, through practices aligned with agile development's underlying principles (Woods, 2015).

In general, the set-up phase of the project - often called '*iteration 0*' (Abrahamsson, Babar, & Kruchten, 2010) - includes some upfront design, with ongoing architectural refinement during the iterative development. However, how can an architect or developer determine what the correct amount of "just enough up-front design" is, *i.e.*, how can agile teams reduce the up-front effort without sacrificing the benefits of an up-front design (Waterman, Noble, & Allan, 2012)? This work states concepts for reducing the amount of effort in up-front decision making such as "*using predefined architecture*", "*intuitive architecture*", "*having architectural experience simplifies decision making*" and "*being familiar with the architecture*".

Coplien and Bjørnvig present the concept of "Lean Architecture" (Coplien & Bjørnvig, 2011), where the lean perspective focuses on how to develop the overall system form by drawing on experience and domain knowledge. One of the proposals for performing design as concepts and requirements emerge is the approach of a walking skeleton. It is as an architectural prototype (Abrahamsson et al., 2010), referring to a tiny implementation of the system that performs minimum functionality (Farhan, Tauseef, & Fahiem, 2009). Kazman proposes the design of a candidate architecture (Kazman, 2013). Cockburn proposes, for larger projects with unstable requirements, to start by quickly designing a candidate architecture even if it leaves out many details. (Cockburn, 2006). He considers an approach to create a simple architecture that handles all the known "*big rocks*" (requirements that are particularly hard to incorporate late in the project), and handle the "small rocks" as they appear during the project. These works describe some strategies for using a candidate architecture approach and its evolution. However, these approaches lack in guiding the architecture design and evolution process aiming the alignment with the gathered requirements. Namely, they lack in providing inputs for the design process in how requirements are embraced within the architecture evolution and management, starting from the candidate version to a "final" version. The design process must take in consideration that the architecture is not static but rather it evolves, because of enhancement and maintenance requirements (Ali Babar, Brown, & Mistrík, 2013). Architecture design is ASD projects should start by a candidate version that handles the "big rocks", however managing architecture evolution includes refining the candidate version and adding new requirements but also a continuous management of architectural risks (Martini, Pareto, & Bosch, 2014).

Architecture approaches are also present in ASD, where architecture-centric methods such as QAW, ADD, ATAM/CBAM and ARID are potentially used in combination with agile practices such as "Iterative and Incremental Development", "Just Enough Work", and "Continuous Integration" (Yang, Liang, & Avgeriou, 2016). Typically they are performed in parallel with the development iterations (Bellomo, Kruchten, Nord, & Ozkaya, 2014; Farhan et al., 2009; Jeon, Han, Lee, & Lee, 2011; Madison, 2010; R. L. Nord & Tomayko, 2006; R. Nord, Ozkaya, & Kruchten, 2014). These approaches focus in architectural requirements rather than requirements specification from the entire solution, which allow designing a logical architecture able to be used as basis for the entire solution development. Additionally, the initial backlog should include both functional and quality (non-functional) requirements (typically quality ones only emerge during development).

Agile Modeling Process for Logical Architectures (AMPLA)

From business needs to agile logical architecting, this chapter introduces requirements modeling activities and artifacts that are part of an integrated modeling roadmap (Figure 1). This roadmap is proposed as a sequential order of artifacts that relate to the outputs that are used within the *Agile Modeling Process for Logical Architectures* (AMPLA), presented in Figure 2. Requirements modeling, called "*D*ecomposing *U*ser *A*gile *R*equirements Ar*TE*facts" (DUARTE) process uses ASD known techniques for deriving an UML use case diagram. Then, the candidate logical architecture will be derived using as input the diagrams from DUARTE.

Figure 1. Integrated modeling roadmap

Running Example: The Unified Hub for Smart Plants (UH4SP)

The UH4SP project aims developing a platform or integrating data from distributed industrial unit plants, with focus in the cement domain, allowing the use of the data acquired from IoT systems for enterprise-level production management and collaborative processes between plants, suppliers, forwarders and clients. The project aimed at developing new solutions regarding the control of trucks arrival/exit as well as the load/unload activities, and for communicating with the plant's ERP and the industrial hardware. These solutions were validated within a proof of concept performed in an ecosystem of industrial unit

Figure 2. Overview of AMPLA

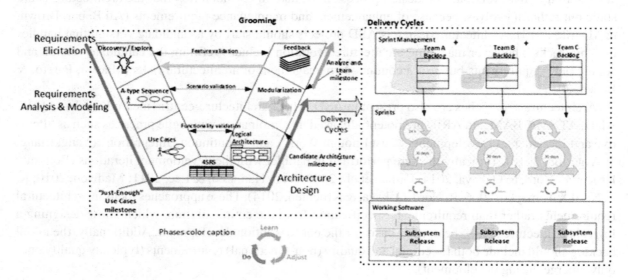

plants using production management systems developed by *Cachapuz Bilanciai Group*, located in Braga, Portugal, as they were the leading entity of the UH4SP project consortium.

The UH4SP project arose with the need of overcoming Cachapuz solution's limitations in adopting IIoT/I4.0 paradigm. Firstly, the current solution is deployed on-premises. It has a considerable scaling and complexity, which made it not adequate and flexible to enable the development and deployment of cloud services based on modules and external access. The on-premises deployment is a difficulty for promoting a corporate-level management, since in order to the industrial group manager to have an integrated analysis of the group's plants, he was only able to access the individual plant's ERP one at a time using a remote virtualized environment. The remote business analysis was also impossible to perform in some contexts, namely within plant's located in poor Internet connectivity spaces. Finally, the current solution was not able to respond to a previous need of enabling third-party access (*e.g.*, forwarders, customers, suppliers) to the inclusion of collaborative tools in process execution and analysis.

In short, the UH4SP project aimed developing:

- New Functionalities for providing management of corporate-level production;
- Tools for supporting new collaborative processes within the supply chain;
- A microservices architecture;
- Production management services, that rely on previous synchronization of Cachapuz's systems (at the industrial unit level)

Emerging Requirements Modeling with DUARTE

This section introduces DUARTE, a requirements-related approach performed within AMPLA, which aims at iteratively elicit and model emerging requirements that will later be used within the 4SRS method in order to derive the candidate logical architecture.

DUARTE is about eliciting and modeling requirements, promoting agility (and hence Agile RE practices) by including practices and mindsets within RE activities from outputs in performing approaches like Lean Startup (Ries, 2011), Design Thinking (Brown, 2009), Domain-driven Design (DDD) (Evans, 2004), Behavior-driven Development (BDD) (Smart, 2015), Kent Beck's 3X and BizDev (Fitzgerald & Stol, 2017). Additionally, uses agile practices in order to deliver small increments (of a requirements package) and to promote continuous customer feedback (Figure 3).

Lean Startup is a hypothesis-driven approach, where a "Build-Measure-Learn" cycle is the basis for supporting product development adequate to the market.

Design Thinking addresses understanding the customer need through systematic exploration. The objective is to understand the right product to develop. This approach encompasses "Empathize", "Define", "Ideate", "Prototype" and "Test" phases.

BDD is an agile practice that consists in defining increments of software behavior and their delivery. Similar to BDD, Test Driven Development (TDD), Acceptance Test Driven Development (ATDD) and Specification by Example (SBE) use testable scenarios as input for the software development. All these have in common to start by defining development based in scenarios and use the "Given, When, Then" (gherkin language).

Figure 3. Overview of DUARTE approach

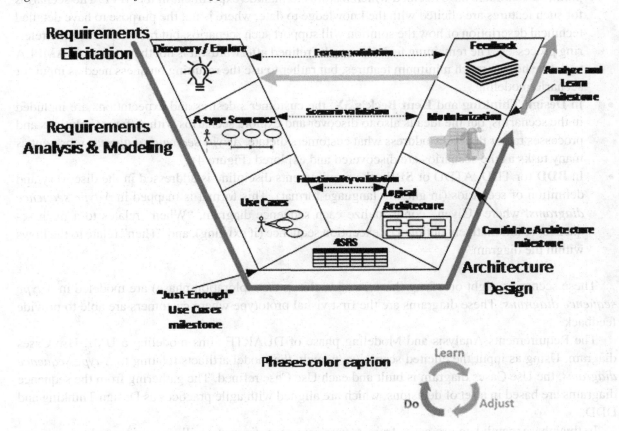

DDD is an approach that proposes the division of concepts by domains, or sub-domains, if applicable. BizDev is continuous linking Business Strategy & Planning and Development. 3X relates to Kent Beck's vision of product development phases: explore, expand, extract.

The elicitation and discovery phase of DUARTE relates to eliciting customer needs, exploring alternatives, discover new requirements, all aligned with current agile practices from ASD frameworks, techniques and philosophies. In AMPLA, this phase outputs a set of scenarios, i.e., processes and activities performed using the solution under development. These scenarios are documented in *A-type sequence diagrams*, a stereotyped version of UML sequence diagrams that only include actors and use cases.

At this stage, the use cases included in these diagrams are not yet composing part of the Use Case model from the next stage. Rather, they are classified as candidate use cases, because they relate to specific activities and tasks that a given actor performs (in software or not) within a given scenario. The flows between actors and candidate use cases relate to the actions performed. The use of these diagrams, instead of UML Activity diagrams, BPMN, or any other process-oriented language, relates to the use of candidate use cases, which help to construct the model in the next stage, because the candidate use cases are input for the use case model.

Applying agile practices in this phase influences:

- In **Lean Startup**, stakeholders define scenarios with the experiment mindset in mind. At this point, stakeholders have decided which features to include/experiment in the MVP. The scenarios for such features are elicited with the knowledge to date, where is not the purpose to have detailed technical description of how the solution will support such scenarios, but rather to define the referring processes. The remaining features may be refined afterwards. It is not the purpose of AMPLA to define how to reach minimum features, but rather to use the resulting business need as input for scenario modeling.
- In **Design Thinking** and **Kent Beck's 3X**, the customer's desires and expectations are included in the scenarios, but the idea is also to discover and explore scenarios with different solutions and processes rather than only address what customers dictate. *A-type sequence diagrams* represent as many tasks as the scenarios are discovered and explored (Figure 4).
- In **BDD** (or TDD, ATDD or SBE), the requirements discipline is addressed in the discovery and definition of scenarios (in gherkin language format). This format is mapped in *A-type sequence diagrams*, where "Given" contextualize each sequence diagram, "When" relates to a main sequence, or alternatively optional or exception sequence (if existing), and "Then" relate to the flows within the diagram.

These scenarios, right or wrong (have in mind this is an exploration phase) are modeled in *A-type sequence diagrams*. These diagrams are the first visual prototype where customers are able to provide feedback.

The Requirements Analysis and Modeling phase of DUARTE aims modeling a UML Use Cases diagram. Using as input the elicited scenarios, namely the model artifacts relating to *A-type sequence diagrams*, the Use Cases diagram is built and each Use Case refined. The gathering from the sequence diagrams are based in a set of decisions, which are aligned with agile practices as Design Thinking and DDD.

In this phase, candidate use cases from *A-type sequence diagrams* will give origin to "typical" use cases, i.e., formal software functional requirements. The idea is to use the gathered information and

Figure 4. Discovery and exploration of the scenarios

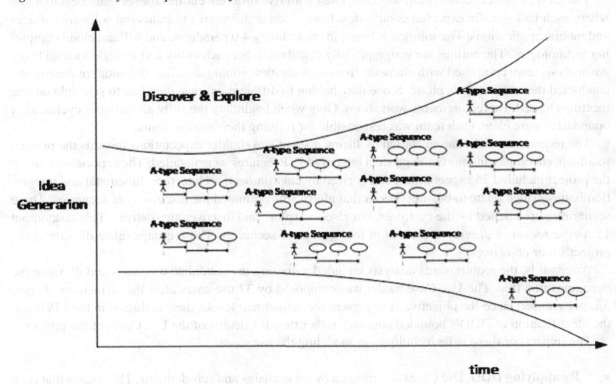

use it to model Use Cases and their refinements. The gathered information allows identifying detailed information about a requirement, which correspond to a use case functionally decomposed in refined use cases. Cruz *et al.* (Cruz, Machado, & Santos, 2014) present such refinement by sub-domains that compose a domain or by splitting a process. They model use case refinement in decomposition trees, and so does this approach. The candidate use cases from *A-type sequence diagrams* are grouped in a logical way, typically grouping them to the scenario from *A-type sequence diagrams* that originated them.

Applying agile practices in this phase influences:

- In **Lean Startup**, as customers define which scenarios to include in an MVP, they are expressed in more detail rather than the scenarios that are left out at this phase. Thus, there is more context to define the models that will compose MMF, which result in more decomposition of those use cases. The remaining requirements that are not refined for the MMF are identified however not afterwards decomposed.
- In **Design Thinking**, Use Cases are used as designed prototypes aiming firsts customer feedbacks
- In **BizDev**, use case models trace back to the scenarios, which support the continuous linking Business Strategy & Planning and Development;
- In **BDD**, the candidate use cases from A-type sequence diagrams are grouped in domains and sub-domains. The refinement "branches" of the decomposition tree hence relate to a single domain or sub-domain, which define bounded contexts for a (sub-)domain. This aspect assures a given team to work on a sub-domain and the independence is assured by the bounded context.

The UH4SP project consortium was composed with five different entities for software development where each had specific expected contributes, from cloud architectures to industrial software services and mobile applications. The solution is based in the Industry 4.0 paradigm, and IoT and cloud computing technologies. The entities are geographically distributed, but each entity had a single located team. An analysis team composed with elements from each entities, aiming to define the initial requirements, conducted the requirements phase. Since they belong to different entities, they had to schedule on-site meetings to perform requirements workshops. Only when beginning the software delivery cycles, after boundaries were clear, each team was responsible for refining their requirements.

The requirements elicitation started by listing a set of stakeholder expectations towards the product roadmap, encompassing the entire product but only MVP features were detailed. The expectations list of the project included 25 expectations, categorized by environment, architecture, functional and integration issues, which relate to business needs that afterwards promoted the discussion of scenarios. These scenarios were elicited by the customer, but also to explore and discover alternatives. This task output 15 *A-type sequence diagrams*, divided in four groups of scenarios. These groups relate directly to the project's four objectives.

Afterwards, the requirements analysis included gathering the candidate use cases and defining the decomposition tree. The Use Case model was composed by 37 use cases after the refinement. *Figure 5* is not zoomed since the objective is to present the refinement levels, their inclusion in the MVP and the identification of DDD's bounded contexts, rather than the details of the Use Cases of the project.

The impacts of these agile techniques in modeling the use cases:

- **By applying DDD**, Use Cases are grouped by the domains and sub-domains. This means that each of the tree's "branches" relate only to a given domain, which also assures that the contexts are properly bounded. Each bounded context is represented like in *Figure 5*. The identified domains relate directly to the four scenario groups. Two of them, "tools for third-party entities" and "system reliability", was afterwards divided in two and three domains, respectively, hence making a total of seven. Two of the "system reliability" bounded context are not even depicted due to MVP decisions.
- **By applying Lean Startup,** the features defined to be included in the MVP are identified in the model by having refined use cases, while the remaining were just identified in the first-level. Use cases {UC.3} and {UC.4} relate to features not addressed in the MVP, hence were not object of further decomposition. The remaining use cases were included in the MVP, where, namely, {UC.1} was decomposed in five use cases, {UC.2} was decomposed in eight use cases, {UC.5} was decomposed in two use cases, {UC.6} was decomposed in five use cases, and {UC.7} was decomposed in ten use cases.

"Just-Enough" Modeling

In this section, the objective is to describe the elicitation of the core requirements, and additionally to include techniques for deciding when the "just-enough" requirements model is complete. In this phase, and namely in agile context, where the requirements are not known upfront, it is very difficult to know in advance how much RE is "just-enough". The vision document, for instance, reflects stakeholder's intentions (*i.e.*, features) towards the entire product, however the main purpose at this time is to assure

Figure 5. Use case decomposition tree of UH4SP, the Use cases from MVP features and for further releases (Lean Startup), and the domain's and sub-domain's bounded contexts (DDD)

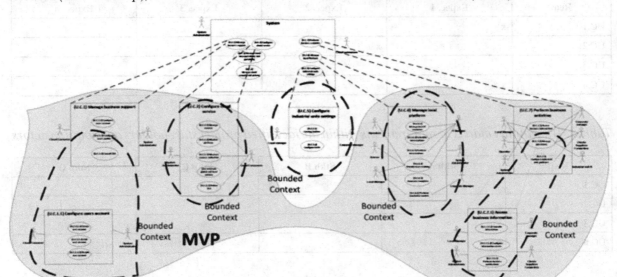

that such features are included. At this point, stakeholders have decided which features to include in the MVP. The requirements that are object of "just-enough" refinement and modeling relate to such features, while the remaining features from the product roadmap may be refined afterwards.

This section illustrates the elicitation process based on stakeholders' expectations. However, every business requirements-related information or document that provide inputs for the software requirements elicitation are useful for validating if high-level requirements were considered. Techniques like interviews, questionnaires, workshops, etc., are additional and complemental approaches of the aforementioned document analysis for gathering inputs on requirements. The use of these techniques is a decision of the requirements engineers as they best fit in a given context.

The elicitation process' goal is to model functional requirements in UML Use Case diagrams, promoting the modeling of the product roadmap by functional decomposition, in compliance with a work-breakdown structure (WBS). Use cases are decomposed once or twice, instead of several times like in upfront contexts. Since the main idea is to model "just-enough" requirements, one decomposition may be sufficient, namely the ones that stakeholders are aware at this point. The use of UML Use Case diagrams is mandatory in this approach, since the 4SRS method for deriving the logical architecture requires Use Cases as input.

To validate if the modeled use cases cover the requirements defined in the product scope, **Table 1** exemplifies the crosschecking between the stakeholders' expectations and the project goals. Since the expectations and goals list emphasizes the MVP features, there is a context for MVP features to be more decomposed than the remaining. The premises is that if all these concerns are included in the Use Case model, with more emphasis in decomposition detail to MVP requirements, one may consider that we have "just-enough" requirements information for this stage.

Like in any requirements process, one of the first critical tasks is to identify all projects stakeholders, as well as the solution's interacting actors. By mapping stakeholders to the use cases (**Table 2**), one

Table 1. Traceability matrix of requirements within the initial expectations

Req.	Expec. 1	Expec. 2	Expec. 3	Expec. n
UC.1	x			
UC.2		x		
UC.3			x	
UC.n	x			x

Table 2. Traceability matrix of requirements within the identified project stakeholders and solution actors

Req.	Stkh A	Stkh B	Stkh C	Stkh D
UC.1	x			
UC.2		x	x	
UC.3				x
UC.n	x			

must assure that every stakeholder/actor has at least a requirement mapped to it, or is a symptom that critical requirements are missing.

The mappings from **Table 1** and **Table 2** validates that the UML Use Cases diagram includes the features for MVP but also the product roadmap, and that all stakeholders have related functionalities. Both tables provide the required traceability to the expectations and stakeholder/actor needs, which hence are the mechanism used to respond to changes. When applied to mid-and long term projects, the approach supports updates of expectations and stakeholder/actor needs over time, as well as the inclusion of new Use Cases, by tracing requirements in **Table 1**. Additionally, the approach is able to lead with organizational changes, by tracing the Use Cases to stakeholder/actor needs in **Table 2**. The approach differs from the segmentation of requirements into different priorities by setting an initial set of Use Cases to the entire solution, refining subsets of the model (section 3.2) and prioritizing them before actually begin the implementation.

Having all the "just-enough" requirements elicited, gathered, modeled and validated, these Use Cases are now able to be used as input for the candidate logical architecture derivation, composed with the "just-enough" architectural components.

Candidate Architecture Design Using the 4SRS Method

This research uses the 4SRS method, by taking advantage from the method's ability to use a functionally decomposed UML Use Case model – so, requirements have been elicited and split in smaller pieces as possible - as input to derive in a stepwise manner a component-based logical architecture (i.e., the software product version of the 4SRS). For this reason, the method evolution is presented and its steps are detailed in this section.

The 4SRS method takes as input a set of use cases in the problem space, describing the requirements for the processes that tackle the initial problem. They are then refined trough successive 4SRS iterations (by recurring to tabular transformations), producing progressively more detailed requirements and a design specification, in the form of a logical architecture representation of the system, representing the intended concerns of the involved business and technological stakeholders. A correct application of the tabular transformations assures alignment and traceability, between the derived logical architecture diagram and the initial use cases representations, and at the same time allows adjusting the results of the transformation to any changing requirements. The usage context of the proposed 4SRS, with "just-enough requirements and deriving the logical architecture with "just-enough" components is depicted in Figure 6. Since in AMPLA the requirements will be later refined and will emerge, the 4SRS method is regularly revisited alongside the development Sprints.

Figure 6. Method for designing the candidate architecture with 4SRS

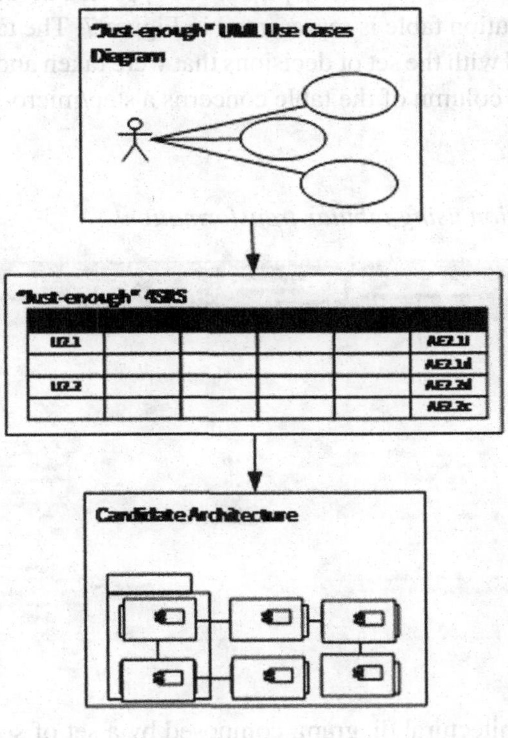

The 4SRS method is composed by four steps: Component Creation; Component Elimination; Packaging and Aggregation; and Component Associations.

The first step regards the creation of software architectural components. The 4SRS method associates, to each component found in analysis, a given category: interface, data, and control. This categorization makes the architectures derived by the 4SRS to be compliant with architectures from object-oriented programming, or by Model-View-Controller (MVC) patterns. Interface components refer to interfaces with users, software or other entities (*e.g.*, devices, etc.); data components refer to generic repositories, typically containing the type of information to be stored in a database; and control components refer to the business logic and programmatic processing.

In the second step, components are submitted to elimination according to pre-defined rules. At this moment, the system architect decides which of the original three components (i, c, d) are maintained or eliminated, firstly taking into account the context of a use case from Step 1, and later compared for redundancy within the entire system. Additionally, each component is named and textually described relating to its behavior.

In the third step, the remaining components (those that were maintained after executing step 2), where there is an advantage in treating them in a unified process, should give the origin to aggregations or packages of semantically consistent components.

The final step refers to the associations between components. The method provides steps for identifying such associations based in descriptions from use cases, as well as from the own components during the components creation.

The execution of the 4SRS transformation steps can be supported in tabular representations. A small part of the 4SRS method execution table is represented in Figure 7. The table is not zoomed due to size limitations. The cells are filled with the set of decisions that were taken and made possible the derivation of a logical architecture. Each column of the table concerns a step/micro-step of the method execution.

Figure 7. 4SRS method execution using tabular transformations

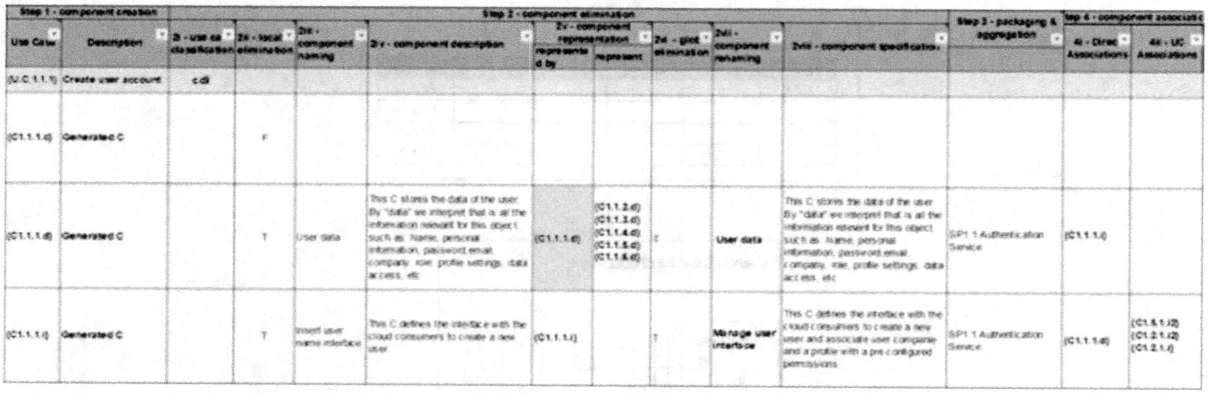

Step 1 - component creation		Step 2 - component elimination									Step 3 - packaging & aggregation	Step 4 - component associations	
Use Case	Description	2i - use case classification	2ii - local elimination	2iii - component naming	2iv - component description	2v - component representation: represented by	2v - component representation: represent	2vi - global elimination	2vii - component renaming	2viii - component specification		4i - Direct Associations	4ii - UC Associations
{U.C.1.1.1}	Create user account	c-d-i											
{C1.1.1.c}	Generated C		F										
{C1.1.1.d}	Generated C		T	User data	This C stores the data of the user. By "data" we interpret that is all the information relevant for this object such as: Name, personal information, password, email, company, role, profile settings, data access, etc	{C1.1.1.d}	{C1.1.2.d} {C1.1.3.d} {C1.1.4.d} {C1.1.5.d} {C1.1.6.d}	F	User data	This C stores the data of the user. By "data" we interpret that is all the information relevant for this object such as: Name, personal information, password, email, company, role, profile settings, data access, etc	SP1.1 Authentication Service	{C1.1.1.i}	
{C1.1.1.i}	Generated C		T	Insert user name interface	This C defines the interface with the cloud consumers to create a new user	{C1.1.1.i}		T	Manage user interface	This C defines the interface with the cloud consumers to create a new user and associate user companies and a profile with a pre configured permissions	SP1.1 Authentication Service	{C1.1.1.d}	{C1.5.1.i2} {C1.2.1.i2} {C1.2.1.i}

The output is a logical architectural diagram, composed by a set of software components and relations/flows between them. The architectural diagram is modeled in UML Components, as depicted in a simple example in Figure 8.

It must be pointed out that AMPLA and the 4SRS supports the logical view (Kruchten, 1995) of the architecture, where namely they support the identification and design of software components referring to functional requirements. Architecture design should also address quality requirements for supporting the logical view. Addressing quality requirements is out of the scope of AMPLA, however AMPLA is able to coexist with other architecture-centric methods such as QAW or ADD.

The use of 4SRS throughout the process, first in the scope of the candidate architecture, and afterwards in the scope of each refinement, provides the traceability between components and the functional requirements in order to identify affected requirements. The number of components or the number of associations between components are possible indicators to determine the architecture's riskiest components.

Figure 8. Simple example of a candidate UML components architecture

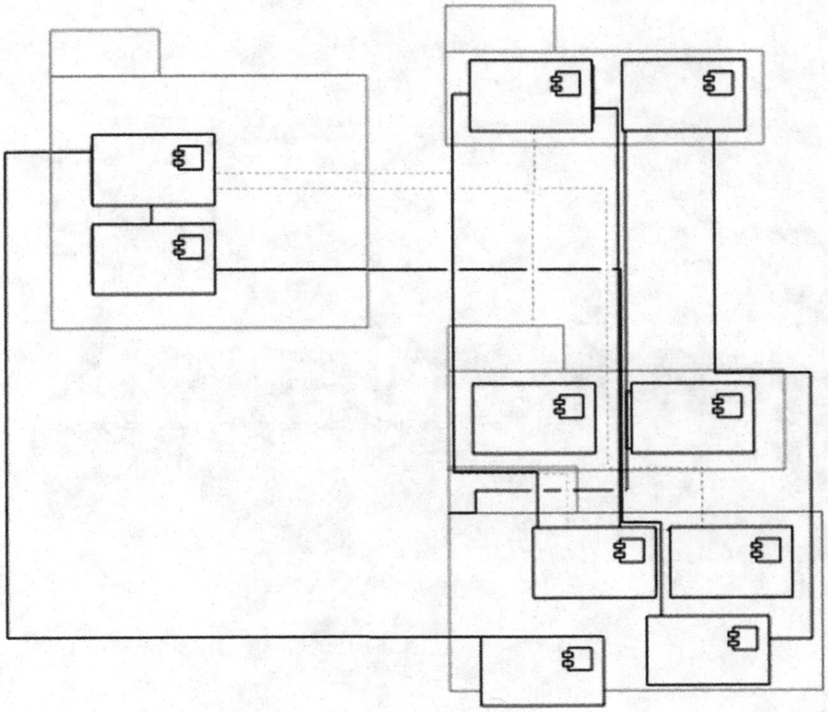

The UH4SP logical architecture had as input 37 use cases and, after executing 4SRS method, was derived with 77 architectural components that compose it (*Figure 9*). It is not the purpose of this diagram to analyze its components, but rather to have a representation to follow the incremental design, thus the

Figure 9. UH4SP logical architecture derived after 4SRS execution

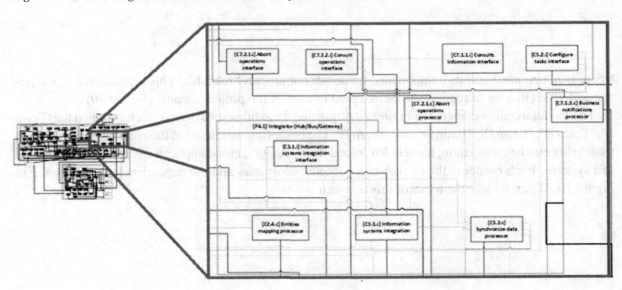

Figure 10. The modularization of the logical architecture

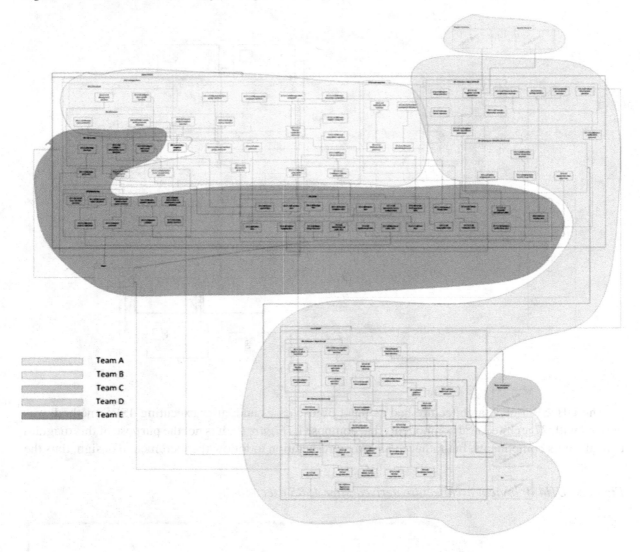

figure is not zoomed and its components' name are not properly readable. This architecture was afterwards divided in a set of modules to be assigned to each of the project's teams (*Figure 10*).

The modularization depicted in *Figure 10* originated 5 modules/subsystems, each assigned for 'Team A', 'Team B', 'Team C', 'Team D' and 'Team E'. The bordering was based in the contributions that each team brings to the consortium, namely IoT, cloud infrastructure, cloud applications and sensors/embedded systems. Each border is thus a part of a complex ecosystem and the dependencies are depicted in *Figure 10*. 'Team B' was the focus of this research.

Incremental Design for Refining the Logical Architecture

As referred in the previous section, the output of performing the 4SRS method during requirements is a candidate logical architectural diagram, composed by a set of software components and relations/flows between them.

The idea is to refine the architecture incrementally, in parallel with the implementation efforts regarding the architectural components that already were refined. Like in most cases, the best approach to issue complex problems is to divide them into smaller ones and address them one by one, ultimately allowing to address the big solution.

With the purpose of modularizing the architecture, the candidate logical architecture is partitioned into sub-systems. AMPLA is able to be performed in parallel within a typical ASD context, however the subsystem bordering is helpful in complex ecosystems contexts. This bordering is likely to reflect the ecosystem, e.g., IoT, cloud, infrastructure, embedded systems, etc., and the dependencies between the subsystems. The sub-system border provides context for modeling more refined Use Cases, as well as context for making technical design decisions that in the initial phase were very difficult to make. The Use Cases may then be used for a new execution of the 4SRS (Figure 11), since they relate to "new" Use Cases that emerged and hence did not exist before the definition of the sub-systems. Within these "new" Use Cases, they may relate to refined use cases from the previous model, as well as relating to new use cases within the same level of refinement. *E.g.*, a sub-system related to a use case {UC1.5} may result in refinements like {UC1.5.1} and {UC1.5.2}, as well as new use cases in the same level of refinement like {UC1.6} and {UC1.7}.

By performing the 4SRS method within this new use case model, the resulting software components relate to refined components for that sub-system that can be "replaced" in the initial candidate architecture, resulting in a more refined version. In order to assure that the defined sub-system, even though composed by more components, is still able to fit in the overall logical architecture, its interfaces must be maintained (system of systems theory). It must be pointed out that the execution of the 4SRS for the new and emerged use cases in Figure 11 are an increment to the previous execution, rather than performing a new 4SRS execution with only the new use cases.

Figure 11. Recursive execution of 4SRS for refining a given example module

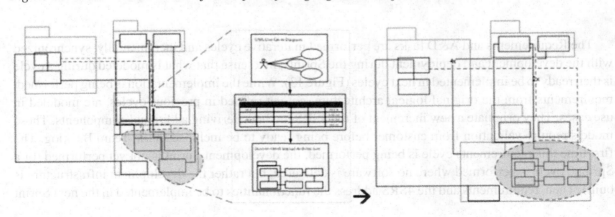

The sub-system requirements are object of analysis within each iterative cycle. In this section is described the refinement process aligned with iterative cycles, e.g., Scrum Sprints. Figure 12 depicts the distribution of the module requirements for refinement and respective implementation tasks to be included as Product Backlog Items (PBI), distributed within the cycles (Sprints).

After each subsystem is defined, the process is then structured as an iterative approach (e.g., Scrum Sprints). Within every iteration, the team performs tasks involving several software engineering disciplines. The terminology from RUP's and AUP's disciplines is used (only for demonstration purposes) to depict the type of effort involved within the Sprints. These efforts are illustrated in Figure 12 by the colored bars within each cycle, where each bar is a software engineering disciplines, and with more or less effort during the cycle, similar to RUP and AUP. The main difference is that, in parallel with carrying out typical disciplines within the Sprints (Implementation, Testing and Deploy) that result in the delivery of a software increment, other team members are responsible for refining requirements regarding the features not yet included in the team's Sprint Backlog, and that are planned to be implemented in further Sprints. These requirements are modeled, hence the Requirements discipline, and then an incremental execution of the 4SRS method, hence the Analysis & Design (A&D) discipline.

Figure 12. Distributed implementation of each architecture module

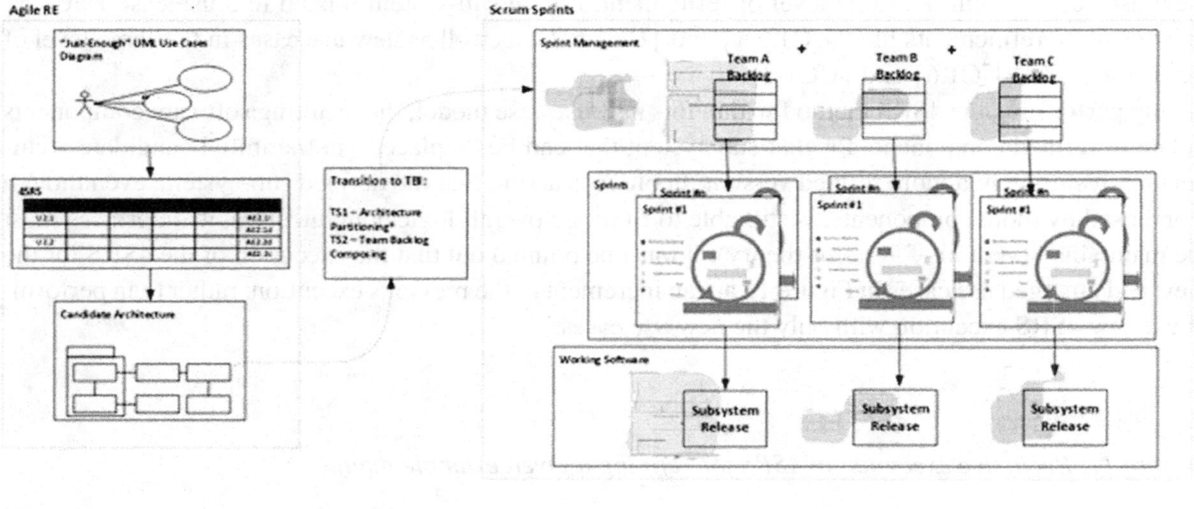

The Requirements and A&D tasks are performed in iterative cycles and incrementally, synchronized with the development and deployment during the Sprints, in a sense that what is modeled during a cycle is then ready to be implemented in next cycles (Figure 13). While the implementation is being performed, requirements from the original logical architecture, not yet refined in previous cycles, are modeled in use cases. They originate a new increment of the 4SRS method, deriving additional components. These models require validation from customer before being ready to be included in the Team Backlog. The first time this requirements cycle is being performed, the development Sprint is not yet performed (or a Sprint 0 cycle is performed where no software is delivered, but rather the development infrastructure is built). Then, requirements and the 4SRS address the functionalities to be implemented in the next Sprint

Figure 13. Incremental requirements and 4SRS execution throughout the Sprints

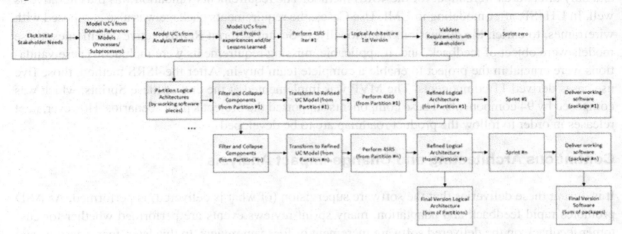

or even more ahead Sprints. It is assumed that, since the components have been refined, they are in an improved situation to be now passed for implementation.

While this refined information is implemented, coded, tested and deployed, ending in a delivery of a software increment to customer, in parallel other model is refined within the same approach (*i.e.*, use cases, 4SRS and architecture). This process is depicted in Figure 14 as a Software Process Engineering Metamodel (SPEM) diagram. This way, when a cycle is finished, it is expectable that new sub-systems were refined and able for implementation.

In the UH4SP project, during the first "Just-enough" modeling, there were 37 use cases and 77 architectural components after performing the 4SRS method. After modularizing, 11 use cases from the 37, and the 15 components from the 77, compose the module under analysis. Finally, the requirements refinement output 29 use cases, *i.e.*, 18 refined functionalities, which then derived 37 architectural components from the 4SRS method. Having in mind the large-scale and complex ecosystem context of the project, these values may be perceived as acceptable. It is an increase of almost three times as the original models. The refinement was performed incrementally and in parallel with team's Sprints (using Scrum), as in *Figure 14*. The requirements were refined, modeled and validated with the consortium,

Figure 14. Parallel tasks within Sprints in SPEM diagram

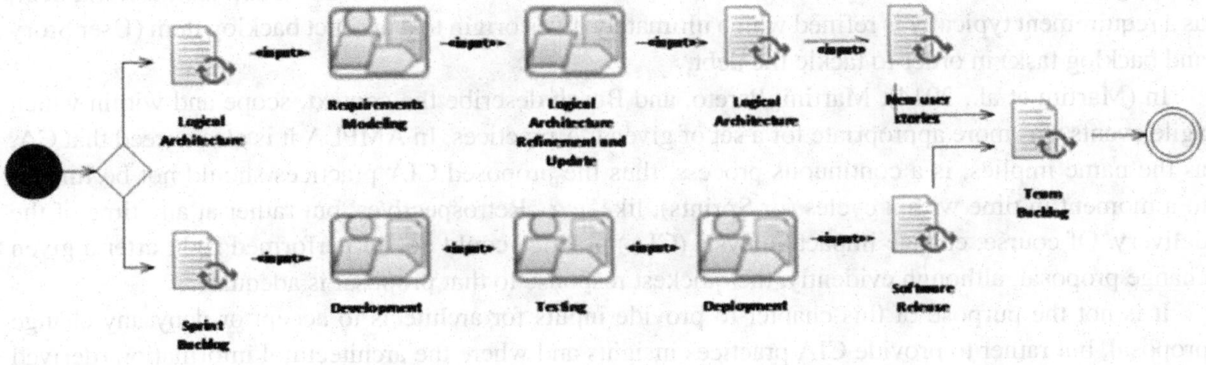

and only afterwards were input for the 4SRS method. The requirements validation was thus iterative as well. In UH4SP, after modeling in UML Use Cases, the requirements package was also composed with wireframes, to enrich the discussion. Additionally, in Scrum's Sprint Retrospective ceremonies, these models were object of feedback, and, if applicable, missing requirements were included. These validations were crucial in the project to enable a complete team buy-in. After the 4SRS method, those five use cases derived 11 components. The MVP was implemented at the end of these Sprints, which was composed by 94 components. These components supported the project's pilot scenarios. However, next releases in order to follow the product roadmap are to be developed.

Continuous Architecting and Change-Impact Analysis

It is during these deliveries that the software supervision (of what is delivered) is performed. As ASD promotes rapid feedback and adaptation, many sprint reviews events are performed whether for customer feedback on the delivered software increment or for team review. In this later, many designs and implementation decisions are made, whether related to the team's perception of the delivered quality, the development process, the adopted technologies or concerning the way the architecture is emerging. And it is based on the customer feedback or team review that changes during the cycles. For both cases, a proper in-depth analysis (especially for safety-critical systems) related to the proposed changes should be performed.

Just like during the refinement process, the remaining sprints the teams perform tasks related to several disciplines. In this section, the "Analysis & Design" discipline is focused.

The architecture should be present at all moments of the development. Whenever new requirements emerge, or a need for change/refactoring of a given component is identified, the architect should carefully analyze the impact before accepting such occurrences.

As described in the previous section, AMPLA provides traceability between requirements models (UML Use Cases), architectural components (UML Components) and the product backlog items. Thus, it is within these three artifacts that impact analysis may be based on.

The architect may analyze the architectural artifact (arrow (a) in *Figure 15*) for a component candidate for refactoring, which remaining components are affected by any change to that component, or depicting which quality characteristic is affected. Alternatively, the architect may trace back to the requirements model for depicting the business value of the requirements that relate to the component affected by the refactoring (arrow (b) in *Figure 15*). Finally, when a new requirement emerges, it is added to the UML Use Cases model and afterward "follows" the AMPLA process flow towards the architecture and product backlog (arrow (a) in *Figure 15*). Arrow (c) may also relate to address technical and architectural debt, as a requirement typically is refined which ultimately gives origin to a product backlog item (User Story and backlog task) in order to tackle the debt.

In (Martini et al., 2014), Martini, Pareto, and Bosch describe the context, scope and within which agile events was more appropriate for a set of given CA practices. In AMPLA it is also agreed that CA, as the name implies, is a continuous process, thus the proposed CIA practices should not be limited to a moment in time within cycles (or Sprints), like, e.g., Retrospectives, but rather at any time of the delivery. Of course, change impact analysis (CIA) practice could not be performed right after a given change proposal, although evidently, the quickest response to that proposal is adequate.

It is not the purpose of this chapter to provide inputs for architects to accept or deny any change proposal, but rather to provide CIA practices insights and where the architectural information (derived

Figure 15. Possible targets of CIA within AMPLA

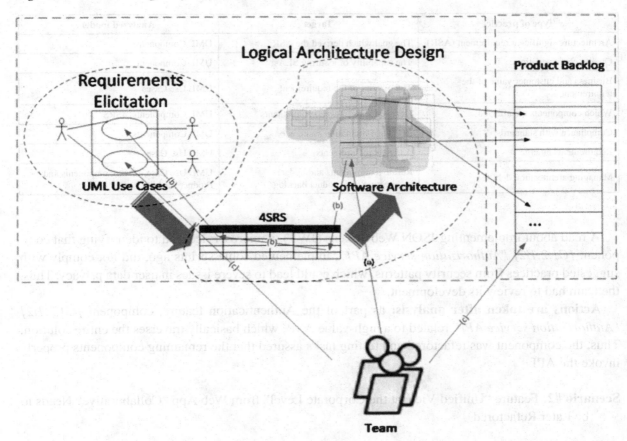

within AMPLA) is located in order for providing the required inputs for an appropriate decision, as listed in *Table 3*. Thus, the proposed CIA practices allow analyzing, monitoring and assessing the architectures in many ways, the architectural value of the sprint increment, sprint business value, increments dependencies, architecture compliance, risk management, architectural debt, controlling architecture erosion are some examples. If analyzed all, or just some of them, the architect is able to provide an appropriate acceptance or denial of a change proposal.

In the UH4SP project, the requirements from the architecture modules were refined in order to have detailed information to specify software services, due to the fact that the goal was to develop microservices that support business processes in a cloud-computing environment.

The architecture module under analysis included developing two microservices: "Authentication" and "Collaborative" services. In next sections are demonstrated examples of change proposals during the Sprints.

Scenario #1: Microservice "Authentication" not Assures Compliance with Security Standards

Table 3. List of CIA practices and their targeted models

Type of practice	Target	Analyzed model
Architecture significant requirement (ASR)	The goal which derived the ASR	UML Component
Quality characteristic	The capability of assuring SLAs	UML Component
Business and customer value of the requirement	The priority of the requirement	UML Use Cases
Which components are affected	Dependencies between components	UML Components, 4SRS
Compliance with standards	Legal and regulation assurance	UML Components
Requirements emerge	Add new requirements	UML Use Case
Managing architectural debt	Refine requirements and update architecture and product backlog	UML Use Case, UML Components and Product Backlog items

A read about implementing JSON Web Tokens (JWT) in microservices led to identifying that component *{C1.2.1i2}* *"Authorization service API"*, implemented some sprints ago, did not comply with suggested practices from security patterns, which could lead to severe issues in user data privacy. Thus, the team had to review its development.

Actions are taken after analysis: as part of the Authentication feature, component *{C1.2.1i2}* *"Authorization service API"* related to a high-value ASR, which basically traverses the entire solution. Thus, the component was refactored and testing tasks assured that the remaining components properly invoke the API.

Scenario #2: Feature "Unified View at the Corporate Level" from Web App "Collaborative" Needs to be Later Refactored

The component {C5.3.1.i} *"Consult operational indicators interface"* is basically responsible for a user interface based on a specific dataset stored in the cloud. Because the dataset sent to the cloud was not stable and still in development, ultimately this component was not retrieving "cleaned" daily production data. While another team was responsible for providing the dataset, the team needed to assure component could interface with that dataset.

Actions are Taken After Analysis: As component {C5.3.1.i} *"Consult operational indicators interface"* related to a high-value feature for the customer in the current release, it was iteratively developed and also work was continuously aligned with the dataset development (with frequent meetings with the other team) in order to follow the dataset structure evolution. When both were implemented, testing needed to be performed to components {C5.3.1.i2}; {C5.3.1.i}; {C1.2.1.i2}; {C1.1.1.i2}, that directly interact with component {C5.3.1.i}.

Scenario #3: Feature "Work tokens" from Web App "Authentication" Needs Refinement

From the initial requirements elicitation, feature "Work tokens" was designed to support a work assignment process. However, when reviewing software increment with the customer, it was identified that the logic of this process was more complex than initially discussed, which required that requirements had to be refined.

Actions are Taken After Analysis: The requirements were refined, namely eliciting and modeling five new UML use cases to the previous diagram. These new use cases were added to the 4SRS method, deriving new components to be added to the logical architecture and items for the future backlog.

DISCUSSION AND FUTURE TRENDS

Applying DUARTE affected use case modeling with the following advantages:

- Overall, the use of agile practices *per se* did not make the process agile, but allowed specifying agilely the right product for the customer's needs. Delivering the product right is promoted by using Scrum, Kanban, XP, SAFe or LeSS, for instance, which is also present in AMPLA.
- Promoting scenarios discovery and exploration allowed defining 15 scenarios from four groups (from the project's objectives). Without the exploring, each groups would probably include one or two scenarios.
- Defining bounded contexts using DDD allowed to clearly understanding boundaries between what requirements different teams could address. The use of the Lean Startup strategy allowed to refine only the use cases from the MVP hypothesis that the project aim validating, rather than refining all use cases, even those that would not been included in the MVP.
- These practices ease customer feedback, which is fundamental in any ASD process.

AMPLA provides a method for deriving a candidate logical architecture based in UML Use Cases, the 4SRS method. The approach also validated the coverage of the elicited "just-enough" model, gathered together with identified key stakeholders. The "just-enough" UML Use Case model allows to early identify main features, which provides an overview of the project and its scope. The design of "just-enough" architecture used an architectural method, the 4SRS, to derive the candidate architecture based in the small set of ("just-enough") UML Use Cases. There is not any difference within the steps of the method, in comparison with the original method, to derive a candidate architecture. Rather, as the input are high-level requirements in opposition to more refined ones, one may experience difficulties in identifying a proper classification of the use case in order to decide the components to be maintained within the second step, since a more refined information helps in better define the component's nature. However, as in AMPLA the requirements will be later refined and will emerge, the 4SRS method is used as in a "living table" that is opened alongside the development Sprints, rather than a waterfall-based and one-time-execution approach, providing traceability between the requirements and the components in order to agilely respond to changes.

Defining a traceability method for supporting the CIA for architectural decision-making from feature adding and changing arose many challenges. The model traceability between architecture and requirements strengthened AMPLA in a sense of architecture maintenance during ASD. However, implementing the method was a learning process, with advantages and disadvantages, which are detailed in this section.

Applying the CIA within AMPLA allowed supporting architectural decision-making with the following **advantages**:

Identify Architecture Value Proposed for Change: Is a feature is proposed for change, traceability to architectural models allows identifying if that change affects components that are ASR's if the requirements relating to a high customer value feature or if it relates to imposition from standards and policies compliance.

Depicting Dependencies: Revisiting the 4SRS method execution allows identifying dependencies with other components from architecture, which are affected by a given change

Adding and Refining Requirements: Either derived from new needs from stakeholders or from technical debts, the decision to add or refine requirements is eased by modeling the new requirements and derive the resulting new components by performing the 4SRS method.

CIA Practices Validation: In this research, the presented scenarios included using all the proposed CIA practices (ASR, Quality characteristic, Business and customer value of the requirement, Which components are affected, Compliance with standards, Requirements emerge, and Managing architectural debt).

However, applying the method faces some obstacles/**disadvantages**, namely:

Quantity of Models for Sprint 0 and Refinements: AMPLA proposes additional activities and artifacts for modeling (sequence, use cases, 4SRS and components diagrams), which may be perceived as a disadvantage. However, the method provides traceability between models, which eases the agility of analyzing changes.

Need for Revisiting a set of Models Within Each Change: Whenever a change is proposed, the CIA may result in considering changes in more than one model (e.g., change use cases, then perform 4SRS and derive new logical architecture), which can be time-consuming.

It also needs to be pointed out some **threats to the validity** of this research, namely:

Method's Learning Curve: AMPLA was only applied by the method's designers, thus it was not possible to depict in the UH4SP project any possible data regarding the adoption of the method by other teams.

Team's Involvement: It was difficult to commit the entire UH4SP consortium towards the approach. The candidate architecture was proposed and the sub-systems delivered to all entities, however, it was not possible to assess CIA and possibly identify new change scenarios besides the one's our team addressed. Other teams used Scrum for their sub-systems but did not follow a refinement approach like AMPLA, hence the traceability was not assured.

Newly-Formed Team: The fact that it was a completely new development team and, mainly, first time implementing microservices architectures, may have led to situations that the team was unable to identify a need for changing in how a microservice should have been implemented and hence reported such change during sprint review events.

Identified Practices: Although the scenarios refer to three different change needs (in fact other changes were proposed during the UH4SP project, but they fell under the scope of these three scenarios, thus for demonstration purposes they were already represented), it is impossible to assure that the additional scenarios may occur in the future that require other CIA practices than the ones proposed in this paper. The proposed CIA practices were based in the scenarios, and the literature review did not perceive the need for additional practices, however, missing practices can not be ruled out.

The initial three phases of AMPLA (Requirements Elicitation, Requirements Analysis & Modeling and Architecture Design) required having dedicated teams for conducting these phases, with more focus in modeling. Only when entering the fourth and final phase, the Delivery Cycles, project teams were included in the process. In projects with more than one team, the dedicated team for conducting the first three phases was composed by representatives from the involved teams. However, in settings of more than one team, each team may start defining requirements from the beginning, rather than start by a "shared" model, like our proposed candidate architecture. There is a need for future research in a proper discussion on the suitability of parallel requirements emerging rather than starting with a single architecture proposal.

The MVP requirements elicitation may be performed by gathering stakeholder's individual needs, also referred as "bespoke", "custom" or "tailor-made" RE (Fernandes & Machado, 2016). Alternatively, it may be oriented to a combination of a number of known customers, or to a mass-market where customers cannot be clearly pinpointed, also referred as "market-driven RE" (MDRE) (Regnell & Brinkkemper, 2005). DUARTE is oriented for requirements elicitation together with a set of key stakeholders (e.g., business owner, product lead, etc.) that have clearly defined their business needs, based on a previously defined market strategy. Hence, this phase is clearly based in Bespoke RE. Alternatively, elicitation could be based in involving customers or other market entities (MDRE). This context will be object of future research. Especially for companies adopting Lean Startup, which aim launching their MVP with no specifically identified customer to bespoke their requirements, MDRE will be for sure the proper adoption for RE.

CONCLUSION

This chapter discusses requirements modeling approaches in ASD settings, where research addressed initial artifact proposal regarding processes of upfront requirements elicitation and modeling, and a later artifact proposal for emerging requirements (DUARTE). Upfront requirements was used towards use case-driven and user story-driven Product Backlogs. DUARTE was used towards user story-driven Product Backlogs based in AMPLA.

While use case-driven Product Backlogs used directly the UML Use Cases from the requirements modeling as backlog items, the inputs for being able to define user story-driven Product Backlogs required a set of models, namely UML Use Cases and logical architecture (UML Components), supported by architectural method 4SRS and V-Model for traceability purposes.

AMPLA is a process for model derivation applicable in an Agile RE and AM context. Firstly, more specifically regarding Agile RE, this research presented the DUARTE approach, which is inspired by a V-Model approach based in successive model derivation, namely referring to sequence, use case and components diagrams, this process aims modeling the same artifacts however using agile practices such as Lean Startup, Design Thinking, DDD, BDD, and others. The model derivation follows typical agile feedback loops, encompassing discovery and exploration, learning from feedbacks and adjusting posterior loops. It also addresses AM so requirements emerge from these loops, by including only core and high-level requirements in early phase of projects, use them for deriving a UML components diagram using the 4SRS method, and further incremental refinements within development cycles (e.g., Scrum Sprints). The approach also validated the coverage of the elicited "just-enough" model, gathered together with identified key stakeholders.

A need for changing a software's code or architecture is getting more frequent in software projects. The customer involvement as proposed by ASD values promotes embracing those changes, requiring decisions from the business but also from architects. Agile architecting is about continuous design and evolution of the solution, by acknowledging the architecture's evolution but assuring such evolution is not endangered by business decisions. Included within the AMPLA method, this research presented how CA is supported during ASD iteration cycles, by supporting CIA practices for eventual changes proposals.

Due to the model traceability supported by AMPLA, impact-analysis could be discussed. This research demonstrated performing CIA practices namely ASR, Quality characteristic, Business and customer value of the requirement, Which components are affected, Compliance with standards, Requirements emerge and Managing architectural debt.

ACKNOWLEDGMENT

This work has been supported by FCT – Fundação para a Ciência e Tecnologia within the R&D Units Project Scope: UIDB/00319/2020.

REFERENCES

Abrahamsson, P., Babar, M. A., & Kruchten, P. (2010). Agility and architecture: Can they coexist? *IEEE Software, 27*(2), 16–22. doi:10.1109/MS.2010.36

Agile Alliance. (2001). *Manifesto for agile software development*. Author.

Ali Babar, M., Brown, A. W., & Mistrík, I. (2013). *Agile Software Architecture: Aligning Agile Processes and Software Architectures*. Elsevier.

Ambler, S. (2002). *Agile modeling: effective practices for extreme programming and the unified process*. John Wiley & Sons, Inc.

Ambler, S. (2007, Feb.). Agile Model Driven Development (AMDD). Xootic Magazine.

Bellomo, S., Kruchten, P., Nord, R., & Ozkaya, I. (2014). How to Agilely Architect an Agile Architecture. *Cutter IT Journal*.

Brown, T. (2009). *Change by Design: How Design Thinking Transforms Organizations and Inspires Innovation*. Harper Collins.

Cao, L., & Ramesh, B. (2008). Agile requirements engineering practices: An empirical study. *IEEE Software, 25*(1), 60–67. doi:10.1109/MS.2008.1

Caroli, P. (2019). Lean Inception: How to Align People and Build the Right Product. Retrieved from https://martinfowler.com/articles/lean-inception/

Cockburn, A. (2006). *Agile software development: the cooperative game*. Pearson Education.

Coplien, J. O., & Bjørnvig, G. (2011). *Lean architecture: for agile software development*. John Wiley & Sons.

Cruz, E. F., Machado, R. J., & Santos, M. Y. (2014). *On the Decomposition of Use Cases for the Refinement of Software Requirements. In 2014 14th International Conference on Computational Science and Its Applications* (pp. 237–240). IEEE; doi:10.1109/ICCSA.2014.54.

Evans, E. (2004). *Domain-driven design : tackling complexity in the heart of software*. Addison-Wesley.

Farhan, S., Tauseef, H., & Fahiem, M. A. (2009). Adding agility to architecture tradeoff analysis method for mapping on crystal. In WRI World Congress on Software Engineering (WCSE'09) (Vol. 4, pp. 121–125). IEEE. doi:10.1109/WCSE.2009.405

Fernandes, J. M., & Machado, R. J. (2016). Requirements in Engineering Projects. Springer International Publishing. doi:10.1007/978-3-319-18597-2

Ferreira, N., Santos, N., Machado, R. J., Fernandes, J. E., & Gasevic, D. (2014). A V-Model Approach for Business Process Requirements Elicitation in Cloud Design. Advanced Web Services, 551–578.

Fitzgerald, B., & Stol, K.-J. (2017). Continuous software engineering: A roadmap and agenda. *Journal of Systems and Software*, *123*, 176–189. doi:10.1016/j.jss.2015.06.063

Grau, B. R., & Lauenroth, K. (2014). Requirements engineering and agile development - collaborative, just enough, just in time, sustainable. International Requirements Engineering Board. IREB.

IIBA. (2017). *Agile Extension to the BABOK Guide v2*. International Institute of Business Analysis.

Jeon, S., Han, M., Lee, E., & Lee, K. (2011). Quality attribute driven agile development. In *9th International Conference on Software Engineering Research, Management and Applications (SERA)* (pp. 203–210). IEEE. 10.1109/SERA.2011.24

Kazman, R. (2013). Foreword - Bringing the Two Together: Agile Architecting or Architecting for Agile? In Agile Software Architecture: Aligning Agile Processes and Software Architectures (pp. xxix–xxx). Elsevier.

Kruchten, P. (1995). The 4+1 View Model of Architecture. *IEEE Software*, *12*(6), 42–50. doi:10.1109/52.469759

Madison, J. (2010). Agile architecture interactions. *IEEE Software*, *27*(2), 41–48. doi:10.1109/MS.2010.35

Martini, A., Pareto, L., & Bosch, J. (2014). Role of Architects in Agile Organizations. In J. Bosch (Ed.), Continuous Software Engineering. Springer Cham. doi:10.1007/978-3-319-11283-1_4

Nord, R., Ozkaya, I., & Kruchten, P. (2014). Agile in distress: architecture to the rescue. In T. Dingsøyr & N. B. Moe (Eds.), *International Conference on Agile Software Development (XP'14)* (pp. 43–57). Springer Verlag; doi:10.1007/978-3-319-14358-3_5.

Nord, R. L., & Tomayko, J. E. (2006). Software architecture-centric methods and agile development. *IEEE Software*, *23*(2), 47–53. doi:10.1109/MS.2006.54

Regnell, B., & Brinkkemper, S. (2005). Market-Driven Requirements Engineering for Software Products. In Engineering and Managing Software Requirements (pp. 287–308). Springer-Verlag., doi:10.1007/3-540-28244-0_13

Ries, E. (2011). *The lean startup: How today's entrepreneurs use continuous innovation to create radically successful businesses*. Crown Books.

Schwaber, K., & Beedle, M. (2001). *Agile Software Development with Scrum*. Prentice Hall.

Smart, J. F. (2015). *BDD in Action: Behavior-driven development for the whole software lifecycle*. Manning.

Waterman, M., Noble, J., & Allan, G. (2012). How much architecture? Reducing the up-front effort. In A. G. I. L. E. India (Ed.), (pp. 56–59). IEEE; doi:10.1109/AgileIndia.2012.11.

Woods, E. (2015). Aligning Architecture Work with Agile Teams. *IEEE Software*, *32*(5), 24–26. doi:10.1109/MS.2015.119

Yang, C., Liang, P., & Avgeriou, P. (2016). A systematic mapping study on the combination of software architecture and agile development. *Journal of Systems and Software*, *111*, 157–184; Advance online publication. doi:10.1016/j.jss.2015.09.028

KEY TERMS AND DEFINITIONS

Agile Logical Architecting: Architecture design practices that allows the logical architecture to emerge throughout the iterations (e.g., Scrum sprints), allowing to derive the scope and functionalities of the system.

Agile Modeling: Agile modeling is the task of developing emerging model-based artifacts, related to requirements and design, properly performed under agile software development. The models emerge as a "just-in-time" need for further implementation.

Bespoke RE: RE elicitation activities performed by gathering stakeholder's individual needs (e.g., interviews, workshops, questionnaires).

Change Impact Analysis (CIA): A technique that identifies the effect of a change or estimates the tasks required to implement a change.

Continuous Architecting: Architecture design practices that evolves iteratively and responds to changes, in order to ease agility and continuous delivery.

Evolutionary Design: Evolutionary design means that the design of the system grows as the system is implemented. As the software solution evolves, the design changes.

Logical Architectures: A logical architecture is an abstraction view of functionality-based elements that support a system's functional requirements, relations between them and with external systems, embodying design decisions. It is typically represented as objects or object classes, or as components.

Minimum Viable Product (MVP): Software release that includes minimum working functionalities, with a hypothesis-driven mindset, in order to get further feedbacks from the market.

Chapter 4
Service–Oriented Computing Applications (SOCA) Development Methodologies:
A Review of Agility–Rigor Balance

Laura C. Rodriguez-Martinez
Tecnológico Nacional de México/IT Aguascalientes, Mexico

Hector A. Duran-Limon
CUCEA, Universidad de Guadalajara, Jalisco, Mexico

Manuel Mora
iD https://orcid.org/0000-0003-1631-5931
Autonomous University of Aguascalientes, Mexico

ABSTRACT

Software development methodologies (SDMs) have had an accepted evolution (i.e., the replacement of SDMs of one era to the next) through the pre-methodology and early-methodology eras to the methodology era. But in the last 20 years, the transition of the methodology era (rigor-oriented) to the post-methodology era (agile-oriented) has led a debate on benefits and drawbacks of rigor vs. agile orientation. Regarding the general software-engineering evolution, the service-oriented software engineering (SOSE) that studies service-oriented computing (SOC) development approaches, which are widely used to develop software-oriented computing applications (SOCA), has emerged. SOSE developers then face the problem of selecting and adapting a SOCA SDM. This chapter compares 11 SOCA SDM on agility-rigor balance by a framework of Boehm and Turner addressing the rigor-agility conflicts by defining three factors and their methodological characteristics. Each characteristic is evaluated for each SDM with a novel agility-rigor 45-point scale. Results suggest three of such SDMs are agility-rigor balanced.

DOI: 10.4018/978-1-7998-4165-4.ch004

INTRODUCTION

Software development tasks have used methodologies that can be tracked from four eras (Avison & Fitzgerald, 2003; Rodriguez et al., 2008). The pre-methodology era where no software engineering methodology was available only supported a generic programming approach. In the early-methodology era the first software engineering methodologies such as Waterfall (Royce, 1970) and SADT (Dickover, McGowan & Ross, 1977) emerged. The methodology era included more comprehensive and rigorous software engineering methodologies such as Spiral (Boehm, 1988), RUP (Kruchten, 2004), and MBASE (Boehm et al., 2004) . Lastly, the post-methodology era involves the agility approach (Dyba & Dingsoyr, 2009), which emerged in the last 20 years with Scrum (Sutherland & Schwaber, 2011) and XP (Beck, 1999) as the main development methodologies.

According to Avison and Fitzgerald (2003) and Rodriguez et al. (2008), the transition and evolution from one era to the next one has been well-accepted from developers and project managers because an era advanced on new development technology paradigms (e.g. object-oriented programming languages) and/ or advanced on new required project management knowledge for a better project control over the previous era. This seamless evolution occurred from the pre-methodology era toward the early-methodology one, as well as from this one toward the methodology era. However, the last transition from the methodology era (based on a rigorous approach) toward the post-methodology era (based on an agile approach) has had some methodological conflicts and debates (Boehm, 2002; de Marco & Boehm, 2002).

The methodology era prescribes the need of rigorous methodologies to control and document practically "everything" that occurred in the project. However, such rigor (also called heavy-process methodologies) approaches imply a heavy weight processes, which can be complex to follow. Such methodological difficulties fostered the emergence of a counter-approach based on agility. Nevertheless, this emergent agile development approach, while reducing drastically the "everything" is in control, has been identified as a hard practice to perform it correctly. According to Beck and Boehm the agile development approaches rely on a "technically premier team" (2003), and thus "agility is only possible through greater discipline on the part of everyone involved." (Beck & Boehm, 2003; pp. 44). Consequently, current software developers and software project managers face on one hand the difficulty to correctly execute an agile development process -regarding its proper characteristics, like implicit quality controls, and the need of high creativity programmers-, and on the other hand the difficulty to execute a rigorist -heavy or highly planed or controlled- development process that emphasizes the documentation and the control of tasks rather than the creativity on the development process and the evolvability of the developed product (Sommerville, 2005). Additionally, Beck & Boehm (2003) reported that a lack of rigor on development methodologies lead to failed software projects although agile development methodologies avoid the bureaucratic documentation issues. Given that both the rigorous and agile approaches have presented benefits and drawbacks, balanced methodologies for software development have been proposed (Beck & Boehm, 2003; Boehm & Turner, 2004). As Beck and Boehm (2003; pp. 46) report, there are required "efforts to synthesize the best from agile and plan-driven methods to address our future challenges of simultaneously achieving high software dependability, agility, and scalability."

This chapter addresses such a topic (i.e. the rigorous-agile balanced software development approach) but from a relatively new development technology perspective of Service-Oriented Software Engineering / Service-Oriented Computing SOSE/SOC (Papazoglou et al., 2006; Rodriguez-Martinez et al., 2012). SOSE research stream investigates systematic, disciplined and quantifiable approaches to develop service-oriented systems (Gu & Lago, 2011). SOC is a computing paradigm which *"utilizes services as the constructs to support the development of rapid, low-cost and easy composition of distributed applications.*

Services are autonomous, platform-independent computational entities that can be used in a platform independent way" (Papazoglou et al., 2006; pp. 224). SOC can be considered a technological driver which has contributed to move from the methodology era toward the post-methodology one. Hence, this chapter presents a study of the level of agility-rigor balance of several software development methodologies that can be used to develop Service-Oriented Computing Applications (SOCA) (i.e. software applications built/assembled from a suite of available computing services).

This article aims to help software engineering academicians and professionals with the provision of a compact but substantive descriptive-comparative guide over agility-rigor balancing of a set of eleven methodologies to develop Service Oriented Computing Applications.

Background

This section provides definitions over a literature review that support the framework for evaluating the agility-rigor balance of the methodologies.

Software Development Methodology Eras

Software development is a highly complex activity and thus several software development methodologies have been proposed from the different evolutive eras (Avison & Fitzgerald, 2003). Each era evolves from other preexisting ones. The early-methodology era pursued to provide a high-level software development life cycle process which was not existent in the pre-methodology era. The methodology era advanced the early-methodology era by providing heavy-process or rigorous methodologies pursuing a more controlled software development life cycle process. This methodology era of rigorous methodologies demands having all the requirements in the early development phases and also requires having minimal or none changes at all in the next phases. In the next post-methodology era appears the agile methodologies that try to simplify the software development life cycle process control by maximizing the possibility to accept and accommodate any required change as well as achieving a faster delivery of a valuable functional software, which can evolve during the next iterations.

Software Development Methodologies in the Methodology Era

Two exemplary cases of software development methodologies in the Methodology era are the Rational Unified Process for Systems Engineering (RUP SE) (Cantor, 2003) (extended from the classic RUP methodology (Kruchten, 2004)) and the Model-based System Architecting and Software Engineering (MBASE) (Boehm et al., 2004). Both methodologies include the flexibility of an iterative and incremental process, both are well-defined methodologies according to the expected structure of phases, activities, roles, artifacts and tools (Oktaba & Ibargüengoita, 1998), and both approaches include relevant activities for modern software projects like Risk Management and Business Modeling activities.

The RUP SE (Cantor, 2003) is a methodology proposed as an enhancement of the well-known object-oriented or component-based RUP methodology (Kruchten, 2004). This methodology incorporates additional diagrams and techniques no reported in the standard RUP such as: context diagrams, system use cases with services, business process, process interaction diagrams and system and sub-system architectures. The RUP SE is also based on an iterative-incremental development approach, which combines activities (that can be repeated in an iterative way), within phases which end with specific control milestones. The phases and activities (named disciplines) in the RUP SE are the same ones reported in other RUP methodologies. These phases are: Inception, Elaboration, Construction and Transition; and the activities are: Business Modeling, Requirements, Analysis and Design, Implementation, Test, Deployment, Configuration and Change Management, Project Management and Environment Management. In particular, the Business Modeling activity is mandatory and not optional as in standard RUP, and it is augmented with additional analysis diagrams (Cantor, 2003).

The MBASE methodology provides a system-based approach for developing integrated software systems (Boehm et al., 2004). MBASE is based on the updated version of the Boehm's Win-Win Spiral Model (Boehm et al., 1998) which proposes a system's specification with six elements: Operational Concept Description (OCD), System and Software Requirements Definition (SSRD), System and Software Architecture Description (SSAD), Life Cycle Plan (LCP), Feasibility Rationale Description (FRD), and Risk-driven prototypes. This methodology combines an incremental approach (with Inception, Elaboration, Construction, and Transition phases) with an iterative strategy (for developing the six core elements previously reported) for developing software systems. Similar to the RUP SE, each phase ends with specific control milestones. In MBASE there are three core control milestones: Life-Cycle Objectives (LCO), Life-Cycle Architecture and Plan (LCA), and an Initial Product ready for Operational use (IOC). In MBASE, the Business Modeling and Risk Analysis activities are also considered core activities and not optional ones as reported in other SDMs.

Software Development Methodologies in the Post-Methodology Era (Agile Era)

Scrum (Sutherland & Schwaber, 2011) and XP (Beck, 1999) are two of the most representative software development methodologies in the post-methodology era (agile era). Scrum and XP are the first agile software development methodologies which emerged in the post-methodology era during the 1995-2001 period and are some of the most used methodologies at present (Hoda, Salleh, & Grundy, 2018). The Scrum methodology is focused on Project Management life cycle processes whereas XP focuses on the Software Development life cycle process, so both are usually combined for their utilization. According to (Abrahamsson, Oza, & Siponen, 2010) the agile software development methodologies promote a frequent and small release of useful software, acceptance of changes during the execution of the project, and the co-responsibility on the software product from the whole team (i.e. developer team, project coordinator and the customer).

One of many distinguishing features between agile and rigorous software development methodologies is the way in which software requirements are managed. It is common in heavy linear software development methodologies to identify and froze the set of software requirements at most as possible during the project initiation and planning phases. Then, software requirements are rigorously controlled. In contrast, in an agile software development process which is incremental, the requirements are managed through the delivery of successive software increments partitioning the software requirements to be implemented in each of the increments. Under these requirement management differences, if the software requirements are rigorously controlled in some methodologies, they are considered heavy-process or rigorous ones, but, if they have some flexibility in revising the software requirements as the software product evolves, they are considered agile software development methodologies. As Bourque and Farley (2014; pp. 8-5) establishes *"Agile models may define product scope and high-level features initially; however, agile models are designed to facilitate evolution of the software requirements during the project. It must be emphasized that the continuum of SDLCs from linear to agile is not a thin, straight line. Elements of different approaches may be incorporated into a specific model; for example, an incremental software development life cycle model may incorporate sequential software requirements and design phases but permit considerable flexibility in revising the software requirements and architecture during software construction.*" This continuous vision from rigor toward agility also suggests the possibility of balanced software development methodologies in the middle part of this continuous line.

Similarly, according with a relatively new survey (Javanmard & Alian, 2015; pp. 1386), "*the key difference between heavyweight and agile methodologies is the adaptability factor. In an agile methodology if any major change is required, the team doesn't freeze its work process; rather it determines how to better handle changes that occur throughout the project. The verification process in agile method occurs much earlier in the development process. On the other hand, heavyweight methods freeze product requirements and disallow change. It implements a predictive process and relies on defining and documenting a stable set of requirements at the beginning of a project*".

Agile methodologies, thus, promote a people-intensive empirical software development process coordination approach vs. a process-intensive well-defined software development process control used in rigorous methodologies. Most of the task coordination of agile methodologies is over the personal-discipline of the developers and of a continuous evaluation-feedback (Javanmard & Alian, 2015). In contrast, in rigorous software development methodologies the people's tasks are strongly controlled and any deviation from planned tasks is avoided.

The Service-Oriented Computing Approach

Service-Oriented Computing (SOC) is an emerging topic regarding Service-oriented Software Engineering (SOSE). SOSE is a software development paradigm which advances on the previous Object-oriented and Component-based Software Engineering (OOSE and CBSE) paradigms (Gu & Lago, 2009). The SOSE paradigm aims to produce high-quality Service-oriented Computing Applications (SOCAs). These SOCAs can be defined as software systems built through a suite of software services. Software services are auto-contained computational work units provided by internal or external parties (service providers) to other parties (service customers) (Miller & Mukerji, 2003). Software services have also been defined as "*autonomous, platform-independent entities that can be described, published, discovered, and loosely coupled in novel ways*" (Papazoglou & Van Den Heuvel, 2007).

According to several authors (Zimmermann et al., 2004; Papazoglou et al., 2006) a Service-oriented Computing (SOC) approach provides new capabilities and technical challenges for designing and building software applications. These main challenges are: 1) a SOC application (i.e. a SOCA or Service-Oriented Computing Application) is built with the use of a set of services in a way that multiple SOCAs could simultaneously use the same set of services; 2) the set of services are platform-independent which increases the SOCA inter-operability; 3) the set of services can be provided for different heterogeneous and external computational platforms to the service customer SOCA; 4) SOCAs should dynamically re-configure their contracted services (e.g. some consumed services can be supplied from one services supplier during some period of time, and the service can also be supplied from another alternative service providers during another period of time); 5) SOCAs demand the utilization of new SOC programming technologies although older technologies can be adapted via wrappers; and 6) a new conceptual layer on business processes is added and thus this one must be considered mandatory in the Requirements and Design phases of SOC development methodologies.

A SOCA can also be defined as a distributed and loosely coupled software system represented and constructed as a main customer control code calling a suite of computational services (Arsanjani et al., 2008). A SOCA differs from an Object-Oriented Computing Application (OOCA) and a Component-based Computing Application (CBCA) in several ways. In the Table 1 are reported these differences (Korbyn, 2000; Hopkins, 2000). In particular, two critical differences regard coupling and interoperability. In the case of a SOCA (Reyes-Delgado, et al., 2015), loosely coupling and a high interoperability in their building blocks, involve their main benefits.

Table 1. Comparative Table of OOCA, CBCA and SOCA

Attribute	Object-oriented Computing Application	Component-based Computing Application	Service-oriented Computing Application
Main entity for analysis	Class	Business component	Business service
Main entity for design	Object (conceptual)	Component (conceptual)	Business computing service
Main entity for runtime	Object (local runtime)	Component (local or distributed runtime)	ICT computing service
Coupling level	Tightly	Medium	Loosely
Cohesion level	Normal	High	Very high
Platform Independence	Minimal or null	Medium to high	Very high
Interoperability	Minimal or null	Medium to high	Very high
Example Technology	C++	JavaBeans	Web services from several languages (Java, C#, PHP)

According to Dumas, O'Sullivan, Hervizadeh, Edmond & Hofstede (2001), the services -as a broad concept- can be classified in *Business Services* and *Computing Services*. In addition, *Computing Services* can be divided in: 1) *Computing Service of Business* when it implements a *Business Service*, and 2) *Information and Communication Technologies (ICT) Computing Service* when it provides a service to another software system. Based on these concepts, a SOCA can be also conceptualized as a composition of *Business Computing Services* (Rodriguez-Martinez et al., 2012). Table 2, adapted from (Dumas et al., 2001) summarizes this typology of services.

Hence, the SOC approach introduces and demands new concerns for the development of SOCAs, which must be considered in their proposed development engineering methodologies. Thus, research in SOSE investigates *"systematic, disciplined and quantifiable approaches to develop service-oriented systems"* (Gu & Lago, 2007). In particular (Kontogiannis et al., 2007) indicates that one of the core research challenges in the SOSE paradigm is the proposal of "development processes and methodologies for service-oriented systems".

The development of SOCAs has been identified with a greater complexity process than those found in previous OOSE and CBSE paradigms (Avison & Fitzgerald, 2003; Boehm & Turner, 2004; Papazoglou & Van Den Heuvel; 2007; Rodriguez-Martinez et al., 2012). This complexity includes: 1) the need to

Table 2. Topology of Services

Type of Service	Sub-type of Service	Definition	Service Composition Issues
Business Service	*Business services*	A human-based service provided to clients.	A business service composition constitutes a workflow in an enterprise, which is perceived as a functional unit and it is composed for several *Business Computing Services*.
Computing Service	*Business computing services*	A machine-based service provided to clients.	A *Business Computing Service* provides a full work-unit which is part of a *Business Service* and it is composed from *Computing Services*.
	Computing services	A machine-based service provided to *Business Computing Services*.	A *Computing Service* is a single auto-contained functionality. It might include the utilization of other internal *Computing Services*.

achieve an agility-rigor balance (Boehm & Turner, 2004); 2) the novelty to realize a more appropriate fit of the methodological analysis and design techniques, with the final implementation tools (Papazoglou & Van Den Heuvel; 2007); 3) and a vast variety of single techniques already reported for supporting the analysis and design of SOCAs (Rodriguez-Martinez et al., 2012). Furthermore, (Boehm & Turner, 2004) reported that a lack of rigor on development methodologies has led to failed software projects; and while agile development methodologies avoid the bureaucratic documentation issues which exist in rigor-oriented development (West & Grant, 2010), these development methodologies introduce more software project risks than rigor-oriented ones (Boehm & Turner, 2004). Thus, a balanced agility-rigor development paradigm has been recommended (Boehm & Turner, 2004). Additionally, for building SOCAs there have been a wide variety of available development tools in the last decade (Papazoglou & Van Den Heuvel, 2006; Gu & Lago, 2007; Rodriguez-Martinez et al., 2012). This variety of development tools provides more computational capabilities for software developers, but they simultaneously demand more technical skills to be acquired by the software developers, which incurs in higher learning costs and associated learning curves (Rodriguez-Martinez et al., 2012).

Also, a study on SOCA development methodologies (Gu & Lago, 2011) revealed that while several methodologies have been reported in academic and industrial settings, none of them has gained its total acceptance, few of them (four out of the eleven reviewed methodologies) have addressed the full lifecycle process, and none satisfied the expected characteristics for a well-structured methodology. In addition, it has been acknowledged that SOCAs demand specific development methodologies with a SOSE approach (Papazoglou & Van Den Heuvel, 2007). According to these authors (Rodriguez-Martinez et al., 2012) *"older software development paradigms for object-oriented and component-based development cannot be blindly applied to SOA and Web services as they do not address SOA's key elements: services, information flows, and components realizing services"*. Thus, SOCA developers and academicians must adapt such development methodologies in an ad-hoc manner because they provide fragmented SOSE features. After 2011, there is a lack of proposals regarding SOCA methodologies, instead, there are several studies for specific questions on SOA methodologies like (Reyes-Delgado, et al., 2015) and others, and new specific ways of developing-deployed services -or even microservices- (Familiar, 2015; Zimmermann, 2016). However, a recent methodology was proposed in 2019 (Rodriguez-Martinez, Duran-Limon, Mora & Alvarez-Rodriguez, 2019), given that this topic is still relevant.

Finally, all methodologies to develop SOCAs tend to be agile, and this chapter aims to address agility versus rigor by measuring the level of agility-rigor balance of several of the potential SOCA development methodologies reported in the literature. Most related studies present the characteristics of heavy methodologies -regarding rigorous development processes- as well as characteristics of agile software development methodologies but no study was found focused on measuring the agility-rigor balance of them (Javanmard & Alian, 2015).

AGILITY-RIGOR BALANCE OF SOCA DEVELOPMENT METHODOLOGIES

The proposal of this chapter is to discuss how can the balance between Agility-Rigor be achieved when adopting or proposing new SDCLs, and the need of emerging Service-Oriented Computing approaches that also require such a balance. Thus, this chapter evaluates the level of agility-rigor balance of some selected methodologies that can be applied to develop SOCAs.

Boehm and Turner (2004) recommend incorporating an Agility-Rigor balance to the software development processes. These authors define *a framework for agility-rigor balance* that enables or facilitates the evaluation of software development processes. This framework defines three factors whereby each one divided into some characteristics, which can be measured for a SDLC.

This chapter presents an analysis regarding these two trends: (1) agility-rigor balance and (2) service-oriented computing approaches. Agility-rigor balance refers to a traditional debate on using agile or rigorous –heavy weight- methodologies. Plan-driven (or heavy weight) methodologies *"work best when developers can determine the requirements in advance ... and when the requirements remain relatively stable, with change rates on the order of one percent per month"* (Boehm, 2002; pp. 66). In contrast, agile methodologies are created to easily adopt changes based on new requirements. The agility-rigor balance advances such a traditional debate that posits that a methodology should be either agile or rigorous, but never combined.

Agility-Rigor Evolution of SDLCs

Rodriguez-Martinez et al. (2012) present a possible location for rigor-agility balanced methodologies. Such a location is based on an SDLC evolution map that uses three concepts: (i) methodological era, (ii) rigor level of SDLCs, (iii) and agility level of SDLCs. The methodological era is presented by Avison & Fitzgerald (2003) who provides a chronological four period evolution-classification scheme (e.g., pre-methodology era, early methodology era, methodology era, and post-methodology era). The rigor level of an SDLC represents the extent of detailed specifications to be achieved in each phase, activity and task before proceeding to the next phase. Agility level of an SDLC accounts for the extent of a system developer's freedom to complete phases, activities and tasks in the application of the SDLC. Agility and Rigor were assessed by using ordinal scales of four and two values, respectively (for rigor: null, low, medium, and high; and for agility: low and high).

Then, the work in (Rodriguez-Martinez et al., 2012) supports the notion of an intersection of SDLC rigor and agility sets of scales in the evolution map, and a non-trivial inference about that the utilization of these scales asserts that the both concepts -rigor and agility- do not represent disjoint sets. This means that an SDLC can be balanced when it has either medium or high assessment in both rigor and agility levels. It is also possible to identify a partially balanced SDLC when the assessments are high and medium or vice versa for both rigor and agility levels. Hence, in this research the two concepts are not considered antonymous. In Figure 1, the SLDC evolution map is presented. For each SDLC, the following items are reported: (i) year of origin, (ii) its main change force (a methodological knowledge gap or the emergence of a new technology), and (ii) its extent of rigor and agility.

Rodriguez-Martinez et al. (2012) suggests the need for a new SDLC approach for two events: "(i) new available computational and informatic-technology development-tools oriented to services, and (ii) existence of critical knowledge gaps about service-oriented software engineering (SOSE)". Then, such SDLCs might have some characteristics like the need to be agility-rigor balanced, among others. So, in Figure 1, symbols "●"and "◑" suggest the suitable locations for balanced and partially balanced SDLCs, respectively.

Figure 1. Evolution map of SDLCs with possible locations of rigor-agility SDLCs. (Quoted by Rodríguez-Martinez et al., 2012, pp. 96)

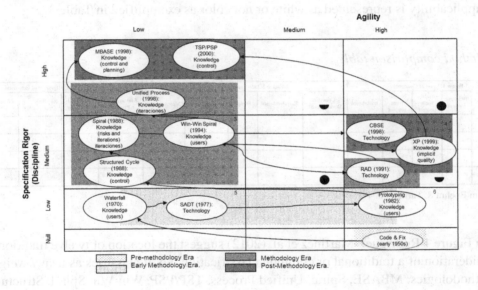

Characteristics of Agility-Rigor on SDLCs

Boehm & Turner (2004) present a framework toward Agility-Rigor balance on SDLCs. This framework defines three factors (Factor1: Level of Concerns; Factor 2: Life-Cycle Coverture; and Factor 3: Sources of Constraints). Each factor is divided into some concerns, that can be measured for each SDLC. From the Boehm & Turner (2004) evaluation of RUP and other methodologies it may be concluded that RUP is balanced in terms of agility-rigor. Such factors are: Factor 1. Level of Concerns identifies the enterprise scope for which the SDLC proposes specific guidelines (not assumptions), i.e. it refers to the control of the project and business aligning. More assumptions imply more agility. Its characteristics are Business Enterprise, Business System, Multi-team project, Single team, individual, e.g. if the SDLC guides for managing Business Enterprise, or for some other characteristic of this factor. Factor 2. Life-Cycle Coverture identifies the activities of the process of the development process for which the SDLC proposes specific guides (cycle coverture). (i.e. it refers to structural activities). When an SDLC covers and details more phases of software development, it is considered more rigorous. The characteristics of this factor are Concept Development, Requirements, Design, Development, Maintenance, e.g. if the SDLC covers to certain extent the activities of the phase Requirements, or some other characteristic (i.e. details the activities for each characteristic phase of this factor). Factor 3. Sources of Constraints if the SDLC proposes constraints to the implementer. When an SDLC is less constrained it is considered more agile. Also, the source of the constraint indicates the characteristic that it covers. (i.e. it refers to the umbrella activities, or protective activities). Its characteristics are Management Process, Technical Practices, Risk/Opportunity, Measurement Practices, Customer Interface, e.g. if the SDLC include practices, guides or activities for the quality or usability on the design of the Customer Interface, or for some other characteristics of this factor.

Each characteristic was assessed for each methodology as "partial applicability", "full applicability" or "non applicability". Such assessing was showed in a comparison table similar to Table 3, where the "partial applicability" is represented by gray squares "full applicability" is represented by black squares, and "non applicability is represented as white or not color as exemplified in Table 3.

Table 3. Method comparison table

DSM	Factor 1. Level of Concerns					Factor 2. Life-Cycle Coverture					Factor 3. Sources of Constraints				
	Business Enterprise	Business System	Multi-team project	Single-team project	Individual	Concept Development	Requirements	Design	Development	Maintenance	Management Process	Technical Practices	Risk/ Opportunity	Measurement Practices	Customer Interface
XP															
...															
RUP															

(adapted from Boehm & Turner, 2004)

Also, in Figure 1 Rodriguez-Martinez et al. (2012) suggest the location of twelve traditional SDLCs under consideration of a traditional or common classification, i.e. it classifies as heavy weight the following methodologies: MBASE, Spiral, Unified Process, TSP/PSP, Win-Win Spiral, Structured Cycle, Waterfall y SADT, and it classifies as agile the following ones: CBSE, XP, RAD, Prototyping, Code & Fix. But, Boehm & Turner (2004) report that RUP is agility-rigor balanced based on their proposed concerns of agility and rigor.

Comparison and Agility-Rigor Evaluation of Eleven SOCA Development Methodologies

Ten of the selected SOCA development methodologies (or SOC approaches) are proposed between 2003 to 2008, where the SOC research area emerges. According to (Gu & Lago, 2011), several SOCA methodologies have been reported in the decade from 2000 to 2010, but none has gained sufficient acceptance for SOCA academic and professional community, as it happened in the previous OOSE and CBSE paradigms. These authors (Gu & Lago, 2011) presented several generic process-related properties of SOCA development methodologies. This permits to compare the SOCA methodologies. Also, the

Table 4. List of eleven SOC development methodologies under study

ID	SDLC Name, Source	General description	Type
M1	WSbBP (Web services-based business processes methodology), (Karastoyanova, 2003)	"While this SDLC is strong through its contribution of web services code generation automation, it also lacks of specific process guidance on requirements definition, system architecture design, and system evolution... Contributes with one of the first generic methodologies to define, build and reach an executable business process based on web services." (Rodriguez-Martinez et al., 2012)	3
M2	COMPOSE (COMPonent-oriented software engineering), (Kotonya, Hutchinson & Bloin, 2005)	"COMPOSE, focuses on the requirements definition activity. It provides a framework for mapping requirements to a hybrid component and service-oriented architecture. According to authors, the proposed method incorporates negotiation as a key process to balance aspects of systems requirements and of business constraints, with assumptions and capacities of the architecture that are implicated in the component and services software." (Rodriguez-Martinez et al., 2012)	5
M3	Toward an SODM (Toward a service-oriented development methodology), (Ivanyukovich, Gangadharad, D'Andrea & Marchese, 2005)	"Main findings of each dimension related to existent SDLCs are (a) the use of some characteristics of XP for an agile development, (b) characteristics of RUP to specify the development process, and (c) selection of two goal-oriented approaches for the requirements specification as stakeholders' goals (TROPOS and MAP). Four existent SDLCs (XP, RUP, TROPOS and MAP) are reviewed and authors conclude that all of them contribute to service domain, but adaptations for addressing specific domain characteristic are required. However, none specific proposals are reported for implementing such adaptations." (Rodriguez-Martinez et al., 2012)	5
M4	Toward an SODM for the orchestration and validation of cooperative e-business components, (Kühne, Thränert & Speck, 2005)	"T-SODM proposes system-orchestration of distributed cooperative components by using semi-automation tools to build part of SoSS. In TSODM three activities are proposed: (1) structured analysis of requirements, (2) validation, and (3) transformation. The last delivered product by this SDLC is an orchestrated model skeleton (i.e., a model based requirements specification) which by manual development is completed into an executable orchestration model. It can be considered as a weakly completed SDLC." (Rodriguez-Martinez et al., 2012)	1
M5	SOA-LC management (Service-oriented architecture life cycle management), (Cox & Kreger, 2005)	"Authors [28] pose that the development and deployment of SOA relies on a real world viewpoint, in which a set of services are assembled and reused for adapting to new business needs. This flexibility is pursued by organizations as a core value of SOA trying to reach wide transformations over how software is constructed. In particular, this SDLC proposes two set of activities: (1) Preproduction and (2) Production. It also adds control points in each activity of these sets." (Rodriguez-Martinez et al., 2012)	5
M6	Automatic derivation of BPEL4WS from IDEF0 process models, (Karakostas, Zorgios & Alevizos)	"This approach permits a top-down analysis for business process and their web services. This also avoids inconsistency things between the web service process and its corresponding business process toward maintenance of architectural integrity. Hence, the specification of complex scenarios is limited to the expressivity power of the IDEF0 diagrams and the translator of such diagrams to the execution code." (Rodriguez-Martinez et al., 2012)	3
M7	BP-DLC (Business process development life cycle), (Papazoglou & Van den Heuvel, 2007)	It "...is a well-defined SDLC (from a more traditional viewpoint than a service-oriented view) with six activities: (1) planning, (2) service and process analysis and design, (3) construction and testing, (4) provisioning, (5) deployment, (6) execution and monitoring. Its definition of BP-DLC is also the most complete SDLC because in an explicit/implicit way it proposes for each of the six phases: its description, a few sets of activities, deliverables and tools. Also BP-DLC includes some emergent activities such as service requirements, business modeling, service architecture design, and service orchestration. Transition through these activities tends to be incremental and iterative by nature and can imply reviews in situations where their scope cannot be defined totally a priori." (Rodriguez-Martinez et al., 2012)	1
M8	A stakeholder-driven SOA-LC model (SOA-LC – Service-oriented architecture life-cycle model), (Gu & Lago, 2007)	It "...proposes that SoSS can be developed in two parts like two applications: (i) a service provider that provides the services to their use, and (ii) a service consumer that is composed of several workflows, service compositions and user interfaces that access the services published by the service provider (as end-user application). ..SOA-LC does not define phases, only proposes particular SDLC activities for the 'SOA stakeholders' " (Rodriguez-Martinez et al., 2012)	3
M9	Rational unified process for systems engineering (RUP-SE), (Cantor, 2003)	"RUP-SE is focused on designing generic engineering systems (which can or not include software). In this study, RUP-SE is considered explicitly for SoSS development. RUP-SE considers (i) modeling of system architecture, (ii) details concerning with all system components (hardware, workers, information components), this is to say, not just software concerning (iii) multiple teams in concurrent way, (not just individual or a single team work), and (iv) redesign of IT infrastructure to support evolving business processes. RUP-SE proposes a suite of abstraction levels for modeling the system..." (Rodriguez-Martinez et al., 2012)	1
M10	SOMA (Service-oriented modeling and architecture – method for developing service-oriented solutions), (Arsanjani, Ghosh, Allam, Abdollah, Ganapathy & Holley, 2008)	"SOMA is a software development life-cycle method invented and initially developed in IBM for designing and building SOA-based solution. This method defines key techniques and provides prescriptive tasks and detailed normative guidance for analysis, design, implementation, testing, and deployment of services, components, flows, information, and policies needed to successfully design and build a robust and reusable SOA solution in an enterprise." (Arsanjani et al., 2008). It focuses in the implementation of services by designing the SOA. Nor the choreography neither the choreography.	2
M11	MDA-based SOCA-DSEM (Service-Oriented Computing Approach – Development Software Engineering Methodology), (Rodriguez-Martinez et al., 2019)	It considers: (i) concerns of business, architecture and system (application) along the whole development process; and (ii) the analysis and design of services, composition, orchestration, and choreography. Also, it covers all the software system development life-cycle in a well-structured manner and includes phases, activities, models, and products as well as roles and an iterative development process. This is similar to other methodologies or models such as RUP and Spiral that enable the use of specific methods. (Rodriguez-Martinez et al., 2019)	1

last selected methodology is from 2019 (Rodriguez-Martinez, et al., 2019). Hence, this chapter presents a comparison of eleven SOCA development methodologies currently reported in the literature. First, Table 4 presents the list of such methodologies, their source and a short description. Also, Table 4 also classifies each one of them as type 1, 2, 3, 4, or 5 regarding the objective/scope of the methodology according to the distinguished five types (Rodriguez-Martinez, et al., 2019) as follow: 1) focused on a full development process, 2) focused only in analysis and design, 3) focused on service composition, 4) focused on migration of SOA, and 5) focused on project management. This categorization matches with different levels of abstraction of the methodology, from the management project, passing through the architecture perspective and process engineering, to the service composition.

Comparison of the Eleven Methodologies

In this chapter, an MDA-based SOCA-DSEM is used as a methodology of reference for the comparison and evaluation of agility-rigor balance of the methodologies under study. Since, according to (Rodriguez-Martinez et al., 2019), such a methodology of reference is considered that it covers all SDLCs in a well-manner and also, it is agility-rigor balanced.

Figure 2 shows the generic MDA-based SDEM to develop SOCAs, in two dimensions, it presents: 1) in the vertical axis, the levels of abstraction of MDA models, namely CIM – Computation Independent Model, PIM – *Platform Independent Model*, PSM – *Platform Specific Model* and PM – *Platform Executable Model* (or E-PM – *Executable Platform Model*); 2) in the horizontal axis, the Macro-Phases

Figure 2. Generic MDA-based Software Development Engineering Methodology for SOCAs (Quoted by Rodriguez-Martinez et al., 2019)

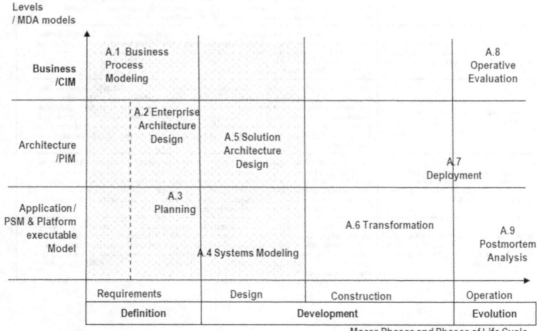

of the generic SDLC, namely Definition Development, and Evaluation; 3) also in the horizontal axis, the Phases of the generic SDLC, namely Requirements, Design, Construction, and Operation; and located over the map, the nine generic activities of the generic SDLC.

The activities of the MDA-based SOCA-DSEM are used as the general activities for comparing the how each methodology meets the evaluated aspects. Since the evaluation of an SDLC (e.g. degree of meeting phases, activities and delivered artifacts) as a main factor to be considered on the agility or rigor of a methodology, here it is presented a comparison of the eleven methodologies based on its proposed activities.

Table 5 presents such a comparison. In the headers of the columns, the M1 to M11 labels represent the SOCA development methodologies. The first column has three sub-tables corresponding to the Definition, Development and Evolution of the Macro-phases that categorizes the activities of the SDLCs. The second column presents the MDA-based SOCA-DSEM phases ***Requirements, Design, Construction and Operation***. The third column is for the generic artifacts of MDA-based SOCA development methodologies, i.e. ***CIM, PIM & PSM, PM*** and ***Evaluation & Evolution Plan***. The fourth column is for the Business, Architectural and Application domains. Finally, the fifth column is for the MDA-based SOCA-DSEM activities (this column shows some cells marked as "None proposed activity" when in some development methodologies are not considered or are not required since they are already covered in other activities). The remainder columns are for the activities defined on each SOCA development methodology.

Figure 3 complements this comparison from a graphical perspective. This figure presents what SOCA development methodologies cover regarding the generic activities of the SDLC of reference -i.e. the activities of the generic MDA-based SOCA development methodology-.

Figure 3. Generic MDA-based SDLC and the eleven SOC development methodologies

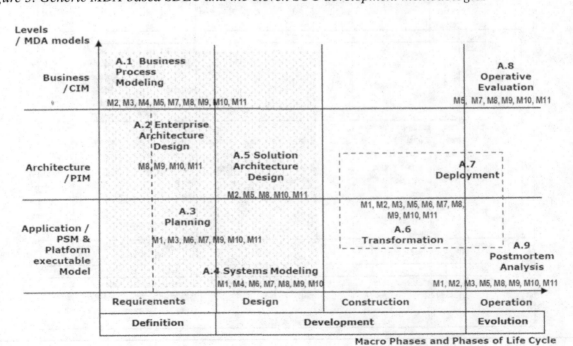

Table 5. Comparative view of the eleven SOC development methodologies (extended from Rodriguez-Martinez et al., 2012)

Macro-Phase	Phase	Domain	Artifact	M1 (Karastoyanova, 2003)	M2 (Kotonya et al. 2004)	M3 (Ivanyukovich et al. 2005)	M4 (Kühne et al. 2005)	M5 (Cox & Kreger, 2005)	M6 (Karakostas et al., 2006)	M7 (Papazoglou & Van Den Heuvel, 2007)	M8 (Gu & Lago, 2009)	M9 (Cantor, 2003)	M10 (Arsanjani, 2008)	M11 (Rodriguez-Martinez et al., 2019)
Definition	Requirements	CIM	Business		X — System Requirements Definition: 1. Requirements elicitation. 2. Requirements scope. 3. Requirements modeling.	Business Modeling	Structured analysis of requirements. Requirements validation.	Business Process Model (BPM)	X	Scenario analysis. Analysis and design of services. Process identification	Market scan Requirements Engineering Business Modeling	Business Process Model (BPM)	Business modeling and transformation	Business Process Model (BPM)
			Architecture	X	X	X	X	X	X	X	System base-architecture model X		Solution management: Hybrid solution type selection, method adoption and integration, project management, enterprise architecture.	Enterprise Architecture Design
			Application		X	Requirements X	X	X	Service definition	Gap analysis	X	Requirements	Identification: Identifying services, components, flows and information	Planning
Development	Design	PIM & PSM	Business	X	X	X	X	X	X	X	Service Design	X	X	X
			Architecture	X	Mapping requirements to architectural design: 1. Dividing service descriptions in logic subsystems. 2. Establish subsystems interfaces. X	X	X	Definition SOA. X	X	X	X	X	Specification of services, flows and information. Analyse subsystems Specify components	Solution Architecture Design (services, processes, workflows - choreography and orchestration + database design)
			Application	Modeling and assembling process models.	X	Analysis and Design	Transformation (orchestration)	X	Service definition and orchestration	Service specifications. Process specifications.	Application Design	Modeling and assembling of process model	X	System Modeling (Composition and Orchestration)
	Construction	PM	Business	X	X	Integration	X	X	X	X		X	X	X
			Architecture	X	X	Integration	X	X	X	X	Service Orchestration /Composition Registry selection	X	Realization: Decisions, solutions templates and patterns, detailed SOA reference architecture, technical feasibility prototyping	X
			Application	Generating process definition. Pre-processing Deployment	System composition: 1. Replacing subsystem definition with components and services. 2. Adapting components and services.	Implementation Test Deployment Integration	X	Service implementation and work flows. Interfaces implementation.	Executable Transformation.	Code Web services Code business process Provisioning Deployment	Service Development Service Testing Service publishing Application Implementation Module Testing	Implementation Test Deployment Integration	Implementation build/assembly & Testing	Transformation Deployment
Evolution	Operation	Operation	Business	X	X	X	X	Operation, monitoring and optimization.	X	Execution Monitoring	Service Management	X	Execute user-acceptance test.	Operative Evaluation
	Evaluation & Evolution Plan		Architecture	X	X	X	X		X		Registry maintenance	X	Deployment	Deployment
			Application	Run-time Post-execution time	Verification	Configuration management, Project management and Environment	X	Maintenance and growing.	X	X	Service monitoring Application testing and maintenance	Configuration management Project management Environment	Monitoring, and management processes and performance	Deployment Postmortem Analysis

Table 6. Rigor-Agility Score of the eleven SOC development methodologies (extended from Rodriguez-Martinez et al., 2012)

SOCA Development Methodology	Factor 1. Level of Concerns					Factor 2. Life-Cycle Coverture					Factor 3. Sources of Constraints					RIGOR TOTAL SCORE
	Business Enterprise	Business System	Multi-team project	Single-team project	Individual	Concept Development	Requirements	Design	Development	Maintenance	Management Process	Technical Practices	Risk/ Opportunity	Measurement Practices	Customer Interface	
M1	1	1	0	0	0	0	0	2	1	0	0	1	0	0	0	6
M2	1	1	0	0	0	0	1	1	1	0	0	2	1	0	1	9
M3	0	2	2	2	0	3	2	3	2	2	2	1	2	1	2	26
M4	1	1	0	0	0	0	1	2	0	0	0	1	0	0	0	6
M5	1	0	0	0	0	0	0	1	1	1	1	0	0	0	0	5
M6	0	1	0	0	0	1	0	2	1	0	0	1	1	0	0	7
M7	1	0	0	0	0	1	1	1	1	2	1	1	0	1	0	10
M8	0	1	0	0	0	0	1	1	1	1	1	0	0	0	0	6
M9	1	2	2	2	0	3	2	3	2	2	2	1	2	1	2	27
M10	1	0	1	0	0	0	1	1	2	2	1	2	0	1	0	12
M11	1	2	2	1	0	3	2	2	2	1	1	1	2	0	2	22

From the results reported in the Table 7 and Figure 3, it can be inferred that some SOCA development methodologies are concentrated on the Application Domain (e.g. M1 and M6 are generally focused on the Application domain with little or no specific attention to the Business and Architectural domains) and others cover the three MDA layers (CIM, PIM, PSM). The more traditional SOCA development methodologies are also primarily located in the Development Macro-phase, and partially located in the Definition and Evolution Macro-phases. Other relevant findings are the following ones: 1) emergent SOCA development methodologies (like M2 and M5) have also a similar structure of activities but they

Table 7. Rigor-Agility Balance Assessment of the eleven SOC Development Methodologies (extended from Rodriguez-Martinez et al., 2012)

SOCA Development Methodology	Rigor – Agility			
	Agility	Rigor	Rigor-Agility Balance (in %)	Rigor-Agility Balance Index min(R,A)/max(R,A)
M11	23/45	27/45	51%-49%	(49/51) = .96
M9	18/45	27/45	40%-60%	(40/60) = .67
M3	18/45	27/45	40%-60%	(40/60) = .67
M10	12/45	33/45	27%-73%	(27/73) = .36
M7	35/45	10/45	22%-77%	(22/77) = .29
M2	36/45	9/45	20%-80%	(20/80) = .25
M6	38/45	7/45	16%-84%	(16/84) = .19
M1	39/45	6/45	13%-87%	(13/87) = .15
M4	39/45	6/45	13%-87%	(13/87) = .15
M8	39/45	6/45	13%-87%	(13/87) = .15
M5	40/45	5/45	11%-88%	(11/88) = .13

Figure 4. Localization of eleven SDLCs over a map of Agility-Rigor

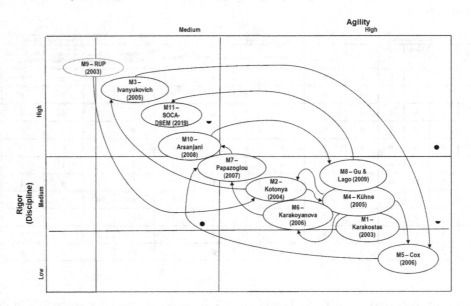

still lack some important activities (like System Planning); 2) some emergent SOCA development methodologies (like M7, M8, M9 and M10) are the most complete from a SOCA point of view, however, none of them can be considered fully complete under the framework reported in the Figure 3. Nevertheless, the proposed M11 methodology (i.e. SOCA-DSEM) can be considered as the most complete of them, because meets various aspects of both, SOCA concerns and SDLC concerns, but with an agility-rigor balance. In addition, M3 covers all SDLC and SOCA concerns, both tend to be more rigorous because it does not propose the SDLC since considers using RUP with SOC; but the concerns of SOCA includes also many assumptions, i.e. SOC tends to be agile.

Measuring Agility-Rigor Balance of the Eleven Methodologies

Eleven methodologies numbered in Table 4 are evaluated for each agility-rigor characteristic proposed by Boehm and Turner (2004) Table 6 presents the results of the measures. The evaluation was executed as described as follows.

The authors of this chapter evaluated the scientific literature of each methodology under study considering as a base reference the traditional RUP, which is considered agility-rigor balanced as explained in the subsection "Characteristics of Agility-Rigor on SDLCs ". Then, each agility-rigor characteristic was evaluated for each SOCA development methodology under study. In Table 6, a score for each constraint was assigned for each M1..M11 methodology and each concern of agility-rigor balance, by using an ordinal scale (null, low, medium, and high consideration) from the values 0 to 3 in a similar as represented in Table 3, but with numbers instead black, gray and white colors-. Thus, the maximum rigor score in this analysis, for each SOCA development methodology is 45 points (15 items x 3 points). Thus, the rigor score for each SOCA engineering methodology is derived directly from the scores assigned in Table 6. The agility score is calculated from the maximum rigor score (45 points) minus the rigor score reached in this review by the SOCA development methodology. For instance, the M2 methodology has a rigor score of 9 points and its agility score is 36 points (i.e. 45-9). Here, the maximum score (45 points) is considered as the maximum rigor of a SOCA engineering methodology, and thus a rigor score between 20 to 25 points must be considered as a balanced development methodology.

Three methodologies could be considered balanced, the first, would be the most balanced, and the second and third less balanced, respectively. Such methodologies are M11 (SOCA-DSEM), M3 and M9 (RUP) that have the total rigor scores of 22, 26 and 27, accordingly. Some of the methodologies are considered as agile proposals (ordered from more agile to less agile): M10, M7, M2, M6, M8, M4, M1, M5 with the following total scores 12, 10, 9, 7, 6, 6, 6 and 5, respectively. Also, M1, M4 and M8 have the same level of rigor. Then, the most agility-rigor balanced methodology was M11 (SOCA-DSEM, i.e. the methodology of reference). It can be characterized as both moderately agile and rigorous. Regarding RUP (i.e. M9), it has a good agility-rigor balance, although it is the most rigorous of the eleven methodologies under study.

Next, the overall assessment of the Agility-Rigor balance of each SOCA development methodology is reported in the Table 7. Then the percentages of agility and rigor issues presented in the fourth column in Table 7 are divided to calculate an index. Such an index of Agility-Rigor balance is calculated as the rate of the minimum percentage value on agility or rigor issue divided into the maximum percentage value them. For instance, for M9 such index is 67% and for SOCA-DSEM is 96%. These 30 points of difference between 96% of SOCA-DSEM and 67% of M6 allows us to conclude that SOCA-DSEM is balanced in agility-rigor, while M9 can be classified as more rigorous than agile (i.e. a non balanced development methodology).

Finally, this chapter considers some changes over the location of RUP-SE (i.e. M9) in these two Rigor and Agility axis and the other ten SDLCs under evaluation in this work, as shown in Figure 4. We can observe in this figure that around half of the reviewed methodologies (M1, M2, M4, M6, and M7) are grouped in the second quadrant of the right column. This group of methodologies has a high level of rigor while they maintain a medium level of agility. There are a few approaches (M3, M9, M10, and M11) that have a low and a medium level of rigor while they preserve a high level of agility. Only two approaches have a high level of rigor and only a low level of agility.

The question now is how to measure the agility of the SDLCs or equate the level of rigor and agility to reach SDLCs that could be located over the full moons.

FUTURE RESEARCH DIRECTIONS

Future and emerging trends are the following:

- The first SOC approaches that were proposed have low rigor since they have few details on their definitions, and they tended to not cover all the SDLC. As new proposals were appearing, they tended to have more rigor, when they increasingly covered both the SDLC and aspects of organization and quality. Such a methodologies try to address more the SOCA concerns rather than the SDLC concerns. Then, it is expected that the concerns of SDLC, business and quality, will be included in new SOC approaches.
- Also, as future work, many practical experiments need to be carried out to ensure that different emerging studies on agility rigor balance are feasible and practical when they are applied to SOC approaches.

- A possible trend is the emergence of more balanced methodologies in the SOC domain having a medium level of both rigor and agility. Also, future efforts can investigate the benefits and drawbacks of such emergent balanced methodologies.
- Other emerging trends regards the emergence of service-oriented approaches for development and deployment like Lean development and DevOps (Familiar, 2015), or new proposals for developing service systems like microservices (Zimmermann, 2016) and the distributed paradigm "edge and fog service" computing for large amounts of data (Romana, 2018). Hence, the authors of this chapter claim that such approaches (1) require new methods that could be applied with the same methodologies for SOCA, and (2) this implies that *agile and rapid development-deployment* requires a newer or higher levels control regarding configuration management issues.

CONCLUSION

The evolution of the SDLC models tend to Service Orientation and to achieve a better balance on Agility-Rigor. Currently, most of the SDLC proposals on SOSE are incomplete and are commonly not labeled as agile or rigorous methodologies. This fact makes it is difficult to know if such methodologies are suitable or not to dynamic and rapid changes. Hence, this work gives some light about the level of agility-rigor balance of eleven SOC development approaches.

This study shows that the index of rigor-agility balance of most of the eleven SOC approaches is less than 67%. The lack of rigor of such approaches is mainly due to the fact that they do not cover all phases of the SDLC. Further research is required to propose more balanced methodologies in the SOC domain. We believe the emergence of more balanced approaches will help to consolidate SOC development practices. Although the concept of agility-rigor balance is not explicitly addressed by the SOCA engineering methodologies reviewed in this chapter -except by the methodology M11-, a recent study of SOCA/SOA research issues (Keith, Demirkan & Goul, 2013) strongly suggests the inclusion of this relevant concept for SOCA development methodologies.

REFERENCES

Abrahamsson, P., Oza, N., & Siponen, M. (2010). Agile software development methods: a comparative review. In T. Dingsøyr, T. Dybå, & N. Moe (Eds.), *Agile Software Development* (pp. 31–59). Springer. doi:10.1007/978-3-642-12575-1_3

Arsanjani, A., Ghosh, S., Allam, A., Abdollah, T., Ganapathy, S., & Holley, K. (2008). SOMA: A method for developing service-oriented solutions. *IBM Systems Journal, 47*(3), 377–396. doi:10.1147j.473.0377

Arsanjani, A., Hailpern, B., Martin, J., & Tarr, P. L. (2003). Web Services: Promises and compromises. *ACM Queue; Tomorrow's Computing Today*, 48–58.

Avison, D., & Fitzgerald, G. (2003). Where now for development methodologies? *Communications of the ACM, 46*(1), 78–82. doi:10.1145/602421.602423

Beck, K. (1999). Embracing change with extreme programming. *Computer, 32*(10), 70–77. doi:10.1109/2.796139

Beck, K., & Boehm, B. (2003). Agility through Discipline: A Debate. *IEEE Computer, 36*(6), 44–46. doi:10.1109/MC.2003.1204374

Boehm, B. (2002). Get ready for agile methods, with care. *IEEE Computer, 35*(1), 64–69. doi:10.1109/2.976920

Boehm, B., Egyed, A., Kwan, J., Port, D., Shah, A., & Madachy, R. (1998). Using the WinWin spiral model: A case study. *IEEE Computer, 31*(7), 33–44. doi:10.1109/2.689675

Boehm, B., Klappholz, D., Colbert, E., Puri, P., Jain, A., Bhuta, J., & Kitapci, H. (2004). *Guidelines for Model-Based (System) Architecting and Software Engineering (MBASE)*. Center for Software Engineering, University of Southern California.

Boehm, B., & Turner, R. (2004). Balancing agility and discipline: Evaluating and integrating agile and plan-driven methods. In *Proceedings of the 26th International Conference on Software Engineering (ICSE'04)* (pp. 718-719). Edinburgh, UK: IEEE 10.1109/ICSE.2004.1317503

Boehm, B. W. (1988). A spiral model of software development and enhancement. *Computer, 21*(5), 61–72. doi:10.1109/2.59

Bourque, P., & Farley, R. E. (2014). *SWEBOK: Guide to the Software Engineering Body of Knowledge Versión 3.0*. IEEE, Computer Society.

Cantor, M. (2003). *Rational Unified Process for Systems Engineering*. Rational Brand Services IBM Software Group.

Cox, D. E., & Kreger, H. (2005). Management of the service oriented-architecture life cycle. IBM Corporation. *IBM Systems Journal, 44*(4), 709–726. doi:10.1147j.444.0709

DeMarco, T., & Boehm, B. (2002). The agile methods fray. *Computer, 35*(6), 90–92. doi:10.1109/MC.2002.1009175

Dickover, M. E., McGowan, C. L., & Ross, D. T. (1977, January). Software design using: SADT. In *Proceedings of the 1977 annual conference* (pp. 125-133). ACM. 10.1145/800179.810192

Dumas, M., O'Sullivan, J., Hervizadeh, M., Edmond, D., & Hofstede, A. (2001). Towards a semantic framework for service description. In *Proceedings of the IFIP TC2/WG2.6 Ninth Working Conference on Database Semantics: Semantic Issues in E-Commerce Systems* (pp. 277-291). Kluwer, B.V.

Dyba, T., & Dingsoyr, T. (2009). What do we know about agile software development? *IEEE Software, 26*(5), 6–9. doi:10.1109/MS.2009.145

Familiar, B. (2015). Microservices, IoT, and Azure: Leveraging DevOps and Microservice Architecture to Deliver SaaS Solutions. Apress Ed.

Gu, Q., & Lago, P. (2007). A stakeholder-driven service life cycle model for SOA. In *Proceedings of 2nd international workshop on Service oriented software engineering: in conjunction with the 6th ESEC/FSE joint meeting (IW-SOSWE'07)* (pp. 1-7). Dubrovnik, Croatia: ACM 10.1145/1294928.1294930

Gu, Q., & Lago, P. (2011). Guiding the selection of service-oriented software engineering methodologies. SpringerLink. *Service Oriented Computing and Applications*, 5(4), 203–223. doi:10.100711761-011-0080-0

Hoda, R., Salleh, N., & Grundy, J. (2018). The rise and evolution of agile software development. *IEEE Software*, 35(5), 58–63. doi:10.1109/MS.2018.290111318

Hopkins, J. (2002). Component Primer. *ACM Communications*, 43(10), 27–30. doi:10.1145/352183.352198

Ivanyukovich, A., Gangadharan, G. R., D'Andrea, V., & Marchese, M. (2005). Toward a service-oriented development methodology. *Journal of Integrated Design & Process Science*, 9(3), 53–62.

Javanmard, M., & Alian, M. (2015). Comparison between Agile and Traditional software development methodologies. Science Journal, 36(3), 1386-1394.

Karakostas, B., Zorgios, Y., & Alevizos, C. C. (2006). Automatic derivation of BPEL4WS from IDEF0 process models. *Software & Systems Modeling*, 5(2), 208–218. doi:10.100710270-006-0003-2

Karastoyanova, D. (2003). *A methodology for development of Web Services-based Bussines Processes*. Thechnische Universität Darmstadt.

Keith, M., Demirkan, H., & Goul, M. (2013). Service-oriented methodology for systems development. *Journal of Management Information Systems*, 30(1), 227–260. doi:10.2753/MIS0742-1222300107

Kontogiannis, K., Lewis, G. A., Smith, D. B., Litoiu, M., Muller, H., Schuster, S., & Stroulia, E. (2007). The landscape of service-oriented systems: A research perspective. In *International Workshop on Systems Development in SOA Environments (SDSOA'07: ICSE Workshops 2007)*. Minneapolis, MN: IEEE Computer Society. 10.1109/SDSOA.2007.12

Korbyn, C. (2000). Modeling components and frameworks with UML. *ACM Communications*, 43(10), 31–38. doi:10.1145/352183.352199

Kotonya, G., Hutchinson, J., & Bloin, B. (2005). A method for formulating and architecting component and Service-oriented Systems. In Z. Stojanovic & A. Dahanayake (Eds.), *Service-Oiented Software Systems Engineering: Challenges and Practices* (pp. 155–181). IGI-Global. doi:10.4018/978-1-59140-426-2.ch008

Kruchten, P. (2004). *The rational unified process: an introduction*. Addison-Wesley Professional.

Kühne, S., Thränert, M., & Speck, A. (2005). Towards a methodology for orchestration and validation of cooperative e-business components. In *Proceedings of 7th GPCE Young Researchers Workshop, GPCE YRW 2005* (pp. 29-34). Tallinn, Estonia: Institute of Cybernetics at Tallinn Technical University.

Miller, J., & Mukerji, J. (2003). *MDA guide version 1.0.1. Object Management Group*. OMG.

Oktaba, H., & Ibargüengoitia, G. (1998). Software process modeled with objects: Static view. *Computación y Sistemas*, 1(4), 228-238.

Papazoglou, M. P., Traverso, P., Schahram, D., Leymann, F., & Bernd, J. (2006). Service-oriented Computing: Research roadmap. *Dagstuhl Seminar Proceedings 05462 Service Oriented Computing (SOC)*.

Papazoglou, M. P., & Van Den Heuvel, W. (2007). Business process development life cycle methodology. *Communications of the ACM*, *50*(10), 79–85. doi:10.1145/1290958.1290966

Reyes-Delgado, P. Y., Mora, M., Duran-Limon, H. A., Rodriguez-Martinez, L. C., Mendoza-González, R., & Rodríguez-Díaz, M. A. (2015). State of the Art of Software Architecture Design Methods Used in Main Software Development Methodologies. In M. Khosrow-Pour (Ed.), *Encyclopedia of Information Science and Technology* (3rd ed., pp. 7359–7370). IGI-Global.

Rodriguez, L. C., Mora, M., & Alvarez, F. J. (2008) Process Models of SDLCs: Comparison and evolution. In M.R. Syed, & Syed, S.N. (Ed.), Handbook of Research on Modern Systems Analysis and Design Technologies and Applications (pp. 76-89). Minnesota State University.

Rodriguez-Martinez, L. C., Duran-Limon, H. A., Mora, M., & Alvarez-Rodriguez, F. (2019). SOCA-DSEM: A Well-Structured SOCA Development Systems Engineering Methodology. *Computer Science and Information Systems*, *16*(1), 19–44. doi:10.2298/CSIS170703035R

Rodriguez-Martinez, L. C., Mora, M., Alvarez, F., Garza, L. A., Duran, H. A., & Muñoz, J. (2012). State of the art analysis of the System Development Life Cycle (SDLC) in Service-oriented Software Engineering (SOSE). *Journal of Applied Research and Technology*, *10*(2), 94–113. doi:10.22201/icat.16656423.2012.10.2.396

Romana, R., Lopeza, J., & Mambob, M. (2018). *Future Generation Computer Systems. Elsevier.* doi:10.1016/j.future.2016.11.009

Royce, W. (1970). Managing the development of large software systems: Concepts and techniques. In *Technical Papers of Western Electronic Show and Convention (WesCon). Academic Press.

Sommerville, I. (2005). *Software Engineering*. Addison-Wesley.

Sutherland, J., & Schwaber, K. (2011). *The Scrum Papers: Nuts, Bolts and Origins of an Agile Process.* Academic Press.

West, D., & Grant, T. (2010). *Agile Development: Mainstream Adoption Has Changed Agility - Trends In Real-World Adoption Of Agile Methods*. Forrester Study.

Zimmermann, O. (2016). Microservices Tenets: Agile Approach to Service Development and Deployment. *SummerSoc 2016 Proceedings Conference.*

Zimmermann, O., Krogdahl, P., & Gee, C. (2004). Elements of Service Oriented Analysis and Design: an approach of interdisciplinary modeling for SOA projects. *IBM Developer Works*. Retrieved from https://www.ibm.com/developerworks/library/ws-soad1/

KEY TERMS AND DEFINITIONS

CBSE Paradigm: Component-Based Software Engineering paradigm is a way to construct software systems whose building blocks are components.

Choreography: Define the service collaboration at service-computing level.

DevOps: It is a way to work were the software is rapidly developed and immediately deployed for operating in a computational productive environment. It is continuous delivery product development lifecycle. It must automate the development process. DevOps is both a culture and a set of technologies and tools used for automation.

Edge and Fog Computing: An early and incipient definition could the following: It is a distributed computing paradigm to provide services by the cloud to the edge of the network.

Lean Development: It is a way to work similar with DevOps. The Lean development (or engineering) cycle promotes Continuous Delivery, Continuous Analytics, and Continuous Feedback.

MDA: Model-Driven Architecture regards to some levels of abstraction of the models to construct software systems, and that facilitates the transformations of ones into others. Such models are Computation Independent Model (CIM), Platform Independent Model (PIM), Platform Specific Model (PSM) and Executable Platform Model (E-PM).

Microservices: It is a specific way of decomposition of services in a greater granularity. Also, microservice represents a capability of the business process in a lesser level of abstraction than a service, Then, a microservice is a service but with greater granularity or in a lesser level of abstraction.

OOSE Paradigm: Object-Oriented Software Engineering paradigm is a way to construct software systems whose building blocks are objects.

Orchestration: It defines the service collaboration at business process level.

Service Composition: Regards a suite of services that as a set and under a defined collaboration, conforms a service or a complete workflow.

SOA: Service-Oriented Architecture expresses an architecture that define the use of software services.

SOC: Service-Oriented Computing is an emerging paradigm for distributed computing.

SOC Approach: Is a methodology or process model for developing service-oriented software systems.

SOCA: Service-Oriented Computing Applications is synonymous of SOSS.

SOSE Paradigm: Service-Oriented Software Engineering paradigm. Is a way to construct systems whose building blocks are services.

SOSS: Service-Oriented Software System is a system constructed as a set of distributed services with loose coupling. Also defined as a software system based on SOA or SOC Application.

Workflow: It defines the tasks and its order to complete a business process.

Chapter 5
Managing Contradictory Tensions in Agile Distributed Development:
An Ambidextrous Approach

Ashay Saxena
Indian Institute of Management, Bangalore, India

Shankar Venkatagiri
Indian Institute of Management, Bangalore, India

Rajendra K Bandi
https://orcid.org/0000-0002-1872-3587
Indian Institute of Management, Bangalore, India

ABSTRACT

Increasingly, agile approaches are being followed in a distributed setup to develop software. An agile approach is characterised by the need to regularly welcome change requests and update the software artefact accordingly whereas distributed teams prefer to work towards following a plan to fulfil project objectives defined upfront. This results in contradictory tensions when agile is practised with teams operating in a globally distributed format. This chapter focuses on exploring the central conflict and discuss approaches to manage the conflicting forces in an agile distributed development setup. Furthermore, it presents an industry case study to provide more clarity on conflict management in such settings.

INTRODUCTION

Over the last decade, agile approaches have become the *de facto* standard owing to their promise of iterative and incremental software development. Unlike traditional approaches, Agile recognizes the need for software requirements to evolve with and thrive on frequent changes to the product definition

DOI: 10.4018/978-1-7998-4165-4.ch005

(Paetsch et al., 2003). In essence, agile offers *flexibility* to continuously update the software artefact and deliver relevant functionality, with work being coordinated by self-managing teams (Boehm & Turner, 2003; Moe et al., 2010). Heretofore, this necessitated the co-location of the software team, a mode which promoted extensive face-to-face communication so that developers could collaborate efficiently on project-related tasks.

To meet the demands of globalized development, software teams are increasingly operating in a distributed setup. Their main objective is to develop high-quality software in multiple time-boxed iterations by optimizing resources that are available globally (Jiménez et al., 2009; Shrivastava & Date, 2010). In direct contrast to flexibility, teams working in a distributed setup seek *stability* to predictably meet the objectives of a project plan. They prefer to operate with clarity on what needs to be delivered upfront in order to ensure that the project progresses in a smooth manner.

There is, therefore, a conflict between flexibility and stability when the promise of agile meets the reality of a distributed setup.

In an Agile Distributed Development (ADD) model, projects are implemented by teams located across multiple geographies and following an agile approach (Ramesh et al., 2012). Depending upon the contingencies presented by different variants of ADD setup, which are described in the next section, the conflicting forces between flexibility and stability surface in a nuanced form. A holistic view of the contingencies experienced by software teams in varied setups has received scant attention within existing literature (Jalali & Wohlin, 2011). This chapter elaborates on the potential drivers of the flexibility-stability conflict across different types of ADD setup.

Dealing with such a conflict is not unique to the ADD setting. Researchers (e.g., Gibson & Birkinshaw, 2004) have examined other domains that involve demands of similar nature across an entire business unit. Invariably, organizational settings have demonstrated the need for the simultaneous pursuit of trade-off decisions rather than strictly selecting one over another. In this regard, the capability of organizational ambidexterity provides guidance in managing the conflicting forces. This chapter dwells on the potential drivers of ambidexterity, which enable teams to manage the tensions posed in the ADD setting. We also present findings from a case study to provide evidence from the field.

BACKGROUND

This section outlines the basic principles of agile software development and the fundamentals of distributed teamwork. We focus on the foundational aspects of agile approaches (i.e., theoretical underpinnings) and the constraints induced when teams operate in a distributed setup. These elements are essential to uncover conflicting experiences in ADD settings.

Agile Software Development

Agile practices picked up pace since the enunciation of a manifesto in 2001. The academic community began to take note of this new approach towards developing software starting 2005, and their contributions have steadily increased since then (Dingsøyr et al., 2012). Over the last decade, the domain of agile software development (ASD) has generated a significant amount of literature uncovering theoretical underpinnings, among many other themes (Hoda et al., 2018).

Fundamental to the notion of agility is the capacity to embrace and respond to change (Conboy & Fitzgerald, 2004; Dingsøyr et al., 2012; Dybaᵒ & Dingsøyr, 2008; Cohen et al., 2004; Highsmith & Cockburn, 2001). Agility has been defined as the ability of an information systems development (ISD) organization or a team to sense and respond swiftly to technical changes and new business opportunities (Lyytinen & Rose, 2006; Lee & Xia, 2010). Conboy (2009) defines agility as "the continual readiness of an ISD method to rapidly or inherently create change, proactively or reactively embrace change, and learn from change while contributing to perceived customer value (economy, quality, and simplicity), through its collective components and relationships with its environment". Conboy's (2009) definition is widely regarded as the most comprehensive.

A traditional software development approach like the waterfall model facilitates an environment with prediction, verifiability, and control, and minimised change by freezing the requirements prior to commencing development. Agile recognizes the need for these requirements to evolve and thrive on frequent changes (Paetsch et al., 2003). The short time-boxed iterations of Scrum projects admit multiple review points, with the customer being allowed to modify requirements at the beginning of the Sprint planning phases. Daily Scrum meetings follow a two-pronged approach of inspect (progress towards the goal) and adapt (to change) (Schwaber & Beedle, 2001).

Traditional approaches are heavily dependent on a faithful and efficient execution of the project plan and mandate a command-and-control style of management (Nerur & Balijepally, 2007). In the agile approach, work is coordinated by self-managing teams (Boehm & Turner, 2003; Moe et al., 2010), with command-and-control being replaced by leadership-and-collaboration (Nerur et al., 2005). Agility requires that teams can organize themselves in various configurations so as to address the emerging challenges as they arise. Individual competence helps enhance team competence via continuous collaboration and self-organization (Cockburn & Highsmith, 2001).

Distributed Teams

Distributed teams are gaining importance in organizations due to the rise in outsourcing, globalization, alliances and joint ventures (Upadhyaya & Krishna, 2007). Recent years have seen an upsurge in distributed teams within organizations; consequently, research has begun to focus on this versatile form of teamwork execution (Jimenez et al., 2017). Despite the growing body of literature, the exact definition of a distributed team is manifold. Distilling from previously published research, Powell et al. (2004) highlight multi-dimensional characteristics: "These are groups of geographically, organizationally and/or time dispersed workers that are assembled using a combination of information and telecommunication technologies (ICTs) to accomplish an organizational task".

The setting of a globally distributed project is characterized by spatial, temporal, configurational (O'Leary & Cummings, 2007) and socio-cultural differences (Holmström et al., 2006). Generally, dispersed team members develop weak ties (Wong & Burton, 2000); they rely on ICT-mediated interactions to coordinate their tasks. As a result, they prefer to work towards delivering what they know has been finalized upfront. Table 1 presents a description of these dimensions.

Thus far, literature has taken a dichotomous and unidimensional approach to dispersion, with studies that focus on either full colocation versus full dispersion (O'Leary & Cummings, 2007). As Hinds and Mortenson (2005) note, "little work has yet examined different dimensions of distributed work and how these dimensions shape team dynamics". However, there is some evidence that temporal and configurational dimensions of dispersion have distinct effects (O'Leary & Cummings, 2007). Specifically,

Table 1. Dimensions of distributedness

Dimension	Definition
Spatial dispersion (O'Leary & Cummings, 2007)	o Separation, in terms of distance, between sites at which the team members are located
Temporal dispersion (O'Leary & Cummings, 2007)	o Extent to which there is an overlap in working hours between the team members across sites
Configurational dispersion (O'Leary & Cummings, 2007)	o Specific arrangement in which the teams are dispersed. For instance, 6 member teams can be spread across two sites in numerous ways
Socio-cultural dispersion (Holmström et al., 2006)	o Separation faced by the team members due to the different cultural background and the language issues across sites

configurational dimension concerns the subgroup dynamics. In the context of software development, the role of configurational dimension is equally vital to establish the team dynamics. Generally, the nature of work demands that distributed teams de-couple modules and take up work on independent features or components across sites (Ebert & De Neve, 2001; Sahay, 2003). In an alternate arrangement, the work is specified in such a way that there are specific interfaces that distinguish "require" and "provide" layer of the architecture (Crnkovic et al., 2005).

CONTRADICTORY TENSIONS IN AGILE DISTRIBUTED DEVELOPMENT

Having fleshed out the notions of agility and distributedness, this section describes the core constructs of flexibility and stability in the context of an ADD setup. We then go on to provide insights beyond earlier conceptualizations of the central conflict between the two constructs in an ADD setting.

Flexibility

The philosophy of agile approaches mandates the demand for *flexibility* from software teams. Agile principles profess a self-organized team, and underscore the need for motivated and skilled human resources. They emphasize that customer and developers must collaborate closely while developing software. A second set of principles emphasises customer satisfaction and the need to accommodate changing business requirements. A third set of principles focuses on creating value by frequently delivering working software in time-boxed intervals. These principles implicitly demand teams to adopt a nimble approach to software development. In line with Conboy's arguments (2009), flexibility for this setting concerns the *ability of the software teams to continuously update the software artefact and deliver functionality.* The teams tend to rely on informal mechanisms in terms of exercising control, modes of communication and interpersonal collaboration (Ramesh et al. 2006).

This notion of flexibility is nuanced further by the nature of the project effort. Product-focused engagements involve developing the software artefact for the market at large, with the marketing team or a carefully constituted product management group playing the role of a "proxy customer". This facilitates negotiations regarding the feasibility of requirement updates on an ongoing basis. In contrast, services-oriented engagements involve developing the software artefact for a real customer, thus warranting a more committed and less negotiable handling of requests.

Stability

The realities of a distributed setup necessitate the need for *stability* in the project environment. We build on the conceptualization of stability by Vinekar et al. (2006), which situates it in the context of traditional software development approaches. For instance, the waterfall method relies on minimising changes during the course of a project via rigorous upfront requirements gathering, analysis and design. Such linear approaches prosper on a tradition of predictability and control (Vinekar et al., 2006). Predictability demands team members to anticipate and follow the future steps of execution. The intent of control is to adhere to a pre-defined project plan (Tiwana, 2010). This ensures stable conditions for the teams to execute their project, which leads to assurance of timely project delivery (Boehm & Turner, 2004).

Distributed teams employ ICT-mediated interactions to coordinate their tasks across multiple geographies and time zones. As a result, dispersed team members generally develop weak ties (Wong & Burton, 2000). Thus, there is a push for clear specification of requirements and design upfront, and a big picture product definition. Consequently, teams across sites prefer to work towards executing a clearly defined project charter. In line with the arguments supplied by Vinekar et al. (2006), stability for this setting concerns the *need for software teams to predictably meet the objectives of a pre-defined project plan*. The teams tend to rely on formal mechanisms, such as coordination by standardisation, in order to exploit detailed technical documentation and address the impediments to communication induced due to the geographical separation of team members (Ramesh et al., 2006; Ågerfalk & Fitzgerald, 2006).

This notion of stability is nuanced by the "configurational" dimension of distributedness experienced in a project setup. Teams working in a dependent mode across sites require regular coordination and clarity in deliverable dates. In contrast with this, teams working in an independent split can operate in a self-contained mode, after they have engaged in detailed planning upfront. Such contingencies fundamentally make a difference as to how teams organise themselves in the project setup. This has the potential to impact boundary spanning decisions and the manner in which team-level objectives are defined for a given duration.

Conflict Between Flexibility and Stability

Given the opposing nature of flexibility and stability, it is but natural for a conflict to arise in ADD settings when the demand for managing frequent requirement changes competes with the need to work predictively following a plan. This central conflict has received some attention in the literature. Lee et al. (2006) emphasize that agile methods, which encourage teams to embrace change, must be modified to incorporate more rigor and discipline in globally distributed contexts. Ramesh et al. (2006; 2012) highlight competing demands between the tenets of agile and distributedness in ADD projects; whereas an agile setting relies on informal processes to facilitate coordination, distributed settings typically embrace formal mechanisms.

Our analysis (captured by Figure 1) suggests that the nature of agile project engagement will influence the manner in which teams handle updated requirements. Moreover, the type of distributed team configuration will impact the way teams organise their work on a regular basis.

Figure 1. Conflict in agile distributed development projects

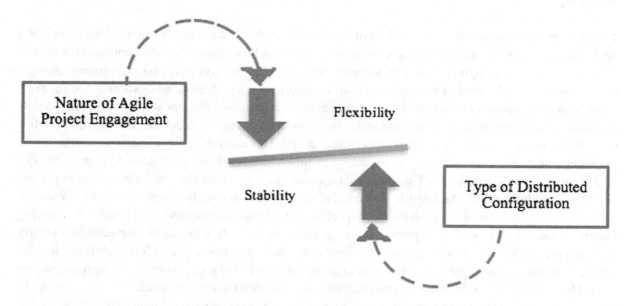

Managing the Conflict Between Flexibility and Stability

The conflicting tensions being explored in this chapter are not unique to ADD project settings. Organizational studies have focused on the effective management of conflicts experienced at multiple levels. One illustration would be the dilemma between social responsibility and profit-making. As internal organizational processes tend to become more complex, especially while dealing with competitive global environments, such tensions become more pervasive (Lewis, 2000). Contingency theory offers one response to alleviating these tensions (Smith & Lewis, 2011). This approach focuses on finding the right "fit" between internal and external conditions (Donaldson, 2001). Researchers have leveraged this notion to elaborate on leadership choices (such as, Vroom & Jago, 2007), structural approaches (such as, Morton & Hu, 2008), and strategic decision-making choices (such as, Tarter & Hoy, 1998).

In their bid for survival and continued growth, organizations generally strive to strike a balance between opposing demands: (1) exploring new markets versus exploiting existing assets and capabilities, or (2) adapting to future environmental changes versus aligning with current business demands. In particular, information systems studies continue to expand on the second trade-off, generally experienced at a business unit level. For instance, evidence has been provided from the context of software development (Cao et al., 2013; Ramesh et al., 2012; Tiwana, 2010), innovation-seeking project alliances (Tiwana, 2008), business units of R&D organizations (McCarthy & Gordon, 2011), software organizations (Napier et al., 2011), mobile communities of practice (Kietzmann et al., 2013) and the social media influence on communication in organizations (Huang et al., 2015).

A unifying theme across these studies has been the need for the simultaneous pursuit of trade-off decisions. Contingency theory does not offer actionable insights in this regard; the literature points at following an "ambidextrous" approach. Ambidexterity refers to specific ways adopted by an organization and/or business unit to reconcile the tensions faced upon dealing with conflicting choices. One suggestion would be to create separate units to handle the duality (Duncan, 1976; Tushman & O'Reilly, 1996). An exemplar of this approach comes from the newspaper industry, which faced competing demands to sustain the print business and at the same time thrive on an online presence in the wake of the internet boom. Faced with this situation, *USA Today* chose to explore the online business through an independent division, while it simultaneously exploited its existing print business through an existing division.

An alternative approach could be to provide an appropriate context for a business unit (Gibson & Birkinshaw, 2004). A real-life example is presented by *Toyota Production Systems*, which harnesses a work context that involves a mix of 'forces of expansion' as well as 'forces of integration' (Takeuchi et al., 2008). Forces of expansion deals with setting impossible goals, local customization and experimentation, whereas forces of integration involve inculcating values from the founders, up-and-in people management and open communication. Amalgamation of such forces enables contradictions to co-exist in the setting. The emphasis is then put on individuals to divide their time between the "opposing" activities (i.e., efficiency vs problem-solving).

The contextual approach is ideal in ADD settings when the tenets of agile development as well as distributedness are warranted by a single software project (Ramesh et al., 2012). Typically, global ADD teams are faced with regular demands for altering work objectives at each of the development sites; the teams prefer to individually take on a portion of the accountability on the requirements, through a business analyst or product owner. When faced with multiple change requests in a given time horizon, the individual sites choose to negotiate their scope. Thus, an appropriate context is necessitated to ensure that the team at a given site can take adequate decisions to manage the trade-off.

This favourable context is characterized by performance and social elements, for individuals to carry out their work (Schulze et al., 2008). Performance elements are defined by the behaviour-framing attributes of *discipline* and *stretch*, whereas social elements are described via the attributes of *support* and *trust* (Gibson & Birkinshaw, 2004; Ghoshal & Bartlett, 1994). On the one hand, 'discipline' induces the team members to voluntarily strive to meet all the expectations generated by their explicit or implicit commitments, while 'stretch' induces them to voluntarily strive for more, rather than less, ambitious objectives. On the other hand, 'support' induces the members to lend assistance and countenance to others, while 'trust' induces them to rely on the commitments of each other.

The interaction between these variables leads to the development of ambidextrous capabilities. Several studies (Barlatier et al., 2015; Havermans et al., 2015) have established their significance in organizational settings. This approach has direct implications for the ADD setting, where the project context for software teams should allow them to embrace agility and distributedness together. In the next section, we present our findings from a case study and elaborate on the enabling mechanisms.

CASE STUDY: A RETAILER WEBSITE OPERATIONS

Our case project is focused on the retail sector. Multiple software teams are engaged in developing a web interface for the client, which will be accessed by end consumers. Examining a page from any global retailer's website tells us that typically the end consumer will have the option to make relevant purchases across categories (such as grocery, floral items etc.) by creating an account with the merchant.

The project work involves three sets of activities: (1) rewrite existing services, (2) develop a set of enhancements or new features, and (3) change the order flow. The software team in India focuses on the enhancements, while the on-site team, in collaboration with the client representatives (sitting in USA), focuses on micro-service re-write and order flow related work.

Figure 2 illustrates the project structuring. Teams at independent sites work in a self-contained mode, so that they can take complete responsibility of the specific module handled by them. The customer view stems from the associates, who regularly interact with the onsite software team regarding project relevant matters.

Figure 2. Project structure

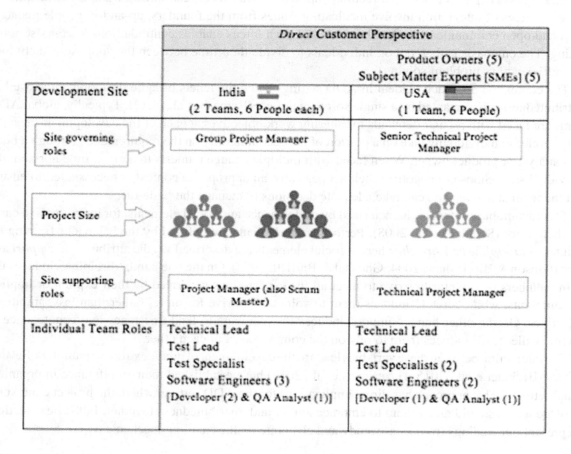

	Direct Customer Perspective	
		Product Owners (5) Subject Matter Experts [SMEs] (5)
Development Site	India (2 Teams, 6 People each)	USA (1 Team, 6 People)
Site governing roles	Group Project Manager	Senior Technical Project Manager
Project Size		
Site supporting roles	Project Manager (also Scrum Master)	Technical Project Manager
Individual Team Roles	Technical Lead Test Lead Test Specialist Software Engineers (3) [Developer (2) & QA Analyst (1)]	Technical Lead Test Lead Test Specialists (2) Software Engineers (2) [Developer (1) & QA Analyst (1)]

Stability in this case setting manifests in software teams functioning independently from the India and USA sites, a particular specialisation for the project to predictably meet its objectives. The onsite software teams take primary responsibility to coordinate the requirements between the client and off-shore teams. They work closely with the product owner (PO) and other stakeholders onsite to develop an understanding of what needs to be done. Subsequently, they negotiate on behalf of the offshore teams to ensure that a reasonable workload gets allotted for a given time frame.

The offshore software teams are responsible to develop services application programming interfaces (API) for the project. They are primarily focused on development and must regularly demonstrate progress to the client. The teams segregate relevant stories among themselves in a manner that allows them to function independently at the site. When responding to queries and/or clarifications, they allow the project manager to work in conjunction with the onsite teams to elicit the client response.

This case setting follows the notion of (1) Core and (2) Feature team members. At a broad level, core team members are responsible for supporting the developmental activities undertaken by the feature team members. Although software teams follow the practice of core and feature team members at both the sites, we witness that the onsite teams are still primarily accountable for fetching appropriate requirements. In the words of the technical lead:

The only difference [onsite] is that the core team will be looking at requirements for future iterations and the feature team will look at requirements and any support on the development effort related to the current iteration.

Despite teams working in such a self-contained mode at a given site, they must wrestle to accommodate any updated requirements from the client. Given the services mode of operation, *flexibility* manifests in teams handling sporadic reliance on each other in response to the regular direction offered by the client. Increasingly, teams are faced with ad-hoc requests from the client, which needs to be fulfilled in a committed manner. As the Scrum Master explains:

Ad-hoc tasks do come up. Something like during a release activity, some defects might pop up in integration support; then the focus must shift to them. The stories currently under execution will take a back seat. And the chief Scrum Master actually gives confidence to the team in that regard.

Such unplanned requests result in an intermittent reliance across sites to complete the work. As the offshore team might be involved with closing other stories, they expect the onsite team to help them out. Although the onsite team is primarily concerned with handling requirements management, they end up creating bandwidth to accommodate the work. Explaining the rationale, the onsite technical manager remarks:

As the codebase is shared, whenever we receive an unplanned request [from the client] and the offshore team cannot take it up completely, then the work is passed to the onsite team to make sure that they complete it [because the sprint will be closed]. We can't just carry forward the stories.

Moreover, when we held a discussion with one of the QA personnel, we realized that changes to the backlog are not that common. In fact, teams seldom experience movement on the stories, which are part of the backlog. The changes are experienced at the API level, where there could be a lack of complete clarity during the sprint conception.

Overall, we witness that the teams are regularly stretched, having to align with their specific work specializations, and at the same time having to respond to the sporadic reliance on their counterpart for project related matters to accommodate updated client expectations.

To manage these conflicting forces, we witness a novel project context involving the interaction between performance and social elements. Performance elements enable teams to manage their responsibilities effectively, whereas social elements facilitate them to handle cross-site relations adequately.

The teams demonstrate practices that suggest an interplay between these elements resulting in an ambidextrous response.

As an exemplar, teams rely upon complete visibility of work progression, in terms of story status, dependencies and trends. Consequently, the teams prefer to conduct formal meetings (such as sprint planning and review) in a disciplined manner following a time-boxed approach. The teams follow a set agenda and prefers to have fixed duration for the meetings. As the intermittent dependencies are already shared over the tool, the teams attempt to engage only in relevant discussions on the dependent stories and provide a status update in the formal meetings. Subsequently, they are able to work with autonomy to deliver on the target dates. Such practices result in teams adopting a nimble approach to ensure the smooth progression of project work in an ADD setup.

FUTURE RESEARCH DIRECTIONS

Future research should analyse alternate forms of ADD setups to derive insightful conclusions. As an illustration, the setting might involve globally dispersed members from a single software team. Such a setup allows individual teams to gain exposure to multiple areas of expertise from across the globe. One could explore such settings and offer a nuanced understanding of the conflict between flexibility and stability, with pointers to manage it.

Future research also needs to build upon existing work (such as Ramesh et al., 2012) and dwell further on the performance and social elements relevant for the setup. There is a powerful discourse in ambidexterity literature that emphasizes uncovering practices that enable creation of a suitable context. Such insights will provide recommendations to practitioners which could serve to inform ADD practice in the long run.

CONCLUSION

This chapter has focused on tensions that arise in projects that follow agile methodologies in a setup with multiple teams working in geographically distributed locations. It provides nuanced clarity on the notion of the conflict between flexibility and stability in an agile distributed development setup. We dwell on the drivers of this conflict and uncover tenets pertaining to an agile setup and distributed configuration. For managing such forces, we propose contextual ambidexterity as the theoretical basis and provide some insights regarding the constituents of this approach.

REFERENCES

Ågerfalk, J., & Fitzgerald, B. (2006). Flexible and distributed software processes: Old petunias in new bowls? *Communications of the ACM*, *49*(10), 27–34.

Barlatier, P. J., & Dupouët, O. (2015). Achieving contextual ambidexterity with communities of practice at GDF SUEZ. *Global Business and Organizational Excellence*, *34*(3), 43–53. doi:10.1002/joe.21603

Boehm, B., & Turner, R. (2003). *Balancing Agility and Discipline: A Guide for the Perplexed*. Addison-Wesley.

Boehm, B., & Turner, R. (2004). Balancing agility and discipline: Evaluating and integrating agile and plan-driven methods. In *Proceedings of 26th International Conference on Software Engineering (ICSE)* (pp. 718-719). IEEE. 10.1109/ICSE.2004.1317503

Cao, L., Mohan, K., Ramesh, B., & Sarkar, S. (2013). Evolution of governance: Achieving ambidexterity in IT outsourcing. *Journal of Management Information Systems*, *30*(3), 115–140. doi:10.2753/MIS0742-1222300305

Cockburn, A., & Highsmith, J. (2001). Agile Software Development: The People Factor. *Computer, IEEE*, *34*(11), 131–133. doi:10.1109/2.963450

Cohen, D., Lindvall, M., & Costa, P. (2004). An Introduction to Agile Methods. In M. Zelkowitz (Ed.), *Advances in Computers, Advances in Software Engineering*. Elsevier. doi:10.1016/S0065-2458(03)62001-2

Conboy, K. (2009). Agility from First Principles: Reconstructing the Concept of Agility in Information Systems Development. *Information Systems Research*, *20*(3), 329–354. doi:10.1287/isre.1090.0236

Conboy, K., & Fitzgerald, B. (2004). Toward a Conceptual Framework of Agile Methods. In *Proceedings of ACM Workshop on Interdisciplinary Software Engineering Research* (pp. 37-44). Newport Beach, CA: Academic Press. 10.1145/1029997.1030005

Crnkovic, I., Chaudron, M., & Larsson, S. (2005). Component-based Development Process and Component Lifecycle. *CIT. Journal of Computing and Information Technology*, *13*(4), 321–327. doi:10.2498/cit.2005.04.10

Dingsøyr, T., Nerur, S., Balijepally, V., & Moe, N. (2012). A Decade of Agile Methodologies: Towards Explaining Agile Software Development. *Journal of Systems and Software*, *85*(6), 1213–1221. doi:10.1016/j.jss.2012.02.033

Donaldson, L. (2001). The contingency theory of organizations. *Sage (Atlanta, Ga.)*.

Duncan, R. B. (1976). The ambidextrous organization: Designing dual structures for innovation. *The Management of Organization*, *1*, 167–188.

Dyba°, T., & Dingsøyr, T. (2008). Empirical studies of agile software development: A systematic review. *Information and Software Technology*, *50*(9-10), 833–859. doi:10.1016/j.infsof.2008.01.006

Ebert, C., & De Neve, P. (2001). Surviving global software development. *IEEE Software*, *18*(2), 62–69. doi:10.1109/52.914748

Ghoshal, S., & Bartlett, C. A. (1994). Linking organizational context and managerial action: The dimensions of quality of management. *Strategic Management Journal*, *15*(2), 91–112.

Gibson, C. B., & Birkinshaw, J. (2004). The antecedents, consequences, and mediating role of organizational ambidexterity. *Academy of Management Journal*, *47*(2), 209–226.

Havermans, L. A., Den Hartog, D. N., Keegan, A., & Uhl-Bien, M. (2015). Exploring the role of leadership in enabling contextual ambidexterity. *Human Resource Management*, *54*(1), 179–200. doi:10.1002/hrm.21764

Highsmith, J., & Cockburn, A. (2001). Agile software development: The business of innovation. *Computer, IEEE*, *34*(9), 120–127. doi:10.1109/2.947100

Hinds, P. J., & Mortensen, M. (2005). Understanding conflict in geographically distributed teams: The moderating effects of shared identity, shared context, and spontaneous communication. *Organization Science*, *16*(3), 290–307. doi:10.1287/orsc.1050.0122

Hoda, R., Salleh, N., & Grundy, J. (2018). The rise and evolution of agile software development. *IEEE Software*, *35*(5), 58–63. doi:10.1109/MS.2018.290111318

Holmström, H., Conchúir, E. Ó., Ågerfalk, P. J., & Fitzgerald, B. (2006). Global software development challenges: A case study on temporal, geographical and socio-cultural distance. In *Proceedings of International Conference on Global Software Engineering (ICGSE)* (pp. 3-11). IEEE. 10.1109/ICGSE.2006.261210

Huang, J., Baptista, J., & Newell, S. (2015). Communicational ambidexterity as a new capability to manage social media communication within organizations. *The Journal of Strategic Information Systems*, *24*(2), 49–64. doi:10.1016/j.jsis.2015.03.002

Jalali, S., & Wohlin, C. (2011). Global software engineering and agile practices: A systematic review. *Journal of Software: Evolution and Process*, *24*(6), 643–659.

Jimenez, A., Boehe, D. M., Taras, V., & Caprar, D. V. (2017). Working across boundaries: Current and future perspectives on global virtual teams. *Journal of International Management*, *23*(4), 341–349. doi:10.1016/j.intman.2017.05.001

Jiménez, M., Piattini, M., & Vizcaíno, A. (2009). Challenges and improvements in distributed software development: A systematic review. *Advances in Software Engineering*, 3.

Kietzmann, J., Plangger, K., Eaton, B., Heilgenberg, K., Pitt, L., & Berthon, P. (2013). Mobility at work: A typology of mobile communities of practice and contextual ambidexterity. *The Journal of Strategic Information Systems*, *22*(4), 282–297. doi:10.1016/j.jsis.2013.03.003

Lee, G., DeLone, W., & Espinosa, J. A. (2006). Ambidextrous coping strategies in globally distributed software development projects. *Communications of the ACM*, *49*(10), 35–40. doi:10.1145/1164394.1164417

Lee, G., & Xia, W. (2010). Toward Agile: An Integrated Analysis of Quantitative and Qulaitative Field Data on Software Development Agility. *Management Information Systems Quarterly*, *34*(1), 87–114. doi:10.2307/20721416

Lewis, D. (2000). *Promoting socially responsible business, ethical trade and acceptable labour standards*. Social Development Department, Department for International Development.

Lyytinen, K., & Rose, G. M. (2006). Information system development agility as organizational learning. *European Journal of Information Systems*, *15*(2), 183–199. doi:10.1057/palgrave.ejis.3000604

McCarthy, I. P., & Gordon, B. R. (2011). Achieving contextual ambidexterity in R&D organizations: A management control system approach. *R & D Management*, *41*(3), 240–258. doi:10.1111/j.1467-9310.2011.00642.x

Moe, N. B., Dingsøyr, T., & Dybå, T. (2010). A teamwork model for understanding an agile team: A case study of a Scrum project. *Information and Software Technology*, *52*(5), 480–491. doi:10.1016/j.infsof.2009.11.004

Morton, N. A., & Hu, Q. (2008). Implications of the fit between organizational structure and ERP: A structural contingency theory perspective. *International Journal of Information Management*, *28*(5), 391–402. doi:10.1016/j.ijinfomgt.2008.01.008

Napier, N. P., Mathiassen, L., & Robey, D. (2011). Building contextual ambidexterity in a software company to improve firm-level coordination. *European Journal of Information Systems*, *20*(6), 674–690. doi:10.1057/ejis.2011.32

Nerur, S., & Balijepally, V. (2007). Theoretical reflections on agile development methodologies. *Communications of the ACM*, *50*(3), 79–83. doi:10.1145/1226736.1226739

Nerur, S., Mahapatra, R., & Mangalaraj, G. (2005). Challenges of Migrating to Agile Methodologies. *Communications of the ACM*, *48*(5), 72–78. doi:10.1145/1060710.1060712

O'Leary, M. B., & Cummings, J. N. (2007). The spatial, temporal, and configurational characteristics of geographic dispersion in teams. *Management Information Systems Quarterly*, *31*(3), 433–452. doi:10.2307/25148802

Paetsch, F., Eberlein, A., & Maurer, F. (2003). Requirements Engineering and Agile Software Development. In *Proceedings of 12th IEEE International Workshops on Enabling Technologies: Infrastructure for Collaborative Enterprises (WET ICE)* (pp. 308-313). IEEE.

Powell, A., Piccoli, G., & Ives, B. (2004). Virtual Teams: Team Control Structure, Work Processes, and Team Effectiveness. *Information Technology & People*, *17*(4), 359–379. doi:10.1108/09593840410570258

Ramesh, B., Cao, L., Mohan, K., & Xu, P. (2006). Can distributed software development be agile? *Communications of the ACM*, *49*(10), 41–46. doi:10.1145/1164394.1164418

Ramesh, B., Mohan, K., & Cao, L. (2012). Ambidexterity in agile distributed development: An empirical investigation. *Information Systems Research*, *23*(2), 323–339. doi:10.1287/isre.1110.0351

Sahay, S. (2003). Global software alliances: The challenge of 'standardization'. *Scandinavian Journal of Information Systems*, *15*(1), 11.

Schulze, P., Heinemann, F., & Abedin, A. (2008). Balancing Exploitation and Exploration. In *Academy of Management Proceedings* (Vol. 2008, No. 1, pp. 1-6). Academy of Management. doi:10.5465/ambpp.2008.33622934

Schwaber, K., & Beedle. (2001). *Agile Software development with Scrum*. Prentice Hall.

Shrivastava, S. V., & Date, H. (2010). Distributed Agile Software Development: A Review. *Journal of Computing Science and Engineering: JCSE*, *1*(1), 10–17.

Smith, W. K., & Lewis, M. W. (2011). Toward a theory of paradox: A dynamic equilibrium model of organizing. *Academy of Management Review, 36*(2), 381–403.

Takeuchi, H., Osono, E., & Shimizu, N. (2008). The contradictions that drive Toyota's success. *Harvard Business Review, 86*(6), 96–104. PMID:18411967

Tarter, C. J., & Hoy, W. K. (1998). Toward a contingency theory of decision making. *Journal of Educational Administration, 36*(3), 212–228. doi:10.1108/09578239810214687

Tiwana, A. (2008). Do bridging ties complement strong ties? An empirical examination of alliance ambidexterity. *Strategic Management Journal, 29*(3), 251–272. doi:10.1002mj.666

Tiwana, A. (2010). Systems development ambidexterity: Explaining the complementary and substitutive roles of formal and informal controls. *Journal of Management Information Systems, 27*(2), 87–126. doi:10.2753/MIS0742-1222270203

Tushman, M. L., & O'Reilly, C. A. III. (1996). Managing evolutionary and revolutionary change. *California Management Review, 38*(4), 8–28. doi:10.2307/41165852

Upadhyaya, A., & Krishna, S. (2007). Antecedents of knowledge sharing in globally distributed software development teams, In *Proceedings of European Conference of Information Systems (ECIS)* (pp. 727-738). St. Gallen, Switzerland: Academic Press.

Vinekar, V., Slinkman, C. W., & Nerur, S. (2006). Can agile and traditional systems development approaches coexist? An ambidextrous view. *Information Systems Management, 23*(3), 31–42. doi:10.1201/1078.10580530/46108.23.3.20060601/93705.4

Vroom, V. H., & Jago, A. G. (2007). The role of the situation in leadership. *The American Psychologist, 62*(1), 17–24. doi:10.1037/0003-066X.62.1.17 PMID:17209676

Wong, S. S., & Burton, R. M. (2000). Virtual teams: What are their characteristics, and impact on team performance? *Computational & Mathematical Organization Theory, 6*(4), 339–360. doi:10.1023/A:1009654229352

KEY TERMS AND DEFINITIONS

Agile Distributed Development: Software projects that are implemented by teams located across multiple geographies and following an agile approach.

Contextual Ambidexterity: Behavioral capacity of the organizational unit to simultaneously manage contradictory demands in the setting.

Flexibility: Ability of the software team to continuously update the software artifact and deliver functionality.

Project Context: Systems, processes, and beliefs that shape individual-level behaviour within a team.

Stability: Need for a software team to predictably meet the objectives of a pre-defined project plan.

Chapter 6
Adapting Agile Practices During the Evolution of a Healthcare Software Product

Danilo F. S. Santos
Embedded Lab, Federal University of Campina Grande, Brazil

André Felipe A. Rodrigues
Embedded Lab, Federal University of Campina Grande, Brazil

Walter O. Guerra Filho
Embedded Lab, Federal University of Campina Grande, Brazil

Marcos Fábio Pereira
Embedded Lab, Federal University of Campina Grande, Brazil

ABSTRACT

Agile Software Development (ASD) can be considered the mainstream development method of choice worldwide. ASD are used due to features such as easy management and embrace of changes, where change in requirements should be taken as a positive feature. However, some domain verticals, such as medical-healthcare, are classified as critical-safety system, which usually requires traditional methods. This chapter presents a practical use case describing the evolution of a software product that was conceived as a wellness software for end-users in mobile platforms to a medical-healthcare product restricted to regulatory standard recommendations. It presents the challenges and how the ASD is compatible to standards such as ISO/IEC 82304-1.

DOI: 10.4018/978-1-7998-4165-4.ch006

INTRODUCTION

Agile methods can be considered one of the most adopted methodologies for software development nowadays. When considering the development of consumer-based services and applications, which are mostly focused for end-users in mobile and cloud platforms, Agile Software Development (ASD) is the de-facto methodology. ASD are used due features such easily management and embrace of changes, where change in requirements should be taken as a positive feature. However, some domain verticals, such as medical-healthcare, are classified as critical-safety system, which usually requires traditional methods where requirements are well stablished before development, and validation and verification are usually executed in the end of development.

When considering new paradigms such as the Internet of Things (IoT) and Industry 4.0 revolution, new conflicts appears between market needs and safety regulations. In this new world, the need for fast development for market fit purposes is a reality, and that´s where ASD fits (Kumari, 2018) (Laukkarinen, 2018). These challenges appear in almost all domains, such as healthcare (Gupta, 2019) (Laukkarinen, 2017).

In this context, we present a practical use case describing how was the evolution of a software product that was conceived as a wellness software for end-users in mobile platforms. The product evolved to be a medical-healthcare product, restricted to regulatory standard recommendations, where agile software practices were adopted to fulfill such guidelines.

As most Minimum Viable Products (MVP), the presented target software was firstly developed using a standard agile process. As the product requirements changed due to integration with medical devices, its regulatory requirements also increased, including the need to be complaint to standards such as ISO 82304-1 (ISO/IEC 82304, 2012) and ISO 62304-1 (ISO/IEC 62304, 2006). Therefore, the previously adopted agile methodology was adapted to fulfill these new requirements, balancing recommendations required by regulatory standards, such as requirement traceability, with agile features such as the embrace of changes.

In this chapter we show that it is possible to use standard agile methodologies in the first stages of development, when creating an MVP, and then, reuse already developed artifacts and adapt the process to be complaint with regulatory rules for safety-critical systems in the healthcare domain. The chapter shows how Scrum artifacts were adapted to enhance traceability, as also, as automated management tools were customized and integrated, and finally, how new requirements for validation and verification were introduced into the agile process due regulatory standards.

The remainder of this chapter is organized as follows: In *Background* section we present a review of agile Software Development (ASD) main features, a literature review about the main challenges in ASD for health care, and the main standards used in our work. The next section presents the adopted software development process, highlighting the main challenges and decisions made during the process adaptation. In the *Future Research Directions* section, we discuss how intelligent tools could help in software engineering process as whole. Finally, in the *Conclusion*, an overall discussion and current challenges are presented.

Background

Traditional plan-based software development processes, or disciplined processes, are based on a sequence-based linear approach, where each phase is exhaustive executed before the next one. Disciplined methodologies, such as Waterfall or V-Process (Sommerville, 2011), are usually used in the development of systems that need extensive quality assurance processes, where verification and validation activities are one of the main drivers of the product release. Although they are well suited for healthcare product development, as they usually deal with the validation of critical requirements, nowadays new market needs in healthcare demand new innovations and fast time-to-market releases. Based on this new scenario, disciplined processes present challenges for embrace of changes, especially when facing the need for new products and features.

Talking about Agile Software Development (ASD), nowadays it can be considered the "the mainstream development method of choice worldwide" (Hoda, 2018). ASD arose from dissatisfaction with the overloads of development methods in the 1980s and 1990s. The main features of ASD can be listed as, (i) focus on code instead of project documentation, and (ii) interactive approach to development, where planning is carried iteratively, and project scope is continuously refined and prioritized (Ramesh, 2010).

Therefore, the main goal of ASD is to deliver software quickly, and deal with volatile requirements (Hoda, 2017). The goal is to reduce development process overloads, and to be able to respond quickly to requirements changing without excessive rework. One of the main features of ASD is that specification, design and implementation phases are interspersed. The system is developed in a series of versions or increments with business stakeholders involved in (almost) all phases. To achieve this, frequent delivery of new versions is executed, and extensible use of support tools are encouraged, such as automated testing, continuous integration, and management tools, etc.

When dealing with safety regulations, as the ones applied to software for healthcare, new challenges appears. Well stablished standards define how medical device software should follow, namely ISO/IEC 62304 (ISO/IEC 62304, 2006) and ISO/IEC 82304 (ISO/IEC 82304, 2012) family of standards. They are international standards that "provides a lifecycle with activities and tasks necessary for the safe design and maintenance of software for medical devices". Although it is not itself a regulation, it is recognized by many regulatory agencies as good standards for medical device software development. Therefore, companies and regulatory agencies are continuously discussing how to concretely meet the requirements from those standards.

ISO/IEC 62304 family of standards describes and provides guidance on development processes to be applied according to each classification. All these documents recommend that the risk associated with a software product be assessed to establish a development process with the appropriate level of rigor and robustness.

In general, they recommend manufacturers to show traceability between system requirements, software requirements, and tests, and to verify and document traceable software requirements to system requirements and other sources (Martins, 2018). Traceability is the degree to which a relationship can be established between two or more products of the development process. Several approaches exist that focus on establishing traces among different types of artifacts, such as requirements traceability, requirements-to-architecture, requirements-to-code, and others (Bianchini, 2019). Some works presented approaches about how to map requirements and enhance traceability in healthcare software development (Barbosa, 2018), however, they do not detail a practical case for the industry, mostly focusing on academic trials.

Mostly of these challenges are common in disciplined methodologies and ASD. However, when dealing with ASD, new challenges appears when managing requirements for traceability (Barbosa, 2018). For example, in (Heager, 2018), it is performed a systematic literature review about agile Requirements Engineering. The authors expose evidences about how agile practices respond to the traditional challenges from the Requirements Engineering and how to manage development teams in this context.

To easily the adoption of agile in these scenarios, initiatives were created to help the adaptation of ASD for safety critical systems development. For example, the SafeScrum approach (Hanssen, 2018) split the software development from the process of design, develop, deploy and maintain safety-related systems, as defined in the IEC 61508 standard. That way, the software development uses Scrum, and the decision making for safety are done in a separated process. Another initiative was presented by (AAMI, 2012), defining practice guidelines for medical device software development using ASD. The adaptation of an ASD process for healthcare software development presented in this chapter, although share similar points, was defined and executed independently of those initiatives, and our experience is presented in the following sections.

Healthcare Software Product Development

The first developed MVP, namely Personal HealthCare System (PHC), was focused on monitoring newborns babies through mobile platforms and personal health devices. The goal was the consumer market in a B2C (Business to Consumer) chain. The system was composed by a cloud-hosted service and a mobile frontend application used to input vital signals such as temperature, weight and height. In this sense, a simple agile approach, strongly based on Scrum, was used for development. The product backlog was defined through standard User Stories, focusing only on user requirements, as illustrated in the following Table 1.

Table 1. Example of Simple User Stories for the MVP

User Story	Points
As a parent, I want to store height information using a web page	5
As a parent, I want to store height information using my Android phone	5
As a parent, I want to follow the evolution of my baby's height over the months through a line graph	13
As a system administrator, I want to register and unregister users from the system	3
As a physician, I want to access data from my patients and register comments	5

Short sprints were defined (two weeks), where about 80% of tasks were focused on feature development, and the remaining 20% on testing and validation activities for Quality Assurance (QA). Backlog was maintained through online management tools, and tasks were daily controlled through a wallboard and post-its. As a result, the MVP was developed into 6 months with the first product market fit release.

Some highlights are important to mention:

- Requirements were stored in a separated document, most as business requirements from stakeholders.
- QA activities were managed separated from the Backlog and Requirements, such as Bug management, test plans, and simple continuous integration systems.

Evolution to HealthCare Platform

As the product business requirements changed, new challenges appeared due a new goal of the system:

- Integration with personal and clinical health devices, such as thermometers, blood pressure devices, weight scales, etc.

The need for interoperability was an additional feature besides this integration. Therefore, as a new requirement, the need to be compliant with Continua Health Alliance Guidelines (Wartena, 2010), as also, Bluetooth SIG specifications (Bluetooth SIG, 2020) for wireless connectivity.

As a result, the HealthCare platform was conceived (Santos, 2016). The platform offers services for remote monitoring and management of patient health data. It allows the user to receive data from Personal Health Devices independently and automatically, and securely synchronize this data with Cloud services. The Cloud platform therefore shares this information as healthcare professionals or family members and offers value-added services such as a threshold alert system, appointment scheduling, user classification by health status, among others. In addition to offering personal patient monitoring solutions in their homes, the HealthCare platform enables continuous patient monitoring through its connection to multi-parameter monitors, enabling healthcare professionals to remotely monitor patient progress 24/7 and in real time.

The HealthCare Platform is divided into 3 main modules:

- Service Platform.
- Application Portals.
- Health Data Aggregators (HDA).

The Service Platform offers web services and stores data. In conjunction with Application Portals, which provide the application vision for the customer domain, the Service Platform provides a 24/7 online infrastructure for patients, healthcare professionals and system administrators.

Health Data Aggregators (HDA) can be considered as the modules where information flow is initiated, thus a health data collector. An HDA can work on a mobile device, such as a tablet or smartphone, or on a dedicated device, a health hub. HDA collects data from Personal Health Devices (DPS) or Medical Devices through communication interfaces such as Bluetooth, Bluetooth Smart, Wi-Fi, or Ethernet. An HDA can communicate with Personal Health Devices such as oximeters, blood pressure meters, glucometers, and more, or communicate with Medical Devices for continuous monitoring, such as a Multi-parameter Monitor. HealthCare Platform can be described using the diagram of Figure 1.

Adopted Agile Software Development

Adopting an ASD process, as expected, added a list of benefits for the product development, such as fast requirement review and update due to earlier releases; better interaction with stakeholders and users; fast adaptation of product specification due new market demands. However, as dealing with a healthcare product submitted for conformance rules, it was necessary to review all quality assurance processes to be compliant with international standards.

Figure 1. Diagram of HealthCare System.

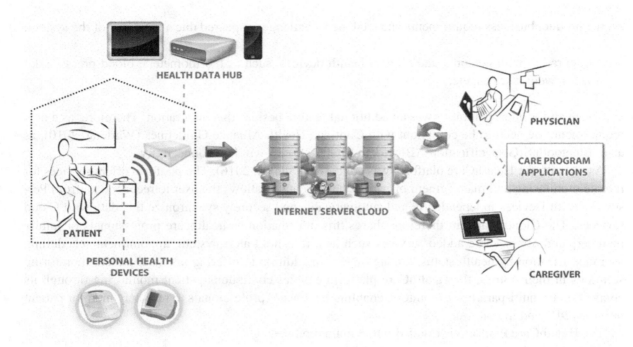

In order to achieved better conformance and QA metrics, the development process was reviewed. As before, the new software product development procedure adopted follows an agile approach. In this procedure, all phases required for project development are fulfilled, where records and artifacts are generated for each phase.

In general, project development goes through four phases: (i) Proposal, (ii) Planning, (iii) Execution and (iv) Closure. In the development process the following actors participate:

- **Product Owner:** Is the customer representative for the software product. Its responsibilities include defining features / requirements, maintaining Product Backlog, prioritizing, risk analysis, and accepting / validating results.
- **Development Team:** A team of engineers, architects and software developers responsible for product development, testing, verification.
- **Scrum Master:** Responsible for keeping the development process in compliance with its rules and following the development team.

The following Figure 2 illustrates this process, and the artifacts delivered in each phase.

In particular, during implementation, the Scrum agile development approach is used. In the Scrum approach, you define a list of features that will be validated according to the provided specifications (requirements). The list describes a user story that forms what is called a product backlog. This list is developed in the Planning phase and continuously updated during Execution. Each story contains a description of the requirements and use cases that must be met by the product (validation).

Figure 2. Adopted agile procedure

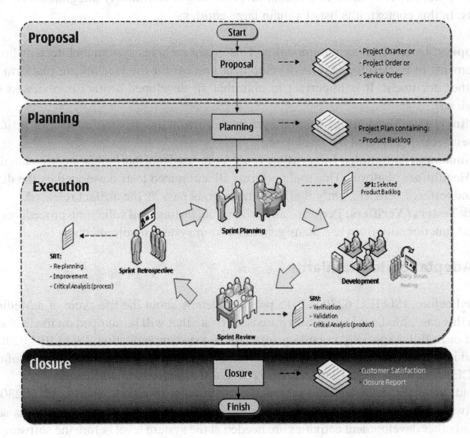

During the Execution phase the stories, which reveal features / requirements, are implemented according to priorities and at equal time intervals ranging from 2 to 4 weeks. These time intervals are called Sprints. During a Sprint cycle 4 phases are performed:

- Sprint Planning, where the Product Backlog features to be developed are chosen.
- Development of features / requirements. In this phase verification and validation tests are performed continuously.
- Sprint Review, where features are reviewed and validated by the Product Owner.
- Sprint Retrospective, where a critical analysis of Sprint's development and results is performed. These results serve to improve the development process and the software product.

In the last phase, the Closure phase, the Customer (Product Owner) certifies that all functionality has been validated and that the final product is ready for its intended use. To perform this attestation, the Product Owner makes use of the acceptance results of the validation tests used during the development phase. At the end, the Product Owner signs a closure and acceptance report, validating and certifying that the software product is ready for its intended use.

In the new process, verification and validation procedure is continually integrated into the development process. In this context, it is listed 4 main large entities:

1. **Developers:** Develop all system modules. This group includes system architects, who define the requirements to be developed. The development process for the HealthCare platform is detailed in another document. It is important to note that all developed artifact is reviewed by another professional.
2. **Repository with Versioning:** Central system that maintains version control of artifacts (code, documents, etc.) generated by developers.
3. **Continuous and Automated Integration Tool:** Automated tool that builds and launches the modules of the HealthCare platform. This tool performs all automated tests developed by the development team and testers / verifiers. Only if all automated tests pass, is the artifact released.
4. **Quality Testers / Verifiers:** Performs all verification, testing, and validation procedures for system data and functionality from test plans generated from system requirements.

Process Adaptation to Standards

As introduced before, ISO/IEC 62304: 2015 provides details about the life cycle of a Medical Device Software. In this case, Medical Device Software is software that will be shipped on medical equipment, either in part or in full. Especially regarding software and system validation, ISO / IEC 62304: 2015 is clear in detail in its section 1.2: "This standard does not cover validation and final release of the MEDICAL DEVICE, even when the MEDICAL DEVICE consists entirely of software."

To this end, ISO / IEC 62304-2015 suggests the use of other standards, such as IEC 82304-1: 2015, "Health Software - Part 1: General requirements for product safety", as mentioned in its section 1.2: Validation and other development activities are needed at the system level before the software and medical device can be placed into service. These system activities are not covered by this standard but can be found in related product standards (e.g., IEC 60601-1. IEC 82304-1, etc.).

As the HealthCare platform is entirely a software product (software system). Therefore, the requirements required in a validation report should be in accordance with the recommendations of ISO/IEC 82304-1:2015. ISO/IEC 82304-1:2015 focuses on safety requirements for healthcare software products designed to operate on computing platforms. Thus, the intended use of these products is independent of hardware. Therefore, ISO/IEC 82304: 2015 covers the software product life cycle with respect to design, development, VALIDATION, installation and maintenance.

ISO / IEC 82304-1: 2015 defines VALIDATION as a process that aims to show that a healthcare software product meets the functionalities (or requirements) defined in the project for its intended use.

The VALIDATION report provides evidence that the process has been performed and that the product meets its requirements for its intended use. To this end, ISO / IEC 82304-1: 2015 defines that the following information should be presented in a validation report:

1. The "manufacturer" shall identify the individuals responsible for validation.
2. The validation report shall provide evidence that the health software product meets its requirements and intended use.
3. The validation report shall include a summary of the results of the validation process.

4. The validation report shall provide evidence that the validation results are traceable to the health software product requirements.

Practical Activities

As introduced before, as the product evolved to medical/healthcare domain, the development process was adapted to meet requirements of international standards. In addition, it was necessary to integrate new tools and create new testing, verification and validation processes.

The Product Backlog has been modified for each story to include references to the requirements to be met. These references were intended to increase the traceability of Sprint requirements. Risk analysis and mitigation activities were also considered in the Done definition of all Product Backlog stories.

To operationalize this process, a new project lifecycle management tool was used. Initially, all requirements and stories were registered in the tool. Sprints were recorded as they were executed with their respective user stories, description and effort estimation (points), as shown in Table 2.

Table 2. Example of simple user stories for the MVP

User Story	Description	Points
As a doctor, I want to see the main bed information in the main screen.	Short Description: Create the "reduced bed widget" which must be placed in the main screen. This "reduced bed widget" is dynamic, and must adapt to the number of lines available. Evaluate how to support horizontal scroll It is desirable, must not mandatory, to support the expansion of lines. Reference Use Cases: US011, US012 Acceptance Requirements: REQ-1002, REQ-1003, REQ-1004	8
As a doctor, I want to see vital signal information in the main screen	Short Description: Create integrated/connected monitor widget. The widget can have a "fixed" design for the alpha. Reference Use Cases: US101, US103 Acceptance Requirements: REQ1102, REQ1103, REQ1104	5

Throughout the Sprint, artifacts resulting from risk analysis of the executed stories were stored also in the tool. At the end of the project, it was possible to track exactly which Sprint a given requirement was met, including the risk analyzes performed for it.

A new Continuous Integration process has been incorporated to ensure quality deliveries. Daily, the latest project code was compiled to generate a new version. Automatic tests were performed to check for potential problems with each generation. In addition, source code anomalies were always checked using static analysis tools across generations. This way, problems were detected and fixed before the version was released.

The automation tool was used to deploy the Continuous Integration process. A task was set up to compile the latest version of the project at the end of each day with static analysis checks and automated

Figure 3. Example of static problems found.

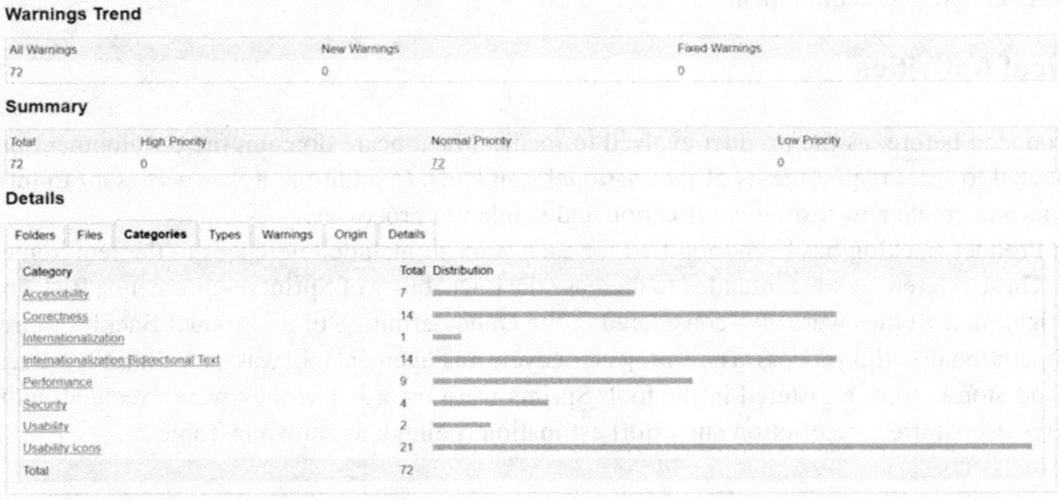

Warnings Trend

All Warnings	New Warnings	Fixed Warnings
72	0	0

Summary

Total	High Priority	Normal Priority	Low Priority
72	0	72	0

Details

Folders | Files | **Categories** | Types | Warnings | Origin | Details

Category	Total	Distribution
Accessibility	7	
Correctness	14	
Internationalization	1	
Internationalization Bidirectional Text	14	
Performance	9	
Security	4	
Usability	2	
Usability Icons	21	
Total	72	

test runs. In this tool, static analysis problems found in each project module were stored and presented as shown in Figure 3.

The testing process was rigorously modified to ensure that the released requirements were as expected. Tests are now planned for each release requirement. The test plan was always fully executed before

Figure 4. Example of requirements registration

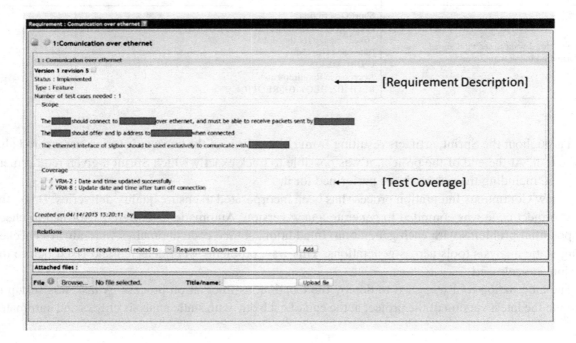

releasing the production version. Some tests were performed manually and others automatically. The person responsible for applying the test plan recorded the result (success or failure) and date of execution.

The Testlink tool was used to perform test management. Initially, all project requirements were registered in the tool as exemplified in Figure 4. It is important to notice that all requirements have a test coverage for validation.

And, each the test case is described in detail, including its definition of criticality, preconditions, planned execution steps as shown in Figure 5.

Figure 5. Example of test case traced to requirement

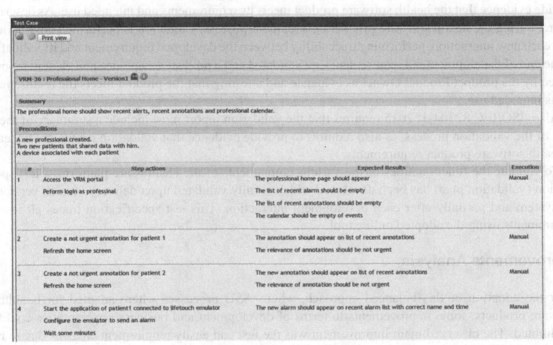

Prior to each release, the test plan was fully executed in the candidate version. If the success percentage was less than 90% or a critical test case failed, the release was canceled. Finally, in order to speed up the execution of the test plan, tools were used to automate test cases whenever possible, such as automatic robot scripts to test external medical devices.

Compliance Validation Documentation

For software product validation, the following procedures and artifacts are used:

- During Sprint Review features are accepted by the Product Owner. These functionalities (requirements) presented in Product Backlog are mapped to test cases, which are executed, logged, and their results reviewed by the Product Owner for validation.

- At the end of software product development, the Product Owner makes a general acceptance of the product, thereby making a statement that the product meets the requirements for its intended use.

For example, ISO / IEC 82304-1: 2015 requires the "manufacturer" to identify the individuals responsible for validation. The tests performed within the previously presented software development process are performed by the testing team and developers, which are always identified in the documentation.

Acceptance and validation of requirements (functionalities) are performed by the project Product Owner upon delivery of new functionalities at each interaction, and at the end of each released version.

Another important feature is that ISO / IEC 82304-1: 2015 requires that the validation report must provide evidence that the health software product meets its requirements and intended use. As described before, during the health software product development process, validation is performed continuously with each new interaction, performing traceability between the developed requirement and its validation. At the end of development, all requirements are validated and a product acceptance and closure report is signed by the product Product Owner as evidence and attesting that the product meets the requirements for its intended use.

Also, ISO/IEC 82304-1: 2015 requires that the validation report must include a summary of the results of the validation process, as also requires to provide evidence that validation results are traceable to health software product requirements.

To validate the functionalities of the various components of the HealthCare platform, a test specification (validation plan) has been developed which is fully validated upon delivery of each version of the system and partially after each development interaction. This test specification traces all tests to requirements using the adopted online tool.

Improvements Analysis

After the adoption of this balanced approach, where ASD processes where adapted for healthcare software products, some improvements in terms of development and business opportunities could be highlighted. The observed main improvement was the fast and easily requirement changes due to new business opportunities and market changes.

For example, during the development process new clinical devices were added to the supported device list due new business opportunities, for example, support chronic disease patients. These devices were rapidly integrated into the system keeping all regulatory and compliance requirements. For instance, one new glucometer device was integrated into the system in 6 weeks, including all validation and verification processes. This example, which was motivated by business opportunities, was rapidly embraced by the development team and, as a proof of its efficient, the software product was registered into the Brazilian regulatory agency, showing that all adopted processes were in conformance with the required standards.

Comparing with a traditional disciplined process, the insertion of a new requirement, such as support a new device, would require a new planning phase for requirement elicitation and validation, a new architecture revision phase, then a new development phase, which could result in a few months of work.

FUTURE RESEARCH DIRECTIONS

As future trends, we can highlight the use of intelligent tools for software engineering. In (Perkusich, 2019) is presented a systematic review of Intelligent Software Engineering tools and methods applied to ASD. In this context, we can foresee the use of intelligent tools and artificial intelligence to map requirements for medical device software in the specification phase. This mapping would reduce the need of rework due missing specifications. Also, artificial intelligence tools would help in the mapping of requirements and implemented features, easing the traceability task.

CONCLUSION

For the last few years, we developed a process to adapt ASD to regulations requirements into the healthcare domain. Our experience proved that it is possible to use agile methodologies in different domains, especially considering the fast-growing business opportunities that are appearing in the last few years. As result of our experience, it was proved that regulation requirements can meet agile development, keeping the software products updated and safety, and still fit the market time windows for business opportunities.

Although the development is fast, still, all the processes for registration with regulation agencies are necessary for every main update, making the ASD process even more important. As one of the main results of this adaptation process, we can highlight the fast release of new increments that were registered into regulatory agencies, attesting that all adopted procedures are in conformance with regulatory standards and recommendations.

REFERENCES

AAMI. (2012). TIR45:2012 - Guidance on the use of agile practices in the development of medical device software. Association for the Advancement of Medical Instrumentation, 21, 22-78.

Barbosa, P., Leite, F., Santos, D., Figueiredo, A., & Galdino, K. (2018, June). Introducing Traceability Information Models in Connected Health Projects. In *2018 IEEE 31st International Symposium on Computer-Based Medical Systems (CBMS)* (pp. 18-23). IEEE. 10.1109/CBMS.2018.00011

Barbosa, P., Queiroz, J., Santos, D., Figueiredo, A., Leite, F., & Galdino, K. (2018, June). RE4CH: Requirements Engineering for Connected Health. In *2018 IEEE 31st International Symposium on Computer-Based Medical Systems (CBMS)* (pp. 292-297). IEEE.

Bianchini, E., Francesconi, M., Testa, M., Tanase, M., & Gemignani, V. (2019). Unique device identification and traceability for medical software: A major challenge for manufacturers in an ever-evolving marketplace. *Journal of Biomedical Informatics*, 93, 103150. doi:10.1016/j.jbi.2019.103150 PMID:30878617

Bluetooth, S. I. G. (2020). *Bluetooth SIG specifications*. Retrieved February 20, 2020, from https://www.bluetooth.com/specifications/

Gupta, R. K., Venkatachalapathy, M., & Jeberla, F. K. (2019, May). Challenges in adopting continuous delivery and DevOps in a globally distributed product team: a case study of a healthcare organization. In *Proceedings of the 14th International Conference on Global Software Engineering* (pp. 30-34). IEEE Press. 10.1109/ICGSE.2019.00020

Hanssen, G. K., Stålhane, T., & Myklebust, T. (2018). *SafeScrum®-Agile Development of Safety-Critical Software*. Springer International Publishing. doi:10.1007/978-3-319-99334-8

Heeager, L. T., & Nielsen, P. A. (2018). A conceptual model of agile software development in a safety-critical context: A systematic literature review. *Information and Software Technology*, *103*, 22–39. doi:10.1016/j.infsof.2018.06.004

Hoda, R., Salleh, N., & Grundy, J. (2018). The rise and evolution of agile software development. *IEEE Software*, *35*(5), 58–63. doi:10.1109/MS.2018.290111318

Hoda, R., Salleh, N., Grundy, J., & Tee, H. M. (2017). Systematic literature reviews in agile software development: A tertiary study. *Information and Software Technology*, *85*, 60–70. doi:10.1016/j.infsof.2017.01.007

ISO/IEC 62304. (2006). 62304:2006 Medical Device Software—Software Life Cycle, Assoc. Advancement Medical Instrumentation, 2006.

ISO/IEC 82304. (2012). IEC 82304-1: Health Software–Part 1: General Requirements for Product Safety.

Kumari, A., Tanwar, S., Tyagi, S., & Kumar, N. (2018). Fog computing for Healthcare 4.0 environment: Opportunities and challenges. *Computers & Electrical Engineering*, *72*, 1–13. doi:10.1016/j.compeleceng.2018.08.015

Laukkarinen, T., Kuusinen, K., & Mikkonen, T. (2017, May). DevOps in regulated software development: case medical devices. In *Proceedings of the 39th International Conference on Software Engineering: New Ideas and Emerging Results Track* (pp. 15-18). IEEE Press. 10.1109/ICSE-NIER.2017.20

Laukkarinen, T., Kuusinen, K., & Mikkonen, T. (2018). Regulated software meets DevOps. *Information and Software Technology*, *97*, 176–178. doi:10.1016/j.infsof.2018.01.011

Martins, L. E. G., & Gorschek, T. (2017). Requirements engineering for safety-critical systems: Overview and challenges. *IEEE Software*, *34*(4), 49–57. doi:10.1109/MS.2017.94

Perkusich, M., Silva, L. C., Costa, A., Ramos, F., Saraiva, R., Freire, A., ... Almeida, H. (2019). Intelligent Software Engineering in the Context of Agile Software Development: A Systematic Literature Review. *Information and Software Technology*.

Santos, D. F., Rodrigues, A. F. A., Pereira, M. F., Almeida, H. O., & Perkusich, A. (2016). An interoperable and standard-based end-to-end remote patient monitoring system. In *Encyclopedia of E-Health and Telemedicine* (pp. 260–272). IGI Global. doi:10.4018/978-1-4666-9978-6.ch022

Sommerville, I. (2011). Software engineering (9th ed.). Academic Press.

Wartena, F., Muskens, J., Schmitt, L., & Petkovic, M. (2010, July). Continua: The reference architecture of a personal telehealth ecosystem. In *The 12th IEEE International Conference on e-Health Networking, Applications and Services* (pp. 1-6). IEEE.

KEY TERMS AND DEFINITIONS

Agile Software Development: Discipline that studies a set of behaviors, processes, practices, and tools used to create products and their subsequent availability to end users.

Connected Health: It is a new way for delivery of healthcare services using mobile and internet technologies.

Medical Device Software: Software intended to be part of a hardware medical device.

Medical Informatics: Also called Health Information Systems, Health Care Informatics, Healthcare Informatics, Medical Informatics, Nursing Informatics, Clinical Informatics, or Biomedical Informatics, is a discipline at the intersection of information science, computer science, social science, behavioral science, and healthcare.

Personal Health Device: It is a health device that is maintained by the patient.

Personal Health Record: It is a health record where health data and information related to the care of a patient is maintained by the patient.

Software Engineering: Is an area of computing focused on the specification, development, maintenance, and creation of software, with the application of technologies and project management practices and other disciplines, aiming at organization, productivity and quality.

Chapter 7
Disciplined or Agile?
Two Approaches for Handling Requirement Change Management

Danyllo Wagner Albuquerque
Federal University of Campina Grande, Brazil

Everton Tavares Guimarães
Pennsylvania State University, USA

Felipe Barbosa Araújo Ramos
iD https://orcid.org/0000-0002-0937-811X
Federal University of Campina Grande, Brazil

Antonio Alexandre Moura Costa
Federal Institute of Paraiba, Brazil

Alexandre Gomes
Federal University of Campina Grande, Brazil

Emanuel Dantas
Federal University of Campina Grande, Brazil

Mirko Perkusich
VIRTUS, Brazil

Hyggo Almeida
Federal University of Campina Grande, Brazil

ABSTRACT

Software requirements changes become necessary due to changes in customer requirements and changes in business rules and operating environments; hence, requirements development, which includes requirements changes, is a part of a software process. Previous studies have shown that failing to man-

DOI: 10.4018/978-1-7998-4165-4.ch007

age software requirements changes well is a main contributor to project failure. Given the importance of the subject, there is a plethora of efforts in academia and industry that discuss the management of requirements change in various directions, ways, and means. This chapter provided information about the current state-of-the-art approaches (i.e., Disciplined or Agile) for RCM and the research gaps in existing work. Benefits, risks, and difficulties associated with RCM are also made available to software practitioners who will be in a position of making better decisions on activities related to RCM. Better decisions can lead to better planning, which will increase the chance of project success.

INTRODUCTION

The acceptance of changes is low in disciplined software development due to detailed planning, extensive design, and documentation (Awad, 2005). In contrast, as stated in the Agile Manifesto, agile software development continually "welcomes changing requirements, even late in development" due to its characteristic of incrementally elaborating the product as a means to assure customer satisfaction (Stålhane et al., 2014)(Cao & Ramesh, 2008). Therefore, it promotes constant feedback and communication between stakeholders.

In agile software development, changes in requirement are frequent, occurring due to several causes such as organizational, market demand, customer need, or increase in the knowledge of the software engineers. As a result, it can be a challenge to identify, analyze and evaluate the consequences and impacts of these changes (Eberlein & Leite, 2002). Therefore, Requirements Change Management (RCM) is a challenging task, and neglecting it might lead a project failure (Cohn, 2004).

More recently, there is an increasing number of reported studies on research topics such as identifying change causes (Bano et al., 2012), change taxonomies (Saher et al., 2017)(McGee & Greer, 2012) and requirements change process models (Bano et al., 2012). From a researcher's perspective, the diversity of requirements change management makes it hard to develop general theories. Empirical research in RCM thereby becomes a crucial and challenging task (Wagner et al., 2019). Empirical studies of all kinds, ranging from classical action research through observational studies to broad exploratory surveys, are necessary to understand the practical needs and improvement goals in RCM to guide problem-driven research and to empirically validate new research proposals (Wagner et al., 2019).

To the extent of our knowledge, there is no precise definition of an RCM in agile context or even a catalog of agile practices to support the various steps that comprise the ARCM process. In order to address this research gap, the present chapter book focuses on (i) defining a process to agile requirement change management and (ii) identifying the agile practices used to support the steps that comprise the ARCM process.

The authors conducted an exploratory study where 21 research papers have been analyzed. As result, we identified and classified 11 distinct agile practices that provide support for RCM in the context of agile development. For doing so, the present chapter book study followed the guidelines described by (Kitchenham & Charters, 2007)(Petersen et al.., 2015). For the sake of simplicity, to identify the primary studies, we performed a hybrid search strategy procedure (Mourão et al., 2017). Although agile practices seem to have a very efficient way of managing change, we were able to identify practical challenges in some of the practices described in this study. This study provided information related to many aspects of ARCM, giving a holistic view to handle this process. Additionally, we described the key features, as well as some research gaps in existing work for ARCM. Benefits, risks, and difficulties associated with ARCM are also made available to software researchers and practitioners making better decisions on processes and practices to support ARCM.

The remainder of this chapter is structured as follows. Section 2 presents the main related studies. Section 3 presents the main causes of requirement changes pointed out in the literature. Section 4 describes in details the disciplined requirement change management. Section 5 point out the definition of agile requirement change whereas Section 6 describes the proposed agile requirement change management process. Section 7 outlines the main research gaps in RCM. Finally, Section 8 presents the final remarks and future work.

RELATED WORK

More recently, there is an increasing number of reported work on research topics such as identifying change causes (Bano et al., 2012), change taxonomies (Saher et al., 2017)(McGee & Greer, 2012) and requirement change process models (Bano et al., 2012). In what follows, the authors will describe some these works.

Identifying Causes of Requirement Change: The study of Bano *et al..* (2012) identifies the causes of requirement change and groups these causes into two main categories: (i) essential and (ii) accidental. Similarly, the study of McGee *et al..* (2012) identifies various causes of requirement change and uses taxonomy to group these causes for better understanding and future identification. In regards to identifying change causes, we mention the study of Saher *et al..* (2017) identifies the requirement change and further categorizes the requirement change element based on reason and origin of change, for a better understanding of change request. Finally, the study of Spichkova and Schimidt (2019) investigated how to manage the diversity of cultural and technical aspects to optimize the process of requirements specification and the corresponding change management.

Requirement Change Process Models: The study of Ramzan *et al..* (2006) brings together various requirement management models, identifying their key features and challenges. Similarly, the study of Inayat *et al..* (2015) mapped the evidence about requirements engineering practices adopted and challenges faced by agile teams to understand how traditional requirements engineering issues are resolved using agile requirements engineering. Finally, the study of Melegati *et al.* (2019) showed how requirements engineering practices are performed in the context of startups context. They constructed a model to show that software startups do not follow a single set of practices. Although requirements engineering activities in software startups are similar to those in agile context, some steps vary as a consequence of the lack of an accessible customer.

Requirements Change Management: First, Schon *et al.* (2017) concluded a study aims to capture the current state of art of the literature related to Agile RE with focus on stakeholder and user involvement. In particular, the authors investigated what existing approaches involve stakeholder in the process, which methodologies are commonly used to present the user perspective and how requirements management is been carried out. Second, Jayatilleke and Lai (2018) presented a systematic review of research in Requirements Change Management (RCM) as reported in the literature. They used a systematic review method aims to answer four key research questions related to causes of requirements changes, as well as process and techniques providing support to requirements change management. They have also investigated how organizations make decisions regarding requirements changes. These questions are aimed at studying the various directions in the field of requirements change management and at providing suggestions for future research work. Finally, Curcio *et al.* (2018) conducted a systematic mapping study resulting 2171 papers. These papers were initially identified and further narrowed to 104 by applying exclusion criteria and analysis. The authors identified 15 areas of research of which 13 are document in the SWEBOK). Five of such areas points to the need of future researches, among them are requirement elicitation, change management, measuring requirements, software requirements tools and comparative studies between traditional and agile requirements.

In contrast to the studies above, the present chapter book investigates the process as well as the agile practices to support ARCM. It explores in-depth the techniques used in ARCM and provides a critical analysis of the agile practices extracted by identifying the key features, significant challenges, and research gaps. In summary, this chapter book provides information related to many aspects of ARCM in more detail, giving a holistic view for researchers and practitioners.

WHAT ARE THE CAUSES OF REQUIREMENTS CHANGE?

Requirements can change during a project life cycle. Whilst this fact is a constant, delayed discovery of such changes poses a risk to the cost, schedule and quality of the software (McGee & Greer, 2012) and such volatility constitutes one of the top ten risks to successful project development McGee and Greer (McGee & Greer, 2012). Pfleeger (2008) recommends that a method needs to be developed to understand and anticipate some of the inevitable changes during the development process in order to reduce these risks.

The identification of factors that cause requirements uncertainty is a necessity. The recognition of such factors will support requirements change risk visibility and also facilitate better recording of change data. Change cause factors were collected from Jayatilleke and Lai (2017) exploratory study. Most literature extracted mentioned/indicated the reasons for requirement changes. Of the literature extracted, there were three studies that formally classify the causes of RCs.

Weiss and Basili (1985) divide changes into two categories: *error correction and modifications*. This classification appears to be simplistic and categorizing all the identified change causes may not create an in-depth understanding.

Bano et al.. (2012) classifies change causes also under two categories; *essential and accidental*. They further classify the change causes based on their origin: within the project, from the client organization and from the business environment.

McGee and Greer (2012) use five areas/domains to classify change causes. The five change areas are: external market, customer organization, project vision, requirement specification and solution.

For this chapter book, we use the classification presented by McGee and Greer (2012) as it has a more comprehensive categorization. Within the five change areas, they distinguish between two causes of change: trigger and uncertainty. The difference between these two categories is that an event can cause a change without pre- or post-uncertainty. However, uncertainty cannot cause a change to occur without an event that is triggered to manage the risk of the uncertainty. The factors that were identified as causes of requirements change were sorted into five areas as follows:

External Market: In this category, the changes to the requirements are triggered by the events and uncertainties that occur in the external market which also include stakeholders. These stakeholders include parties such as customers, government bodies and competitors. Therefore, events such as changes in government policy regulations (Van Lamsweerde, 2009), fluctuations in market demands and response to competitors can be considered (Wiegers & Beatty, 2013). Also, uncertainties such as the stability of the market and the changing needs of the customers (Daneva et al., 2013) are also part of this category.

Customer Organization: In this category, changes to the requirements are triggered by the events and the uncertainties that arise from a single customer and their organizational changes. Although the changes occur within the customer's organization, such changes have a tendency to impact the needs of the customer and as a result, impact the design and requirements of the software project. Therefore, events such as strategic changes within the organization (Bano et al., 2012), restructuring of the organization, changes in organizational hierarchy and changes in software/hardware in the organization should be considered (Wiegers & Beatty, 2013). The stability of the customer's business environment can create uncertainties that may lead to changes and these are also part of this category.

Project Vision: In this category, the changes to the requirements are triggered by changes in the vision of the project. These changes are in response to a better understanding of the problem space from a customer point-of-view and the emergence of new opportunities and challenges. Events such as improvements to business processes (Sommerville, 2011), changes to business cases due to return on investment (Bano et al., 2012), overrun in cost/schedule of the project (Van Lamsweerde, 2009), identification of new opportunities (Saher et al., 2017) and more participation from the stakeholder (Stålhane et al., 2014) should be considered (Wiegers & Beatty, 2013). Uncertainties, such as the involvement of all stakeholders, novelty of application, clarity in product vision, improved knowledge development team in the business area, identification of all stakeholders, experience and skill of analyst, size of the project can also cause changes under this category (Christel & Kang, 1992).

Requirement Specification: In this category, changes in the requirements are triggered by events and uncertainties related to requirements specification. These trigger events are based on a developer's point-of-view and their improved understanding of the problem space and resolution of ambiguities related to requirements. Events such as increased understanding of the customer (Wiegers & Beatty, 2013), resolution of misunderstandings and miscommunication (Curtis et al., 1988) and resolution of incorrect identification of requirements (Nurmuliani et al., 2004) can be considered as change triggers. Uncertainties, such as the quality of communication within the development team (Bano et al., 2012), insufficient sample of user representatives (Bano et al., 2012), low staff morale, quality of communication between analyst/customer (Christel & Kang, 1992), logical complexity of problem (Boehm, 2000, techniques used for analysis (Van Lamsweerde, 2009), development teams' knowledge of the business area (Boehm, 2000), involved customers' experience of IT, quality of requirement specification (Bano et al., 2012), and the stability of the development team (Bano et al., 2012) can contribute towards change under this category.

Table 1. Comparison between classifications.

Bano et al.'s Classification	Mc Gee and Greer's Classification		
Essential	External Market	Customer Organization	
Accidental	Porject Vision	Requirement Specification	Solution

Solution: In this category, changes in the requirements are triggered by events and uncertainties related to the solution of the customer's requirements and the techniques used to resolve this. Events such as increased understanding of the technical solution (Bano et al., 2012), introduction of new tools/technology (Curtis et al., 1988) and design improvement (Van Lamsweerde, 2009) should be are considered as change triggers. Technical uncertainty and complexity can also be considered under this category as a cause of change (Bano et al., 2012).

The five change areas listed above can be mapped to the classification proposed by Bano et al.. (2012). According to this study, change causes under the essential category are those that are inherent in nature and cannot be controlled i.e. "fluctuating market demand" cannot be controlled or avoided by the development team or the organization. In comparison, accidental causes can be controlled and avoided i.e. "overrun in cost/schedule of the project" can be avoided or at least controlled by putting better techniques and mechanisms in place. Being able to categorize change causes under these two categories has added benefits in managing RCs. With essential causes, the focus should be to deal with their impact and therefore use techniques that will reduce time and effort for their management. With the accidental causes, the focus should be to use techniques that avoid such occurrences. Table 1 show how these five categories in McGee and Greer's classification (2012) can be mapped to Bano et al..'s classification (Bano et al., 2012) of essential and accidental categories.

DISICIPLINED REQUIREMENT CHANGE MANAGEMENT

Change is an intrinsic characteristic of the software engineering discipline compared to other engineering disciplines. In real-world scenarios, it is difficult to specify all the requirements for software as the need and the circumstance of the scenario is subject to change. According to described in previous section, factors such as customer needs, market change among others contribute profoundly to the changing nature of requirements. The need for increasingly complex software is in high demand as organizations struggle to survive in a highly competitive market. Therefore, managing change in software development is not just important but crucial for the success of the final product.

Nurmuliani (2004) defines requirements volatility as "the tendency of requirements to change over time in response to the evolving needs of customers, stakeholders, the organization and the work environment". Requirements, in principle, are the needs and wants of the users and stakeholders of the system captured by an analyst through an elicitation process. These requirements change throughout the system development and maintenance process, which includes the whole lifecycle of a system: requirement formation, analysis, design, evaluation and learning (Curtis et al., 1988). Therefore, requirements change management (RCM) can be defined as the management of such changing requirements during the requirements engineering process, system development and the maintenance process (Sommerville, 2011). This definition of RCM is an adaptation of the definition provided by Sommerville (2011) who states RCM is a process of "managing changing requirements during the requirements engineering process and system development".

According to Jayatilleke and Lai (2017), there are three key areas of a practical approach to managing change (i.e. change identification, change analysis and change cost estimation). It is important to understand how these areas can be practically implemented and what best practices are available in an organizational setting. As shown in Fig. 1, none of these areas are standalone. They need to communicate with each other in terms of updates and verifications. The reason for this is that each area has the ability to feed information to another area. For example, although change analysis can be undertaken once the change has been identified, the cost estimation may provide additional information for the analysis step that may not have been identified previously. A good RCM process does not have steps that are stand alone, rather they are interconnected with information following to and fro from the steps.

Change Identification: This step is important for the rest of the management process as the steps to follow will be based on the correct identification of the problem space as well as the change requirement. According to Fig. 1, the change management process starts with change identification. Within this identification, there are two major activities, i.e. change elicitation and change representation. In order to ensure the correct elicitation of changes, the change requirements need to be identified. The correct elicitation should then lead to identifying further details of the change and if possible, where in the system the change has to be made. This signifies the representation part of the identification step. In most situations, the personnel involved in this step will need to have continuous communication with the stakeholders in order to verify that identification is done correctly, as illustrated in Fig. 1. Through the literature, we identified two methods of change identification: taxonomies and classification. The following sections describe these two methods and several other methods that do not fall under these categories.

Figure 1. Change management process based on Jayatilleke and Lai (2017).

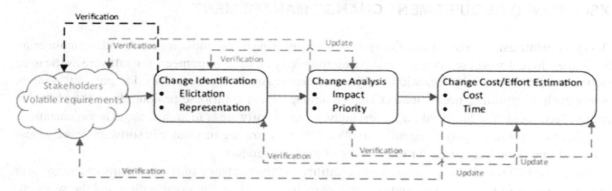

Change Analysis: Once a change has been identified, it needs to be further analyzed to understand its impact on the software system so that informed decisions can be made. One of the key issues is that seemingly small changes can ripple throughout the system and cause substantial impact elsewhere (Ibrahim et al., 2005). As stated in the literature, the reason for such a significant impact is that the requirements of a system have very complex relationships. Therefore, the way to realize this is to undertake change impact analysis, which according to Bohner (1998) is defined as "the activity of identifying the potential consequences, including side effects and ripple effects, of a change, or estimating what needs to be modified to accomplish a change before it has been made". Change impact analysis provides visibility into the potential effects of the proposed changes before the actual changes are implemented (Ibrahim et al., 2005). The ability to identify the change impact or potential effect will help decision makers to determine the appropriate actions to take with respect to change decisions, schedule plans, cost and resource estimates.

Software cost/effort estimation is referred to as the process of predicting the effort required to develop a software system. It is noteworthy that although effort and cost are closely related, they are not a simple transformation of each other (Leung & Fan, 2002). Effort is often measured in person-months of the development team whilst cost (dollars) can be estimated by calculating payment per unit time for the required staff and then multiplying this by the estimated effort (Leung & Fan, 2002). Cost estimation is usually carried out at the beginning of a project but as we have demonstrated, changes to the system can occur at any stage of the project. Therefore, there is a need to estimate the additional cost for implementation of the change. There are some basic factors to be considered when estimating, regardless as to whether it is for the entire project or just for a change. The first step in cost/effort calculation is the calculation of the size of the software, which is considered to be the most important factor affecting estimation (Leung & Fan, 2002). Therefore, it is essential to understand the popular software sizing methods used and their suitability for estimating the cost/effort of implementing requirements changes.

DEFINING AGILE REQUIREMENT CHANGE MANAGEMENT

Aims to properly defining the notion of Agile Requirement Change Management (ARCM), the authors conducted an exploratory study. This research method allows categorizing relevant solutions and concepts in a specific field, as well as visualizing the coverage and maturity of an entire research field. For doing so, the authors followed the guidelines proposed by Kitchenham and Charters (2007) and specific guidelines proposed by Petersen et al.. (2015).

The authors seek identify the practices that have been proposed in the scientific literature to handle Agile Requirements Change Management (ARCM). To achieve this goal, the following steps were derived from the objective to characterize the identified agile practices further.

What are the key steps that make up the requirements change management process in the agile context? This step aims at getting a holistic view of the ARCM and understanding how to handle this process.

What are the agile practices that support the various steps of the ARCM process? This step aims to identify the specific agile practices that address the steps of ARCM process. While it is not our intention to analyze particular requirements engineering practices, this categorization helps in understanding the purpose of the agile practices.

In fewer words, whereas the first one shall structure the process and steps of the ARCM, the last one shall provide a catalog of agile practices to support ARCM. From the conclusion of these research steps, the authors can provide a foundation to discuss the current state of evidence and implications for future research in ARCM.

Search Strategy - The exploratory study employed a hybrid search strategy (Mourão et al., 2017) that involves conducting a string-based search on the Scopus digital library. Next, the authors complemented the set of papers with backward and forward snowballing using Google Scholar. This strategy allows us to identify studies indexed in other digital libraries. As shown in (Mourão et al., 2017), the employed strategy generally tends to provide similar results as when conducting searches on several digital libraries. The hybrid search strategy allows a simplified string supporting reproducibility and replicability.

Study Selection - The primary inclusion criterion was on papers that describe how to handle Requirements Change Management in the context of agile development. When several papers reported the same agile practice (e.g., in the case of journal extensions), only the most recent one was included. When multiple studies were reported in the same paper, each relevant study was considered separately. The exclusion criteria applied for filtering the papers are: (i) Papers that do not have information about agile practices or how they handle the ARCM process, (ii) Papers not written in English, (iii) Grey literature, including white papers, theses, and papers that were not peer-reviewed and (iv) Papers only available in the form of abstracts/posters and presentations.

Figure 2. Search Strategy conducted to identify the primary papers.

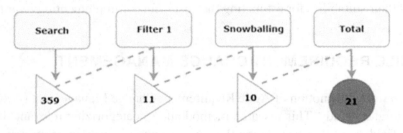

Fig. 2 presents the search procedure steps and results. The first step (Search) consisted of searching for papers using the search string in the digital library selected for this study. For this purpose, we used the string "Requirement change management AND agile". This search returned 359. In the second step (Filter 1), the first filtering took place by applying the exclusion criteria. As a result, we reduced the set of candidate papers to 11. All exclusions were peer-reviewed and agreed by an independent researcher. In the third step (Snowballing), we applied backward and forward snowballing iteratively following the snowballing guidelines in (Wohlinl, 2014). For the sake of work simplification, only one backward snowballing and forward snowballing iterations were applied. The backward snowballing involved analyzing 124 papers (including duplicates) and allowed included six papers. The forward snowballing iterations involved analyzing 89 papers (including duplicates) and allowed identifying included four papers. The StArt tool (Fabri et al.., 2016) aided the execution of this study. It is worthy to mention the snowballing process was peer-reviewed.

PROPOSED AGILE REQUIREMENT CHANGE MANAGEMENT

The agile manifesto suggests to value working software over comprehensive documentation as well as individuals and interactions over processes and tools. To extend of our knowledge, the documentations and formalization of Agile Requirement Change Management remains unclear (Kleebaum et al., 2019). It occurs due to the requirement documentation in agile context is non-intrusive in comparison to disciplined context. The challenges are that the documented requirement might be hard to access and exploit for developers since it can be distributed and might be not fully formalized. Further, decisions related to requirement changes can rapidly be changed which might lead to inconsistent and outdated requirement documentation (Kleebaum et al., 2019). Therefore, Agile Requirements Change Management (ARCM) is a challenging task, and neglecting it might lead a project failure

In what follows, this section outlines the results of the exploratory study regarding the Agile Requirement Change Management (ARCM). First, the authors provided an overview of the ARCM process in Section 6.1. Similarly, the authors addressing pointed out the practices which provide support to some step of the ARCM process in Sections 6.2, 6.3, and 6.4.

THE PROCESS OF ARCM

Examining the processes introduced in Section 3, the authors have identified three key steps of a practical approach for managing requirements change. Fig. 3 illustrates these steps (i.e., change identification, change analysis, and cost/effort estimation) which will be described as follows.

Figure 3. ARCM process

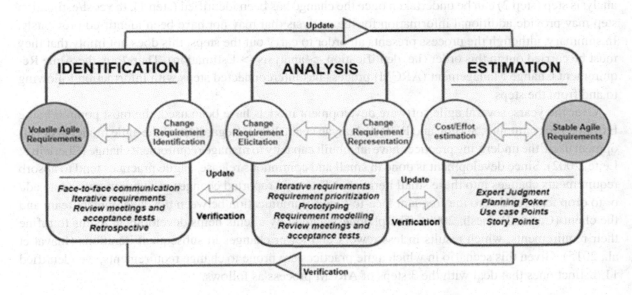

Change Identification: As depicted in Fig. 3, the ARCM process starts with the "*Change identification*" step. Within this step, there are two major activities: change elicitation and change representation. The changing must be identified to ensure its correct elicitation, leading to the identification of more details about the change and its impact on the system. In most situations, the personnel involved in this step needs to have continuous communication with the stakeholders aims to verify that identification is made correctly, as illustrated in Fig. 3.

Change Analysis: Once a change has been identified, it needs to be further analyzed to understand its impact on the software system. One of the critical issues is that seemingly small changes can ripple throughout the system and cause a substantial impact elsewhere (Ibrahim et al., 2005). As stated in the literature, the reason for such a significant impact relies on the complex relationships between system requirements (Dahlstedt & Persson, 2005). This step provides visibility into the potential effects of the proposed changes before the actual changes are implemented (Ibrahim et al., 2005). The ability to identify the change impact or potential effect assists the decision-making process, determining the appropriate actions to take concerning schedule plans, change decisions, cost, and resource estimates.

Cost/effort Estimation: The "Software cost/effort estimation" step includes the set of activities aiming at predicting the cost/effort required to implement the change (Leung & Fan, 2002). Effort is often estimated in person-months of the development team whereas cost can be measured by calculating payment per unit time for the required staff and then multiplying this by the estimated effort (Leung & Fan, 2002). Cost/effort estimation is usually carried out at the beginning of a software project, but in the context of agile projects, it is common, and expected, that they occur at any stage of the project, including late stages. Therefore, due to the constraints of the project, such as time, cost, and scope, there is a need to estimate the additional cost/effort for the implementation of the change.

It is important to understand how these steps can be practically implemented and what practices are available to address them. In the agile development context, none of these steps are standalone, given that each one can feed another with information (e.g. update and verification). For example, although analysis step (step 2) can be undertaken once the change has been identified (step 1), the cost/estimation step may provide additional information for the analysis that may not have been identified previously. In summary, although the process presents an order to carry out the steps, this does not imply that they must be carried out in this order (i.e. dentification -> analysis -> Estimation). Therefore, the Agile Requirement Change Management (ARCM) process has interconnected steps with information following to and from the steps.

Over the years, several agile software development models have been used, the most popular being Extreme Programming, Scrum, and RUP (Bilgaiyan et al., 2016). Regardless of the agile model of development used, the underlying practices have an inbuilt capacity to manage requirement change (Eberlein & Leite, 2002). Since development is done in small and continuous releases, agile practices tend to absorb requirements changes into these small iterations. The main reported changes in requirements are to add or to drop features due to the frequent face-to-face communication between the development team and the client (Cao & Ramesh, 2008). The plainness gained by clients helps development teams to refine their requirements, which results in less rework and fewer changes in subsequent iterations (Inayat et al., 2015). Given this scenario in which agile practices are prone to change requirements, we identified 11 distinct ones that deal with the 3 steps of ARCM process as follows.

PRACTICES FOR CHANGE IDENTIFICATION IN ARCM

In contrast to traditional requirement engineering methods, agile development welcomes changes in various stages (Inayat et al., 2015). As discussed, changes can be identified in several different phases of the development process. In what follows, the authors present the different characteristics of agile development that contribute to the identification of requirements changes, the challenges faced, and solutions, as suggested by the scientific literature.

Face-to-Face Communication: In agile development, this is a frequent activity between the client and the development team (Cao & Ramesh, 2008)(Wagner et al., 2017). The frequency of this activity helps clients to steer the project in their direction as the understanding of needs tends to develop and evolve the requirements (Inayat et al., 2015)(Jun et al., 2010). The success rate of the change identification at this stage is dependent on customer availability. However, this dependency is often unrealistic and a challenge, as confirmed by studies (Ramesh et al., 2010). The major challenge from this practice is that the frequency of the communication depends on the availability and willingness of the team members. Customers may not be familiar with this agile technique, or available to apply it (Daneva et al., 2013).

Iterative Requirements: In contrast to traditional software development, in agile development, the requirements are identified throughout the entire project lifecycle through the feedback of stakeholders (Ramesh et al., 2010). The feedback loops make this an iterative process, allowing the requirements to evolve with less volatility (Cao & Ramesh, 2008). This practice can create budget and schedule overruns as initial estimations might be affected by the requirement changes (Ramesh et al., 2010). Inayat et al.. (2015) suggest frequent communication to identify as many requirements as possible at early iterations to keep these overruns to a minimum.

Prototyping: Prototype is a model of the software application that supports the evaluation of design alternatives and communication. This is a simple technique to review the specification of the requirements with clients to obtain timely feedback before moving to subsequent iterations (De Lucia & Qusef, 2010). This assists in the ARCM process by identifying (i) what new additions are required and (ii) what current requirements are to be changed or removed. Since this is a review phase of the development, the client may have a large number of changes to be included based on the prototype; consequently, schedule overruns can be created (Inayat et al., 2015). Some actions, like frequent communication, high customer involvement, and interaction in stages before prototyping, can mitigate the problem, as mentioned earlier (Inayat et al., 2015).

Review Meetings and Acceptance Tests: During review meetings, which occur at the end of every iteration on Scrum, the stakeholders inspect the delivered product increment to ensure that it satisfies their expectations. During this meeting, the stakeholders might also adapt the requirements to address their updated needs, causing an influx of changes (Carlson & Matuzic, 2010), as with prototyping. Also, if the product backlog is not maintained in detail, finding information related to changes made during the iterations is challenging. Daneva et al.. (2013) suggest maintaining a detailed artifact called delivery stories aims to cope with the previously mentioned challenge. This artifact provide additional information to user stories, helping developers to make the right implementation choices in the coding stage of a sprint. On the other hand, acceptance tests are similar to a unit test, resulting in a pass or a fail for a user story (Ramesh et al., 2010)

Retrospective: In the context of agile development, this practice comprises meetings that are held after the completion of an iteration (Carlson & Matuzic, 2012). These meetings inspects and adapt the team process. In terms of ARCM, this meeting can trigger changes such as refactoring in the product (Carlson & Matuzic, 2012) (Ramesh et al., 2010). If there are many changes identified Agile Requirements Change Management: A Systematic Mapping Study in the completed user story at this stage, there might be a considerable amount of rework to be done, causing budget and schedule overruns (Inayat et al., 2015). Increase customer involvement and interaction in the stages before the completion of user stories is essential to mitigate previously mentioned challenges (Inayat et al., 2015).

PRACTICES FOR CHANGE ANALYSIS IN ARCM

In agile development, requirement engineering activities are less explicit compared to traditional software development. Partially, this is due to lack of documentation that could assist in the traceability of activities and serve as a milestone for marking its beginning and end (Abdullah et al., 2011). As minimal documentation is a characteristic, there are only two main documents: user stories (US) and product backlog (Cohn, 2012). This characteristic becomes a problem when there is a communication lapse or project representatives are unavailable (Daneva et al., 2013). It is also problematic when requirements must be communicated to stakeholders in distributed geographical locations (Ramesh et al., 2010).

Similar to change identification, the change analysis in agile development is not restricted to a particular phase of the development, being addressed by a mixture of techniques used interactively. Following, we point out agile practices identified in this exploratory study that can be applied to the "Change analysis" step.

Iterative Requirements: As previously depicted, not all the requirements related to a user story are properly detailed (or identified) at the beginning of a project. Requirements are built on iterations which allow stakeholders to gain a better understanding of what is required and therefore analyze and understand the need for changes (Jun et al., 2010).

Requirement Prioritization: This is a part of each iteration in the context of agile development (Inayat et al., 2015). In each iteration, requirements are prioritized by customers who focus on some factors such as risk or business value, technical dependency and effort (Ramesh et al., 2010). Iterative requirement prioritization helps in ARCM by comparing the need for the change with the current requirements and then placing it an appropriate priority location for implementation (Daneva et al., 2013). In each iteration, the identified requirements are prioritized. This means that any changes that occur during the iterations are compared to current requirements and are assigned a place in the hierarchy of implementation. The iterative nature of this activity ensures that the priority of requirements remains current.

Prototyping: As previously mentioned, this is a simple way to review the specification of the requirements with clients (De Lucia & Qusef, 2010). This technique allows the agile team to review the requirement specifications with clients to obtain feedback. However, prototyping problems may occur if there a high influx in client requirements at a particular iteration. It highlights issues with the changes identified so far and prompts the development team to find better solutions (Cao & Ramesh, 2008).

Requirement Modeling: This practice identifies the requirements that a software application must meet to solve the business problem. The goal-sketching is a technique used in requirement modeling in the agile development context. This technique provides goal graphs that are easy to understand and evolve (Boness & Harrison, 2007). The outcome is an easy-to-read goal graph that allows stakeholders to refine the goals, making them well defined. Changes that are introduced in the iterations can be mapped to goals, and this can help with decision making in the implementation of changes (Ernst et al., 2014).

Review Meetings and Acceptance Tests: As previously depicted, the developed requirements and product backlogs are reviewed to identify if user stories have been completed. In terms of change analysis, this evaluates if changes have been implemented correctly and satisfy the end goal.

PRACTICES FOR COST/EFFORT ESTIMATION IN ARCM

There are many popular practices for estimating cost/effort in agile development. Regardless of the used practice, none of them discussed in this section can be used off-the-shelf. One of the key findings in this section is to identify the appropriateness of these practices for estimating the cost/effort of implementing ARCM. Following, we describe several popular Cost/Effort estimation practices associated with agile development:

Expert Judgment: The developers look to past of the iterations or projects and use their own experiences to produce estimates for the user stories (Abrahamsson et al., 2011). The primary challenge associated with this practice is the dependence on experts, in which human error is a significant risk, and there can be bias. This practice can be suitable since it is fast and can be quickly adapt to various circumstances. However, the limitation carries a lot of risk (Ceschi et al., 2005).

Planning Poker: This practice is a variation of the Wideband Delphi, in which all the team members of the agile team use cards to estimate effort and reveal their estimates simultaneously (Haugen, 2006). The highest and lowest estimates need to be justified by their estimator. The group continues the discussion until they agree with the estimation value. The primary challenge from this practice in the case the estimation process is unstructured, factors such as group pressure, company politics, anchoring, and dominant personalities, may reduce estimation performance. This practice has similar suitability as expert judgment but is still dependent on the skill and experience of the team members (Mahnič & Hovelja, 2012).

Use Case Points (UCP): Once the use cases are identified from the user stories, UCPs are calculated based on (i) the number and complexity of use cases, (ii) actors of the system, (iii) non-functional requirements and (iv) characteristics of the development environment (Khatri et al., 2016). The UCP can then be used to calculate the estimated effort for a particular project. The primary challenge from this practice is that UCP can be used only when the design is done using RUP or UML. Finally, this technique can be suitable for changes during the early stages of the development process. Changes in the latter phases require more effort due to size of the backlog. Therefore, this practice may not be suitable (Nunes et al., 2010) in this particular case.

Story Points: Story point is a measure for expressing the overall size of a user story. The value of the story point is dependent on (i) development complexity, (ii) the effort involved, (iii) the inherent risk, among other factors (Cohn, 2004). The major challenge from this practice is story points create lots of vagueness to the agile development. For every team, depending on what baseline they chose, story size could mean different things. Story points do not relate to hours. Accordingly, this practice may only be suitable for teams that are collocated, based on the challenges of the practice. Also, it may not be suitable for effort calculation in hours as it will take additional calculations to convert story points to hours (Panda et al., 2015).

RESEARCH GAPS IN RCM

Research Gaps in Change Identification: Accurate change identification not only leads to a better understanding of the required change but also the impact it can cause on the entire system and project. The techniques discussed in change identification can be divided into two categories: change taxonomies and change classification as discussed in previous section. Given the existence of these methods, their still remains several major gaps that need to be addressed:

1. The parties involved in the elicitation and identification process of changes are from a variety of backgrounds and experience levels. Common knowledge for one group may be completely foreign for another. This is especially true in the case of communication between the analyst and the stakeholder(s).
2. The language and terminology used to communicate the changes to and from the stakeholder to the analyst and then to software practitioners (designers, developers, testers, etc.) may be either too formal or informal to meet the needs of each party involved.
3. There will be a large amount of information gathered that is part of one single change. Not having a common structure to categorize this information may lead to misinterpretation of the need for the change and the change itself.
4. Information gathered at one level of the organization could be biased based on the parties involved if one form of structure is not used to capture the changes at all levels.
5. The methods already in existence provide minimal guidance in terms of applying them to identify changes.

Research gaps in Change Analysis:As seen in the previous section on change analysis, it is clear that traceability is one of the most popular techniques to analyses the impact of changes on a system, either in existence or in the design phase. Several other non-conventional methods were also identified that contribute to change analysis. Through these methods and the existing knowledge on the volatility of requirements, several gaps in the research are identified:

1. Although traceability is a common method of identifying impact, it can be costly and time consuming, and in most cases, the benefits (of traceability) are realized immediately. This gives rise to a need for another method that addresses these limitations.
2. In most existing methods of change impact analysis, the priority of changes is not established. Understanding priority benefits the decision-making process by allowing software practitioners to establish which change to implement first and also how critical the change is to the existing system and hence, resources can be allocated accordingly.
3. The existing literature is unclear on ways to identify the difficulty of implementing a change in an early phase of the change request process. Understanding the difficulty associated with a change leads to better decision making in two ways: firstly, if the difficulty of implementing the change is too high and the delivery of the product is time sensitive, the change could be held back for a consecutive version; secondly, the difficulty can be used as a gauge of the effort required to implement the change.

Research Gaps in Change Cost Estimation: The cost estimation methods discussed in the previous section were not explicit for the estimation of implementing changes. In practice, these methods can still be applied for this purpose yet there is still much room for improvement. Based on the information discussed earlier and in the other related literature, several gaps in the research were identified:

1. No significant work in the existing literature caters explicitly for estimating the cost of implementing RCs. As demonstrated in the previous sections, changes occur for a plethora of reasons and can occur during any phase of the software development life cycle. Therefore, it would be beneficial if there was a dedicated method by which to estimate the cost of such changes as the implication of these changes based on the project's timeline results in different outcomes.
2. Estimation done at an early stage of the development process is usually based on expert judgement with less precise input and less detailed design specification. In some cases, this may result in effort estimation which is too low which leads to issues such as delayed delivery, budget overrun and poor quality while high estimates may lead to loss of business opportunities and the inefficient use of resources.
3. Estimating the cost in the early stages of development depends on expert judgment and historical data which can be biased and inconsistent. There needs to be ways to eliminate these ambiguities in change cost estimation.

The research gaps identified indicate the importance of having a full-scale model that increases the efficiency of managing change with better accuracy. The review highlights that although the concept of change management has been in existence for many years, the applicability of the available methods has many limitations and has room for improvement. With challenges such as poor communication, impact identification issues and no dedicated method for change cost calculation, the avenues for future research is promising.

Finally, we highlight the use of ML-based approaches to support the aforementioned RCM activities. For instance, The study of Binkhonain et al. (2019) showed ML-based approaches have generally performed well, achieving an accuracy of more than 70% in detecting and classifying NFRs. Therefore, hopefully these results can be achieved in RCM activities.

FINAL REMARKS

It is evident that changes in requirements can be caused by multiple stakeholders or may occur for many reasons. Regardless of who or what cause these changes, the need for appropriate management is great due to the undesirable consequences if left unattended. However, through this chapter book, it was discovered change management is an elusive target to achieve and that there are two main ways to tackle it. The main objective of this chapter book was to collate information and techniques related to RCM and critically analyze the functionality of such techniques in managing change. This also led to identifying strengths and limitations of these techniques, which signifies the need to enhance the existing change management approaches.

This chapter book is also a guide for future researchers on change management in terms of what major work has been undertaken thus far. In this study, the section on factors that cause change in requirements provides an understanding on how vast and constant these changes can be. There is no one root cause for changes which makes change management a challenging task. Therefore, even with an abundance of research on change management, there is still room for improvement. Given the complexity of changes, it is important to identify the processes in place to manage them. It is clear from the available literature that there is no consensus on how to manage change. In some instances, it is based on the type of organization and the environment and in many cases, it is based on the type of changes. Through the available process steps, three common processes were identified; identification, analysis and cost estimation of change.

Significant work has been done in each of these areas and disciplined and agile models that encompass these steps have been developed in an effort to provide a full-scale solution for change management. It is also important to understand that the approaches vary depending on the level of the organization managing the change. When identifying future work in RCM, we deemed it useful to focus on the three areas of RQ3 where the majority of the techniques have been discussed. We do not directly suggest future work but identify the research gaps in the areas of change identification, analysis and cost estimation where the possibility for new research lies.

Although agile development seems to have a very efficient way of managing change requirements, we were able to identify practical challenges in some of the agile practices. This paper provided information about the key features, challenges, and some research gaps in existing work related to ARCM. The results described on this study can benefit: (i) Researchers who are interested in knowing the state of the art of ARCM and (ii) Practitioners who may be interested in understanding the reported solutions in terms of practices for support the ARCM process.

REFERENCES

Abdullah, N. N. B., Honiden, S., Sharp, H., Nuseibeh, B., & Notkin, D. (2011). Communication patterns of agile requirements engineering. In *Proceedings of the 1st workshop on agile requirements engineering*. ACM.

Abrahamsson, P., Fronza, I., Moser, R., Vlasenko, J., & Pedrycz, W. (2011). Predicting development effort from user stories. In *2011 International Symposium on Empirical Software Engineering and Measurement*, (pp. 400–403). IEEE. 10.1109/ESEM.2011.58

Awad, M. (2005). *A comparison between agile and traditional software development methodologies*. University of Western Australia.

Bano, M., Imtiaz, S., Ikram, N., Niazi, M., & Usman, M. (2012). *Causes of requirement change - A systematic literature review*. Academic Press.

Bilgaiyan, S., Mishra, S., & Das, M. (2016). A review of software cost estimation in agile software development using soft computing techniques. In *2016 2nd international conference on computational intelligence and networks (CINE)*, (pp. 112–117). IEEE. 10.1109/CINE.2016.27

Binkhonain, M., & Zhao, L. (2019). A review of machine learning algorithms for identification and classification of non-functional requirements. *Expert Systems with Applications*, *10*. doi:10.1016/j.eswax.2019.100001

Boehm, B. (2000). Requirements that handle IKIWISI, COTS, and rapid change. *Computer*, *33*(7), 99–102. doi:10.1109/2.869384

Bohner, S. A., & Arnold, R. S. (1996). *Software change impact analysis* (Vol. 6). IEEE Computer Society Press.

Boness, K., & Harrison, R. (2007). Goal sketching: Towards agile requirements engineering. In *International Conference on Software Engineering Advances (ICSEA 2007)*, (pp. 71–71). IEEE. 10.1109/ICSEA.2007.36

Cao, L., & Ramesh, B. (2008). Agile requirements engineering practices: An empirical study. *IEEE Software*, *25*(1), 60–67. doi:10.1109/MS.2008.1

Carlson, D., & Matuzic, P. (2010). Practical agile requirements engineering. *Proceedings of the 13th Annual Systems Engineering Conference.*

Carlson, R., Matuzic, P., & Simons, R. (2012). Applying scrum to stabilize systems engineering execution. *Crosstalk*, 1–6.

Ceschi, M., Sillitti, A., Succi, G., & De Panfilis, S. (2005). Project management in plan-based and agile companies. *IEEE Software*, *22*(3), 21–27. doi:10.1109/MS.2005.75

Christel, M. G., & Kang, K. C. (1992). *Issues in requirements elicitation (No. CMU/SEI-92-TR-12).* Carnegie-Mellon Univ Pittsburgh Pa Software Engineering Inst.

Coelho, E., & Basu, A. (2012). Effort estimation in agile software development using story points. *International Journal of Applied Information Systems*, *3*(7), 7–10. doi:10.5120/ijais12-450574

Cohn, M. (2004). *User stories applied: For agile software development.* Addison Wesley Professional.

Curcio, K., Navarro, T., Malucelli, A., & Reinehr, S. (2018). Requirements engineering: A systematic mapping study in agile software development. *Journal of Systems and Software*, *139*, 32–50. doi:10.1016/j.jss.2018.01.036

Curtis, B., Krasner, H., & Iscoe, N. (1988). A field study of the software design process for large systems. *Communications of the ACM*, *31*(11), 1268–1287. doi:10.1145/50087.50089

Dahlstedt, Å. G., & Persson, A. (2005). Requirements interdependencies: state of the art and future challenges. In *Engineering and managing software requirements* (pp. 95–116). Springer. doi:10.1007/3-540-28244-0_5

Daneva, M., Van Der Veen, E., Amrit, C., Ghaisas, S., Sikkel, K., Kumar, R., Ajmeri, N., Ramteerthkar, U., & Wieringa, R. (2013). Agile requirements prioritization in large-scale outsourced system projects: An empirical study. *Journal of Systems and Software*, *86*(5), 1333–1353. doi:10.1016/j.jss.2012.12.046

De Lucia, A., & Qusef, A. (2010). Requirements engineering in agile software development. *Journal of Emerging Technologies in Web Intelligence*, *2*(3), 212–220. doi:10.4304/jetwi.2.3.212-220

Eberlein, A., & Leite, J. (2002). Agile requirements definition: A view from requirements engineering. *Proceedings of the International Workshop on Time Constrained Requirements Engineering (TCRE '2002)*, 4–8.

Ernst, N. A., Borgida, A., Jureta, I. J., & Mylopoulos, J. (2014). Agile requirements engineering via paraconsistent reasoning. *Information Systems*, *43*, 100–116. doi:10.1016/j.is.2013.05.008

Fabbri, S., Silva, C., Hernandes, E., Octaviano, F., Di Thommazo, A., & Belgamo, A. (2016). Improvements in the StArt tool to better support the systematic review process. In *Proceedings of the 20th International Conference on Evaluation and Assessment in Software Engineering* (pp. 1-5). 10.1145/2915970.2916013

Haugen, N. C. (2006). An empirical study of using planning poker for user story estimation. In AGILE 2006 (AGILE'06). IEEE. doi:10.1109/AGILE.2006.16

Ibrahim, S., Idris, N. B., Munro, M., & Deraman, A. (2005). A requirements traceability to support change impact analysis. *Asian Journal of Information Tech, 4*(4), 345–355.

Inayat, I., Salim, S. S., Marczak, S., Daneva, M., & Shamshirband, S. (2015). A systematic literature review on agile requirements engineering practices and challenges. *Computers in Human Behavior, 51,* 915–929. doi:10.1016/j.chb.2014.10.046

Jayatilleke, S., & Lai, R. (2018). A systematic review of requirements change management. *Information and Software Technology, 93,* 163–185. doi:10.1016/j.infsof.2017.09.004

Jun, L., Qiuzhen, W., & Lin, G. (2010). Application of agile requirement engineering in modest-sized information systems development. In *2010 Second world congress on software engineering*, (vol. 2, pp. 207–210). IEEE.

Khatri, S. K., Malhotra, S., & Johri, P. (2016). Use case point estimation technique in software development. In *2016 5th international conference on reliability, infocom technologies and optimization (trends and future directions) (ICRITO)*, (pp. 123–128). IEEE. 10.1109/ICRITO.2016.7784938

Kitchenham, B., & Charters, S. (2007). Guidelines for performing systematic literature reviews in software engineering version 2.3. *Engineering, 45*(4ve), 1051.

Kleebaum, A., Johanssen, J. O., Paech, B., & Bruegge, B. (2019). How do Practitioners Manage Decision Knowledge during Continuous Software Engineering? In *31st International Conference on Software Engineering and Knowledge Engineering, SEKE* (pp. 735-740). Academic Press.

Kotonya, G., & Sommerville, I. (1998). *Requirements engineering: processes and techniques.* Wiley Publishing.

Leung, H., & Fan, Z. (2002). Software cost estimation. In Handbook of Software Engineering and Knowledge Engineering: Volume II: Emerging Technologies, (pp. 307–324). World Scientific. doi:10.1142/9789812389701_0014

Mahnič, V., & Hovelja, T. (2012). On using planning poker for estimating user stories. *Journal of Systems and Software, 85*(9), 2086–2095. doi:10.1016/j.jss.2012.04.005

McGee, S., & Greer, D. (2012). Towards an understanding of the causes and effects of software requirements change: Two case studies. *Requirements Engineering, 17*(2), 133–155. doi:10.100700766-012-0149-0

Melegati, J., Goldman, A., Kon, F., & Wang, X. (2019). A model of requirements engineering in software startups. *Information and Software Technology, 109,* 92–107. doi:10.1016/j.infsof.2019.02.001

Mourão, E., Kalinowski, M., Murta, L., Mendes, E., & Wohlin, C. (2017). Investigating the use of a hybrid search strategy for systematic reviews. In *2017 ACM/IEEE International Symposium on Empirical Software Engineering and Measurement (ESEM)*, (pp. 193–198). IEEE. 10.1109/ESEM.2017.30

Nunes, N. J., Constantine, L., & Kazman, R. (2010). Iucp: Estimating interactivesoftware project size with enhanced use-case points. *IEEE Software*, 28(4), 64–73. doi:10.1109/MS.2010.111

Nurmuliani, N., Zowghi, D., & Powell, S. (2004, April). Analysis of requirements volatility during software development life cycle. In *2004 Australian Software Engineering Conference. Proceedings* (pp. 28-37). IEEE. 10.1109/ASWEC.2004.1290455

Panda, A., Satapathy, S. M., & Rath, S. K. (2015). Empirical validation of neural network models for agile software effort estimation based on story points. *Procedia Computer Science*, 57, 772–781. doi:10.1016/j.procs.2015.07.474

Petersen, K., Vakkalanka, S., & Kuzniarz, L. (2015). Guidelines for conducting systematic mapping studies in software engineering: An update. *Information and Software Technology*, 64, 1–18. doi:10.1016/j.infsof.2015.03.007

Pfleeger, S. L. (2008). Software metrics: Progress after 25 years? *IEEE Software*, 25(6), 32–34. doi:10.1109/MS.2008.160

Ramesh, B., Cao, L., & Baskerville, R. (2010). Agile requirements engineering practices and challenges: An empirical study. *Information Systems Journal*, 20(5), 449–480. doi:10.1111/j.1365-2575.2007.00259.x

Ramzan, S., & Ikram, N. (2006). Requirement change management process models: Activities, artifacts and roles. In *2006 IEEE International Multitopic Conference*, (pp. 219–223). IEEE. 10.1109/INMIC.2006.358167

Saher, N., Baharom, F., & Ghazali, O. (2017). Requirement change taxonomy and categorization in agile software development. In *2017 6th International Conference on Electrical Engineering and Informatics (ICEEI)*, (pp. 1–6). IEEE. 10.1109/ICEEI.2017.8312441

Schön, E.-M., Thomaschewski, J., & Escalona, M. J. (2017). Agile requirements engineering: A systematic literature review. *Computer Standards & Interfaces*, 49, 79–91. doi:10.1016/j.csi.2016.08.011

Sommerville, I. (2011). Software engineering (9th ed.). Addison-Wesley/Pearson.

Spichkova, M., & Schmidt, H. (2019). *Requirements engineering for global systems: cultural, regulatory and technical aspects*. arXiv preprint arXiv:1910.05008

Stålhane, T., Katta, V., & Myklebust, T. (2014). *Change impact analysis in agile development*. EHPG Røros.

Van Lamsweerde, A. (2009). *Requirements engineering: From system goals to UML models to software* (Vol. 10). John Wiley & Sons.

Wagner, S., Fernández, D. M., Felderer, M., & Kalinowski, M. (2017). Requirements engineering practice and problems in agile projects: Results from an international survey. CIbSE 2017, 85–98.

Wagner, S., Fernández, D. M., Felderer, M., Vetrò, A., Kalinowski, M., Wieringa, R., Pfahl, D., Conte, T., Christiansson, M.-T., Greer, D., Lassenius, C., Männistö, T., Nayebi, M., Oivo, M., Penzenstadler, B., Prikladnicki, R., Ruhe, G., Schekelmann, A., Sen, S., ... Winkler, D. (2019). Status quo in requirements engineering: A theory and a global family of surveys. *ACM Transactions on Software Engineering and Methodology*, *28*(2), 1–48. doi:10.1145/3306607

Weiss, D. M., & Basili, V. R. (1985). Evaluating software development by analysis of changes: Some data from the software engineering laboratory. *IEEE Transactions on Software Engineering*, *SE-11*(2), 157–168. doi:10.1109/TSE.1985.232190

Wiegers, K., & Beatty, J. (2013). *Software requirements*. Pearson Education.

Wohlin, C. (2014). Guidelines for snowballing in systematic literature studies and a replication in software engineering. *Proceedings of the 18th international conference on evaluation and assessment in software engineering*, 38. 10.1145/2601248.2601268

KEY TERMS AND DEFINITIONS

Agile Software Development: Agile Software Development or Agile Method is a discipline that studies a set of behaviors, processes, practices, and tools used to create products and their subsequent availability to end users.

Disciplined Software Development: Disciplined (or Traditional) software development methodologies are based on pre-organized phases/stages of the software development lifecycle. Here the flow of development is unidirectional, from requirements to design and then to development, then to testing and maintenance.

Planning Poker: Planning poker, also called Scrum poker, is a consensus-based, gamified technique for estimating, mostly used to estimate effort or relative size of development goals in software development.

Requirement: The software requirements are description of features and functionalities of the target system. Requirements convey the expectations of users from the software product. The requirements can be obvious or hidden, known or unknown, expected or unexpected from client's point of view.

Requirement Change Management: Requirement change management is defined as a process of managing changing requirements during the requirements engineering process and system development. A requirement change management process in the organization not only improves the organizational processes but success and predictability of projects as well.

Requirement Management: Requirements management is a systematic approach to finding, documenting, organizing, and tracking the changing requirements of a system.

Use Case: A use case is a methodology used in system analysis to identify, clarify and organize system requirements. The use case is made up of a set of possible sequences of interactions between systems and users in a particular environment and related to a particular goal. The method creates a document that describes all the steps taken by a user to complete an activity.

User Story: User Story is a concise description of a user's need for the product (that is, a "requirement") from that user's point of view. User Story seeks to describe this need in a simple and light way.

Chapter 8
Disciplined Teams
vs. Agile Teams:
Differences and Similarities in Software Development

Antonio Alexandre Moura Costa
Federal Institute of Paraiba, Brazil

Felipe Barbosa Araújo Ramos
https://orcid.org/0000-0002-0937-811X
Federal Institute of Paraiba, Brazil

Dalton Cézane Gomes Valadares
Federal University of Campina Grande, Brazil & Federal Institute of Pernambuco, Brazil

Danyllo Wagner Albuquerque
Federal University of Campina Grande, Brazil

Emanuel Dantas Filho
Federal University of Campina Grande, Brazil

Alexandre Braga Gomes
Federal University of Campina Grande, Brazil

Mirko Barbosa Perkusich
VIRTUS, Brazil

Hyggo Oliveira de Almeida
Federal University of Campina Grande, Brazil

ABSTRACT

Software development has been considered a socio-technical activity over the past decades. Particularly, in the case of software engineering, the necessity to communicate effectively with stakeholders and team

DOI: 10.4018/978-1-7998-4165-4.ch008

members has been progressively emphasized. Human resources play a critical role in the success of software projects. Many techniques, methods, tools, models, and methodologies have been proposed, applied, and improved in order to help and ease the management of the software development process. Regardless of the software development methodology adopted, delivering a quality product in a predictable, efficient, and responsive manner is the objective for every team. Disciplined and Agile teams have different characteristics, but also share common aspects when working to accomplish their goals. The main motivation of this chapter is to present the differences and similarities of both teams in the context of software development.

INTRODUCTION

Delivering high-quality products in time and without budget overrun is still a significant struggle for most software organizations. Among the most common reasons are inaccurate estimates of needed resources, unmanaged risks, sloppy development practices, poor project management, commercial pressures, among others (Charette, 2005; Macnab & Doctolero, 2019). Software projects failures have a major negative impact on the organizations and can deeply compromise its future.

Projects continue to proliferate in society today, in both the public and private sectors of the economy. Investments in projects number in the trillions of dollars annually. Just as ubiquitous as these projects, unfortunately, are their significant failure rates. The CHAOS reports have identified the current state of project success rates across organizations, noting that in spite of much higher visibility and importance placed on project performance, failure rates have remained high and relatively stable across over a decade of research. (Serrador & Pinto, 2015)

When a software project fails, it jeopardizes an organization's prospects. If the failure is large enough, it can steal the company's entire future. In one stellar meltdown, a poorly implemented resource planning system led FoxMeyer Drug Co., a $5 billion wholesale drug distribution company in Carrollton, Texas, to plummet into bankruptcy in 1996. (Charette, 2005)

For a long time, Disciplined approaches had been used to increase project success. These approaches, also known as plan-driven or heavyweight methodologies, are conducted in a linear way, whereas process activities of specification, development, validation, and evolution must be performed in sequential order, which means that an activity must be completed before the next one begins. Due to the heavy aspect of the Disciplined approaches, several consultants have developed methodologies and practices with more emphasis on people, collaboration, customer interaction, and working software, rather than on processes, tools, documentation, and plans. These approaches, known as Agile methods, have been gained popularity over the past years, especially after the advent of the Agile Manifesto in 2001 (Fowler & Highsmith, 2001). Unlike Discipline approaches such as the Waterfall model, the Agile ones promote continuous iteration of development and testing throughout the software development lifecycle.

Agile methods are based on adaptive software development, while Disciplined approaches are derived from the predictive approach. Disciplined teams work with a detailed plan and have a complete list of requirements that must be implemented in the next months or in the entire lifecycle of the product. Predictive approaches entirely depend on the requirement analysis and detailed planning at the beginning of the cycle. Any change must go through a rigorous change control management and prioritization. In adaptive methods, there is no extensive planning and only clear tasks are related to the features that must be developed. Agile teams are more adaptable to dynamic changes in product requirements. Communication and minimal documentation represent ordinary characteristics of agile software development. Also, customer interaction is another strong suit for these approaches. While Agile methods are indicated for small and medium projects, disciplined approaches are more suitable to the large ones.

Once Disciplined and Agile approaches are highlighted by different aspects, their teams also have different characteristics regarding size, roles, planning, executions, and others. For instance, Disciplined teams are composed of dozens of professionals, not necessarily co-located, usually divided into teams of specialists. For example, the project may have a programmer team, a quality assurance team, and a design team. Each of them focusing on specific phases and goals. As mention before, these kinds of projects are focused on processes and tools, thus their teams are document-driven and less flexible to change. In contrast, Agile teams are smaller, usually three to nine people, and preferably co-located. Agile projects prioritize communication over documentation; therefore, teams are more collaborative and work together on features to delivering value to the customer. Agile teams are cross-functional which means that the team must have all competencies required to fulfill the work without depending on others not part of the team. Despite the differences, these Disciplined and Agile teams present similarities under several points. Both teams work to deliver a quality product in a predictable, efficient, and responsive manner.

Human resources represent a fundamental asset in the software development cycle. They are directly involved in all process activities and can contribute to both success or failure of the company and its projects. Human resource allocation in software development is a unique challenge due to the specific characteristics of software projects and their teams. Therefore, the desired team profiles may vary depending on the development methodology adopted in the software project.

Many investigations recognize that human resources play a critical role in software project success or failure. However, people continue to be the least formalized factor in process modeling, which tends to focus more on the technical side. Defective people assignment and problems among project team members have been identified as two of the main human factor-related issues affecting software project success. (André et al., 2011)

This chapter addresses the topic of software development teams in the context of Disciplined and Agile approaches. The main idea is to present the differences and similarities of both teams in the software development lifecycle.

Background

In this section, the authors describe the basic principles of Disciplined and Agile approaches, including common practices and methods of both software development methodologies.

Discipline is the foundation for any successful endeavor. Athletes train, musicians practice, craftsmen perfect techniques, and engineers apply processes. Without these basic skills, there may be an occasional success using natural talent, but professional consistency and long term prospects are limited. The strength and comfort which come from discipline support the endeavor when things are difficult, when the body or mind is under the weather, or when something new or unexpected arises and a response is required. Discipline creates well-organized memories, history, and experience. (Boehm & Turner, 2004)

Traditional software development comprises Disciplined approaches such as the Waterfall model (Petersen et al, 2009), V-Model (Mathur & Malik, 2010), and Rational Unified Process (RUP) (Kruchten, 2004). They demand the definition and documentation of a set of requirements at the initial stage of a project. According to Sommerville (2015), there are four phases that belong to traditional software development.

- Software specification: the objective is to capture and understand a complete description of how the system is expected to perform.
- Software design and implementation: this phase represents the process of transforming a system specification into an executable system.
- Software validation: the objective is to show that the system follows its specification and that it meets the desires of the customer.
- Software evolution: this phase includes the initial development of the system and its maintenance and updates.

Disciplined approaches depend on a set of pre-established processes and documentation which is written as the work evolves and guides further development. In Disciplined projects, success relies on knowing all the requirements before the development begins. Consequently, this also means that implementing changes during the development lifecycle can be quite problematic. On the other hand, it is easier to estimate the costs of the project, set a schedule, and allocate resources accordingly (Leau et al., 2012).

The Waterfall is one of the most popular methods of traditional software development. It has been used worldwide since the 1950s when it was presented by Herbert D. Benington at the Symposium on Advanced Programming Methods for Digital Computers. During the years of its use, the model became the golden standard of this industry. This approach is based on three main principles: low customer involvement, strong documentation, and sequential structure of projects. One of the main advantages of the Waterfall model is that it does not allow overlapping phases. The phases are linear which means that the next phase only starts after the previous one is completed. This reduces the chance of having model application failures during the project. It is worthy to mention that, all phases are equally important. If at least one of them is not correctly followed, the whole structure can be compromised. Each phase is well defined and makes it clear to understand what needs to be done to get through it.

Regarding the disadvantages of this model, some practitioners argue that it is very inflexible, the Waterfall leaves almost no room for unexpected changes or revisions. Moreover, no working software is produced until late during the development lifecycle, i.e. the customer only accesses the features when the phases are already well advanced, almost at the end of the project. There is no mandatory feedback between phases, and it is not possible simply to go back to correct possible mistakes. Once an application is in the testing phase, it is very difficult to go back and change something that was not well defined in the design phase. Another disadvantage is that when the model is executed by a team, not all members may keep pace. In this case, it is necessary to wait for everyone to align their progress and then advance.

Agile methods emerged as a reaction to traditional software development, with the goal of reducing the overhead inherent in disciplined approaches and trying to meet market demand for more productivity, flexibility, and shorter deadlines (Tam et al., 2020; Dhir et al., 2019; Girma et al., 2019).

In Agile approach to software development, work is carried out in small phases, based on collaboration, adaptive planning, early delivery, continuous improvement, regular customer feedback, frequent redesign resulting into development of software increments being delivered in successive iterations in response to the everchanging customer requirements. Agile methodologies are increasingly being adopted by companies worldwide to meet increased software complexity and evolving user demands. (Matharu et al., 2015)

Agile software development is a simpler and more efficient way to build software that seeks to maximize customer satisfaction, focusing on the results and collaboration of all stakeholders. This process gained notoriety in 2001 based on the precepts of the Agile Manifesto, which was developed by several experienced professionals of the software industry, according to the following values:

- Individuals and interactions more than processes and tools;
- Working software more than comprehensive documentation;
- Collaboration with the customer rather than contract negotiation;
- Responses to change more than following a plan.

Among the most common Agile approaches are Kanban (Ahmad et al., 2018), Extreme Programming (XP) (Hameed, 2016), and Scrum (Permana, 2015). The latter is a framework created by Ken Schwaber and Jeff Sutherland (Schwaber & Sutherland, 2017) in the early 1990s to maintain and develop complex products. Scrum is used to potentialize the teamwork and to control product evolution effectively, always keeping in mind quality and deadlines. It encompasses a set of values, principles, and practices that provide the basis for an iterative and incremental process for project management and agile development. Also, this framework is an alternative to optimizing and organizing the development team. By structuring the demands and stages of the project, allow us to improve performance and deliver better results quickly and in an organized manner.

Scrum includes scheduled activity cycles, the Sprints, task planning and specific start, and end dates. The duration of each sprint can vary, but they are often short, which explains the agile denomination. During the sprint, there is a daily meeting called the daily scrum to ensure that everyone involved in the project is aware of the previous day's activities. This meeting aims to identify impediments and problems that team members may be suffering. Unlike the Waterfall model, Scrum's process is flexible and can be very adaptable to work with other approaches. Having a good Scrum team is crucial in determining how to implement the business strategy, which directly contributes to the success or failure of the initiative.

Scrum includes several artifacts, usually textual or graphic elements, which are used to provide transparency and opportunities for inspection and adaptation. The main artifacts are Product Backlog, Sprint Backlog, and Increment. The Product Backlog is an ordered list of the requirements to be developed in order to satisfy customer needs. The Sprint Backlog represents a set of Backlog items that must be delivered in the final of a Sprint. During Sprint Planning these items are broken down into technical tasks to be implemented during the Sprint. The Increment represents the sum of all Backlog Items developed in a specific Sprint. It is worthy to mention that there are other artifacts that are commonly used by Scrum teams such as Burndown Chart, Task Board, and User Stories.

Scrum is an agile team-centered methodology in which its members work collaboratively to achieve a common goal. The framework promotes effective interaction between team members, allowing them to focus on delivering business value. The Scrum Team is comprised of three key roles:

- The Product Owner (PO) is the person responsible for bridging the gap between the business area and the Development Team. The PO is a key part of an agile project, as it is responsible for designing, managing, and maintaining the Product Backlog, i.e. he decides which features will be implemented and in which order they should be done.
- The Development Team which is responsible for turning Backlog Items into potentially usable software increment. According to the Scrum Guide, the Development Team should consist of 3 to 9 members, regardless of the PO and Scrum Master.
- The Scrum Master acts as a facilitator and enhancer of teamwork. He is responsible for ensuring that the team respects and follows Scrum's values and practices. In addition, it is his job to remove any and all impediments that may interfere with the team's goal.

Disciplined and Agile approaches have aspects that help their followers to achieved specifics objectives. Table 1 summarizes the mains characteristics of each approach.

Table 1. Comparison of the characteristics of Disciplined and Agile approaches

Characteristic	Disciplined approaches	Agile approaches
Customer involvement	Requirement and delivery phases	Throughout project
Documentation	Extensive	Minimal
Focus	Process	People
Project Scale	Large	Small and medium
Requirements	Defined at the beginning of the project	Interactive input
Structure	Linear	Iterative
Testing	Completed at the end of the development cycle	Throughout the project

HUMAN RESOURCES IN SOFTWARE DEVELOPMENT

The main assets of any organization are its human resources (intellectual capital) (Hilorme et al., 2019; Macke & Genari, 2019). Therefore, organizations need to understand that cultivate people means building a successful path, since these resources are the ones responsible for conducting all the operations of the company. A successful business depends on the individual and collective triumph of its employees, which is a concrete representation of the return on investment that is made in hiring. The corporate environment requires companies and their employees to being in constant improvement. Nowadays, the reality of the market demands a high degree of dynamism, which increases the need for transformation and adaptation.

Software development has been considered a socio-technical endeavor for some time. Particularly in the case of software engineering, the need to communicate effectively with users and team members has been increasingly emphasized. Software is a by-product of human activities, such as problem-solving capabilities, cognitive aspects, and social interaction. Human beings, however, are more complicated and less predictable than computers. Therefore, the complexity of human personality gives rise to intricate dynamics in software development, ones that cannot be ignored but which have often been overlooked. (Ahmed et al., 2015)

Given the above, it is clear that software development is a human-centered activity and the people factor has a great impact on the process and its performance. In order to meet the requirements of the globalized market, companies seek to optimize their processes by balancing cost, time, and quality. To achieve this goal effectively and efficiently, the project managers need to understand the constituent elements of their processes, which are identified as procedures, technologies, and people.

Project managers can assist their organizations to improve the way the projects are implemented by reducing risks. However, this requires much more than just recognizing organizational priorities. It is necessary to have a deeper understanding of how each software development methodology can create the greatest positive impact, and at the same time, how each of these methodologies can make it unlikely that the project will be successful in the organization. Consequently, choosing the proper software development methodology, according to the project needs is the first step to success. Thereafter, it is necessary to choose the most appropriate team which must be composed of members who possess characteristics that match the software development methodology adopted.

Differences Between Disciplined and Agile Teams

In this subsection the authors present the differences between Disciplined and Agile Approaches, focusing on three main characteristics: team sizes and the roles played by their member; the customer involvement during the project execution, and how the teams participate in the planning and execution of the project.

Team Sizes and Roles

Different software development methodologies have different structures of teams. Some of these teams are quite large, others are small. Furthermore, the typical roles of their members also differ. Disciplined teams are usually composed of dozens of professionals performing several roles such as analysts, designers, testers, developers, managers, and others. For instance, the structure of Waterfall teams includes four roles: a developer, a tester, a business analyst, and a project manager. Each member is responsible for a specific part of the work and some of them act only at particular phases of the project. The overall amount of work is subdivided between the members at the beginning of the phase. After the conclusion of the design phase, every Waterfall team member knows exactly what he or she should do at the next stages of project execution. Unlike Agile teams, the Disciplined ones do not comprise the customers or their representatives, and their members are not interchangeable. Moreover, a project manager is one true leader, i.e. he or she is the principal person, responsible for the success of the project.

Agile teams are significatively smaller than the disciplined ones. They are generally composed of less than ten people, however, there is no consensus on the optimal Agile team size. Agile experts argue that smaller teams tend to be more focused, organized, transparent, and productive. For instance, communication skills are very important in Agile teams. If a team is composed of five people, there will be ten different combinations of team members interacting with another team member. Agile teams need to have strong relationships between each of the team members to achieve high performance. Therefore, each new member adds some individual level of productivity to the team. On the other hand, each new person also raises the communication overhead. Therefore, as the team size grows, the communication costs to manage those relationships increases.

Regarding the roles, Agile teams are cross-functional which means that their members are individuals with different functional and domain expertise. Each developer is a tester and an analyst at the same time. Additionally, there are no formal leaders, because they are self-organized. Potential project issues are figured out through communication between team members.

Customer Involvement

In disciplined approaches such as Waterfall, the customers negotiate the requirements of the product before any development activity starts, i.e., they do not participate in the project execution. There are two meetings the customers take part in: the initial stage of the project, in which occurs the definition and documentation of the requirements, and the product delivering, in which the product is ready to be used. In this case, it is not rare to have to low customer acceptance of the software products, since it is very difficult to have requirement changes.

Requirement changes are one of the major drawbacks of the disciplined approaches. Constant changes demand close collaboration between the customer and the development team. According to the Agile Manifesto, the customer must collaborate throughout the whole development process, making it easier for the development team to meet the needs of the customer. This increases the chances of having customer satisfaction in the early deliverables and continual feedback the later ones. In Agile approaches, the customer is represented by the Product Owner, which is part of the team, attending all meetings, and ensuring the product satisfies the business expectations.

Planning and Execution

Traditional software development is based on pre-defined phases and each of them has specific deliverables and extensive documentation that are submitted to the review process. The participation of the team is usually only focused on the execution of the project, leaving the planning to project managers and other stakeholders. For instance, the tasks that must be developed to build features of the product, are assigned without the team. The group of people responsible for the planning decides which tasks and when they need to be done, i.e. the team is simply there to produce the outcomes when necessary. Therefore, the participation of the team is very restricted during the planning stage.

In Agile approaches, the execution is quite different. The development lifecycle is done through iterations and there is no detailed plan from the beginning to the end of the project. The planning is performed throughout the development process and the team is directly involved in both planning and execution. For instance, each team member decides which tasks he or she will implement and when to complete. To facilitate this process, the tasks are selected from a prioritized list, which is limited to a specific number of tasks, but the final choice is always up to the team.

Similarities Between Disciplined and Agile Teams

In this Section, we present similarities that can be found in both types of teams, Disciplined and Agile, focusing on the commitment of the team to provide quality in every developed task, the necessity of continuous self-improvement to be up to date with market demands, and problem-solving skills which are an intrinsic characteristic of the software development.

Commitment to Quality

The concept of quality is present directly or indirectly in any product or service available at the market. When customers buy some products or hire some services, often they will be judging the product or service by its quality. In general, quality can be defined as the conformance level regarding the product or service requirements/specification. It is intrinsically related to customer's satisfaction: how good or bad a product or service is according to customer's needs and expectations. When a product or service meets or surpasses the customer's expectation, its quality is considered good, since it reaches the customer satisfaction.

Regardless of the sector's productivity, every production line has or should have a quality control program, to verify the quality of its products, keeping an acceptable level of quality for the customers. Even a company that works with services, instead of products, should care about their quality. Since software can be considered and negotiated as a product or service, every software engineering team should care about software quality during the development process, checking the compliance of the produced artifacts according to specified functional and non-functional requirements. Besides, software quality can also consider features like usability, efficiency, reliability, flexibility, and portability.

Despite more than 30 years of effort to improve its quality, software is still released with many errors. Many major products are known to have thousands of bugs. It is not for lack of trying; all major software developers have a software quality assurance effort and attempt to remove bugs before release. The problem is the complexity of the code. It is very easy to review code but fail to notice significant errors. (Parnas & Lawford, 2003)

To manage software quality, regardless of the adopted model is the Disciplined/Traditional or the Agile, it is necessary to establish a process responsible for controlling and assuring the conformance of software artifacts regarding their specifications, whatever if the specifications are well documented in a Waterfall model artifact (e.g. requirements document) or are just well described in the sprint's user stories. This way, the Software Quality Management deals with processes and practices to ensure the required quality levels in software products and services, defining and establishing quality standards and making these standards applied.

Software Quality Management (Yahaya, 2020; Stepanova, 2019; Nistalaet al., 2019) can be composed of two sub-processes: Quality Assurance (QA) and Quality Control (QC). The Quality Assurance process is directly related to quality process execution, assuring that the performance of the process and the development of the software are following the planned quality requirements/standards. The Quality

Control process is responsible to inspect the quality of the final products, analyzing the outcomes. While Quality Assurance aims in avoiding defects in the software during its development process, the Quality Control aims in identifying and analyzing possible defects when the software is finished, ready to be delivered. To summarize, the focus of Quality Assurance is the software quality during the development process, being a process more proactive and preventive, while the focus of Quality Control is the quality of the developed software, being a process more reactive and corrective.

Thus, even considering the differences between the two models, Disciplined and Agile, every team that concerns the success of its developed software must introduce some Software Quality Management process in its development methodology. Producing high-quality software is an essential objective in the Software Engineering field, which offers methods, techniques, and tools to accomplish this objective. Both Disciplined and Agile teams must demonstrate a commitment to improving the software quality following the steps of their respective approaches. This will increase the possibilities of delivering software with better quality, reducing the number of software defects, maximizing the probabilities of good customer satisfaction, and thus increasing the chances of success in the overall process.

Common Practices and Continuous Self-Improvement

In general, both Disciplined and Agile models have the same goal, which is related to deliver software with quality, satisfying the needs of the customers/users. This way, common operations such as planning, activities/tasks definition, coding, testing, verification, and validation, etc. are all considered by teams working with any of the models. For instance, planning the work (activity, task, use case, user story, or some other term according to the adopted model nomenclature) before it starts is a highly recommended good practice for every software engineering team. Good planning will always increase the chances of success in any project and it should always consider budget available, scope delimitation, time estimation, possible risks and mitigations (or avoidances), and quality assurance/control. This process commonly includes requirements prioritization, risk assessment, deliverables definition along the time, among other operations.

Another good practice recommended in both models is the requirements elicitation and analysis, which is directly related to the scope delimitation of the software project. The requirements are responsible to guide the software development process. Besides, based on the requirements is that the testing analysts elaborate on the different kinds of tests (functional, performance, and usability, for instance) and organize the execution of the tests plan. Furthermore, if the requirements are well documented, the verification and validation of them in the Quality Assurance Quality Control processes will tend to be easier and smoother.

The following technical workflow can be also considered when summarizing the project execution in both models:

1. Analyze the requirements and architect the solution;
2. Implement the functionalities accordingly and verify them through testing execution;
3. Validate the requirements conformance, checking software quality;
4. Deploy the software artifacts.

Once the software project is planned and its development starts, the test/quality teams have also similarities as they are always interested in finding and reporting possible problems regarding the established requirements. No matter what kind of test or process is being executed and adopted, the focus of the team will be the same: avoiding the deployment and delivery of software out of specified quality standards.

This way, although both Disciplined and Agile models differ regarding how their processes are executed, when abstractly analyzing both regarding their processes' aims, some similarities can be found, mainly because both have the same objective that is the successful software delivery, achieving the quality levels specified by the quality standards.

Regardless of the approach chosen to carry out software development, team members play roles for which they are naturally suited for. For instance, some professionals are better at focusing on team goals and delegating work, while others are more effective at checking for errors in the final work. The continuous growth of the team allows each member to develop and focus on what he or she is best and permit each member to find his/her niche so that they can contribute better as an individual while still working together.

Since each model has specific approaches to conduct the execution of the software development process, the teams can be divided according to the specific tasks in each development phase/cycle and established roles (e.g. developer, tester, analyst, project manager, etc.). Once every software development team member has a specific role, it becomes easier to improve his/her skills by focusing on what is more relevant for performing better his/her work.

Problem-Solving Skills

Software development is a problem-solving profession in which the customer highlights an issue in the current mode of operations and the software developer aims at providing a computer-oriented solution. Analytical and problem-solving skills means that one has the ability to view and look into a situation from a very logical, systematic perspective and come up with a solution fitted to the scenario. In the process of software development each role, to a certain extent, has to make decisions which directly and indirectly have impact on the overall software cost, quality, and productivity. While he or she is making decisions some choices are challenging and take careful thought and consideration. (Ahmed et al., 2015)

Many people when face a problem tend to procrastinate or avoid it completely. However, avoiding problems is a short-term solution. Having the skills and the tools to solve problems effectively and efficiently helps to accomplish the objectives of the project in faster and more viable way. Generally, software development teams from both approaches (Disciplined and Agile) have two distinct types of mental skills, analytical and creative, which are directly related to problem solving. Analytical thinking provides a logical framework for problem solving and assist to select the best option from those available by narrowing down the range of possibilities. Creativity is simply being able to find a unique solution. This means not responding to problems with a knee-jerk reaction, or some safe solution that will likely bring unsatisfactory results. These problem-solving skills provides the pathway through the problem, so the teams can develop effective solutions to resolve their issues.

FUTURE TRENDS

Over the past few decades, Agile methods have been gaining more and more space in the industry over Disciplined ones. Thereafter, there was a frequent discussion in the agile community about which is the best agile method. Scrum stands out as the most widely used agile approach However, being the most popular is different from being the best one. Many organizations choose to begin their software development journey with Scrum, but teams tend to look for other methods to complement software development and be able to deliver a higher quality product closer to customer requirements. However, by using other methods, conflicts with the terminology, team roles, and goals come to light. To mitigate these challenges, Scott Ambler, the former head of Information Technology methodology at IBM Rational, proposed in 2009 the Disciplined Agile Delivery (DAD) (Ambler et al, 2012; Lines & Ambler, 2015).

DAD uses practices and strategies from a variety of methods, including traditional software methodologies, with a focus on delivering a subset of the product life cycle, which is comprised of the following phases:

- **Inception:** It includes initiation activities. Most teams do some initial survey work at the beginning of a project that takes about a month. Therefore, at this early stage of DAD, some very light vision activities are done to frame the product correctly.
- **Construction:** In this phase, a DAD team will implement a potentially consumable solution on an incremental basis. The team can do this through a set of iterations or through a lean and continuous flow approach. In addition, members can utilize hybrid approaches with Scrum, XP, Agile Modeling, Agile Data practices, and other methods to provide the solution.
- **Transition:** DAD recognizes that for agile projects in large organizations, deploying the solution to stakeholders is often not a trivial task. This explains why it is important for teams to try to simplify their deployment processes so that over time this phase lasts less and less time until it ideally disappears.

In DAD, the member roles are suggested according to team size, from teams that have up to 10 people to teams of 50 or more. It is worthy to mention that the roles are not unchangeable, anyone can perform one or more roles over the project duration. In addition, any role can have zero or many people for certain periods. Basically, the roles are divided into primary roles, which are present in all teams regardless of the project scale, and secondary roles that exist in large scale projects and only for a specific period. They are primary roles:

- Team Lead is the person responsible for facilitating team ceremonies, removing impediments, promoting collaboration, and ensuring that the process is correctly followed. This role is similar to the Scrum Master.
- Product Owner represents the interests of the Customer. This is the only person on a team who is responsible for the list of prioritized work items, for making timely decisions, and for providing product information.
- Team Member is the person responsible for developing the deliverable increment and performs activities such as modeling, programming, testing, and release activities.
- Architecture Owner is the Architect Decision Maker. This role differs from that of a traditional architect, as it is not solely responsible for defining the direction of architecture, but rather facilitating its creation and evolution.
- Stakeholders represent the people who affect or are affected by the success of the system.

They are secondary roles:

- Specialist is the person who has one or more technical skills that can directly impact the team's work. The specialist should have at least a more general knowledge of software development and the business domain. In addition, one of its most important characteristics is proactivity, as the expert must actively pursue new skills, including in other areas.
- Independent Tester is the one responsible for conducting tests that validate teamwork throughout the process lifecycle. It is an optional role, usually adopted only in large scale projects.
- Domain-expert is a person who knows in detail information that is often not known to the end user or stakeholders.
- Technical Expert is the one with specialized knowledge who works temporarily to help the team with complex problems. During his or her participation in team time, he or she transfers his skills to one or more team members.
- Integrator is the person responsible for the integration of complex systems and/or subsystems.

Previous activities performed by project managers or business analysts on traditional projects exist and tend to be increasingly done by people in agile roles as companies adopt a new way to speed up software delivery or improve their ability to change their capabilities. priorities. Moving to agile requires a paradigm shift, and part of that change is the acceptance that people's roles have changed for the better.

CONCLUSION

In corporate environments, there is a high probability of having project failures. Even minor errors can directly interfere with adherence to deadlines or even make execution costs excessively high. Additionally, the inability to assess the proper way to conduct processes can impair the productivity of professionals, generating a series of bottlenecks. All these factors contribute to the choice of the methodology being a key factor in optimizing the manager's ability to deliver what was promised in the planning stages.

There is no magic formula to define whether one methodology is better suited for one organization than another. Prior to its adoption, some details should be analyzed, such as the profile of the project to be developed, the team's capacity, and the client's availability for joint goal setting. Both methodologies can be used when the company understands which one is most productive for its projects. For this, qualified professionals are essential in identifying and directing the enterprises, according to the appropriate method.

The agile methodology adds the most present values in contemporary ways of work, focusing on innovation, creativity, and collaboration. Although some stakeholders avoid using the disciplined one, it can be very well applied in specific cases where the rules are stricter, and the client company structure does not fit the agile practice. This will greatly depend on the type of project and company culture. The company itself may prefer the traditional methodology, even more so if the project stakeholders are not used to working with an agile methodology, even if it applies to that project. The traditional methodology is suitable for more specific cases, such as something that needs to be planned and decided from the start. If the project is unlikely to change and is at low risk, it is best to have a more detailed project plan before you start.

Remember that the choice of methodology is important not only to be successful in the process, but especially in the delivery of the product. Both methodologies have advantages and can be used even together, coexisting perfectly well, even because the focus of both is on project optimization. The choice between traditional and agile methodology need not be a conflict. One must respect the premises of both methodologies and know what each can add to the objectives of each project.

ACKNOWLEDGMENT

This research was financed in part by the Coordenação de Aperfeiçoamento de Pessoal de Nível Superior – Brasil (CAPES) – Finance Code 001.

REFERENCES

Ahmad, M. O., Dennehy, D., Conboy, K., & Oivo, M. (2018). Kanban in software engineering: A systematic mapping study. *Journal of Systems and Software*, *137*, 96–113. doi:10.1016/j.jss.2017.11.045

Ahmed, F., Capretz, L. F., Bouktif, S., & Campbell, P. (2015). *Soft skills and software development: A reflection from the software industry*. arXiv preprint arXiv:1507.06873

Ambler, S. W., & Lines, M. (2012). *Disciplined agile delivery: A practitioner's guide to agile software delivery in the enterprise*. IBM Press.

André, M., Baldoquín, M. G., & Acuña, S. T. (2011). Formal model for assigning human resources to teams in software projects. *Information and Software Technology*, *53*(3), 259–275. doi:10.1016/j.infsof.2010.11.011

Boehm, B., & Turner, R. (2004). Balancing agility and discipline: Evaluating and integrating agile and plan-driven methods. In *Proceedings. 26th International Conference on Software Engineering* (pp. 718-719). IEEE.

Charette, R. N. (2005). Why software fails. *IEEE Spectrum*, *42*(9), 42–49. doi:10.1109/MSPEC.2005.1502528

Dhir, S., Kumar, D., & Singh, V. B. (2019). Success and failure factors that impact on project implementation using agile software development methodology. In *Software Engineering* (pp. 647–654). Springer. doi:10.1007/978-981-10-8848-3_62

Fowler, M., & Highsmith, J. (2001). The agile manifesto. *Software Development*, *9*(8), 28–35.

Girma, M., Garcia, N. M., & Kifle, M. (2019, May). Agile Scrum Scaling Practices for Large Scale Software Development. In *2019 4th International Conference on Information Systems Engineering (ICISE)* (pp. 34-38). IEEE. 10.1109/ICISE.2019.00014

González-Cruz, T. F., Botella-Carrubi, D., & Martínez-Fuentes, C. M. (2020). The effect of firm complexity and founding team size on agile internal communication in startups. *The International Entrepreneurship and Management Journal*, 1–21. doi:10.100711365-019-00633-1

Hameed, A. (2016). Software Development Lifecycle for Extreme Programming. *International Journal of Information Technology and Electrical Engineering*, *5*(1).

Hilorme, T., Perevozova, I., Shpak, L., Mokhnenko, A., & Korovchuk, Y. (2019). *Human capital cost accounting in the company management system.* Academy of Accounting and Financial Studies Journal.

Kruchten, P. (2004). *The rational unified process: an introduction.* Addison-Wesley Professional.

Leau, Y. B., Loo, W. K., Tham, W. Y., & Tan, S. F. (2012). Software development life cycle AGILE vs traditional approaches. In *International Conference on Information and Network Technology* (*Vol. 37*, No. 1, pp. 162-167). Academic Press.

Lines, M., & Ambler, S. W. (2015). *Introduction to Disciplined Agile Delivery: A Small Agile Team's Journey from Scrum to Continuous Delivery.* CreateSpace Independent Publishing Platform.

Macke, J., & Genari, D. (2019). Systematic literature review on sustainable human resource management. *Journal of Cleaner Production*, *208*, 806–815. doi:10.1016/j.jclepro.2018.10.091

Macnab, C. J. B., & Doctolero, S. (2019, May). The role of unconscious bias in software project failures. In *International Conference on Software Engineering Research, Management and Applications* (pp. 91-116). Springer.

Matharu, G. S., Mishra, A., Singh, H., & Upadhyay, P. (2015). Empirical study of agile software development methodologies: A comparative analysis. *Software Engineering Notes*, *40*(1), 1–6. doi:10.1145/2693208.2693233

Mathur, S., & Malik, S. (2010). Advancements in the V-Model. *International Journal of Computers and Applications*, *1*(12), 29–34.

Nistala, P., Nori, K. V., & Reddy, R. (2019, May). Software quality models: A systematic mapping study. In *2019 IEEE/ACM International Conference on Software and System Processes (ICSSP)* (pp. 125-134). IEEE. 10.1109/ICSSP.2019.00025

Parnas, D. L., & Lawford, M. (2003). The role of inspection in software quality assurance. *IEEE Transactions on Software Engineering*, *29*(8), 674–676. doi:10.1109/TSE.2003.1223642

Permana, P. A. G. (2015). Scrum method implementation in a software development project management. *International Journal of Advanced Computer Science and Applications*, *6*(9), 198–204.

Petersen, K., Wohlin, C., & Baca, D. (2009, June). The waterfall model in large-scale development. In *International Conference on Product-Focused Software Process Improvement* (pp. 386-400). Springer. 10.1007/978-3-642-02152-7_29

Schwaber, K., & Sutherland, J. (2017). *The Scrum Guide - The Definitive Guide to Scrum: The Rules of the Game, 2017.* Academic Press.

Serrador, P., & Pinto, J. K. (2015). Does Agile work?— A quantitative analysis of agile project success. *International Journal of Project Management*, *33*(5), 1040–1051. doi:10.1016/j.ijproman.2015.01.006

Sommerville, I. (2015). *Software Engineering* (10ᵗʰ ed.). Academic Press.

Stepanova, V. (2019). Quality Control Approach in Developing Software Projects. *International Journal of Computer Science and Software Engineering*, *8*(1), 1–5.

Stoica, M., Mircea, M., & Ghilic-Micu, B. (2013). Software Development: Agile vs. Traditional. *Informatica Economica, 17*(4).

Tam, C., da Costa Moura, E. J., Oliveira, T., & Varajão, J. (2020). The factors influencing the success of on-going agile software development projects. *International Journal of Project Management, 38*(3), 165–176. doi:10.1016/j.ijproman.2020.02.001

Yahaya, J. H. (2020). Software quality and certification: Perception and practices in Malaysia. *Journal of Information and Communication Technology, 5*, 63–82.

KEY TERMS AND DEFINITIONS

Agile Software Development: Is an umbrella term for a set of frameworks and practices based on the values and principles expressed in the Manifesto for Agile Software Development and the 12 Principles behind it.

Plan-Driven: Are processes where all of the process activities are planned in advance and progress is measured against this plan.

Project Manager: A project manager is a professional responsible for leading a project from its inception to execution, which includes planning, execution and managing the people, resources, and scope of the project.

Software Developers: The person who is responsible for creating the technical specification and write the software.

Software Development Methodology: Is the process of dividing software development work into distinct phases to improve design, product management, and project management.

Software Engineering: The application of a systematic, disciplined, quantifiable approach to the development, operation, and maintenance of software, and the study of these approaches.

Software Organization: Is a company whose primary products are various forms of software, software technology, distribution, and software product development.

Software Product: Is a product, software, which is usually made to be sold to users, and users pay for license which allows them to use it.

Chapter 9
Building an Ambidextrous Software Security Initiative

Daniela Soares Cruzes
SINTEF Digital, Norway

Espen Agnalt Johansen
VISMA, Norway

ABSTRACT

Improving software security in software development teams is an enduring challenge for software companies. In this chapter, the authors present one strategy for addressing this pursuit of improvement. The approach is ambidextrous in the sense that it focuses on approaching software security activities both from a top-down and a bottom-up perspective, combining elements usually found separately in software security initiatives. The approach combines (1) top-down formal regulatory mechanisms deterring breaches of protocol and enacting penalties where they occur and (2) bottom-up capacity building and persuasive encouragement of adherence to guidance by professional self-determination, implementation, and improvement support (e.g., training, stimulating, interventions). The ambidextrous governance framework illustrates distinct, yet complementary, global and local roles: (1) ensuring the adoption and implementation of software security practices, (2) enabling and (3) empowering software development teams to adapt and add to overall mandates, and (4) embedding cultures of improvement.

INTRODUCTION

Today, nearly all sectors of society depend on software systems to operate efficiently. As the dependency on software has grown, so have the threats towards these systems and the potential consequences of incidents (Tøndel, Jaatun, Cruzes, & Moe, 2017). Though network security measures (such as firewalls and anti-virus software) can improve the security of the software systems, these only address the symptoms of the real problem: software that is crippled with vulnerabilities (McGraw, 2006).

Building security into the software through adopting software security activities and measures in the development process is a direct and effective way of dealing with cyber threats towards software systems

DOI: 10.4018/978-1-7998-4165-4.ch009

(Tøndel, Jaatun, Cruzes, & Moe, 2017). This, however, adds to the development time and cost, and this addition needs to be well implemented to be effective. In many ways, security can be considered to be in conflict with the current trend of "continuous development" (Fitzgerald & Stol, 2017), reducing efficiency by delaying delivery of new features (at least in the shorter term, though costs may be saved through having to provide fewer fixes later).

Many researchers affirm that it may be more difficult to establish a working process for software security activities in agile development compared to waterfall-based development, where you could more easily have mandatory or recommended security activities for the different software development phases (Ben Othmane, Angin, Weffers, & Bhargava, 2014) (Ambler, 2008) (Microsoft, 2019). (Oyetoyan, Jaatun, & Cruzes, 2017) provide a brief overview of secure SDLs (Secure Development Lifecycle) and conclude that traditional approaches to software security do not necessarily work well with agile development processes. Additionally, security, as a non-functional requirement (NFR), is largely a systemic property, and with agile development it can be more of a challenge to have a complete view of the final system (Ben Othmane, Angin, Weffers, & Bhargava, 2014).

Non-functional requirements (NFRs) focus on aspects that typically involve or crosscut several functional requirements (Ambler, 2008). Although considered important and crucial to project success, it is common to see non-functional requirements losing attention in comparison to functional requirements. (Crispin & Gregory, 2009) argue that with that business partners might assume that the development team will take care of non-functional requirements such as performance, reliability, and security. But in reality, due to the agile philosophy that stimulates delivering user value early and often, the prioritization of quality attributes can be hard in early deliverable increments, resulting in hard-to-modify, unreliable, slow, or insecure systems (Baca, Boldt, Carlsson, & Jacobsson, 2015) (Bellomo, Gorton, & Kazman, 2015) (Wäyrynen, Bodén, & Boström, 2004). It is not rare to observe in software organizations that security practices are not prioritized, either because the practitioners are not able to see the relevance and importance of the activities to the improvement of the security in the project (Camacho, Marczak, & Cruzes, 2016) or because non-functional or cross-functional issues are perceived as a low risk for many systems (Jaatun, Cruzes, Bernsmed, Tøndel, & Røstad, 2015). Another issue is that agile development teams are generally composed of a small number of developers, and many times are composed of generalists. However, the proper handling of software security requires specialized tools and might need specialized knowledge. Given this need for specialized knowledge, a team member with specialized security skills might be required to avoid issues in production (Gregory & Crispin, 2014). As it is nowadays, there are usually not designated roles for security in the software development teams.

At the same time, agile development may come with some opportunities regarding security, e.g., to adapt to new security threats and to maintain the interaction with customers about security. (Tøndel, Jaatun, Cruzes, & Moe, 2017) propose a risk-centric approach to security. The authors found that the observed software security practices in software organizations were not based on an assessment of software security risks, but rather driven by compliance. Additionally, their practices could in many cases be characterized as arbitrary, late, and error driven, with limited follow up on any security issues throughout their software development projects. Based on the results of the study, the authors identified the need for improvements in three main areas: responsibilities and stakeholder cooperation, risk perception and competence, and practical ways of doing risk analysis in agile projects.

Still, to be effective, the software security initiative needs a good governance. In the agile software development world, a security engineering process is unacceptable if it is perceived to run counter to the agile values, and agile teams have thus approached software security activities in their own way. To improve security within agile settings requires that management understands the current practices of software security activities within their agile teams and to appropriately influence the adoption of these practices. Many roles in an organization can have major influences on a development project's approach to security and can have important parts to play when it comes to identifying and understanding risk, making risk-based decisions in the projects, and having a proper security focus (Tøndel, Jaatun, Cruzes, & Moe, 2017). In this chapter, the focus is on another angle of the establishment of a software security program: the top-down and bottom-up approach, an ambidextrous approach to build and maintain a software security initiative, which is very much related to the way developers address security in projects.

This chapter is based on results from the ongoing project named SoS-Agile, which investigates how to meaningfully integrate software security into agile software development activities (Cruzes, Jaatun, & Oyetoyan, 2018) (SoS-Agile Project (2015-2020), u.d.). The method of choice for the project is Canonical Action Research (Greenwood & Levin, 2006) which is one of the many forms of action research (Davison, Martinsons, & Kock, 2004) (Davison, Martinsons, & Ou, 2012); it is iterative, rigorous, and collaborative, involving focus on both organizational development and the generation of knowledge. The combination of scientific and practical objectives aligns with the basic tenet of action research, which is to merge theory and practice in a way such that real-world problems are solved by theoretically informed actions in collaboration between researchers and practitioners (Greenwood & Levin, 2006).

SOFTWARE SECURITY AND AGILE

Software security or security engineering is the idea of engineering a software system so that it keeps working correctly even under malicious attack (McGraw, Software Security, 2004). The (ISO/IEC 25010, 2011) defines security as a capability of the software to protect information and functionalities while allowing authorized users to access information and functionality to which they have permission. (Firesmith, 2003) from the Software Engineering Institute (SEI) published a technical note where he presents information models providing a standard terminology and set of concepts that explain the similarities between the asset-based, risk-driven methods for identifying and analysing safety, security, and survivability requirements as well as a rationale for the similarity in architectural mechanisms that are commonly used to fulfil these requirements. Firesmith's definition of security is, *"the degree to which malicious harm to a valuable asset is prevented, detected, and reacted to. Security is the quality factor that signifies the degree to which valuable assets are protected from significant threats posed by malicious attackers."* (Firesmith, 2003) decomposes security into many different quality subfactors:

- **Access control** is the degree to which the system limits access to its resources only to its authorized externals (e.g., human users, programs, processes, devices, or other systems). The following are quality subfactors of the access-control quality subfactor:
- **Identification** is the degree to which the system identifies (i.e., recognizes) its externals before interacting with them.
- **Authentication** is the degree to which the system verifies the claimed identities of its externals before interacting with them. Thus, authentication verifies that the claimed identity is legitimate and belongs to the claimant.
- **Authorization** is the degree to which access and usage privileges of authenticated externals are properly granted and enforced.

- **Attack/harm detection** is the degree to which attempted or successful attacks (or their resulting harm) are detected, recorded, and notified.
- **Availability protection** is the degree to which various types of Denial of Service (DoS) attacks are prevented from decreasing the operational availability of the system. This is quite different from the traditional availability quality factor, which deals with the operational availability of the system when it is not under attack.
- **Integrity** is the degree to which components are protected from intentional and unauthorized corruption. Integrity includes data, hardware, personnel and software integrity.
- **Nonrepudiation** is the degree to which a party to an interaction (e.g., message, transaction, or transmission of data) is prevented from successfully repudiating (i.e., denying) any aspect of the interaction.
- **Physical protection** is the degree to which the system protects itself and its components from physical attack.
- **Privacy** is the degree to which unauthorized parties are prevented from obtaining sensitive information. Privacy includes confidentiality, defined as the degree to which sensitive information is not disclosed to unauthorized parties (e.g., individuals, programs, processes, devices, or other systems).
- **Prosecution** is the degree to which the system supports the prosecution of attackers.
- **Recovery** is the degree to which the system recovers after a successful attack.
- **Security auditing** is the degree to which security personnel are enabled to audit the status and use of security mechanisms by analyzing security-related events.
- **System adaptation** is the degree to which the system learns from attacks in order to adapt its security countermeasures to protect itself from similar attacks in the future.

Once that all these factors shall be addressed during the software development lifecycle, security cannot be treated as an add-on functionality or isolated product feature (McGraw, 2006), and it is thus important that security is a "built-in" in the process and the product. However, a traditional security engineering process is often associated with additional development efforts and is likely to invoke resentment among agile development teams (Ben Othmane, Angin, Weffers, & Bhargava, 2014). A software security approach tailored to the agile mind-set thus seems necessary.

Some approaches have been proposed to integrate security activities into agile development, e.g., the Microsoft SDL for Agile (Microsoft, 2019). The Building Security in Maturity Model (BSIMM) (McGraw, 2006) has been used to measure security practices in different organizations and to give advice on which practices are more commonly adopted by organizations. BSIMM is useful for measuring the software security maturity of an organization and helping them formulate an overall security strategy. Recently, the OWASP organization also released a new version of their Software Assurance Maturity Model (SAMM 2.0) (Deleersnyder, 2019), which provides an effective and measurable way for organizations to analyse and improve their software security posture. While these activities could be argued to be beneficial and cost-effective to integrate, there are still gaps between what is "preached" and what is "practiced" in software organizations. These approaches have been criticized for looking similar to the traditional versions in terms of workload (e.g., performing a long list of security verification and validation tasks) (Ben Othmane, Angin, Weffers, & Bhargava, 2014). As a result, "agile" organizations have approached software security in a way that fits their processes and practices.

Thus, regardless of whether agile is perceived to be incompatible with any particular secure software development lifecycle, the major discussion we should have is how to improve security within the agile context (Bartsch, 2011). Previous studies (Ayalew, Kidane, & Carlsson, 2013) (Baca & Carlsson, 2011) have investigated which security activities are practiced in different organizations, and which are compatible with agile practices from cost and benefit perspectives. A set of challenges of developing secure software using the agile development approach and methods are reported in the literature (Oueslati H., Rahman, ben Othmane, & Ghani, 2016). (Oueslati, Rahman, & Othmane, 2015) performed a systematic review in which they identified 20 challenges for developing secure software using the agile approach, classified into 5 categories. A summary of the challenges is provided in Table 1.

Table 1 . Classification of the security challenges by (Oueslati, Rahman, & Othmane, 2015)

Challenge
Software development life-cycle challenges
Security requirements elicitation activity is not included in the agile development methods
Risks assessment activity is not included in the agile development methods
Security related activities need to be applied for each development iteration
Iteration time is limited and may not fit time-consuming security activities
Incremental development challenges
Refactoring practice breaks security constraints
Changes of requirements and design breaks system security requirements
Continuous code changes hinder assurance activities
Requirement changes makes the trace of the requirements to security objectives difficult
Security assurance challenges
Security assessment favours detailed documentation
Tests are, in general, insufficient to ensure the implementation of security requirements
Tests do no cover in general, all vulnerability cases
Security tests are in general difficult to automate
Continuous changing of the development processes (to support lesson learned) conflicts with audit needs of uniform stable processes
Awareness and collaboration challenges
Security requirements are often neglected
Developers lack experience on secure software
Customers lack security awareness
Developer role must be separate from security reviewer role to have objective results
Security management challenges
Security activities increases the cost of the software
There is no incentive for organizations to develop security features in early increments
Organizations compromise security activities to accommodate accelerated releasing schedule

AN AMBIDEXTROUS SECURITY INITIATIVE

Research on ambidexterity represents a major effort to address the management of paradoxical tensions, contrasting efficiency, control, and incremental improvement on one hand, and flexibility, autonomy, and experimentation on the other (Xiao, Witschey, & Murphy-Hil, 2014). Ambidexterity as a capability for resolving organizational tensions has been studied in a variety of forms. Some forms focus on the alignment of disparate organizational processes in relatively static operating conditions, while other forms focus on dynamic re-alignments that adapt to changing demands (Xiao, Witschey, & Murphy-Hil, 2014).

Creative Industry Organizations' (CIOs') achieve ambidexterity in different ways. (Wu & Wu, 2016) performed a systematic review on how CIOs achieve alignment ambidexterity and adaptability ambidexterity. The authors found there is a dominance of contextual approaches and the prevalence of external engagements specific to CIO ambidexterity. It also reveals different solutions adopted for alignment ambidexterity and adaptability ambidexterity. Contextual approaches involve top-down system arrangements that coordinate individuals' actions and interactions to achieve organizational goals that would otherwise be conflicting on a daily and continuous basis. Creative production requires a close alignment of all goals for one product (alignment ambidexterity) and a constant pursuit of new creativity over time (adaptability ambidexterity).

(McDermott, Hamel, Steel, Flood, & Mkee, 2015), motivated by the need to improving healthcare governance, studied two national healthcare regulators who were adopting novel "hybrid" regulatory control strategies in pursuit of improvement, which combines: (1) top-down formal regulatory mechanisms deterring breaches of protocol and enacting penalties where they occur (e.g. standard-setting, monitoring, and accountability); and (2) bottom-up capacity building and persuasive encouragement of adherence to guidance by professional self-determination, implementation, and improvement support (e.g. training, stimulating interventions). (McDermott, Hamel, Steel, Flood, & Mkee, 2015) identify socio-historical contextual factors constraining and enabling regulatory hybridity, whether and how it can be re-created, and circumstances when the approaches might be delivered separately. They developed a goal-oriented governance framework illustrating distinct, yet complementary, national and local organizational roles: (1) ensuring the adoption and implementation of best practice, (2) enabling and (3) empowering staff to adapt and add to national mandates, and (4) embedding cultures of improvement.

This model, although designed in relation to healthcare governance, resonated very well to the context of governance for a software security initiative for agile software development teams. Adapted from the model from (McDermott, Hamel, Steel, Flood, & Mkee, 2015), Figure 1 details distinct, yet complementary, roles in the security program. It provides a framework for identifying potential company-improvement supporting roles to deliver together in pursuit of an ambidextrous program (e.g. combining top-down and bottom-up supporting roles). It also identifies supporting local roles in the development team. The approach assumes that the teams are self-managed agile teams that need leadership on security but must retain the continuity and self-management of their software development: (1) ensuring the adoption and implementation of software security practices, (2) enabling and (3) empowering software development teams to adapt and add to overall mandates, and (4) embedding cultures of improvement. The following subsections explain how the model from Figure 1 was instantiated in the Visma software security initiative.

Figure 1. Ambidextrous governance model
Source: Adapted from (McDermott, Hamel, Steel, Flood, & Mkee, 2015)

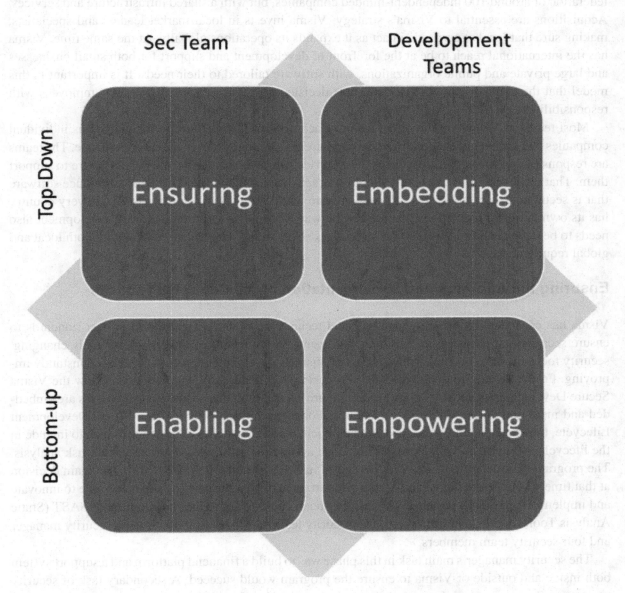

About Visma

Visma is a software company headquartered in Norway that delivers software that simplifies and digitizes core business processes in the private and public sector. Visma believes in empowering people through technology. Since Visma was founded in 1997, it has grown to become a family of more than 11000 employees. Today Visma has a local presence in more than 16 countries and over 200 offices. By taking advantage of opportunities in a fast-moving market characterized by rapid development in technology, Visma has turned into an international leader in cloud software delivery.

Visma is not a monolithically hierarchical organization; Visma is easier to understand if viewed as a federation of around 100 independent-minded companies, but with a shared infrastructure and services. Acquisitions are essential to Visma's strategy; Visma invests in local market leaders and specialists, making sure that local expertise is intact as it expands its operations globally. At the same time, Visma has the international reach to be at the forefront of development and support for both small businesses and large private and public organizations, with software tailored to their needs. It is important in this model that the company moves fast, has short decision processes, and empowers its employees with responsibilities.

Most teams in Visma are the direct result of acquisitions. The teams are maintained as individual companies and are not under centralized, strong governance, apart from financial governance. The teams are responsible for the entire lifecycle of their service, while the rest of the overhead is there to support them. That means the software teams should stay self-managed, but they still have to produce software that is secure and does not expose Visma software and customers to security risks. As every country has its own laws and regulations that impact the way a business is run, the software development also needs to be done in such a way that the software is always up to date and compliant with both local and global requirements.

Ensuring the Adoption and Implementation of the Security Practices

Visma has established processes, methods, and technologies, and has embraced proven standards to ensure security and accessibility for their customers. As the nature of threats is constantly changing, security focus needs to become a natural part of Visma's development process, which is constantly improving. From planning to deployment of new services or features. Visma products follow the Visma Secure Development Lifecycle (Figure 2 and Figure 3), meaning that security requirements are embedded and measured during the service's lifetime. For the definition of the Visma Secure Development Lifecycle, the security team, in a top-down approach, made an analysis of which activities to include in the lifecycle, agreeing on what needed to be done at the time, starting with some simple risk analysis. The program was inspired by activities described in BSIMM and OWASP SAMM. The main decision at that time was to figure out what was most important and what the security team was able to innovate and implement as soon as possible. The security team chose to start with the adoption of SAST (Static Analysis Tools) and extend from there. The security team was then composed by the security manager and four security team members.

The security manager's main task in this phase was to build a financial platform and a support system both inside and outside of Visma to ensure the program would succeed. A secondary task of security management was to embed the security program into the already-existing quality management systems (QMSs) to ensure the existing command line executes on the guidance from security management. This was chosen to avoid building a separate governance structure from the rest of the company and to enable the line managers to take an active part in security management. The rest of the security team focused on the services. Clearly the investment required in compiling and sharing best practice evidence, as well as engaging in scrutiny to ensure its adoption, makes it appropriate for a top-down organization to lead this role. After two years, the lifecycle evolved to what is shown in Figure 3.

Figure 2. First instantiation of the Visma secure software development lifecycle (2015-2018)

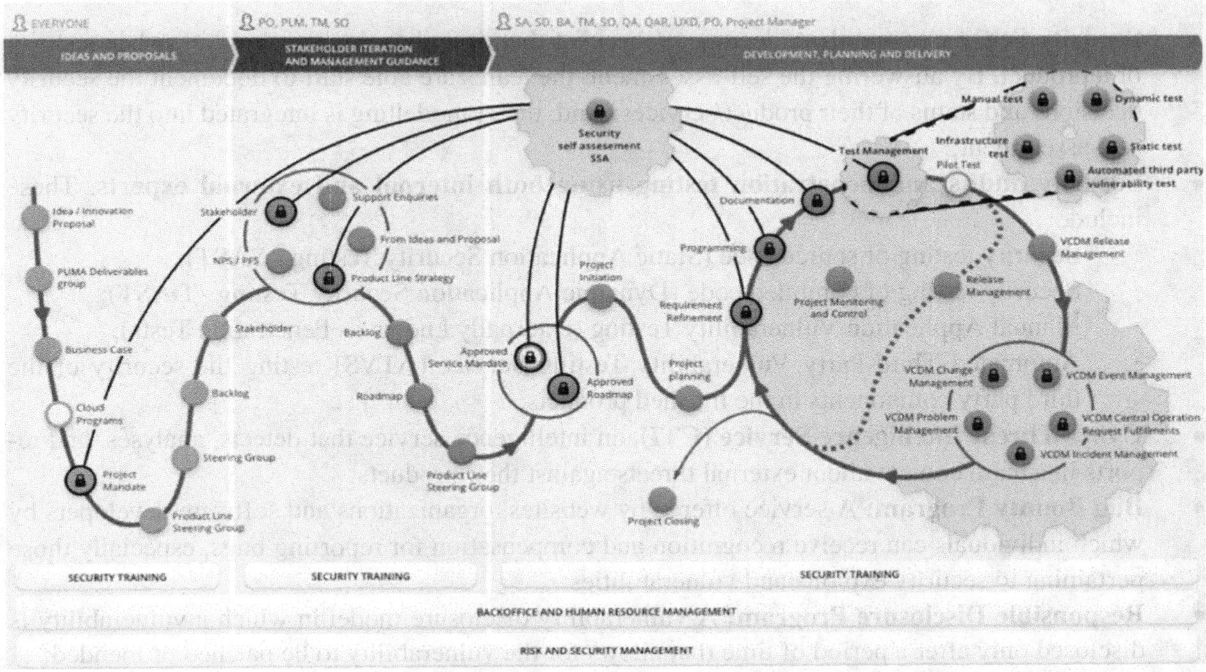

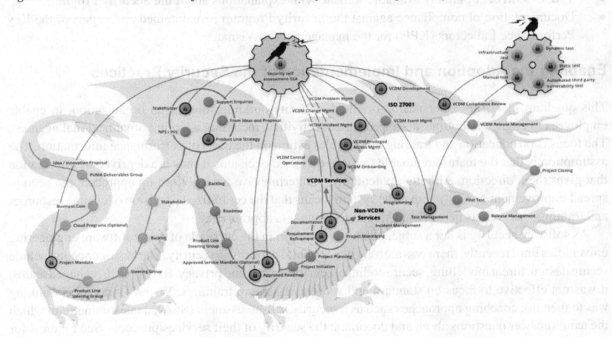

Figure 3. Second instantiation of the Visma secure software development lifecycle

Some of the software security activities that are executed in Visma are:

- **Security Self-Assessment:** A document/checklist that describes the high level of cyber security of a product. By answering the self-assessment, the teams are able start to document the security decisions and status of their product/services. And, threat modelling is integrated into the security self-assessment;
- **Security audits and penetration testing using both internal and external experts**. These include:
  - Security testing of source code (Static Application Security Testing - SAST);
  - Security testing of compiled code (Dynamic Application Security Testing - DAST);
  - Manual Application Vulnerability Testing (externally known as Penetration Tests);
  - Automated Third-Party Vulnerability Testing Service (ATVS) testing the security of the third party components in the finished products;
- **Cyber Threat Intelligence Service (CTI)**, an intelligence service that detects, analyses, and reports in a team context about external threats against their products;
- **Bug Bounty Program:** A service offered by websites, organizations and software developers by which individuals can receive recognition and compensation for reporting bugs, especially those pertaining to security exploits and vulnerabilities;
- **Responsible Disclosure Program:** A vulnerability disclosure model in which a vulnerability is disclosed only after a period of time that allows for the vulnerability to be patched or mended;
- **Red Teaming Service**, a service the teams may use to get a Red Team exercise delivered to their service;
- **Trust Centre:** A publicly available website with explanations about the Security Program.
- Documentation of compliance against the Security Program is maintained and is part of the Key Performance Indicators (KPIs) for the management of Visma.

Enabling the Adoption and Implementation of the Security Practices

This quadrant identifies a persuasion-oriented, capacity-building role for an organization, to enable employees to engage in bottom-up improvement activities, including adapting organizational agendas. The focus is on education and training that enables action on the basis of performance information. The assumption is that the teams are unable to make qualified decisions if they are deprived of information that gives them direction. Although potentially counterintuitive for a bottom-up approach, the need to spread improvement capacity across the system means that the centralized provision of change resources and training—as well as networks to spread learning—is appropriate.

As software security is not a subject that was common in the curricula of many software engineering universities until recently, there was a strong need to build capacity in security. The basic concepts include secure design, threat modelling, secure coding, security testing, and privacy. But, for self-managed teams, it was not effective to focus on standard and generic classroom trainings. Visma's strategical thinking was to then use coaching approaches such as a security self-assessment (SSA), a questionnaire in which the teams answer questions about and document the security of their services/products. See Figure 4 for an example of questions that the teams have to answer on the use of up to date components and libraries. The purpose/background of the SSA is described in Visma as to:

- Provide teams with a documented way to assess the security of their service/product according to a common checklist;
- Identify improvements regarding the security of the service and decide how to prioritize them;
- Have a common approach on how to work with proactive security measures;
- Educate and increase awareness of security topics for team members;
- Place responsibility of security inside the teams;

Figure 4. Example of question from the self-assessment questionnaire

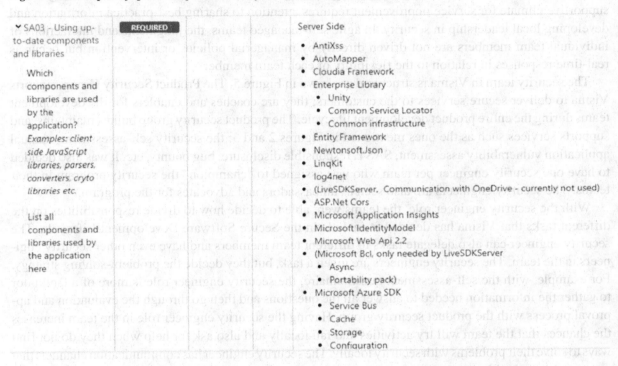

Another strategy to enable the teams was the provision of the whole infrastructure and licensing of the static analysis tools (SAST). Visma has decided to have one official SAST and configure it as a centralized resource that the software development teams could use. This enabled the teams to start as soon as possible with the use of the tools. The purpose/background defined in the security initiative was to:

- Prevent security problems due to implementation defects in source code;
- Support automation so it can be done more often and by more teams;
- Give teams visibility into the potential implementation defects and a way to manage them;
- Provide a capability to identify potential security defects early in the development cycle;
- Provide support for the majority of languages and compilers used in Visma; and
- Provide in-context remediation advice to developers to help them fix defects and learn.

In addition, as seen in Figure 2 and 3, all additional security activities are placed inline and the main effort is to control the leadership and enable the teams to make decisions themselves by reducing control elements to be rational and descriptive for the process they use.

Empowering the Teams

Quadrant 3 notes the important persuasive organizational role in empowering employees to utilize their bottom-up improvement capacity in their own teams—adding to organizational efforts via trial and error and innovative problem-solving and sharing findings from local evaluation efforts. Creating such a supportive climate for service improvement requires attention to sharing best-practice information and developing local leadership in security. In agile self-managed teams, the judgments and interactions of individual team members are not driven directly by managerial policies or intervention but occur as real-time responses in relation to the flexibility of each team member.

The security team in Visma is structured as shown in Figure 5. The Product Security Group supports Visma to deliver secure services to the customers; they are coaches and enablers for the development teams during the entire product development lifecycle. The product security group builds, maintains, and supports services such as the ones mentioned in Figures 2 and 3: the security self-assessment, manual application vulnerability assessment, SAST, responsible disclosure, bug bounty, etc. It was also decided to have one security engineer per team who was assigned to "champion" the security program in their teams. The security engineers are also seen as ambassadors and advocates for the program.

With the security engineer role, the teams were able to decide how to divide responsibilities on the different tasks that Visma has decided to include in the Secure Software Development Lifecycle. The security engineer can also delegate tasks to different team members and have even other security engineers in the team. The security engineers are given a task, but they decide the problem-solving strategy. For example, with the self-assessment questionnaire, the security engineer role is more of a facilitator to gather the information needed to answer all the questions and then go through the evaluation and approval process with the product security group. Having the security engineer role in the team increases the chances that the team will try activities and fail locally and also ask for help when they do not find ways to solve their problems with security locally. The security engineer has communication channels that were established with the product security group; through these communication channels, the security engineers can share information about the teams, hear about other teams' approaches, get informed about diverse threats and incident cases, and ask for help. To summarize, the security engineers are defined to have the following purpose/background:

- Spread and increase security awareness/culture;
- Share knowledge on the security program and how to use it;
- Scale security work in an efficient and tested way; and
- Be a point of contact to the security team—for example, for upcoming changes in the Security Program or sharing information, best practices, or questions among teams.

Additionally, empowering can be fostered by giving flexibility to the teams to adapt the way they adopt the practices/tools/techniques that are ensured by the top-down management. For example, for the SAST (Static Analysis Tools), the teams are given flexibility to decide how to implement the tools in their pipelines and how to follow up with the vulnerabilities that are disclosed by the tools. The

Figure 5. Security team configuration in Visma

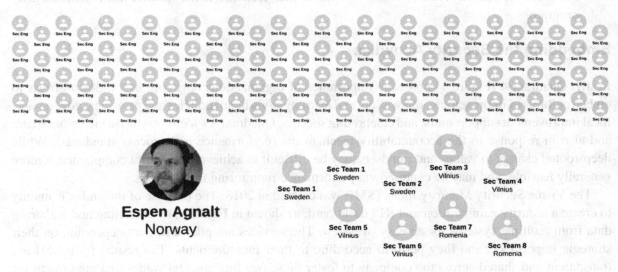

teams also have the power to decide and reason the use of other tools in addition to the one that Visma has chosen to adopt company wide. In this way, the teams can foster local improvements to the use of the SAST by adding extra checks in their code and improving confidence in the security of their code. Many teams have done that. Many teams have also innovated in the way they have followed up with the compliance to use the SAST; in cases where the SAST chosen by Visma was too slow for their code base (sometimes up to a week), they have, for example, decided to conduct an incremental analysis of the code base using another tool and then running the Visma's SAST on a monthly basis. The teams report that the Visma's SAST takes longer but goes more thoroughly into the code and uncovers issues that other free tools do not.

Annually, the Product Security group holds feedback sessions to get feedback from the teams on the security program and also to foster improvement actions on the program. These feedback sessions are called Security Chartering and provide a good channel to empower the security engineers giving them voice to raise their concerns, success cases, and experiences with the program. In addition, the Security Chartering meetings created an arena for them to talk with each other and share experiences. We have noticed that these meetings have triggered motivation to start some activities that they have not started. The sessions are run in 1,5 hours, and the structure consists of asking the security engineers to talk freely about the security program. As an example of one of these sessions was structured as follows:

- Around the table, getting to know each other (10 min);
- Rating the confidence of the team in software security (from 1-10) (10min);
- List the tasks that makes us great on security (30 min) (Things the team does already, Things that the team does but not part of the program, Things that the team wishes to have focus in Visma, Thing that the team are doing for security and it is meaningful, painful but meaningful, doing only because the team has to, not meaningful);
- Describing the motivation for performing security work - we used the technique of "Thumbs-up-thumbs-down-new-ideas-and-recognition" (30 min);

- Feedback for Security team (10 min) – giving written feedback to the security team on the security program.

Embedding the Security Activities

Lastly, Quadrant 4 (Figure 1) notes the importance of organizations engaging in top-down efforts to embed cultures of improvement, innovation, and learning—via board policies and priorities, governance, local improvement support units, and celebrating success. Quadrant 4's focus may arise via voluntarism, and also in response to the accountability mechanisms (performance and process standards). While deep-rooted change to values and mindsets may be difficult to achieve, behavioral compliance is more generally feasible, and may be captured via performance-monitoring mechanisms.

The Visma Security Maturity Index (SMI) was created in 2018. The purpose of this index is mainly to create a security gamification and KPI dashboard, as shown in Figure 6, by collecting and gathering data from multiple systems for an easy overview. The services are placed in tiers depending on their strategic importance, and they perform according to their measurements. The results from SMI are transparent and shared across the company to foster these two fundamental values that are critical for Agile/DevOps teams to work. The index is based on penalty points, depending on how serious the lack of compliance is. The initial priority for was to create a performance-monitoring mechanism based on the initial services of the Visma Secure software development lifecycle, such as the self-assessment, SAST, dependency checking, manual security testing, and triaging of the issues and how much this shows maturity in self-managing of the security issues. For example, security group in Visma recommends that each team will perform the self-assessment of their service/product once a year, and when the validity of the self-assessment expires, there is a penalty of 3,000 points. The same rule applies for the manual security testing, but the penalty is 1,000 points. The strategy in Visma was to initially only have in the

Figure 6a. Security maturity index Visma

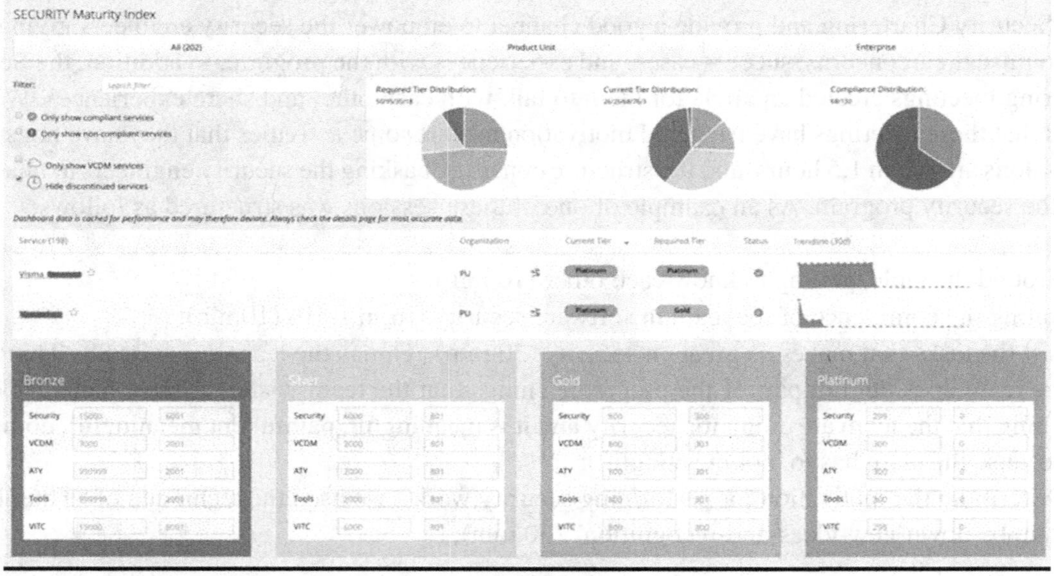

Figure 6b. Security maturity index Visma

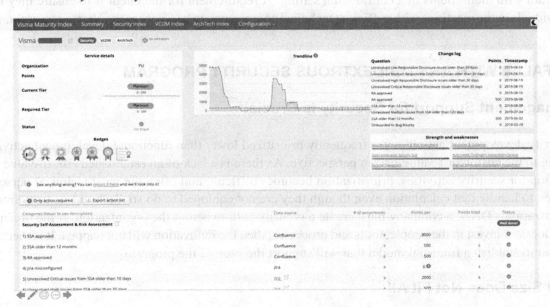

SMI items that were easy to automate and to follow up on, and later on adding other, more qualitative, items. The gamification happens when internally the teams try to work their way up to the required tier and to keep their status, as well as across teams when the different service owners compare their services to others and work/prioritize work that will lead them to the required tier in the maturity index.

Transparency is very important for the SMI to work, first because it fosters the visibility of the internal working practices of the teams, and second because if there is manipulation of the data that are plotted by the SMI, the whole system loses credibility and effect. It was communicated to the development teams that the goals of the SMI are to have a tool for fostering and tracking improvement, and it is very important that this goal is shared in all levels of the organization, so the SMI is used as it should be and not misused for other reasons than it was originally intended for. It happens sometimes that the teams do not improve over time, and they do not advance in tiers, and then the motivation of the team goes down. The reasons for non-improvement can be various, but one recurrent reason is the lack of prioritization of the activities that will make an effect on the numbers and ultimately on the tier upgrade. When teams change tiers (e.g., from Silver to Gold), the teams can celebrate improvements, and this has been a good motivator for people to keep focusing on security over time. The teams that have leaders that base their motivational schemes on stimulating good behavior seem to be more focused on celebrations, while the individual leaders that base their motivation on fear seem to focus on "deviation from norm". From our observations it seem like the reinforcement of positive behavior trough celebrations and similar gives the most lasting results.

In the Trust Centre, the customer is provided an explanation on how the security program works and what to expect from their chosen product with regards to security. This effort is top down but designed in such a way that it only reflects externally what is possible to support with evidence for clients by the development teams. The teams are given an expectation to perform direct, one-on-one meetings with their clients and, in these, share details of how they have chosen to solve the security issues in their context. The meetings are called "Level 3 meetings" and require the team to share all outputs from the security program with their clients in a confidential setting. A requirement for the client is to ensure they have individuals in the meetings with sufficient technical competency to be a peer to the Visma representative.

PITFALLS WITH AN AMBIDEXTROUS SECURITY PROGRAM

Management Support for Security is Crucial

Security development activities are frequently prioritized lower than functional development activities owing to the customer's value-driven perspective. As there is a lack of an established risk-to-value calculation for security activities, prioritization becomes difficult, and often the most technical person is chosen to handle that calculation even though they are not equipped to do so. To build security into an organization's DNA, a company must create a security culture across the organization. If the organization does not invest in the people, tools and processes, then the innovation will not happen. It is therefore crucial to stablish a financial model that will support the pace of the program.

One Size Does Not Fit All

Implicit in the framework is a suggestion of a variety of contextually responsive ways of achieving the company's goal of continuous, proactive improvement. Therefore, an "one size fits all" approach does not work, and to achieve a uniform level of success overall with the teams, there is a need for customization of the approach to the different software development teams. Some teams are open for innovation in their way of working; others are not so open to changes. In addition, the teams have different levels of maturity in software development or with previous experiences with security incidents, also impacting their level of receptiveness for top-down demands. For some teams, the approach to security will have to be adopted first from the bottom-up and then top-down.

We have also faced differences in cultures in the different countries, which also deserves appropriate measures to balance the top-down or bottom-up approach. Cultural differences in leadership styles often create unexpected misunderstandings and, many times, conflicts and barriers against top-down decisions. Approaches to authority and decision making are not the only ways in which cultures differ, but they are quite important in the leadership context. When impacting the practices of the development teams on a daily basis, it is very important that the security group leaders are aware of these differences and address them appropriately.

In the case of Visma, the cultural bias was clearly identified by management. To create effective management of these units, the chosen approach was to use different people to relate to the various teams. Some teams seem to respond better to coaching from top management, while others seem to respond better to coaching from individuals seen more as peers to them. To achieve this, a very flat organizational structure, with a focus on self-management, was chosen by security management. Current evidence shows that this works if the trust is established and frequent communication is available to sort out differences in opinion.

The second part of this was to establish the client as the most powerful entity in the organizational chart. This change gives more power to the teams, allowing them to establish direct relations to the client and enabling to harvest, among other things, security requirements, directly from the client (as opposed to getting them from a rather large policy collection).

A Security Engineer/Champion is Not Always Easy to Find

An innovation can be any idea, product, process, or object that is perceived as new to an individual or group (Rogers, 1995). In the case of the software security initiative, it is any new software security task that the software development team will start performing. But the innovation needs a champion to survive. Traditionally, "champion" has not been part of anybody's job description; rather, this is a role that some people in the right place of the organization have taken informally upon themselves. The agile software development teams are not usually composed with one security expert or a security leader. (Howell, 2005) studied 72 innovations in 38 companies, and discovered there are personal characteristics and behaviors that differentiate effective champions from ineffective ones. This observation was also true in the security program in Visma. In order to function effectively, a champion must have access to the required resources (including intra-organizational networking skills), as well as past experience with the innovation process (Weidman, Young-Corbett, Fiori, Koebel, & Montague, 2015). He also needs to have other characteristics as also stated by (Howell, 2005):

- Convey confidence and enthusiasm about the innovation;
- Enlist the support and involvement of key stakeholders;
- Persist in the face of adversity;
- Scout widely for new ideas and information and rely on personal networks;
- Have wide general knowledge, breadth of experience, and diverse interests;
- View the role broadly, are well informed about issues that affect the organization;
- Frame ideas as opportunities and tie ideas to positive organizational outcomes such as profitability, enhanced reputation, or strategic advantage;
- Use both formal and informal selling channels; and
- Are high self-monitors: They analyze potential reactions of influence targets and tailor their selling strategies to be maximally persuasive.

It is not every software development team that will have a team member with all these characteristics. Sometimes the security engineer/champion will be appointed to the role without much predisposition to the role or pursuing the characteristics that it takes to perform a good job in championing the security program in the team. In those cases, these security champions/engineers need to be coached closely and supported in the role.

It is Easy to Forget to be Bottom Up

The model shown in this chapter involves top-down system arrangements that coordinate individuals' actions and interactions to achieve organizational goals that would otherwise be conflicting on a daily and continuous basis. There is a dynamic shifting between the poles of top-down and bottom-up. And sometimes it is hard to remember to do this shift. There is a tendency to focus only on one over the other because of leadership styles. Our observation leads us to conclude that forcing the teams, produces small, short-term achievements, but by creating interest and making it easy to use the security activities in context, it becomes a part of the everyday lives of the security leaders, but it also demands more time and new ways of thinking.

Teams' Motivation Towards Security Can Vary

Motivating the team is a prerequisite for a successful result. Ensuring application security is not a trivial task, especially for developers who are often mistaken as security experts. We have observed many different occasions when the developer's motivation to keep up with the work in software security went down. But also, other stakeholders have their motivators and demotivators for software security. (Assal & Chiasson, 2018) conducted an interview study with software developers to explore factors influencing their motivation towards security, and they identified both intrinsic and extrinsic motivations, as well as different factors that led participants to lack motivation towards software security. Intrinsic motivation is when an activity is voluntarily performed for the pleasure and enjoyment it causes. Intrinsic motivations are driven by humans' "inherent tendency to seek out novelty and challenges, to extend and exercise one's capacities, to explore, and to learn". In contrast, extrinsic motivation is when a person is engaged in an activity for outcomes separate from those innate to the activity itself. They have found that when the motivation stems from the developer, rather than external factors, their participants exhibited better attitudes towards software security.

FUTURE DIRECTIONS

Ambidexterity is seldom observed in organizations the same way. The framework described in this chapter depicts parts of the strategies used in Visma. It might be that it will be difficult to replicate the results from this context to other contexts. But with so many software development teams involved in Visma's initiative, we are confident that the results can be generalized but further studies could help to understand more of the confound effects of the context variables. Further research is needed to investigate further the model used in this chapter in more contexts. Other pitfalls can also emerge from other contexts as well as other strategies to deal with security in the context of self-managed teams. There is also a need for further research on how to measure the effectiveness and efficacy of this framework over a long period of time, and what needs to be focused on from a long-term perspective.

CONCLUSION

In this chapter, we have instantiated an ambidextrous approach for a software security initiative for self-managed software development teams. The approach is ambidextrous in the sense that it focuses on approaching software security activities both from a top-down and a bottom-up perspective, combining elements usually found separately in software security initiatives. This chapter illustrates distinct, yet complementary, global and local roles for a software security initiative: (1) ensuring the adoption and implementation of software security practices, (2) enabling and (3) empowering software development teams to adapt and add to overall mandates, and (4) embedding cultures of improvement.

ACKNOWLEDGMENT

This work was supported by the SoS-Agile project: Science of Security in Agile Software Development, funded by the Research Council of Norway (grant number 247678).

REFERENCES

Ambler, S. W. (2008). Beyond functional requirements on agile projects. *Dr. Dobb's Journal*, *33*(10).

Assal, H., & Chiasson, S. (2018). Security in the software development lifecycle. In *SOUPS @ USENIX Security Symposium* (pp. 281-296). Springer.

Ayalew, T., Kidane, T., & Carlsson, B. (2013). Identification and Evaluation of Security Activities in Agile Projects. *NordSec*, *2013*, 139–153.

Baca, D., Boldt, M., Carlsson, B., & Jacobsson, A. (2015). A Novel Security-Enhanced Agile Software Development Process Applied in an Industrial Setting. *ARES*, *2015*, 11–19.

Baca, D., & Carlsson, B. (2011). Agile development with security engineering activities. *ICSSP*, *2011*, 149–158.

Bartsch, S. (2011). Practitioners' Perspectives on Security in Agile Development. *ARES*, *2011*, 479–484.

Bellomo, S., Gorton, I., & Kazman, R. (2015). Toward Agile Architecture: Insights from 15 Years of ATAM Data. *IEEE Software*, *32*(5), 38–45. doi:10.1109/MS.2015.35

Ben Othmane, L., Angin, P., Weffers, H., & Bhargava, B. K. (2014). Extending the Agile Development Process to Develop Acceptably Secure Software. *IEEE Transactions on Dependable and Secure Computing*, *11*(6), 497–509. doi:10.1109/TDSC.2014.2298011

Camacho, C. R., Marczak, S., & Cruzes, D. S. (2016). Agile Team Members Perceptions on Non-functional Testing: Influencing Factors from an Empirical Study. *ARES*, *2016*, 582–589.

Crispin, L., & Gregory, J. (2009). Agile Testing: A Practical Guide for Testers and Agile Teams. Addison-Wesley Professional.

Cruzes, D. S., Jaatun, M. G., Bernsmed, K., & Tøndel, I. (2018). Challenges and Experiences with Applying Microsoft Threat Modeling in Agile Development Projects. *ASWEC*, *2018*, 111–120.

Cruzes, D. S., Jaatun, M. G., & Oyetoyan, T. D. (2018). Challenges and approaches of performing canonical action research in software security: research paper. *HotSoS 2018*, 8:1-8:11.

Davison, R. M., Martinsons, M. G., & Kock, N. (2004). Principles of canonical action research. *Information Systems Journal*, *14*(1), 65–86. doi:10.1111/j.1365-2575.2004.00162.x

Davison, R. M., Martinsons, M. G., & Ou, C. X. (2012). The roles of theory in canonical action research. *MIS Q*, *36*(3), 763-786.

Deleersnyder, S. W. (2019). *Software Assurance Maturity Model - How To Guide - A Guide to Building Security Into Software Development*. Retrieved from https://owaspsamm.org/

Dingsøyr, T., Moe, N. B., Fægri, T., & Seim, E. A. (2018). Exploring software development at the very large-scale: A revelatory case study and research agenda for agile method adaptation. *Empirical Software Engineering Journal*, 23(1), 490–520. doi:10.100710664-017-9524-2

Eclipse. (2016). *Eclipse Process Framework (EPF)*. Retrieved from http://www.eclipse.org/epf/

Fenz, S., & Ekelhart, A. (2011). Verification, Validation, and Evaluation in Information Security Risk Management. *IEEE Security and Privacy*, 9(2), 58–65. doi:10.1109/MSP.2010.117

Firesmith, D. (2003). *Common Concepts Underlying Safety Security and Survivability Engineering. No. CMU/SEI-2003-TN-033*. Carnegie-Mellon UNIV Pittsburgh Pa Software Engineering Inst. doi:10.21236/ADA421683

Fitzgerald, B., & Stol, K.-J. (2017). Continuous software engineering: A roadmap and agenda. *Journal of Systems and Software*, 123, 176–189. doi:10.1016/j.jss.2015.06.063

Greenwood, D. J., & Levin, M. (2006). *Introduction to Action Research: Social Research for Social Change*. Sage Publications, Inc.

Gregory, J., & Crispin, L. (2014). *More Agile Testing: Learning Journeys for the Whole Team* (1st ed.). Addison-Wesley Professional.

Howell, J. M. (2005). The right stuff: Identifying and developing effective champions of innovation. *The Academy of Management Perspectives*, 19(2), 108–119. doi:10.5465/ame.2005.16965104

ISO/IEC. (2011). *ISO/IEC 27005: 2011 Information technology–Security techniques–Information security risk management*.

ISO/IEC 25010. (2011). *Systems and software Quality Requirements and Evaluation (SQuaRE) — System and software quality models. Iso/Iec Fdis 25010:2011*, 2010, 1-34.

Jaatun, M. G., Cruzes, D. S., Bernsmed, K., Tøndel, I., & Røstad, L. (2015). Software Security Maturity in Public Organisations. *ISC*, 2015, 120–138.

Jaatun, M. G., & Tøndel, I. (2008). Covering Your Assets in Software Engineering. *ARES*, 2008, 1172–1179.

McDermott, A. M., Hamel, L. M., Steel, D., Flood, P. C., & Mkee, L. (2015). Hybrid health care governance for improvement? Combining top-down and bottom-up approaches to public sector regulation. *Public Administration*, 93(2), 324–344. doi:10.1111/padm.12118

McGraw, G. (2004). Software Security. *IEEE Security and Privacy*, 2(2), 80–83. doi:10.1109/MSECP.2004.1281254

McGraw, G. (2006). Software Security: Building Security. *ISSRE 2006*. http://bsimm.com

Microsoft. (2019). *Security development lifecycle for agile development*. Retrieved from http://www.microsoft.com/en-us/SDL/Discover/sdlagile.aspx

Oueslati, H., Rahman, M. M., & ben Othmane, L. (2015). Literature Review of the Challenges of Developing Secure Software Using the Agile Approach. *10th International Conference on Availability, Reliability and Security*, 540-547. 10.1109/ARES.2015.69

Oueslati, H., Rahman, M. M., ben Othmane, L., Ghani, I., & Arbain, A. F. B. (2016). Evaluation of the Challenges of Developing Secure Software Using the Agile Approach. *International Journal of Secure Software Engineering*, 7(1), 17–37. doi:10.4018/IJSSE.2016010102

Oyetoyan, T., Jaatun, M. G., & Cruzes, D. S. (2017). A Lightweight Measurement of Software Security Skills, Usage and Training Needs in Agile Teams. *International Journal of Secure Software Engineering*, 8(1), 1–27. doi:10.4018/IJSSE.2017010101

Poller, A., Kocksch, L., Türpe, S., Epp, F. A., & Kinder-Kurlanda, K. (2017). Can Security Become a Routine?: A Study of Organizational Change in an Agile Software Development Group. *CSCW*, *2017*, 2489–2503.

Rogers, E. M. (1995). *Diffusion of innovations* (4th ed.). Free Press.

Shostack, A. (2014). *Threat Modeling: Designing for Security*. Wiley.

Smite, D., Moe, N. B., & Torkar, R. (2008). Pitfalls in Remote Team Coordination: Lessons Learned from a Case Study. *PROFES*, *2008*, 345–359.

SoS-Agile Project (2015-2020). (n.d.). Retrieved from Science of Security for Agile Software Development research project, 2015-2020, funded by the Research Council of Norway: http://www.sintef.no/sos-agile

Tøndel, I., Jaatun, M. G., Cruzes, D. S., & Moe, N. B. (2017). Risk Centric Activities in Secure Software Development in Public Organisations. *International Journal of Secure Software Engineering*, 8(4), 1–30. doi:10.4018/IJSSE.2017100101

Tøndel, I., Line, M. B., & Johansen, G. (2015). Assessing Information Security Risks of AMI - What Makes it so Difficult? *ICISSP*, *2015*, 56–63.

Tuma, K., Çalikli, G., & Scandariato, R. (2018). Threat analysis of software systems: A systematic literature review. *Journal of Systems and Software*, *144*, 275–294. doi:10.1016/j.jss.2018.06.073

Wäyrynen, J., Bodén, M., & Boström, G. (2004). *Security Engineering and eXtreme Programming: An Impossible Marriage?* XP/Agile Universe.

Weidman, J., Young-Corbett, D., Fiori, C., Koebel, T., & Montague, E. (2015). Prevention through Design Adoption Readiness Model (PtD ARM): An integrated conceptual model. *Work*.

Wu, Y., & Wu, S. (2016). Managing ambidexterity in creative industries: A survey. *Journal of Business Research*, 69(7), 2388–2396. doi:10.1016/j.jbusres.2015.10.008

Xiao, S., Witschey, J., & Murphy-Hil, E. (2014). Social influences on secure development tool adoption: why security tools spread. In *Proceedings of the 17th ACM conference on Computer supported cooperative work & social computing (CSCW'14)* (pp. 1095-1106). New York, NY: ACM. 10.1145/2531602.2531722

KEY TERMS AND DEFINITIONS

Ambidextrous: Having the ability to use the right and left hands equally well; while few of us are naturally ambidextrous, there is a possibility to train the brain to become more ambidextrous.

Bug Bounty: A deal offered by many websites, organizations, and software developers by which individuals can receive recognition and compensation for reporting bugs, especially those pertaining to exploits and vulnerabilities.

DAST (Dynamic Application Security Testing): A process of testing an application or software product in an operating state.

Penetration Testing: A penetration test, colloquially known as a pen test, or ethical hacking, is an authorized simulated cyberattack on a computer system, performed to evaluate the security of the system.

Responsible Disclosure: A vulnerability disclosure model in which a vulnerability or an issue is disclosed only after a period of time that allows for the vulnerability or issue to be patched or mended. This period distinguishes the model from full disclosure.

SAST (Static Analysis Tools): Static program analysis is the analysis of computer software that is performed without actually executing programs.

Threat Modelling: A process by which potential threats, such as structural vulnerabilities or the absence of appropriate safeguards, can be identified and enumerated, and mitigations can be prioritized.

Chapter 10
Challenges and Trends of Agile

Fayez Salma
Carl von Ossietzky Universität Oldenburg, Germany

Jorge Marx Gómez
Carl von Ossietzky Universität Oldenburg, Germany

ABSTRACT

Rapidly increasing of requirements of business pushed researchers to define new approaches and methodologies to meet marketing needs. Agile methodology has been created and replaced the traditional-driven development methods that focus on soliciting, documenting a complete set of requirements, and take a long time comparing to market change. On the other hand, customers need to be closer to the development process and collaborate with team development. Despite agile advantages, introducing new tools, coordination, and collaboration concepts, some challenges still need to be discussed and improved. These challenges relate to achieve balanced IT service development process in the organization. As a result, new trends have been created to facilitate new changes in software development. This chapter will study agile methodologies and different challenges with suggested solutions generated from agile philosophy itself.

INTRODUCTION

The software development process was developed over several decades, offering many methodologies and aspects according to competitiveness and market, but in general, customer satisfaction and developing a product that meets the basic requirements are foundations. These requirements have direct bearing on the trend of software development methodology, as long as they require more time and various changes during the used development process, thus using more resources to finish the projects (Williams & Cockburn, 2003a). Agile has provided an appropriate solution to rapidly change of marketing and customer requirements; it is based on the iterative enhancement, each iteration represents a small scale and self-contained Software Development Life Cycle (SDLC) by itself (Al-Zewairi et al., 2017; Williams, 2010). In other hand, customers need to be closer to the development process and collaborate with team development to produce high quality software and increasing competitive advantage (Kumar & Bhatia,

DOI: 10.4018/978-1-7998-4165-4.ch010

2012). These kind of relation causes increasing the authority and sharing making decisions including those pertaining to business, process, and systems requirements (Williams & Cockburn, 2003a).

Agile birth was announced as kind of transformation from the old approach when this approach declared its inability to continue; The idea took shape when manifesto was written for agile software development in 2001 (Fowler & Highsmith, 2001; Lous et al., 2018), which is a list of four values and twelve principles that describe the philosophy behind the methodology (Lous et al., 2018). Meanwhile, agile methods such as Scrum, Kanban, Scrumban and Extreme Programming (XP) are widely used in development management in order to add the agility and flexibility to projects.

Despite their advantages which included a new approach, respond to changes quickly, new tools, coordination and collaboration concepts, some challenges emerged, making it necessary to address them in order to find appropriate solutions. These challenges vary according to the nature of each organization and each project.

Basically, applying the appropriate way of agile supposes good understanding the agile methodology in depth. Any lack or gap in any step of agile causes kind of poor management, which affects the product quality. In parallel, understanding project and environment can prevent and overcome challenges when there is lack of documentation and more informal communications which considered as huge amount of information (Altameem, 2015). However, challenges and difficulties relate to achieving a balanced process for developing IT services in the organization by doing many activities. Theoretically, communication is one of the most important factors in agile, thus applying balanced process needs effective communications between the team and the manager to understand the team's dynamics and efficient agile practice. Agile communication should be applied optimally between team members themselves as well in order to share knowledge, passing difficulties and improve product industry. In some cases, good communications cannot prevent failures if management approach conflict with agile methods, this matter imposes some updates on agile characteristics. But failure in team management or to achieve a high-quality product that can be due to the presence of many stakeholders and lack of corporation between them. This limitation requires some updates on agile and make kind of balancing between team development process and stakeholders' preo-pipeline. Externally, agile has been created to react to marketing growth and development techniques changes, but these changes happened frequently so agile should keep up and naturally define new methods and tools.

Challenges always need solutions to evolve agile and its concepts, so new trends will emerge and new technologies in development will now be reflected in Agile. This chapter will highlight two main topics related to agile conceptually:

- As long as agile is in place to contain changes in marketing and business, do they also need adjustments to adapt to changes in the structural domain?
- How is the ability of agile to adapt the challenges?

We aim to demonstrate its ability to overcome challenges and what trends emerged as a result of these challenges. This research will list some challenges based on changes in teams, large organizations and multi-site operations. In parallel, it will review some agile challenges to understand more about how agile can embrace itself for application in organizations and to define other challenges which still open and not covered. Finally, we will review some agile trends to understand better the changes and updated on agile which helped it to keep running and attracted more organizations to use it.

BACKGROUND

Generally, software developments methodologies are mainly classified into two main types: Traditional Methodology (Heavyweight) or Agile Methodology (Awad, 2005). Traditional Methodologies (Heavyweight) follow series of phases which start from gathering requirements and end with deployment, during these phases, documentations play guiding role in creating product features, based on agreement and requirements. Many traditional methodologies were created, some of them were declined while other strongly imposed itself, taking advantage of its characteristics and features such as Waterfall Model, Spiral Model and Unified Process (Awad, 2005).

Waterfall model converts product industry into sequential phases by defining these requirements as an initial step followed by analysis, design, testing and deploying. It can provide an easy way to developed complex systems by defining requirements and designing the implementation afterward into production (Szalvay, 2004). It requires extensive customer interactions in order to understand the functional and non-functional requirements and to determine the features of the required product that creates a lot of documentation. The iterative model uses the waterfall in an iterative fashion by creating a partial implementation of a holistic system, then slowly adding increasing functionality (Alshamrani & Bahattab, 2015). Spiral Model extends waterfall model by defining more phases to each cycle and dividing the life cycle of software development process into four phases: Planning, Risk Analysis, Development/ Engineering and Evaluation Phase (Boehm et al., 1998). Waterfall and other models with all their huge advantages and solutions to build systems and products started to be an old fashion as a result of quick changes in world of business. These changes in business increased ascending and development process became unable to deliver output as same tempo. These feature spotted light on lot of disadvantages, most of them relate to requirements changes, these changes could happen in the middle of development as a result of changing in business process or uncertainty of requirements in the beginning of the project (Cohen et al., 2004).

Beginning in the mid-1990s, many companies found this initial requirements documentation step frustrating and, perhaps, impossible (Williams & Cockburn, 2003a). Developers decided to find another model or methodology can break them away from traditional structured, segmented, bureaucratic approaches to software development and moved towards more flexible one (McCormick, 2012). In real world, changes happen in quick frequency, the development process should be done in flexible and efficient way (Cohen et al., 2004). Actually, markets are changing quickly and pushing more new requirements which are required from customers and business competition with high quality conditions, all of this was accompanied by technological development that seemed to accelerate unpredictably and the need to find new technologies can solve the limitations in current tools and systems (Cockburn & Highsmith, 2001; Dzamashvili Fogelström et al., 2010; Williams & Cockburn, 2003b).

Companies started to find alternative methodologies in order to continuity and competitiveness, many methodologies appeared. The efforts were to define new methodology replace the traditional one with new aspects and style. Historically, the famous meeting happened on February 11–13, 2001, at The Lodge at Snowbird ski resort in the Wasatch mountains of Utah, 17 people met to talk, ski, relax and try to find common ground. It was clear for all participations the necessity to better cope with changing requirements, focusing and starting from people and it should be more flexible (Cohen et al., 2004; Highsmith & Cockburn, 2001). Finally, they defined a new methodology called Agile Methodology (Fowler & Highsmith, 2001).

They analyzed their work habits to make them more lightness which provide more relevant output with customer satisfaction (Williams & Cockburn, 2003a). as a result, they wrote Manifesto for Agile Software Development which focuses on (Fowler & Highsmith, 2001; Turk et al., 2014; Williams & Cockburn, 2003a):

- Individuals and interactions over processes and tools.
- Working software over comprehensive documentation.
- Customer collaboration over contract negotiation.
- Responding to change over following a plan.

Another 12 principle are generated and emphasis on many goals such as customer satisfaction, continuous delivery, value, and early deliveries. adaptability, competitiveness, and customer benefit. Collaboration...etc. (Highsmith & Cockburn, 2001; Laanti et al., 2013).

Agile is a result of traditional methodologies shortcomings which makes it known plan-driven methodology (Cohen et al., 2004), it focuses on people and effective communications between them, customer participate during development stage to improve opportunities and product quality (Cristal et al., 2008). Enormous efforts of software development adaptions hide behind Agile in order to meet the increasing of business requirements.

AGILE METHODS

Agile as framework defines many methods which translate agile principles and provide practical rules to be applied. Describing agile methods reflect their features, but in general it tends to be lightweight comparing to old ones which described as rigorous, disciplined, bureaucratic, heavyweight, and industrial strength (Paulk, 2002). Agile methods like Agile itself promise shorter market time, plus greater flexibility to include changes in requirements that are created from clients and the market (Dzamashvili Fogelström et al., 2010; Williams & Cockburn, 2003b). As mentioned before, there is one of the most restrictive restrictions on waterfall methodology and other traditional methodologies behind changes after the analysis phase, during the design, implementation, or production stage. These changes increased in ascending order. Thus, traditional models should be more flexible to deal with when they arise. Agile methods have brought a new perspective to software development. It can easily adapt to different requirements or environment, to provide value to customers (Janes & Succi, 2012), While more organizations seek to get more competitions in shorter time with keeping developer far away from pressure to produce new or enhanced implementations quickly (Turk et al., 2014).

A number of software development methods have been created such as extreme programming (XP), feature-driven development, crystal clear method, scrum, dynamic systems development, and adaptive software development, fall into this category (Nerur et al., 2005).

AGILE CHALLENGES

As any change in software development, several challenges appeared after using agile in organizations, that prompted researchers to classify them or study specific cases in order to understand and provide solutions to these challenges.

The deliverable of each study is considered as an attempt to develop agile methodology itself and find the best way to merging it in organization. Significantly, reviewing and focusing on group of these challenges in addition to define other challenges are main idea in this section which enable us to aware their features. Organization type is considered the main factor to determine the best way to apply agile. weather agile can be applied smoothly or need update. Nowadays, organizations begin to be larger and larger in parallel with the strong movement of agility, which has proven its strength to respond to rapid changes in the market, and thus adaptation it in companies has become an urgent need and this has created many challenges related to their ability to adapt to the large size of companies.

These challenges were not the only ones, in addition, there are others related to the team itself and what are the frameworks of maneuver the team owns

Team Level

The change in team level can be found in any kind of organization according to several criteria that ranged from team knowledge, skills, organization, management, and ability to change ... etc. For that, focusing on modern team level challenges requires understanding fundamental changes in the work team, regardless of the nature of the organization, so we can move on to know the necessary requirements for the team in large organizations.

Agile method in the organization requires improving team skills to counter this change. Ideally, the team should be able to deal with the new approach and get its advantages without any problems, but this change does not happen smoothly, and the team must be practiced and prepared. Initially, team must understand agile culture to make the organizational environment accept the agile method (Tolfo et al., 2011). The organization should pave the way for the development of specifically designed recruitment practices, use team recruiting to find the right person or hire newly appointed graduates into fast-moving projects (Conboy et al., 2011).

In other hand, team members should aware of business knowledge which means provide small training modules, recruit staff and graduates with a combination of IT and business knowledge and customer company runs training sessions. In addition, team should understand principles of agile and its philosophy by ensuring multiple members get agile training, agile coaching and championing and cross-team observation/validation of agile practices. Furthermore, transferring to agile requires increasing of team motivation to keep high quality work performance and increase productivity. Meanwhile, agile assumes more focusing on decision-making which is achieved by building a sharing and learning environment, implement a democratic voting system and requires that project manager plays the role of facilitator. At the end, there is a challenge about compliant performance evaluation which means more challenges and more need to adapt breadth of skills much higher weighting for mentoring (Conboy et al., 2011).

Skills of team members are not the only challenges a team faces, as by expanding the scope of the vision, it allows us to monitor how the work environment can affect the teams and reduce the quality of production. Therefore, organizations and the team provide the right environment for agility and preparation, and they have found that a lack of understanding of the work environment is an important factor in limiting flexible advantages (Buchan et al., 2019) which cause limitation in communication and coordination between teams.

However, environment of work leads us to think about how team management will be changed and what are the challenges which related to this domain? Beginning of agile concepts, we can realize a lot of changes on management roles and way of management. Some management roles have been changed in agile comparing to traditional methods such as product owner who has difference in responsivity and tasks. Product owner should be available to all team and active in clearing definition of requirements in backlog (Nuottila et al., 2016). Agile assumes that customer and team member should work together with strong communication, thus self-management approach has emerged further as one of the twelve principles behind Agile Manifesto (Fowler & Highsmith, 2001) to display high levels of autonomy (Hoda & Murugesan, 2016; Stray et al., 2018). So as normal result, team needs to be aware how to apply self-management and what are the accompanied difficulties behind it. Self-management requires harmony with the rest of the team and some of the skills in management, especially that some methodologies such as scrum that allow members to choose tasks flexibly from the backlog. Team member should handle some other difficulties like cross-functional (Hoda & Murugesan, 2016) which means working across various technologies and domains in order to achieve organizational tasks (Pinto & Pinto, 1990). Thus team member should share knowledge between each other to learn new things which help achieve cross-functionality to a great extent (Hoda & Murugesan, 2016). Self-management assume any member can measure the required effort to finish tasks in order to organize sprint and work between team members. For that, agile introduced planning meetings with all members to share their views on the estimations and understanding the tasks (Hoda & Murugesan, 2016).

One of the challenges that began to spread as a natural result of the organization' inflation is the increase of the remote dispersed teams, which has become a reality in many companies, and this constituted a clear contradiction with the principles of agile procedure, which pushed towards finding ways and means to overcome them. So many studies emerged that presented ideas and visions centered mostly on how to overcome problems such as communication while confidence in agile practices was an important matter that prompted the necessity of sharing knowledge (Lautert et al., 2019). While there are other keys which are important such as agile servant leader, agile team, trust, virtual work environment, inspect & adapt, and reduce waste (Lous et al., 2018). Because of its apparent inconsistency with the basic principles of agile, and the need for it constantly increasing, it becomes clear that this topic is gripping to further research and realization of the required amendments on agile.

Organization Level

Agile is characterized by many challenges at the enterprise level, and these challenges vary according to the type of organization, for example, its business activity, size or time of rapid approval.

Business can vary between public and non-public organizations, but the challenges are the same in some specific cases. However, in any agile accreditation process, there are common challenges based on the following factors. (Nuottila et al., 2016): Conflict between agile nature and organization process to reduce documentation; Education, experience and commitment; Stakeholder communication and involvement; Roles in agile set-up; Location of the agile teams and Other challenges relate to legislation and permission of information sharing while other focus on the complexity of developed systems.

These challenges have become part of other challenges that have arisen with the expansion of organizations and their large size and their tendency to take advantage of the agile procedure to implement it.

Large-scale agile appeared to refer to the generated changes when agile adoption in large organizations, these changes pushed organizations to rethink their goals and reconfigure their human, managerial, and technology components. it includes many aspects range from using agile methods in large organizations to large projects and how can agile deal with these large projects, also it means using agile in large team to large multi-team projects to making use of principles of agile development in a whole organization (Dingsøyr & Moe, 2014; Fuchs & Hess, 2018). What is mentioned above means focusing more on management, organizational, people, process, and technological issues in adopting agile methodologies (Nerur et al., 2005).

In general, we can distinguish two categories of these challenges, the first, when a large organization decides to shift to agile and replaces the old approach with agile style while the second, examines the challenges of agility after organizations become larger.

Challenges of Large-Scale Agile Adoption

A lot of challenges are studied and analyzed during large-scale agile transformations, the goal was to define main points relate to transformation process and introduce solutions. Some of these challenges fall in following points (Dikert et al., 2016; Paasivaara et al., 2018):

- Change resistance
  People are not willing to change, so any change means time to learn to understand and kind of ambiguity. That applied on management which could be not willing to change as well
- Lack of investment
  Includes lack of training and coaching, too high workload, old commitments kept and rearranging physical spaces
- Agile difficult to implement
  This challenge considered very important to apply agile in organizations as it and not follow old approach with some agile concepts. That means team should not misunderstanding agile concepts or depends on guidance from literature which hard to learn agile. In some cases, Agile customized poorly which means skipping practices, that led to problems. Difficult and challenge of implementation push people revert to the old way of working but at meantime, people should not become too evangelic, in order to avoid making people reluctance of agile development and give up transformation process.
- Coordination challenges in multi-team environment
  Coordinating the work of several agile teams introduced new challenges to organizations, if surrounding organization was not responsive enough. However, another aspect in this point relate to autonomous team model challenging and focusing on own goal instead of striking a balance between team goals and general goals of the organization. Anyway, more coordination problems were appeared when teams are distributed over many geographical locations or when using different scripts in one case which leads to problems in synchronizing and consistency of software interfaces between teams.
- Different approaches emerge in a multi-team environment
  Because of interpretation of agile differs between teams, using old and new methods side by side, management in waterfall mode even after adopting agile
- Hierarchical management and organizational boundaries

- Requirements engineering challenges
  Agile methods like Scrum and XP don not have a quite structured approach to requirements which are required in large development projects in addition estimation time for these requirements are so difficult to Product managers and business analysts while teams need to break them down into small sizes which are able to be estimated.
- Quality assurance challenges
  In some cases, agile methods lack non-functional, continuous integration and automated testing, so applying these kinds of tests is considered as an important challenge to produce high quality product.
- Integrating non-development functions
- Defining team roles
- Challenges in defining the Product Owner role

Another interesting study has been done by (Uludag et al., 2018) and identified 11 categories of challenges as following Communication & Coordination, Software-Architecture, Geographical Distribution, Knowledge Management, Culture & Mindset, Methodology, Requirements Engineering, Enterprise Architecture, Quality Assurance, Tooling and Project Management.

Challenges of Expanding the Organization to Become Larger

Second kind of challenges in large organizations based on expanding small organizations to become larger, which means limitation agile methods to adapt this expanding. Conceptually, Agile assume software projects should be small and include small teams. It effected on organizations and business style by reducing size of software projects and focusing on microservices with its advantages epically in reducing complexity and risks(Dingsøyr et al., 2019; Ebert, 2018; Flyvbjerg et al., 2003).

Many extensions and trends in this domain appeared to coordinate working between customers, teams, departments and other participations in agile. Several of these extensions have been suggested e.g., the Scaled Agile Framework (SAFe), Large-Scale Scrum (LeSS), and Disciplined Agile Delivery (DAD) (Paasivaara et al., 2018).

AGILE TRENDS

Scrum of Scrums

Scrum is used and applied in small teams, while application in large teams is difficult and does not meet the purpose assigned to them. Therefore, large teams need to expand Scrum to meet its characteristics, and from here the trend appeared to offer an expansion of Scrum. Scrum of Scrums (SOS) is a framework for large organizations where many teams work together and coordinate to complete a product. We can say that SOS focus more on structural level. It divides a large team into multiple teams communicate with each other's and work on different sides of the same project (AlMutairi & Qureshi, 2015). These team make daily or weekly meeting by one representative from each team, and these meeting could be after daily stand-up meetings to update other SOS participants, after Release Planning meeting and after the Sprint Planning meeting (Mundra et al., 2013). In general, SOS meetings aim to address team coordination (Paasivaara et al., 2012). SOS team contains product owner attends all meeting related to his product and we have scrum mater in each team who will participate in SOS meeting.

The question remains as to what nature of companies or teams SOS can be applied to. In fact, as long as SOS is to apply the same concepts of Scrum, but on another level of the teams, this means that the teams must be homogeneous and work within the same project and product (Keller et al., 2019). This is evident in the challenges facing the meetings that SOS contains when the meeting period is for a long period or contains a large number of participants or the nature of the meeting itself and therefore it cannot be described as unsuccessful (Keller et al., 2019) but needs controls and conditions that restrict the progress and direction of the nature of the meetings. This gives an indication of the work and development you need to achieve the required adjustment process.

Scaled Agile Framework (SAFe)

Scaled Agile Framework (SAFe) uses agile and lean principles to scale whole organization. It depends and works together with agile methods and other current model such as Scrum, XP, Lean, and Product Development Flow. SAFe consists of three levels: team, program, and portfolio levels in addition to the optional value stream level (Alqudah & Razali, 2016; Turetken et al., 2017; Uludağ et al., 2017):

- The team level basically consists of agile teams, which define, build, and test software in fixed-length iteration and releases. SAFe uses in team level agile project management practices (Scrum) and agile technical practices (XP), it imports concepts from them depending on each stage.
- The program level organizes the agile team, so all roles should be defined, these roles are distributed into System Team, Product Manager, System Architect, Release Train Engineer (RTE), UX and Shared Resources and Release Management Team. Product manager prioritizes the program backlog and works with product owners at the team level to optimize Feature delivery. In this level, the agile release train is the major concept, thus this agile release train produces releases which are releases are planned during a 2-days release planning event with all relevant stakeholders.
- The value stream is long-lived series of system definition, development, and deployment steps, which means insuring that multiple large teams remain aligned.
- Program Portfolio Management team consists of people with fully understand to business strategy, used technology, and financial aspects such as business managers and executives. In this level, the strategy is established and identified, then new features are created and boken down to program level.

SAFe is a solution to large organizations that need to scale agile development by scaling up 'some' of the agile practices and introducing new practices and concepts (such as release train, business, and architecture epics, portfolio backlog). There some criticism for being too prescriptive and team are not much flexible in process decisions. Even these criticisms feel that this framework is not agile because of many upfront planning and some top-down processes which implies lack of flexibility. But in general, it accelerates time-to-market, increases productivity and quality, and reduces risks and project costs. At the same time, SAFe has some weakness during the scaling process relate to project size and need to structural approaches and methodological guidelines for scaling agile in large settings, in particular for SAFe (Turetken et al., 2017).

Disciplined Agile Delivery (DAD)

Disciplined Agile Delivery (DAD), developed by Scott Ambler and Mark Lines. DAD is a framework to adapt the scrum to the organization, when this organization decides to move to agile methodology. Scrum itself does not have the full requirements; it is only part of what is required to provide complex solutions to stakeholders. The team will start using another process to fill in this gap which leads to a lot of confusion and mystery. So DAD is a hybrid approach that provides a coherent approach to delivering a graceful solution that works as a guiding and decision-making including scrum, Agile Modeling (AM), Extreme Programming (XP), Unified Process (UP), Kanban, Lean Software Development, SAFe and LeSS and many other ways.

DAD considers that agile methods focus only on one phase which is "Construction", while large projects need more. For that, it added other two phases (Inceptions and Transitions), while inception phase located before construction, transition phase focus in the stage after construction to prepare for delivery. These phases are achieved during short iterations (Alqudah & Razali, 2016).

Large Scale Scrum (LeSS)

It is an agile framework for scaling Scrum to more than one team in large organizations. So scrum is applied with some extensions like different sprint planning activity which include two members from each team plus the one overall Product Owner to decide which chunk of Product Backlog items to work on (Alqudah & Razali, 2016). In general, It is classified into two types, first one called LeSS framework-1which covers up to ten Scrum teams and another, called LeSS framework-2, has more than ten (Vaidya, 2014).

More practices were established like: Inter-team coordination meeting, a Joint Light Produce Backlog Refinement and Joint Retrospective meeting (Alqudah & Razali, 2016). These practices are mainly applied to LeSS framework-1, while in LeSS framework-2 a new Pre-Sprint Product Team Meeting is introduced in addition to overall Sprint Review meeting and Overall Sprint Retrospective meeting at the product level (Vaidya, 2014).

AGILE FUTURE TRENDS

Software systems change rapidly every day and new trends appear frequently according to many factors include market and requirements. Mobile applications, big data, social and communication media and other top topics pushed software development to find alternatives and extension to old approaches and during this development agile methodology proofed itself as flexible approach can be trusted to keep up business run.

Efforts started to study effect of rapid changes in requirements on agile, and the questions was what agile need to update. One of the essential topics focuses on manifesto and its future whether it should be developed or not, as a result of the discussion, some ideas prompt stop focusing on the future trends of the agile manifest while other supported the distribution of the agile mindset into new fields of application. In parallel, there is discussion about the future of agile methodology and if scrum should be replaced or not. The results found agile train keeps moving and Scrum is not the end of the road, in addition, maintain flexibility, stop doing stupid stuff and focus on delivering value more quickly and be professional (Hohl et al., 2018).

Agile tends to make team more self-organizing and autonomous which was one of the agile challenges as we mentioned before, this direction more important where team should make decision, estimate tasks and ensure the continuity of the organization's system. Studying barriers of autonomous agile team generated some ideas like not having clear and common goals, lack of trust, too many dependencies to others, lack of coaching and organizational support and diversity in norms (Stray et al., 2018), so the effort was to identify these barriers and attempt to understand their related factors. Main domains and related topics were leadership, coordination, organizational context, design of autonomous agile teams and team processes which suggested group of questions in order to draw borders and clear way to make team self-organized (Stray et al., 2018).

On other hands, Teams and organizations started to be bigger and bigger, thus new aspects and techniques should be followed which means update on agile and its methods. Distributed teams are located in different geographical places, taking advantage of technological development to communicate and reduce the costs. But agile has been created to handle small teams, so as we mentioned before, agile has been continuously evolved according to team natural and organization expanding, therefore agile has ability to keep going in this evolution process and this kind of work. Organizations use agile in their distributed teams by making changes on the organizational design, decision making, collaboration and coordination and in agile culture. These changes include splitting teams into specialized groups and replacing face-to-face meeting with other types using the modern communications tools while agile should be learned and understood between team members to solve challenges quickly. In other hand, the adaptions should be applied on agile itself, therefore we can notice multi-team backlog, multiple meetings, scaling the infrastructure and organizational agility (Papadopoulos, 2015).

Agile methodology defined a new extension to support new trends like Business Intelligent (BI). Uncontrolled growth of data generated new domains of manipulating, understating and analyzing data such as Big Data and BI; these domains convert data into information to be used by software systems. BI and analytics provide decisions-making information in supply chain, sales, finance, and marketing, so this necessity met the characteristics that characterize agile and this has led to extend agile to Agile Data Warehousing, Extreme Scoping which focused on the data integration aspect of BI projects (Muntean & Surcel, 2013).

This success of agile adoption encourages asking questions about the future changes and ability of agile to be applied in modern trends such as fulfil the demand of the IoT and AI or if agile can improve data analytics and data sciences. Agile should handle security and support the development of safety critical systems like autonomous vehicles and robotics which are very important in current and futures markets (Hoda et al., 2018).

CONCLUSION

During this research we can identify how agile was able to adapt to the changes that occurred on the structural structure, as it has always found solutions to most challenges at the organizational level and the level of teams. Its development and how it began to extend to departments that are not IT departments, pushes the business to develop and grow, and this is what appears in the development of concepts such as self-management and work in geographically distributed places. It also shows us through the research how the flexibility that it enjoys has always allowed in the first place the organization and the teams and researchers to find solutions to develop software and respond to market and work changes.

Agile succeeded in keeping abreast of developments in the market and business, which are directly reflected in the companies 'performance, as evidenced by the great trend of companies of various kinds towards adopting agility. Agile as others, needs many expansions and activities to be adapted and used in the procedure approved in the organization.

Education, training, and procedural understanding are essential aspects of successful organizations and projects, meanwhile, the communication between the team members, face to face, increases the effectiveness of the performance to achieve high-quality products which meet customer's satisfaction. After reviewing natural and reasons of challenges of agile, we can notice that agile should be applied as it, by understanding its basics and any update or extension should be created based on these principles.

Rapid changes prompted agile to define new trends which are suitable to large organizations or distributed teams. These changes raised questions about future of agile. This discussion about future of agile still open, but in general agile proofed its advantages to adapt new changes in business and market. Agile extensions provide the required techniques to the organization to facilitate work between teams. In the same way, modern phenomenon integrated with agile in some domains, while many questions still open about agile and some aspects relate to the vision and future of agile.

ACKNOWLEDGMENT

We thank the co-editors and IGI for the opportunity to collaborate on this book.

REFERENCES

Al-Zewairi, M., Biltawi, M., Etaiwi, W., & Shaout, A. (2017). Agile software development methodologies: Survey of surveys. *Journal of Computer and Communications*, 5(05), 74–97. doi:10.4236/jcc.2017.55007

AlMutairi, A. M., & Qureshi, M. R. J. (2015). The proposal of scaling the roles in scrum of scrums for distributed large projects. *International Journal of Information Technology and Computer Science*, 7(8), 68–74. doi:10.5815/ijitcs.2015.08.10

Alqudah, M., & Razali, R. (2016). A review of scaling agile methods in large software development. International Journal on Advanced Science. *Engineering and Information Technology*, 6(6), 828–837.

Alshamrani, A., & Bahattab, A. (2015). A comparison between three SDLC models waterfall model, spiral model, and Incremental/Iterative model. *International Journal of Computer Science Issues*, 12(1), 106.

Altameem, E. A. (2015). Impact of Agile methodology on software development. *Computer and Information Science*, 8(2), 9. doi:10.5539/cis.v8n2p9

Awad, M. A. (2005). A comparison between agile and traditional software development methodologies. University of Western Australia.

Boehm, B., Egyed, A., Kwan, J., Port, D., Shah, A., & Madachy, R. (1998). Using the WinWin spiral model: A case study. *Computer*, 31(7), 33–44. doi:10.1109/2.689675

Buchan, J., MacDonell, S. G., & Yang, J. (2019). Effective team onboarding in Agile software development: Techniques and goals. *2019 ACM/IEEE International Symposium on Empirical Software Engineering and Measurement (ESEM)*, 1–11. 10.1109/ESEM.2019.8870189

Cockburn, A., & Highsmith, J. (2001). Agile software development: The people factor. *Computer, 11*(11), 131–133. doi:10.1109/2.963450

Cohen, D., Lindvall, M., & Costa, P. (2004). An introduction to agile methods. *Advances in Computers, 62*(03), 1–66.

Conboy, K., Coyle, S., Wang, X., & Pikkarainen, M. (2011). *People over process: Key people challenges in agile development.* Academic Press.

Cristal, M., Wildt, D., & Prikladnicki, R. (2008). Usage of Scrum practices within a global company. *2008 IEEE International Conference on Global Software Engineering*, 222–226. 10.1109/ICGSE.2008.34

Dikert, K., Paasivaara, M., & Lassenius, C. (2016). Challenges and success factors for large-scale agile transformations: A systematic literature review. *Journal of Systems and Software, 119*, 87–108. doi:10.1016/j.jss.2016.06.013

Dingsøyr, T., Falessi, D., & Power, K. (2019). Agile Development at Scale: The Next Frontier. *IEEE Software, 36*(2), 30–38. doi:10.1109/MS.2018.2884884

Dingsøyr, T., & Moe, N. B. (2014). Towards principles of large-scale agile development. *International Conference on Agile Software Development*, 1–8.

Dzamashvili Fogelström, N., Gorschek, T., Svahnberg, M., & Olsson, P. (2010). The impact of agile principles on market-driven software product development. *Journal of Software Maintenance and Evolution: Research and Practice, 22*(1), 53–80. doi:10.1002pip.420

Ebert, C. (2018). 50 Years of Software Engineering: Progress and Perils. *IEEE Software, 35*(5), 94–101. doi:10.1109/MS.2018.3571228

Flyvbjerg, B., Bruzelius, N., & Rothengatter, W. (2003). *Megaprojects and risk: An anatomy of ambition.* Cambridge University Press. doi:10.1017/CBO9781107050891

Fowler, M., & Highsmith, J. (2001). The agile manifesto. *Software Development, 9*(8), 28–35.

Fuchs, C., & Hess, T. (2018). *Becoming agile in the digital transformation: The process of a large-scale agile transformation.* Academic Press.

Highsmith, J., & Cockburn, A. (2001). Agile software development: The business of innovation. *Computer, 34*(9), 120–127. doi:10.1109/2.947100

Hoda, R., & Murugesan, L. K. (2016). Multi-level agile project management challenges: A self-organizing team perspective. *Journal of Systems and Software, 117*, 245–257. doi:10.1016/j.jss.2016.02.049

Hoda, R., Salleh, N., & Grundy, J. (2018). The rise and evolution of agile software development. *IEEE Software, 35*(5), 58–63. doi:10.1109/MS.2018.290111318

Hohl, P., Klünder, J., van Bennekum, A., Lockard, R., Gifford, J., Münch, J., Stupperich, M., & Schneider, K. (2018). Back to the future: Origins and directions of the "Agile Manifesto"–views of the originators. *Journal of Software Engineering Research and Development, 6*(1), 15. doi:10.118640411-018-0059-z

Janes, A. A., & Succi, G. (2012). The dark side of agile software development. *Proceedings of the ACM International Symposium on New Ideas, New Paradigms, and Reflections on Programming and Software,* 215–228. 10.1145/2384592.2384612

Keller, A., Rössle, A., Sheik, R., Thell, H., & Westmark, F. (2019). *Issues with Scrum-of-Scrums.* Academic Press.

Kumar, G., & Bhatia, P. K. (2012). Impact of agile methodology on software development process. *International Journal of Computer Technology and Electronics Engineering, 2*(4), 46–50.

Laanti, M., Similä, J., & Abrahamsson, P. (2013). Definitions of agile software development and agility. *European Conference on Software Process Improvement,* 247–258. 10.1007/978-3-642-39179-8_22

Lautert, T., Neto, A. G. S. S., & Kozievitch, N. P. (2019). A survey on agile practices and challenges of a global software development team. *Brazilian Workshop on Agile Methods,* 128–143. 10.1007/978-3-030-36701-5_11

Lous, P., Tell, P., Michelsen, C. B., Dittrich, Y., & Ebdrup, A. (2018). From Scrum to Agile: A journey to tackle the challenges of distributed development in an Agile team. *Proceedings of the 2018 International Conference on Software and System Process,* 11–20. 10.1145/3202710.3203149

McCormick, M. (2012). *Waterfall vs. Agile methodology.* MPCS.

Mundra, A., Misra, S., & Dhawale, C. A. (2013). Practical scrum-scrum team: Way to produce successful and quality software. *2013 13th International Conference on Computational Science and Its Applications,* 119–123.

Muntean, M., & Surcel, T. (2013). Agile BI-The Future of BI. *Informatica Economica, 17*(3).

Nerur, S., Mahapatra, R., & Mangalaraj, G. (2005). Challenges of migrating to agile methodologies. *Communications of the ACM, 48*(5), 72–78. doi:10.1145/1060710.1060712

Nuottila, J., Aaltonen, K., & Kujala, J. (2016). Challenges of adopting agile methods in a public organization. *International Journal of Information Systems and Project Management, 4*(3), 65–85.

Paasivaara, M., Behm, B., Lassenius, C., & Hallikainen, M. (2018). Large-scale agile transformation at Ericsson: A case study. *Empirical Software Engineering, 23*(5), 2550–2596. doi:10.100710664-017-9555-8

Paasivaara, M., Lassenius, C., & Heikkilä, V. T. (2012). Inter-team coordination in large-scale globally distributed scrum: Do scrum-of-scrums really work? *Proceedings of the ACM-IEEE International Symposium on Empirical Software Engineering and Measurement,* 235–238. 10.1145/2372251.2372294

Papadopoulos, G. (2015). Moving from traditional to agile software development methodologies also on large, distributed projects. *Procedia: Social and Behavioral Sciences, 175,* 455–463. doi:10.1016/j.sbspro.2015.01.1223

Paulk, M. C. (2002). Agile methodologies and process discipline. *Institute for Software Research, 3,* 15–18.

Pinto, M. B., & Pinto, J. K. (1990). Project team communication and cross-functional cooperation in new program development. *Journal of Product Innovation Management*, 7(3), 200–212. doi:10.1111/1540-5885.730200

Stray, V., Moe, N. B., & Hoda, R. (2018). Autonomous agile teams: Challenges and future directions for research. *Proceedings of the 19th International Conference on Agile Software Development: Companion*, 16. 10.1145/3234152.3234182

Szalvay, V. (2004). *An introduction to agile software development*. Danube Technologies.

Tolfo, C., Wazlawick, R. S., Ferreira, M. G. G., & Forcellini, F. A. (2011). Agile methods and organizational culture: Reflections about cultural levels. *Journal of Software Maintenance and Evolution: Research and Practice*, 23(6), 423–441. doi:10.1002mr.483

Turetken, O., Stojanov, I., & Trienekens, J. J. (2017). Assessing the adoption level of scaled agile development: A maturity model for Scaled Agile Framework. *Journal of Software: Evolution and Process*, 29(6), e1796.

Turk, D., France, R., & Rumpe, B. (2014). *Limitations of agile software processes*. ArXiv Preprint ArXiv:1409.6600

Uludag, Ö., Kleehaus, M., Caprano, C., & Matthes, F. (2018). Identifying and structuring challenges in large-scale agile development based on a structured literature review. *2018 IEEE 22nd International Enterprise Distributed Object Computing Conference (EDOC)*, 191–197.

Uludağ, Ö., Kleehaus, M., Xu, X., & Matthes, F. (2017). Investigating the role of architects in scaling agile frameworks. *2017 IEEE 21st International Enterprise Distributed Object Computing Conference (EDOC)*, 123–132.

Vaidya, A. (2014). Does dad know best, is it better to do less or just be safe? Adapting scaling agile practices into the enterprise. *PNSQC. ORG*, 1–18.

Williams, L. (2010). Agile software development methodologies and practices. *Advances in Computers*, 80, 1–44. doi:10.1016/S0065-2458(10)80001-4

Williams, L., & Cockburn, A. (2003). Agile software development: It's about feedback and change. *IEEE Computer*, 36(6), 39–43. doi:10.1109/MC.2003.1204373

KEY TERMS AND DEFINITIONS

Agile: A software development approach to convey rapid changes in the market and customer requirements on high-quality terms.

Agile Manifesto: An alternative to documentation-driven and heavyweight software development processes.

Kanban: A method in software development which considered as a system for visualizing work and converting it into flow to reduce waste time and maximizing customer value.

Scrum: An iterative and incremental software development to handle drawbacks of traditional development methodologies. It produces many releases in short times based on customer requirements, time pressure, competition, product quality and available resources.

Scrumban: A combination of the benefits of Scrum and Kanban to improve transparency in a short time to release.

Software Development Methodology: A process or series of processes used in software development.

XP: An engineering methodology consisting of code-focused practices to ensure high quality of development.

Chapter 11
A Framework for Analyzing Structural Mechanisms Deployed to Support Traditional and Agile Methods:
Making Sense of "Democratization" in the Software Development Workplace

Michal Dolezel

https://orcid.org/0000-0002-5963-5145
University of Economics, Prague, Czech Republic

Alena Buchalcevova

https://orcid.org/0000-0002-8185-5208
University of Economics, Prague, Czech Republic

ABSTRACT

People rely on structures to make their worlds orderly. This chapter conceptually probes into the problem of the differences between organizational structures deployed in traditional and agile environments. The authors develop an argument that all common forms of organizational entities can be classified by involving a two-dimensional classification scheme. Specifically, they constructed a typology to examine the issues of formal vs. informal authority, and disciplinarity vs. cross-functionality in terms of their significance for traditional and agile software development workplaces. Some examples of concrete organizational forms—including traditional project team, independent test team, self-organizing agile team and developers' community of practice—are discussed. In sum, they argue that by employing this classification scheme, they can theorize the nature of the on-going structural shift observed in conjunction with deploying agile software development methods. They acknowledge that the structures have fundamentally changed, terming the move "democratization" in the software development workplace.

DOI: 10.4018/978-1-7998-4165-4.ch011

INTRODUCTION

Over the last two decades, Agile Software Development Methods (ASDMs) have rapidly grown in popularity. While ASDMs were originally coined by a group of "organizational anarchists" (Fowler & Highsmith, 2001) who wanted to "undo the damage that waterfall had done to ... [the software development] profession" (Schwaber, 2013), the methods seem to be nowadays widely accepted as *the* mainstream way of software development. The shift from the plan-driven methods to ASDMs can be characterized as a move from the rigorous and well-defined processes towards rapid, people-oriented and customer-centered software practices (Cohn, 2010). Indeed, the shift was supposed to also bring some fundamental changes in the overall philosophy and value-orientation with regard to software development activities. These changes were exemplified in the Agile manifesto and its twelve principles (Fowler & Highsmith, 2001). However, despite the huge attention which the Agile manifesto attracted in the past decade, the question whether it is yet making a real, on-going impact remains open. In our view, this may be due to the essential fluidity of the Agile manifesto, despite the fluidity being intentional (Hohl et al., 2018).

In contrast to being fluid and uncertain, in many aspects of their everyday lives people naturally tend to look for tangible guiding principles and structures. In that sense, social psychologists argue that "structure provides people with the means to achieve their desired ends", as "[w]hen the world is orderly and structured, people can make sense of events" and predict the future (Laurin & Kay, 2017). Notably in the world of work, structures play an important role. In this context, a structure means a generic mechanism allowing workers to get their work done. In particular, organizational structures, which are typically over-simplistically represented by corporate organizational charts, are frequently used in practice and examined by management scholars (Daft et al., 2010; Pugh et al., 1969). It is reasonable to expect that software teams are no exception in their need for a structure.

Apparently, due to ASDMs in general, and scaled agile frameworks in particular, the commonly used approaches to organizational structuring within the software world have changed during the last decade or so. It appears that software practitioners hold that the structures which previously worked in plan-driven settings (e.g. silo-ed functional teams) are now partly or fully dysfunctional in agile settings (Noordeloos et al., 2012). Also, emerging structuring mechanisms such as cross-functional teams, communities of practice (Cohn, 2010), agile centers of excellence (Knaster & Leffingwell, 2019), agile chapters and guilds (Smite et al., 2019) etc. have appeared in the organizational repertoires of software development enterprises. One of key drivers for the adoption of these structures seem to be the growing popularity of scaled agile frameworks. These frameworks now play a dominant role by demonstrating how to conduct and structure software development activities in an agile manner at a large scale (Ebert & Paasivaara, 2017; Kalenda et al., 2018). In some of these frameworks, it is possible to find a prescription of the role delineation to be implemented (Smite et al., 2019), which is an important structural aspect of modern organizations (Daft et al., 2010).

In sum, we believe that the issues such as how practitioners structure the fluid world of ASDMs, and whether they do so at all, are of great practical and theoretical relevance. Moreover, the current "restructuring" trend, i.e. the move from certain type of structures to others, is an interesting phenomenon *per se*. In particular, a deeper understanding of the emerging agile organizational structures may help software leaders and managers to understand the nature of the shift from traditional to agile methods. Also, it may help them to choose an appropriate structure by finding a fit between their context and available organizational options. In addition, we propose that the present theory-founded analysis can stimulate further research on this currently under-researched topic. Therefore, the question we pose herein is:

What is the impact of the shift from plan-driven to agile methods on the selected structural aspects of the software development organization? In this chapter, we conceptualize this problem by introducing a typology of organizational arrangements through demonstrating the influence of two important dimensions – namely, functional orientation and authority.

The chapter is organized as follows. Section 2 reviews the theoretical foundations. Then, Section 3 introduces the typology. Next, Section 4 discusses the selected aspects of the typology and its application. After that, Section 5 demonstrates how the typology can be used. Finally, Section 6 provides concluding remarks.

THEORETICAL PRELIMINARIES

Below we provide the starting point for our typology construction effort by presenting theoretical foundations. Specifically, Section 2.1 outlines three core concepts. Expanding on them, Sections 2.2 and 2.3 define the role of authority and functional orientation, respectively.

Examining the Context Beyond a Particular Software Team

We theoretically frame the core of the organizational structuring activities outlined in Section 1 as the issue of designing effective inter- and intra-team Communication, Coordination and Integration mechanisms (Daft et al., 2010), further abbreviated as **CCI**. The definitions of these fundamental concepts are provided in Table 1.

Table 1. Definitions of core concepts

Concept	Definition
Communication	The process of "imparting or interchanging thoughts, opinions, or information by speech, writing, or sign" (Mishra & Mishra, 2008)
Coordination	The process of "managing dependencies between activities" (Malone & Crowston, 1994) The process of "harmonious adjustment or interaction of different people or things to achieve a goal or effect" (Mishra & Mishra, 2008)
Integration	The process of "achieving unity of effort among the various subsystems in the accomplishment of the organization's task" (Lawrence & Lorsch, 1967)

In general, software development is a concord of activities occurring not only between software workers seen as individual players, but many times also between whole organizational entities (i.e. software teams) seen as uniform people aggregates. To elaborate on the latter abstract notion, not only individual people, but also whole teams, are expected to interact with their counterparts in order to get the work done (Begel et al., 2009). Stated more accurately, for an effective performance of their work duties, software workforce must implement and utilize effective inter and intra-team CCI mechanisms, supplemented with appropriate decision-making patterns and management responsibilities (Kalliamvakou et al., 2017).

In a pursuit of consistency, the actions of individual team members are expected to be aligned with a collective will of the aggregate they are members of. Among the CCI aspects, integration seems to be a salient set of mechanisms for preventing conflicts among software professionals. For example, a "silo mentality" among various software professions is an issue claimed to be resolvable by introducing more integrated organizational models (Jesse, 2018). Similarly, some companies experiment with a software role re-definition by integrating previously separated roles together, naming such model "Combined Software Engineering" (Dolezel & Felderer, 2018).

It is important to note that, in principle, a number of possible CCI patterns and means are available for use alongside organizational structures. To briefly illustrate the richness and broadness of the repertoire, the work of Bick et al. (2018) stresses the importance of inter-team planning meetings. Next, Šmite et al. (2017) identified six distinct mechanisms for networking, one of them being associated with software workforce's participation in forums and communities of practice. Finally, Bjørnson et al. (2018) propose that there are three crucial enabling mechanisms at the inter-team level: shared mental models, closed-loop communication and trust.

Aside from the above less-tangible, mostly informal aspects of CCI, research literature in the field of management studies and information systems commonly use the term "structural overlays" to denote a more formalized organizational arrangement (Balaji & Brown, 2014). Along this line of research, structural overlays are understood as a broad concept, encompassing, for example, also governance committees and various liaison roles. Similarly, in the software engineering field, Bannerman (2009) introduced the concept of Software Development Governance (SDG). In his understanding, governance means "managing the management function of the organization" (Bannerman, 2009). A similar view is particularly popular in research literature focusing on IT Governance (Brown & Grant, 2005). Accordingly, SDG's main purpose is "to establish how the organization's software development capability is sustained (in terms of structures, processes and relational mechanisms) to meet its engineering and business needs" (Bannerman, 2009).

In line with the cited research, we assume that in order to analyze organizational mechanisms and patterns holistically, it is necessary to look beyond the immediate horizon, i.e. beyond individual software teams. That means, an individual or single-team centered perspective seems to be insufficient when trying to gather a complete snapshot of the CCI vehicles implemented in a software enterprise. Therefore, our main aim is to contrast these entities against each other, and inductively derive certain conclusions about their essential features. We expect that those conclusions should be generalizable to a broader population of CCI entities encountered in the software industry. Such analysis is to provide important insights about the nature of the shift from traditional methods to ASDMs. In this case, we mostly rely on two important aspects: (i) authority, a concept adopted from sociology; (ii) functional orientation, a concept adopted from management and organizational studies.

Authority

The on-line Cambridge dictionary[1] defines authority as "the moral or legal right or ability to control". In our everyday lives, we have been greatly influenced by numerous authorities. For example, obeying parental authority was a natural act during certain parts of our lives. As adults, we respect both formal and informal authorities, attributable to concrete people and institutions. Here we draw upon the concept of authority as defined by the European sociologist Max Weber (Shepard, 2013). Weber distinguished among three types of authority: (i) traditional, which is based on long-established norms, customs and patterns in society, (ii) legal-rational, which "derives from legal norms" (Spencer & Spencer, 1970), and

(iii) charismatic, which can be associated with a concrete person and his/her behavior strongly appealing to others. See Table 2 for a summary with examples.

Table 2. Forms of authority in the societal and organizational context (adapted from Shepard, 2013)

Type of authority	Essential mechanism	Example
Charismatic	Based on a leader's personal qualities	*Society:* Power of charismatic and influential figures of the public life, e.g. Dalai Lama or Nelson Mandela
		Modern organizations: Power of informal influencers (i.e. people with trust and respect) within an organization
Traditional	Rooted in customs, habits and rituals	*Society:* Power of early kings based on divine right (i.e. a belief that power is given to them by God)
		Modern organizations: Significant decision-making authority in an area, which is exercised by a person or department for a number of years or even decades, while not being formally mandated
Rational-legal	Associated with a formally defined standing or position	*Society:* Power of the political representation of a country with a democratic constitution
		Modern organizations: Power of the board of directors

In reality, the above types of authority can be commonly mixed. For example, the Queen of the United Kingdom holds both rational-legal and traditional, and perhaps also charismatic authority.

In the realm of organizations, authority is one of the essential mechanisms which most organizations are enacted by. In that sense, Weber's framework is accepted as a theoretical basis which his successors in the field of organizational sociology frequently build upon (Graham, 1991). Naturally, for the purpose of organizational analysis, the framework needs to be conceptually adapted. To give an example, rational-legal organizational authority can be viewed as "employees' belief in the legality of [organizational] rules and the right of those elevated to positions of authority to issue commands" (Daft et al., 2010). Similarly, charismatic authority can serve as a conceptual basis for contrasting charismatic, transformational and servant leadership in organizations (Graham, 1991). We consider the remaining type of Weberian authority, i.e. traditional authority, as unsuitable for the analysis of modern software organizations.

Software Disciplines and Their Functional Orientation (i.e. "Silo-ism")

Within the broad field of computing (Denning, 2018), it is possible to recognize contours of several software engineering (SE) *disciplines*. (Note that the term "discipline" was introduced by RUP (Kroll & Kruchten, 2003) and as such it is used in a different, less encompassing sense than in the case of academic disciplines.) Their role has been commonly seen as fundamentally structuring the software development landscape. In metaphorical terms, particular SE disciplines can be thought of as abstract *containers* for various SE activities, roles, responsibilities and resulting artefacts within a given domain of expertise. Put simply, one SE discipline groups those SE activities that have a common denominator. Examples of the SE disciplines include software testing and software architecture. These are also commonly treated as two distinct SE professions in industry, despite the fact that both are often subsumed into the generic profession of software engineering (Miller & Voas, 2008). Importantly, not all roles found within software development methods always exist in the reality of software development companies (Borges et al., 2012).

In the following text, for the sake of simplicity, we do not draw a clear-cut separator between the SE disciplines defined in the software development methods vs. practice-based professions. While their mutual relationship is complex and certainly not 1-to-1, the extent of this chapter does not allow a more nuanced discussion than a few notes below.

Regarding the issue of functional orientation in software development, creating a functional organizational structure means putting professionals with alike responsibilities together in an organizational sense (Quinnan, 2010). Management theory suggests that the key benefit of this type of structuring is in having "all human knowledge and skills with respect to specific activities ... consolidated, providing a valuable depth of knowledge" (Daft et al., 2010). Until recently, functional organizational structures had been arguably the most popular way of organizing the SE activities, resonating greatly with the disciplinary separation. Specifically, functional organizational structures were used to introduce a set-up when "several discipline-oriented departments" provided their professionals into software programs, with each of these professionals being "highly qualified in a fairly narrow area" (Quinnan, 2010).

With the advent of agile development, however, this thinking has been fundamentally reconsidered. In essence, the proponents of agile approaches argue that functional structures are being materialized as unwanted silos, which moreover results in a "deep-rooted dependency on the organizational hierarchy" (Schatz & Abdelshafi, 2005). This contrarian logic drives presently the boom of organizational efforts that are to "break down organizational silos" in order to introduce agility in software organizations (Motingoe & Langerman, 2019). However, breaking down silos should be followed by looking for new forms of structural mechanisms. This is due to the silos having not only unwanted aspects, but also a number of positive. In particular, they serve as a home base for disciplinary professionalism.

TYPOLOGY DEVELOPMENT

In this section, we develop a typology of basic organizational structures seen in traditional and agile environments.

Essentials

Researchers typically use typologies as means for contrasting complex relationships among various instances of a concept. In that sense, typologies are considered to be effective means for theory-building (Reynolds, 2016), although many scholars do not consider typologies being theories *per-se* (Stol & Fitzgerald, 2015). Typology-development efforts can commonly be found in many areas of the social sciences, including management studies (Cornelissen, 2017). Aside from typologies, taxonomies have been frequently used for presenting a similar type of research outputs (Pugh et al., 1969). In the software engineering domain, the latter term seems to be more common than the former, especially when the presented output is based on empirical research results (Ralph, 2018).

In our case, we followed the idea that typologies and taxonomies can result from various theory-building endeavors, both empirical (Pugh et al., 1969) and conceptual (Cornelissen, 2017). Being the latter case, our approach to theory-building was driven by two underlying notions. Firstly, the discussions that revolve around the role of formal and informal authority in software development teams have intensified recently, mainly thanks to the popularity of the self-organization notion (Hoda et al., 2010). We thus held that distinguishing between formally organized and self-organized teams is an important aspect of the analysis of organizational structures in software development. Secondly, functional specialization is among the top discriminating attributes that have been traditionally used to characterize organizational structures in management studies (Pugh et al., 1969). We thus chose this criterion as the second discriminator.

In sum, our initial position is that every organizational structure can be defined in terms of a unique combination of the authority and functional orientation modes. Moreover, it can be characterized by a set of three CCI mechanisms we have defined in Table 1. The reason for distinguishing among different authority and functional orientation modes is to demonstrate that managers and administrators carrying out their duties have a possibility to choose from a number of fundamentally different organizational means. Illustrating the nature of the choice, Morgan (2006) argued that one's preference of a concrete organizational mechanism is closely related with his/her inner beliefs about the world of work, and that the chosen mechanism also says something about his/her own personality. For example, in the software engineering domain, many professionals might tend to prefer largely mechanistic views of organizations based on the fact they imagine ideal organizations as, stated metaphorically, *well-oiled machines*. To the contrary, the proponents of agile methods have been strong advocates of seeing organizations as living organisms or, more precisely, complex adaptive systems (Kautz & Zumpe, 2008).

Typology

The resulting typology is portrayed in Figure 1, distinguishing four ideal types of organizational entities. The view proposed is that there are two fundamental decisions which must be made when organizing activities within the domain of software engineering. Put differently, there are two important variables for characterizing any organizational entity related to software development.

First, the type of authority discussed in Section 2 determines a number of distinct organizational features. How authority is exercised in a particular organizational entity is closely related to the issues of power and control, both being bound to the matter of formal chain of command. Interestingly, self-management modes of organizing seem to presently outgrow hierarchical modes, which were considered the dominant way in the past (Nalebuff & Brandenburger, 1997). Based on this finding, the dichotomy portrayed by the poles of *Ad-hoc* or non-formalized authority and *Rational-legal* or formalized authority has been chosen as the first discriminator. (Note that the term "ad-hoc authority" refers not only to the concept of charismatic authority defined in Section 2.2, but also to additional hypothetical forms of authority that are principally different from the ratio-legal one – e.g. *consensus-based authority*.)

Second, it should be considered whether the organizational entity is to promote segregation among different SE disciplines/professions. As suggested in Section 2, certain traces indicate the possibility that many SE professionals identify with a certain SE discipline (e.g. software testing, software architecture etc.). However, little consensus exists whether a discipline-oriented approach should be prioritized over cross-functionality when organizing software teams. Hence, it is meaningful to treat this criterion as an important discriminator.

Together, combining the above two variables, the typology matrix results in four possible organizational modes, which are discussed in detail below. A brief description of the entities commonly belonging to the four quadrants is also provided.

Figure 1. Typology matrix of organizational entities in traditional and agile organizational settings

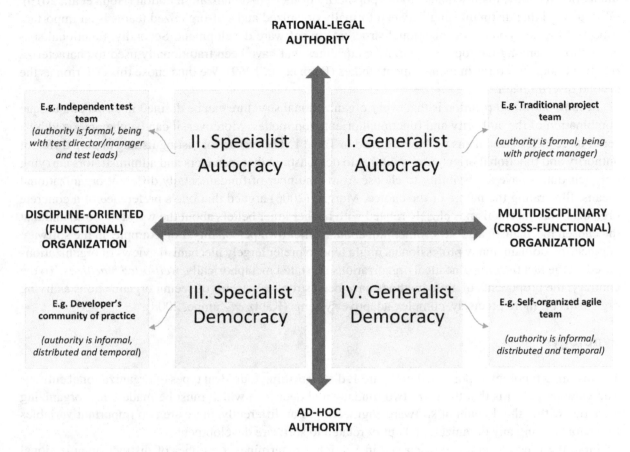

Generalist autocracy (Quadrant I). For organizational entities in Quadrant I, *rational-legal authority* and *multidisciplinarity* are the key characteristics. These entities can be called *Generalist autocracies*. This is to say authority and decision-making are predominantly associated with a single person or a small subgroup of people (i.e. a single manager or a few managers), and this person (subgroup) is expected to be a generalist in terms of his/her ability of making sense of a wide range of problems brought by more specialized members of the entity. In general, forming a single organizational entity by putting together a team of specialists with a different background and work focus is to achieve synergies through their multidisciplinary collaboration (Quinnan, 2010). Arguably, based on this central promise, such an approach has become a de-facto standard in the domain of software project management during the past decades. By contrast, the potential disadvantage of this approach is differing expectations and espoused values of the team members, possibly resulting in conflicts (Zhang et al., 2014).

Despite the strong bonds of this organizational mode to the general project management principles, additional organizational entities falling under this category can be certainly identified. These may include, for example, a cross-functional Systems & Software Capability Board that govern the activities of engineering councils (Bannerman, 2009); static product development teams led by a product development manager in product-focused development organizations – i.e. when individual projects led by project managers are spawned only for customer-centric customizations (Vähäniitty & Rautiainen, 2005); and some Software Process Improvement (SPI) initiatives carried-out through bureaucratic organizational infrastructures – e.g. when a generalist SPI department with a broad process focus is created (Ngwenyama & Nielsen, 2013).

Generalist Democracy (Quadrant IV)

These organizational entities are defined by the combination of *ad-hoc authority* and *multidisciplinarity*. We call these entities *Generalist democracies*, as they do not exhibit a centralized authority. Instead, authority may be less obvious – either evenly distributed among the members of the entity, or even highly volatile. Being in this configuration principally on their own, specialists must find a common ground to be able to work effectively together. In other words, there is no central authority to negotiate and translate meanings among the members involved, or to solve their conflicts. This organizational mode will typically be associated with ASDMs and the concept of team self-organization (Cohn, 2010).

However, it is worth mentioning that while the concept of self-organization (i.e. ad-hoc authority) has been heavily popularized in connection with ASDMs, it has not come out of nowhere. For example, Humphrey introduced a very similar concept of self-directed teams in his work on *Team Software Process* in the late 1990s (Humphrey, 1998). Tracing the roots even more to the past, the concept of self-managed, voluntarism-driven quality circles was introduced by Kaoru Ishikawa as a part of the "Japanese way" to quality control in manufacturing in 1985 (Lillrank, 1995). While partly forgotten, these seminal organizational concepts (entities) are infrequently mentioned in the software engineering domain even nowadays.

Specialist Autocracy (Quadrant II)

The entities labeled *Specialist autocracies* and located in Quadrant II are those with the key attributes of *rational-legal authority* and *discipline-oriented organization*. Similarly to *Generalist autocracy*, authority is expected to be in the hands of a single person or a small subgroup of people. In contrast to *Generalist autocracy*, the entities are uniform in terms of the profession or specialization they are dominantly formed by.

During the typology development process, we expected to see these entities being associated primarily with plan-driven or traditional methods. Nevertheless, exploring the state of knowledge regarding these entities, we found that extant SE research literature says surprisingly little about the structural organization of software-developing enterprises working in the plan-driven methods paradigm (see also Bannerman, 2009). Nonetheless, an implicit assumption seemed to be that organizational functions responsible for software development and software operations were frequently separated (Quinnan, 2010), at least in large enterprises. Moreover, software development professionals (e.g., developers, testers, architects) were frequently organized within additional disciplinary "silos" (Motingoe & Langerman, 2019). While the size of the silo could be variable (e.g. a team, group, department, functional division etc.), the key principle (i.e. putting alike skills together) remained the same. As explained in Section 2, similar organizational mechanisms were implemented largely with the aim to effectively and efficiently collect, keep and share specialized domain expertise (Daft et al., 2010). In addition, the mechanism might contribute to an increase in job satisfaction by offering staff members more diverse career opportunities (C. Jones, 2010).

Specialist Democracy (Quadrant III)

Finally, within the last type of entities called *Specialist democracy*, *ad-hoc authority is* combined with *discipline-oriented organization*. In essence, authority is informal, possibly being repeatedly negotiated through various mechanisms. This may provide opportunities for charismatic leaders to get into power (see Section 2.2). Also, other means of acquiring power or reaching group consensus are possible in these entities (e.g., via polling).

We speculate that these entities may be slightly less common. In any case, examples in the software development world include some profession-oriented communities of practice (CoPs), for example Developer CoPs (Paasivaara & Lassenius, 2014) and CoPs focused on particular technologies (e.g. a programming language). Also, Architecture Councils, where cross-team decisions are expected to be formed on a peer-to-peer basis (Clerc et al., 2011) can be mentioned.

TYPOLOGY APPLICATION

This section illustrates how the typology can be used for demonstrating the importance of differences between formal and informal authority, and functional and non-functional orientation of selected organizational entities. For this purpose, we selected four examples: (i) Traditional project team (Section 4.1); (ii) Self-organizing Scrum team (Section 4.2); Independent test team (Section 4.3); Developer's Community of Practice (Section 4.4). By doing so, we also demonstrate the usability and viability of the typology.

Traditional Project Team as a Generalist Autocracy

Historically, software development activities were structured through defining tasks and responsibilities, which together formed a conceptual basis of the first software development lifecycle models (Kneuper, 2017). Moreover, the domain of software engineering took a lot of inspiration from the project management world. This fact is quite apparent from the review of certain fundamental software engineering sources. For example, our reading of the Software Engineering Body of Knowledge (SWEBOK; IEEE, 2014) suggests the existence of a strong conceptual bridge to the Project Management Body of Knowledge (PMBOK). The former source notes that, in general, many professionals understand the term "software engineering management" as a synonym for the execution of project management activities within a software development context. In essence, such an understanding strongly promotes the view that a central figure (a project manager) should be designated, and a multidisciplinary entity directed by him/her (a project team) should be formed.

It is therefore not surprising that the organization of software teams has been rooted in common project management principles. Within the project management paradigm, every project is led by a project manager; he/she is "the leader of the team, regardless of what authority the project manager may have over its members" (PMI, 2013). A project team is then "comprised of individuals from different groups with specific subject matter knowledge or with a specific skill set to carry out the work of the project" (ibid.). For the sake of simplicity we assume that the project team works within a "projectized" organization structure, as defined by the PMBOK (PMI, 2013). The term "projectized" is used to denote a set-up in which skills from different domains are brought into the project team by people with different specialization. Hence traditional project teams can be labelled as *Generalist autocracies*.

Communication, Coordination and Integration

First and foremost, it should be noted that while different project managers may certainly exhibit very different management styles, a common belief is that many organizations appoint "a project manager (PM) with 'command and control' responsibilities" (Taylor, 2016). Without doubts, such a mentality would influence the atmosphere in the team to a great extent. Therefore, a typical project team will be mobilized by directive means of rational-legal authority. This management style fundamentally influences all CCI mechanisms, and it can be expected that those mechanisms will typically be centralized (Schwaber, 2004). For example, some project managers may insist on being the "hubs" in the majority of communication occurring within the project team, authorizing all key decisions. However, it is increasingly recognized that a number of common issues in the modern organizational world can be sorted-out by decentralizing decision-making through empowering people (Daft et al., 2010).

What we consider interesting is that previous research in management studies clearly shows that the project management profession represented a field with quite a convergent view on what constitutes appropriate professional knowledge, having strong roots in Tayloristic organizational notions (Hodgson, 2002) and the above mentioned command&control management styles. Yet, this mechanistic view seems to be significantly re-defined today (Fontana et al., 2014). This development opens up a possibility to move software development activities to another quadrant of our typology.

Self-Organizing Scrum Team as a Generalist Democracy

As already stated in Section 1, the Agile Manifesto, published in 2001, articulated 4 values and 12 principles. Among the principles, team self-organization took a prominent position. For the proponents of this philosophy, relying on a directive project manager role is hardly acceptable (Cohn, 2010; Schwaber, 2004). In their research, Hoda, Noble and Marshall (2010) compare agile leadership with traditional project management. They argue that "Leadership in Agile teams is distributed, providing *subtle control and direction* to the team … in contrast to *centralized management* in traditional [project] teams" (italics ours).

Speaking about the popularity of different agile methods, Scrum and its derivates are among the most popular (Dolezel et al., 2019). While Scrum can be classified as a project management framework (Schwaber, 2004), it is important to clarify certain substantial differences between the concept of software project management exemplified above and Scrum. Notably, practitioner literature covering Scrum argues for a new type of leadership role – the Scrum Master (McKenna, 2016):

A Scrum Master is the servant leader of the Scrum team. … [But, note that the] Scrum Master is not a development manager with a cool, new name. In Scrum, the team is supposed to be self-managed. In other words, they manage themselves.

According to the presented perspective, Scrum teams (and more broadly agile teams) are enacted by invoking a different form of authority than in the previous case. Our typology labels such a democratic type of authority as *ad-hoc authority*. As such, this authority would be based on entirely different mechanisms than in the case of rational-legal authority. Namely, it may be the charisma of natural born leaders (be it or not the Scrum Master) or functional competencies of development team members. Given the broad spectrum of the roles involved, and the reliance on ego-less principles, we see self-organizing Scrum teams as *Generalist Democracies*.

Communication, Coordination and Integration

A number of CCI mechanisms are relevant for self-organizing agile teams. For example in Scrum, a set of ceremonies is defined to facilitate coordination among team members (Schwaber, 2004). Aside from that, team members may coordinate themselves and others through informal communication means. Therefore, it is virtually impossible to put a strict borderline between the concepts of communication and coordination in agile teams. Importantly, communication and personal interactions are key, so that individual team members "can no longer sit in their cubicles and wait to be told exactly what to do" (Cohn, 2010). Naturally, large-scale software development that is based on agile principles brings its own set of additional CCI challenges (Bick et al., 2018).

Regarding integration, agile teams achieve unity, which is the central attribute of integration, primarily through the mechanism of cross-functionality. As Cohn puts it: "the team needs to include everyone necessary to go from idea to implementation" (Cohn, 2010). In other words, the team needs to be integrated, being not dependent on other teams in terms of basic development activities. Another aspect of cross-functionality is put forward by Schwaber: "in situations where everyone is chipping in to build the functionality, you don't have to be a tester to test, or a designer to design" (Schwaber, 2004). Nevertheless, this comes with a price: "When you ask a team to be cross-functional, you are asking them to set aside some of their expertise to become more versatile" (McKenna, 2016). Both these theses seem to be in quite a stark contrast with the view of traditional project teams, representing a total of expertise acquired through involving various SE disciplines/professions.

Independent Test Team as a Specialist Autocracy

The past few decades have seen establishing of certain software engineering professions as fully or partly autonomous. Software testing is an example of such a progress, resulting in many test professionals' believing that a certain level of autonomy in software testing is desirable. For example, the Test Maturity Model Integration (TMMi; TMMi Foundation, 2012) strongly promotes the idea of centralizing the test expertise within the boundaries of a formal organizational entity. As the TMMi convincingly puts it: "Establishing a test organization implies a commitment to better testing and higher-quality software" (TMMi Foundation, 2012). Despite the fact that the proponents of ASDMs call for removing the tester-developer gap by including software testers into self-organized agile teams (Cohn, 2010), independent test teams are still common in many enterprises (TMMi Foundation, 2012).

While some test teams may be very flat, practitioner literature mostly argues that larger test teams are typically organized in a hierarchical manner (J. A. Jones et al., 2009).

Industry specialists often recommend a more hierarchical structure for the testing team. At the top of the hierarchy is a test manager. (In some organizations there may also be a test director who is the managerial head of the test organization.) A typical testing team assigned to a project will consist of 3–4 or more test specialists with a test team leader at the head of each team.

In test organizations and test teams respectively, test directors, test managers, and test team leaders are usually appointed based on their previous experience within the field. Therefore, the entity is ruled by specialists, hence independent testing teams can be called *Specialist Autocracies*.

Communication, Coordination and Integration

In such an environment, designing effective CCI mechanisms may be tricky. In principle, there are two commonly used alternatives. First, work can be carried out within the test organizations (i.e. a silo-ed functional department), which "throw-over-the-wall" their outputs when they are "done" with their part. Arguably, this configuration is quite inflexible. Interestingly, while it brings significant challenges related to effective CCI, it is still being used (J. A. Jones et al., 2009), expectedly due to the alignment with plan-driven and functionally-oriented software development methods (Borges et al., 2012), or due to estimated cost benefits (J. A. Jones et al., 2009).

Second, project teams may be assembled by "borrowing" testers from their functional departments led by a different line manager (e.g. test director/manager) (Daft et al., 2010). The model in which specialists of certain kind formally share an organizational unit while factually working elsewhere is titled "Matrix organization" (Kolodny, 1979). (Imagine the core functional unit of software workers as their *home harbor*, while most of the *real work* happens during frequent *trips* to project teams.)

Broadly speaking, this is a frequent model. For example, C. Jones (2010) argues that

In the software world, matrix organizations are found most often in large companies that employ between perhaps 1,000 and 50,000 total software personnel. These large companies tend to have scores of specialized skills and hundreds of projects going on at the same time.

In this model, one important aspect strongly influences the CCI mechanism. Namely, the line managers still exercise certain level of power and authority over the workers. As there are a number of possible configurations (e.g. weak matrix, balanced matrix, strong matrix), distribution of authority between the line manager and the project manager generally differs (PMI, 2013).

An additional problem factor may arise when different line managers have different work-related goals driven by the corporate hierarchy (Palm & Lindahl, 2015). Then, looking at the project team as an aggregate of people, the goals inherited from their managers may be significantly misaligned. Also, further misalignments between the project goals and line-unit goals may occur (Kolodny, 1979). In sum, despite matrix organization being used for a number of decades, it is not entirely clear up to date how to effectively resolve potential organizational conflicts between the line manager and the project manager in real-world organizations.

Developer's Community of Practice as a Specialist Democracy

Communities of practice (CoP) is a concept that have attracted a particular attention of SE researchers (Paasivaara & Lassenius, 2014). In agile environments, communities of practice are established to help professionals working in cross-functional teams, in which they have limited possibility to deepen their disciplinary knowledge (McKenna, 2016). (This situation can be directly contrasted with the functional organization described in Section 3.4.) Alternatively, the communities are deployed to help solving certain coordination challenges (Bick et al., 2018).

In this section, we examine the situation when communities of practice arise as discipline-centered – i.e. there is one community for Scrum Masters, another for developers working with a specific technology, and yet other for testers (McKenna, 2016). While some of these communities may be officially sanctioned and formalized, the very essence of the concept as used within the SE domain seems to emphasize informal relations and personal authority stemming from individual expertise. In other words, communities of practice have a different purpose than "getting the work done"; they are primarily about personal development, passion and enjoyment (Gilley & Kerno, 2010). Yet, in most organizations they need to be cultivated by managers to survive in the long-run, because voluntarism may clash with formal authority (Wenger et al., 2002).

Stressing the knowledge management aspect of CoPs, Cohn (2010) argues that as communities span development teams they are

a primary mechanism for spreading good ideas among teams and for ensuring desirable levels of consistency or commonality across a set of development teams.

As sharing "good ideas" is often done primarily among members of the same profession, such communities may be labeled *Specialist Democracies*. That means, the community mostly consists of the *equal* members of a particular profession, so that it promotes a peer-to-peer organizational philosophy (Wenger et al., 2002). Nonetheless, some communities may be supported by competency leads or coaches (Paasivaara & Lassenius, 2014).

Communication, Coordination and Integration

As suggested above, communities may be used as a home-base for nurturing diverse CCI mechanisms. When communities are used as a voluntary, personal-development platform, they typically stimulate communication among workers with the same interest. Community meetings may be quite relaxed, having "a loose agenda with discussion items collected by the participants to wiki pages" (Paasivaara & Lassenius, 2014). This suggests highly informal CCI mechanisms. By contrast, when communities have a more formalized role, typically in the coordination of large-scale software development, the CCI mechanism may be more rigorous.

DISCUSSION

Below, we firstly summarize the key theses of this chapter (Section 5.1). Then, in Section 5.2, we sketch how the proposed typology can be used for theorizing. Finally, in Section 5.3, we suggest that the typology highlights an additional, *bigger* idea – that of workplace democratization.

Short Summary

This chapter dealt with selected structural aspects of the software development organization in light of the shift from plan-driven to agile software development methods (ASDMs). To explore this issue, we introduced the novel classification schema of traditional and agile organizational structures, and briefly analyzed four concrete organizational entities which have been commonly implemented by the software industry in relation to software development activities. Our overall goal was to demonstrate that such entities represent an important element of the organizational life of software professionals, who rely on various Communication, Coordination and Integration (CCI) mechanisms in order to get their work done.

Further, we postulated that the type of authority and the level of disciplinary (functional) orientation are the important discriminators when examining the current forms of organizational entities in software development companies. To reiterate, authority can be either rational-legal or ad-hoc, and the entities can be either disciplinary-oriented or multidisciplinary. Our analysis affirmed that the software industry seems to be on a continuing move from the rational-legal/disciplinary organizational configurations towards their ad-hoc/multidisciplinary cousins, as exemplified by the changing nature of organizational structures selected as the examples.

In the next section, we aim to briefly demonstrate how the typology can be used as an analytical vehicle for researchers and practitioners. Aside from demonstrating the usefulness of the typology, we also aim to formulate a rudiment of an emerging theory (Reynolds, 2016) of agile transformations.

Using the Typology to Understand and Predict the Process of Agile Transformation/Transition

To answer the question posed in Introduction, i.e. *What is the impact of the shift from plan-driven to agile methods on the selected structural aspects of the software development organization?*, we now put our findings into the context of a hypothetical agile transformation and adoption. These are two common terms to denote the necessity to change organizational culture and software development practices respectively (Diebold et al., 2019).

Using the proposed typology, we postulate that agile transformations and adoptions will go along the vertical line, following the top-to-bottom direction (i.e. Q.I -> Q.IV portrayed in green and Q.II -> Q.III portrayed in red, see Figure 2). So, in the course of an agile transformation and transition, *autocratic* organizational entities are to become *democratic* organizational entities. To this end, two transformation efforts will typically occur. First, at the individual team level, *Generalist Autocracies* (i.e. traditional project teams, Q.I) will be transformed to *Generalist Democracies* (i.e. self-organized agile teams, Q.IV). Second, at the enterprise level – i.e. with an expected impact on the existing organizational structures, *Specialist autocracies* (i.e. functional departments/divisions, Q.II), which previously served as specialist home-bases for knowledge exchanges, will be dissolved due to not being a fit for purpose in the agile world. Then, *Specialist Democracies* (Q.III) will become the key mechanism for coordination and knowledge sharing among software professionals. Based on the described scenario, we assume that the latter type of transition will be triggered by the former type of transition.

Nevertheless, our typology clearly counts only with ideal instances of the four archetypes, being primarily a theoretical tool (Reynolds, 2016). Therefore, it does not explicitly cover a real-word possibility such as an enterprise is to be transformed from traditional project management to Scrum, while the fact that the underlying management philosophy and culture must be changed as well is being ignored (Taylor, 2016). In principle, the result of such a situation could be a hybrid team entity, which contains fragments of both formal and ad-hoc authority. Then, it is for a careful consideration whether the resulting organizational entity belongs to either of the quadrants (Q.I and Q.IV), or rather overlaps them both. In that sense, it is important to reiterate that real-word reality is complex. Even if a company pursues a "faithful" agile transformation, ASDMs are rarely implemented in their "pure" form (Dolezel et al.,

Figure 2. Agile transformation/transition in light of the typology

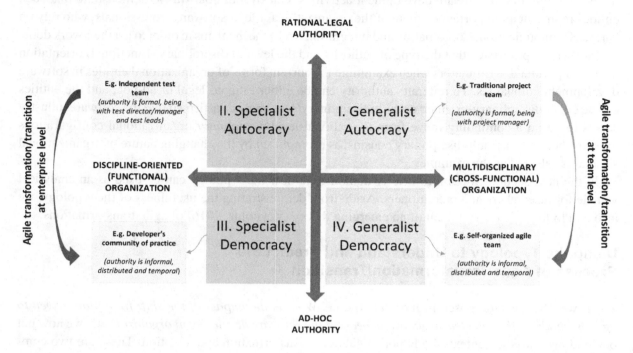

2019). As a result, existing management hierarchies may be preserved, which may result in autonomy and self-organization being merely an illusion (Hodgson & Briand, 2013).

Elaborating on these issues, we believe that a number of academic disciplines have a lot to offer to software engineering at present days. In the following section we thus briefly turn to the phenomenon we term "democratization in the workplace".

Democratization in the Workplace – Insights from other Disciplines

By "democratization" we mean the fundamental change we have conceptualized as a move from the autocratic to democratic archetypes (Figure 2). In general, our perspective has been so far limited to organizational entities which are directly involved in software development. Along this line of thought, the original ideas about agility were formulated by a dissenting group of organizational contrarians (Hohl et al., 2018) . Then, after two decades, the impact of the agile philosophy crossed the borderline of computing. This has become quite obvious recently, looking at the current headlines such as "What to expect from Agile?", which can today be found in respected business administration magazines (Birkinshaw, 2018). Importantly, we suggest that the "democratization process" is a phenomenon catching a significant interest not only in the domain of software engineering. An additional insight from different disciplines can portray a more complete picture. We therefore aim to conceptually connect our observations regarding organizational entities analyzed in this chapter to a global, on-going shift in the world of work.

Doing so, we are able to articulate that the idea of agility resonates well with certain concepts within that domain. Focusing only on a few selected concepts, we firstly mention the catchy ideas of *holacracy* and *empowering organization*, being used by well-known companies such as Zappos and W. L. Gore & Associates respectively. (A particularly convincing story of a working experience in the "lattice" or flat organization, as deployed in the latter company, was given by Pacanowsky (1988) three decades ago). Both these ideas resonate with the seminal thoughts of Laloux presented in his work titled *Reinventing Organizations* (Laloux, 2014), where the concept of *teal organizations*, being "less driven by ego" and more by democratic principles, was introduced. Next, the inception of Lean startup has also attracted a significant scholarly and practitioner interest (Blank, 2013). Finally, Eckstein has recently introduced the concept of *sociocracy* to software engineering researchers by defining it as "an organizational model for scaling agile development" that "do not hinder, but foster agility" (Eckstein, 2016). It seems that both academia and industry currently exhibit quite a high level of enthusiasm with regards to these models.

However, despite all their promising aspects, the "SALT organizational models" (Sociocracy, Agile, Lean startup and Teal) seem to have a number of downsizes too. For example, some Human Resources professionals suggest to remain cautious when it comes to the discussion about the applicability of these models at large scale (Østergaard, 2020).

The SALT group of organizational models ... is really interesting and seductive, and clearly a great codification of how to embrace organizational democracy, personal engagement and business adaptability. They work, and cases of successful implementation keep popping up. And, yes, those models do have a scaling issue. They work very well in small teams or clusters of five, 25, or maybe even 80 employees, but applying that thinking to an organization of thousands of employees is overwhelming.

The present chapter does not give a clear-cut answer on whether the above opinion holds true. In any case, we agree that scalability of every organizational model is a crucial aspect deserving a serious attention.

CONCLUSION

In this chapter, we proposed an approach to analyzing key structural aspects associated with entities commonly used for the organization of software development activities. Furthermore, we highlighted the importance of selected formal and semi-formal organizational arrangements, being a crucial element of software development enterprises nowadays. Broadly speaking, structures are to establish order, which many people naturally look for, and therefore it is important to understand how structures are created, maintained and collapsed. In that sense, we offered a thesis that the software development workplaces seem to presently be "democratizing" themselves through redefining their structural portfolio.

While we believe we have added an important piece to the software engineering body of knowledge, we need to clarify that our work has three important limitations. First, it does not cover the problems of large-scale ASDMs in an adequate level of detail. Still, the presented typology can certainly be used to categorize emerging entities such as squads, guilds, chapters (Smite et al., 2019), and agile centers of excellence (Knaster & Leffingwell, 2019) etc., which are increasingly popular. Second, as we briefly noted in Section 3.2, certain structures support professional development of specialists better than others. While we did not intend to cover aspects such as personnel motivation, we point out to the fact that a future exploration of such factors against the backdrop of structures is of foremost importance. Third, our discussion of the impact with regards to hybrid software development methods (Kuhrmann et al., 2019) was very limited. Given that the representation of hybrid software development methods is significant (Marinho et al., 2019), it would therefore be very reasonable to explore questions such as how hybrid models of authority could look like. Together, these are important stimuli for future work. Overall, we expect to see a growing number of research initiatives focused on structural issues of software development soon, because creating effective organizational structures is an issue of central importance in large-scale ASDMs (Paasivaara & Lassenius, 2014; Smite et al., 2019).

ACKNOWLEDGMENT

This research was supported by the University of Economics, Prague [internal grant number F4/23/2019].

REFERENCES

Balaji, S., & Brown, C. V. (2014). Lateral coordination mechanisms and the moderating role of arrangement characteristics in information systems development outsourcing. *Information Systems Research*, *25*(4), 747–760. doi:10.1287/isre.2014.0556

Bannerman, P. L. (2009). Software development governance: A meta-management perspective. *ICSE Workshop on Software Development Governance (SDG)*, 3–8.

Begel, A., Nagappan, N., Poile, C., & Layman, L. (2009). Coordination in large-scale software teams. *ICSE Workshop on Cooperative and Human Aspects on Software Engineering (CHASE)*, 1–7.

Bick, S., Spohrer, K., Hoda, R., Scheerer, A., & Heinzl, A. (2018). Coordination Challenges in Large-Scale Software Development: A Case Study of Planning Misalignment in Hybrid Settings. *IEEE Transactions on Software Engineering*, *44*(10), 932–950. doi:10.1109/TSE.2017.2730870

Birkinshaw, J. (2018). What to Expect From Agile. *MIT Sloan Management Review*, *59*(2), 39–42.

Bjørnson, F. O., Wijnmaalen, J., & Stettina, C. J. (2018). Inter-team Coordination in Large-Scale Agile Development: A Case Study of Three Enabling Mechanisms. *XP*, 216–231.

Blank, S. (2013). Why the Lean Start-Up Changes Everything. *Harvard Business Review*, *91*(5), 64–68.

Borges, P., Monteiro, P., & MacHado, R. J. (2012). Mapping RUP roles to small software development teams. *Software Quality Days*, 59–70.

Brown, A., & Grant, G. (2005). Framing the frameworks: A review of IT governance research. *Communications of the Association for Information Systems*, *15*, 696–712. doi:10.17705/1CAIS.01538

Clerc, V., Lago, P., & Van Vliet, H. (2011). Architectural knowledge management practices in agile global software development. *6th IEEE International Conference on Global Software Engineering Workshops*, 1–8. 10.1109/ICGSE-W.2011.17

Cohn, M. (2010). *Succeding with Agile*. Addison Wesley.

Cornelissen, J. (2017). Editor's comments: Developing propositions, a process model, or a typology? Addressing the challenges of writing theory without a boilerplate. *Academy of Management Review*, *42*(1), 1–9. doi:10.5465/amr.2016.0196

Daft, R. L., Murphy, J., & Willmott, H. (2010). *Organization Theory and Design*. Cengage Learning.

Denning, P. J. (2018). The profession of IT: The computing profession. *Communications of the ACM*, *61*(3), 33–35. doi:10.1145/3182108

Diebold, P., Theobald, S., Wahl, J., & Rausch, Y. (2019). Stepwise transition to agile: From three agile practices to Kanban adaptation. *Journal of Software: Evolution and Process*, *31*(5), e2167.

Dolezel, M., Buchalcevova, A., & Mencik, M. (2019). The State of Agile Software Development in the Czech Republic: Preliminary Findings Indicate the Dominance of "Abridged" Scrum. *International Conference on Research and Practical Issues of Enterprise Information Systems*, 43–54. 10.1007/978-3-030-37632-1_4

Dolezel, M., & Felderer, M. (2018). Organizational Patterns Between Developers and Testers: Investigating Testers' Autonomy and Role Identity. *Proceedings of the 20th International Conference on Enterprise Information Systems*, *2*, 336–344. 10.5220/0006783703360344

Ebert, C., & Paasivaara, M. (2017). Scaling Agile. *IEEE Software*, *34*(6), 98–103. doi:10.1109/MS.2017.4121226

Eckstein, J. (2016). *Sociocracy - An organization model for large-scale agile development*. XP Workshops.

Fontana, R. M., Fontana, I. M., Da Rosa Garbuio, P. A., Reinehr, S., & Malucelli, A. (2014). Processes versus people: How should agile software development maturity be defined? *Journal of Systems and Software*, *97*, 140–155. doi:10.1016/j.jss.2014.07.030

Fowler, M., & Highsmith, J. (2001). The Agile Manifesto. *Dr. Dobb's Journal*. http://www.drdobbs.com/open-source/the-agile-manifesto/184414755

Gilley, A., & Kerno, S. J. Jr. (2010). Groups, teams, and communities of practice: A comparison. *Advances in Developing Human Resources*, *12*(1), 46–60. doi:10.1177/1523422310365312

Graham, J. W. (1991). Servant-leadership in organizations: Inspirational and moral. *The Leadership Quarterly*, *2*(2), 105–119. doi:10.1016/1048-9843(91)90025-W

Hoda, R., Noble, J., & Marshall, S. (2010). Organizing Self-Organizing Teams. *International Conference on Software Engineering*, 285–294.

Hodgson, D. (2002). Disciplining the professional: The case of Project Management. *Journal of Management Studies*, *39*(6), 803–821. doi:10.1111/1467-6486.00312

Hodgson, D., & Briand, L. (2013). Controlling the uncontrollable: "Agile" teams and illusions of autonomy in creative work. *Work, Employment and Society*, *27*(2), 308–325. doi:10.1177/0950017012460315

Hohl, P., Klünder, J., van Bennekum, A., Lockard, R., Gifford, J., Münch, J., Stupperich, M., & Schneider, K. (2018). Back to the future: Origins and directions of the "Agile Manifesto" – views of the originators. *Journal of Software Engineering Research and Development*, *6*(1), 1–27. doi:10.118640411-018-0059-z

Humphrey, W. S. (1998). Why don't they practice what we preach? *Annals of Software Engineering*, *6*(1/4), 201–222. doi:10.1023/A:1018997029222

IEEE. (2014). *Guide to the Software Engineering Body of Knowledge - v3.0*. IEEE.

Jesse, N. (2018). Organizational Evolution - How Digital Disruption Enforces Organizational Agility. *IFAC PapersOnLine*, *51*(30), 486–491. doi:10.1016/j.ifacol.2018.11.310

Jones, C. (2010). *Software Engineering Best Practices*. McGraw Hill.

Jones, J. A., Grechanik, M., & Van der Hoek, A. (2009). Enabling and enhancing collaborations between software development organizations and independent test agencies. *ICSE Workshop on Cooperative and Human Aspects on Software Engineering (CHASE)*, 56–59. 10.1109/CHASE.2009.5071411

Kalenda, M., Hyna, P., & Rossi, B. (2018). Scaling agile in large organizations: Practices, challenges, and success factors. *Journal of Software: Evolution and Process*, *30*(10), e1954.

Kalliamvakou, E., Bird, C., Zimmermann, T., Begel, A., DeLine, R., & German, D. M. (2017). What Makes a Great Manager of Software Engineers? *IEEE Transactions on Software Engineering*, *45*(1), 87–106. doi:10.1109/TSE.2017.2768368

Kautz, K., & Zumpe, S. (2008). Just Enough Structure at the Edge of Chaos: Agile Information System Development in Practice. *Agile Processes in Software Engineering and Extreme Programming*, 137–146.

Knaster, R., & Leffingwell, D. (2019). *SAFe Distilled*. Scaled Agile, Inc.

Kneuper, R. (2017). Sixty years of software development life cycle models. *IEEE Annals of the History of Computing*, *39*(3), 41–54.

Kolodny, H. F. (1979). Evolution to a Matrix Organization. *Academy of Management Review*, *4*(4), 543–553. doi:10.5465/amr.1979.4498362

Kroll, P., & Kruchten, P. (2003). *Rational Unified Process Made Easy: A Practitioner's Guide to the RUP*. Addison Wesley.

Kuhrmann, M., Diebold, P., Munch, J., Tell, P., Trektere, K., Mc Caffery, F., Vahid, G., Felderer, M., Linssen, O., Hanser, E., & Prause, C. (2019). Hybrid Software Development Approaches in Practice: A European Perspective. *IEEE Software*, *36*(4), 20–31. doi:10.1109/MS.2018.110161245

Laloux, F. (2014). *Reinventing Organizations: A Guide to Creating Organizations Inspired by the Next Stage in Human Consciousness*. Nelson Parker.

Laurin, K., & Kay, A. C. (2017). The Motivational Underpinnings of Belief in God. In Advances in Experimental Social Psychology (Vol. 56, pp. 201–257). Academic Press. doi:10.1016/bs.aesp.2017.02.004

Lawrence, P. R., & Lorsch, J. W. (1967). Differentiation and Integration in Complex Organizations. *Administrative Science Quarterly*, *12*(1), 1–47. doi:10.2307/2391211

Lillrank, P. (1995). The Transfer of Management Innovations from Japan. *Organization Studies*, *16*(6), 971–989. doi:10.1177/017084069501600603

Malone, T. W., & Crowston, K. (1994). The Interdisciplinary Study of Coordination. *ACM Computing Surveys*, *26*(1), 87–118. doi:10.1145/174666.174668

Marinho, M., Noll, J., Richardson, I., & Beecham, S. (2019). Plan-Driven Approaches Are Alive and Kicking in Agile Global Software Development. *International Symposium on Empirical Software Engineering and Measurement (ESEM)*. 10.1109/ESEM.2019.8870168

McKenna, D. (2016). *The Art of Scrum*. CA Technologies. doi:10.1007/978-1-4842-2277-5

Miller, K. W., & Voas, J. (2008). Computer Scientist, Software Engineer, or IT Professional: Which Do You Think You Are? *IT Professional*, *10*(4), 4–6. doi:10.1109/MITP.2008.64

Mishra, D., & Mishra, A. (2008). Workspace environment for collaboration in small software development organization. *International Conference on Cooperative Design, Visualization and Engineering*, 196–203. 10.1007/978-3-540-88011-0_27

Morgan, G. (2006). *Images of Organization* (3rd ed.). Sage.

Motingoe, M., & Langerman, J. J. (2019). New Organisational Models That Break Silos in Organisations to Enable Software Delivery Flow. *International Conference on System Science and Engineering (ICSSE)*, 341–348. 10.1109/ICSSE.2019.8823257

Nalebuff, B., & Brandenburger, A. (1997). Self-organization: The irresistible future of organizing. *Strategy and Leadership*, *25*(6), 28–33. doi:10.1108/eb054655

Ngwenyama, O., & Nielsen, P. A. (2013). Using organizational influence processes to overcome IS implementation barriers: Lessons from a longitudinal case study of SPI implementation. *European Journal of Information Systems*, *23*(2), 205–222. doi:10.1057/ejis.2012.56

Noordeloos, R., Manteli, C., & Van Vliet, H. (2012). From RUP to Scrum in global software development: A case study. *7th International Conference on Global Software Engineering (ICGSE)*, 31–40. 10.1109/ICGSE.2012.11

Østergaard, E. K. (2020, Jan.). Organisations of the future. *HR Future*, 14–15.

Paasivaara, M., & Lassenius, C. (2014). Communities of practice in a large distributed agile software development organization - Case Ericsson. *Information and Software Technology*, *56*(12), 1556–1577. doi:10.1016/j.infsof.2014.06.008

Pacanowsky, M. (1988). Communication in the Empowering Organization. In J. A. Anderson (Ed.), *Communication yearbook 11* (pp. 356–379). Sage.

Palm, K., & Lindahl, M. (2015). A project as a workplace - Observations from project managers in four R&D and project-intensive companies. *International Journal of Project Management*, *33*(4), 828–838. doi:10.1016/j.ijproman.2014.10.002

PMI. (2013). *A Guide to the Project Management Body of Knowledge* (5th ed.).

Pugh, D. S., Hickson, D. J., & Hinings, C. R. (1969). An Empirical Taxonomy of Structures of Work Organizations. *Administrative Science Quarterly*, *14*(1), 115–126. doi:10.2307/2391367

Quinnan, R. E. (2010). The management of software engineering, Part V: Software engineering management practices. *IBM Systems Journal*, *19*(4), 466–477. doi:10.1147j.194.0466

Ralph, P. (2018). Toward Methodological Guidelines for Process Theories and Taxonomies in Software Engineering. *IEEE Transactions on Software Engineering*, *45*(7), 712–735. doi:10.1109/TSE.2018.2796554

Reynolds, P. D. (2016). *Primer in Theory Construction*. Routledge.

Schatz, B., & Abdelshafi, I. (2005). Primavera gets Agile: A successful transition to Agile development. *IEEE Software*, *22*(3), 36–42. doi:10.1109/MS.2005.74

Schwaber, K. (2004). *Agile Project Management with Scrum*. Microsoft Press.

SchwaberK. (2013). *unSAFe at any speed*. https://kenschwaber.wordpress.com/2013/08/06/unsafe-at-any-speed/

Shepard, J. (2013). Sociology (11th ed.). Wadsworth, Cengage Learning.

Smite, D., Moe, N. B., Levinta, G., & Floryan, M. (2019). Spotify Guilds: How to Succeed With Knowledge Sharing in Large-Scale Agile Organizations. *IEEE Software*, *36*(2), 51–57. doi:10.1109/MS.2018.2886178

Šmite, D., Moe, N. B., Šāblis, A., & Wohlin, C. (2017). Software teams and their knowledge networks in large-scale software development. *Information and Software Technology*, *86*, 71–86. doi:10.1016/j.infsof.2017.01.003

Spencer, M. E., & Spencer, M. E. (1970). Weber on Legitimate Norms and Authority. *The British Journal of Sociology*, *21*(2), 123–134. doi:10.2307/588403 PMID:4928951

Stol, K. J., & Fitzgerald, B. (2015). Theory-oriented software engineering. *Science of Computer Programming*, *101*, 79–98. doi:10.1016/j.scico.2014.11.010

Taylor, K. J. (2016). Adopting Agile software development: The project manager experience. *Information Technology & People*, *29*(4), 670–687. doi:10.1108/ITP-02-2014-0031

TMMi Foundation. (2012). *Test Maturity Model Integration R1.2*. https://www.tmmi.org/tmmi-documents/

Vähäniitty, J., & Rautiainen, K. (2005). Towards an Approach for Managing the Development Portfolio in Small Product-Oriented Software Companies. *38th Hawaii International Conference on System Sciences*. 10.1109/HICSS.2005.636

Wenger, E., McDermott, R., & Snyder, W. M. (2002). *Cultivating Communities of Practice*. Harvard Business School Press.

Zhang, X., Stafford, T. F., Dhaliwal, J. S., Gillenson, M. L., & Moeller, G. (2014). Sources of conflict between developers and testers in software development. *Information & Management*, *51*(1), 13–26. doi:10.1016/j.im.2013.09.006

KEY TERMS AND DEFINITIONS

Ad-Hoc Authority: A form of authority enacted and exercised without a formal basis.

Cross-Functionality: An organizational principle that follows the idea of putting *diverse* competencies and expertise together, expectedly resulting in a synergistic effect.

Democratization: A metaphorical term used to characterize the move from traditional to agile organizational structures and management principles (here examined within the context of software development activities).

Functional Orientation: An organizational principle that follows the idea of intensifying *alike* competencies in terms of their segregation from competencies of a different nature (e.g. software analysis from software testing).

Rational-Legal Authority: A form of authority that stems from a formal position or standing.

Structure: An arrangement that is to introduce stability and/or order.

Typology: A form of classification schema with possible theoretical implications.

ENDNOTE

[1]   https://dictionary.cambridge.org/

Chapter 12
Aligning Strategic-Driven Governance of Business IT Services With Their Agile Development:
A Conceptual Modeling-Based Approach

Konstantinos Tsilionis

https://orcid.org/0000-0001-9702-6941
Katholieke Universiteit Leuven, Belgium

Yves Wautelet

https://orcid.org/0000-0002-6560-9787
Katholieke Universiteit Leuven, Belgium

ABSTRACT

Large organizations often describe IT needs in terms of services. IT governance mechanisms ensure investments lead to systems aligned with the long-term objectives. This business and IT alignment is often evaluated at the early stages when a service development decision needs to be taken. Evaluating such an alignment nevertheless requires knowledge and details on the tasks, activities, and requirements that the service is supposed to support. This is incompatible with agile development principles that prescribe to focus on an ad-hoc design built during a sprint. The latter indeed uses an operational approach where value delivered to stakeholders is the driver. This chapter advocates that investment decisions based on (coarse-grained) services is reconcilable with their agile development. It proposes Agile-MoDrIGo, a model-driven IT governance framework using services as scope elements and relying on agile to determine run-time behavior. To this end, the framework uses parallel top-down and bottom-up approaches based on conceptual models where integration is ensured by a middle layer.

DOI: 10.4018/978-1-7998-4165-4.ch012

INTRODUCTION

For years now, IT departments have been structuring themselves as service providers to appear as profit centers rather than as cost centers in modern organizations. Inherently they have started proposing IT services to other departments or other organizations together with a defined consumption price and a service level agreement. IT services encapsulate some complex behavior that is seldom the concern of the consumer that does not want to take any ownership of the costs and risks. IT Services have nevertheless evolved over the years in order to better align with organizational requirements to abstractions like Business Process as a Service (BPaaS). The latter aims to furnish services supporting or automating entire (or parts of) the business processes of the organizations. In such cases understanding the internal behavior of the service in order to understand its alignment with the long term organizational strategy turns out to be useful.

Indeed, organizations deploy governance structures where development related decisions are taken by C-level executives that need to have an understanding of the impact of a service or software development notably on the long-term business and IT strategies to ensure proper business and IT alignment. The latter can be achieved through the use of goal-oriented conceptual modeling as it is proven to be a valuable tool for eliciting and articulating business, user and IT requirements (Wand & Weber, 2002; Ullah & Lai, 2011), thereby assisting top-level managers in IT governance decisions. Engelsman et al., (2011) define a 'goal' as the desired effect by some stakeholder which should be achieved. Goals can be formulated as more abstract (business) objectives and/or more concrete (IT) objectives.

Accordingly, Wautelet (2019) proposes MoDrIGo, a model-driven corporate and IT governance process allowing to evaluate the alignment of so called business IT services[1] (i.e. custom services developed to support business processes and that can be deployed on premise or in the cloud) with strategic (business and IT) objectives. The approach allows to integrate the governance level as a (graphical) (business and IT) strategic layer made of long-term objectives that organizational services potentially contribute or hamper to attain. The strategic layer is custom developed for each organization and linked with organizational representations of services in order to study their alignment.

The agile initiative is nowadays taking a lot of importance in the software development industry in order to better understand user requirements, the business environment and to cope with change. Often software developed in an agile fashion is driven by user stories (Wautelet et al., 2014), which are structured natural language artefacts recording user desiderata and immediate operational improvements to be implemented without taking into account long-term expectations. Development can nevertheless not be driven by operational aspects only like the agile initiative implicitly prescribes and needs at least partial alignment with long-term business and IT objectives. We thus face a mismatch between agile practices allowing high uncertainty at the level of system behavior and traditional governance requiring an evaluation of Business IT Alignment (BITA) leading to two different development approaches.

Wautelet et al. (2016) propose a graphical approach for structuring user-story sets. User stories (US) are short, simple descriptions of a feature told from the perspective of the person who desires the new capability, usually a user or customer of the system. US are generally used in agile methods (like Scrum) to represent all of the user and stakeholders requirements. They are very important in the sense that they define what problem should be solved. The Rationale Tree proposed by Wautelet et al. (2016) specifically links the operational elements described in user stories with stakeholder goals to provide a rationale to the functions described in user stories.

This paper intends to introduce the Agile-MoDrIGo framework. The latter suggests to merge the approaches of Wautelet (2019) and Wautelet et al. (2016). Concretely, top-level executives define the business and IT objectives of the organization. Business IT services are then defined in a top-down fashion and a set of goals to be met for their development are cascaded in the form of epic user story associated with acceptance tests. A bottom-up approach allows to collect user requirements, structure them into user stories and link each user story to a specific epic to distinguish independent sets. Basically, the development of the user stories attached to a particular epic should allow to meet his acceptance test. Then, the functions to be developed for a particular epic user story can be attached to a specific business IT service. All along the line, operational functions' (depicted in user stories) development contribute or hamper the realization of strategic objectives. The contribution of user stories to business and IT objectives can then be evaluated in during each sprint in order to determine the functions that are best aligned. The latter offer maximal long-term value to the business and receive highest development priority in release planning. This middle-out approach represents the layer where we evaluate the strategic value offered by functional elements identified (by operators) as providing user value (classically called 'business value' in agile development).

As a summary, the approach allows to integrate the service-based governance-level with the management one driven by agile development. The strategic layer is custom developed for each organization and linked with operational functions (defined in the user stories) grouped under each epic itself as part of a (business IT) service. The strength of the approach is to:

- Ensure proper governance of services in agile settings using traceable entities from strategic (business IT services) to tactical (epic user story) to operational levels (user stories) and vice-versa;
- Allow to inherit the benefits of a service-oriented architecture. Services are loosely coupled elements which inherently allow to apprehend the complexity of large systems through independent sub-entities where the consequences of the denial of a particular service remains local. The top-down definition of services allows to have loose coupling and high cohesion in their implementation and deployment;
- Keep the benefits of agile practices: the bottom-up approach allows to address user desiderata in a more customized manner and allows co-creation;

Deal with scalability since each business IT service can be developed independently allowing different agile teams to work in parallel after setting-up deployment constraints. Scalability is enhanced by using loosely coupled elements. High cohesion need to be ensured but at the same time, services can be developed separately so that different teams can work in parallel. This improves the scalability within an agile approach.

BACKGROUND

From IT Governance to Business and IT Alignment Evaluation

De Haes & Van Grembergen (2008) acknowledge the pervasive use of IT within corporations as an enabler of the achievement of organizational objectives. Illustratively, Dahlberg & Kivijärvi (2006) remark that large organizations have been using IT since the late 1950s for internal and external purposes. They observe, however, that the concept of IT governance has emerged much later on as organizations have started to strive on how to use IT resources responsibly and how to ensure that IT delivers value to the business overall.

Every IT-engaging organization applies some form of IT governance. However, the conception and development of an IT governance model might actually prove to be easier than its sustainable implementation within the organization. Accordingly, the quality of an IT organization and its service delivery may differ among various enterprises. The performance of an IT governance model is measured - among others - by the quality of the services that the IT organization delivers, as seen from a business point of view (De Haes & Van Grembergen, 2008; Simonsson, Johnson, & Ekstedt, 2010). IT service delivery presupposes all the decision-making on the services a corporation should adopt and their corresponding functionalities. Consequently, these decisions have a direct impact on the entirety of the organization and this is why services can be seen as the 'scope elements' that assist in evaluating if the correct IT assets and capabilities are provided to sustain an alignment between the defined business and IT strategies which is one of the ultimate goals of IT governance (Wautelet, 2019).

A proper IT governance mechanism should encompass broad corporate governance principles, structures and processes along with more explicit managerial behaviors and use of IT capabilities in the effort to achieve strategic organizational objectives (Weill & Ross, 2011; De Haes & Van Grembergen, 2008). Strategic objectives can be represented graphically through the use of conceptual models that enable to visualize short or longer-term (up to 5 years) organizational objectives (Wautelet, 2009). They are essentially a high level depiction of the business and/or IT strategy pursued by the organization. In addition, the use of goal-oriented modeling tools can provide direct traceability from abstract strategic concerns to concrete operational realization to evaluate the Business and IT Alignment (BITA). The latter is a crucial aspect of IT governance (Van Lamsweerde, 2001; Wautelet & Kolp, 2019).

Even though BITA has been extensively researched since the early 1980s, findings remain inconclusive. This is mainly due to the existence of multiple definitions of BITA as well as different organizational expectations of what BITA aims to accomplish (Dahlberg & Kivijärvi, 2006). Despite these differences, BITA refers essentially to the level of integration between the overall corporate strategy and its encompassing IT technologies (Avison et., 2004). The pivot of BITA research was originally focused on ways to align the (business and IT) strategic layer (Coltman et al., 2015) of an organization. However, Henderson & Venkatraman (1993) introduced a cross-domain perspective detailing the integration of the strategic layer with operational activities as an exemplary path towards alignment. Luftman, Papp & Brier (1999) viewed BITA as a dynamic and evolving process in which certain organizational and managerial activities act as enablers (while others act as inhibitors) but Reich and Benbasat (2000) argue that BITA can be perceived both as a process and as an outcome. A process-oriented perspective includes setting up milestones and planning activities which evaluate the current stage of BITA and establish goals for the next milestone. An outcome-oriented approach on the other hand involves the assessment of the realized strategies (Avison et al., 2004).

In this paper, any reference to the concept of BITA will signify that an organization has the potential to set-up the appropriate IT capabilities, processes and infrastructure in order to realize its current and future strategic objectives; these elements are encapsulated in the notion of business IT service. Wautelet (2019) indeed explains that MoDrIGo distinguishes a strategic layer for the representation of strategic business and IT objectives while synchronizing the organizational governance and management layers through the use of business IT services. These are services intensively supporting the business processes and needs of the organization through the use of IT. MoDrIGo thus allows the board of director and other C-level employees that participate in governance boards to evaluate the alignment of their service acquisition or development decisions with regards to the overall business and IT strategies.

IT Governance within the Agile Transformation

Some authors emphasize on the gap between high-level IT governance practices that can be exercised on large, bureaucratic organizations with well-established conventional software development processes and the general notion of agility (Talby & Dubinsky, 2009; Dubinsky et., 2011). However, agile software development methods and governance practices do not have to be mutually excluding. De O'Luna, Kruchten, & de Moura (2013) report an increasing number of organizations that try to apply large-scale agile approaches to their businesses. In that way, they try to benefit from the ability of agile methods to respond to ongoing challenges and changes in a quicker and a more sustainable way. A scaled-up agile approach intertwined with elements of traditional IT governance would infuse elements of organizational ambidexterity allowing a firm to focus on business process optimization during times of environmental stability while seeking to exploit new opportunities to become competitive in times of environmental volatility (Vejseli et al., 2018).

Nonetheless, an agile transformation presupposes that the organizations' governance mechanisms and business operations keep evolving in order to converge with the mindset that the agile methodology requires. Agile practices require the set-up of enterprise-wide, top-down and bottom-up collaboration and communication mechanisms that identify, promote and reinforce initiatives that encourage self-assessment and self-improvement of agile teams (de O'Luna, Marinho, & de Moura, 2019). By definition, agile practices perform quite well on small and lightweight projects in which the customer can be directly involved due to the flexibility that they can induce within a software development process that faces high uncertainty, changing requirements and short development cycles. In such environments, empowered agile teams can be effective at decision-making or providing valuable input crucial to decision takers (Qumer & Henderson-Sellers, 2008).

However the notion of agility does not necessarily constitute a panacea to every issue related to organizational effectiveness and efficiency. For one thing, agility is by nature a multipurposed conceptual term, open to many definitions and strategies even within the same organization (Abbas et al., 2008). Sambamurthy et al. (2003) illustrate its multidimensionality by differentiating between customer agility (leveraging customer insights to expedite innovation), partnering agility (exploiting strategic partnerships and business networks to discover competitive opportunities) and operational agility (swift redesign and cocreation of business processes with the synergies of customers/developers for maximized business value delivery). Adding up to this ambiguity, Hobbs & Petit (2017) report that there is a lack of practical guidelines on how to utilize and scale-up agile processes to large and complex project-oriented organizational settings.

Despite the existence of such challenges, Qumer (2007) negotiated the basic components of an agile governance framework. The author emphasized that such a framework should allow agile teams, managers and customers to take upon themselves the responsibility and accountability of facilitating the achievement of agile goals. Nonetheless, this particular framework is purely descriptive and does not elaborate on what processes are needed. Qumer & Henderson-Sellers (2008) continued with this line of research and presented the Agile Software Solution Framework (ASSF). Even though the framework is described in full detail and contains important components such as the capability to assees the agility level for each organization, still the framework is limited to establishing governance formations bottom-up, emphasizing essentially the need for an in-between collaboration and empowerment of agile teams. Cheng et. al (2009) manage to classify IT governance between software development governance and agile governance. The authors emphasize on control mechanisms (i.e. specific KPIs and 'interventions') that both approaches should consider but there is no description of a holistic agile governance framework. Vlietland et al. (2016) propose an agile governance framework intending to coordinate 300 Scrum teams within a multinational financial institution in order to enable a faster business value delivery. However, their interventions are aiming at better alignment and coordination among the agile teams while little is mentioned about the assessment of agile goals compared to long term strategic objectives. To sum up, we share the viewpoint of Vejseli et al. (2018) stating that research in agile governance seems to be lagging since the current state-of-the-art offers faint insights about the contribution and impact of agile strategies in a governance setting.

THE RISING NEED OF A SERVICE-ORIENTED FRAMEWORK INTEGRATING AGILE AND TRADITIONAL GOVERNANCE APPROACHES

Cummings (2007) and Verlaine (2017) converge that in their effort to become agile, modern enterprises turn to service-oriented architecture and service-oriented computing. The former depicts a business design paradigm using flexible architectures that simplify business processes by modularizing large applications into services. No matter the device, the operating system or the programming language used, a client can demand and access a service as a loosely coupled element to create a new (or extend an existing) business process (Papazoglou & van den Heuvel, 2007). The latter refers to organization-wise service-oriented developments (Schroth, 2007) enabling increases in the agility of hardware and software components of IT services so companies can manage IT projects in a quicker and a more outcome-oriented manner (Verlaine, 2017).

Despite the rising importance of agility in IT service-orientation/management and delivery, the instruments and governance mechanisms used so far depend on models and frameworks which are considered either too theoretical or plainly too 'bureaucratic' and 'labor-intensive' to be applied in an agile setting (De O'Luna, Kruchten & De Moura, 2013; Qumer, 2007). Illustratively, COBIT - one of the most renowned IT service governance frameworks - consists of 5 governance and 35 management processes. COBIT is a heavily process-centered framework that treats software development activities as a supporting practice in a business value chain rather than a central business activity in itself (Dahlberg & Kivijärvi, 2006; Dubinsky et al., 2011). At the same time, ITIL (a framework focused on IT service management) consists of 7 guiding principles including 34 management practices and while it receives massive support from IT practitioners globally, the framework itself has traditionally provided little support for mapping strategic IT concerns (Simonsson, Johnson & Ekstedt, 2010; Dubinsky et al., 2011).

Summarizing, Verlaine (2017) ideates a novel agile framework in which service-oriented developments act as a catalyst towards the achievement of operational agility. Wautelet (2019) describes a framework where services are considered on a more abstract level as governance-assisting entities encapsulating relevant business behavior that needs to be supported and on which their alignment with the business and IT strategies can be evaluated. On the other side, Hobbs & Petit (2017) and Qumer (2007) describe the requirements of an agile framework that would have the ability to exercise control and to scale-up agile software development methods for large and complex projects while focusing on performance and maximizing business value at all levels without jeopardizing the ability to respond quickly to change.

Vlietland et al. (2016) state that such a framework should also alleviate collaboration and communication hurdles among agile teams.

To this end, Agile-MoDrIGo offers a multilayered governance approach that can support on one hand large project-based organizations with a traditional IT governance setting. Since such organizations rely mostly on command and control mechanisms to ensure efficiency and project deliverability (Peterson, 2004), Agile-MoDrIGo can assist in monitoring the actualization of organizational strategic objectives through specific Key Performance Indicators (KPIs) and trace their operational execution representations through business IT services. On the other hand, agile governed organizations desire the maximization of business value by controlling large agile software development environments and ensuring the alignment of business and agile software development goals (Qumer, 2017). Agile-MoDrIGo ensures this alignment by assessing simultaneously the user value offering and the strategic value of operational functions at the end of each sprint. In other words, Agile-MoDrIGo acts as multiscale approach that can assist a plethora of organizational compositions to instill flexible governance structures without compromising their long term strategic viewpoint.

Hereafter we refer to agility as an attribute of the software development methodology that makes use of the principles that prescribe to focus on an ad-hoc design built when a sprint is conducted. This induces a very operational approach where the value delivered to stakeholders acts as the primary driver. The operational user support is provided through the utilization of user stories which are very operational documents describing user functionalities on a low-level basis. They represent essentially all of the user and stakeholder requirements in agile development methodologies such as eXtreme Programming (XP) and Scrum (Wautelet et al., 2014). Moreover, epic user story define more abstract features that need to be satisfied by the system, require several sprints to be fulfilled, and are fully decomposed into a set of operational US (Wautelet et al., 2017). These epic user stories will serve in the framework defined in these pages as pivot elements linking business IT services with operational US. The contribution of user stories to the business strategy can then be determined to evaluate if the service development attributes (or not) to strategy realization. Implicitly, this leads us to evaluate the contribution of the service development in terms of BITA.

ALIGNING AGILE DEVELOPED SERVICES WITH STRATEGIC OBJECTIVES

This section describes the Agile-MoDrIGo meta-model (it can be visualized in Figure 1) and further depicts the approach. Indeed, we first describe the top-down approach for the definition of strategic objectives, business IT services and epic user stories together with their acceptance test. Then we describe the bottom-up approach for user-centered definition of requirements into user stories. The middle-out approach allows to center the defined user stories around the epic ones defined under the scope of a business IT service. Finally, we overview an applicative example validating the ideas depicted in the novel approach.

Top-Down Approach: Distinguishing the Strategic Objectives and the Business IT Services

Service-oriented computing is characterized as a holistic paradigm for organizations (Schroth, 2007). Taking a decision on the services to acquire or implement is the responsibility of the governance level

Figure 1. Merging service-based IT governance and agile Development: A meta-model

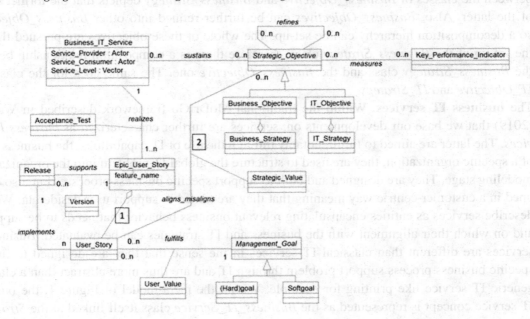

and has an immediate impact on the entire organization in terms of structures, processes and people. From a technical point of view, services are presented as encapsulated and loosely coupled software entities (Krafzig et al., 2005) of which the design and implementation is ensured by the IT management level. Because they do play an important role in how an IT provider structures itself, services are often used as the scope elements for business and IT alignment (Wautelet & Kolp, 2016). This means that we can use services as elements to evaluate if the adequate IT assets and capabilities are put in practice to support the business and IT strategies (Wautelet, 2019). Indeed, the service as a whole and its constituting actions/activities provide or hamper value at strategic level.

Classically, 3 types of elements are defined top-down in Agile-MoDrIGo; more specifically:

- **The strategic objectives**. We define them as the objectives that an organization aims to achieve over a defined period to fulfill the strategic plan. They express long-term (up to 5 years) strategic aspirations and, by hypothesis in our framework, they are established in a top-down fashion, i.e. by the board of directors and C-level executives. Strategic objectives can also be determined bottom-up through stakeholder-based governance (Freeman, 2010); this will be studied in future work. We mention in brief that the notion of a stakeholder is much broader than the one of a shareholder; the first can include employees, clients, suppliers, local communities, government, unions, etc. Hence, proper stakeholder-based governance means that when fixing strategic objectives and taking decisions to fulfill them, all of these individual groups should be taken into account to maximize shared value (Wautelet, 2019). A strategic objective is represented as the class *Strategic_Objective* in the meta-model. It is an abstract class meaning that it should necessarily be instantiated as a *Business_Objective* or an *IT_Objective* which are traditional classes in the meta-model. Typically, these two types of *Strategic_Objectives* realization can be measured by *Key_Performance_Indicators*; this is why the two former classes are linked. The relationship between the classes of *Business_Objective* and *Business_Strategy* depicts that the former is part of the latter. Also, *Business_Objectives* can be further refined into other *Business_Objectives,* so a decomposition hierarchy can be set-up. The whole of these objectives are pursued through the set-up of the *Business_Strategy* class; therefore there is a composition relationship between the *Business_Strategy* class and the *Business_Objective* one. The same goes for the classes of *IT_Objective* and *IT_Strategy*.

- The **business IT services**. Within the traditional MoDrIGo framework described in Wautelet (2019) that we base our developments on, services are further characterized as *business IT services*. The latter are aimed to fulfill, notably through the use of IT capabilities, the business needs of a specific organization; they are used to structure the global IT problem into the organizational modeling stage. They are designed and built to support specific business processes but also developed in a customer-centric way meaning that they are aimed to support user desiderata. We thus describe services as entities encapsulating relevant business behavior that needs to be supported and on which their alignment with the business and IT strategies can be evaluated. Business IT services are different than classical IT services in the sense that they are designed to fulfill a specific business process support problem through IT and are thus more abstract than a classical generic IT service like printing for example. Within the meta-model of Figure 1, the business IT service concept is represented as the *Business_IT_Service* class itself linked to the *Strategic_Objective* class to represent the ability of the former to impact the latter. Therefore, the behavior of particular services can be constantly reevaluated with respect to the business and IT strategies. Illustratively, business and IT strategies impact the organizational behavior of pipeline services while for catalog services the strategies serve for the evaluation of the current situation leading to a continuous modification whenever deemed necessary; even small modifications in terms of infrastructure (hardware, software) or processes can be dynamically made in order to better align (or realign) particular business IT services with the business or IT strategies (Wautelet, 2019).

- The **epic user story** and its **acceptance test**. Epic user stories (represented as the class *Epic_User_Story* in the meta-model) describe large functions of the system to be estimated, implemented and tested at once. Typically, one or more epic user stories are defined for the development of a *Business_IT_Service* and an epic encompasses several other US containing elements described in a more concrete (operational) manner. An epic user story is too large to be developed in a single iteration so requires several iterations to build a *Release*. A release is a deployable software package built over several iterations and – as can be seen in the meta-model – that can be validated through an *Acceptance_Test*. The latter defines the minimum system behavior that needs to be fulfilled to validate the epic user story. In our meta-model, we also relate the notion of release (class *Release*) to the one of epic user story showing that one of them supports a specific epic user story. The evolution in releases is supported through different versions (class *Version* in the meta-model).

Bottom-Up Approach: Building Up User Stories and Mapping Them to an Epic

User stories are typically defined by the to-be system users under the responsibility of the Product Owner. In that sense, user stories express elements that need to be defined in a bottom-up fashion. They are represented by the class *User_Story* in the meta-model of Figure 1. User stories are generally structured around 3 dimensions, i.e. the WHO, the WHAT and (possibly) the WHY and are usually expressed in the format: As a *<type of user>*, I want *<some goal>* so that *<some reason>* (Cohn, 2004; Wautelet et al., 2014). The WHAT dimension specifies a functional or non-functional element desirable by the end-user or a stakeholder. The meta-model of figure 1 illustrates short or middle-term organizational objectives incorporated in the class *Management_Goal*. The latter represents an abstract class where it can be further instantiated as the traditional classes of *(Hard)Goal* and *SoftGoal*. The i* modeling language differentiates between the two as *(hard)goal* defines a state that is sought to be achieved whereas *softgoal* represents a goal whose satisfaction is subject of interpretation (Franch et al., 2016). Typically, a *Management_Goal* can be fulfilled by zero or many user stories but it is the responsibility of management to place each user story within the scope of an epic user story; User Story Mapping is a well-known technique (Patton, 2014) but in our case we recommend using the rationale tree approach of Wautelet et al. (2017) to ensure future traceability with the strategic level using conceptual models. Indeed, a rationale tree can be created on the basis of a user story set tagged to use the concepts of the unified US template described by Wautelet et al. (2014). The rationale tree uses parts of the constructs and visual notation of an i* Strategic Rationale Diagram to build various trees of relating US elements in a single project. The benefits of sculpturing such a rationale diagram is to identify depending US, identifying epic ones and group them around common user story themes. Therefore, a diagram furnishing a consistent visual representation of an existing US set thus providing a graphical representation of the system-to-be only provides added value and is in line with agile expectations (Wautelet et al., 2016).

Middle-Out Approach: Merging Service-Based IT Governance and Agile Development

After having presented the governance approach based on business IT services and the agile one based on user stories, we present a middle layer for merging both approaches. To this aim, Agile-MoDrIGo distinguishes two different perspectives taken in parallel. On the one side, the decision of delimitating and demarcating the business IT service is taken by top-management but more specifically, it is their responsibility to take an acquisition or implementation decision. To do so, once the business IT service is defined, a few epic user stories are written to depict the main element that need to be covered for its fulfillment as well as a contract for their fulfillment in terms of acceptance tests. As large functions, one might say that epic user stories formally decompose and depict the behavior to be met by a specific business IT service. On the other side, user stories are written by operators under the responsibility of the Product Owner in a full bottom-up manner; user story sets are then mapped under the scope of an epic user story defined top-down.

To summarize, two important alignment activities need to be taken in a middle-out fashion for Agile-MoDrIGo to be applied successfully:

1. Each user story defined in a bottom-up-fashion needs to be mapped to an epic user story defined top-down. This is the responsibility of the Product Owner. Roughly speaking, the most important element is that the group of user stories defined for a specific epic user story allows to meet the acceptance test as defined by the governance-level for validation and inclusion as a release. This is marked with a squared 1 in the meta-model;

2. Each function depicted in an individual user story needs to be aligned with the strategic objectives in order to evaluate if the implementation of the former contributes or hampers the realization of the latter. This evaluation can be the responsibility of the Strategy Manager where during each sprint he/she can decide the contribution of user stories to business and IT objectives; This allows

the resolution whether the development of new IT is aligned with the long-term aspirations of the business. This is marked with a squared 2 in the meta-model.

Finally, one could say that, in our proposal, epic user stories are envisaged as tactical and pivot elements between the top strategic objective definition and bottom user requirements definition so they serve as a middle out approach for evaluating business and IT alignment. Typically a decision can be rooted in the difference in Business and IT Alignment (BITA) between the current situation and the situation when an epic user story have been developed and furnished as a new release. Support links between the user stories depending on a specific epic and the strategic objectives can be used, in a diagram, to highlight the contribution of the (to-be) business IT service in terms of BITA. More formally we define that a user story has a positive impact on a strategic objective if the functionality expressed in that user story and implemented within business IT service has a positive impact on the Key Performance Indicators (KPI) associated to that strategic objective.

Applicative Example of Agile-MoDrIGo

The applicative example used in this section further develops the case of a Belgian hospital as depicted in (Wautelet et al., 2018; Wautelet, 2019). The example is fictional for some parts and taken from a real case for some others. Even though the application is only partial, it is meant to be realistic and relevant. Saint-Romain is a Belgian hospital which activities have grown exponentially in the last few years; available IT budgets have nevertheless only grown in a linear way. After the successful commissioning of an emergency unit five years ago and the building of new spaces devoted to care, Saint-Romain rapidly tripled its patient base and administrative activities became more and more complex. This nevertheless generated cash and momentum to expand and rethink the entire organization.

Today, Saint-Romain is a group of divisions, delivering healthcare services supported by a administration and logistics departments. To manage the new configuration, Saint-Romain has transformed itself into a divisional structure. Each division has a director responsible for the particular domain. Saint-Romain as a whole is managed by a central staff, consisting of the CEO and staff services such as finance, human resources and procurement. Decisions on what business strategy should be followed and on (business) IT services to develop are thus taken by a central authority: the Hospital Governance Board that governs the hospital at its highest level and thus elaborates the strategies to put in practice.

At management level, Saint-Romain has implemented ITIL for service provision. No standard framework has been formally adapted for IT governance. Although the business IT services as modeled in Agile-MoDrIGo can be smoothly interfaced with the ITIL *Service Portfolio Management*, our framework adoption does not presuppose the existing implementation of any other global IT governance or management framework.

As an applicative example we depict, in Figure 2, the business strategy of the hospital (as fully depicted in Wautelet et al., 2018) and study the alignment of functions developed in the context of the *Online Patient Appointment* business IT service. As can be seen in the graphical representation, the latter service is further divided in 3 epic user stories determined top-down. Defining acceptance tests and justifying their satisfaction/fulfilment by the collected operational user stories is left for future work. For illustration purposes, we further decompose the second epic user story in operational user stories following the guidance of the rational tree. Finally, the detailed functions present in the user stories are represented as decompositions from the further developed epic user story. The traces (positive contributions in this case) from these functions to the business objectives are finally represented to show their (so transitively also the second epic user story and finally the business IT service) contribution to the business strategy in terms of strategic value. These contributions are determined in discussion with middle managers and presented to top managers under the responsibility of the Strategy Manager to be formally adapted. The full explanation of the impacted KPIs and justification of the obtained contributions is left for future work.

Computer-Aided Software Engineering Tool Support for Diagram Edition and Process Handling

We are currently extending the Descartes Architect Computer Aided Software Engineering (CASE) tool (Kolp & Wautelet, 2019) to furnish support to the Agile-MoDrIGo approach. Basically, we use a user story view where all of the user stories are depicted. The graphical view allows to build and edit diagram as the one presented in Figure 2. Consistency between both views is ensured using the same conceptual elements depicted in the user story view and the graphical view. In other words if we update or delete a user story in one view, the other is automatically updated. Moreover, after the impact of a user story onto a strategic objective (i.e. strategic value) has been set-up, the narrative (the WHAT dimension) of

Figure 2. User Story support of business Objectives: An illustrative example in the medical field

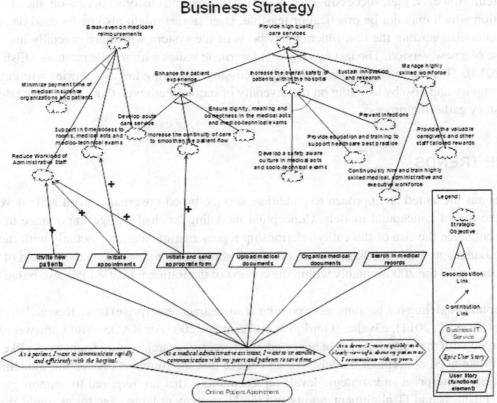

239

an individual user story can be updated in the user story view to reflect this impact. Exposing the entire set of functionalities through screenshots is left for future work.

Threats to Validity

This section discusses the validity threats attributed to our proposal. As with any other approach within the design science domain, there is always the issue of various modelers perceiving the elements of the model in a different manner than the intended model definition. This threat to the construct validity can be bypassed by arranging meetings between modelers and other involved parties to communicate their viewpoints and corresponding modeling concepts/notations.

Our framework specifies that the knowledge acquisition on the organizations' strategy takes place in a top-down approach where interviews utter the strategic objectives. At the level of governance, a potential threat can be that interviewees include their own opinion on what strategy should be followed into the knowledge repository rather than the entire governance board agreed upon. In such a case the modeled strategy would not be consistent with the objectives of the organization. Moreover, the specific role and perception of an interviewee could have an influence on the answers in the sense that he/she could emphasize/overrate/minimize specific objectives. This shortcoming can be dealt with through multiple interviews and cross-examination of multiple viewpoints when building the strategic representations (Wautelet, 2019).

At the user level, user stories present an effortless method to elicit requirements and features of the to-be system. However, their successful representation depends on customer access on-site and constant participation which may not be practical or feasible. User stories might also be focused on functional requirements disregarding the non-functional aspects of the system which are crucially important for the release of a new version. The last two represent intrinsic issues within agile methods (Elshandidy & Mazen, 2013). This threat can be dealt with by discussing/validating the user stories within the entire user community and also by insisting on the diversity of requirement type that can be expressed during the user story gathering process.

FUTURE TRENDS

The paper has presented an approach to conciliate service-based governance with agile development through the use of conceptual models. Conceptual modeling has had a huge importance in software development since the rise of the entity-relationship representation and after notably with the Unified Modeling Language. Building diagrams out of models was a *de facto* practice in the context of software developments until the 2000s notably within the context of the Rational Unified Process-based developments.

Conceptual modeling has become more popular at an abstract (enterprise) level. Research frameworks like i-star (Yu et al., 2011), e3value (Gordijn & Akkermans, 2003) or KAOS (Van Lamsweerde, 2009) have emerged with the years but also industry-adopted enterprise architecture frameworks like TOGAF and ArchiMate need conceptual models. We do believe that the future of conceptual modeling lies in more abstract (enterprise and strategic-level) representations that are required to support governance decisions, business and IT alignment, audits and the IT strategy at large - see for example Wautelet & Kolp (2019) for a state of the art. Another aspect of the business strategy are the commercial dependencies in which the company is involved (e.g., outsourcing, strategic alliances, joint ventures, etc.; - see Kolp, Wautelet & Faulkner (2011) for the representation of these commercial dependencies through conceptual modeling. Similarly, Pant & Yu (2016) and Pant & Yu (2018) represent coopetition of different organizations using conceptual models to align inter-organizational dependencies with a series of IT related design choices.

Since the emergence of the agile initiative this importance has considerably decreased. Agile methods do indeed not prescribe to build conceptual models in development but rather to implement the solution (or release) as fast as possible without focusing on the software design nor the documentation practices. Scientific communities active in the development of conceptual models have little by little started to question themselves about the utility of such models especially after the emergence of the DevOps approach. Different researches have nevertheless tried to incorporate and show the added value of conceptual models in agile development. The work of Wautelet, Heng, Kolp, Mirbel & Poelmans (2016) aims to transform user stories into a decomposition tree in order to understand the dependencies among user story elements. The work of Trkman, Mendling, & Krisper (2016) and Trkman, Mendling, Trkman, & Krisper (2019) has introduced the use of workflows in order to better understand user stories and their constituting elements. Also, Lucassen et al. (2017) propose to build a conceptual model using natural language processing out of a user story set. There are thus several research work that are aimed to further support agile methods and more particularly user stories lists with conceptual models.

The rationale tree approach described in the work of Wautelet et al. (2016) links the operational elements described in user stories with stakeholder goals to provide a justification to the functions that user stories describe. However, the work of Wautelet (2019) discusses the concept of stakeholder-based governance (Freeman, 2010) meaning that when fixing strategic objectives and taking decisions to fulfill them, stakeholders rather than shareholders should be taken into account so as to maximize shared value. Stakeholder can be anyone belonging to the following groups: employees, clients, suppliers, local communities, government, unions, etc. (Wautelet & Kolp, 2019). For an optimal application of stakeholder-based governance, the strategic objectives should also be set-up (or at least completed) by a bottom-up approach. As presented in this paper this process is not taken into account and objectives are fixed in the classical way. Indeed, by its conception, Agile-MoDrIGo models strategic objectives in a top-down fashion, i.e. by the board of directors and C-level executives that could include or not a broad consultation of stakeholders. Nonetheless, the goal-driven modeling approach within MoDrIGo can support such an approach where the high-end governance level is set-up on the basis of input from the operational and tactical level in the form of a set of management goals (providing classical user or business value) from all of the involved stakeholders. Future work will study the determination of strategic objectives in a bottom-up fashion for pure stakeholder-based governance in agile settings.

CONCLUSION

The need to conjunctly use a software development model based on services with an agile development path has progressively risen in the industry. Service science notably prescribes to structure and profile the IT department as a profit center. Also, structuring the IT solution around consistent business processes supported and automated as a package allows to furnish an input for modular implementation using a service-oriented architecture. Finally, the services – as coarse-grained entities – can support governance mechanisms because they are easy to use as scope elements for business and IT alignment evaluation and development decision. Agility, on the other hand, is very useful to cope with the true requirements of users; it offers the flexibility to cope with change while its iterative approach and short delivery cycles aim to bring value at the earliest stages of the development process.

This paper has introduced the Agile-MoDrIGo framework. The latter asserts that software development should not be driven by enforcing a choice between considering either strategic or operational aspects; it reconciles both venues counterbalancing possible vulnerabilities when only one of them is considered. The framework uses a parallel a top-down and bottom-up approach based on conceptual modeling where integration is ensured middle-out by the use of goal and objective-driven models. Specifically, Agile-MoDrIGo allows:

- A top-down delineation of custom Business/IT strategies and their representation as strategic organizational objectives. These are the drivers facilitating the formation of business IT services as the scope elements that assist in evaluating the alignment between business and IT. Following their definition, business IT services can be then decomposed in a few epic user stories along with their acceptance tests as contracts transcribing minimum system behavior required to validate the epic user story;
- A bottom-up collection of user requirements; their structuring into user stories and their aggregation under the scope of a specific epic user story to distinguish independent sets. This agile approach regards user stories as operational-level elements representing system functionalities while proposing improvements within the development process without considering (yet) long-term organizational objectives;
- A middle-level reconciliation between the top-down and bottom-up approach; firstly, user stories (determined at an operational level) are mapped to the (tactical-level) epic user stories refining a business IT service. Secondly, the contribution of user stories to business and IT objectives can be evaluated during each sprint in order to determine user driven functions that best align with strategic aspects.

The framework depicted in this chapter represents a graphical approach detailing the convergence of upper-level service-based governance and bottom-up agile development practices. The applicative example of the hospital provides directions on how to the model certain strategic elements that Agile-MoDrIGo describes in detail. However, actual case studies are needed so that Agile-MoDrIGo can gain maturity. The contribution of agile professionals and strategists can yield significant insight that can facilitate its smooth implementation.

REFERENCES

Abbas, N., Gravell, A. M., & Wills, G. B. (2008). Historical roots of agile methods: Where did "Agile thinking" come from? *Lecture Notes in Business Information Processing, 9*, 94–103.

Avison, D., Jones, J., Powell, P., & Wilson, D. (2004). Using and validating the strategic alignment model. *The Journal of Strategic Information Systems, 13*(3), 223–246. doi:10.1016/j.jsis.2004.08.002

Beck, K., Beedle, M., Bennekum, A. V., Cockburn, A., Cunningham, W., Fowler, M., Grenning, J., Highsmith, J., Hunt, A., Jeffries, R., Kern, J., Marick, B., Martin, R., Mellor, S., Schwaber, K., Sutherland, J., & Thomas, D. (2001). *Manifesto for Agile Software Development*. Retrieved from: http://agilemanifesto.org

Cheng, T. H., Jansen, S., & Remmers, M. (2009). Controlling and monitoring agile software development in three dutch product software companies. *2009 ICSE Workshop on Software Development Governance*, 29-35. 10.1109/SDG.2009.5071334

Cohn, M. (2004). *User Stories Applied: For Agile Software Development*. Addison Wesley Longman Publishing Co., Inc.

Coltman, T., Tallon, P. P., Sharma, R., & Queiroz, M. (2015). Strategic IT alignment: Twenty-five years on. *JIT*, *30*(2), 91–100.

Cummings, F. (2009). *Building the Agile Enterprise. With SOA, BPM and MBM*. Morgan Kaufmann.

Dahlberg, T., & Kivijärvi, H. (2006). An integrated framework for IT governance and the development and validation of an assessment instrument. *Proceedings of the Annual Hawaii International Conference on System Sciences, 8*(C), 1–10. 10.1109/HICSS.2006.57

De Haes, S., & Van Grembergen, W. (2008). Analysing the relationship between IT governance and business/IT alignment maturity. *Proceedings of the Annual Hawaii International Conference on System Sciences*.

De O'Luna, A. J. H., Kruchten, P., & De Moura, H. P. (2013). GAME: Governance for Agile management of enterprises a management model for agile governance. *Proceedings - 2013 IEEE 8th International Conference on Global Software Engineering Workshops, ICGSEW 2013*, 88–90.

De O'Luna, A. J. H., Marinho, M. L. M., & de Moura, H. P. (2019). Agile governance theory: Operationalization. *Innovations in Systems and Software Engineering*.

Dubinsky, Y., Yaeli, A., Feldman, Y., Zarpas, E., & Nechushtai, G. (2011). Governance of Software Development. *Software Applications*, 309–327.

Elshandidy, H., & Mazen, S. (2013). Agile and Traditional Requirements Engineering: A Survey. *International Journal of Scientific and Engineering Research*, *4*(9), 473–482.

Engelsman, W., Quartel, D. A. C., Jonkers, H., & van Sinderen, M. (2011). Extending enterprise architecture modelling with business goals and requirements. *Enterprise IS*, *5*(1), 9–36. doi:10.1080/17517575.2010.491871

Franch, X., López, L., Cares, C., & Colomer, D. (2016). The i* Framework for Goal-Oriented Modeling. In D. Karagiannis, H. Mayr, & J. Mylopoulos (Eds.), *Domain-Specific Conceptual Modeling: Concepts, Methods and Tools* (pp. 485–506). Springer. doi:10.1007/978-3-319-39417-6_22

Gordijn, J., & Akkermans, J. M. (2003). Value-based requirements engineering: Exploring innovative e-commerce ideas. *Requirements Engineering*, *8*(2), 114–134. doi:10.100700766-003-0169-x

Henderson, J. C., & Venkatraman, H. (1993). Strategic alignment: Leveraging information technology for transforming organizations. *IBM Systems Journal*, *32*(1), 472–484. doi:10.1147j.382.0472

Hobbs, B., & Petit, Y. (2017). Agile Methods on Large Projects in Large Organizations. *Project Management Journal, 48*(3), 3–19. doi:10.1177/875697281704800301

International Publishing Switzerland. (2016). *Strategic management: A stakeholder approach*. Cambridge University Press.

Kolp, M., & Wautelet, Y. (2019). *Descartes Architect: Design Case Tool for Agent-Oriented Repositories, Techniques, Environments and Systems*. Louvain School of Management, Université catholique de Louvain, Louvain-la-Neuve, Belgium. https://www.isys.ucl.ac.be/descartes/

Kolp, M., Wautelet, Y., & Faulkner, S. (2011). Sociocentric design of multi-agent architectures. In E. Yu, P. Giorgini, N. Maiden, & J. Mylopoulos (Eds.), *Social Modeling for Requirements Engineering*. MIT Press.

Krafzig, D., Banke, K., & Slama, D. (2005). *Enterprise SOA: service-oriented architecture best practices*. Prentice Hall Professional.

Lucassen, G., Robeer, M., Dalpiaz, F., van der Werf, J. M. E., & Brinkkemper, S. (2017). Extracting conceptual models from user stories with Visual Narrator. *Requirements Engineering, 22*(3), 339–358. doi:10.100700766-017-0270-1

Luftman, J., Papp, R., & Brier, T. (1999). Enablers and inhibitors of business-IT alignment. *Communications of the AIS, 1*(3).

Pant, V., & Yu, E. (2016). Coopetition with frenemies: Towards modeling of simultaneous cooperation and competition among enterprises. *The Practice of Enterprise Modeling - 9th IFIP WG 8.1. Working Conference, PoEM 2016, Proceedings*, 164–178.

Pant, V., & Yu, E. (2018). Modeling simultaneous cooperation and competition among enterprises. *Business & Information Systems Engineering, 60*(1), 39–54. doi:10.100712599-017-0514-0

Papazoglou, M., & van den Heuvel, W. J. (2007). Service oriented architectures: Approaches, technologies and research issues. *The VLDB Journal, 16*(3), 389–415. doi:10.100700778-007-0044-3

Patton, J. (2014). User story mapping: discover the whole story, build the right product. O'Reilly Media, Inc.

Peterson, R. R. (2004). Integration Strategies and Tactics for Information Technology Governance. In Strategies for Information Technology Governance (pp. 37–80). IGI Global. doi:10.4018/978-1-59140-140-7.ch002

Qumer, A. (2017). Defining an Integrated Agile Governance for Large Agile Software Development Environments. *International Conference on Extreme Programming and Agile Processes in Software Engineering*, 157-160.

Qumer, A., & Henderson-Sellers, B. (2008). A framework to support the evaluation, adoption and improvement of agile methods in practice. *Journal of Systems and Software, 81*(11), 1899–1919. doi:10.1016/j.jss.2007.12.806

Reich, B. H., & Benbasat, I. (2000). Factors That Influence the Social Dimension of Alignment Between Business and Information Technology Objectives. *Management Information Systems Quarterly, 24*(1), 81–113. doi:10.2307/3250980

Sambamurthy, V., Bharadwaj, A., & Grover, V. (2003). Shaping agility though digital options: Reconceptualizing the role of information technology in contemporary firms. *Management Information Systems Quarterly, 27*(2), 237–263. doi:10.2307/30036530

Schroth, C. (2007). The service-oriented enterprise. *Journal of Enterprise Architecture, 3*(4), 73-80.

Simonsson, M., Johnson, P., & Ekstedt, M. (2010). The effect of IT governance maturity on IT governance performance. *Information Systems Management, 27*(1), 10–24. doi:10.1080/10580530903455106

Talby, D., & Dubinsky, Y. (2009). Governance of an agile software project. *Proceedings of the 2009 ICSE Workshop on Software Development Governance, SDG 2009*, 40–45. 10.1109/SDG.2009.5071336

Trkman, M., Mendling, J., & Krisper, M. (2016). Using business process models to better understand the dependencies among user stories. *Information and Software Technology, 71*, 58–76. doi:10.1016/j.infsof.2015.10.006

Trkman, M., Mendling, J., Trkman, P., & Krisper, M. (2019). Impact of the conceptual model's representation format on identifying and understanding user stories. *Information and Software Technology, 116*, 106169. doi:10.1016/j.infsof.2019.08.001

Ullah, A., & Lai, R. (2011). Modeling Business Goal For Business/It Alignment Using Requirements Engineering. *Journal of Computer Information Systems, 51*(3), 21–28.

Van Lamsweerde, A. (2001). Goal-oriented requirements engineering: A guided tour. *Proceedings of the IEEE International Conference on Requirements Engineering*, 249–261.

Van Lamsweerde, A. (2009). *Requirements engineering: From system goals to UML models to software* (Vol. 10). John Wiley & Sons.

Vejseli, S., Proba, D., Rossmann, A., & Reinhard, J. (2018). The Agile Strategies In It Governance: Towards A Framework Of Agile It Governance In The Banking Industry. *Twenty-Sixth European Conference on Information Systems (ECIS2018)*.

Verlaine, B. (2017). Toward an Agile IT Service Management Framework. *Service Science, 9*(4), 263–274. doi:10.1287erv.2017.0186

Vlietland, J., Van Solingen, R., & Van Vliet, H. (2016). Aligning codependent Scrum teams to enable fast business value delivery: A governance framework and set of intervention actions. *Journal of Systems and Software, 113*, 418–429. doi:10.1016/j.jss.2015.11.010

Wand, Y., & Weber, R. (2002). Research Commentary: Information Systems and Conceptual Modeling - A Research Agenda. *Information Systems Research, 13*(4), 363–376. doi:10.1287/isre.13.4.363.69

Wautelet, Y. (2019). A model-driven IT governance process based on the strategic impact evaluation of services. *Journal of Systems and Software, 149*, 462–475. doi:10.1016/j.jss.2018.12.024

Wautelet, Y., Heng, S., Kiv, S., & Kolp, M. (2017). User-story driven development of multi-agent systems: A process fragment for agile methods. *Computer Languages, Systems & Structures*, *50*, 159–176. doi:10.1016/j.cl.2017.06.007

Wautelet, Y., Heng, S., Kolp, M., & Mirbel, I. (2014). Unifying and extending user story models. In *International Conference on Advanced Information Systems Engineering* (pp. 211-225). Springer.

Wautelet, Y., Heng, S., Kolp, M., Mirbel, I., & Poelmans, S. (2016). Building a rationale diagram for evaluating user story sets. In *2016 IEEE Tenth International Conference on Research Challenges in Information Science (RCIS)* (pp. 1-12). IEEE. 10.1109/RCIS.2016.7549299

Wautelet, Y., & Kolp, M. (2016). Business and model-driven development of BDI multi-agent systems. *Neurocomputing*, *182*, 304–321. doi:10.1016/j.neucom.2015.12.022

Wautelet, Y., & Kolp, M. (2019). Conceptual Modeling as a Tool for Corporate Governance Support : State of the Art and Research Agenda. *Research & Innovation Forum*, *2019*, 1–16. doi:10.1007/978-3-030-30809-4_49

Wautelet, Y., Kolp, M., Heng, S., & Poelmans, S. (2018). Developing a multi-agent platform supporting patient hospital stays following a socio-technical approach: Management and governance benefits. *Telematics and Informatics*, *35*(4), 854–882. doi:10.1016/j.tele.2017.12.013

Weill, P., & Ross, J. W. (2011). *IT Governance on One Page*. SSRN Electronic Journal. doi:10.2139srn.664612

Yu, E., Giorgini, P., Maiden, N., & Mylopoulos, J. (2011). *Social Modeling for Requirements Engineering*. MIT Press.

KEY TERMS AND DEFINITIONS

Agility: The term itself can be defined in multiple ways pending on the context; it usually describes a methodology aligned with the values, principles, and practices as they were established by the 'Agile Manifesto' in 2001.

Business IT Alignment: A state in which an organization is able to set-up the appropriate IT capabilities, processes and infrastructure in order to realize its current and future strategic (business) objectives.

Business IT Services (BITA): Services that are defined in a top-down fashion and designed to fulfill a specific business process support problem through IT.

Conceptual Modeling: A formal technique that uses abstractions of organizational settings, user requirements, software system behavior/structure (among others) in order to help stakeholders build, document and improve a modeled reality.

Epic User Stories: User stories with a high-level of abstraction which means that they must be refined/decomposed into smaller user stories to describe the user requirements more precisely.

IT Governance: The structures, processes, and mechanisms by which the current and future use of ICT is directed and controlled.

Model-Driven IT Governance (MoDrIGo): A model-based, service-oriented framework that furnishes support to the evaluation of the business IT service portfolio by highlighting the alignment of the business IT services with the business and/or IT strategies.

Service-Oriented Architectures: A flexible enterprise architectural design whose primary purpose is to allow software resources to be packaged as 'services'.

ENDNOTE

[1]   The concept of 'business IT service' is formally defined later. See section: "Top-Down Approach: Distinguishing the Strategic Objectives and the Business IT Services".

Chapter 13
A Review of the IT Service Design Process in Agile ITSM Frameworks

Manuel Mora

https://orcid.org/0000-0003-1631-5931

Autonomous University of Aguascalientes, Mexico

Jorge Marx Gómez

Carl von Ossietzky Universität Oldenburg, Germany

Fen Wang

Central Washington University, USA

Edgar Oswaldo Díaz

National Institute of Statistics and Geography, Mexico

ABSTRACT

The current and most used IT Service Management (ITSM) frameworks (ITIL v2011, CMMI-SVC, and ISO/IEC 20000) correspond to a rigor-oriented paradigm. However, the high dynamism in business requirements for IT services has fostered the emergence of agile-assumed ITSM frameworks. In contrast with the Software Engineering field where the rigorous and agile development paradigms co-exist because both paradigms are well-known and well-accepted, in the ITSM field, agile ITSM frameworks are practically unknown. This chapter, thus, reviews the main emergent proffered agile ITSM frameworks (Lean IT, FitSM, IT4IT, and VeriSM) focusing on the IT service design process category. This process category is relevant because an IT service is designed after its business strategic authorization and the IT service design determines the future warranty and utility metrics for the IT service. The main findings suggest the need for clear and effortless agile ITSM frameworks with agile design practices to guide potential ITSM practitioners to cope with the new digital business environment.

DOI: 10.4018/978-1-7998-4165-4.ch013

INTRODUCTION

The modern management of the IT area in business organizations relies on the Service Paradigm (Keel et al., 2007; Gallup et al. 2009; Schiesser, 2010; Iden & Eikebrokk, 2013; Pilorget & Schell, 2018). IT area was traditionally managed with a technological resource view (i.e. focused on the technical operation of mainframes, networking, databases, applications, end-user equipment, and facilities) complemented with a functional specific view (i.e. operations, development, staffing, human resource, procurement, and administration) (Keel et al. 2007; Schiesser, 2010; Pilorget & Schell, 2018). However, in the last decade, a Service Paradigm (Gallup et al. 2009; Iden & Eikebrokk, 2013), which emerged mainly from Industrial Engineering and Operations Management (Levitt, 1976; Chase & Apte, 2007), and Marketing (Lovelock, 1983; Vargo & Lusch, 2004) fields, has permeated the IT management domain (Gallup et al., 2009).

A Service Paradigm from Industrial Engineering and Operations Management view (Levitt, 1976; Chase & Apte, 2007) proposes an updated concept of *service* from a non-designed and free-process and low-valued human activity framed in a boss-servant relationship, towards the new concept as a high-valued human activity that requires a previous design and structured process-supported implementation. In the Marketing field (Lovelock, 1983; Vargo & Lusch, 2004), a Service Paradigm occurred also as an update on the economic relevance from the diverse services sectors (i.e. Healthcare, Education, Financial, Legal, Transportation, and other ones) regarding the manufacturing ones (i.e. Automotive Manufacturing, Machinery Manufacturing, and in general any Goods Manufacturing), as well as a shift from a Goods-Centered Dominant Logic to a Services-Centered Dominant Logic, where a *service* is the primary unit of economic exchanges. In this stream of research, a *service* can be defined as the application of specialized knowledge and skills from some entities for producing valued outcomes in other entities (Vargo & Lusch, 2004).

From these two domains of influence, the IT management domain has adopted the Service Paradigm under the conceptual umbrella of IT Service Management (ITSM) (Gallup et al., 2009; Schiesser, 2010; Iden & Eikebrokk, 2013; Pilorget & Schell, 2018). However, ITSM focused initially on technical IT operation processes (i.e. IT service support and IT service delivery processes) (Gallup et al., 2009), but it evolved in a few years towards the full IT management area (Schiesser, 2010; Iden & Eikebrokk, 2013; Pilorget & Schell, 2018). Entire books on modern IT management topics (Schiesser, 2010; Pilorget & Schell, 2018) account for the inclusion of a Service Paradigm, as well as the emergence of specific ITSM frameworks such as ITIL v3/v2011, CMMI-SVC, and ISO/IEC 20000 (Iden & Eikebrokk, 2013). Service Management, in the ITSM domain, refers to the organizational capabilities used and applied to provide value to customers through the delivery of services (itSMF UK, 2012).

Services are *"means of delivering value to customers by facilitating outcomes customers want to achieve without the ownership of specific costs and risks"* (itSMF UK, 2012; p. 5). ITSM is defined as *"the implementation and management of quality IT services that meet the needs of the business"* (itSMF UK, 2012; p. 7). An IT Service is a service made up of IT, people and processes, and it is delivered by an IT service provider. Thus, ITSM provides IT services *"through an appropriate mix of people, process and information technology"* (itSMF UK, 2012; p. 7). Value is realized in the IT service delivery when the IT service impacts the achieved utility (*fit for purpose*) and received warranty (*fit for use*) on the customer business process supported by the IT service. The utility of an IT service corresponds to what service does and warranty to how-well it is delivered (itSMF UK, 2012). The utility of an IT service is manifested when a performance improvement and/or a reduction of constraints occur on a customer's business process using the IT service. Warranty of an IT service is received when the customer obtains the expected levels of availability, capacity, continuity, and security from the contracted IT service. Thus, ITSM can essentially be summarized as an IT Service-Centered management approach to provide value (i.e. utility and warranty) to the IT service customers.

In the last decade (Iden & Eikebrokk, 2013), several ITSM frameworks such as ITIL v3/v2011 (itSMF UK, 2012), CMMI-SVC v1.3 (Software Engineering Institute, 2010), and ISO/IEC 20000:2005 (ISO/IEC, 2005a, 2005b, 2010) emerged. ITIL v3/v2011, CMMI-SVC v1.3, and ISO/IEC 20000 have been recently updated to ITIL v4 (TSO, 2019), CMMI-SVC v2 (CMMI Institute, 2018), and ISO/IEC 20000:2018 (ISO/IEC, 2018) but the majority of ITIL, CMMI-SVC and ISO/IEC 20000 implementations correspond at present to the previous versions of these ITSM frameworks (Marrone & Kolbe, 2011; Iden & Eikebrokk, 2013; Marrone et al., 2014; Cots et al., 2016). Table 1 summarizes the main structure of these relevant ITSM frameworks.

Table 1. Summary of the essential structure of main ITSM frameworks

ITSM Process Framework	Concept and Purpose	Overall Structure and Service Design Issues	Size of Official Documentation
ITIL v3/v2011	• An ITSM framework of best practices organized in lifecycle service stages, processes, functions, and other capabilities (principles, activities, procedures, tools, and others) • To provide guidance for implementing and performing ITSM through a tested suite of best practices	• 5-Stage Service lifecycle (Strategy, Design, Transition, Operation, Continual Improvement) • Process-oriented approach with 26 processes and 4 functions • Over 30 roles (6 roles in average by Service lifecycle stage) • IT service design includes 7 processes plus 5 activities (none agile practice is reported)	• 5 books • Over 1,500 pages (300 pages on average by Service lifecycle stage book)
ISO/IEC 20000:2005	• An ITSM standard organized as an integrated process approach • To effectively deliver managed services to meet the business and customer requirements	• 7-Process Category • Process-oriented approach with 26 processes • Over 21 roles (3 roles in average by process category) • IT service design includes 3 processes with 9 specific activities (none agile practice is reported)	• 2 documents (ISO/IEC 20000-1 Specification; ISO/IEC 20000-2 Code of Practice) • 3 Technical Reports (ISO/IEC 20000-3, 2000-4 and 20000-5) • Over 125 pages (25 pages in average by Service lifecycle stage book)
CMMI-SVC v1.3	• An ITSM framework of best practices that help organizations to improve their processes • To provide a comprehensive integrated set of guidelines for providing superior services	• 24-process areas (16 core one, 1 shared one, and 7 service-specific ones) • Over 72 roles (3 roles in average by process area) • IT service design includes 1 process with 3 specific goals and 12 specific practices (none agile practice is reported)	• 1 official document • Over 500 pages (a single official document)

Source: (authors, 2020)

These main ITSM frameworks (i.e. ITIL v3/v2011, CMMI-SVC v1.3, and ISO/IEC 20000), whereas they have differences, they also shared a rigorous heavy process-oriented approach with a relatively large number of processes, roles, and documentation pages. From Table 1, it can be also noted that these three ITSM frameworks contain specific processes for the design of IT services, but none of them includes agile practices.

However, in the last decade, the high dynamism of business requirements for IT services, as well as the growing utilization of agile practices in another closely related domain (i.e. software development), has pushed the ITSM professional and academic communities to propose and elaborate agile versions of ITSM frameworks (Verlaine, 2017). Four main ITSM frameworks that claim to be agile are Lean IT v1.03 (Lean IT Association, 2015), FitSM (FitSM, 2016a; 2016b; 2016c), IT4IT v2.1 (The Open Group, 2017), and VeriSM (Agutter et al., 2017). Agile practices are also lightweight ones but not vice versa. Lightweight practices are shortened but still useful practices regarding the original heavy-oriented ones. Agile practices are also lightweight ones but they need to be also flexible (i.e. to embrace changes), responsive (i.e. reactive to changes), rapid (i.e. applicable in relatively short periods), lean-seeking (i.e. simple, high-quality and waste minimizing), and improvable (i.e. continually improved) (Conboy & Fitzgerald, 2004; Qumer & Henderson-Sellers, 2008). Additionally, the ITSM literature on the agile approach is still scarce, and consequently, ITSM practitioners lack informative references on the applicability, benefits, and limitations of using agile ITSM frameworks. Hence, the two opposite approaches (i.e. rigor-oriented ITSM and the emergent agile-assumed ITSM) exhibit conflicts and tensions in their tenets (aim, values, principles, and practices) (Mora et al., 2020), and thus a conciliated transition from the former to the latter is an open practical and research question.

This chapter applies a Conceptual Research method adapted from Mora et al. (2008) using the following steps: 1) depicting research goal; 2) selection of conceptual documents of analysis; 3) analysis of documents; and 4) discussion and agreement of findings. It focuses on the goal to review the essential structure (i.e. aim, overall content, and IT service design issues) as well as the alignment from their specific IT service design practices to a rigor-oriented and an agile-oriented framework from the four agile-assumed ITSM frameworks (Lean IT, FitSM, IT4IT, and VeriSM). This chapter complements this review goal with a discussion of gained insights and trends on agile ITSM frameworks. IT service design processes and practices are relevant because they determine the future warranty and utility metrics for the IT service. Thus, this chapter contributes to the ITSM literature and ITSM practitioners with the insights derived from the analysis of the four agile-assumed ITSM frameworks and the formulation of potential trends related to agile ITSM frameworks.

The remainder of this chapter continues as follows. In the next section Background, a review is presented on the essential structure of three main rigor-oriented ITSM frameworks (ITIL v3/v2011, ISO/IEC 20000, and CMMI-SVC), as well as an evaluative IT service design process framework derived from an ISO/IEC systems engineering standard applicable to the rigor-oriented ITSM approach. In this section an evaluative agile-oriented framework derived from first studies on agile ITSM domain is also reported, which relies on the agile Software Engineering literature. The following section, Review of Agile ITSM Frameworks and their IT Service Design Processes and Practices, uses the last two conceptual tools to evaluate the essential structure and expected elements in the four agile-assumed ITSM frameworks and their respective IT service design processes and practices. Then, in the subsequent section, Discussion and Future Trends, several insights on potential trends on agile ITSM frameworks and their specific IT service design process and practices are reported. Finally, in the last section Conclusion, the main findings, limitations, and recommendations for further research are reported.

BACKGROUND

In this section, an evaluation process scheme derived from the ISO/IEC 15288:2002 standard is reported with the corresponding evaluations for the IT service design processes in the main rigor-oriented ITSM frameworks (ITIL v3/v2011, ISO/IEC 20000, and CMMI-SVC v1.3). This evaluation framework illustrates the expected process elements in a reference model for developing general man-made systems. Here, it is also reported an agile development model from the Software Engineering literature, which is used as a reference model on the expected elements in the agile IT service design process and practices included in the four agile-assumed ITSM frameworks.

IT Service Design Processes in Rigor-Oriented ITSM Frameworks

This section is based on the thorough review and analysis of the IT service design process included in the main rigor-oriented ITSM frameworks reported in Mora et al. (2014; 2015). The ISO/IEC 15288:2002 Systems Engineering - System Life Cycle Processes standard (ISO/IEC, 2002) – was used as a process reference model for engineering man-made systems. This standard *"encompasses the life cycle of man-made systems, spanning the conception of the ideas through to the retirement of the system"* and it can be used for the assessment and improvement of the system project lifecycle. In the System Engineering field, a system is *"an integrated set of elements that accomplish a defined objective. These elements include products (hardware, software, firmware), processes, people, information, techniques, facilities, services, and other support elements."* (INCOSE, 2004; p. 10). An IT service, thus, fits this definition for the inclusion of the diverse configuration items such as hardware components, base software components, database components, networking components, environment components, data components, application components, external IT services, service teams, and service suppliers (itSMF UK, 2011).

The ISO/IEC 15288:2002 standard provides four processes categories: Enterprise, Project, Technical and Agreement. Each one includes respectively 5, 7, 11, and 2 processes. However, due to the disparity of views in the analyzed IT service design processes and the extension of the ISO/IEC 15288:2002 standard, a compacted scheme was elaborated (Mora et al., 2015). In this chapter, we selected the following compacted ISO/IEC 15288 processes: Acquisition and Supply processes (from Agreement category); Project Planning, Project Control, Decision-Making, and Risk Management (from Project category); and Stakeholder Requirements Definition, Requirement Analysis, and Architectural Design (from Technical category). The Appendix reports the main characteristics (aim, artifacts, and activities) of these selected processes. Table 2 (from Mora et al., 2015) reports the overall evaluation obtained on the IT service design processes from the rigor-oriented ITSM frameworks considered in this analysis (ITIL v3/v2011, ISO/IEC 20000, and CMMI-SVC v1.3).

A basic but illustrative ordinal scale with the values *weak, moderate* and *strong* was used. A *weak* level refers to a lack of fit between the expected activities, roles, and artifacts from the ISO/IEC 15288:2002 processes and the related ones in the ITSM framework. Similarly, a *moderate* level refers to a partial fit between the expected activities, roles, and artifacts from the ISO/IEC 15288:2002 processes and the related processes in the ITSM framework. Finally, a *strong* level refers to a high fit between the expected activities, roles, and artifacts from the ISO/IEC 15288:2002 processes and the associated ones in the ITSM framework.

Evaluations against the three categories of processes derived from the ISO/IEC 15288 standard show that only the IT service design processes in the CMMI-SVC v1.3 ITSM framework cover strongly the

Table 2. Overall evaluation of the IT service design process in the main rigor-oriented ITSM frameworks

ISO/IEC 15288:2002 Standard Processes	ITIL v3/v2011	ISO/IEC 20000	CMMI-SVC v1.3
PROJECT AND AGREEMENT PROCESSES			
Acquisition / Supply	*strong*	*strong*	*strong*
Project planning / Project control	*strong*	*strong*	*strong*
Decision-making / Risk management	*strong*	*strong*	*strong*
TECHNICAL PROCESSES			
Stakeholder requirements definition	*moderate*	*moderate*	*strong*
Requirements analysis	*strong*	*strong*	*strong*
Architectural design	*weak*	*weak*	*strong*
OVERALL RIGOR LEVEL EVALUATION	*moderate-strong*	*moderate-strong*	*strong*

Source: (adapted from Mora et al., 2015)

expected ones in the ISO/IEC 15288 standard. For the cases of ITIL v3/v2011 and ISO/IEC 20000, both were evaluated as overall moderate-strong levels, due to the *weak* levels in Technical Processes, particularly in the Architectural Design process.

The Agile Development Approach

The Agile Development paradigm emerged in the Software Engineering field from about 20 years ago (Beck et al., 2001). Main literature on the Agile Development paradigm (Highsmith & Cockburn, 2001; Dyba & Dingsøyr, 2008; Abrahamsson et al., 2010; Dingsøyr et al., 2012; Hoda et al., 2018) grew as a response to the inadequacy of the current rigor-oriented development paradigm regarding the high dynamic business requirements demanding effective and efficient responses to the fast changes and a kind of uncertain or even uncompleted full description of requirements. Additionally, there were also strong disappointment with current bureaucratic development methods provoking long-time delivery of a useful software release. Consequently, several senior software engineering practitioners (rather than academic scholars) formed the *Agile Alliance* organization and declared the well-known Agile Manifesto with one overall aim, four values, and twelve principles (Beck et al., 2001).

This software development paradigm has permeated strongly in both small, medium and large organizations (Hoda et al., 2018), and co-exists with traditional rigor-oriented development paradigm (Boehm & Turner, 2005; Batra et al., 2010; Ahimbisibwe et al., 2015). Several agile software development methodologies have been proposed (Abrahamsson et al., 2010) such as Scrum, Extreme Programming (best known as XP), Crystal, and Feature Driven Development (FDD). A relevant study (Qumer & Henderson-Sellers, 2008) evaluated the adherence to the Agile Manifest components (i.e. aim, values, principles) from the phases and practices of several agile software development methodologies, and XP, Crystal, and Scrum resulted as the best ones. However, Scrum and Hybrid Scrum-XP are identified as the most widely used methods in the last decade comparing to the other ones (Stavru, 2014; VersionOne, 2018).

In the ITSM domain, despite the existence of similar organizations like itSMF International (https://www.itsmfi.org), there are no commonly shared frameworks and unique agile ITSM manifesto has been elaborated. An ITSM literature review, however, identified (Mora et al., 2020) an initial proposal for an agile ITSM framework (Verlaine, 2017) based on the Agile Manifesto from the Software Engineering domain (Beck et al., 2001). Table 3 shows a summarized adaptation from the components (aim, values, and principles) of this proposal of the agile ITSM framework as reported in Mora et al. (2020). Table 3 adds also a list of the most used agile practices based on diverse current studies in the Software Engineering (SwE) domain (Kurapati et al., 2012; Alahyari et al., 2017; VersionOne, 2018; Vallon et al., 2018), as well as the 7 ones proposed by Verlaine (2017).

REVIEW OF AGILE ITSM FRAMEWORKS AND THEIR IT SERVICE DESIGN PROCESSES AND PRACTICES

In this section, the main identified four agile-assumed ITSM frameworks (Lean IT v1.03 (Lean IT Association, 2015), FitSM (FitSM, 2016a;2016b; 2016c), IT4IT v2.1 (The Open Group, 2017), and VeriSM (Agutter et al., 2017)) are reviewed. The aim is to report their essential structure (i.e. concept, purpose, overall structure, size of official documentation), as well as the adherence from their specific

Table 3. Basic agile ITSM framework

Aim. *Providing business value to its customers and users.*
Values.   *V1. Individuals and interactions over processes and tools.*   *V2. Working IT services over comprehensive documentation.*   *V3. Whole team collaboration over contracts.*   *V4. Responses to changes over the following plans.*
Principles.   **Outcome Principles.** *P1. Customer satisfaction as the highest priority. P7. Customer value provided as a primary measure of success.*   **Project Principles.** *P2. Embrace changes. P3. Deliver frequently useful and warranted IT service.*   **Team Principles.** *P4. Business and technical people work together daily. P5. Adequate work environment. P6. Face-to-face conversations within teams. P8. Keep sustainable work. P12. Break-times for reflection. P11. Self-organized team.*   **Design Principles.** *P9. Simplicity with technical excellence. P10. Value simplicity—the art of maximizing the amount of work not necessary—.*
Practices.   **Agile ITSM Practices.**   *Pr.1A Self-Organized Teams. Pr.1B Coaching.*   *Pr.2A Work Monitoring. Pr.2B Team Decision-Making.*   *Pr.3A Focus on User Value. Pr.3B User concerns in SLA.*   *Pr.4A Business Alignment.*   *Pr.5A Work Integrated Teams. Pr.5B Work Face-to-Face Coordination.*   *Pr.6A Simple Knowledge Management System.*   *Pr.7A Operational and Project Dual Roles.*   **Agile SwE Practices.**   *Pr.1 Daily Stand-Up Meetings. Pr.2 Sprint Planning. Pr.3 Sprint/Iteration.*   *Pr.4 Short-Releases. Pr.5 Retrospectives. Pr.6 Face-to-Face Communication.*   *Pr.7 Unit Testing. Pr.8 Tracking Monitoring. Pr.9 Continuous Integration.*   *Pr.10 User Stories / Backlog. Pr.11 Team Working. Pr.12 Sprint Review.*   *Pr.13 Coding Standards. Pr.14 Refactoring. Pr.15 Collective Ownership.*   *Pr.16 40-hour per week. Pr.17 Simple Incremental Design. Pr.18 Simple Documentation.*   *Pr.19 Burn-Down Charts. Pr.20 Release Planning Game. Pr.21 Backlog Grooming.*   *Pr.22 Agile Dev-Test Team. Pr. 23 Acceptance Testing. Pr.24 Scrum of Scrums.*   *Pr.25 Kanban. Pr.26 Dedicated Customer/Product Owner. Pr.27 Short Releases.*   *Pr.28 Test-Driven Development. Pr.29 One Team Office. Pr.30 Agile UX.*   *Pr.31 Scrum Master. Pr.32 Niko-Niko Calendar.*

Source: (adapted and extended from Verlaine, 2017, and Mora et al., 2020)

IT service design practices to the rigor-oriented and agile-oriented evaluation frameworks reported in the Background section.

Overall Description of the Agile ITSM Frameworks

Lean IT

Lean IT v1.03 (Lean IT Association; 2015) is not defined properly as an agile ITSM process or practices framework but as a Quality System. Lean IT v1.03 pursues the application of Lean Manufacturing and Services Principles to improve IT people, IT processes/practices, and IT products/services regarding customer value. Lean process and practices refer to ones that have been improved (i.e. feasible optimized ones regarding process/practice simplicity; process/practice time, space and cost minimization; and maximization of the expected product or service quality) (Lean IT Association; 2015). Lean IT approach claims, thus, that it can be applied to any ITSM process or practices framework either it is rigor-oriented or agile-oriented. Lean IT aim can be indicated as *the continual improvement of the value delivered by*

IT areas to their customers. Value is generated when there are a reduction in costs, and/or periods, and/or quality accomplishment in the customer business process, by the IT service delivery. Lean IT refers to a *"way to thinking and behaving"* (Lean IT Association, 2015; p. 9) relying in the following core concepts: customer value improvement, progressive continual improvement in small steps, reduction of process/production variability (peaks and valleys), waste minimization or full elimination, all people/teams involvement and development, and long-term business goals.

Lean IT is essentially structured with one aim – previously reported-, five principles, three types of activities, five dimensions, and one improvement process known as DMAIC. The five principles are Customer Value, Value Stream, Flow, Pull, and Perfection. The three types of activities are Valued-Add Activities, Non-Value Add Activities, and Necessary Non-Value Add Activities. The five dimensions are Customer, Process, Performance, Organization, and Behavior & Attitude. The improvement process DMAIC corresponds to Define, Measure, Analyze, Improve, and Control phases.

The Customer Value principle refers to the focus on the *Voice of the Customer*, and on delivering a product or service which produces the expected value. The Value Stream principle refers to create a whole system of activities, tasks, tools, materials, information, and people for delivering value to customers in the fastest feasible time to market period. Flow principle refers to establish a development/production with the minimal of unnecessary interruptions causing delays and waste of materials and time resources. Pull principle refers to a *Make to Order* production approach where the products/services are started to be developed until customers demand them. Perfection principle refers to empower the people for enabling them to do things right for the first time. Lean IT classifies all activities in three types (Valued-Add Activities, Non-Value Add Activities, and Necessary Non-Value Add ones). The first type refers to those that add value from a customer perspective. The second type refers to those that do not add value from a customer perspective. The third type refers to those that do not add value from a Customer perspective but are mandatory to be conducted in the organization usually required by external or internal regulations.

The customer dimension proposes to understand their points of view and their expected values from the delivered products and/or services. The process dimension proposes to create effective and efficient value streams. The organization dimension proposes to make the required organizational structures to assure people's cooperation. The performance dimension proposes to define adequate and realistic metrics based on the understanding of the previous dimensions of Customer, Process, and Organization. Behavior and Attitude dimension propose the development of the human resources seeking human virtues such as patience, reflection, trust, respect, and objectivity among other ones. The Lean IT DMAIC improvement process is conducted through the phases of Define, Measure, Analyze, Improve, and Control. In the Define phase, it is structured a problem-improvement project (problem, goals, costs, teams, resources, schedule, and stakeholders' support). In the Measure phase, a plan to study the problem-improvement situation is elaborated and applied. In the Analyze phase, the collected performance metrics and other informative cues are studied to understand the underlying generation system from the problem-improvement situation. In the Improve phase, potential specific solutions are elaborated, and a decision-making process is applied to select the most feasible ones to be implemented. In the Control phase, the selected solutions are implemented, and their results are monitored, expecting they are positive ones. Learning lessons are also shared, and project reports and closure are elaborated.

A specific process for IT service design is not reported in Lean IT.

FitSM

FitSM (FitSM, 2016a) is defined as "*a lightweight standards family*" in the ITSM domain compatible with the ISO/IEC 20000 standard and ITIL v3/v2011 ITSM framework. FitSM aims "*to maintain a clear, pragmatic, lightweight and achievable standard that allows for effective IT service management (ITSM)*" (FitSM, 2016a; p. 1). FitSM is composed of seven documents. FitSM-0 Overview and vocabulary, FitSM-1 Requirements, FitSM-2 Objectives and Activities, FitSM-3 Role Model, FitSM-4 Selected Templates and Samples, FitSM-5 Selected Implementation Guides, and FitSM-6 Maturity and Capability Assessment Scheme. FitSM claims its application in any type of organization and IT area.

In FitSM-1 are reported 7 categories of General Requirements for a Service Management System which include 16 items, as well as the 14 FitSM processes with their 69 Specific Requirements. The 7 categories of General Requirements are Top Management Commitment & Responsibility, Documentation, Defining the Scope of Service Management, Planning Service Management, Implementing Service Management, Monitoring and Reviewing Service Management, and Continually Improving Service Management.

The 14 processes of FitSM are Service Portfolio Management (SPM), Service Level Management (SLM), Service Reporting Management (SRM), Service Availability and Continuity Management (SACM), Capacity Management (CAPM), Information Security Management (ISM), Customer Relationship Management (CRM), Supplier Relationship Management (SUPPM), Incident and Service Request Management (ISRM), Problem management (PM), Configuration Management (CONFM), Change Management (CHM), Release and Deployment Management (RDM), and Continual Service Improvement Management (CSI). These 14 processes of FitSM are claimed to comply with the ISO/IEC 20001-1 standard (FitSM, 2016b). Each process in FitSM is structured with an objective, set-up activities, inputs, ongoing activities, and outputs. Additionally, there are 7 objectives for the respective 7 categories of General Requirements for a Service Management System. FitSM defines also 7 generic roles and about three specific-process roles for each one of the 14 FitSM processes. The 7 generic roles are SMS owner, SMS manager, Service owner, Process owner, Process manager, Case owner, and Member of process staff (process practitioner). FitSM reports over 60 artifacts in an ITSM Documentation Checklist guide.

FitSM claims to be an ITSM lightweight with the reduction to four core documents with a total of 38 pages compared with the extensive official documentation of full ITSM frameworks such as ITIL v3/v2011 and the ISO/IEC 20000. The concept of *agile* is not explicitly reported in the four core documents.

On the IT service design process and practices applicable in FitSM, this contains a specific guide on how to specify them. FitSM locates this guide to be used in the Service Portfolio Management (SPM) and Service Level Management (SLM) processes. Additionally, due FitSM claims to be compatible with ITIL v3/v2011, consequently, the related process of Service Availability and Continuity Management (SACM), Capacity Management (CAPM), and Information Security Management (ISM) must be also considered. An IT service design package is not reported explicitly in FitSM. Thus, the IT service descriptor elaborated with the previous guide can be considered the IT service design package in FitSM. This descriptor must contain Service Basic Information (name, service description, user of the service); Service Management Information (service owner, internal contact, external contact, service status, service area/category, service agreements); Detailed Makeup (core service buildings blocks, additional service building blocks, service packages, dependencies); and Business Case (service cost, funding source, service price, value to customer, risks, competitors).

IT4IT

IT4IT v2.1 (The Open Group, 2017) is *a standard reference architecture for managing the IT area as a business covering IT end-to-end from plan, through build and operate*. As standard, the IT4IT implies that is a prescriptive reference with mandatory shall and shall not statements, as well as optional ones (may) and recommended ones but not mandatory (should). As reference, the IT4IT architecture it can be used for organizations to map their current IT areas (structure, roles, functions, information) with the aim *"to manage the business of IT, enable business insight across the IT value chain, increase focus on business outcomes, and improve agility"* (The Open Group, 2017; p. viii). As architecture, the IT4IT provides a model composed of one IT Value Chain, four IT Primary Activities (denominated IT Value Streams), five IT Supporting Activities, and four core models (Service, Information, Functional, and Integration). IT4IT reference architecture also reports its main objective as *"to convey, in a prescriptive fashion, the key data objects, relationships, and components that are foundational for all IT organizations"* (The Open Group, 2017; p. 27).

IT4IT architecture does not prescribe a specific set of ITSM processes but they are supported and included in additional guides (outside of the standard) referred like Capability Disciplines. Instead, the IT4IT architecture provides IT-based building blocks that can be used in any ITSM process framework such as ITIL v3/v2011, ISO/IEC 20000, or CMMI-SVC. Thus, the IT4IT architecture claims to be complementary to these ITSM process frameworks on the missing IT-based building blocks to enable an ITSM approach using IT components, so its name regarding IT components usable for supporting IT service management.

IT4IT IT Value Chain is *"the series of activities that IT performs to add value to a service"* (The Open Group, 2017; p. 7). IT4IT IT Value Chain is composed of two groups of activities. Primary activities (known as Value Streams) account for the IT service planning, building, delivering, and operation. Primary activities in IT4IT Value Chain are Strategy to Portfolio, Requirements to Deploy, Request to Fulfill, and Detect to Correct. In Strategy to Portfolio value stream are evaluated strategic demands for new or improved IT services, and if authorized, the conceptual service description is elaborated. In Requirements to Deploy value stream, the conceptual service description is transformed by design in a logical service and built as a service release and a service release blueprint. In Request to Fulfill value stream, the service release blueprint (and the built IT service) is transitioned from IT test to the IT production environment, and a service catalog entry is created as the desired service. In Detect to Correct value stream, the desired service becomes in a realized service, and it is operated (i.e. monitored, managed, and remedied). Supporting activities in IT4IT Value Chain are Governance Risk & Compliance, Sourcing & Vendor, Intelligence & Reporting, Finance & Assets, and Resource & Project. Thus, the IT service design activities in IT4IT are accounted for the Requirements to Deploy value stream. The description of each one of the four IT Value Streams includes objectives, business value propositions, key performance indicators, and their service data objects and functional components.

IT4IT IT Value Chain is supported by four models (Service, Information, Functional, and Integration). Service Model defines the specific service lifecycle status as conceptual, logical, release, blueprint release, catalog entry, desired, and realized service. Information Model defines the IT service data objects with their attributes and interrelationships. These data objects can be key and auxiliary types. Some key data objects (32 items) describe how services are created, delivered and consumed, and others (3 groups of conceptual, logical and release service models) describe what services attributes are delivered (denominated Service Model Backbone). Auxiliary data objects (8 items) describe why, where, when, and how many attributes of the IT service. There are 11, 10, 13, and 15 service data objects respectively in the four value streams of Strategy to Portfolio, Requirements to Deploy, Request to Fulfill, and Detect to Correct. The Functional Model defines the functional components for supporting the IT value streams. A functional component is not an activity or process but a functional generic processing unit of IT with the capability or capabilities to provide the referred function through a particular executable implementation. A functional component creates and/or consumes service data objects. Functional components can be key and auxiliary types. There are 6, 9, 9, 9 functional components respectively in the four value streams of Strategy to Portfolio, Requirements to Deploy, Request to Fulfill, and Detect to Correct.

The overall IT service design is supported in the Requirements to Deploy (R2D) value stream. Its main objective can be reported as designing predictable, cost-effective, and high quality IT services. Its business value proposition can be stated as achieving that *IT organizations can better control the quality, utility, schedule, and cost of services regardless of the delivery model*. There are reported also about 12 critical success factor categories with about 3-5 key performance indicators by each category. Its 10 service data objects are IT initiative, logical service, requirements, source, service release, service release blueprint, test case, defect, build, and build package. Their 9 functional components are Project, Requirements, Service Design, Source Control, Build, Build Package, Release, Test, and Defect. The specific IT service design is accounted for the Requirements and Service Design functional components. In the Requirements functional component, the service-level requirements are collected, refined, scoped, and tracked. In Requirements functional component, it is created a requirements data object which must include id, type, summary, logical service id, requirements source, owner, and service release id. Requirements functional component shall provide the functional capabilities of being the system of record for all requirements, managing the requirements lifecycle, capturing service-level requirements, collecting, refining, scoping, and tracking requirements, permitting traceability to test cases and source, and providing requirements information to the Service Design functional component. In the Service Design functional component, the logical service and logical service blueprint data objects are created. The logical service data object must report id, name, description, conceptual service id, budgeted spend, and actual spend. The logical service blueprint data object must report id, name, description, version, logical service id, and architecture design. Service Design functional component shall provide the functional capabilities of being of the system of record for all logical services, designing a logical service that meets the requirements, defining required architectural artifacts, elaborating the logical service blueprint, identifying the service delivery model, identifying suppliers, enabling interrelationships with IT operations, assuring the compliance with policies and regulations, assuring security issues, enabling service performance collecting tools, and assuring the service architecture meets the SLAs and KPIs specified in the requirements data object.

VeriSM

VeriSM (Agutter et al., 2017; p. 376) is defined as a *"value-driven, evolving, responsive, and integrated service management approach"* for the entire organization in the digital era, and not only for the IT area. A service management approach is *a management approach to deliver value to customers through quality products and services*. VeriSM indicates that whereas the ITSM best practices frameworks have provided value to organizations in the last decade, the new digital business era demands a broader IT-based or digital transformation approach for the entire organization, and thus, these ITSM frameworks are insufficient to cope with the business demands in this digital era. VeriSM aims *to help organizations on how they can use integrally a mesh of best management practices in a flexible way to deliver the right product or service at the right time to their customers.*

VeriSM is documented with a service management operating model composed of Consumers, Governance, Service Management Principles, and the Management Mesh. The implementation of VeriSM approach enables organizations to define governance requirements, service management principles, a management mesh of best practices, and the service or product stages from their definition, production, responding, and provision.

Customers provide the product or service requirements, pay, receive and give feedback for the products or services. Governance provides the background system to direct and regulate the activities of an organization, and Management provides the foreground system which manages the activities of an organization into the boundaries and regulations fixed by Governance. Governance consists of three main activities (evaluate, direct, and monitor). Evaluate refers to compare the overall current organizational status vs the future forecasted or planned ones. Direct refers to create organizational principles, policies, and strategies. Monitor refers to assure that policies comply as they were planned, and the strategic performance reaches the expected one. Service Management Principles are statements that define *how the organization wants to perform and what is valued*. Service Management Principles, thus, help to define the specific best practices to include in the Management Mesh. Service Management Principles address usually assets/resources utilization, change, continuity, financial, knowledge, measurement and reporting, performance, quality, regulations, risk, and security issues.

Management Mesh refers to the integral and flexible fabric composed of organizational resources, management practices, current and emergent technologies, and environmental conditions. This Management Mesh enables a flexible and agile management service approach in organizations to define, produce, provide and respond to their products and services. The definition of a particular Management Mesh happens after the definition of Governance strategies and policies, and Service Management Principles. In particular, the environmental conditions in the Management Mesh include the called service stabilizers (processes, tools, and measurements). This Management Mesh lately defines four functional areas/stages for developing and providing the products and services of the organization. These are Define, Produce, Provide and Respond. There are 4, 3, 3, and 2 high-level activities respectively in the four stages. The 4 activities of the Define stage are consumer need, required outcome, solution, and service blueprint. The 3 activities of the Produce stage are build, test, and implement and validate. The 3 activities of Provide are protect, measure and maintain, and improve. The 2 activities of Respond stage are record and manage.

The IT service design issues in VeriSM corresponds to the Define stage. Its objective is providing the activities and outcomes (artifacts) related to the service or product design in conformance with the Governance policies and Service Management Principles to meet the performance, security, risk and quality requirements. The 4 high-level activities are consumer need, required outcome, solution, and service blueprint. In consumer need, a demand for a product or service is presented and authorized or rejected. In the required outcome, the service or product requirements of diverse types (functional and non-functional ones) are gathered. In solution, a design plan is elaborated which includes service attributes (capacity, availability, continuity, security), risk issues, testing issues, training issues, implementation plan, people involved, supply chain, facilities, infrastructure and technology, metrics, knowledge for ongoing and improvement activities, and support processes and tools for delivering the service or product. Finally, in service blueprint, the details for the service or product delivering/production are generated. In this Define stage, the implicit outcomes (artifacts) to generate are service/product proposal, service/product requirements, service/product solution, and service/product blueprint.

Overall Evaluation of the Agile ITSM Frameworks vs the Rigor-Oriented ITSM Framework

Based on the previous reviews for the four ITSM frameworks, Table 4 presents a high-level evaluation of their content provided regarding the expected processes in the ISO/IEC 15288 standard. Table 4 utilizes the same ordinal scale from *weak, moderate* to *strong* levels as used in Table 2. Table 4 includes the previous evaluations done on the rigor-oriented ITSM process frameworks (ITIL v3/v2011, ISO/IEC 20000, and CMMI-SVC) for comparative purposes. Lean IT v1.03 (Lean IT Association; 2015) is not defined properly as an agile ITSM processes or practices framework but as a Quality System. Lean IT v1.03 pursues the application of Lean Manufacturing and Services Principles to improve IT people, IT processes/practices, and IT. Thus, Table 4 reports only the evaluation of the other three reviewed agile-assumed ITSM frameworks/approaches.

Table 4. Overall evaluation of the IT service design process in the main rigor-oriented ITSM Frameworks and emergent agile service management approaches/frameworks

ISO/IEC 15288:2002 Standard Processes	ITIL v3/v2011	ISO/IEC 20000	CMMI-SVC v1.3	FitSM	IT4IT	VeriSM
PROJECT AND AGREEMENT PROCESSES	*strong*	*strong*	*strong*	*moderate*	*moderate*	*weak*
Acquisition / Supply	*strong*	*strong*	*strong*	*moderate*	*weak*	*weak*
Project planning / Project control	*strong*	*strong*	*strong*	*weak*	*strong*	*weak*
Decision-making / Risk management	*strong*	*strong*	*strong*	*mod*	*weak*	*weak*
TECHNICAL PROCESSES	*moderate*	*moderate*	*strong*	*moderate*	*strong*	*weak*
Stakeholder requirements definition	*strong*	*strong*	*strong*	*moderate*	*strong*	*moderate*
Requirements analysis	*strong*	*strong*	*strong*	*moderate*	*strong*	*weak*
Architectural design	*weak*	*weak*	*strong*	*moderate*	*strong*	*weak*
OVERALL RIGOR EVALUATION	*moderate-strong*	*moderate-strong*	*strong*	*moderate*	*moderate-strong*	*weak*

Source: (adapted and extended from Mora et al., 2015)

It must be also clarified that this evaluation should be interpreted as an overall approximation of how these management service frameworks (including the IT area) fit a normative rigor-oriented process framework (i.e. the ISO/IEC 15288 standard). Thus, for the agile-assumed ITSM frameworks (i.e. FitSM, IT4IT, and VeriSM) it should be expected as *weak* levels. FitSM and IT4IT were assessed with *moderate* and *moderate-strong* levels, and thus these ITSM frameworks can be considered lightweight but not as agile types. VeriSM, in contrast, was assessed with a *weak* level, and hence, it qualifies as an agile ITSM framework. This evaluation is an approximation due to the identified limitations including 1) Lean IT is a generic approach for ITSM process improvement rather an ITSM framework; 2) IT4IT does not provide process for ITSM but functional components and data objects for supporting and enabling any ITSM process framework; and 3) VeriSM does not provide ITSM processes but it provides a service management model (which includes the IT area) which helps to integrate diverse specific ITSM process and best practices frameworks. FitSM does qualify as an ITSM process framework. However, these four service management (two generic ones - Lean IT and VeriSM-, and two for IT area - FitSM and IT4IT -) frameworks were included in this review as ITSM were reported in literature as service management frameworks which embrace an agile approach.

Additionally, none particular agile ITSM process framework has been already reported, and thus, this review is useful to report an initial approximation to the concerns regarding the realization of an agile ITSM approach and how far they are from a rigor-oriented ITSM approach assessed with the ISO/IEC 15288 standard.

Overall Evaluation of the Agile ITSM Frameworks vs the Agile-Oriented ITSM Framework

Table 5 reports the evaluation of the four reviewed agile-assumed ITSM frameworks/approaches. As it indicates, Lean IT is a Quality System applicable to many domains (and thus to ITSM), FitSM and IT4IT are focused on IT area, and VeriSM claims to be a whole organizational service management approach, and consequently, this is also applicable to IT area. The ordinal scale used is as follows: 1) *weak*: agile statements are scarcely supported; 2) *moderate*: agile statements are supported but not explicitly included; and 3) *strong*: agile statements are supported and explicitly included.

Table 5. Initial Evaluation of the emergent agile service management approaches/frameworks

AGILE DIMENSION	Lean IT	FitSM	IT4IT	VeriSM
Core Concepts	*moderate-strong*	*weak-moderate*	*moderate*	*strong*
- Aim	*strong*	*weak*	*strong*	*strong*
- Values	*moderate*	*moderate*	*weak*	*strong*
Principles	*moderate-strong*	*weak-moderate*	*weak*	*strong*
- Outcome Principles	*strong*	*weak*	*strong*	*strong*
- Project Principles	*moderate*	*moderate*	*weak*	*moderate*
- Team Principles	*moderate*	*weak*	*weak*	*strong*
- Design Principles	*strong*	*moderate*	*weak*	*strong*
Practices	*moderate*	*moderate*	*weak*	*strong*
- Agile ITSM Practices	*moderate*	*moderate*	*weak*	*strong*
- Agile SwE Practices	*moderate*	*weak*	*weak*	*moderate*
- Agile IT service design	*moderate*	*moderate*	*weak*	*strong*
OVERALL AGILITY LEVEL EVALUATION	*moderate-strong*	*weak-moderate*	*weak*	*strong*

Source: (adapted and extended from Verlaine, 2017, and Mora et al., 2020)

Relevant insights from Tables 4 and 5 indicate that IT4IT exhibits a weak agility level and consistently a moderate-strong rigor level. Similarly, FitSM exhibits a weak-moderate agility level and a moderate rigor level. VeriSM exhibits a strong agility level and consistently a weak rigor level. Finally, Lean IT is also evaluated with a moderate-strong fit to agility approach.

DISCUSSION AND FUTURE TRENDS

This chapter aims to report an initial review on emergent ITSM frameworks and approaches that have been used in the context of Agile Paradigm, and in particular to identify their IT service design processes and practices. Consequently, the four main ITSM frameworks were reviewed essentially on 1) their IT service design coverage regarding a rigor-oriented process evaluation framework derived from the ISO/IEC 15288 Systems Engineering standard (Table 4); and 2) their adherence to supporting and explicitly including agile tenets (i.e., aim, values, principles, and practices) derived from an initial reported agile ITSM framework and core agile Software Engineering literature, as well as on their specific agile IT service design phase (Table 5).

Firstly, from Table 4, it can be identified that the three reported rigor-oriented ITSM frameworks (ITIL v3/v2011, ISO/IEC 20000, and CMMI-SVC) fit very well with the expected rigor-oriented elements from the ISO/IEC 15288 Systems Engineering standard, and thus, they qualify correctly as rigor-oriented (process-heavy) ITSM process frameworks. Regarding the three initially agile-assumed ITSM frameworks, it can be identified that only the VeriSM is assessed congruently with a weak level regarding its adherence to a rigor-oriented ITSM framework. In contrast, the IT4IT reference architecture standard was assessed with a moderate to strong level of adherence to being a rigor-oriented ITSM framework. Accordingly, the IT4IT is less likely to be considered as an agile framework. The assessment result of FitSM is unexpected. FitSM is a lightweight ITSM process framework with its strong reduction in processes, roles, and artifacts required regarding the rigor-oriented ITSM process frameworks such as ITIL v3/v2011, ISO/IEC 20000, and CMMI-SVC. Although a lightweight attribute is necessary for agile practices, it is not sufficient. As it was previously indicated, besides being lightweight, agile practices are also required to be flexible (i.e. to embrace changes), responsive (i.e. reactive to changes), rapid (i.e. applicable in relatively short periods), lean-seeking (i.e. simple, high-quality and waste minimizing), and improvable (i.e. continually improved). FitSM official documentation is just 38-page long, but it fits still moderately the expected elements in a rigor-oriented ITSM process framework.

Secondly, from Table 5, the results of the assessment on the adherence to agile ITSM tenets for the four agile-assumed ITSM frameworks indicate. congruently with results from Table 4, that VeriSM can be considered with strong adherence to agile tenets, IT4IT at a weak level, and FitSM at a moderate level. These results are also congruent with their reasons to be proposed. VeriSM has emerged to cope with the dynamic demands caused by the digital transformation era, as well as by the multiple availabilities of management approaches, frameworks, practices, and methodologies. Accordingly, its concept of Management Mesh is to elaborate an ITSM fabric customized. VeriSM, thus, does not impose mandatory low-level activities to be followed (though recommended), while its four high-level phase model on how services or products are developed is expected to be followed. VeriSM official documentation includes emergent ITSM management practices such as Lean, DevOps, and Customer/User Experience, as well as emergent technologies such as Cloud Computing, Machine Learning, and the Internet of Things. Thus, VeriSM can be recognized as an "open-mind alike" service management approach that can glue all particular management approaches and emergent technologies.

The case of IT4IT was relatively unexpected. IT4IT claims to be usable for an agile approach, but despite its strong adherence to the delivering value to customers as a maximum priority, IT4IT does not explicitly support the remainder agile tenets (according to Table 5). It can be argued that IT4IT does not provide process, activities or practices, but functional components (computationally executable building blocks) and data objects for enabling the particular Capability Disciplines (i.e. the specific ITSM processes) used for an organization. However, the diverse agile tenets reported in Table 5 are not explicitly considered and fostered to be used in the official IT4IT documentation. An additional guide (The Open Group, 2016), specific on Agile Scenarios for IT4IT, reports complex architectural design recommendations, unlikely to be applied by agile ITSM practitioners. Thus, its assessment was weak, implying great difficulty for small and medium-sized organizations interested in using IT4IT for enabling an agile ITSM framework. IT4IT has been designed, actually, *"for large enterprise IT organizations"* (The Open Group, 2016; p. 16). Thus, the IT4IT weak assessment regarding its adherence to agile tenets is congruent with its moderate to strong assessment regarding its adherence to rigor-oriented ITSM frameworks. The assessment for FitSM was from weak to moderate. Some agile tenets (aim, outcome principles, team principles, and agile SwE practices) are weak and the remaining ones are moderate. FitSM official four documents do not report the concept of agility. FitSM emerged in the context of scientific data centers (cloud, grid, and federation types), providing scientific computing services to a wide global community. Consequently, while an ITSM process framework was required, the available ones (ITIL v3/v2011 and ISO/IEC 20000) were considered quite bureaucratic with excessive required documentation, most likely useful for business organizations. FitSM, thus, emerges with the need to lighten this heavy-process approach rather than to provide an agile one.

Thirdly, regarding the specific IT service design issues reported in the four agile-assumed ITSM frameworks, the results are strong, moderate, moderate, and weak, respectively for VeriSM, FitSM, Lean IT, and IT4IT. VeriSM, consistent with its support to an agile approach, presents a flexible IT service design phase (first one of Define), with four activities (consumer need, required outcome, solution, and service blueprint) that can effortlessly include agile practices. FitSM is considered moderate because it reports a specific 6-page guide (complementary document FitSM-5, 2014), which is lightweight regarding ITIL v3/v2011 or ISO/IEC 20000 IT service design specifications but does not include agile practices. Similarly, the IT service design interpretation from Lean IT is evaluated at a moderate level regarding agile practices. The IT service design in IT4IT is assessed as weak from an agile perspective and in moderate to strong level from a rigor-oriented one. The second Value Stream of Requirements to Deploy (R2D) accounts for the IT service design. This R2D Value Stream has respectively 12, 3-5, 10, and 9 critical success factor categories, key performance indicators by each category, service data objects, and functional components (besides their particular Capability Disciplines that must be associated to realize this Value Stream). Among them, just two Functional Components (Requirements and Service Design) and three data objects (requirements, logical service, and logical service blueprint) were identified as directly associated with the IT service design purpose. Despite the reduced number of Functional Components and data objects associated with IT service design, they report quite prescriptive statements (with minimal flexibility to omit some of them), enduring a rigor-oriented approach rather than an agile one. Additionally, none references to agile practices from Capability Disciplines are reported.

Rigor-oriented ITSM process frameworks have been successfully implemented in the last two decades in multiple organizations (Marrone & Kolbe, 2011; Marrone et al., 2014), with the need of coping with IT-silos in IT areas, and a technological-centered perspective instead of a user-centered one, where the concepts of service and service value were omitted in IT management approaches. However, in the last five years, the arisen of the digital transformation business demands, and the highly dynamic business environment, the emergence and convergence of disruptive IT such as Cloud Computing, Internet of Things, and Machine Learning among others, and the cultural-social and IT professional movement to reject bureaucratic management approach toward an agile perspective, have led to the emergence of new agile-assumed ITSM frameworks.

This chapter reviewed four agile-assumed ITSM frameworks (Lean IT, FitSM, IT4IT, and VeriSM) from the literature, and with a thorough analysis has revealed that strictly only one of them qualifies as an agile ITSM framework. Lean IT is a generic process improvement methodology that can be applied to any ITSM framework. FitSM can be considered as a lightweight ITSM process framework but it is insufficient to be considered as an agile one. IT4IT, as a standard, prescribes a vast set of mandatory statements to be realized, and no specific references on the utilization of agile practices are reported. VeriSM qualifies as the best available agile one but it claims to be focused on the entire organization. Thus, VeriSM is a service management approach rather than an ITSM framework. Additionally, in contrast with the Software Engineering field where a well-recognized agile framework existed since two decades ago, in the ITSM field, an agile framework with a global acceptance is missing.

Based on the previous analysis, the following trends for future research and practical work in agile ITSM management emerge: 1) clear agile ITSM frameworks will be demanded by the business organizations; 2) an adequate agile version of FitSM can be elaborated; 3) detailed implementation guides on how Lean IT and/or IT4IT can be applied with an agile approach can be generated; 4) VeriSM will expand their application in multiple global organizations; 5) specific agile versions of ISO/IEC 20000 standard, ITIL v3/v2011, and CMMI-SVC can be generated; 6) the new version of ITIL v4, which claims to embrace agile and other emergent management approaches must be studied together with empirical cases of successful implementation of agile ITSM using ITIL v4; and 7) a globally accepted agile ITSM framework with specific agile tenets, comparable to the existing one in the Software Engineering field since two decades ago can be agreed jointly by top ITSM organizations of practitioners and ITSM academic scholars.

CONCLUSION

This chapter reviewed the main four agile-assumed ITSM frameworks (Lean IT, FitSM, IT4IT, and VeriSM) reported in the current ITSM literature, to assess their coverage to both rigor-oriented and agile-oriented paradigms. This assessment is imperative and worthy given the current growing needs and interest in implementing successful agile ITSM approaches to cope with the new business environment driven by digital transformation pressures. With this thorough review and evaluation, it was identified that Lean IT does not qualify as an ITSM framework but it can be used for improving any existent one toward its *agilization*. FitSM is properly an ITSM process framework that qualifies as lightweight but moderately as agile one. IT4IT, while its complementary guides include the ITSM processes (named Capability Disciplines in IT4IT), provides rather computational and executable functional components and data objects organized in four value streams, to enable any ITSM framework. IT4IT is a reference architecture standard, and thus, provides a core set of mandatory statements to be achieved. Additionally, no clear specifications to agile practices are reported. Thus, it was assessed as weak from an agile perspective. Finally, VeriSM, as a generic service management approach, which can be used also for the

IT area, presents an adequate flexible approach that can accommodate effortlessly an agile approach, and thus it was assessed as strong in its adherence to agile tenets.

These evaluations were conducted using the official documents from the four ITSM frameworks by the first two authors and reviewed by the third one. The fourth author reviewed the logical consistency of this chapter from an ITSM practitioner perspective. Thus, the evaluation and analysis were performed from multiple perspectives but with a quality control mechanism for caring the research rigor. A possible limitation of the research is that it did not involve a larger number of experts through focus groups or interviews, which can be also one of the possible directions for future research. Finally, an integrated need derived from this analysis is the joint formulation of an agile ITSM framework by ITSM experts from both the practice and the academy that can be globally accepted, like the existing one in the Software Engineering discipline.

ACKNOWLEDGMENT

The authors thank their respective academic institutions for the academic support provided for the realization of this research.

REFERENCES

Abrahamsson, P., Oza, N., & Siponen, M. T. (2010). Agile Software Development Methods: A Comparative Review. In T. Dingsøyr, T. Dybå, & N. Moe (Eds.), *Agile Software Development* (pp. 31–59). Springer. doi:10.1007/978-3-642-12575-1_3

Agutter, C., van Hove, S., Steinberg, R., & England, R. (2017). *VeriSM - A service management approach for the digital age*. Van Haren.

Ahimbisibwe, A., Cavana, R. Y., & Daellenbach, U. (2015). A contingency fit model of critical success factors for software development projects: A comparison of agile and traditional plan-based methodologies. *Journal of Enterprise Information Management*, 28(1), 7–33. doi:10.1108/JEIM-08-2013-0060

Alahyari, H., Svensson, R. B., & Gorschek, T. (2017). A study of value in agile software development organizations. *Journal of Systems and Software*, 125, 271–288. doi:10.1016/j.jss.2016.12.007

Batra, D., Xia, W., VanderMeer, D. E., & Dutta, K. (2010). Balancing agile and structured development approaches to successfully manage large distributed software projects: A case study from the cruise line industry. CAIS, 27(21), 379-394.

Beck, K., Beedle, M., Van Bennekum, A., Cockburn, A., Cunningham, W., Fowler, M., . . . Kern, J. (2001). *The agile manifesto*. Available from https://agilemanifesto.org/

Boehm, B., & Turner, R. (2005). Management challenges to implementing agile processes in traditional development organizations. *IEEE Software*, 22(5), 30–39. doi:10.1109/MS.2005.129

Chase, R. B., & Apte, U. M. (2007). A history of research in service operations: What's the big idea? *Journal of Operations Management*, 25(2), 375–386. doi:10.1016/j.jom.2006.11.002

Conboy, K., & Fitzgerald, B. (2004). Toward a Conceptual Framework of Agile Methods. In C. Zannier, H. Erdogmus, & L. Lindstrom (Eds.), *Extreme Programming and Agile Methods - XP/Agile Universe 2004, LNCS* (Vol. 3134, pp. 105–116). Springer. doi:10.1007/978-3-540-27777-4_11

Cots, S., Casadesús, M., & Marimon, F. (2016). Benefits of ISO 20000 IT service management certification. *Information Systems and e-Business Management, 14*(1), 1–18. doi:10.100710257-014-0271-2

Dingsøyr, T., Nerur, S., Balijepally, V., & Moe, N. B. (2012). A decade of agile methodologies. *Journal of Systems and Software, 85*(6), 1213–1221. doi:10.1016/j.jss.2012.02.033

Dybå, T., & Dingsøyr, T. (2008). Empirical studies of agile software development: A systematic review. *Information and Software Technology, 50*(9-10), 833–859. doi:10.1016/j.infsof.2008.01.006

Fit, S. M. (2016a). *FitSM-1: Requirements, The FitSM Standard Family: Standard for lightweight IT service management 1, version 2.1*. Available from https://www.fitsm.eu/downloads/

Fit, S. M. (2016b). *FitSM-2: Objectives and activities, The FitSM Standard Family: Standard for lightweight IT service management 1, version 2.2*. Available from https://www.fitsm.eu/downloads/

Fit, S. M. (2016c). *FitSM-3: Role model, The FitSM Standard Family: Standard for lightweight IT service management, version 2.2*. Available from https://www.fitsm.eu/downloads/

Galup, S. D., Dattero, R., Quan, J. J., & Conger, S. (2009). An overview of IT service management. *Communications of the ACM, 52*(5), 124–127. doi:10.1145/1506409.1506439

Highsmith, J., & Cockburn, A. (2001). Agile software development: The business of innovation. *Computer, 34*(9), 120–127. doi:10.1109/2.947100

Hoda, R., Salleh, N., & Grundy, J. (2018). The rise and evolution of agile software development. *IEEE Software, 35*(5), 58–63. doi:10.1109/MS.2018.290111318

Iden, J., & Eikebrokk, T. R. (2013). Implementing IT Service Management: A systematic literature review. *International Journal of Information Management, 33*(3), 512–523. doi:10.1016/j.ijinfomgt.2013.01.004

INCOSE. (2004). *Systems Engineering Handbook*. International Council in Systems Engineering.

ISO/IEC. (2002). *ISO/IEC 15288-2002 - Systems Engineering - System Life Cycle Processes*. International Organization for Standardization.

ISO/IEC. (2005a). *ISO/IEC 20000-1:2005 Information technology - Service management - Part 1: Specification*. International Organization for Standardization.

ISO/IEC. (2005b). *ISO/IEC 20000-1:2005 Information technology — Service management — Part 2: Code of practice*. International Organization for Standardization.

ISO/IEC. (2010). *ISO/IEC TR 20000-4:2010 Information technology — Service management — Part 4: Process reference model*. International Organization for Standardization.

itSMF UK. (2012). *ITIL Foundation Handbook*. London, UK: The Stationery Office.

Keel, A. J., Orr, M. A., Hernandez, R. R., Patrocinio, E. A., & Bouchard, J. (2007). From a technology-oriented to a service-oriented approach to IT management. *IBM Systems Journal, 46*(3), 549–564. doi:10.1147j.463.0549

Kurapati, N., Manyam, V. S. C., & Petersen, K. (2012). Agile Software Development Practice Adoption Survey. In C. Wohlin (Ed.), *Agile Processes in Software Engineering and Extreme Programming, XP 2012, LNBIP* (Vol. 111, pp. 16–30). Springer. doi:10.1007/978-3-642-30350-0_2

Lean I. T. Association. (2015). Lean IT Foundation - Increasing the Value of IT. Newark, NJ: Lean IT Association.

Levitt, T. (1976). Industrialization of service. *Harvard Business Review, 54*(5), 63–74.

Lovelock, C. H. (1983). Classifying services to gain strategic marketing insights. *Journal of Marketing, 47*(3), 9–20. doi:10.1177/002224298304700303

Marrone, M., Gacenga, F., Cater-Steel, A., & Kolbe, L. (2014). IT service management: A cross-national study of ITIL adoption. CAIS, 34(49), 865-892.

Marrone, M., & Kolbe, M. (2011). Impact of IT Service Management Frameworks on the IT Organization: An Empirical Study on Benefits, Challenges, and Processes. *Business & Information Systems Engineering, 1*(1), 5–18. doi:10.100712599-010-0141-5

Mora, M., Gelman, O., Paradice, D., & Cervantes, F. (2008). The case for conceptual research in information systems. CONF-IRM 2008 Proceedings, 1-10.

Mora, M., Gomez, J. M., O'Connor, R. V., Raisinghani, M., & Gelman, O. (2015). An extensive review of IT service design in seven international ITSM processes frameworks: Part II. *International Journal of Information Technologies and Systems Approach, 8*(1), 69–90. doi:10.4018/ijitsa.2015010104

Mora, M., Raisinghani, M., O'Connor, R. V., Gomez, J. M., & Gelman, O. (2014). An extensive review of IT service design in seven international ITSM processes frameworks: Part I. *International Journal of Information Technologies and Systems Approach, 7*(2), 83–107. doi:10.4018/ijitsa.2014070105

Mora, M., Wang, F., Gómez, J. M., & Díaz, O. (2020). A Comparative Review on the Agile Tenets in the IT Service Management and the Software Engineering Domains. In Trends and Applications in Software Engineering, CIMPS 2019, Advances in Intelligent Systems and Computing (Vol. 1071, pp. 102-115). Berlin, Germany: Springer. doi:10.1007/978-3-030-33547-2_9

Pilorget, L., & Schell, T. (2018). *IT Management: The art of managing IT based on a solid framework leveraging the company's political ecosystem.* Springer. doi:10.1007/978-3-658-19309-6

Qumer, A., & Henderson-Sellers, B. (2008). An evaluation of the degree of agility in six agile methods and its applicability for method engineering. *Information and Software Technology, 50*(4), 280–295. doi:10.1016/j.infsof.2007.02.002

Schiesser, R. (2010). *IT Systems Management.* Prentice-Hall.

Software Engineering Institute. (2010). *CMMI for Service Version 1.3, CMMI-SVC v1. 3. CMU/SEI-2010-TR-034.* Software Engineering Institute.

Stavru, S. (2014). A critical examination of recent industrial surveys on agile method usage. *Journal of Systems and Software*, *94*, 87–97. doi:10.1016/j.jss.2014.03.041

The Open Group. (2016). *IT4IT Agile Scenario Using the Reference Architecture*. Available from https://publications.opengroup.org/w162

The Open Group. (2017). *The Open Group IT4IT™ Reference Architecture, Version 2.1*. The Open Group.

Vallon, R., da Silva Estacio, B. J., Prikladnicki, R., & Grechenig, T. (2018). Systematic literature review on agile practices in global software development. *Information and Software Technology*, *96*, 161–180. doi:10.1016/j.infsof.2017.12.004

Vargo, S. L., & Lusch, R. F. (2004). The four service marketing myths: Remnants of a goods-based, manufacturing model. *Journal of Service Research*, *6*(4), 324–335. doi:10.1177/1094670503262946

Verlaine, B. (2017). Toward an agile IT service management framework. *Service Science*, *9*(4), 263–274. doi:10.1287erv.2017.0186

VersionOne. (2018). *CollabNet 13th Annual State of Agile Report*. Available from https://www.stateofagile.com/#ufh-i-521251909-13th-annual-state-of-agile-report/473508

KEY TERMS AND DEFINITIONS

Agility: The property of an entity to be flexible, responsive, quick, lightweight, and lean.

IT Service: A service delivered mandatory with IT.

ITSM: Information Technology Service Management is a management approach for managing the IT area with a service-centered focus.

Lightweight: The property of an entity to be small or short in its core content.

Rigor-Oriented Framework: A framework whose content must be mandatory followed and that is relatively extenso.

Service: A valued functionality received from a service provider.

Service Value: An objective or subjective benefit appreciated exclusively by the beneficiary from a service.

APPENDIX

Table 6. Characteristics from the main process in the ISO/IEC 15288:2002 standard

PROJECT AND AGREEMENT PROCESSES
Acquisition / Supply
Aim. *Acquisition process accounts for the activities for conducting a systematic acquisition of products or services required for a system with a supplier. Supply process concerns with the provision to an acquirer with a product or service that meets the agreed requirements.*
Main Artifacts. *Acquisition.* *(i) a set of potential suppliers, (ii) an agreement of acquisition with acceptance criteria, and (iii) the product or service in compliance with the agreement.* ***Supply.*** *(i) an acquirer for a product or service, (ii) an agreement of acquisition with acceptance criteria, and (iii) the product or service in compliance with the agreement.*
Main Activities. *Acquisition.* *(i) prepare the acquisition, (ii) advertise the acquisition and select the supplier, (iii) initiate an agreement, (iv) monitor the agreement, and (v) accept the product or service.* ***Supply.*** *(i) identify opportunities, (ii) respond to a tender, (iii) initiate an agreement, (iv) execute the agreement, (v) deliver and support the product or service, and (vi) close the agreement.*
Project Planning / Project Control
Aim. *Project Planning process basically defines the scope, roles, activities, deliverables, schedules, and resources required for conducting an effective and efficient project. Project Control process refers to monitoring and corrective activities required to fit the planned schedules, budgets and technical objectives of the product or service.*
Main Artifacts. *Project Planning.* *(i) project plans, (ii) list of resources, and (iii) list of roles.* ***Project Control.*** *(i) project performance and deviation metrics, (ii) corrective actions, and (iii) realization of project objectives.*
Main Activities. *Project Planning.* *(i) define the project, (ii) plan the project resources, (iii) plan the project technical and quality management, and (iv) activate the project. . **Project Control.** (i) assess the project, (ii) control the project, and (iii) close the project.*
Decision Making / Risk Management
Aim. *Decision-Making process provides activities to select most adequate course of action when relevant alternatives appear during the execution of the system life cycle processes. Risk Management process is used for identify, analyze, treat and monitor the risks continuously.*
Main Artifacts. *Decision Making.* *(i) a decision-making method, (ii) a decision-making situation is structured, and (iii) decisions with their rationale.* ***Risk Management.*** *(i) scope of risk management, (ii) risk management methods, (iii) risk management actions.*
Main Activities. *Decision Making.* *(i) plan and define decisions, (ii) analyze the decision information, (iii) track the decision.* ***Risk Management.*** *(i) plan risk management, (ii) manage the risk profile, (iii) analyze the risks, (iv) treat the risks, (v) monitor the risks, and (v) evaluate the risk management processes.*
TECHNICAL PROCESSES
Stakeholder Requirements Definition
Aim. *Stakeholder Requirements Definition process refers to identification of stakeholders and their needs, expectations and desires which must be specified in technical feasible requirements.*
Main Artifacts. *(i) context and stakeholders description, (ii) needs and constraints for the system, and (iii) feasible stakeholders requirements.*
Main Activities. *(i) elicit stakeholder requirements, (ii) define stakeholder requirements, and (iii) analyze and maintain stakeholder requirements.*
Requirements Analysis
Aim. *Requirement Analysis is the process where stakeholders requirements are technically specified.*
Main Artifacts. *(i) technical requirements (functional, performance, security, and others), (ii) constraints, and (iii) acceptance criteria.*
Main Activities. *(i) define systems requirements, and (ii) analyze and maintain system requirements.*
Architectural Design
Aim. *Architectural design process concerns with synthesizing a solution that can fit the technical requirements.*
Main Artifacts. *(i) a baseline system architecture design, (ii) a description of the elements of the system architecture and their interrelationships, and (iii) acceptance criteria.*
Main Activities. *(i) define the architecture, (ii) analyze and evaluate the architecture, and (iii) document and maintain the architecture.*

Source: (authors, 2020)

Chapter 14
Requirements on Dimensions for a Maturity Model for Smart Grids Based on Two Case Studies:
Disciplined vs. Agile Approach

Agnetha Flore
Oldenburger OFFIS, Germany

Jorge Marx Goméz
Carl von Ossietzky Universität Oldenburg, Germany

ABSTRACT

This contribution describes two different types of requirements engineering analysis of the necessary dimensions of a possible maturity model for Smart Grids to be implemented for utilities. For the first case study, the requirements engineering for necessary dimensions for a Smart Grid maturity model was elicited using a systematic literature research. On the contrary a more agile approach is used for the second requirements engineering. For this more agile approach, interviews with energy suppliers were conducted, taking into account the analysis of the literature research. Various energy suppliers from Germany took part in the survey. The results were used to develop the basic framework for a maturity model for Smart Grids, which can still be tailored if necessary. Finally, future research activities for the application and further development of maturity models for Smart Grids in the energy industry are explained as well as the different procedural variants in the requirements analysis.

DOI: 10.4018/978-1-7998-4165-4.ch014

INTRODUCTION

At present, the issue of energy system transformation and climate targets is of crucial importance for politics and society. In order to be a successful utility in the future, it is important to move from a previously centrally controlled grid infrastructure to a decentralized, dominated structure. Only through a decentralized grid infrastructure is it possible to guarantee increasing feed-in from renewable energy into the grid (Appelrath, Mayer, & Rohjans, 2012).

This decentralization of the grid can be achieved through increased measurement, control and automation of the electricity flow, as well as regional high-resolution monitoring and control of the electricity grid. To achieve this, the electricity grid is to be modernized and made more intelligent through new information and communication technologies (ICT) (Projekt Green Access, 2019).

More and more research and development projects are dealing with the topics of the energy grid of the future, innovative technologies, the addition of storage facilities, etc. This shows that the subject is of great interest for practice and science.

In this contribution, a maturity model will be applied as an evaluation model for utilities. Through the use of evaluation models, the continuous improvement of a company is aimed at, whereby the focus is on comparison, i.e. "learning from the best" (Uebernickel, Stölzle, Lennerts, Lampe, & Hoffman, 2015). This maturity model should be specific to the energy domain in order to analyse the specific dimensions there. This analysis is necessary for a utility to know its status quo. Only when the status quo is known can the goal of making the own grid more modern and intelligent be pursued.

Due to the strong change in the energy domain that demands a high degree of change from utilities – in processes, procedures, methods and technologies – flexibility, adaptability, changeability and willingness to company-wide change processes play an increasingly important role.

A domain-specific maturity model has to be developed for two research projects in Germany, each of which uses different approaches and ideas to research and test new technological solutions for an intelligent power grid. Both case studies involve distribution system operators.

In this chapter we report on how the requirements for the dimensions of the maturity model to be developed were determined in these two research projects - case studies "utility 1" and "utility 2".

Due to the increasing importance of agility in business, the approach of requirements elicitation will be conducted with two different methods: a disciplined and an agile approach.

The following research questions are to be answered:

RQ1: Is there already a suitable maturity model in the literature that can be used for this case studies?
RQ2: If a new maturity model is necessary, which dimensions of a utility have to be considered?
RQ3: Which approach is the better one for collecting the requirements for the dimensions, a disciplined or an agile one?

This contribution is structured as follows: The section "Introduction" briefly presents the motivation for dealing with the topic. Section "Background" represents the basic terminologies and section "Disciplined Maturity Models vs. agile Maturity Models" describes the differences between these kinds of maturity models. The research methodologies of the two case studies are presented in section "Research Methodology" and the results are presented and interpreted in section "Results".

Based on the results, a maturity model for Smart Grids will be developed (section "Dimension for a European Smart Grid Maturity Model) and the chapter will be concluded with a summary in section "Conclusion" (Mehmann, Frehe, & Teuteberg, 2015).

BACKGROUND

Energy Sector

History and Grid Infrastructure

Since the 19th century, energy has been made available to companies in industrially highly developed countries. This should be as technically convenient as possible and the energy should be easily controllable for their own consumption.

Since the beginning of electrification, the world's energy demand has risen steadily. Since then, the main task of utilities has been to ensure the supply of energy for consumers (Crastan, 2000).

Today the utility grids are divided into low, medium, high and extra-high voltage. The distribution system operators (DSO) are responsible for low, medium and high voltage grids and the transmission system operators (TSO) for the extra-high voltage grids (Heuck, Dettmann, & Schulz, 2010).

Unbundling

Unbundling in the energy sector describes the legal requirement for a separation of grids and sales for utilities. The aim is to ensure neutral grid operation (Bundesnetzagentur, 2011).

This unbundling applies to the German and European electricity markets, but not to the US electricity market. In the US market, this separation does not exist and American utilities are therefore positioned differently from European or specifically German utilities.

Centralized vs. Decentralized Power Supply

A central energy supply usually provides for a large power plant of the utility, from which the power supply to all consumers via the power grid is made.

With a decentralized energy supply, there is no longer just one power plant as the electricity feeder, but many other feeders of renewable energies (e.g. wind turbines, biogas plants, and photovoltaic plants). The utility must now additionally take the electricity from many small and often distant feeders into the distribution grid and make it available to the consumers. This requires a much greater planning and control effort on the part of the utility, since the integration of renewable energies means that there is a very strongly fluctuating supply of electricity, which is counterbalanced by strongly fluctuating demand. The utility has to manage this problem and guarantee security of supply at all times (Bauknecht & Funcke, 2013).

Maturity

Maturity can be understood as an evolutionary process at the end of which there is evidence of a special ability or the fulfilment of a desired or normally regarded target state (Mettler, 2011). Simpson (1989) describes maturity as a state of perfection, completeness or complement (Simpson & Weiner, 1989).

Maturity Model

Becker et al. (Becker, Knackstedt, & Poeppelbuss, 2008) understand maturity models as instruments that serve to determine one's position with regard to one's own performance. A maturity model describes successive development stages for objects (e.g. processes, project management, organization) (Hevner, March, Park, & Ram, 2004).

Maturity models are also described as a special form of the competence model (Ahlemann, Schroeder, & Teuteberg, 2005).

In other words, a maturity model is a tool that can be used to measure the abstract quantity "maturity". This size can be described by a vector in an n-dimensional maturity space. The individual dimensions are subdivided into arbitrarily freely but permanently selected scales, the maturity levels.

Maturity models are recognized tools that are used in strategy development both as a basis for planning and for its evaluation. Maturity levels (i.e. competence, ability, level of complexity) are measured within several dimensions of a selected domain.

Dimensions

According to (Marx, Wortmann, & Mayer, 2012) dimensions include specific skills, process areas and other design objects to structure an area of interest. Dimensions should be complete and well distinguishable. According to (De Bruin, Freeze, Kaulkarni, & Rosemann, 2005) they are specified either by means of evaluation elements / measurement criteria (practices, objects or activities) or qualitative descriptions.

An example of possible dimensions for a maturity model in process management can be configuration management, measurement and analysis, product integration, project monitoring and control, requirements management, risk management and validation (Software Engineering Institute, 2010b).

For an agile maturity model the following dimensions are conceivable: developer information, team and work planning, feedback culture and technical excellence (Packlick & Sabre Airline Solutions Southlake, 2007).

Basically, there are also many possibilities to select dimensions. There must simply be areas or categories where a company is interested in taking a closer look at them and experiencing its maturity.

Metrics must then be defined for the selected dimensions, which can be used to define and record different levels of maturity. The definition of the maturity levels is usually done by literature research and expert interviews and the subsequent query of the maturity of an organization by means of questionnaires specially designed for this purpose. From the answers to the questionnaires, it is then clear which maturity an organization has in the respective dimension.

Disciplined Approach

A disciplined approach means all efforts to secure and expand knowledge through analysis and theory building.

In the context of this paper, this means that a chosen approach is disciplined if it is based on theories and models or if they are applied to them.

AGILE APPROACH

Agility

Agility is understood as maneuverability, alertness, flexibility and adaptability, as well as speed and creativity. Agility also includes skills and values that individuals or whole organizations have or believe to be important.

Agility is said to enable organizations to act adequately in times of change and uncertainty. Actions of agile individuals and companies are characterized by a high degree of energy which is also used effectively. This is what makes them stand out from the crowd with the ease of generating added value. This bundle of properties and settings is also called an agile mindset (Oswald & Müller, 2019), and (Oswald, Köhler, & Schmitt, 2017).

Agile Management

The cornerstones of agile Management 4.0 are therefore an agile mindset, meta-competence, leadership, self-organization, learning, fluid organization, transformation and complex systems (Oswald & Müller, 2019).

An organization is agile if it uses agile techniques (e.g. from Scrum, Kanban), if learning and leading are subject to constant evaluation cycles (P-D-C-A cycle), if it has the ability for self-reflection, if there is an agile mindset among employees and managers that is guided by self-organization and if classical methods are also used (Oswald & Müller, 2019).

Because speed times flexibility creates agility, agile Management 4.0 consists of the product of appropriate agile mindset (factor 1000), governance (factor 100) and technology (factor 1).

From this it can be deduced that the mindset is most important and can be represented by a DILTS pyramid and governance and technology play only subordinate roles (Oswald & Müller, 2019).

Disciplined Maturity Models vs. Agile Maturity Models

After the previous section outlined what is meant by maturity and maturity models, this section will highlight the difference between disciplined and agile maturity models. At the end of this chapter it will be shown which form of maturity model is best suited for a certain situation or for a domain or process to be measured.

With disciplined maturity models, companies have a widely used tool for assessing **processes** (e.g. PEMM (Uslar & Masurkewitz, 2015), and SPICE/ ISO 15504-5 (Garcia, 1997), and (Paulk, Konrad, & Garcia, 1995)), **software development** (e.g. CMMI (Software Engineering Institute, 2010b), (Software

Engineering Institute, 2010a), and (Software Engineering Institute, 2010c)), **business skills** (e.g. OPM3 (Knowledge Foundation, 2013)), **cyber security** (e.g. ES-C2M2 (U.S. Department of Energy, 2014)), and other relevant issues. In total, there are more than 100 maturity models and more than 1000 (Mettler & Rohner, 2009) scientific papers that analyze, refine or develop maturity models (Poeppelbuss, Niehaves, Simons, & Becker, 2011).

Basically, the disciplined maturity models can be divided into two different types of models where the difference lies in the focus. On the one hand, there are models that refer to cross-company topics such as processes or business skills (Akkasoglu, 2013). The dimensions of the process and business maturity models to be analyzed are so general that they can be found in all companies and domains and are therefore applicable everywhere. On the other hand, there are models that have been developed to evaluate specific issues such as the Smart Grid or interoperability in the Smart Grid. Therefore, these models are only relevant for a few companies and usually only for one domain.

Although the well-known maturity models such as CMMI and SPICE are still maintained and adapted by the developers, these disciplined maturity models split the minds of representatives of the agile faction: basically there are already representatives who believe that these models can also be used in agile organizations to measure the achievement of higher levels or the improvement of software processes, but many find the support of these models insufficient (Software Engineering Institute, 2010a), and (Garcia, 1997).

For this reason, there have been about 40 published agile maturity models with very different characteristics in recent years. Some of the agile maturity models are similar to the maturity level structure of CMMI and some do not use maturity level structures (Schweigert, Vohwinkel, Korsaa, Nevalainen, & Biro, 2013), and (Schweigert, Vohwinkel, Korsaa, & Nevalainen, 2013), but are otherwise quite different in their domains, backgrounds, structures, and contents (Leppänen, 2013).

But all these models have a common starting point, which has been a goal of the BOOTSTRAP methodology over 20 years ago, namely changing and reorganizing software development and maintenance activities so that software production as a whole meets business needs better (Similä, Kuvaja, & Krzanik, 1994). There are different methods for the different agile maturity models, but the goal always remains the same (Schweigert, Vohwinkel, Korsaa, Nevalainen, et al., 2013).

With agile maturity models, it is fundamentally important that the improvement of development and management is not only a question of formal skills and maturity levels, but also a question of values, emotions and culture.

Leppänen (2013) has carried out an analysis of agile maturity models in his paper. He compared the maturity models AMM ((Ambler, 2010), and (Patel & Ramachandran, 2009)), Road map (Lui & Chan, 2005), XPMM (Nawrocki, Walter, & Wojciechowski, 2001), Agility maturity map (Packlick & Sabre Airline Solutions Southlake, 2007), Agile maturity model (Pettit, 2006), AIIM (Qumer & Henderson-Sellers, 2008) (Sidky, Arthur, & Bohner, 2007) and Agile Adoption framework. Basically, all agile maturity models try to measure **improvements of agility** in the company. They are not, for example, process-oriented like many disciplined maturity models, but rather business goal-oriented. The Road map measures e.g. the XP practices of an enterprise, the XPMM specific agile practices in key process areas, the Agility maturity map in general the agile goals and the AIIM and Agile Adoption framework the agile objects and applications (Leppänen, 2013).

There is no fundamental contradiction between the agile maturity models and the CMMI (exemplary for a disciplined maturity model). With agile maturity models, certain processes and practices are prescribed with agile methods. CMMI requires a company to codify its processes and practices. However, no statement is made as to what these processes and practices should be like. And with the application of agile methods one could qualify in CMMI just as well as with disciplined methods (Meyer, 2014).

The Poppendieks (2003) have raised two major objections – from the point of view of the agile representatives – to CMMI: firstly, that the introduction of standardization has shaped a strong prejudice against change, and secondly they assume that these requirements will increase bureaucracy and inhibit the individuality of developers (Poppendieck & Poppendieck, 2003), and (Meyer, 2014).

As it was important for the utilities in the case studies in a first step to measure different domain specific topics in order to be able to develop further in them, the maturity model to be developed should basically be a disciplined maturity model.

In the next section, therefore, the method is to be presented, how it was proceeded with the development of the maturity model and in the special case with the requirement engineering of the dimensions to be used.

RESEARCH METHODOLOGY

In this section the research methodology for two different case studies is presented. As already briefly mentioned in the introduction, we will look at requirements engineering for determining dimensions for a maturity model to be developed for the Smart Grid domain on the basis of two case studies.

These case studies are two different research projects, each claiming to have developed a maturity model and migration paths. Therefore, from a scientific point of view, the first step is to investigate whether a suitable maturity model already exists, what can be applied to these research projects or whether a new one needs to be developed (**RQ1**). The second research question (**RQ2**) then deals with the issue of what dimensions a maturity model must have, in the case where a separate one needs to be developed for these research projects.

The two research projects took place at different times and the findings from the procedure for the first project were useful for the procedure in the second project.

As an evaluation method of the research results, the case study according to R.K. Yin (Yin, 2016) was used as the evaluation method. The research design follows five components:

- Research question
- Research proposal
- Analysis unit - "the case"
- Linking data to the proposal
- Criteria for the interpretation of the results

A disciplined approach to requirements management for the first project - case study "utility 1" - should be chosen. This means that requirements management should be based on theories and models (as defined in the "Background" section).

For the second project - case study "utility 2" - which took place afterwards, a more agile approach should be chosen in order to check which approach is more suitable or delivers better results.

To make the approach for case study "utility 2" more agile, the user story method was used. Although (Meyer, 2014) has written that the use of user stories as a basis for the requirement survey requires a high level of abstraction. And they can be used to check the requirements for completeness, but should not be used as a basis alone there are there are other authors who advocate the use for user stories for requirements management.

Wautelet et al.(Wautelet, Heng, Kolp, & Mirbel, 2014) say, for example, that user stories can be used for requirements elicitation to express requirements at a low level of abstraction using simple language. In order to make the design and understanding of user stories more consistent and therefore qualitatively better, they present a framework for standardization in their work. Furthermore, they also suggest visualizing the user stories, especially in projects with a large number of user stories, in order to better plan their hierarchy and the content of the iterations (Wautelet, Heng, Kolp, Mirbel, & Poelmans, 2016).

This means that in case study "utility 2" no completely agile approach was chosen, but rather built on the insights from case study "utility 1" (which were gained with a disciplined approach) and supplemented by agile components - here the user stories.

With these two different approaches to requirements engineering in the two case studies, the third research question is to be answered (**RQ3**).

Approach for Case Study "Utility 1"

For the first Case Study, a disciplined approach has been chosen for the requirement assessment. First a systematic literature analysis based on (Fettke, 2006) in order to gather scientific knowledge about maturity models for Smart Grids and their dimensions was performed. In his contribution, Fettke describes five phases of review research:

Phase 1: Formulation of problems
Phase 2: Literature search
Phase 3: Literature evaluation
Phase 4: Analysis and interpretation
Phase 5: Presentation

In the first phase, the question to be answered by the review is formulated. The second phase is for the research of suitable literature. In the third phase, the literature found is checked for its relevance.

The subsequent fourth phase is concerned with the interpretation of the results with regard to the question posed at the beginning. The last fifth phase is devoted to the preparation and presentation of the research results to the public.

The first phase of problem formulation was already completed with the introduction and the research questions formulated therein.

For the literature search in phase 2, the keyword phrase <maturity model AND Smart Grid> and the databases EBSCOhost (all fields) and Google Scholar (only title) has been used, which resulted in seven papers.

In the next step, the phase 4, these papers has been checked for their relevance. Three of the five papers has been identified as relevant. The other paper do not focus so much on maturity models or do not mentioned the word "dimension".

After this search one more report has been added: a maturity model with focus on Smart Grid and future energy grid designed in OFFIS[1] before. It is not published in that way, so that it was not possible to find it in the literature search. This unpublished maturity model from OFFIS was added because it came from the right domain (energy domain), it was already developed in OFFIS for a utility (from

Germany) and can be seen as a kind of "preliminary work", it is still relatively up-to-date (2016) and the data for this work could be made available.

These eight papers represent the database for the analysis, four of which are relevant for this case (Mehmann et al., 2015). The analysis and interpretation - phase 4 - can be found in the "Results" section below. The final phase 5, the presentation, is the preparation of the literature results and their presentation in an online survey to German utilities in order to obtain feedback from them regarding the importance of the researched dimensions.

Approach for Case Study "utility 2"

The procedure for the second Case Study has been carried out in two steps. In the first step, the systematic literature search from Case Study "utility 1" has been used as a basis for the requirement analysis. This process was explained in detail in the previous section.

Building on this knowledge and using the agile technique of "user stories", a second step was taken in the requirements elicitation process. A uniform template was chosen for the creation of the user stories, which describes the role, the function and the use/advantage. The structure of the user stories using a uniform framework is presented in more detail in the subsection "Dimensions for Case Study "utility 2"". In this case study, the user stories has been developed alongside the stakeholders in order to check the completeness of the database obtained through the literature research and to evaluate whether the result corresponds to the actual requirements of the stakeholders or whether it still needs to be improved.

RESULTS

This section first gives an overview of the results of the literature review, which was used for both case studies.

Systematic Literature Analysis for both Case Studies

First, Table 1 gives an overview of all search hits in addition to the one from OFFIS. The literature review was conducted using the databases of EBSCOhost (all fields) and Google Scholar (only title). The search phrase <maturity mode AND Smart Grid> was used.

Our previously constructed database has produced four relevant articles, and in these four articles, four different maturity models for Smart Grids are mentioned:

- Smart Grid Maturity Model (SGMM)
- Smart Grid Interoperability Maturity Model (SG IMM)
- Electricity Subsector Cybersecurity Capability Maturity Model (ES-C2M2)
- OFFIS Maturity Model with Focus Smart Grid and Future Energy Grid

After the literature was found, these were generally looked at in terms of their origin, domain, topicality, and then the dimensions used in these maturity models were compiled. Table 2 shows the dimensions of these four maturity models. This list is needed to be able to answer the research question **RQ2** later.

Table 1. Results of literature research

No.	Paper	Maturity Model	Comment	Relevant
1	International Smart Grid Roadmaps and their Assessment; Specht, M., Rohjans, S., Trefke, J., Uslar, M., González, J.M.; 2013 (Specht, Rohjans, Trefke, Uslar, & González, 2013)	SGMM	Referred to the SGMM because of standardization in the Smart Grid environment.	YES
2	In the face of Cybersecurity: How the Common Information Model Can Be Used; Skare, P., Falk, H., Rice, M., Winkel, J.; 2016 (Skare, Falk, Rice, & Winkel, 2016)	ES-C2M2	Based on ES-C2M2.	YES
3	Cybersecurity Governance and Management for Smart Grids in Brazilian Energy Utilities; Pardini, D., Heinisch, A., Parreiras, F.; 2018 (Pardini, Heinisch, & Parreiras, 2018)		Based only on the ES-C2M2 on the edge but it is not a maturity model. It uses the word dimensions, but too specialized on cybersecurity.	NO
4	A Smart Grid Interoperability Maturity Model Rating System; Mater, J., Drummond, R.; 2009 (Mater & Drummond, 2009)	SG IMM	Based on SG IMM. The term dimension is not used. It is called categories, which can be regarded as dimensions.	YES
5	Research of Smart Grid IT Capability Maturity Model and Its Fuzzy Comprehensive Evaluation; Cai, Z., Shu, H.; 2013 (Z. Cai & Shu, 2013)	Smart Grid IT CMM	Not specific and no dimensions.	NO
6	Research of the IT capability maturity models and its Extension evaluation of Smart Grid; Cai, Z., Shu, H., Zhang, W.; 2013 (Z. L. Cai, Shu, & Zhang, 2013)	Smart Grid IT CMM	The CMM was used and extended by a mathematical model for the Smart Grid domain. No relation to dimensions.	NO
7	Research on Model and Method of Maturity Evaluation of Smart Grid Industry; He, Y. Wu, J. Yi, G., Li, D., Yan, H.; 2017 (Li et al., 2017)	Model of Smart Grid Industry Maturity	Is not called dimension, but aspects for an index. Very generic.	NO
8	Technische Reifegradmodelle für EWE – Fokus Smart Grids@ EWE und BMWi Future Energy Grid; Uslar, M., Dänekas, C., Specht, M.; 2012 (Uslar, Dänekas, & Specht, 2012)	OFFIS Maturity Model Focus Smart Grid and Future Energy Grid	19 fields of technology that can be regarded as dimensions.	YES

For the research question **RQ1** it is important to know for which market the maturity model is developed. The reasons for this have already been given in the "Background" section with the sub-item "Unbundling". Just one of the four maturity model is for the German market. Table 3 illustrates this.

Interpretation of the Literature Analysis

All the papers considered have dimensions or something comparable. The number of dimensions but also the dimensions themselves are different. Some terms occur more frequently at least in similar form. The focus of the maturity model is also decisive.

Table 2. Dimensions of the identified maturity models

No.	Maturity Model	Number of Dimensions	Dimensions
1	SGMM (Software Engineering Institute, 2011)	8	• Strategy, Management and Regulatory • Organization and Structure • Grid Operations • Work and Asset Management • Technology • Customer • Value Chain Integration • Societal and Environmental
2	ES-C2M2 (U.S. Department of Energy, 2014)	10	• Risk Management • Asset, Change and Configuration Management • Identity and Access Management • Threat and Vulnerability Management • Situational Awareness • Information Sharing and Communication • Event and Incident Response; Continuity of Operations • Supply Chain and External Dependencies Management • Workforce Management • Cybersecurity Program Management

4	SG IMM (The GridWise Architecture Council, 2011)	8	• Technical (Syntax):
			  o Basic Connectivity
			  o Grid Interoperability
			  o Syntactic Interoperability
			• Informational (Semantics):
			  o Semantic Understanding
			  o Business Context
			• Organizational (Pragmatics):
			  o Business Procedures
			  o Business Objectives
			  o Economic/ Regulatory Policy

8	OFFIS Maturity Model (not published)	19	• Asset Management for Grid Components • Grid Control Systems • Wide Area Management System (WAMS) • Grid Automation • Flexible-AC-Transmission-System (FACTS) • Information Communication Technology (ICT) Connectivity • Asset Management for Decentralized Generation Plants • Regional Energy Marketplaces • Trading Guidance Systems • Forecasting Systems • Business Services • Virtual Power Plant Systems • Plant Communication and Control Modules • Advanced Metering Infrastructure • Smart Appliances • Industrial Demand Side Management/ Demand Response • Integration Techniques • Data Management • Security

The ES-C2M2 focuses very strongly on cybersecurity and the SG IMM very strongly on interoperability. Therefore, the dimensions have a definite focus on a small topic area of a company and ignore other areas.

Table 3. Maturity models and their origin

No.	Maturity Model	Market/Country
1	SGMM	USA
2	ES-C2M2	USA
4	SG IMM	USA
8	OFFIS Maturity Model	Germany

Most of the articles come from the USA, i.e. have been produced for the American electricity market. Only one of the models comes from Germany and is for the German electricity market.

As a result, these US-designed models fit perfectly into the US energy sector and its specific needs but are basically not applicable to the European market. Particularly noteworthy here is the difference in the legally required unbundling for the European energy market (Rohjans, Uslar, Cleven, Winter, & Wortmann, 2011) (Uslar & Masurkewitz, 2015).

For the maturity model to be created, it is now decisive which focus it should have. This is because the analysis shows that the dimensions also vary greatly due to the focus of what is to be evaluated.

By analyzing and interpreting the results, we have established that only one of the known maturity models originates from Europe and can therefore also be used for the European market without problems. The other models are originally intended for the American market. Expert interviews or surveys with utilities should be conducted to determine whether any of these dimensions are also useful for the maturity model to be developed.

But since this remaining model for the German market is a model created by OFFIS and not published more public and also very specifically designed for a utility of a special order, we conclude that a new and generally valid maturity level model for Smart Grids is needed to been developed for the European market.

This statement thus answers research question **RQ1** and leads us to research question **RQ2**. So if a new maturity model is to be developed, what dimensions are necessary? This is shown in the next section.

Dimensions for a European Smart Grid Maturity Model

In this section, the further procedure for requirements elicitation for the selection of dimensions for the maturity model to be developed for both case studies is presented.

Dimensions for Case Study "Utility 1"

On the basis of the literature research, the dimensions found are clustered. The same topics are bundled, duplications avoided and omitted to special dimensions (since they, for example, merge with other dimensions). To find out which dimensions are considered important for the European and thus also for the German energy market, an online survey has been conducted among German grid operators. The results are used to determine 18 dimensions for the future maturity model.

Since the number of dimensions at 18 is very large – in comparison with other known maturity models – the term "subject area" has been introduced for better clarity. The term "subject area" refers to dimensions that belong to the same theme. It is a kind of generic term for the bundle of dimensions. The term "subject area" was chosen because, according to the definition, it expresses a part of the problem from a certain field of interest. It was decided to explore and analyse this topic in more detail. And this wish is exactly what should be done in the dimensions of a maturity model and therefore appropriate (Sachs & Hauser, n.d.).

The result can be found in Table 4. With this result **RQ2** was answered in case study "utility 1".

Table 4. Dimensions for the European smart grid maturity model case study "utility 1"

Subject Area	Dimensions
Organization & Strategy	• General Information about the Organization • Strategy, Management and Regulation • Asset Management for Decentralized Generation Plants • Value Chain • Plant, Change and Configuration Management
Grid	• Grid Operations • Grid Components • Grid Control Systems • Grid Automation
Technology & Communication	• Technology in General • Information and Communication Technology (ICT) - Connectivity • Data Management • Forecasting Systems • Plant Communication and Control Modules • Information Exchange and Communication
Security	• Event and Incident Response; Continuity of Operations • Threat and Vulnerability Management • Risk Management

Dimensions for Case Study "Utility 2"

For the second Case Study, the results from the first Case Study "utility 1" have been taken and presented at a workshop with seven German distribution system operators (DSO).

The aim is to evaluate the results and to jointly create user stories in order to examine the results for their completeness. The section "Research Methodology" has already explained in more detail why the agile technique "User Stories" is used here.

A user story should always be structured as follows:

Together with the DSO, the following user stories have been developed:

Table 5. Template user story

As a	…(role)
I want	… (function)
so that	… (use/advantage)

1. As a utility, I would like to have a model with which the current maturity can be measured in a special dimension.
2. As a utility, I would like to have a model with which I can place a special focus on the topics of grids, technology and security.
3. As a utility, I would like to have a model that queries the latest topics from the areas of grids, technology and security.

After the development of the user stories and the discussion about the dimensions arising from the literature research, there are four points to which the dimensions were adapted.

- The dimension "Grid Operation" is extended by the topic "Fault Clearance Management".
- The additional dimension "Grid Planning" is introduced.
- The dimension "Event and Incident Response; Continuity of Operations" from ES-C2M2 is re-named in "Business Continuity Management".
- The additional dimension "Information Security Management System" is introduced.

The adapted list of dimensions is compared with the requirements from the user stories.

Table 6. Dimensions for the European Smart Grid Maturity Model Case Study "utility 2"

Subject Area	Dimensions
Organization & Strategy	• General Information about the Organization • Strategy, Management and Regulation • Asset Management for Decentralized Generation Plants • Value Chain • Plant, Change and Configuration Management
Grid	• Grid Operations / Fault Clearance Management • Grid Components • Grid Control systems • Grid Automation • Grid Planning
Technology & Communication	• Technology in General • Data Management • Forecasting Systems • Plant Communication and Control Modules (incl. ICT) • Information Exchange and Communication
Security	• Business Continuity Management (BCM) • Threat and Vulnerability Management • Risk Management • Information Security Management System (ISMS)

User Story 1: The utility wants a model with which the current maturity of a specific dimension can be measured.
- This is possible with maturity models as already explained in the section **"Terminology"**.

User Story 2: The utility wants a model with which he can place a special focus on the topics of grids, technologies and security.

○ In the defined list there are five dimensions on the topic of grids, five dimensions on the topic of technologies and four dimensions on the topic of security.

User Story 3: The utility wants a model with which the latest topics in the areas of grids, technologies and security can be queried.

○ Existing dimensions in the subject area grid have been extended (grid operation by fault clearance management) and a new dimension has been added (grid planning). Two dimensions have been combined in the Technology & Communication topic area (ICT connectivity and communication and control modules have been combined in the dimension Plant Communication and Control Modules (incl. ICT)).

For this reason, the further development of the maturity model should concentrate in particular on these three topic areas. This focus must also be considered when developing questionnaires and defining metrics to determine the maturity level. For example, that there are many and varied questions for particularly important dimensions and that the state of the art is always available.

For case study "utility 2", **RQ2** was answered based on the user stories, the discussion of results and the resulting table 6.

CONCLUSION

The purpose of this chapter was to investigate whether there is a maturity model for the Smart Grid domain in the literature and whether it can be applied to utility in Germany (**RQ1**). If this is not the case, the question should be answered, which dimensions of a utility are important for a maturity model – which is still to be worked out (**RQ2**)? A further question is whether one should proceed with disciplined or agile methods in the requirement collection of necessary forms. This has been be investigated by means of two case studies (**RQ3**).

A literature research shows that there are only three known maturity models for Smart Grids and an unpublished one from OFFIS. These three known maturity models all come from the USA and are made for the American electricity market. As explained in the chapter "Background", there is no unbundling in the USA, but there it is in Europe and especially Germany. As a result, the fundamentals for utilities, their orientation and their business are very different and therefore, these maturity models are not 1:1 adaptable for the German market.

Now, either an attempt can be made to extend existing maturity models, as suggested by (Rohjans et al., 2011), or a new one can be designed. This paper discussed that the topic of maturity models in the energy domain is still much underrepresented in Europe and Germany and leaves much room for further research.

In order to investigate which dimensions are necessary for a new maturity level model, in a first step all dimensions of the existing models are selected for both case studies by means of structured literature research, examined and clustered? For Case Study "utility 1", an online survey of grid operators has been carried out regarding the importance of dimensions for the German and European energy market and, based on this, 18 dimensions for the European Smart Grid Maturity Model are determined.

For the second Case Study "utility 2", the results of the first Case Study "utility 1" have been used as the basis for a workshop with seven German grid operators. There, the results have been evaluated with the experts and user stories for a maturity model to be developed have been created together with them.

The evaluation and comparison of the three developed user stories with the results leads to a European Smart Grid maturity model with 19 dimensions.

Looking at the results of the two case studies and considering the different approaches, it can be seen that in the second Case Study "utility 2" the combination of disciplined and agile methods results in an even better, more up-to-date and more individual maturity model with regard to the choice of dimensions.

An interesting finding from this article is that also in the area of requirements elicitation an agilization of the techniques makes sense and improves the results. This is therefore a further confirmation of the research of Wautelet et al. (Wautelet et al., 2016), who have also had positive experiences with the use of user stories in requirements engineering in the projects they examined. This statement answers **RQ3** in the end.

This is precisely where further research work begins, namely the further development of the European Smart Grid Maturity Model. For this maturity model, the next research steps are to determine metrics and key performance indicators and to develop questionnaires. The metrics are used to measure and determine various maturity levels (often 1 – 5) in the dimensions. Based on the metrics, questionnaires will be developed to determine the status quo of utilities in each dimension. A process model for the further development of maturity models is presented in (Flore & Uslar, 2019).

FUTURE RESEARCH DIRECTIONS

Basically, it has to be said that the utilities and thus the entire energy industry are facing a time of great change. The development from a centralized to a decentralized energy supply – in order to do justice to the politically prescribed energy turnaround – requires a transformation of the grid. If the utilities do not want to replace the lines with expensive copper lines for a significant amount of money, which takes a lot of time, they must make the grid more intelligent using ICT. The grid must therefore become a Smart Grid.

Due to the large and far-reaching changes that utilities are facing and the limited time available for these changes, the idea of meeting these rapid times with more agile management methods and techniques suggests itself. Only if companies acquire an agile mindset is it guaranteed that they will be able to react flexibly, adaptably, quickly and creatively to all new economic and political challenges in the future. There are already first experience reports of agile transformations of energy supplies which are valuable as experience values for other utilities (Eggers & Hardt, 2019).

However, since it has already been shown in this article that the techniques and governance have only a minor influence on how agile a company is or whether a company becomes agile, it seems indispensable for utilities in the future to deal with the topic of agile mindsets: how do employees and managers achieve an agile mindset (which has a major influence on the agility of the organization). In their book chapter "Learning and Guidance for the Implementation of Agility", (Oswald & Müller, 2019) describe the gross mistakes that occur when introducing agility and how to deal with them. Another issue for utilities is how they will manage the transformation in the enterprise due to the major changes they are facing. Basically, a bottom-up or top-down transformation is possible (Oswald et al., 2017).

In the specific case of the application of maturity models by utilities, it is therefore also important in future to measure the agility of a company.

Two approaches are conceivable for the implementation: either the existing European Smart Grid Maturity Model can be extended to include agility dimensions, or two different maturity models can be applied (one being the European Smart Grid Maturity Model in its existing form, and the other the European Agile Smart Grid Maturity Model in its new form) (Schweigert, Vohwinkel, Korsaa, Nevalainen, et al., 2013), (Henriques & Tanner, 2017) (Schweigert, Nevalainen, Vohwinkel, Korsaa, & Biro, 2012), (Leppänen, 2013), and (Schweigert, Vohwinkel, Korsaa, & Nevalainen, 2013).

REFERENCES

Ahlemann, F., Schroeder, C., & Teuteberg, F. (2005). Kompetenz- und Reifegradmodelle für das Projektmanagement: Grundlagen, Vergleich und Einsatz. ISPRIArbeitsbericht. Osnabrück.

Akkasoglu, G. (2013). *Methodik zur Konzeption und Applikation anwendungsspezifischer Reifegradmodelle unter Berücksichtigung der Informationsunsicherheit*. Academic Press.

Ambler, S. W. (2010). *The Agile Maturity Model (AMM)*. Retrieved from https://www.drdobbs.com/architecture-and-design/the-agile-maturity-model-amm/224201005

Appelrath, H.-J., Mayer, C., & Rohjans, S. (2012). Future Energy Grid - Migrationspfade ins Internet der Energie. In Energy Talks Ossiach 2011. Berlin: Springer Verlag. doi:10.1007/978-3-642-27864-8

Bauknecht, D., & Funcke, S. (2013). Dezentralisierung oder Zentralisierung der Stromversorgung: Was ist darunter zu verstehen? *Energiewirtschaftliche Tagesfragen*, *63*(8), 14–17.

Becker, J., Knackstedt, R., & Poeppelbuss, J. (2008). Dokumentationsqualität von Reifegradmodellentwicklungen. *Arbeitsbericht Des Instituts Für Wirtschaftsinformatik*, (121), 1–50. Retrieved from https://www.ifib-consult.de/publikationsdateien/2009.pdf

Bundesnetzagentur. (2011). *Entflechtung/Konzessionen*. Retrieved from https://www.bundesnetzagentur.de/DE/Sachgebiete/ElektrizitaetundGas/Unternehmen_Institutionen/EntflechtungKonzessionenVerteilernetze/entflechtungkonzessionenverteilernetze-node.html

Cai, Z., & Shu, H. (2013). Research of Smart Grid IT Capability Maturity Model and its Fuzzy Comprehensive Evaluation. *Journal of Kunming University of Science and Technology (Natural Science Edition)*, (6), 68–73.

Cai, Z. L., Shu, H. C., & Zhang, W. (2013). Research of the IT Capability Maturity Model and its Extension Evaluation of Smart Grid. *Applied Mechanics and Materials*, *423–426*, 2693–2702. . doi:10.4028/www.scientific.net/AMM.423-426.2693

Crastan, V. (2000). *Elektrische Energieversorgung 1*. Berlin: Springer Berlin/Heidelberg.

De Bruin, T., Freeze, R., Kaulkarni, U., & Rosemann, M. (2005). Understanding the Main Phases of Developing a Maturity Assessment Model. In *Australasian Conference on Information Systems (ACIS)* (pp. 8–19). 10.1108/14637151211225225

Eggers, T., & Hardt, D. (2019). Agile Transformation eines kommunalen Energiedienstleisters - ein Erfahrungsbericht. In Realisierung Utility 4.0 (pp. 465–492). Academic Press.

Fettke, P. (2006). State-of-the-art des state-of-the-art: Eine Untersuchung der Forschungsmethode "review" innerhalb der Wirtschaftsinformatik. *Wirtschaftsinformatik*, *48*(4), 257–266. doi:10.100711576-006-0057-3

Flore, A., & Uslar, M. (2019). Organisationsentwicklung mit Smart Grid Reifegradmodellen für Versorger. In O. D. Doleski (Ed.), *Realisierung Utility 4.0* (pp. 675–692). Springer Vieweg.

Garcia, S. (1997). Paradigms : Capability Maturity Models and ISO / IEC 15504 (PDTR). *Software Process Improvement and Practice*, *3*(1), 47–58. doi:10.1002/(SICI)1099-1670(199703)3:1<47::AID-SPIP64>3.0.CO;2-5

Henriques, V., & Tanner, M. (2017). A systematic literature review of agile and maturity model research. *Interdisciplinary Journal of Information, Knowledge, and Management*, *12*, 53–73. doi:10.28945/3666

Heuck, K., Dettmann, K.-D., & Schulz, D. (2010). Elektrische Energieversorgung. Wiesbaden: Vieweg+Teubner Verlag. doi:10.1007/978-3-8348-9761-9

Hevner, A. R., March, S. T., Park, J., & Ram, S. (2004). Information Design Science Systems. *Management Information Systems*, *28*(1), 75–105. doi:10.2307/25148625

Knowledge Foundation. (2013). Organizational Project Management Maturity Model (OPM3) (3rd ed.). Project Mgmt Inst.

Leffingwell, D., & Widrig, D. (1999). *Managing Software Requirements. A Unified Approach*. Addison-Wesley.

Leppänen, M. (2013). A Comparative Analysis of Agile Maturity Models. In Information Systems Development (Vol. 35, pp. 329–343). New York: Springer. doi:10.1007/978-1-4614-4951-5_27

Li, K., Xue, Y., Cui, S., Niu, Q., Yang, Z., & Luk, P. (2017). Research on Model and Method of Maturit Evaluation of Smart Grid Industry. *Communications in Computer and Information Science*, *763*(3), 633–642. doi:10.1007/978-981-10-6364-0

Lui, K. M., & Chan, K. C. C. (2005). A Road Map for Implementing eXtreme Programming. In *International Software Process Workshop* (pp. 474–481). Beijing: Springer.

Marx, F., Wortmann, F., & Mayer, J. H. (2012). Ein Reifegradmodell für UnternehmenssteuerungssystemeA Maturity Model for Management Control Systems. *Wirtschaftsinformatik*, *54*(4), 189–204. doi:10.100711576-012-0325-3

Mater, J., & Drummond, R. (2009). A Smart Grid Interoperability Maturity Model Rating System. Development.

Mehmann, J., Frehe, V., & Teuteberg, F. (2015). Crowd Logistics – A Literature Review and Maturity Model. *Innovations and Strategies for Logistics and Supply Chains*.

Mettler, T. (2011). Maturity assessment models: A design science research approach. *International Journal of Society Systems Science*, *3*(12), 81–98. doi:10.1504/IJSSS.2011.038934

Mettler, T., & Rohner, P. (2009). Situational maturity models as instrumental artifacts for organizational design. In *Proceedings of the 4th International Conference on Design Science Research in Information Systems and Technology - DESRIST '09* (p. 1). 10.1145/1555619.1555649

Meyer, B. (2014). *Agile! The Good, the Hype and the Ugly*. Springer International Publishing.

Nawrocki, J., Walter, B., & Wojciechowski, A. (2001). Toward maturity model for extreme programming. *Conference Proceedings of the 27th EUROMICRO*, 233–239. 10.1109/EURMIC.2001.952459

Oswald, A., Köhler, J., & Schmitt, R. (2017). *Projektmanagement am Rande des Chaos. Projektmanagement am Rande des Chaos.* Springer Vieweg., doi:10.1007/978-3-662-55756-3

Oswald, A., & Müller, W. (2019). Management 4. 0 - Handbook for Agile Practices (A. Oswald & W. Müller, Eds.). Nürnberg: BoD.

Packlick, J., & Sabre Airline Solutions Southlake. (2007). The Agile Maturity Map A Goal Oriented Approach to Agile Improvement. In *Proceedings of AGILE 2007 conference* (pp. 266–271). 10.1109/AGILE.2007.55

Pardini, D. J., Heinisch, A. M. C., & Parreiras, F. S. (2018). Cyber Security Governance and Management for Smart Grids in Brazilian Energy Utilities. *Journal of Information Systems and Technology Management*, *14*(3), 385–400. doi:10.4301/S1807-17752017000300006

Patel, C., & Ramachandran, M. (2009). Agile Maturity Model (AMM): A software process improvement framework for agile software development practices. *International Journal of Synthetic Emotions*, *2*(I), 3–28. doi:10.4304/jsw.4.5.422-435

Paulk, M., Konrad, M., & Garcia, S. (1995). CMM Versus SPICE Architectures. *Software Process Newsletter,* (3), 7–11.

Pettit, R. J. (2006). *Agile Processes: Making Metrics Simple*. Retrieved from https://www.agileconnection.com/article/agile-processes-making-metrics-simple-0

Poeppelbuss, J., Niehaves, B., Simons, A., & Becker, J. (2011). Maturity Models in Information Systems Research : Literature Search and Analysis. *Communications of the Association for Information Systems*, *29*(1), 30. doi:10.17705/1CAIS.02927

Poppendieck, M., & Poppendieck, T. (2003). *Lean Software Development: An Agile Toolkit*. Academic Press.

Projekt Green Access. (2019). Abschlussbericht.

Qumer, A., & Henderson-Sellers, B. (2008). A framework to support the evaluation, adoption and improvement of agile methods in practice. *Journal of Systems and Software*, *81*(11), 1899–1919. doi:10.1016/j.jss.2007.12.806

Rohjans, S., Uslar, M., Cleven, A., Winter, R., & Wortmann, F. (2011). Towards an Adaptive Maturity Model for Smart Grids. *17th international Power Systems Computation Conference*.

Sachs & Hauser. (n.d.). *Definition: Themenfeld*. Retrieved from https://www.repetico.de/card-70811769

Schienmann, B. (2002). *Kontinuierliches Anforderungsmanagement prozesse-Techniken-Werkzeuge.* Addison-Wesley.

Schwaber, K., & Sutherland, J. (2017). Der Scrum Guide - DEUTSCH. *Scrumguides.Org*, 22. Retrieved from https://www.scrumguides.org/docs/scrumguide/v2016/2016-Scrum-Guide-German.pdf

Schweigert, T., Nevalainen, R., Vohwinkel, D., Korsaa, M., & Biro, M. (2012). Agile maturity model: Oxymoron or the next level of understanding. *Communications in Computer and Information Science, 290*(6), 289–294. doi:10.1007/978-3-642-30439-2_34

Schweigert, T., Vohwinkel, D., Korsaa, M., & Nevalainen, R. (2013). Agile Maturity Model : A Synopsis as a First Step. In EuroSPI 2013 (pp. 214–227). doi:10.1007/978-3-642-39179-8_19

Schweigert, T., Vohwinkel, D., Korsaa, M., Nevalainen, R., & Biro, M. (2013). Agile maturity model: Analysing agile maturity characteristics from the SPICE perspective. *Journal of Software: Evolution and Process, 25*(7), 513–520. doi:10.1002mr

Sidky, A., Arthur, J., & Bohner, S. (2007). A disciplined approach to adopting agile practices: The agile adoption framework. *Innovations in Systems and Software Engineering, 3*(3), 203–216. doi:10.100711334-007-0026-z

Similä, J., Kuvaja, P., & Krzanik, L. (1994). BOOTSTRAP: A Software Process Assessment and Improvement Methodology. In *1st Asia-Pacific Conference* (pp. 183–196). 10.1109/APSEC.1994.465261

Simpson, J., & Weiner, E. (1989). *The Oxford English Dictionary.* OUP.

Skare, P., Falk, H., Rice, M., & Winkel, J. (2016). In the Face of Cybersecurity: How the Common Information Model Can Be Used. *IEEE Power & Energy Magazine, 14*(1), 94–104. doi:10.1109/MPE.2015.2485899

Software Engineering Institute. (2010a). CMMI for Acquisition, Version 1.3: Improving processes for acquiring better products and services. *Technical Report, 1.3*(November).

Software Engineering Institute. (2010b). CMMI for Development, Version 1.3: Improving Processed for Better Products and Services. *Technical Report, 1.3*(November). ESC-TR-2010-033.

Software Engineering Institute. (2010c). CMMI for Services, Version 1.3: Improving processes for providing better services. *Technical Report, 1.3*(November). doi:10.1002/adem.201100259

Software Engineering Institute. (2011). SGMM Model Definition - Technical Report. Pittsburgh: Author.

Specht, M., Rohjans, S., Trefke, J., Uslar, M., & González, J. M. (2013). International smart grid roadmaps and their assessment. *EAI Endorsed Transactions on Energy Web, 13*(1–6). Advance online publication. doi:10.4108/trans.ew.2013.01-06.e2

The GridWise Architecture Council. (2011). Smart Grid Interoperability Maturity Model Beta Version. *Architecture*, 1–46. https://www.gridwiseac.org/pdfs/imm/sg_imm_beta_final_12_01_2011.pdf

Uebernickel, F., Stölzle, W., Lennerts, S., Lampe, K., & Hoffman, C. P. (2015). *Das St. Galler Business-Innovation-Modell. Business Innovation: das St. Galler Modell.* doi:10.1007/978-3-658-07167-7

U.S. Department of Energy. (2014). *Electricity subsector cybersecurity capability maturity model.* Retrieved from http://energy.gov/sites/prod/files/2014/02/f7/ES-C2M2-v1-1-Feb2014.pdf

Uslar, M., Dänekas, C., & Specht, M. (2012). Technische Reifegradmodelle für EWE – Fokus Smart Grids @ EWE und BMWi Future Energy Grid. Academic Press.

Uslar, M., & Masurkewitz, J. (2015). A Survey on Application of Maturity Models for Smart Grid: Review of the State-of-the-Art. In Proceedings of Enviroinfo and Ict for Sustainability 2015 (Vol. 22, pp. 261–270). Kopenhagen: Academic Press.

Vázquez, J. M. G. (2012). *Ein Referenzmodellkatalog für die Energiewirtschaft.* Academic Press.

Wautelet, Y., Heng, S., Kolp, M., & Mirbel, I. (2014). Unifying and Extending User Story Models. In *Advanced Information Systems Engineering* (pp. 211–225). Springer. doi:10.1007/978-3-319-07881-6_15

Wautelet, Y., Heng, S., Kolp, M., Mirbel, I., & Poelmans, S. (2016). Building a rationale diagram for evaluating user story sets. In *International Conference on Research Challenges in Information Science* (pp. 1–12). Grenoble: IEEE. 10.1109/RCIS.2016.7549299

Yin, R. K. (2016). Case Study Research Design and Methods (5th ed.). Washington, DC: SAGE Publications. doi:10.3138/cjpe.30.1.108

KEY TERMS AND DEFINITIONS

Dimension: Dimensions include specific skills, process areas, and other design objects to structure an area of interest. Dimensions should be complete and well distinguishable. They are specified either by means of evaluation elements/measurement criteria (practices, objects, or activities) or qualitative descriptions.

Domain: In knowledge management, a domain is a specialist area, i.e. a subject area of content specialization. It can also be described as a field of knowledge.

Energy Sector: The energy sector is an umbrella term for companies that perform tasks in different economic sectors (such as the electricity or gas industries) for the provision of energy services. This includes various activities from extraction to transport to conversion into useful energy (heat, mechanical work, light, sound, etc.) for consumers.

Maturity Model: Maturity can be understood as an evolutionary process at the end of which there is evidence of a special ability or the fulfilment of a desired or normal target state. Therefore a maturity level model is a special competence model that defines different levels of maturity in order to be able to assess the extent to which a competence object fulfils a generally defined qualitative requirement for a class of competence objects.

Requirements: According to the Institute of Electrical and Electronics Engineers - Glossary (1990), a requirement has two meanings. First, a condition or functionality that a user needs to solve a problem or achieve an objective. Second, a condition or functionality that an application system or application system components must address or fulfill in order to fulfill a contract, standard, specification or condition from other formal documents. For both cases, a documented description of the formulated conditions or functionality is required.

Requirements Engineering: The term requirements management is used as a comprehensive term for all tasks in dealing with requirements and therefore includes requirements management and requirements engineering (Schienmann, 2002; Leffingwell & Widrig, 1999). As a result, requirements management is understood on the one hand as a structured approach to the collection, organization, and documentation of requirements for a system. On the other hand, requirements management also includes the process of defining and ensuring the joint agreement of the customer and the project team regarding the changing requirements on the system.

Smart Grid: The term Smart Grid (also known as SmartGrid or Smart Grids [plural]) refers to the vision of an intelligent (electricity) grid. The various Smart Grid definitions are based on the integration of various generators, consumers and other systems and devices using IT to improve the control, management and monitoring of the grid (Vázquez, 2012). The German "Bundesnetzagentur" says that conventional grids will become a Smart Grid if they are upgraded with communication, measurement, control and automation technology as well as IT components. According to the definition of the "Bundesnetzagentur", a Smart Grid leads to better utilization of the existing grid, which dampens its expansion requirements or improves grid stability at the same capacity utilization.

Unbundling: Unbundling refers to the legal, organizational, and accounting separation of the functions of generation, transmission and distribution, trading and other activities of a utility in accordance with EnWG (2008) Part 2.

User Story: From the user's perspective, the product owner formulates the requirements for a software product or a business solution (processes/methods) in user stories (Schwaber & Sutherland, 2017).

Utility: A utility is responsible for the safe and reliable operation of the electrical grid in a given area and for connections to other grids. In this context, system services must be provided to ensure the reliability of supply.

ENDNOTE

[1]   OFFIS – Institute for Information Technology – Oldenburg, Germany.

Chapter 15
Transforming Disciplined IT Functions:
Guidelines for DevOps Integration

Anna Wiedemann
Neu-Ulm University of Applied Sciences, Germany

Manuel Wiesche
https://orcid.org/0000-0003-0401-287X
Technical University of Dortmund, Germany

Heiko Gewald
https://orcid.org/0000-0003-2107-2217
Neu-Ulm University of Applied Sciences, Germany

Helmut Krcmar
https://orcid.org/0000-0002-2754-8493
Technical University of Munich, Germany

ABSTRACT

In today's fast-changing environment, many organizations are applying the DevOps (Development and Operations) concept to transform their IT functions and establish cross-functional IT teams to deliver software services quickly, reliably, and safely with end-to-end responsibility. The results of an empirical study on which this chapter is based presents platform-oriented, application-oriented, and mobile-oriented DevOps setups, outlining areas of potential collaboration between these DevOps setups and the importance of aligning the aims of development (process agility) and operations (process rigor). Based on the study, six indicators of successful DevOps integration formulated as recommendations for successful IT function transformation were identified.

DOI: 10.4018/978-1-7998-4165-4.ch015

INTRODUCTION

In response to the many opportunities and challenges of this digital era, many large companies have been rethinking the organizational setups of their IT functions. Digital innovators such as Google and Amazon regularly release information about the newest trends in technology and serve as role models for other companies. Furthermore, large organizations manage their departments as organizational silos in which development and operations employees tend to be highly specialized. As a result of the silo setup, strict managerial hierarchies and clearly defined work environments often make communication across IT subunits rare. A key task of IT departments is to provide new software while ensuring smooth operations and functionality. In the silo setup, software updates are typically planned, constructed and executed as waterfall-style command-and-control projects (Dery, Sebastian, & van der Meulen, 2017), new software functionalities are seldom provided and large-scale error-prone releases are often executed on the weekend to avoid extensive system outages during peak business times.

As companies adopt enhanced development processes to make projects successful, it has become clear that providing complete service lifecycle support is most efficient when operations and development activities are combined. Developing capabilities and collaboration across internal IT subunits is necessary for both clear intra-organizational communication and improved performance (Dhaliwal, Onita, Poston, & Zhang, 2011). As organizations realize that silo IT functions are less able to leverage digitalization to maximize business value, they are more frequently integrating cross-functional IT teams in their IT departments to ensure fast and stable IT services (Wiedemann, 2017). The concept of DevOps is widely used to structure cross-functional teams with end-to-end responsibility for one or more IT services (Debois, 2011). In fact, a 2017 global conducted DevOps benchmark study by the market research institute Forrester presents that more than 50% of the participating organizations have implemented DevOps by end of 2017 (Stroud, 2017).

DevOps combines agility and rigor in cross-functional teams. Agility is defined as a method that enables rapid reaction to changing user requirement in an iterative way (Hemon, Monnier-Senicourt, & Rowe, 2018). The architecture of established IT departments often yields monolithic IT system with tightly coupled centralized application systems and bulky, often rigid legacy systems. Although this structure worked very well for a long time, progressive organizations following DevOps principles are striving for greater agility. For example, by creating internal IT ecosystems with loosely coupled IT infrastructures like microservices for managing frontend systems that run on digital service platforms serving as backend systems (Ross et al., 2016). Process rigor is defined as the stringent enforcement of and adherence to compliance and formal, structured IS processes. Process rigor builds upon formal, clearly defined, and detailed explanations of tasks, roles, activities, work products, measures, and methods related to IS software processes. An example of a plan-driven software development approach based on process rigor is the Capability Maturity Model Integrated (CMMI) (Lee, DeLone, & Espinosa, 2010). One way to achieve process rigor in software operation is by implementing the highly formalized Information Technology Infrastructure Library (ITIL)[1].

Within DevOps teams, people from software development and software operations work together to enhance the speed of delivery of new software features. This cross-departmental cooperation helps to solve communication barriers and shorten communication routes across departments. Furthermore, the team members develop a broader understanding of the software delivery lifecycle and an appreciation of what everyone is doing to ensure successful delivery of the service. This chapter presents the results of a qualitative research study based on 80 interviews with people experienced in DevOps setups and thought leaders (for more information see Appendix 1.). The study investigates how large companies redesign their IT functions to integrate DevOps efficiently. The findings show that companies take different approaches and adopt various DevOps team constellations to achieve this goal. Furthermore, DevOps integration depends on the IT structure and context of the individual organizations. In what follows, this chapter presents an overview of the major indicators of the investigation.

Background

DevOps and Agile Software Development

Since the Agile Manifesto was published in 2001, agile software development methods have become increasingly popular (Beck et al., 2001). Unlike disciplined plan-driven software development approaches, agile software development responds to unplanned failure and changes, provides iterative planning opportunities due to changing requirements, and fosters project progress transparency through final product delivery (Boehm & Turner, 2005; Hemon et al., 2018). In DevOps, where software development and software operations experts collaborate closely as a single cross-functional team with common responsibility, agility needs to expand to include software operations tasks (Hemon et al., 2018; Krancher, Luther, & Jost, 2018; Wiedemann, Wiesche, Thatcher, & Gewald, 2019). Although the way the DevOps concept is best implemented depends on the context of the individual organization, the common aim is to resolve agile bottlenecks by providing faster, more stable and safer software delivery through continuous delivery and deployment and implementing end-to-end responsibility (Hemon et al., 2018; Wiedemann & Wiesche, 2018).

DevOps is described by the acronym "CALMS": Culture, Automation, Lean, Measurement, Sharing. Culture refers to the cultural change in team members' mindsets regarding service responsibility. Automation refers to the automated planning, building, and running of new processes and the avoidance of repeating manual process steps. Lean refers to the application of lean principles in the area of software delivery. Measurement refers to the implementation of metrics to monitor performance. Sharing refers to knowledge sharing over different organizational levels in order to bring team members closer together (Humble & Farley, 2011; Wiedemann, Forsgren, Wiesche, Gewald, & Krcmar, 2019). DevOps complements and extents Continuous Integration (CI) as well release management of agile methods through making new software functionalities rapidly available to customers. DevOps teams can use agile software development methods to collaborate and manage their release strategies. More and more companies integrate DevOps to enhance customer satisfaction, collaboration and monitoring as well as foster innovation (Lwakatare et al., 2016; Wiedemann, 2017).

Process Rigor and Agility in DevOps Teams

As mentioned above, successful DevOps implementation requires both process rigor and agility, while literature on organizational ambidexterity outlines the benefits of combining exploration and exploitation (Gupta, Smith, & Shalley, 2006). Exploitation aims at utilizing and improving available resources through established processes (Lee, Sambamurthy, Lim, & Wei, 2015; March, 1991). Exploration includes team behaviors and actions aimed at finding new and alternative tasks, opportunities, and principles to extend the existing knowhow of an organization into novel domains (Kang & Snell, 2009; Lee et al., 2015). In DevOps integration, this concept needs to be broadened to IS operations, focusing on developing ambidextrous capabilities for development and operations within the organization (Andriopoulos & Lewis, 2009). Implementing a DevOps culture could enable organizations to achieve faster innovation cycles and better dynamics to stay ahead of competitors (Yoo, Boland Jr, Lyytinen, & Majchrzak, 2012). Thus, to maximize innovation potential, companies not only need to develop ambidextrous capabilities, they also need to exploit and strengthen their internal IT capabilities.

DevOps Integration

Company leaders have begun to recognize how DevOps teams can be leveraged to maximize the benefits of digitalization. This chapters outlines various approaches to DevOps integration in organizations as a means of transforming processes and technology. On way to begin the DevOps journey is to organize a single innovative IT service according to DevOps principles as a model for further integration. The people responsible for this IT service thus demonstrate the potential benefits of DevOps and advocate for wider application. For example, a company wishing to apply new technology to modernizing their processes may develop customized technological solutions and innovations that benefit its IT department and customers.

After identifying a suitable IT service for DevOps transformation, is helpful to adopt structural guidelines. Many of the companies organized their DevOps teams based on the value stream, in which value is specified from the perspective of the end-customer. Applying lean value stream mapping to software development and operation processes helps to detect potential bottlenecks in software delivery lifecycle activities while retaining focus on customer value. Generally, a value stream is a flowchart method and consists of several streams producing products seen by the customer and contributing to end-customer value (Janz, Meek, Nichols, & Oglesby, 2016). Value stream mapping manages the information flow to bring a product to the client. In particular, value stream mapping concentrates on identifying hand-offs and repetitive processes that can be automated with the help of continuous delivery.

Three DevOps Team Setups

Our study reveals three unique patterns of DevOps setup based on the type of software developed and how they contributed to IT convergence. As summarized in Table 1 below, with the help of the empirical study platform-oriented, application-oriented, and mobile-oriented DevOps setups were identified.

Table 1. DevOps Setups

	Platform-oriented DevOps	Application-oriented DevOps	Mobile-oriented DevOps
Aim	• Basis of application-oriented DevOps • Create an internal IT ecosystem • Limited code writing	• Interface between end-user and platform-oriented DevOps • Manage services for end-customer • Extensive code writing	• Make application work on different mobile operating systems and web browsers • Support smartphone and tablet use
Type of product	Platform (cloud-based)	Application (software)	Mobile apps
Background	Operations knowledge	Development knowledge	Mobile development knowledge
Tasks	• Design, construct, configure and run a platform • Provide infrastructure for applications • Create program scripts and automate platform tasks	• Design, construct, configure and run software application • Service operation and on-call duty for trouble-shooting activities	• Design, construct, configure and run a mobile app • Combine platform and application knowledge for app management
Technology	Cloud-based platform with open-source operating systems	Microservice architecture with Application programming interfaces (APIs)	Mobile operating systems
Responsibility	Platform development, operation, and on-call duty for troubleshooting activities.	Development and operation tasks for an application-based service during the complete lifecycle.	Development and operation tasks for mobile apps during the complete lifecycle.

Platform-oriented DevOps teams have a centralized organizational structure. Typically, a DevOps team develops, maintains and supervises the platform, such as a cloud, and potentially collaborates with one or more application-oriented DevOps teams. The platform contains a tool chain that enables continuous integration/delivery and flexible runtime. This gives the platform the maximal benefits of scalability and automation in terms of developing platform-based applications. In the analyzed organizations, management and stakeholders decided together to implement a platform in-house and set guidelines about what infrastructure can be use by the application teams. Close cooperation between platform-oriented and application-oriented DevOps teams facilitate internal IT ecosystems. For example, application-oriented DevOps teams can use a platform as a basis. In addition, other DevOps teams of development/operations with mixed expertise and backgrounds can use APIs to enable self-service, potentially including system administration and software development. Platforms can also be set up to enable all development and operational entities to develop and deploy an application. This end-to-end digital infrastructure enables monitoring, reporting, service management, and application-oriented DevOps teams using self-services to achieve more development speed.

Application-oriented DevOps teams are organized decentrally within the IT organization. Typically, an application-oriented DevOps team is responsible for developing, operating and maintaining one or more software product-oriented services. Such teams integrate infrastructure and IT processes within their team setup to deliver a functional application-based software product. To ensure end-to-end service, developers must ensure IT software and architecture compatibility and operational knowledge must be integrated in the DevOps team. In the studied organizations, such application-oriented DevOps teams were relatively small (three to ten members) and organized according to agile principles. Sometimes DevOps teams use microservices to modernize legacy systems and the team is responsible for one or more of these microservices. Microservices decouple dependencies between complex software applications, enabling independent processes to work together through APIs and giving DevOps team greater autonomy in their work environment.

Mobile-oriented DevOps teams are also organized decentrally within the IT function. Organizations commonly use apps externally, for example as a sales or service platform for customers, and/or internally, for instance to manage internal services or product delivery. In addition to working closely with application-oriented DevOps teams, mobile-oriented DevOps teams often interface with other DevOps teams in the organization for the purpose of data exchange, especially when the app draws on data from software that another team is responsible for. In order to ensure smooth app functionality, close collaboration and communication regarding data scope and modification is essential. Thus, it is necessary to collaborate closely with other teams and to achieve a high level of exchange and communication. Furthermore, given their innate position at the intersection between frontend and backend processes, mobile-oriented DevOps teams must ensure compatibility with the organization's overall setup. Finally, mobile-oriented DevOps teams must also follow relevant app store rules and regulations, especially often strict restrictions on release frequency. Hence, the responsibility for the services lies within the company, and firms achieve a reduction in their dependence on suppliers. The application-oriented DevOps team manages application-based products that usually run on a platform, but these teams can also work without an internal platform.

In summary, these three types of DevOps setups can run alone and independently from the rest of the IT function, such as a platform-oriented DevOps team managing a cloud while the rest of the IT function operates disciplinary. This would present a hybrid solution for integrating DevOps teams and running a disciplined IT function simultaneously. However, in order to build an internal IT ecosystem structure using the DevOps concept, a high degree of collaboration is necessary by combining interdependent DevOps teams to design, develop and operate a platform. For example, a platform-oriented DevOps team responsible for a cloud on which an application-oriented DevOps team runs its internal services, and a mobile-oriented DevOps team depends on both teams for data exchange.

The Software Delivery Lifecycle in DevOps Teams

Implementing DevOps teams facilitates self-management as recommended by agile software development and delivers consistent feedback along the complete software delivery lifecycle (Krancher et al., 2018). From the value stream perspective, certain processes and tools are recommended in adopting DevOps and transforming the IT function effectively. Table 2 aligns value stream processes and supportive DevOps processes and tools.

Table 2. Process Steps of DevOps Teams

	Description	Supporting Processes
Plan	The team does regular planning and the team lead is responsible for meeting business department requirements and attending planning sessions. All team members plan the development and operations work. The team estimates the time needed for unplanned work.	The backlog is usually represented on a Kanban board including development and operations epics and user stories. The team members use different tools to manage their backlog.
Build	Software development includes the building and compiling of new software code. New deployments run automatically through the different stages of the environment.	To support the build process, the implementation of version control tools is recommended. The team members do code review in order to control the accuracy of new features.
Test	Continuous integration enables automatic testing of new code when a team member provides it to the build environment. This approach helps continuously merge different software components.	Continuous integration improves detection of failures. Software is used to support the automation processes.
Deploy	Deployments include the packaging and deploying of new software features across all environments to production. When the software code is in the production environment, it is visible for the end customer.	Continuous delivery builds upon continuous integration and enables the automatic integration and delivery processes that are necessary for iterative deployment. Moreover, configuration management helps to achieve a high level of traceability. Using configuration management tools to document and track changes makes the changes comprehensible to all team members.
Operate	Software operations processes begin with the deployment of new software features in the production environment. Operations processes include the monitoring of running software, solving problems, and automatically logging data through protocols.	Monitoring the activities of running software supports a DevOps teams. Dashboards are used to visualize such items as software performance and metrics. Logging protocols facilitates application management.

Six Indicators as Recommendations for Successful DevOps Integration

While the DevOps concept establishes certain principles of service provision in the digital era, integrating DevOps successfully in existing IT function depends on the context in which a given organization operates. This section outlines six key indicators of effective DevOps integration, translated into recommendations for effective DevOps management based on observed practical adoption of DevOps.

Enable Product-Oriented DevOps Teams Through End-to-End Responsibility

Building on value stream mapping, the first step in DevOps integration is to assign software products for end-to-end delivery. Ideally, the assignment should capture at least 90 to 99 percent of the tasks and activities for which the team is responsible. Once suitably competent people are assigned to DevOps teams, the first challenge is to achieve cultural alignment between development and operations. Developers must learn to consider the deployment of new software features beyond the development or test environment and develop an overall view of the software delivery processes, including potentially high-volume information and data exchange. For their part, operations people must broaden their view of the development process to include the challenges involved in providing new software code. In addition to developing a comprehensive understanding of lead time and end-to-end processes, the team must foster a willingness to collaborate and align their priorities along common goals. This requires transparent communication to avoid conflicts of interests.

The cultural shift from a project-oriented to a product-oriented setup is significant. Projects have start and end dates, whereas products have lifecycles. With DevOps teams responsible for the entire software delivery lifecycle, developers and operations people help each other to understand the processes involved in and share responsibility for production, deployment and problem management, using control mechanisms to review code, evaluate product performance and guarantee process rigor. This can be an eye-opening experience for everyone involved.

Enable Speed and Stability in Software Delivery to Increase Customer Satisfaction

Companies typically only rarely provide new releases and customers often have to wait a long time for new software features. Software releases with a huge number of new features are often implemented on release weekends. Such massive releases are prone to error and lead to customer disappointment. DevOps principles help speed up new software feature provision, enabling more frequent new releases through new technology, new processes, and cultural adaptation. Digital innovators such as Google and Netflix deploy several thousand times per day over a vast array of services (Forsgren, Humble, Kim, Brown, & Kersten, 2018). Many other companies already operate at a very high level and can deploy daily if necessary. DevOps teams achieve greater speed by:

1. Uniting people with development and operations backgrounds in one team to improve communication, facilitate rapid collaboration and foster a productive culture of feedback.
2. Using tools to automate manual processes and simplify the provision of new software features.

These benefits are only possible if DevOps teams have the collective competencies along the entire software delivery lifecycle of the specific products assigned to it, including planning, development, operational, and testing knowledge.

Integrate Agility into Support Processes

The benefits of agile software development, including rapid software delivery and feedback circles can be maximized by combining DevOps principles with agile methods in software development and operations. Bringing software development and operations closer together empowers the incorporation of operational strategy at an earlier stage in the software delivery process (Edberg, Ivanova, & Kuechler, 2012). For example, some Kanban principles are common in lean management (Conboy, 2011) have been used to foster agility in DevOps teams, because Scrum sprints are sometimes too long for DevOps teams to deploy a new software feature as soon as it is ready. Some teams combine Scrum and Kanban principles in order to achieve maximum benefits. Most of the DevOps teams had daily stand-ups or bi-weekly review meetings, which is typical for Scrum, often combined with Kanban principles such as visualizing work-in-progress and using the Kanban board as necessary to plan software development and operations tasks. By thus broadening agility to include operations, DevOps teams improve performance along the entire software delivery lifecycle, including system infrastructure and support processes. In disciplined IT functions, operations work is often unplanned and reactive. In contrast, DevOps teams delivering an IT service schedule such interruptions into their Kanban board as time for unplanned work.

For many years, companies have structured their operations processes successfully using highly formalized ITIL processes as guidelines for structuring groups that deal with incident or problem management, as well as other expert groups organizing service strategy, design, transition, and operations. These structures have often made IT functions act like IT service management functions, which has often been appropriate (Trusson, Doherty, & Hislop, 2014). Managing digital trends and new software products with ITIL often entails high process rigor, which can also be helpful in the context of modern architectures, including microservices. Interconnected DevOps teams with monitoring and service responsibility may find it difficult to determine which service is causing a problem. This is especially true with seemingly independent microservices, which communicate with each other and often have underlying data content or other similar dependencies. Some ITIL principles supporting process rigor in DevOps teams include incident management and version control processes. Following the three-tiered ITIL organization, incidents are grouped into and managed according to first, second and third tiers. This organization establishes strict guidelines and clearly defined rules for incident management, such as reaction times. With DevOps teams responsible for monitoring software operations, such incident management guidelines are helpful when incidents are not recognized by the team.

Such ITIL processes can be successfully combined with new approaches such as using incident swarming as a guideline for managing incidents in DevOps teams. Incident swarming is similar to collective intelligence as known from agile method. Incident swarming is based on network principles, assigning a single group to managing incidents. The group identifies the person most qualified to solve the incident and he or she leads the effort. One type of swarm is the "severity swarm", which handles only the most critical incidents, thus fewer incidents than in traditional major incident management. Another type of swarm is the "dispatch swarm", which handles incidents that can be resolved very quickly. The "backlog swarm" handle the most difficult backlog incidents requiring subject matter expertise (Hall, 2018).

Adopt Transformational Leadership Style to Inspire Collaboration

DevOps team management fosters an enabling culture of collaboration among members, but also between the team and the leader. Whereas disciplined command-and-control management styles have worked well in the past, our analysis indicates that transformational leadership style is preferable in DevOps team management. Rafferty and Griffin (2004) identify five principles of transformational leadership: vision, inspirational leadership, intellectual stimulation, supportive leadership style, and personal recognition. In contrast to traditional waterfall phase-gate project management, DevOps leadership style revolves around practice leaders responsible for keeping people together, bringing new people on board and fostering a DevOps mindset.

As discussed above, an important feature of DevOps management is end-to-end responsibility for the delivery lifecycle of one or more software services. When team members are given the authority to make decisions, they can better define and fulfill their responsibilities, chose appropriate technology, organize their work, and identify managers responsible for decisions that impact other teams or the organization at large, such as decisions with organizational impact. Traditional management models based on strict rules are not flexible enough to respond to the ever-changing needs of the current high-speed IT environment enabled by microservices. Transformational leadership builds up on agile management styles. Nevertheless, agile is often managed in project set ups with determined start and end date and project budget etc. (Cram & Newell, 2016) which is different comparted DevOps. Through the product orientation of DevOps, the leadership style should develop from directive to collaborative and consensual.

Leverage Modularization in IT Architecture

Implementing DevOps often requires a significant shift in IT architecture. Some of the DevOps teams analyzed in this research have integrated a digital service platform as a basis for other services to enable digital innovation (Ross et al., 2016). APIs facilitate automated self-services, enabling a web shop DevOps team, for example, to access databases more quickly. Disciplined monolithic software systems make it difficult to develop and implement new technology and detach individual services. Apps and frontend development can be managed more efficiently on digital platforms with loosely coupled modular microservices and APIs linking frontend and backend systems and teams, especially because the microservice architecture allows backend and frontend services to be scaled separately. Microservices thus make frontend services more independent and easier to scale as needed.

Automation is another key principle of DevOps. In keeping with agile software development, DevOps enables continuous testing, integration and delivery of new software code in different software environments. Using modular automation in a continuous delivery environment, developers can deploy new software code and immediately run tests to detect errors and failures at a very early stage, well before the customer sees the new software feature.

Balance Process Rigor and Agility in DevOps Teams

While cross-functional DevOps team members have allocated roles, each team member should be able to take over various tasks along the software delivery lifecycle. For instance, DevOps teams that mainly include software engineers must also handle all operations tasks related to their service. One method of ensuring sufficient cross-functional expertise is to rotate the role of "Operation Duty Manager" weekly among team members. This not only encourages programmers to consider the operational functionality of their code, but enables all team members to fill in for each other temporarily as needed. From a human capital perspective, team members must develop both specialized and cross-disciplinary knowledge.

Many of the examined DevOps teams have developed social networks to share knowledge internally and across the company, including communication and knowledge sharing model such as lightning and tech talks as well as interest groups for further education in special areas. Some companies also have coaches responsible for standardizing development processes and tools, implementing incident swarming and promoting these processes within the teams to avoid inefficiencies and encourage process rigor.

In summary, the ambidexterity of process rigor and agility within DevOps teams facilitates successful DevOps integration. Most organizations are heavily invested in exploiting existing static technological environments, structures and process capabilities, but also recognize the potential benefits of exploring new technologies like CI and cloud solutions to enhance rigor and agile process capabilities within the organization.

FUTURE RESEARCH

As more and more organizations integrate DevOps teams into their established IT functions, this research identifies patterns of successful DevOps integration and makes recommendations on solving common challenges arising during organizational transformation. Our study points to areas of potentially fruitful further research with highly practical implications, including the relative suitability of certain IT services for DevOps management, a deeper analysis of the relationship between process rigor and process agility, best practices in aligning development and operations, and how DevOps teams can best support the integration of cloud platforms to modernize legacy systems. Furthermore, the empirical results focus on internal DevOps teams. Hence, other sourcing relationships such as outsourcing, near-, and offshoring relationships will provide opportunities for further investigations. In addition, the DevOps concepts is extended by security issues and more and more organization are dealing with DevSecOps. This concept includes topics such as information security and compliance processes and tasks. We leave it to future research to investigate characteristics of security in DevOps setups.

CONCLUSION

This chapter offers guidelines for integrating DevOps management in disciplined IT functions to maximize business value. DevOps enables faster provision of new software components, alignment of development and operations tasks, as well as a rapid feedback cycle. Our study finds that while platform-oriented, application-oriented and mobile-oriented DevOps IT service teams can operate alone and independently, efficient collaboration can be achieved by combining interdependent DevOps teams to leverage synergies and ensure compatibility in an overall IT ecosystem structure based on the DevOps concept.

Our study also identifies six indicators of effective DevOps integration, which are recommendations guiding DevOps transformation in disciplined IT functions. First, give cross-functional DevOps teams end-to-end responsibility for and decision-making authority over one or more IT services. Second, integrate DevOps teams to ensure fast and stable software delivery and high customer satisfaction. Third, expand agile software development methods to agility in operations as well to achieve fast code delivery and feedback. Fourth, adopt a transformational leadership style to inspire collaboration, motivation and responsibility. Fifth, maximize the benefits of modularization, APIs, microservices and automation during IT architecture transformation. Sixth, balance rigor and agility in managing development and operations tasks to facilitate greater cross-functional awareness and understanding, better collaboration and less frictional loss. As organizations strive to leverage new technologies and maximize the business value of their IT investments, hence it is encouraged to explore the potential benefits of integrating cross-functional DevOps teams to achieve continuous delivery and deployment with end-to-end responsibility, progress transparency and fast, stable and safe IT service delivery.

ACKNOWLEDGMENT

This research was supported by the German Federal Ministry of Education and Research (BMBF) [grant number 13FH005PX4].

REFERENCES

Andriopoulos, C., & Lewis, M. W. (2009). Exploitation-Exploration Tensions and Organizational Ambidexterity: Managing Paradoxes of Innovation. *Organization Science*, *20*(4), 696–717. doi:10.1287/orsc.1080.0406

Beck, K., Beedle, M., Bennekum, A., Cockburn, A., Cunningham, W., & Fowler, M. (2001). Manifesto for Agile Software Development. Academic Press.

Boehm, B., & Turner, R. (2005). Management Challenges to Implementing Agile Processes in Traditional Development Organizations. *IEEE Software*, *22*(5), 30–39. doi:10.1109/MS.2005.129

Conboy, K. (2011). *Comparing Apples with Oranges? The Perceived Differences between Agile and Lean Software Development Processes*. Paper presented at the International Conference on Information Systems, Shanghai, China.

Cram, A., & Newell, S. (2016). Mindful Revolution or Mindless Trend? Examining Agile Development as a Management Fashion. *European Journal of Information Systems*, *25*(2), 154–169. doi:10.1057/ejis.2015.13

Debois, P. (2011). Opening Statement. *Cutter IT Journal*, *24*(8), 3–5.

Dery, K., Sebastian, I. M., & van der Meulen, N. (2017). The Digital Workplace is Key to Digital Innovation. *MIS Quarterly Executive*, *16*(2), 135–152.

Dhaliwal, J., Onita, C. G., Poston, R., & Zhang, X. P. (2011). Alignment within the Software Development Unit: Assessing Structural and Relational Dimensions between Developers and Testers. *The Journal of Strategic Information Systems*, *20*(4), 323–342. doi:10.1016/j.jsis.2011.03.001

Edberg, D., Ivanova, P., & Kuechler, W. (2012). Methodology Mashups: An Exploration of Processes Used to Maintain Software. *Journal of Management Information Systems*, *28*(4), 271–304. doi:10.2753/MIS0742-1222280410

Forsgren, N., Humble, J., Kim, G., Brown, A., & Kersten, N. (2018). *Accelerate: State of DevOps Strategies for a New Economy*. Puppet + DORA.

Gupta, A. K., Smith, K. G., & Shalley, C. E. (2006). The Interplay Between Exploration and Exploitation. *Academy of Management Journal*, *49*(4), 693–706. doi:10.5465/amj.2006.22083026

Hall, J. (2018). *Swarming Support vs Tiered Support: What's the Difference?* Retrieved from https://www.bmc.com/blogs/swarming-support-tiered-support-differences/

Hemon, A., Monnier-Senicourt, L., & Rowe, F. (2018). *Job Satisfaction Factors and Risks Perception: An Embedded Case Study of DevOps and Agile Teams*. Paper presented at the International Conference on Information Systems, San Francisco, CA.

Humble, J., & Farley, D. (2011). *Continuous Delivery: Reliable Software Releases through Build, Test, and Deployment Automation*. Pearson Education, Inc.

Janz, B., Meek, T., Nichols, E., & Oglesby, J. (2016). How Buckman's Value Stream Initiative Re-Visioned IT for Value. *MIS Quarterly Executive*, *15*(3), 215–229.

Kang, S. C., & Snell, S. A. (2009). Intellectual Capital Architectures and Ambidextrous Learning: A Framework for Human Resource Management. *Journal of Management Studies*, *46*(1), 65–92. doi:10.1111/j.1467-6486.2008.00776.x

Krancher, O., Luther, P., & Jost, M. (2018). Key Affordances of Platform-as-a-Service: Self-Organization and Continuous Feedback. *Journal of Management Information Systems*, *35*(3), 776–812. doi:10.1080/07421222.2018.1481636

Lee, G., DeLone, W., & Espinosa, A. (2010). *The Main and Interaction Effects of Process Rigor, Process Standardization, and Process Agility on System Performance in Distributed IS Development: An Ambidexterity Perspective*. Paper presented at the International Conference on Information Systems, St. Louis, MO.

Lee, O.-K., Sambamurthy, V., Lim, K. H., & Wei, K. K. (2015). How Does IT Ambidexterity Impact Organizational Agility? *Information Systems Research*, *26*(2), 398–417. doi:10.1287/isre.2015.0577

Lwakatare, L. E., Karvonen, T., Sauvola, T., Kuvaja, P., Olsson, H. H., Bosch, J., & Oivo, M. (2016). *Towards DevOps in the Embedded Systems Domain: Why is it so Hard?* Paper presented at the Hawaii International Conference on System Sciences, Kauai, HI. 10.1109/HICSS.2016.671

March, J. D. (1991). Exploration and Exploitation in Organizaitonal Learning. *Organization Science*, *2*(1), 71–87. doi:10.1287/orsc.2.1.71

Rafferty, A. E., & Griffin, M. A. (2004). Dimensions of Transformational Leadership: Conceptual and Empirical Extensions. *The Leadership Quarterly*, *15*(3), 329–354. doi:10.1016/j.leaqua.2004.02.009

Ross, J. W., Sebastian, I., Beath, C., Mocker, M., Moloney, K., & Fonstad, N. (2016). *Designing and Executing Digital Strategies*. Paper presented at the International Conference on Information Systems, Dublin, Ireland.

Stroud, R. (2017). *2018: The Year Of Enterprise DevOps*. Retrieved from https://go.forrester.com/blogs/2018-the-year-of-enterprise-devops/

Trusson, C. R., Doherty, N. F., & Hislop, D. (2014). Knowledge Sharing Using IT Service Management Tools: Conflicting Discourses and Incompatible Practices. *Information Systems Journal*, *24*(4), 347–371. doi:10.1111/isj.12025

Wiedemann, A. (2017). *A New Form of Collaboration in IT Teams - Exploring the DevOps Phenomenon*. Paper presented at the Pacific Asia Conference on Information Systems, Langkawi, Malaysia.

Wiedemann, A., Forsgren, N., Wiesche, M., Gewald, H., & Krcmar, H. (2019). Research for Practice: The DevOps Phenomenon. *Communications of the ACM, 62*(8), 44–49. doi:10.1145/3331138

Wiedemann, A., & Wiesche, M. (2018). *Are You Ready For DevOps? Required Skill Set for DevOps Teams*. Paper presented at the European Conference on Information Systems, Portsmouth, UK.

Wiedemann, A., Wiesche, M., Thatcher, J. B., & Gewald, H. (2019). *A Control-Alignment Model for Product Orientation in DevOps Teams–A Multinational Case Study*. Paper presented at the International Conference on Information Systems, Munich, Germany.

Yoo, Y., Boland, R. J. Jr, Lyytinen, K., & Majchrzak, A. (2012). Organizing for Innovation in the Digitized World. *Organization Science, 23*(5), 1398–1408. doi:10.1287/orsc.1120.0771

KEY TERMS AND DEFINITIONS

DevOps: People from software development and operations work together to enhance the speed of delivery of new software features. It is a concept for bridging the gap between software development and software operations and integrating the logic of common responsibility for the complete software delivery lifecycle into one cross-functional team.

Incident Swarming: Based on network principles, a single group is responsible for managing incidents. The person most qualified to resolve the incident is identified within the group. Different "swarms" support individual responses to specific levels of incidents.

ITIL: The Information Technology Infrastructure Library (ITIL) presents pre-defined processes for IT service management. The fourth edition of ITIL depicts two key elements ITIL Service-Value-System (SVS) and a four dimensions model.

Microservices: Are an IT architectural pattern for decoupling dependencies between complex software applications and enabling independent processes that than work together through independent APIs.

Process Rigor: The stringent enforcement and adherence to compliance to given formal and structured IS processes.

Transformational Leadership: Is a form of leadership that encourages and inspiring employees. The leader works in the group and guided the team in accordance with the group's commitment.

Value Stream Mapping: Is a lean management technique for analyzing, designing, and managing the flow of data and information from an end-customer perspective to achieve value for them.

ENDNOTE

[1]   Registered Trademark by Axelos.

APPENDIX

Over 80 DevOps experts from more than 25 companies and thought leaders in the DevOps area from Germany, USA, Canada, Africa and Australia participated in this multiple case study. The qualitative research approach was suitable by virtue of the novelty of DevOps integration in established companies. DevOps is a phenomenon that presents great potential for further research and it is challenging to find representative organizations with high performing DevOps teams.

The aim was to understand how firms successfully integrate DevOps principles by analyzing examples of successful DevOps transformation. We focused on disciplined organized companies which are over ten years old and have worked with DevOps principles for at least six months. Start-ups were excluded. In addition, many research activities support the main data collection. The aim was to better understand incumbent firms' DevOps journeys. Literature reviews of both research and practice literature were performed, and we confirmed the validity of our core data and findings in discussions with numerous DevOps experts at scientific and practice conferences. At these practice conferences, we also identified outstanding DevOps transformations in large companies and potential case study participants. Finally, we visited several companies in Germany, the USA, and Australia to broaden our view and better understand DevOps team's set up.

Compilation of References

AAMI. (2012). TIR45:2012 - Guidance on the use of agile practices in the development of medical device software. Association for the Advancement of Medical Instrumentation, 21, 22-78.

Abbas, N., Gravell, A. M., & Wills, G. B. (2008). Historical roots of agile methods: Where did "Agile thinking" come from? *Lecture Notes in Business Information Processing, 9*, 94–103.

Abdullah, N. N. B., Honiden, S., Sharp, H., Nuseibeh, B., & Notkin, D. (2011). Communication patterns of agile requirements engineering. In *Proceedings of the 1st workshop on agile requirements engineering*. ACM.

Abrahamsson, P., Babar, M. A., & Kruchten, P. (2010). Agility and architecture: Can they coexist? *IEEE Software, 27*(2), 16–22. doi:10.1109/MS.2010.36

Abrahamsson, P., Fronza, I., Moser, R., Vlasenko, J., & Pedrycz, W. (2011). Predicting development effort from user stories. In *2011 International Symposium on Empirical Software Engineering and Measurement*, (pp. 400–403). IEEE. 10.1109/ESEM.2011.58

Abrahamsson, P., Oza, N., & Siponen, M. (2010). Agile software development methods: a comparative review. In T. Dingsøyr, T. Dybå, & N. Moe (Eds.), *Agile Software Development* (pp. 31–59). Springer. doi:10.1007/978-3-642-12575-1_3

Ågerfalk, J., & Fitzgerald, B. (2006). Flexible and distributed software processes: Old petunias in new bowls? *Communications of the ACM, 49*(10), 27–34.

Agile Alliance. (2001). *Manifesto for agile software development*. Author.

Agile Business Consortium. (2019). *Chapter 10: MoSCoW Prioritisation*. Retrieved from https://www.agilebusiness.org/page/ProjectFramework_10_MoSCoWPrioritisation

Agutter, C., van Hove, S., Steinberg, R., & England, R. (2017). *VeriSM - A service management approach for the digital age*. Van Haren.

Ahimbisibwe, A., Cavana, R. Y., & Daellenbach, U. (2015). A contingency fit model of critical success factors for software development projects: A comparison of agile and traditional plan-based methodologies. *Journal of Enterprise Information Management, 28*(1), 7–33. doi:10.1108/JEIM-08-2013-0060

Ahlemann, F., Schroeder, C., & Teuteberg, F. (2005). Kompetenz- und Reifegradmodelle für das Projektmanagement: Grundlagen, Vergleich und Einsatz. ISPRIArbeitsbericht. Osnabrück.

Ahmad, M. O., Dennehy, D., Conboy, K., & Oivo, M. (2018). Kanban in software engineering: A systematic mapping study. *Journal of Systems and Software, 137*, 96–113. doi:10.1016/j.jss.2017.11.045

Ahmed, F., Capretz, L. F., Bouktif, S., & Campbell, P. (2015). *Soft skills and software development: A reflection from the software industry*. arXiv preprint arXiv:1507.06873

Akkasoglu, G. (2013). *Methodik zur Konzeption und Applikation anwendungsspezifischer Reifegradmodelle unter Berücksichtigung der Informationsunsicherheit.* Academic Press.

Alahyari, H., Svensson, R. B., & Gorschek, T. (2017). A study of value in agile software development organizations. *Journal of Systems and Software, 125,* 271–288. doi:10.1016/j.jss.2016.12.007

Ali Babar, M., Brown, A. W., & Mistrík, I. (2013). *Agile Software Architecture: Aligning Agile Processes and Software Architectures.* Elsevier.

AlMutairi, A. M., & Qureshi, M. R. J. (2015). The proposal of scaling the roles in scrum of scrums for distributed large projects. *International Journal of Information Technology and Computer Science, 7*(8), 68–74. doi:10.5815/ijitcs.2015.08.10

Alqudah, M., & Razali, R. (2016). A review of scaling agile methods in large software development. International Journal on Advanced Science. *Engineering and Information Technology, 6*(6), 828–837.

Alshamrani, A., & Bahattab, A. (2015). A comparison between three SDLC models waterfall model, spiral model, and Incremental/Iterative model. *International Journal of Computer Science Issues, 12*(1), 106.

Altameem, E. A. (2015). Impact of Agile methodology on software development. *Computer and Information Science, 8*(2), 9. doi:10.5539/cis.v8n2p9

Al-Zewairi, M., Biltawi, M., Etaiwi, W., & Shaout, A. (2017). Agile software development methodologies: Survey of surveys. *Journal of Computer and Communications, 5*(05), 74–97. doi:10.4236/jcc.2017.55007

Ambler, S. (2007, Feb.). Agile Model Driven Development (AMDD). Xootic Magazine.

Ambler, S. W. (2010). *The Agile Maturity Model (AMM).* Retrieved from https://www.drdobbs.com/architecture-and-design/the-agile-maturity-model-amm/224201005

Ambler, S. (2002). *Agile modeling: effective practices for extreme programming and the unified process.* John Wiley & Sons, Inc.

Ambler, S. W. (2008). Beyond functional requirements on agile projects. *Dr. Dobb's Journal, 33*(10).

Ambler, S. W., & Lines, M. (2012). *Disciplined agile delivery: A practitioner's guide to agile software delivery in the enterprise.* IBM Press.

Andersen, E. (1996). Warning: Activity planning is hazardous to your project's health! *International Journal of Project Management, 14*(2), 89–94. doi:10.1016/0263-7863(95)00056-9

Andersen, E., Grude, K., & Haug, T. (2009). *Goal directed project management* (4th ed.). Kogan Page.

André, M., Baldoquín, M. G., & Acuña, S. T. (2011). Formal model for assigning human resources to teams in software projects. *Information and Software Technology, 53*(3), 259–275. doi:10.1016/j.infsof.2010.11.011

Andriopoulos, C., & Lewis, M. W. (2009). Exploitation-Exploration Tensions and Organizational Ambidexterity: Managing Paradoxes of Innovation. *Organization Science, 20*(4), 696–717. doi:10.1287/orsc.1080.0406

Appelrath, H.-J., Mayer, C., & Rohjans, S. (2012). Future Energy Grid - Migrationspfade ins Internet der Energie. In Energy Talks Ossiach 2011. Berlin: Springer Verlag. doi:10.1007/978-3-642-27864-8

Arsanjani, A., Ghosh, S., Allam, A., Abdollah, T., Ganapathy, S., & Holley, K. (2008). SOMA: A method for developing service-oriented solutions. *IBM Systems Journal, 47*(3), 377–396. doi:10.1147j.473.0377

Arsanjani, A., Hailpern, B., Martin, J., & Tarr, P. L. (2003). Web Services: Promises and compromises. *ACM Queue; Tomorrow's Computing Today,* 48–58.

Assal, H., & Chiasson, S. (2018). Security in the software development lifecycle. In *SOUPS @ USENIX Security Symposium* (pp. 281-296). Springer.

Avison, D., & Fitzgerald, G. (2003). Where now for development methodologies? *Communications of the ACM*, *46*(1), 78–82. doi:10.1145/602421.602423

Avison, D., Jones, J., Powell, P., & Wilson, D. (2004). Using and validating the strategic alignment model. *The Journal of Strategic Information Systems*, *13*(3), 223–246. doi:10.1016/j.jsis.2004.08.002

Awad, M. A. (2005). A comparison between agile and traditional software development methodologies. University of Western Australia.

Awad, M. (2005). *A comparison between agile and traditional software development methodologies*. University of Western Australia.

Ayalew, T., Kidane, T., & Carlsson, B. (2013). Identification and Evaluation of Security Activities in Agile Projects. *NordSec*, *2013*, 139–153.

Baca, D., Boldt, M., Carlsson, B., & Jacobsson, A. (2015). A Novel Security-Enhanced Agile Software Development Process Applied in an Industrial Setting. *ARES*, *2015*, 11–19.

Baca, D., & Carlsson, B. (2011). Agile development with security engineering activities. *ICSSP*, *2011*, 149–158.

Balaji, S., & Brown, C. V. (2014). Lateral coordination mechanisms and the moderating role of arrangement characteristics in information systems development outsourcing. *Information Systems Research*, *25*(4), 747–760. doi:10.1287/isre.2014.0556

Ballard, H. (2000). *The last planner system of production control* (Dissertation). Birmingham: University of Birmingham.

Bannerman, P. L. (2009). Software development governance: A meta-management perspective. *ICSE Workshop on Software Development Governance (SDG)*, 3–8.

Bano, M., Imtiaz, S., Ikram, N., Niazi, M., & Usman, M. (2012). *Causes of requirement change - A systematic literature review*. Academic Press.

Barbosa, P., Leite, F., Santos, D., Figueiredo, A., & Galdino, K. (2018, June). Introducing Traceability Information Models in Connected Health Projects. In *2018 IEEE 31st International Symposium on Computer-Based Medical Systems (CBMS)* (pp. 18-23). IEEE. 10.1109/CBMS.2018.00011

Barbosa, P., Queiroz, J., Santos, D., Figueiredo, A., Leite, F., & Galdino, K. (2018, June). RE4CH: Requirements Engineering for Connected Health. In *2018 IEEE 31st International Symposium on Computer-Based Medical Systems (CBMS)* (pp. 292-297). IEEE.

Barlatier, P. J., & Dupouët, O. (2015). Achieving contextual ambidexterity with communities of practice at GDF SUEZ. *Global Business and Organizational Excellence*, *34*(3), 43–53. doi:10.1002/joe.21603

Bartsch, S. (2011). Practitioners' Perspectives on Security in Agile Development. *ARES*, *2011*, 479–484.

Batra, D., Xia, W., VanderMeer, D. E., & Dutta, K. (2010). Balancing agile and structured development approaches to successfully manage large distributed software projects: A case study from the cruise line industry. CAIS, 27(21), 379-394.

Bauknecht, D., & Funcke, S. (2013). Dezentralisierung oder Zentralisierung der Stromversorgung: Was ist darunter zu verstehen? *Energiewirtschaftliche Tagesfragen*, *63*(8), 14–17.

Beck, K., Beedle, M., Bennekum, A. V., Cockburn, A., Cunningham, W., Fowler, M., Grenning, J., Highsmith, J., Hunt, A., Jeffries, R., Kern, J., Marick, B., Martin, R., Mellor, S., Schwaber, K., Sutherland, J., & Thomas, D. (2001). *Manifesto for Agile Software Development*. Retrieved from: http://agilemanifesto.org

Beck, K., Beedle, M., Bennekum, A., Cockburn, A., Cunningham, W., & Fowler, M. (2001). Manifesto for Agile Software Development. Academic Press.

Beck, K., Beedle, M., Van Bennekum, A., Cockburn, A., Cunningham, W., Fowler, M., . . . Kern, J. (2001). *The agile manifesto*. Available from https://agilemanifesto.org/

Beck, K., Beedle, M., van Bennekum, A., Cockburn, A., Cunningham, W., Fowler, M., . . . Thomas, D. (2001). Manifesto for agile software development. Retrieved from: www.agilemanifesto.org/

Becker, J., Knackstedt, R., & Poeppelbuss, J. (2008). Dokumentationsqualität von Reifegradmodellentwicklungen. *Arbeitsbericht Des Instituts Für Wirtschaftsinformatik*, (121), 1–50. Retrieved from https://www.ifib-consult.de/publikationsdateien/2009.pdf

Beck, K. (1999). Embracing change with extreme programming. *Computer*, *32*(10), 70–77. doi:10.1109/2.796139

Beck, K., & Boehm, B. (2003). Agility through Discipline: A Debate. *IEEE Computer*, *36*(6), 44–46. doi:10.1109/MC.2003.1204374

Begel, A., Nagappan, N., Poile, C., & Layman, L. (2009). Coordination in large-scale software teams. *ICSE Workshop on Cooperative and Human Aspects on Software Engineering (CHASE)*, 1–7.

Bellomo, S., Gorton, I., & Kazman, R. (2015). Toward Agile Architecture: Insights from 15 Years of ATAM Data. *IEEE Software*, *32*(5), 38–45. doi:10.1109/MS.2015.35

Bellomo, S., Kruchten, P., Nord, R., & Ozkaya, I. (2014). How to Agilely Architect an Agile Architecture. *Cutter IT Journal*.

Ben Othmane, L., Angin, P., Weffers, H., & Bhargava, B. K. (2014). Extending the Agile Development Process to Develop Acceptably Secure Software. *IEEE Transactions on Dependable and Secure Computing*, *11*(6), 497–509. doi:10.1109/TDSC.2014.2298011

Bianchini, E., Francesconi, M., Testa, M., Tanase, M., & Gemignani, V. (2019). Unique device identification and traceability for medical software: A major challenge for manufacturers in an ever-evolving marketplace. *Journal of Biomedical Informatics*, *93*, 103150. doi:10.1016/j.jbi.2019.103150 PMID:30878617

Bick, S., Spohrer, K., Hoda, R., Scheerer, A., & Heinzl, A. (2018). Coordination Challenges in Large-Scale Software Development: A Case Study of Planning Misalignment in Hybrid Settings. *IEEE Transactions on Software Engineering*, *44*(10), 932–950. doi:10.1109/TSE.2017.2730870

Bilgaiyan, S., Mishra, S., & Das, M. (2016). A review of software cost estimation in agile software development using soft computing techniques. In *2016 2nd international conference on computational intelligence and networks (CINE)*, (pp. 112–117). IEEE. 10.1109/CINE.2016.27

Binkhonain, M., & Zhao, L. (2019). A review of machine learning algorithms for identification and classification of non-functional requirements. *Expert Systems with Applications*, *10*. doi:10.1016/j.eswax.2019.100001

Birkinshaw, J. (2018). What to Expect From Agile. *MIT Sloan Management Review*, *59*(2), 39–42.

Bjørnson, F. O., Wijnmaalen, J., & Stettina, C. J. (2018). Inter-team Coordination in Large-Scale Agile Development: A Case Study of Three Enabling Mechanisms. *XP*, 216–231.

Blank, S. (2013). Why the Lean Start-Up Changes Everything. *Harvard Business Review*, *91*(5), 64–68.

Bluetooth, S. I. G. (2020). *Bluetooth SIG specifications*. Retrieved February 20, 2020, from https://www.bluetooth.com/specifications/

Boehm, B., & Turner, R. (2004). Balancing agility and discipline: Evaluating and integrating agile and plan-driven methods. In *Proceedings. 26th International Conference on Software Engineering* (pp. 718-719). IEEE.

Boehm, B. (2000). Requirements that handle IKIWISI, COTS, and rapid change. *Computer, 33*(7), 99–102. doi:10.1109/2.869384

Boehm, B. (2002). Get ready for agile methods, with care. *IEEE Computer, 35*(1), 64–69. doi:10.1109/2.976920

Boehm, B. W. (1988). A spiral model of software development and enhancement. *Computer, 21*(5), 61–72. doi:10.1109/2.59

Boehm, B., Egyed, A., Kwan, J., Port, D., Shah, A., & Madachy, R. (1998). Using the WinWin spiral model: A case study. *IEEE Computer, 31*(7), 33–44. doi:10.1109/2.689675

Boehm, B., Klappholz, D., Colbert, E., Puri, P., Jain, A., Bhuta, J., & Kitapci, H. (2004). *Guidelines for Model-Based (System) Architecting and Software Engineering (MBASE)*. Center for Software Engineering, University of Southern California.

Boehm, B., & Turner, R. (2003). *Balancing Agility and Discipline: A Guide for the Perplexed*. Addison-Wesley.

Boehm, B., & Turner, R. (2004). Balancing agility and discipline: Evaluating and integrating agile and plan-driven methods. In *Proceedings of the 26th International Conference on Software Engineering (ICSE'04)* (pp. 718-719). Edinburgh, UK: IEEE 10.1109/ICSE.2004.1317503

Boehm, B., & Turner, R. (2005). Management challenges to implementing agile processes in traditional development organizations. *IEEE Software, 22*(5), 30–39. doi:10.1109/MS.2005.129

Bohner, S. A., & Arnold, R. S. (1996). *Software change impact analysis* (Vol. 6). IEEE Computer Society Press.

Boness, K., & Harrison, R. (2007). Goal sketching: Towards agile requirements engineering. In *International Conference on Software Engineering Advances (ICSEA 2007)*, (pp. 71–71). IEEE. 10.1109/ICSEA.2007.36

Borges, P., Monteiro, P., & MacHado, R. J. (2012). Mapping RUP roles to small software development teams. *Software Quality Days*, 59–70.

Bourque, P., & Farley, R. E. (2014). *SWEBOK: Guide to the Software Engineering Body of Knowledge Versión 3.0*. IEEE, Computer Society.

Brechner, E. (2015). *Agile project management with Kanban*. Microsoft Press.

Brown, A., & Grant, G. (2005). Framing the frameworks: A review of IT governance research. *Communications of the Association for Information Systems, 15*, 696–712. doi:10.17705/1CAIS.01538

Brown, T. (2009). *Change by Design: How Design Thinking Transforms Organizations and Inspires Innovation*. Harper Collins.

Buchan, J., MacDonell, S. G., & Yang, J. (2019). Effective team onboarding in Agile software development: Techniques and goals. *2019 ACM/IEEE International Symposium on Empirical Software Engineering and Measurement (ESEM)*, 1–11. 10.1109/ESEM.2019.8870189

Bundesnetzagentur. (2011). *Entflechtung/Konzessionen*. Retrieved from https://www.bundesnetzagentur.de/DE/Sachgebiete/ElektrizitaetundGas/Unternehmen_Institutionen/EntflechtungKonzessionenVerteilernetze/entflechtungkonzessionenverteilernetze-node.html

Cai, Z., & Shu, H. (2013). Research of Smart Grid IT Capability Maturity Model and its Fuzzy Comprehensive Evaluation. *Journal of Kunming University of Science and Technology (Natural Science Edition)*, (6), 68–73.

Cai, Z. L., Shu, H. C., & Zhang, W. (2013). Research of the IT Capability Maturity Model and its Extension Evaluation of Smart Grid. *Applied Mechanics and Materials*, *423–426*, 2693–2702. . doi:10.4028/www.scientific.net/AMM.423-426.2693

Camacho, C. R., Marczak, S., & Cruzes, D. S. (2016). Agile Team Members Perceptions on Non-functional Testing: Influencing Factors from an Empirical Study. *ARES*, *2016*, 582–589.

Cantor, M. (2003). *Rational Unified Process for Systems Engineering*. Rational Brand Services IBM Software Group.

Cao, L., Mohan, K., Ramesh, B., & Sarkar, S. (2013). Evolution of governance: Achieving ambidexterity in IT outsourcing. *Journal of Management Information Systems*, *30*(3), 115–140. doi:10.2753/MIS0742-1222300305

Cao, L., & Ramesh, B. (2008). Agile requirements engineering practices: An empirical study. *IEEE Software*, *25*(1), 60–67. doi:10.1109/MS.2008.1

Carlson, D., & Matuzic, P. (2010). Practical agile requirements engineering. *Proceedings of the 13th Annual Systems Engineering Conference*.

Carlson, R., Matuzic, P., & Simons, R. (2012). Applying scrum to stabilize systems engineering execution. *Crosstalk*, 1–6.

Caroli, P. (2019). Lean Inception: How to Align People and Build the Right Product. Retrieved from https://martinfowler.com/articles/lean-inception/

Castillo Salinas L., Sanchez-Gordón S., Villarroel-Ramos J. & Sánchez-Gordón M. (2020) Evaluation of the implementation of a subset of ISO/IEC 29110 Software Implementation process in four teams of undergraduate students of Ecuador. An empirical software engineering experiment. Journal of Computer Standards & Interfaces, 70.

Ceschi, M., Sillitti, A., Succi, G., & De Panfilis, S. (2005). Project management in plan-based and agile companies. *IEEE Software*, *22*(3), 21–27. doi:10.1109/MS.2005.75

Charette, R. N. (2005). Why software fails. *IEEE Spectrum*, *42*(9), 42–49. doi:10.1109/MSPEC.2005.1502528

Chase, R. B., & Apte, U. M. (2007). A history of research in service operations: What's the big idea? *Journal of Operations Management*, *25*(2), 375–386. doi:10.1016/j.jom.2006.11.002

Cheng, T. H., Jansen, S., & Remmers, M. (2009). Controlling and monitoring agile software development in three dutch product software companies. *2009 ICSE Workshop on Software Development Governance*, 29-35. 10.1109/SDG.2009.5071334

Chetankumar, P., & Ramachandran, M. (2009). Agile maturity model (AMM). (2009). A software process improvement framework for agile software development practices. *International Journal of Software Engineering*, *2*(1), 3–28.

Christel, M. G., & Kang, K. C. (1992). *Issues in requirements elicitation (No. CMU/SEI-92-TR-12)*. Carnegie-Mellon Univ Pittsburgh Pa Software Engineering Inst.

Clerc, V., Lago, P., & Van Vliet, H. (2011). Architectural knowledge management practices in agile global software development. *6th IEEE International Conference on Global Software Engineering Workshops*, 1–8. 10.1109/ICGSE-W.2011.17

Cockburn, A. (2004). *Crystal clear: A human-powered methodology for small teams*. Addison Wesley.

Cockburn, A. (2006). *Agile software development: the cooperative game*. Pearson Education.

Cockburn, A., & Highsmith, J. (2001). Agile Software Development: The People Factor. *Computer, IEEE, 34*(11), 131–133. doi:10.1109/2.963450

Coelho, E., & Basu, A. (2012). Effort estimation in agile software development using story points. *International Journal of Applied Information Systems, 3*(7), 7–10. doi:10.5120/ijais12-450574

Cohen, D., Lindvall, M., & Costa, P. (2004). An introduction to agile methods. *Advances in Computers, 62*(03), 1–66.

Cohen, D., Lindvall, M., & Costa, P. (2004). An Introduction to Agile Methods. In M. Zelkowitz (Ed.), *Advances in Computers, Advances in Software Engineering*. Elsevier. doi:10.1016/S0065-2458(03)62001-2

Cohn, M. (2004). *User Stories Applied: For Agile Software Development*. Addison Wesley Longman Publishing Co., Inc.

Cohn, M. (2004). *User stories applied: For agile software development*. Addison Wesley Professional.

Cohn, M. (2010). *Succeding with Agile*. Addison Wesley.

Cohn, M. (2010). *Succeeding with Agile*. Addison Wesley.

Coltman, T., Tallon, P. P., Sharma, R., & Queiroz, M. (2015). Strategic IT alignment: Twenty-five years on. *JIT, 30*(2), 91–100.

Conboy, K. (2011). *Comparing Apples with Oranges? The Perceived Differences between Agile and Lean Software Development Processes*. Paper presented at the International Conference on Information Systems, Shanghai, China.

Conboy, K., Coyle, S., Wang, X., & Pikkarainen, M. (2011). *People over process: Key people challenges in agile development*. Academic Press.

Conboy, K. (2009). Agility from First Principles: Reconstructing the Concept of Agility in Information Systems Development. *Information Systems Research, 20*(3), 329–354. doi:10.1287/isre.1090.0236

Conboy, K., & Fitzgerald, B. (2004). Toward a Conceptual Framework of Agile Methods. In *Proceedings of ACM Workshop on Interdisciplinary Software Engineering Research* (pp. 37-44). Newport Beach, CA: Academic Press. 10.1145/1029997.1030005

Conboy, K., & Fitzgerald, B. (2004). Toward a Conceptual Framework of Agile Methods. In C. Zannier, H. Erdogmus, & L. Lindstrom (Eds.), *Extreme Programming and Agile Methods - XP/Agile Universe 2004, LNCS* (Vol. 3134, pp. 105–116). Springer. doi:10.1007/978-3-540-27777-4_11

Coplien, J. O., & Bjørnvig, G. (2011). *Lean architecture: for agile software development*. John Wiley & Sons.

Cornelissen, J. (2017). Editor's comments: Developing propositions, a process model, or a typology? Addressing the challenges of writing theory without a boilerplate. *Academy of Management Review, 42*(1), 1–9. doi:10.5465/amr.2016.0196

Cots, S., Casadesús, M., & Marimon, F. (2016). Benefits of ISO 20000 IT service management certification. *Information Systems and e-Business Management, 14*(1), 1–18. doi:10.100710257-014-0271-2

Cox, D. E., & Kreger, H. (2005). Management of the service oriented-architecture life cycle. IBM Corporation. *IBM Systems Journal, 44*(4), 709–726. doi:10.1147j.444.0709

Cram, A., & Newell, S. (2016). Mindful Revolution or Mindless Trend? Examining Agile Development as a Management Fashion. *European Journal of Information Systems, 25*(2), 154–169. doi:10.1057/ejis.2015.13

Crastan, V. (2000). *Elektrische Energieversorgung 1*. Berlin: Springer Berlin/Heidelberg.

Crispin, L., & Gregory, J. (2009). Agile Testing: A Practical Guide for Testers and Agile Teams. Addison-Wesley Professional.

Cristal, M., Wildt, D., & Prikladnicki, R. (2008). Usage of Scrum practices within a global company. *2008 IEEE International Conference on Global Software Engineering*, 222–226. 10.1109/ICGSE.2008.34

Crnkovic, I., Chaudron, M., & Larsson, S. (2005). Component-based Development Process and Component Lifecycle. *CIT. Journal of Computing and Information Technology*, *13*(4), 321–327. doi:10.2498/cit.2005.04.10

Cruz, E. F., Machado, R. J., & Santos, M. Y. (2014). *On the Decomposition of Use Cases for the Refinement of Software Requirements. In 2014 14th International Conference on Computational Science and Its Applications* (pp. 237–240). IEEE; doi:10.1109/ICCSA.2014.54.

Cruzes, D. S., Jaatun, M. G., & Oyetoyan, T. D. (2018). Challenges and approaches of performing canonical action research in software security: research paper. *HotSoS 2018*, 8:1-8:11.

Cruzes, D. S., Jaatun, M. G., Bernsmed, K., & Tøndel, I. (2018). Challenges and Experiences with Applying Microsoft Threat Modeling in Agile Development Projects. *ASWEC, 2018*, 111–120.

Cummings, F. (2009). *Building the Agile Enterprise. With SOA, BPM and MBM*. Morgan Kaufmann.

Curcio, K., Navarro, T., Malucelli, A., & Reinehr, S. (2018). Requirements engineering: A systematic mapping study in agile software development. *Journal of Systems and Software*, *139*, 32–50. doi:10.1016/j.jss.2018.01.036

Curtis, B., Krasner, H., & Iscoe, N. (1988). A field study of the software design process for large systems. *Communications of the ACM*, *31*(11), 1268–1287. doi:10.1145/50087.50089

Daft, R. L., Murphy, J., & Willmott, H. (2010). *Organization Theory and Design*. Cengage Learning.

Dahlberg, T., & Kivijärvi, H. (2006). An integrated framework for IT governance and the development and validation of an assessment instrument. *Proceedings of the Annual Hawaii International Conference on System Sciences, 8*(C), 1–10. 10.1109/HICSS.2006.57

Dahlstedt, Å. G., & Persson, A. (2005). Requirements interdependencies: state of the art and future challenges. In *Engineering and managing software requirements* (pp. 95–116). Springer. doi:10.1007/3-540-28244-0_5

Daneva, M., Van Der Veen, E., Amrit, C., Ghaisas, S., Sikkel, K., Kumar, R., Ajmeri, N., Ramteerthkar, U., & Wieringa, R. (2013). Agile requirements prioritization in large-scale outsourced system projects: An empirical study. *Journal of Systems and Software*, *86*(5), 1333–1353. doi:10.1016/j.jss.2012.12.046

Davison, R. M., Martinsons, M. G., & Ou, C. X. (2012). The roles of theory in canonical action research. *MIS Q, 36*(3), 763-786.

Davison, R. M., Martinsons, M. G., & Kock, N. (2004). Principles of canonical action research. *Information Systems Journal*, *14*(1), 65–86. doi:10.1111/j.1365-2575.2004.00162.x

De Bruin, T., Freeze, R., Kaulkarni, U., & Rosemann, M. (2005). Understanding the Main Phases of Developing a Maturity Assessment Model. In *Australasian Conference on Information Systems (ACIS)* (pp. 8–19). 10.1108/14637151211225225

De Haes, S., & Van Grembergen, W. (2008). Analysing the relationship between IT governance and business/IT alignment maturity. *Proceedings of the Annual Hawaii International Conference on System Sciences*.

De Lucia, A., & Qusef, A. (2010). Requirements engineering in agile software development. *Journal of Emerging Technologies in Web Intelligence*, *2*(3), 212–220. doi:10.4304/jetwi.2.3.212-220

De O'Luna, A. J. H., Kruchten, P., & De Moura, H. P. (2013). GAME: Governance for Agile management of enterprises a management model for agile governance. *Proceedings - 2013 IEEE 8th International Conference on Global Software Engineering Workshops, ICGSEW 2013*, 88–90.

De O'Luna, A. J. H., Marinho, M. L. M., & de Moura, H. P. (2019). Agile governance theory: Operationalization. *Innovations in Systems and Software Engineering*.

Debois, P. (2011). Opening Statement. *Cutter IT Journal*, 24(8), 3–5.

Deleersnyder, S. W. (2019). *Software Assurance Maturity Model - How To Guide - A Guide to Building Security Into Software Development*. Retrieved from https://owaspsamm.org/

DeMarco, T., & Boehm, B. (2002). The agile methods fray. *Computer*, 35(6), 90–92. doi:10.1109/MC.2002.1009175

Denning, P. J. (2018). The profession of IT: The computing profession. *Communications of the ACM*, 61(3), 33–35. doi:10.1145/3182108

Dery, K., Sebastian, I. M., & van der Meulen, N. (2017). The Digital Workplace is Key to Digital Innovation. *MIS Quarterly Executive*, 16(2), 135–152.

Dhaliwal, J., Onita, C. G., Poston, R., & Zhang, X. P. (2011). Alignment within the Software Development Unit: Assessing Structural and Relational Dimensions between Developers and Testers. *The Journal of Strategic Information Systems*, 20(4), 323–342. doi:10.1016/j.jsis.2011.03.001

Dhir, S., Kumar, D., & Singh, V. B. (2019). Success and failure factors that impact on project implementation using agile software development methodology. In *Software Engineering* (pp. 647–654). Springer. doi:10.1007/978-981-10-8848-3_62

Díaz, A., De Jesús, C., Melendez, K., & Dávila, A. (2016). ISO/IEC 29110 Implementation on two Very Small Software Development Companies in Lima. Lessons Learned. IEEE Latin America Transactions Journal, VOL., 14(5), 2504–2510. doi:10.1109/TLA.2016.7530452

Dickover, M. E., McGowan, C. L., & Ross, D. T. (1977, January). Software design using: SADT. In *Proceedings of the 1977 annual conference* (pp. 125-133). ACM. 10.1145/800179.810192

Diebold, P., Theobald, S., Wahl, J., & Rausch, Y. (2019). Stepwise transition to agile: From three agile practices to Kanban adaptation. *Journal of Software: Evolution and Process*, 31(5), e2167.

Dikert, K., Paasivaara, M., & Lassenius, C. (2016). Challenges and success factors for large-scale agile transformations: A systematic literature review. *Journal of Systems and Software*, 119, 87–108. doi:10.1016/j.jss.2016.06.013

Dingsøyr, T., Falessi, D., & Power, K. (2019). Agile Development at Scale: The Next Frontier. *IEEE Software*, 36(2), 30–38. doi:10.1109/MS.2018.2884884

Dingsøyr, T., & Moe, N. B. (2014). Towards principles of large-scale agile development. *International Conference on Agile Software Development*, 1–8.

Dingsøyr, T., Moe, N. B., Fægri, T., & Seim, E. A. (2018). Exploring software development at the very large-scale: A revelatory case study and research agenda for agile method adaptation. *Empirical Software Engineering Journal*, 23(1), 490–520. doi:10.100710664-017-9524-2

Dingsøyr, T., Nerur, S., Balijepally, V., & Moe, N. (2012). A Decade of Agile Methodologies: Towards Explaining Agile Software Development. *Journal of Systems and Software*, 85(6), 1213–1221. doi:10.1016/j.jss.2012.02.033

Dolezel, M., Buchalcevova, A., & Mencik, M. (2019). The State of Agile Software Development in the Czech Republic: Preliminary Findings Indicate the Dominance of "Abridged" Scrum. *International Conference on Research and Practical Issues of Enterprise Information Systems*, 43–54. 10.1007/978-3-030-37632-1_4

Dolezel, M., & Felderer, M. (2018). Organizational Patterns Between Developers and Testers: Investigating Testers' Autonomy and Role Identity. *Proceedings of the 20th International Conference on Enterprise Information Systems*, 2, 336–344. 10.5220/0006783703360344

Donaldson, L. (2001). The contingency theory of organizations. *Sage (Atlanta, Ga.)*.

Dubinsky, Y., Yaeli, A., Feldman, Y., Zarpas, E., & Nechushtai, G. (2011). Governance of Software Development. *Software Applications*, 309–327.

Dumas, M., O'Sullivan, J., Hervizadeh, M., Edmond, D., & Hofstede, A. (2001). Towards a semantic framework for service description. In *Proceedings of the IFIP TC2/WG2.6 Ninth Working Conference on Database Semantics: Semantic Issues in E-Commerce Systems* (pp. 277-291). Kluwer, B.V.

Duncan, R. B. (1976). The ambidextrous organization: Designing dual structures for innovation. *The Management of Organization*, *1*, 167–188.

Dyba°, T., & Dingsøyr, T. (2008). Empirical studies of agile software development: A systematic review. *Information and Software Technology*, *50*(9-10), 833–859. doi:10.1016/j.infsof.2008.01.006

Dyba, T., & Dingsoyr, T. (2009). What do we know about agile software development? *IEEE Software*, *26*(5), 6–9. doi:10.1109/MS.2009.145

Dzamashvili Fogelström, N., Gorschek, T., Svahnberg, M., & Olsson, P. (2010). The impact of agile principles on market-driven software product development. *Journal of Software Maintenance and Evolution: Research and Practice*, *22*(1), 53–80. doi:10.1002pip.420

Eberlein, A., & Leite, J. (2002). Agile requirements definition: A view from requirements engineering. *Proceedings of the International Workshop on Time Constrained Requirements Engineering (TCRE ' 2002)*, 4–8.

Ebert, C. (2018). 50 Years of Software Engineering: Progress and Perils. *IEEE Software*, *35*(5), 94–101. doi:10.1109/MS.2018.3571228

Ebert, C., & De Neve, P. (2001). Surviving global software development. *IEEE Software*, *18*(2), 62–69. doi:10.1109/52.914748

Ebert, C., & Paasivaara, M. (2017). Scaling Agile. *IEEE Software*, *34*(6), 98–103. doi:10.1109/MS.2017.4121226

Eckstein, J. (2016). *Sociocracy - An organization model for large-scale agile development*. XP Workshops.

Eclipse. (2016). *Eclipse Process Framework (EPF)*. Retrieved from http://www.eclipse.org/epf/

Edberg, D., Ivanova, P., & Kuechler, W. (2012). Methodology Mashups: An Exploration of Processes Used to Maintain Software. *Journal of Management Information Systems*, *28*(4), 271–304. doi:10.2753/MIS0742-1222280410

Eggers, T., & Hardt, D. (2019). Agile Transformation eines kommunalen Energiedienstleisters - ein Erfahrungsbericht. In Realisierung Utility 4.0 (pp. 465–492). Academic Press.

Elshandidy, H., & Mazen, S. (2013). Agile and Traditional Requirements Engineering: A Survey. *International Journal of Scientific and Engineering Research*, *4*(9), 473–482.

Engelsman, W., Quartel, D. A. C., Jonkers, H., & van Sinderen, M. (2011). Extending enterprise architecture modelling with business goals and requirements. *Enterprise IS*, *5*(1), 9–36. doi:10.1080/17517575.2010.491871

Eppinger, S., & Browning, T. (2012). *Design structure matrix methods and applications.* MIT Press. doi:10.7551/mitpress/8896.001.0001

Ernst, N. A., Borgida, A., Jureta, I. J., & Mylopoulos, J. (2014). Agile requirements engineering via paraconsistent reasoning. *Information Systems, 43*, 100–116. doi:10.1016/j.is.2013.05.008

Evans, E. (2004). *Domain-driven design : tackling complexity in the heart of software.* Addison-Wesley.

Fabbri, S., Silva, C., Hernandes, E., Octaviano, F., Di Thommazo, A., & Belgamo, A. (2016). Improvements in the StArt tool to better support the systematic review process. In *Proceedings of the 20th International Conference on Evaluation and Assessment in Software Engineering* (pp. 1-5). 10.1145/2915970.2916013

Familiar, B. (2015). Microservices, IoT, and Azure: Leveraging DevOps and Microservice Architecture to Deliver SaaS Solutions. Apress Ed.

Farhan, S., Tauseef, H., & Fahiem, M. A. (2009). Adding agility to architecture tradeoff analysis method for mapping on crystal. In WRI World Congress on Software Engineering (WCSE'09) (Vol. 4, pp. 121–125). IEEE. doi:10.1109/WCSE.2009.405

Fenz, S., & Ekelhart, A. (2011). Verification, Validation, and Evaluation in Information Security Risk Management. *IEEE Security and Privacy, 9*(2), 58–65. doi:10.1109/MSP.2010.117

Fernandes, J. M., & Machado, R. J. (2016). Requirements in Engineering Projects. Springer International Publishing. doi:10.1007/978-3-319-18597-2

Ferreira, N., Santos, N., Machado, R. J., Fernandes, J. E., & Gasevic, D. (2014). A V-Model Approach for Business Process Requirements Elicitation in Cloud Design. Advanced Web Services, 551–578.

Fettke, P. (2006). State-of-the-art des state-of-the-art: Eine Untersuchung der Forschungsmethode "review" innerhalb der Wirtschaftsinformatik. *Wirtschaftsinformatik, 48*(4), 257–266. doi:10.100711576-006-0057-3

Firesmith, D. (2003). *Common Concepts Underlying Safety Security and Survivability Engineering. No. CMU/SEI-2003-TN-033.* Carnegie-Mellon UNIV Pittsburgh Pa Software Engineering Inst. doi:10.21236/ADA421683

Fit, S. M. (2016a). *FitSM-1: Requirements, The FitSM Standard Family: Standard for lightweight IT service management 1, version 2.1.* Available from https://www.fitsm.eu/downloads/

Fit, S. M. (2016b). *FitSM-2: Objectives and activities, The FitSM Standard Family: Standard for lightweight IT service management 1, version 2.2.* Available from https://www.fitsm.eu/downloads/

Fit, S. M. (2016c). *FitSM-3: Role model, The FitSM Standard Family: Standard for lightweight IT service management, version 2.2.* Available from https://www.fitsm.eu/downloads/

Fitzgerald, B., & Stol, K.-J. (2017). Continuous software engineering: A roadmap and agenda. *Journal of Systems and Software, 123*, 176–189. doi:10.1016/j.jss.2015.06.063

Flora, H. K., & Chande, S. V. (2014). A Systematic Study on Agile Software Development Methodologies and Practices. *International Journal of Computer Science and Information Technologies, 5*(3), 3626–3637.

Flore, A., & Uslar, M. (2019). Organisationsentwicklung mit Smart Grid Reifegradmodellen für Versorger. In O. D. Doleski (Ed.), *Realisierung Utility 4.0* (pp. 675–692). Springer Vieweg.

Flyvbjerg, B., Bruzelius, N., & Rothengatter, W. (2003). *Megaprojects and risk: An anatomy of ambition.* Cambridge University Press. doi:10.1017/CBO9781107050891

Fontana, R. M., Fontana, I. M., Da Rosa Garbuio, P. A., Reinehr, S., & Malucelli, A. (2014). Processes versus people: How should agile software development maturity be defined? *Journal of Systems and Software, 97*, 140–155. doi:10.1016/j.jss.2014.07.030

Forsberg, K., Mooz, H., & H., C. (2005). *Visualizing project management: Models and frameworks for mastering complex systems* (3rd ed.). Hoboken, NJ: Wiley.

Forsgren, N., Humble, J., Kim, G., Brown, A., & Kersten, N. (2018). *Accelerate: State of DevOps Strategies for a New Economy*. Puppet + DORA.

Fowler, M., & Highsmith, J. (2001). The Agile Manifesto. *Dr. Dobb's Journal*. http://www.drdobbs.com/open-source/the-agile-manifesto/184414755

Fowler, M., & Highsmith, J. (2001). The agile manifesto. *Software Development, 9*(8), 28–35.

Franch, X., López, L., Cares, C., & Colomer, D. (2016). The i* Framework for Goal-Oriented Modeling. In D. Karagiannis, H. Mayr, & J. Mylopoulos (Eds.), *Domain-Specific Conceptual Modeling: Concepts, Methods and Tools* (pp. 485–506). Springer. doi:10.1007/978-3-319-39417-6_22

Fuchs, C., & Hess, T. (2018). *Becoming agile in the digital transformation: The process of a large-scale agile transformation*. Academic Press.

Galup, S. D., Dattero, R., Quan, J. J., & Conger, S. (2009). An overview of IT service management. *Communications of the ACM, 52*(5), 124–127. doi:10.1145/1506409.1506439

Garcia, S. (1997). Paradigms : Capability Maturity Models and ISO / IEC 15504 (PDTR). *Software Process Improvement and Practice, 3*(1), 47–58. doi:10.1002/(SICI)1099-1670(199703)3:1<47::AID-SPIP64>3.0.CO;2-5

Ghoshal, S., & Bartlett, C. A. (1994). Linking organizational context and managerial action: The dimensions of quality of management. *Strategic Management Journal, 15*(2), 91–112.

Gibson, C. B., & Birkinshaw, J. (2004). The antecedents, consequences, and mediating role of organizational ambidexterity. *Academy of Management Journal, 47*(2), 209–226.

Gilley, A., & Kerno, S. J. Jr. (2010). Groups, teams, and communities of practice: A comparison. *Advances in Developing Human Resources, 12*(1), 46–60. doi:10.1177/1523422310365312

Girma, M., Garcia, N. M., & Kifle, M. (2019, May). Agile Scrum Scaling Practices for Large Scale Software Development. In *2019 4th International Conference on Information Systems Engineering (ICISE)* (pp. 34-38). IEEE. 10.1109/ICISE.2019.00014

González-Cruz, T. F., Botella-Carrubi, D., & Martínez-Fuentes, C. M. (2020). The effect of firm complexity and founding team size on agile internal communication in startups. *The International Entrepreneurship and Management Journal*, 1–21. doi:10.100711365-019-00633-1

Gordijn, J., & Akkermans, J. M. (2003). Value-based requirements engineering: Exploring innovative e-commerce ideas. *Requirements Engineering, 8*(2), 114–134. doi:10.100700766-003-0169-x

Graham, J. W. (1991). Servant-leadership in organizations: Inspirational and moral. *The Leadership Quarterly, 2*(2), 105–119. doi:10.1016/1048-9843(91)90025-W

Grau, B. R., & Lauenroth, K. (2014). Requirements engineering and agile development - collaborative, just enough, just in time, sustainable. International Requirements Engineering Board. IREB.

Greenwood, D. J., & Levin, M. (2006). *Introduction to Action Research: Social Research for Social Change*. Sage Publications, Inc.

Gregory, J., & Crispin, L. (2014). *More Agile Testing: Learning Journeys for the Whole Team* (1st ed.). Addison-Wesley Professional.

Gupta, A. K., Smith, K. G., & Shalley, C. E. (2006). The Interplay Between Exploration and Exploitation. *Academy of Management Journal*, *49*(4), 693–706. doi:10.5465/amj.2006.22083026

Gupta, R. K., Venkatachalapathy, M., & Jeberla, F. K. (2019, May). Challenges in adopting continuous delivery and DevOps in a globally distributed product team: a case study of a healthcare organization. In *Proceedings of the 14th International Conference on Global Software Engineering* (pp. 30-34). IEEE Press. 10.1109/ICGSE.2019.00020

Gu, Q., & Lago, P. (2007). A stakeholder-driven service life cycle model for SOA. In *Proceedings of 2nd international workshop on Service oriented software engineering: in conjunction with the 6th ESEC/FSE joint meeting (IW-SOSWE'07)* (pp. 1-7). Dubrovnik, Croatia: ACM 10.1145/1294928.1294930

Gu, Q., & Lago, P. (2011). Guiding the selection of service-oriented software engineering methodologies. SpringerLink. *Service Oriented Computing and Applications*, *5*(4), 203–223. doi:10.100711761-011-0080-0

Hall, J. (2018). *Swarming Support vs Tiered Support: What's the Difference?* Retrieved from https://www.bmc.com/blogs/swarming-support-tiered-support-differences/

Hameed, A. (2016). Software Development Lifecycle for Extreme Programming. *International Journal of Information Technology and Electrical Engineering*, *5*(1).

Hanssen, G. K., Stålhane, T., & Myklebust, T. (2018). *SafeScrum®-Agile Development of Safety-Critical Software*. Springer International Publishing. doi:10.1007/978-3-319-99334-8

Haugan, D. (2008). *Work reakdown Structures for Projects, Programs, and Enterprises*. Management Concepts.

Haugen, N. C. (2006). An empirical study of using planning poker for user story estimation. In AGILE 2006 (AGILE'06). IEEE. doi:10.1109/AGILE.2006.16

Havermans, L. A., Den Hartog, D. N., Keegan, A., & Uhl-Bien, M. (2015). Exploring the role of leadership in enabling contextual ambidexterity. *Human Resource Management*, *54*(1), 179–200. doi:10.1002/hrm.21764

Heeager, L. T., & Nielsen, P. A. (2018). A conceptual model of agile software development in a safety-critical context: A systematic literature review. *Information and Software Technology*, *103*, 22–39. doi:10.1016/j.infsof.2018.06.004

Hemon, A., Monnier-Senicourt, L., & Rowe, F. (2018). *Job Satisfaction Factors and Risks Perception: An Embedded Case Study of DevOps and Agile Teams*. Paper presented at the International Conference on Information Systems, San Francisco, CA.

Henderson, J. C., & Venkatraman, H. (1993). Strategic alignment: Leveraging information technology for transforming organizations. *IBM Systems Journal*, *32*(1), 472–484. doi:10.1147j.382.0472

Henriques, V., & Tanner, M. (2017). A systematic literature review of agile and maturity model research. *Interdisciplinary Journal of Information, Knowledge, and Management*, *12*, 53–73. doi:10.28945/3666

Heuck, K., Dettmann, K.-D., & Schulz, D. (2010). Elektrische Energieversorgung. Wiesbaden: Vieweg+Teubner Verlag. doi:10.1007/978-3-8348-9761-9

Hevner, A. R., March, S. T., Park, J., & Ram, S. (2004). Information Design Science Systems. *Management Information Systems*, *28*(1), 75–105. doi:10.2307/25148625

Highsmith, J., & Cockburn, A. (2001). Agile software development: The business of innovation. *Computer, IEEE, 34*(9), 120–127. doi:10.1109/2.947100

Hilorme, T., Perevozova, I., Shpak, L., Mokhnenko, A., & Korovchuk, Y. (2019). *Human capital cost accounting in the company management system.* Academy of Accounting and Financial Studies Journal.

Hinds, P. J., & Mortensen, M. (2005). Understanding conflict in geographically distributed teams: The moderating effects of shared identity, shared context, and spontaneous communication. *Organization Science, 16*(3), 290–307. doi:10.1287/orsc.1050.0122

Hobbs, B., & Petit, Y. (2017). Agile Methods on Large Projects in Large Organizations. *Project Management Journal, 48*(3), 3–19. doi:10.1177/875697281704800301

Hoda, R., & Murugesan, L. K. (2016). Multi-level agile project management challenges: A self-organizing team perspective. *Journal of Systems and Software, 117,* 245–257. doi:10.1016/j.jss.2016.02.049

Hoda, R., Noble, J., & Marshall, S. (2010). Organizing Self-Organizing Teams. *International Conference on Software Engineering,* 285–294.

Hoda, R., Salleh, N., & Grundy, J. (2018). The rise and evolution of agile software development. *IEEE Software, 35*(5), 58–63. doi:10.1109/MS.2018.290111318

Hoda, R., Salleh, N., Grundy, J., & Tee, H. M. (2017). Systematic literature reviews in agile software development: A tertiary study. *Information and Software Technology, 85,* 60–70. doi:10.1016/j.infsof.2017.01.007

Hodgson, D. (2002). Disciplining the professional: The case of Project Management. *Journal of Management Studies, 39*(6), 803–821. doi:10.1111/1467-6486.00312

Hodgson, D., & Briand, L. (2013). Controlling the uncontrollable: "Agile" teams and illusions of autonomy in creative work. *Work, Employment and Society, 27*(2), 308–325. doi:10.1177/0950017012460315

Hohl, P., Klünder, J., van Bennekum, A., Lockard, R., Gifford, J., Münch, J., Stupperich, M., & Schneider, K. (2018). Back to the future: Origins and directions of the "Agile Manifesto"–views of the originators. *Journal of Software Engineering Research and Development, 6*(1), 15. doi:10.118640411-018-0059-z

Holmström, H., Conchúir, E. Ó., Ågerfalk, P. J., & Fitzgerald, B. (2006). Global software development challenges: A case study on temporal, geographical and socio-cultural distance. In *Proceedings of International Conference on Global Software Engineering (ICGSE)* (pp. 3-11). IEEE. 10.1109/ICGSE.2006.261210

Hopkins, J. (2002). Component Primer. *ACM Communications, 43*(10), 27–30. doi:10.1145/352183.352198

Howell, J. M. (2005). The right stuff: Identifying and developing effective champions of innovation. *The Academy of Management Perspectives, 19*(2), 108–119. doi:10.5465/ame.2005.16965104

Huang, J., Baptista, J., & Newell, S. (2015). Communicational ambidexterity as a new capability to manage social media communication within organizations. *The Journal of Strategic Information Systems, 24*(2), 49–64. doi:10.1016/j.jsis.2015.03.002

Humble, J., & Farley, D. (2011). *Continuous Delivery: Reliable Software Releases through Build, Test, and Deployment Automation.* Pearson Education, Inc.

Humphrey, W. S. (1998). Why don't they practice what we preach? *Annals of Software Engineering, 6*(1/4), 201–222. doi:10.1023/A:1018997029222

Ibrahim, S., Idris, N. B., Munro, M., & Deraman, A. (2005). A requirements traceability to support change impact analysis. *Asian Journal of Information Tech, 4*(4), 345–355.

Iden, J., & Eikebrokk, T. R. (2013). Implementing IT Service Management: A systematic literature review. *International Journal of Information Management, 33*(3), 512–523. doi:10.1016/j.ijinfomgt.2013.01.004

IEEE. (2014). *Guide to the Software Engineering Body of Knowledge - v3.0*. IEEE.

IIBA. (2017). *Agile Extension to the BABOK Guide v2*. International Institute of Business Analysis.

Inayat, I., Salim, S. S., Marczak, S., Daneva, M., & Shamshirband, S. (2015). A systematic literature review on agile requirements engineering practices and challenges. *Computers in Human Behavior, 51*, 915–929. doi:10.1016/j.chb.2014.10.046

INCOSE. (2004). *Systems Engineering Handbook*. International Council in Systems Engineering.

International Publishing Switzerland. (2016). *Strategic management: A stakeholder approach*. Cambridge University Press.

ISO/IEC 25010. (2011). *Systems and software Quality Requirements and Evaluation (SQuaRE) — System and software quality models. Iso/Iec Fdis 25010:2011, 2010, 1-34*.

ISO/IEC 62304. (2006). 62304:2006 Medical Device Software—Software Life Cycle, Assoc. Advancement Medical Instrumentation, 2006.

ISO/IEC 82304. (2012). IEC 82304-1: Health Software–Part 1: General Requirements for Product Safety.

ISO/IEC. (2002). *ISO/IEC 15288-2002 - Systems Engineering - System Life Cycle Processes*. International Organization for Standardization.

ISO/IEC. (2005a). *ISO/IEC 20000-1:2005 Information technology - Service management - Part 1: Specification*. International Organization for Standardization.

ISO/IEC. (2005b). *ISO/IEC 20000-1:2005 Information technology — Service management — Part 2: Code of practice*. International Organization for Standardization.

ISO/IEC. (2010). *ISO/IEC TR 20000-4:2010 Information technology — Service management — Part 4: Process reference model*. International Organization for Standardization.

ISO/IEC. (2011). *ISO/IEC 27005:2011 Information technology–Security techniques–Information security risk management*.

ISO/IEC. (2011). Software engineering- Lifecycle profiles for Very Small Entities (VSEs) - Part 5-1-2: Management and engineering guide: Generic profile group: Basic profile. ISO/IEC TR 29110-5-1-2:2011. Available at no cost from ISO: http://standards.iso.org/ittf/PubliclyAvailableStandards/index.html

ISO/IEC. (in press). ISO/IEC TR 29110-5-4 - Systems and software engineering — Lifecycle profiles for Very Small Entities (VSEs) — Part 5-4: Agile software development guidelines.

ISO/IEC/IEEE. (2018). International Standard ISO/IEC/IEEE 26515. Systems and software engineering — Developing information for users in an agile environment. Second Edition. 2018-12.

itSMF UK. (2012). *ITIL Foundation Handbook*. London, UK: The Stationery Office.

Ivanyukovich, A., Gangadharan, G. R., D'Andrea, V., & Marchese, M. (2005). Toward a service-oriented development methodology. *Journal of Integrated Design & Process Science, 9*(3), 53–62.

Jaatun, M. G., Cruzes, D. S., Bernsmed, K., Tøndel, I., & Røstad, L. (2015). Software Security Maturity in Public Organisations. *ISC, 2015*, 120–138.

Jaatun, M. G., & Tøndel, I. (2008). Covering Your Assets in Software Engineering. *ARES, 2008*, 1172–1179.

Jalali, S., & Wohlin, C. (2011). Global software engineering and agile practices: A systematic review. *Journal of Software: Evolution and Process, 24*(6), 643–659.

Janes, A. A., & Succi, G. (2012). The dark side of agile software development. *Proceedings of the ACM International Symposium on New Ideas, New Paradigms, and Reflections on Programming and Software*, 215–228. 10.1145/2384592.2384612

Janz, B., Meek, T., Nichols, E., & Oglesby, J. (2016). How Buckman's Value Stream Initiative Re-Visioned IT for Value. *MIS Quarterly Executive, 15*(3), 215–229.

Javanmard, M., & Alian, M. (2015). Comparison between Agile and Traditional software development methodologies. Science Journal, 36(3), 1386-1394.

Jayatilleke, S., & Lai, R. (2018). A systematic review of requirements change management. *Information and Software Technology, 93*, 163–185. doi:10.1016/j.infsof.2017.09.004

Jeon, S., Han, M., Lee, E., & Lee, K. (2011). Quality attribute driven agile development. In *9th International Conference on Software Engineering Research, Management and Applications (SERA)* (pp. 203–210). IEEE. 10.1109/SERA.2011.24

Jesse, N. (2018). Organizational Evolution - How Digital Disruption Enforces Organizational Agility. *IFAC PapersOnLine, 51*(30), 486–491. doi:10.1016/j.ifacol.2018.11.310

Jimenez, A., Boehe, D. M., Taras, V., & Caprar, D. V. (2017). Working across boundaries: Current and future perspectives on global virtual teams. *Journal of International Management, 23*(4), 341–349. doi:10.1016/j.intman.2017.05.001

Jiménez, M., Piattini, M., & Vizcaíno, A. (2009). Challenges and improvements in distributed software development: A systematic review. *Advances in Software Engineering*, 3.

Jones, C. (2010). *Software Engineering Best Practices*. McGraw Hill.

Jones, J. A., Grechanik, M., & Van der Hoek, A. (2009). Enabling and enhancing collaborations between software development organizations and independent test agencies. *ICSE Workshop on Cooperative and Human Aspects on Software Engineering (CHASE)*, 56–59. 10.1109/CHASE.2009.5071411

Jun, L., Qiuzhen, W., & Lin, G. (2010). Application of agile requirement engineering in modest-sized information systems development. In *2010 Second world congress on software engineering*, (vol. 2, pp. 207–210). IEEE.

Jurado, M. (2012). *Visual Planning in Lean Product Development*. KTH Royal Institute of Technology.

Kalenda, M., Hyna, P., & Rossi, B. (2018). Scaling agile in large organizations: Practices, challenges, and success factors. *Journal of Software: Evolution and Process, 30*(10), e1954.

Kalliamvakou, E., Bird, C., Zimmermann, T., Begel, A., DeLine, R., & German, D. M. (2017). What Makes a Great Manager of Software Engineers? *IEEE Transactions on Software Engineering, 45*(1), 87–106. doi:10.1109/TSE.2017.2768368

Kang, S. C., & Snell, S. A. (2009). Intellectual Capital Architectures and Ambidextrous Learning: A Framework for Human Resource Management. *Journal of Management Studies, 46*(1), 65–92. doi:10.1111/j.1467-6486.2008.00776.x

Karakostas, B., Zorgios, Y., & Alevizos, C. C. (2006). Automatic derivation of BPEL4WS from IDEF0 process models. *Software & Systems Modeling, 5*(2), 208–218. doi:10.100710270-006-0003-2

Karastoyanova, D. (2003). *A methodology for development of Web Services-based Bussines Processes*. Thechnische Universität Darmstadt.

Kautz, K., & Zumpe, S. (2008). Just Enough Structure at the Edge of Chaos: Agile Information System Development in Practice. *Agile Processes in Software Engineering and Extreme Programming*, 137–146.

Kazman, R. (2013). Foreword - Bringing the Two Together: Agile Architecting or Architecting for Agile? In Agile Software Architecture: Aligning Agile Processes and Software Architectures (pp. xxix–xxx). Elsevier.

Keel, A. J., Orr, M. A., Hernandez, R. R., Patrocinio, E. A., & Bouchard, J. (2007). From a technology-oriented to a service-oriented approach to IT management. *IBM Systems Journal*, *46*(3), 549–564. doi:10.1147j.463.0549

Keith, M., Demirkan, H., & Goul, M. (2013). Service-oriented methodology for systems development. *Journal of Management Information Systems*, *30*(1), 227–260. doi:10.2753/MIS0742-1222300107

Keller, A., Rössle, A., Sheik, R., Thell, H., & Westmark, F. (2019). *Issues with Scrum-of-Scrums*. Academic Press.

Khatri, S. K., Malhotra, S., & Johri, P. (2016). Use case point estimation technique in software development. In *2016 5th international conference on reliability, infocom technologies and optimization (trends and future directions) (ICRITO)*, (pp. 123–128). IEEE. 10.1109/ICRITO.2016.7784938

Kietzmann, J., Plangger, K., Eaton, B., Heilgenberg, K., Pitt, L., & Berthon, P. (2013). Mobility at work: A typology of mobile communities of practice and contextual ambidexterity. *The Journal of Strategic Information Systems*, *22*(4), 282–297. doi:10.1016/j.jsis.2013.03.003

Kitchenham, B., & Charters, S. (2007). Guidelines for performing systematic literature reviews in software engineering version 2.3. *Engineering*, *45*(4ve), 1051.

Kleebaum, A., Johanssen, J. O., Paech, B., & Bruegge, B. (2019). How do Practitioners Manage Decision Knowledge during Continuous Software Engineering? In *31st International Conference on Software Engineering and Knowledge Engineering, SEKE* (pp. 735-740). Academic Press.

Knaster, R., & Leffingwell, D. (2019). *SAFe Distilled*. Scaled Agile, Inc.

Kneuper, R. (2017). Sixty years of software development life cycle models. *IEEE Annals of the History of Computing*, *39*(3), 41–54.

Kneuper, R. (2018). *Software Processes and Life Cycle Models*. Springer. doi:10.1007/978-3-319-98845-0

Knowledge Foundation. (2013). Organizational Project Management Maturity Model (OPM3) (3rd ed.). Project Mgmt Inst.

Kolodny, H. F. (1979). Evolution to a Matrix Organization. *Academy of Management Review*, *4*(4), 543–553. doi:10.5465/amr.1979.4498362

Kolp, M., & Wautelet, Y. (2019). *Descartes Architect: Design Case Tool for Agent-Oriented Repositories, Techniques, Environments and Systems*. Louvain School of Management, Université catholique de Louvain, Louvain-la-Neuve, Belgium. https://www.isys.ucl.ac.be/descartes/

Kolp, M., Wautelet, Y., & Faulkner, S. (2011). Sociocentric design of multi-agent architectures. In E. Yu, P. Giorgini, N. Maiden, & J. Mylopoulos (Eds.), *Social Modeling for Requirements Engineering*. MIT Press.

Kontogiannis, K., Lewis, G. A., Smith, D. B., Litoiu, M., Muller, H., Schuster, S., & Stroulia, E. (2007). The landscape of service-oriented systems: A research perspective. In *International Workshop on Systems Development in SOA Environments (SDSOA'07: ICSE Workshops 2007)*. Minneapolis, MN: IEEE Computer Society. 10.1109/SDSOA.2007.12

Korbyn, C. (2000). Modeling components and frameworks with UML. *ACM Communications*, *43*(10), 31–38. doi:10.1145/352183.352199

Kotonya, G., Hutchinson, J., & Bloin, B. (2005). A method for formulating and architecting component and Service-oriented Systems. In Z. Stojanovic & A. Dahanayake (Eds.), *Service-Oiented Software Systems Engineering: Challenges and Practices* (pp. 155–181). IGI-Global. doi:10.4018/978-1-59140-426-2.ch008

Kotonya, G., & Sommerville, I. (1998). *Requirements engineering: processes and techniques.* Wiley Publishing.

Krafzig, D., Banke, K., & Slama, D. (2005). *Enterprise SOA: service-oriented architecture best practices.* Prentice Hall Professional.

Krancher, O., Luther, P., & Jost, M. (2018). Key Affordances of Platform-as-a-Service: Self-Organization and Continuous Feedback. *Journal of Management Information Systems, 35*(3), 776–812. doi:10.1080/07421222.2018.1481636

Kroll, P., & Kruchten, P. (2003). *Rational Unified Process Made Easy: A Practitioner's Guide to the RUP.* Addison Wesley.

Kruchten, P. (1995). The 4+1 View Model of Architecture. *IEEE Software, 12*(6), 42–50. doi:10.1109/52.469759

Kruchten, P. (2004). *The rational unified process: an introduction.* Addison-Wesley Professional.

Kühne, S., Thränert, M., & Speck, A. (2005). Towards a methodology for orchestration and validation of cooperative e-business components. In *Proceedings of 7th GPCE Young Researchers Workshop, GPCE YRW 2005* (pp. 29-34). Tallinn, Estonia: Institute of Cybernetics at Tallinn Technical University.

Kuhrmann, M., Diebold, P., Münch, J., Tell, P., Garousi, V., & Felderer, M. (2017). Hybrid Software and System Development in Practice: Waterfall, Scrum, and Beyond. *Proceedings of the 2017 International Conference on Software and System Process.* 10.1145/3084100.3084104

Kuhrmann, M., Diebold, P., Munch, J., Tell, P., Trektere, K., Mc Caffery, F., Vahid, G., Felderer, M., Linssen, O., Hanser, E., & Prause, C. (2019). Hybrid Software Development Approaches in Practice: A European Perspective. *IEEE Software, 36*(4), 20–31. doi:10.1109/MS.2018.110161245

Kumar, G., & Bhatia, P. K. (2012). Impact of agile methodology on software development process. *International Journal of Computer Technology and Electronics Engineering, 2*(4), 46–50.

Kumari, A., Tanwar, S., Tyagi, S., & Kumar, N. (2018). Fog computing for Healthcare 4.0 environment: Opportunities and challenges. *Computers & Electrical Engineering, 72*, 1–13. doi:10.1016/j.compeleceng.2018.08.015

Kurapati, N., Manyam, V. S. C., & Petersen, K. (2012). Agile Software Development Practice Adoption Survey. In C. Wohlin (Ed.), *Agile Processes in Software Engineering and Extreme Programming, XP 2012, LNBIP* (Vol. 111, pp. 16–30). Springer. doi:10.1007/978-3-642-30350-0_2

Laanti, M., Similä, J., & Abrahamsson, P. (2013). Definitions of agile software development and agility. *European Conference on Software Process Improvement,* 247–258. 10.1007/978-3-642-39179-8_22

Laloux, F. (2014). *Reinventing Organizations: A Guide to Creating Organizations Inspired by the Next Stage in Human Consciousness.* Nelson Parker.

Laporte, C. Y., & O'Connor, R. (2016). A Multi-Case Study Analysis of Software Process Improvement in Very Small Companies using ISO/IEC 29110. In 23rd European Software Process Improvement Conference (Euro SPI2 2016). Springer-Verlag.

Laporte, C. Y., & O'Connor, R. (2017, May/June). Software Process Improvement Standards and Guides for Very Small Organizations - An Overview of Eight Implementation. *Crosstalk, 30*(3), 23–27.

Laporte, C., Muñoz, M., Mejía, J., & O'Connor, R. (2018). Applying Software Engineering Standards in Very Small Entities - From Startups to Grownups. *IEEE Software Journal, 35*(1), 99–103.

Larrucea, X., O'Connor, R. V., Colomo-Palacios & R., Laporte, C.Y. (2016). Software Process Improvement in Very Small Organizations. IEEE Software Journal, 33(2), 85-89. Advance online publication. doi:10.1109/MS.2016.42

Laukkarinen, T., Kuusinen, K., & Mikkonen, T. (2017, May). DevOps in regulated software development: case medical devices. In *Proceedings of the 39th International Conference on Software Engineering: New Ideas and Emerging Results Track* (pp. 15-18). IEEE Press. 10.1109/ICSE-NIER.2017.20

Laukkarinen, T., Kuusinen, K., & Mikkonen, T. (2018). Regulated software meets DevOps. *Information and Software Technology*, 97, 176–178. doi:10.1016/j.infsof.2018.01.011

Laurin, K., & Kay, A. C. (2017). The Motivational Underpinnings of Belief in God. In Advances in Experimental Social Psychology (Vol. 56, pp. 201–257). Academic Press. doi:10.1016/bs.aesp.2017.02.004

Lautert, T., Neto, A. G. S. S., & Kozievitch, N. P. (2019). A survey on agile practices and challenges of a global software development team. *Brazilian Workshop on Agile Methods*, 128–143. 10.1007/978-3-030-36701-5_11

Lawrence, P. R., & Lorsch, J. W. (1967). Differentiation and Integration in Complex Organizations. *Administrative Science Quarterly*, 12(1), 1–47. doi:10.2307/2391211

Lean I. T. Association. (2015). Lean IT Foundation - Increasing the Value of IT. Newark, NJ: Lean IT Association.

Leau, Y. B., Loo, W. K., Tham, W. Y., & Tan, S. F. (2012). Software development life cycle AGILE vs traditional approaches. In *International Conference on Information and Network Technology* (Vol. 37, No. 1, pp. 162-167). Academic Press.

Lee, G., DeLone, W., & Espinosa, A. (2010). *The Main and Interaction Effects of Process Rigor, Process Standardization, and Process Agility on System Performance in Distributed IS Development: An Ambidexterity Perspective*. Paper presented at the International Conference on Information Systems, St. Louis, MO.

Lee, G., DeLone, W., & Espinosa, J. A. (2006). Ambidextrous coping strategies in globally distributed software development projects. *Communications of the ACM*, 49(10), 35–40. doi:10.1145/1164394.1164417

Lee, G., & Xia, W. (2010). Toward Agile: An Integrated Analysis of Quantitative and Qulaitative Field Data on Software Development Agility. *Management Information Systems Quarterly*, 34(1), 87–114. doi:10.2307/20721416

Lee, O.-K., Sambamurthy, V., Lim, K. H., & Wei, K. K. (2015). How Does IT Ambidexterity Impact Organizational Agility? *Information Systems Research*, 26(2), 398–417. doi:10.1287/isre.2015.0577

Leffingwell, D., & Widrig, D. (1999). *Managing Software Requirements. A Unified Approach*. Addison-Wesley.

Leppänen, M. (2013). A Comparative Analysis of Agile Maturity Models. In Information Systems Development (Vol. 35, pp. 329–343). New York: Springer. doi:10.1007/978-1-4614-4951-5_27

Leung, H., & Fan, Z. (2002). Software cost estimation. In Handbook of Software Engineering and Knowledge Engineering: Volume II: Emerging Technologies, (pp. 307–324). World Scientific. doi:10.1142/9789812389701_0014

Levitt, T. (1976). Industrialization of service. *Harvard Business Review*, 54(5), 63–74.

Lewis, D. (2000). *Promoting socially responsible business, ethical trade and acceptable labour standards*. Social Development Department, Department for International Development.

Lewis, J. (2008). *Mastering Project Management* (2nd ed.). McGraw-Hill.

Li, K., Xue, Y., Cui, S., Niu, Q., Yang, Z., & Luk, P. (2017). Research on Model and Method of Maturit Evaluation of Smart Grid Industry. *Communications in Computer and Information Science, 763*(3), 633–642. doi:10.1007/978-981-10-6364-0

Lillrank, P. (1995). The Transfer of Management Innovations from Japan. *Organization Studies, 16*(6), 971–989. doi:10.1177/017084069501600603

Lines, M., & Ambler, S. W. (2015). *Introduction to Disciplined Agile Delivery: A Small Agile Team's Journey from Scrum to Continuous Delivery.* CreateSpace Independent Publishing Platform.

Lous, P., Tell, P., Michelsen, C. B., Dittrich, Y., & Ebdrup, A. (2018). From Scrum to Agile: A journey to tackle the challenges of distributed development in an Agile team. *Proceedings of the 2018 International Conference on Software and System Process,* 11–20. 10.1145/3202710.3203149

Lovelock, C. H. (1983). Classifying services to gain strategic marketing insights. *Journal of Marketing, 47*(3), 9–20. doi:10.1177/002224298304700303

Lucassen, G., Robeer, M., Dalpiaz, F., van der Werf, J. M. E., & Brinkkemper, S. (2017). Extracting conceptual models from user stories with Visual Narrator. *Requirements Engineering, 22*(3), 339–358. doi:10.100700766-017-0270-1

Luftman, J., Papp, R., & Brier, T. (1999). Enablers and inhibitors of business-IT alignment. *Communications of the AIS, 1*(3).

Lui, K. M., & Chan, K. C. C. (2005). A Road Map for Implementing eXtreme Programming. In *International Software Process Workshop* (pp. 474–481). Beijing: Springer.

Lwakatare, L. E., Karvonen, T., Sauvola, T., Kuvaja, P., Olsson, H. H., Bosch, J., & Oivo, M. (2016). *Towards DevOps in the Embedded Systems Domain: Why is it so Hard?* Paper presented at the Hawaii International Conference on System Sciences, Kauai, HI. 10.1109/HICSS.2016.671

Lyytinen, K., & Rose, G. M. (2006). Information system development agility as organizational learning. *European Journal of Information Systems, 15*(2), 183–199. doi:10.1057/palgrave.ejis.3000604

Macke, J., & Genari, D. (2019). Systematic literature review on sustainable human resource management. *Journal of Cleaner Production, 208,* 806–815. doi:10.1016/j.jclepro.2018.10.091

Macnab, C. J. B., & Doctolero, S. (2019, May). The role of unconscious bias in software project failures. In *International Conference on Software Engineering Research, Management and Applications* (pp. 91-116). Springer.

Madison, J. (2010). Agile architecture interactions. *IEEE Software, 27*(2), 41–48. doi:10.1109/MS.2010.35

Mahnič, V., & Hovelja, T. (2012). On using planning poker for estimating user stories. *Journal of Systems and Software, 85*(9), 2086–2095. doi:10.1016/j.jss.2012.04.005

Malone, T. W., & Crowston, K. (1994). The Interdisciplinary Study of Coordination. *ACM Computing Surveys, 26*(1), 87–118. doi:10.1145/174666.174668

March, J. D. (1991). Exploration and Exploitation in Organizaitonal Learning. *Organization Science, 2*(1), 71–87. doi:10.1287/orsc.2.1.71

Marinho, M., Noll, J., Richardson, I., & Beecham, S. (2019). Plan-Driven Approaches Are Alive and Kicking in Agile Global Software Development. *International Symposium on Empirical Software Engineering and Measurement (ESEM).* 10.1109/ESEM.2019.8870168

Marrone, M., Gacenga, F., Cater-Steel, A., & Kolbe, L. (2014). IT service management: A cross-national study of ITIL adoption. *CAIS*, 34(49), 865-892.

Marrone, M., & Kolbe, M. (2011). Impact of IT Service Management Frameworks on the IT Organization: An Empirical Study on Benefits, Challenges, and Processes. *Business & Information Systems Engineering*, 1(1), 5–18. doi:10.100712599-010-0141-5

Martini, A., Pareto, L., & Bosch, J. (2014). Role of Architects in Agile Organizations. In J. Bosch (Ed.), Continuous Software Engineering. Springer Cham. doi:10.1007/978-3-319-11283-1_4

Martins, L. E. G., & Gorschek, T. (2017). Requirements engineering for safety-critical systems: Overview and challenges. *IEEE Software*, 34(4), 49–57. doi:10.1109/MS.2017.94

Marx, F., Wortmann, F., & Mayer, J. H. (2012). Ein Reifegradmodell für UnternehmenssteuerungssystemeA Maturity Model for Management Control Systems. *Wirtschaftsinformatik*, 54(4), 189–204. doi:10.100711576-012-0325-3

Mater, J., & Drummond, R. (2009). A Smart Grid Interoperability Maturity Model Rating System. Development.

Matharu, G. S., Mishra, A., Singh, H., & Upadhyay, P. (2015). Empirical study of agile software development methodologies: A comparative analysis. *Software Engineering Notes*, 40(1), 1–6. doi:10.1145/2693208.2693233

Mathur, S., & Malik, S. (2010). Advancements in the V-Model. *International Journal of Computers and Applications*, 1(12), 29–34.

McCarthy, I. P., & Gordon, B. R. (2011). Achieving contextual ambidexterity in R&D organizations: A management control system approach. *R & D Management*, 41(3), 240–258. doi:10.1111/j.1467-9310.2011.00642.x

McCormick, M. (2012). *Waterfall vs. Agile methodology*. MPCS.

McDermott, A. M., Hamel, L. M., Steel, D., Flood, P. C., & Mkee, L. (2015). Hybrid health care governance for improvement? Combining top-down and bottom-up approaches to public sector regulation. *Public Administration*, 93(2), 324–344. doi:10.1111/padm.12118

McGee, S., & Greer, D. (2012). Towards an understanding of the causes and effects of software requirements change: Two case studies. *Requirements Engineering*, 17(2), 133–155. doi:10.100700766-012-0149-0

McGraw, G. (2006). Software Security: Building Security. *ISSRE 2006*. http://bsimm.com

McGraw, G. (2004). Software Security. *IEEE Security and Privacy*, 2(2), 80–83. doi:10.1109/MSECP.2004.1281254

McKenna, D. (2016). *The Art of Scrum*. CA Technologies. doi:10.1007/978-1-4842-2277-5

Mehmann, J., Frehe, V., & Teuteberg, F. (2015). Crowd Logistics – A Literature Review and Maturity Model. *Innovations and Strategies for Logistics and Supply Chains*.

Melegati, J., Goldman, A., Kon, F., & Wang, X. (2019). A model of requirements engineering in software startups. *Information and Software Technology*, 109, 92–107. doi:10.1016/j.infsof.2019.02.001

Mettler, T. (2011). Maturity assessment models: A design science research approach. *International Journal of Society Systems Science*, 3(12), 81–98. doi:10.1504/IJSSS.2011.038934

Mettler, T., & Rohner, P. (2009). Situational maturity models as instrumental artifacts for organizational design. In *Proceedings of the 4th International Conference on Design Science Research in Information Systems and Technology - DESRIST '09* (p. 1). 10.1145/1555619.1555649

Meyer, B. (2014). *Agile! The Good, the Hype and the Ugly*. Springer International Publishing.

Microsoft. (2019). *Security development lifecycle for agile development.* Retrieved from http://www.microsoft.com/en-us/SDL/Discover/sdlagile.aspx

Miller, J., & Mukerji, J. (2003). *MDA guide version 1.0.1. Object Management Group.* OMG.

Miller, K. W., & Voas, J. (2008). Computer Scientist, Software Engineer, or IT Professional: Which Do You Think You Are? *IT Professional, 10*(4), 4–6. doi:10.1109/MITP.2008.64

Miranda, E. (2011). Time Boxing Planning: Buffered Moscow Rules. *Software Engineering Notes, 36*(6), 1–5. doi:10.1145/2047414.2047428

Miranda, E. (2019). Milestone Planning: A Participatory and Visual Approach. *Journal of Modern Project Management, 7*(2).

Mishra, D., & Mishra, A. (2008). Workspace environment for collaboration in small software development organization. *International Conference on Cooperative Design, Visualization and Engineering*, 196–203. 10.1007/978-3-540-88011-0_27

Moe, N. B., Dingsøyr, T., & Dybå, T. (2010). A teamwork model for understanding an agile team: A case study of a Scrum project. *Information and Software Technology, 52*(5), 480–491. doi:10.1016/j.infsof.2009.11.004

Mora, M., Gelman, O., Paradice, D., & Cervantes, F. (2008). The case for conceptual research in information systems. *CONF-IRM 2008 Proceedings*, 1-10.

Mora, M., Wang, F., Gómez, J. M., & Díaz, O. (2020). A Comparative Review on the Agile Tenets in the IT Service Management and the Software Engineering Domains. In Trends and Applications in Software Engineering, CIMPS 2019, Advances in Intelligent Systems and Computing (Vol. 1071, pp. 102-115). Berlin, Germany: Springer. doi:10.1007/978-3-030-33547-2_9

Mora, M., Gomez, J. M., O'Connor, R. V., Raisinghani, M., & Gelman, O. (2015). An extensive review of IT service design in seven international ITSM processes frameworks: Part II. *International Journal of Information Technologies and Systems Approach, 8*(1), 69–90. doi:10.4018/ijitsa.2015010104

Mora, M., Raisinghani, M., O'Connor, R. V., Gomez, J. M., & Gelman, O. (2014). An extensive review of IT service design in seven international ITSM processes frameworks: Part I. *International Journal of Information Technologies and Systems Approach, 7*(2), 83–107. doi:10.4018/ijitsa.2014070105

Morgan, G. (2006). *Images of Organization* (3rd ed.). Sage.

Morton, N. A., & Hu, Q. (2008). Implications of the fit between organizational structure and ERP: A structural contingency theory perspective. *International Journal of Information Management, 28*(5), 391–402. doi:10.1016/j.ijinfomgt.2008.01.008

Motingoe, M., & Langerman, J. J. (2019). New Organisational Models That Break Silos in Organisations to Enable Software Delivery Flow. *International Conference on System Science and Engineering (ICSSE)*, 341–348. 10.1109/ICSSE.2019.8823257

Mourão, E., Kalinowski, M., Murta, L., Mendes, E., & Wohlin, C. (2017). Investigating the use of a hybrid search strategy for systematic reviews. In *2017 ACM/IEEE International Symposium on Empirical Software Engineering and Measurement (ESEM)*, (pp. 193–198). IEEE. 10.1109/ESEM.2017.30

Mundra, A., Misra, S., & Dhawale, C. A. (2013). Practical scrum-scrum team: Way to produce successful and quality software. *2013 13th International Conference on Computational Science and Its Applications*, 119–123.

Muñoz M., Mejia J., Peña A., Lara G. & Laporte, C. Y. (2019). Transitioning international software engineering standards to academia: analyzing the results of the adoption of ISO/IEC 29110 in four Mexican universities. Journal of Computer Standards & Interfaces. Doi:10.1016/j.csi.2019.03.008

Muñoz, M., Mejia, J., Calvo-Manzano, J. A., San Feliu, T., Corona, B., & Miramontes, J. (2017). Diagnostic Assessment Tools for Assessing the Implementation and/or Use of Agile Methodologies in SMEs: An Analysis of Covered Aspects. *Software Quality Professional Journal, 19*(2), 16–27.

Muñoz, M., Mejia, J., & Laporte, C. Y. (2019). Reinforcing Very Small Entities Using Agile Methodologies with the ISO/IEC 29110. In J. Mejia, M. Muñoz, Á. Rocha, A. Peña, & M. Pérez-Cisneros (Eds.), *Trends and Applications in Software Engineering. CIMPS 2018. Advances in Intelligent Systems and Computing* (Vol. 865). Springer.

Muñoz, M., Mejia, J., & Laporte, C. Y. (2019b). *Implementing ISO/IEC 29110 to reinforce four very small entities of Mexico under an agile approach.* IET Software Journal; doi:10.1049/iet-sen.2019.0040

Muñoz, M., Peña, A., Mejia, J., Gasca-Hurtado, G. P., Gómez-Alvarez, M. C., & Laporte, C. (2019). A Comparative Analysis of the Implementation of the Software Basic Profile of ISO/IEC 29110 in Thirteen Teams That Used Predictive Versus Adaptive Life Cycles. In A. Walker, R. O'Connor, & R. Messnarz (Eds.), *Systems, Software and Services Process Improvement. EuroSPI 2019. Communications in Computer and Information Science* (Vol. 1060). Springer.

Muntean, M., & Surcel, T. (2013). Agile BI-The Future of BI. *Informatica Economica, 17*(3).

Nalebuff, B., & Brandenburger, A. (1997). Self-organization: The irresistible future of organizing. *Strategy and Leadership, 25*(6), 28–33. doi:10.1108/eb054655

Napier, N. P., Mathiassen, L., & Robey, D. (2011). Building contextual ambidexterity in a software company to improve firm-level coordination. *European Journal of Information Systems, 20*(6), 674–690. doi:10.1057/ejis.2011.32

Nawrocki, J., Walter, B., & Wojciechowski, A. (2001). Toward maturity model for extreme programming. *Conference Proceedings of the 27th EUROMICRO*, 233–239. 10.1109/EURMIC.2001.952459

Nerur, S., & Balijepally, V. (2007). Theoretical reflections on agile development methodologies. *Communications of the ACM, 50*(3), 79–83. doi:10.1145/1226736.1226739

Nerur, S., Mahapatra, R., & Mangalaraj, G. (2005). Challenges of Migrating to Agile Methodologies. *Communications of the ACM, 48*(5), 72–78. doi:10.1145/1060710.1060712

Ngwenyama, O., & Nielsen, P. A. (2013). Using organizational influence processes to overcome IS implementation barriers: Lessons from a longitudinal case study of SPI implementation. *European Journal of Information Systems, 23*(2), 205–222. doi:10.1057/ejis.2012.56

Nistala, P., Nori, K. V., & Reddy, R. (2019, May). Software quality models: A systematic mapping study. In *2019 IEEE/ACM International Conference on Software and System Processes (ICSSP)* (pp. 125-134). IEEE. 10.1109/ICSSP.2019.00025

Noordeloos, R., Manteli, C., & Van Vliet, H. (2012). From RUP to Scrum in global software development: A case study. *7th International Conference on Global Software Engineering (ICGSE)*, 31–40. 10.1109/ICGSE.2012.11

Nord, R. L., & Tomayko, J. E. (2006). Software architecture-centric methods and agile development. *IEEE Software, 23*(2), 47–53. doi:10.1109/MS.2006.54

Nord, R., Ozkaya, I., & Kruchten, P. (2014). Agile in distress: architecture to the rescue. In T. Dingsøyr & N. B. Moe (Eds.), *International Conference on Agile Software Development (XP'14)* (pp. 43–57). Springer Verlag; doi:10.1007/978-3-319-14358-3_5.

Nunes, N. J., Constantine, L., & Kazman, R. (2010). Iucp: Estimating interactivesoftware project size with enhanced use-case points. *IEEE Software, 28*(4), 64–73. doi:10.1109/MS.2010.111

Nuottila, J., Aaltonen, K., & Kujala, J. (2016). Challenges of adopting agile methods in a public organization. *International Journal of Information Systems and Project Management, 4*(3), 65–85.

Nurmuliani, N., Zowghi, D., & Powell, S. (2004, April). Analysis of requirements volatility during software development life cycle. In *2004 Australian Software Engineering Conference. Proceedings* (pp. 28-37). IEEE. 10.1109/ASWEC.2004.1290455

NYCE. (2020). Companies certified to the ISO/IEC 29110-4-1:2011 standard. Retrieved https://www.nyce.org.mx/wp-content/uploads/2020/01/PADRON-DE-EMPRESAS-CERTIFICADAS-EN-LA-NORMA-ISO-IEC-29110-4-1-16-01-2020.pdf

O'Connor, R. V., & Laporte, C. Y. (2012). Software Project Management in Very Small Entities with ISO/IEC 29110. In D. Winkler, R. V. O'Connor, & R. Messnarz (Eds.), *EuroSPI 2012, CCIS 301* (pp. 330–341). Springer-Verlag.

O'Leary, M. B., & Cummings, J. N. (2007). The spatial, temporal, and configurational characteristics of geographic dispersion in teams. *Management Information Systems Quarterly, 31*(3), 433–452. doi:10.2307/25148802

Oktaba, H., & Ibargüengoitia, G. (1998). Software process modeled with objects: Static view. *Computación y Sistemas, 1*(4), 228-238.

Østergaard, E. K. (2020, Jan.). Organisations of the future. *HR Future,* 14–15.

Oswald, A., & Müller, W. (2019). Management 4. 0 - Handbook for Agile Practices (A. Oswald & W. Müller, Eds.). Nürnberg: BoD.

Oswald, A., Köhler, J., & Schmitt, R. (2017). *Projektmanagement am Rande des Chaos. Projektmanagement am Rande des Chaos.* Springer Vieweg., doi:10.1007/978-3-662-55756-3

Oueslati, H., Rahman, M. M., & ben Othmane, L. (2015). Literature Review of the Challenges of Developing Secure Software Using the Agile Approach. *10th International Conference on Availability, Reliability and Security,* 540-547. 10.1109/ARES.2015.69

Oueslati, H., Rahman, M. M., ben Othmane, L., Ghani, I., & Arbain, A. F. B. (2016). Evaluation of the Challenges of Developing Secure Software Using the Agile Approach. *International Journal of Secure Software Engineering, 7*(1), 17–37. doi:10.4018/IJSSE.2016010102

Oyetoyan, T., Jaatun, M. G., & Cruzes, D. S. (2017). A Lightweight Measurement of Software Security Skills, Usage and Training Needs in Agile Teams. *International Journal of Secure Software Engineering, 8*(1), 1–27. doi:10.4018/IJSSE.2017010101

Paasivaara, M., Behm, B., Lassenius, C., & Hallikainen, M. (2018). Large-scale agile transformation at Ericsson: A case study. *Empirical Software Engineering, 23*(5), 2550–2596. doi:10.100710664-017-9555-8

Paasivaara, M., & Lassenius, C. (2014). Communities of practice in a large distributed agile software development organization - Case Ericsson. *Information and Software Technology, 56*(12), 1556–1577. doi:10.1016/j.infsof.2014.06.008

Paasivaara, M., Lassenius, C., & Heikkilä, V. T. (2012). Inter-team coordination in large-scale globally distributed scrum: Do scrum-of-scrums really work? *Proceedings of the ACM-IEEE International Symposium on Empirical Software Engineering and Measurement,* 235–238. 10.1145/2372251.2372294

Pacanowsky, M. (1988). Communication in the Empowering Organization. In J. A. Anderson (Ed.), *Communication yearbook 11* (pp. 356–379). Sage.

Packlick, J., & Sabre Airline Solutions Southlake. (2007). The Agile Maturity Map A Goal Oriented Approach to Agile Improvement. In *Proceedings of AGILE 2007 conference* (pp. 266–271). 10.1109/AGILE.2007.55

Paetsch, F., Eberlein, A., & Maurer, F. (2003). Requirements Engineering and Agile Software Development. In *Proceedings of 12th IEEE International Workshops on Enabling Technologies: Infrastructure for Collaborative Enterprises (WET ICE)* (pp. 308-313). IEEE.

Palm, K., & Lindahl, M. (2015). A project as a workplace - Observations from project managers in four R&D and project-intensive companies. *International Journal of Project Management, 33*(4), 828–838. doi:10.1016/j.ijproman.2014.10.002

Panda, A., Satapathy, S. M., & Rath, S. K. (2015). Empirical validation of neural network models for agile software effort estimation based on story points. *Procedia Computer Science, 57*, 772–781. doi:10.1016/j.procs.2015.07.474

Pant, V., & Yu, E. (2016). Coopetition with frenemies: Towards modeling of simultaneous cooperation and competition among enterprises. *The Practice of Enterprise Modeling - 9th IFIP WG 8.1. Working Conference, PoEM 2016, Proceedings*, 164–178.

Pant, V., & Yu, E. (2018). Modeling simultaneous cooperation and competition among enterprises. *Business & Information Systems Engineering, 60*(1), 39–54. doi:10.100712599-017-0514-0

Papadopoulos, G. (2015). Moving from traditional to agile software development methodologies also on large, distributed projects. *Procedia: Social and Behavioral Sciences, 175*, 455–463. doi:10.1016/j.sbspro.2015.01.1223

Papazoglou, M. P., Traverso, P., Schahram, D., Leymann, F., & Bernd, J. (2006). Service-oriented Computing: Research roadmap. *Dagstuhl Seminar Proceedings 05462 Service Oriented Computing (SOC)*.

Papazoglou, M. P., & Van Den Heuvel, W. (2007). Business process development life cycle methodology. *Communications of the ACM, 50*(10), 79–85. doi:10.1145/1290958.1290966

Papazoglou, M., & van den Heuvel, W. J. (2007). Service oriented architectures: Approaches, technologies and research issues. *The VLDB Journal, 16*(3), 389–415. doi:10.100700778-007-0044-3

Pardini, D. J., Heinisch, A. M. C., & Parreiras, F. S. (2018). Cyber Security Governance and Management for Smart Grids in Brazilian Energy Utilities. *Journal of Information Systems and Technology Management, 14*(3), 385–400. doi:10.4301/S1807-17752017000300006

Parnas, D. L., & Lawford, M. (2003). The role of inspection in software quality assurance. *IEEE Transactions on Software Engineering, 29*(8), 674–676. doi:10.1109/TSE.2003.1223642

Patel, C., & Ramachandran, M. (2009). Agile Maturity Model (AMM): A software process improvement framework for agile software development practices. *International Journal of Synthetic Emotions, 2*(I), 3–28. doi:10.4304/jsw.4.5.422-435

Patton, J. (2014). User story mapping: discover the whole story, build the right product. O'Reilly Media, Inc.

Paulk, M., Konrad, M., & Garcia, S. (1995). CMM Versus SPICE Architectures. *Software Process Newsletter,* (3), 7–11.

Paulk, M. C. (2002). Agile methodologies and process discipline. *Institute for Software Research, 3*, 15–18.

Perkusich, M., Silva, L. C., Costa, A., Ramos, F., Saraiva, R., Freire, A., ... Almeida, H. (2019). Intelligent Software Engineering in the Context of Agile Software Development: A Systematic Literature Review. *Information and Software Technology*.

Permana, P. A. G. (2015). Scrum method implementation in a software development project management. *International Journal of Advanced Computer Science and Applications, 6*(9), 198–204.

Petersen, K., Vakkalanka, S., & Kuzniarz, L. (2015). Guidelines for conducting systematic mapping studies in software engineering: An update. *Information and Software Technology, 64*, 1–18. doi:10.1016/j.infsof.2015.03.007

Petersen, K., Wohlin, C., & Baca, D. (2009, June). The waterfall model in large-scale development. In *International Conference on Product-Focused Software Process Improvement* (pp. 386-400). Springer. 10.1007/978-3-642-02152-7_29

Peterson, R. R. (2004). Integration Strategies and Tactics for Information Technology Governance. In Strategies for Information Technology Governance (pp. 37–80). IGI Global. doi:10.4018/978-1-59140-140-7.ch002

Pettit, R. J. (2006). *Agile Processes: Making Metrics Simple*. Retrieved from https://www.agileconnection.com/article/agile-processes-making-metrics-simple-0

Pfleeger, S. L. (2008). Software metrics: Progress after 25 years? *IEEE Software, 25*(6), 32–34. doi:10.1109/MS.2008.160

Phillips, D. (2001). *Cards-on-the-Wall Sessions*. Retrieved from Dr. Dobbs: https://www.drdobbs.com/cards-on-the-wall-sessions/184414750

Pilorget, L., & Schell, T. (2018). *IT Management: The art of managing IT based on a solid framework leveraging the company's political ecosystem*. Springer. doi:10.1007/978-3-658-19309-6

Pinto, M. B., & Pinto, J. K. (1990). Project team communication and cross-functional cooperation in new program development. *Journal of Product Innovation Management, 7*(3), 200–212. doi:10.1111/1540-5885.730200

PMI. (2013). *A Guide to the Project Management Body of Knowledge* (5th ed.).

Poeppelbuss, J., Niehaves, B., Simons, A., & Becker, J. (2011). Maturity Models in Information Systems Research : Literature Search and Analysis. *Communications of the Association for Information Systems, 29*(1), 30. doi:10.17705/1CAIS.02927

Poller, A., Kocksch, L., Türpe, S., Epp, F. A., & Kinder-Kurlanda, K. (2017). Can Security Become a Routine?: A Study of Organizational Change in an Agile Software Development Group. *CSCW, 2017*, 2489–2503.

Poppendieck, M., & Poppendieck, T. (2003). *Lean Software Development: An Agile Toolkit*. Academic Press.

Powell, A., Piccoli, G., & Ives, B. (2004). Virtual Teams: Team Control Structure, Work Processes, and Team Effectiveness. *Information Technology & People, 17*(4), 359–379. doi:10.1108/09593840410570258

Projekt Green Access. (2019). Abschlussbericht.

Pugh, D. S., Hickson, D. J., & Hinings, C. R. (1969). An Empirical Taxonomy of Structures of Work Organizations. *Administrative Science Quarterly, 14*(1), 115–126. doi:10.2307/2391367

Quinnan, R. E. (2010). The management of software engineering, Part V: Software engineering management practices. *IBM Systems Journal, 19*(4), 466–477. doi:10.1147j.194.0466

Qumer, A. (2017). Defining an Integrated Agile Governance for Large Agile Software Development Environments. *International Conference on Extreme Programming and Agile Processes in Software Engineering*, 157-160.

Qumer, A., & Henderson-Sellers, B. (2008). A framework to support the evaluation, adoption and improvement of agile methods in practice. *Journal of Systems and Software, 81*(11), 1899–1919. doi:10.1016/j.jss.2007.12.806

Qumer, A., & Henderson-Sellers, B. (2008). An evaluation of the degree of agility in six agile methods and its applicability for method engineering. *Information and Software Technology, 50*(4), 280–295. doi:10.1016/j.infsof.2007.02.002

Radigan, D. (2019). *The Product Backlog: Your Ultimate To Do List*. Retrieved from https://www.atlassian.com/agile/scrum/backlogs

Rafferty, A. E., & Griffin, M. A. (2004). Dimensions of Transformational Leadership: Conceptual and Empirical Extensions. *The Leadership Quarterly*, *15*(3), 329–354. doi:10.1016/j.leaqua.2004.02.009

Ralph, P. (2018). Toward Methodological Guidelines for Process Theories and Taxonomies in Software Engineering. *IEEE Transactions on Software Engineering*, *45*(7), 712–735. doi:10.1109/TSE.2018.2796554

Ramesh, B., Cao, L., & Baskerville, R. (2010). Agile requirements engineering practices and challenges: An empirical study. *Information Systems Journal*, *20*(5), 449–480. doi:10.1111/j.1365-2575.2007.00259.x

Ramesh, B., Cao, L., Mohan, K., & Xu, P. (2006). Can distributed software development be agile? *Communications of the ACM*, *49*(10), 41–46. doi:10.1145/1164394.1164418

Ramesh, B., Mohan, K., & Cao, L. (2012). Ambidexterity in agile distributed development: An empirical investigation. *Information Systems Research*, *23*(2), 323–339. doi:10.1287/isre.1110.0351

Ramzan, S., & Ikram, N. (2006). Requirement change management process models: Activities, artifacts and roles. In *2006 IEEE International Multitopic Conference*, (pp. 219–223). IEEE. 10.1109/INMIC.2006.358167

Regnell, B., & Brinkkemper, S. (2005). Market-Driven Requirements Engineering for Software Products. In Engineering and Managing Software Requirements (pp. 287–308). Springer-Verlag., doi:10.1007/3-540-28244-0_13

Reich, B. H., & Benbasat, I. (2000). Factors That Influence the Social Dimension of Alignment Between Business and Information Technology Objectives. *Management Information Systems Quarterly*, *24*(1), 81–113. doi:10.2307/3250980

Reyes-Delgado, P. Y., Mora, M., Duran-Limon, H. A., Rodriguez-Martinez, L. C., Mendoza-González, R., & Rodríguez-Díaz, M. A. (2015). State of the Art of Software Architecture Design Methods Used in Main Software Development Methodologies. In M. Khosrow-Pour (Ed.), *Encyclopedia of Information Science and Technology* (3rd ed., pp. 7359–7370). IGI-Global.

Reynolds, P. D. (2016). *Primer in Theory Construction*. Routledge.

Ries, E. (2011). *The lean startup: How today's entrepreneurs use continuous innovation to create radically successful businesses*. Crown Books.

Rodriguez, L. C., Mora, M., & Alvarez, F. J. (2008) Process Models of SDLCs: Comparison and evolution. In M.R. Syed, & Syed, S.N. (Ed.), Handbook of Research on Modern Systems Analysis and Design Technologies and Applications (pp. 76-89). Minnesota State University.

Rodriguez-Martinez, L. C., Duran-Limon, H. A., Mora, M., & Alvarez-Rodriguez, F. (2019). SOCA-DSEM: A Well-Structured SOCA Development Systems Engineering Methodology. *Computer Science and Information Systems*, *16*(1), 19–44. doi:10.2298/CSIS170703035R

Rodriguez-Martinez, L. C., Mora, M., Alvarez, F., Garza, L. A., Duran, H. A., & Muñoz, J. (2012). State of the art analysis of the System Development Life Cycle (SDLC) in Service-oriented Software Engineering (SOSE). *Journal of Applied Research and Technology*, *10*(2), 94–113. doi:10.22201/icat.16656423.2012.10.2.396

Rogers, E. M. (1995). *Diffusion of innovations* (4th ed.). Free Press.

Rohjans, S., Uslar, M., Cleven, A., Winter, R., & Wortmann, F. (2011). Towards an Adaptive Maturity Model for Smart Grids. *17th international Power Systems Computation Conference*.

Romana, R., Lopeza, J., & Mambob, M. (2018). *Future Generation Computer Systems. Elsevier.* doi:10.1016/j.future.2016.11.009

Ross, J. W., Sebastian, I., Beath, C., Mocker, M., Moloney, K., & Fonstad, N. (2016). *Designing and Executing Digital Strategies.* Paper presented at the International Conference on Information Systems, Dublin, Ireland.

Royce, W. (1970). Managing the development of large software systems: Concepts and techniques. In *Technical Papers of Western Electronic Show and Convention (WesCon).* Academic Press.

Sachs & Hauser. (n.d.). *Definition: Themenfeld.* Retrieved from https://www.repetico.de/card-70811769

Sahay, S. (2003). Global software alliances: The challenge of 'standardization'. *Scandinavian Journal of Information Systems, 15*(1), 11.

Saher, N., Baharom, F., & Ghazali, O. (2017). Requirement change taxonomy and categorization in agile software development. In *2017 6th International Conference on Electrical Engineering and Informatics (ICEEI)*, (pp. 1–6). IEEE. 10.1109/ICEEI.2017.8312441

Sambamurthy, V., Bharadwaj, A., & Grover, V. (2003). Shaping agility though digital options: Reconceptualizing the role of information technology in contemporary firms. *Management Information Systems Quarterly, 27*(2), 237–263. doi:10.2307/30036530

Sánchez-Gordon, M.-L., de Amescua, A., O'Connor, R. V., & Larrucea, X. (2017, November). A standard-based framework to integrate software work in small settings. *Journal of Computer Standards & Interfaces, 54*(Part 3), 162–175. doi:10.1016/j.csi.2016.11.009

Santos, D. F., Rodrigues, A. F. A., Pereira, M. F., Almeida, H. O., & Perkusich, A. (2016). An interoperable and standard-based end-to-end remote patient monitoring system. In *Encyclopedia of E-Health and Telemedicine* (pp. 260–272). IGI Global. doi:10.4018/978-1-4666-9978-6.ch022

Schatz, B., & Abdelshafi, I. (2005). Primavera gets Agile: A successful transition to Agile development. *IEEE Software, 22*(3), 36–42. doi:10.1109/MS.2005.74

Schienmann, B. (2002). *Kontinuierliches Anforderungsmanagement prozesse-Techniken-Werkzeuge.* Addison-Wesley.

Schiesser, R. (2010). *IT Systems Management.* Prentice-Hall.

Schön, E.-M., Thomaschewski, J., & Escalona, M. J. (2017). Agile requirements engineering: A systematic literature review. *Computer Standards & Interfaces, 49,* 79–91. doi:10.1016/j.csi.2016.08.011

Schroth, C. (2007). The service-oriented enterprise. *Journal of Enterprise Architecture, 3*(4), 73-80.

Schulze, P., Heinemann, F., & Abedin, A. (2008). Balancing Exploitation and Exploration. In Academy of Management Proceedings (Vol. 2008, No. 1, pp. 1-6). Academy of Management. doi:10.5465/ambpp.2008.33622934

Schwaber, K., & Beedle. (2001). *Agile Software development with Scrum.* Prentice Hall.

Schwaber, K., & Sutherland, J. (2017). Der Scrum Guide - DEUTSCH. *Scrumguides.Org,* 22. Retrieved from https://www.scrumguides.org/docs/scrumguide/v2016/2016-Scrum-Guide-German.pdf

Schwaber, K., & Sutherland, J. (2017). *The Scrum Guide - The Definitive Guide to Scrum: The Rules of the Game, 2017.* Academic Press.

Schwaber, K. (2004). *Agile Project Management with Scrum.* Microsoft Press.

SchwaberK. (2013). *unSAFe at any speed.* https://kenschwaber.wordpress.com/2013/08/06/unsafe-at-any-speed/

Schwaber, K., & Beedle, M. (2001). *Agile Software Development with Scrum*. Prentice Hall.

Schweigert, T., Nevalainen, R., Vohwinkel, D., Korsaa, M., & Biro, M. (2012). Agile maturity model: Oxymoron or the next level of understanding. *Communications in Computer and Information Science, 290*(6), 289–294. doi:10.1007/978-3-642-30439-2_34

Schweigert, T., Vohwinkel, D., Korsaa, M., & Nevalainen, R. (2013). Agile Maturity Model : A Synopsis as a First Step. In EuroSPI 2013 (pp. 214–227). doi:10.1007/978-3-642-39179-8_19

Schweigert, T., Vohwinkel, D., Korsaa, M., Nevalainen, R., & Biro, M. (2013). Agile maturity model: Analysing agile maturity characteristics from the SPICE perspective. *Journal of Software: Evolution and Process, 25*(7), 513–520. doi:10.1002mr

Serrador, P., & Pinto, J. K. (2015). Does Agile work?— A quantitative analysis of agile project success. *International Journal of Project Management, 33*(5), 1040–1051. doi:10.1016/j.ijproman.2015.01.006

Shepard, J. (2013). Sociology (11th ed.). Wadsworth, Cengage Learning.

Shostack, A. (2014). *Threat Modeling: Designing for Security*. Wiley.

Shrivastava, S. V., & Date, H. (2010). Distributed Agile Software Development: A Review. *Journal of Computing Science and Engineering: JCSE, 1*(1), 10–17.

Sidky, A., Arthur, J., & Bohner, S. (2007). A disciplined approach to adopting agile practices: The agile adoption framework. *Innovations in Systems and Software Engineering, 3*(3), 203–216. doi:10.100711334-007-0026-z

Similä, J., Kuvaja, P., & Krzanik, L. (1994). BOOTSTRAP: A Software Process Assessment and Improvement Methodology. In *1st Asia-Pacific Conference* (pp. 183–196). 10.1109/APSEC.1994.465261

Simonsson, M., Johnson, P., & Ekstedt, M. (2010). The effect of IT governance maturity on IT governance performance. *Information Systems Management, 27*(1), 10–24. doi:10.1080/10580530903455106

Simpson, J., & Weiner, E. (1989). *The Oxford English Dictionary*. OUP.

Skare, P., Falk, H., Rice, M., & Winkel, J. (2016). In the Face of Cybersecurity: How the Common Information Model Can Be Used. *IEEE Power & Energy Magazine, 14*(1), 94–104. doi:10.1109/MPE.2015.2485899

Smart, J. F. (2015). *BDD in Action: Behavior-driven development for the whole software lifecycle*. Manning.

Smite, D., Moe, N. B., Levinta, G., & Floryan, M. (2019). Spotify Guilds: How to Succeed With Knowledge Sharing in Large-Scale Agile Organizations. *IEEE Software, 36*(2), 51–57. doi:10.1109/MS.2018.2886178

Šmite, D., Moe, N. B., Šāblis, A., & Wohlin, C. (2017). Software teams and their knowledge networks in large-scale software development. *Information and Software Technology, 86*, 71–86. doi:10.1016/j.infsof.2017.01.003

Smite, D., Moe, N. B., & Torkar, R. (2008). Pitfalls in Remote Team Coordination: Lessons Learned from a Case Study. *PROFES, 2008*, 345–359.

Smith, W. K., & Lewis, M. W. (2011). Toward a theory of paradox: A dynamic equilibrium model of organizing. *Academy of Management Review, 36*(2), 381–403.

Software Engineering Institute. (2010). *CMMI for Service Version 1.3, CMMI-SVC v1. 3. CMU/SEI-2010-TR-034*. Software Engineering Institute.

Software Engineering Institute. (2010a). CMMI for Acquisition, Version 1.3: Improving processes for acquiring better products and services. *Technical Report, 1.3*(November).

Software Engineering Institute. (2010b). CMMI for Development, Version 1.3: Improving Processed for Better Products and Services. *Technical Report, 1.3*(November). ESC-TR-2010-033.

Software Engineering Institute. (2010c). CMMI for Services, Version 1.3: Improving processes for providing better services. *Technical Report, 1.3*(November). doi:10.1002/adem.201100259

Software Engineering Institute. (2011). SGMM Model Definition - Technical Report. Pittsburgh: Author.

Sommerville, I. (2011). Software engineering (9th ed.). Academic Press.

Sommerville, I. (2011). Software engineering (9th ed.). Addison-Wesley/Pearson.

Sommerville, I. (2015). *Software Engineering* (10th ed.). Academic Press.

Sommerville, I. (2005). *Software Engineering*. Addison-Wesley.

SoS-Agile Project (2015-2020). (n.d.). Retrieved from Science of Security for Agile Software Development research project, 2015-2020, funded by the Research Council of Norway: http://www.sintef.no/sos-agile

Specht, M., Rohjans, S., Trefke, J., Uslar, M., & González, J. M. (2013). International smart grid roadmaps and their assessment. *EAI Endorsed Transactions on Energy Web, 13*(1–6). Advance online publication. doi:10.4108/trans.ew.2013.01-06.e2

Spencer, M. E., & Spencer, M. E. (1970). Weber on Legitimate Norms and Authority. *The British Journal of Sociology, 21*(2), 123–134. doi:10.2307/588403 PMID:4928951

Spichkova, M., & Schmidt, H. (2019). *Requirements engineering for global systems: cultural, regulatory and technical aspects*. arXiv preprint arXiv:1910.05008

Stålhane, T., Katta, V., & Myklebust, T. (2014). *Change impact analysis in agile development*. EHPG Røros.

Stavru, S. (2014). A critical examination of recent industrial surveys on agile method usage. *Journal of Systems and Software, 94*, 87–97. doi:10.1016/j.jss.2014.03.041

Stepanova, V. (2019). Quality Control Approach in Developing Software Projects. *International Journal of Computer Science and Software Engineering, 8*(1), 1–5.

Stoica, M., Mircea, M., & Ghilic-Micu, B. (2013). Software Development: Agile vs. Traditional. *Informatica Economica, 17*(4).

Stol, K. J., & Fitzgerald, B. (2015). Theory-oriented software engineering. *Science of Computer Programming, 101*, 79–98. doi:10.1016/j.scico.2014.11.010

Stray, V., Moe, N. B., & Hoda, R. (2018). Autonomous agile teams: Challenges and future directions for research. *Proceedings of the 19th International Conference on Agile Software Development: Companion*, 16. 10.1145/3234152.3234182

Stroud, R. (2017). *2018: The Year Of Enterprise DevOps*. Retrieved from https://go.forrester.com/blogs/2018-the-year-of-enterprise-devops/

Sutherland, J., & Schwaber, K. (2011). *The Scrum Papers: Nuts, Bolts and Origins of an Agile Process*. Academic Press.

Szalvay, V. (2004). *An introduction to agile software development*. Danube Technologies.

Takeuchi, H., Osono, E., & Shimizu, N. (2008). The contradictions that drive Toyota's success. *Harvard Business Review, 86*(6), 96–104. PMID:18411967

Talby, D., & Dubinsky, Y. (2009). Governance of an agile software project. *Proceedings of the 2009 ICSE Workshop on Software Development Governance, SDG 2009*, 40–45. 10.1109/SDG.2009.5071336

Tam, C., da Costa Moura, E. J., Oliveira, T., & Varajão, J. (2020). The factors influencing the success of on-going agile software development projects. *International Journal of Project Management*, 38(3), 165–176. doi:10.1016/j.ijproman.2020.02.001

Tarter, C. J., & Hoy, W. K. (1998). Toward a contingency theory of decision making. *Journal of Educational Administration*, 36(3), 212–228. doi:10.1108/09578239810214687

Taylor, K. J. (2016). Adopting Agile software development: The project manager experience. *Information Technology & People*, 29(4), 670–687. doi:10.1108/ITP-02-2014-0031

The GridWise Architecture Council. (2011). Smart Grid Interoperability Maturity Model Beta Version. *Architecture*, 1–46. https://www.gridwiseac.org/pdfs/imm/sg_imm_beta_final_12_01_2011.pdf

The Open Group. (2016). *IT4IT Agile Scenario Using the Reference Architecture*. Available from https://publications.opengroup.org/w162

The Open Group. (2017). *The Open Group IT4IT™ Reference Architecture, Version 2.1*. The Open Group.

Tiwana, A. (2008). Do bridging ties complement strong ties? An empirical examination of alliance ambidexterity. *Strategic Management Journal*, 29(3), 251–272. doi:10.1002mj.666

Tiwana, A. (2010). Systems development ambidexterity: Explaining the complementary and substitutive roles of formal and informal controls. *Journal of Management Information Systems*, 27(2), 87–126. doi:10.2753/MIS0742-1222270203

TMMi Foundation. (2012). *Test Maturity Model Integration R1.2*. https://www.tmmi.org/tmmi-documents/

Tolfo, C., Wazlawick, R. S., Ferreira, M. G. G., & Forcellini, F. A. (2011). Agile methods and organizational culture: Reflections about cultural levels. *Journal of Software Maintenance and Evolution: Research and Practice*, 23(6), 423–441. doi:10.1002mr.483

Tøndel, I., Jaatun, M. G., Cruzes, D. S., & Moe, N. B. (2017). Risk Centric Activities in Secure Software Development in Public Organisations. *International Journal of Secure Software Engineering*, 8(4), 1–30. doi:10.4018/IJSSE.2017100101

Tøndel, I., Line, M. B., & Johansen, G. (2015). Assessing Information Security Risks of AMI - What Makes it so Difficult? *ICISSP*, 2015, 56–63.

Trkman, M., Mendling, J., & Krisper, M. (2016). Using business process models to better understand the dependencies among user stories. *Information and Software Technology*, 71, 58–76. doi:10.1016/j.infsof.2015.10.006

Trkman, M., Mendling, J., Trkman, P., & Krisper, M. (2019). Impact of the conceptual model's representation format on identifying and understanding user stories. *Information and Software Technology*, 116, 106169. doi:10.1016/j.infsof.2019.08.001

Trusson, C. R., Doherty, N. F., & Hislop, D. (2014). Knowledge Sharing Using IT Service Management Tools: Conflicting Discourses and Incompatible Practices. *Information Systems Journal*, 24(4), 347–371. doi:10.1111/isj.12025

Tuma, K., Çalikli, G., & Scandariato, R. (2018). Threat analysis of software systems: A systematic literature review. *Journal of Systems and Software*, 144, 275–294. doi:10.1016/j.jss.2018.06.073

Turetken, O., Stojanov, I., & Trienekens, J. J. (2017). Assessing the adoption level of scaled agile development: A maturity model for Scaled Agile Framework. *Journal of Software: Evolution and Process*, 29(6), e1796.

Turk, D., France, R., & Rumpe, B. (2014). *Limitations of agile software processes.* ArXiv Preprint ArXiv:1409.6600

Tushman, M. L., & O'Reilly, C. A. III. (1996). Managing evolutionary and revolutionary change. *California Management Review, 38*(4), 8–28. doi:10.2307/41165852

U.S. Department of Energy. (2014). *Electricity subsector cybersecurity capability maturity model.* Retrieved from http://energy.gov/sites/prod/files/2014/02/f7/ES-C2M2-v1-1-Feb2014.pdf

Uebernickel, F., Stölzle, W., Lennerts, S., Lampe, K., & Hoffman, C. P. (2015). *Das St. Galler Business-Innovation-Modell. Business Innovation: das St. Galler Modell.* doi:10.1007/978-3-658-07167-7

Ullah, A., & Lai, R. (2011). Modeling Business Goal For Business/It Alignment Using Requirements Engineering. *Journal of Computer Information Systems, 51*(3), 21–28.

Uludag, Ö., Kleehaus, M., Caprano, C., & Matthes, F. (2018). Identifying and structuring challenges in large-scale agile development based on a structured literature review. *2018 IEEE 22nd International Enterprise Distributed Object Computing Conference (EDOC)*, 191–197.

Uludağ, Ö., Kleehaus, M., Xu, X., & Matthes, F. (2017). Investigating the role of architects in scaling agile frameworks. *2017 IEEE 21st International Enterprise Distributed Object Computing Conference (EDOC)*, 123–132.

UNCTAD. (2012). *Information Economy Report 2012 - The Software Industry and Developing Countries.* United Nations Publication.

Upadhyaya, A., & Krishna, S. (2007). Antecedents of knowledge sharing in globally distributed software development teams, In *Proceedings of European Conference of Information Systems (ECIS)* (pp. 727-738). St. Gallen, Switzerland: Academic Press.

Uslar, M., & Masurkewitz, J. (2015). A Survey on Application of Maturity Models for Smart Grid: Review of the State-of-the-Art. In Proceedings of Enviroinfo and Ict for Sustainability 2015 (Vol. 22, pp. 261–270). Kopenhagen: Academic Press.

Uslar, M., Dänekas, C., & Specht, M. (2012). Technische Reifegradmodelle für EWE – Fokus Smart Grids @ EWE und BMWi Future Energy Grid. Academic Press.

Vähäniitty, J., & Rautiainen, K. (2005). Towards an Approach for Managing the Development Portfolio in Small Product-Oriented Software Companies. *38th Hawaii International Conference on System Sciences.* 10.1109/HICSS.2005.636

Vaidya, A. (2014). Does dad know best, is it better to do less or just be safe? Adapting scaling agile practices into the enterprise. *PNSQC. ORG*, 1–18.

Vallon, R., da Silva Estacio, B. J., Prikladnicki, R., & Grechenig, T. (2018). Systematic literature review on agile practices in global software development. *Information and Software Technology, 96*, 161–180. doi:10.1016/j.infsof.2017.12.004

Van Lamsweerde, A. (2001). Goal-oriented requirements engineering: A guided tour. *Proceedings of the IEEE International Conference on Requirements Engineering*, 249–261.

Van Lamsweerde, A. (2009). *Requirements engineering: From system goals to UML models to software* (Vol. 10). John Wiley & Sons.

Vargo, S. L., & Lusch, R. F. (2004). The four service marketing myths: Remnants of a goods-based, manufacturing model. *Journal of Service Research, 6*(4), 324–335. doi:10.1177/1094670503262946

Vázquez, J. M. G. (2012). *Ein Referenzmodellkatalog für die Energiewirtschaft.* Academic Press.

Vejseli, S., Proba, D., Rossmann, A., & Reinhard, J. (2018). The Agile Strategies In It Governance: Towards A Framework Of Agile It Governance In The Banking Industry. *Twenty-Sixth European Conference on Information Systems (ECIS2018).*

Verlaine, B. (2017). Toward an Agile IT Service Management Framework. *Service Science, 9*(4), 263–274. doi:10.1287erv.2017.0186

VersionOne. (2018). *CollabNet 13th Annual State of Agile Report.* Available from https://www.stateofagile.com/#ufh-i-521251909-13th-annual-state-of-agile-report/473508

Vinekar, V., Slinkman, C. W., & Nerur, S. (2006). Can agile and traditional systems development approaches coexist? An ambidextrous view. *Information Systems Management, 23*(3), 31–42. doi:10.1201/1078.10580530/46108.23.3.200 60601/93705.4

Vlietland, J., Van Solingen, R., & Van Vliet, H. (2016). Aligning codependent Scrum teams to enable fast business value delivery: A governance framework and set of intervention actions. *Journal of Systems and Software, 113*, 418–429. doi:10.1016/j.jss.2015.11.010

Vroom, V. H., & Jago, A. G. (2007). The role of the situation in leadership. *The American Psychologist, 62*(1), 17–24. doi:10.1037/0003-066X.62.1.17 PMID:17209676

Wagner, S., Fernández, D. M., Felderer, M., & Kalinowski, M. (2017). Requirements engineering practice and problems in agile projects: Results from an international survey. CIbSE 2017, 85–98.

Wagner, S., Fernández, D. M., Felderer, M., Vetrò, A., Kalinowski, M., Wieringa, R., Pfahl, D., Conte, T., Christiansson, M.-T., Greer, D., Lassenius, C., Männistö, T., Nayebi, M., Oivo, M., Penzenstadler, B., Prikladnicki, R., Ruhe, G., Schekelmann, A., Sen, S., ... Winkler, D. (2019). Status quo in requirements engineering: A theory and a global family of surveys. *ACM Transactions on Software Engineering and Methodology, 28*(2), 1–48. doi:10.1145/3306607

Wand, Y., & Weber, R. (2002). Research Commentary: Information Systems and Conceptual Modeling - A Research Agenda. *Information Systems Research, 13*(4), 363–376. doi:10.1287/isre.13.4.363.69

Wartena, F., Muskens, J., Schmitt, L., & Petkovic, M. (2010, July). Continua: The reference architecture of a personal telehealth ecosystem. In *The 12th IEEE International Conference on e-Health Networking, Applications and Services* (pp. 1-6). IEEE.

Waterman, M., Noble, J., & Allan, G. (2012). How much architecture? Reducing the up-front effort. In A. G. I. L. E. India (Ed.), (pp. 56–59). IEEE; doi:10.1109/AgileIndia.2012.11.

Wautelet, Y. (2019). A model-driven IT governance process based on the strategic impact evaluation of services. *Journal of Systems and Software, 149*, 462–475. doi:10.1016/j.jss.2018.12.024

Wautelet, Y., Heng, S., Kiv, S., & Kolp, M. (2017). User-story driven development of multi-agent systems: A process fragment for agile methods. *Computer Languages, Systems & Structures, 50*, 159–176. doi:10.1016/j.cl.2017.06.007

Wautelet, Y., Heng, S., Kolp, M., & Mirbel, I. (2014). Unifying and Extending User Story Models. In *Advanced Information Systems Engineering* (pp. 211–225). Springer. doi:10.1007/978-3-319-07881-6_15

Wautelet, Y., Heng, S., Kolp, M., & Mirbel, I. (2014). Unifying and extending user story models. In *International Conference on Advanced Information Systems Engineering* (pp. 211-225). Springer.

Wautelet, Y., Heng, S., Kolp, M., Mirbel, I., & Poelmans, S. (2016). Building a rationale diagram for evaluating user story sets. In *2016 IEEE Tenth International Conference on Research Challenges in Information Science (RCIS)* (pp. 1-12). IEEE. 10.1109/RCIS.2016.7549299

Wautelet, Y., & Kolp, M. (2016). Business and model-driven development of BDI multi-agent systems. *Neurocomputing, 182,* 304–321. doi:10.1016/j.neucom.2015.12.022

Wautelet, Y., & Kolp, M. (2019). Conceptual Modeling as a Tool for Corporate Governance Support : State of the Art and Research Agenda. *Research & Innovation Forum, 2019,* 1–16. doi:10.1007/978-3-030-30809-4_49

Wautelet, Y., Kolp, M., Heng, S., & Poelmans, S. (2018). Developing a multi-agent platform supporting patient hospital stays following a socio-technical approach: Management and governance benefits. *Telematics and Informatics, 35*(4), 854–882. doi:10.1016/j.tele.2017.12.013

Wäyrynen, J., Bodén, M., & Boström, G. (2004). *Security Engineering and eXtreme Programming: An Impossible Marriage?* XP/Agile Universe.

Weidman, J., Young-Corbett, D., Fiori, C., Koebel, T., & Montague, E. (2015). Prevention through Design Adoption Readiness Model (PtD ARM): An integrated conceptual model. *Work.*

Weill, P., & Ross, J. W. (2011). *IT Governance on One Page.* SSRN Electronic Journal. doi:10.2139srn.664612

Weiss, D. M., & Basili, V. R. (1985). Evaluating software development by analysis of changes: Some data from the software engineering laboratory. *IEEE Transactions on Software Engineering, SE-11*(2), 157–168. doi:10.1109/TSE.1985.232190

Wenger, E., McDermott, R., & Snyder, W. M. (2002). *Cultivating Communities of Practice.* Harvard Business School Press.

West, D., & Grant, T. (2010). *Agile Development: Mainstream Adoption Has Changed Agility - Trends In Real-World Adoption Of Agile Methods.* Forrester Study.

Whittaker, S., & Schwarz, H. (1999). Meetings of the Board: The Impact of Scheduling Medium on Long Term Group Coordination in Software Development. *Computer Supported Cooperative Work, 8*(3), 175–205. doi:10.1023/A:1008603001894

Wiedemann, A. (2017). *A New Form of Collaboration in IT Teams - Exploring the DevOps Phenomenon.* Paper presented at the Pacific Asia Conference on Information Systems, Langkawi, Malaysia.

Wiedemann, A., & Wiesche, M. (2018). *Are You Ready For DevOps? Required Skill Set for DevOps Teams.* Paper presented at the European Conference on Information Systems, Portsmouth, UK.

Wiedemann, A., Wiesche, M., Thatcher, J. B., & Gewald, H. (2019). *A Control-Alignment Model for Product Orientation in DevOps Teams–A Multinational Case Study.* Paper presented at the International Conference on Information Systems, Munich, Germany.

Wiedemann, A., Forsgren, N., Wiesche, M., Gewald, H., & Krcmar, H. (2019). Research for Practice: The DevOps Phenomenon. *Communications of the ACM, 62*(8), 44–49. doi:10.1145/3331138

Wiegers, K., & Beatty, J. (2013). *Software requirements.* Pearson Education.

Williams, L. (2010). Agile software development methodologies and practices. *Advances in Computers, 80,* 1–44. doi:10.1016/S0065-2458(10)80001-4

Williams, L., & Cockburn, A. (2003). Agile software development: It's about feedback and change. *IEEE Computer, 36*(6), 39–43. doi:10.1109/MC.2003.1204373

Wohlin, C. (2014). Guidelines for snowballing in systematic literature studies and a replication in software engineering. *Proceedings of the 18th international conference on evaluation and assessment in software engineering,* 38. 10.1145/2601248.2601268

Wong, S. S., & Burton, R. M. (2000). Virtual teams: What are their characteristics, and impact on team performance? *Computational & Mathematical Organization Theory, 6*(4), 339–360. doi:10.1023/A:1009654229352

Woods, E. (2015). Aligning Architecture Work with Agile Teams. *IEEE Software, 32*(5), 24–26. doi:10.1109/MS.2015.119

Wu, Y., & Wu, S. (2016). Managing ambidexterity in creative industries: A survey. *Journal of Business Research, 69*(7), 2388–2396. doi:10.1016/j.jbusres.2015.10.008

Xiao, S., Witschey, J., & Murphy-Hil, E. (2014). Social influences on secure development tool adoption: why security tools spread. In *Proceedings of the 17th ACM conference on Computer supported cooperative work & social computing (CSCW '14)* (pp. 1095-1106). New York, NY: ACM. 10.1145/2531602.2531722

Yahaya, J. H. (2020). Software quality and certification: Perception and practices in Malaysia. *Journal of Information and Communication Technology, 5*, 63–82.

Yang, C., Liang, P., & Avgeriou, P. (2016). A systematic mapping study on the combination of software architecture and agile development. *Journal of Systems and Software, 111*, 157–184; Advance online publication. doi:10.1016/j.jss.2015.09.028

Yin, R. K. (2016). Case Study Research Design and Methods (5th ed.). Washington, DC: SAGE Publications. doi:10.3138/cjpe.30.1.108

Yoo, Y., Boland, R. J. Jr, Lyytinen, K., & Majchrzak, A. (2012). Organizing for Innovation in the Digitized World. *Organization Science, 23*(5), 1398–1408. doi:10.1287/orsc.1120.0771

Yu, E., Giorgini, P., Maiden, N., & Mylopoulos, J. (2011). *Social Modeling for Requirements Engineering*. MIT Press.

Zhang, X., Stafford, T. F., Dhaliwal, J. S., Gillenson, M. L., & Moeller, G. (2014). Sources of conflict between developers and testers in software development. *Information & Management, 51*(1), 13–26. doi:10.1016/j.im.2013.09.006

Zimmermann, O. (2016). Microservices Tenets: Agile Approach to Service Development and Deployment. *SummerSoc 2016 Proceedings Conference.*

Zimmermann, O., Krogdahl, P., & Gee, C. (2004). Elements of Service Oriented Analysis and Design: an approach of interdisciplinary modeling for SOA projects. *IBM Developer Works.* Retrieved from https://www.ibm.com/developer-works/library/ws-soad1/

About the Contributors

Manuel Mora is a full-time professor and researcher in the Information Systems Department at the Autonomous University of Aguascalientes (UAA), Mexico. Dr. Mora holds a B.S. in Computer Systems Engineering (1984) and an M.Sc. in Computer Sciences (Artificial Intelligence area, 1989) from Monterrey Tech (ITESM), and an Eng.D. in Engineering (Systems Engineering area, 2003) from the National Autonomous University of Mexico (UNAM). He has published about 90 research papers in international top conferences, research books, and research journals. Dr. Mora is an ACM senior member (since 2008), and a member of the Mexican National Research System at Level II. Dr. Mora currently is the EiC of IJITSA journal, and also serves in the ERBs of several international journals focused on DMSS and IT services.

Jorge Marx Gómez studied Computer Engineering and Industrial Engineering at the University of Applied Science in Berlin (Technische Fachhochschule Berlin, Germany). He was a lecturer and researcher at the Otto-von-Guericke-University Magdeburg where he also obtained a PhD degree 2001 in Business Information Systems with a thesis on "Computer-based Approaches to Forecast Returns of Scrapped Products to Recycling". From 2002 until 2003 he was a visiting professor for Business Informatics at the Technical University of Clausthal (Technische Universität Clausthal, Germany) and worked as lecturer in different countries. In 2004 he received his postdoctoral lecture qualification (Habilitation) for his work on "Automated Environmental Reporting through Material Flow Networks" at the Otto-von-Guericke-University Magdeburg. In April 2005 he received the research price of the faculty of computer science at the Otto-von-Guericke-University Magdeburg. Since 2006 Jorge Marx Gómez is a full professor and chair of Business Information Systems / Very Large Business Applications (VLBA) at the Carl von Ossietzky University of Oldenburg.His research interests include Business Information Systems, Federated ERP-Systems, Business Intelligence, Big Data, Interoperability, Environmental Management Information Systems and e- and Mobile-Commerce.

Rory V. O'Connor is an Associate Professor of Computing at Dublin City University (Ireland) where he is currently serving as the Head of the School of Computing. He is also a Senior Researcher with Lero, The Irish Software Research Centre and is currently serving as Ireland's Head of delegation to International Organization for Standardization (ISO) for Software & Systems Engineering (ISO/IEC JCT1/SC7). Dr. O'Connor previously held research positions at both the National Centre for Software Engineering and the Centre for Teaching Computing, and has also worked as a software engineer and consultant for several European technology organizations. His research interests are centered on the processes whereby software intensive systems are designed, implemented, and managed. In particular, researching methods, techniques, standards and tools for supporting the work of software project managers and software developers in relation to software process improvement, software project planning and management of software development projects.

Alena Buchalcevova, Ing. Ph.D., graduated in 1981 at the Prague University of Economics, Faculty of Management, majoring in Information Systems Management. Since then, she has been working at the Faculty of Informatics and Statistics and at present she is an Associate Professor at the Department of Information Technologies. Her research field is focused on Software Development Methods, Software Quality Assurance, Business Informatics Management, and Enterprise Architecture. She is a programme committee member of several international information systems and software engineering conferences and reviewer of several journals. She has authored and co-authored 10 books, a great deal of journal articles and conference papers.

* * *

Danyllo Albuquerque is a PhD student in computer science at Federal University of Campina Grande, Brazil. He is also a member of the Intelligent Software Engineering (ISE) Research Group. His main research interests are software architecture, software quality, software test, agile and the application of intelligent techniques to solve software engineering problems.

Hyggo Almeida is an Associate Professor at Federal University of Campina Grande. He is the head of the Intelligent Software Engineering research group. His current research interests include applying intelligent techniques to solve complex software engineering problems.

Rajendra Bandi is a Professor of Information Systems at the Indian Institute of Management Bangalore. He did his PhD in Computer Information Systems from the J. Mack Robinson College of Business, Georgia State University, Atlanta, Georgia, USA. Prof Bandi has also been a Visiting Professor at University of Cologne Germany, University Carlos III of Madrid Spain, Hanoi School of Business Vietnam, IIM Tiruchirappalli India, IIM Visakhapatnam India and XLRI School of Management, Jamshedpur India.

Daniela S. Cruzes is a senior researcher scientist at SINTEF and Professor at the Norwegian University of Science and Technology (NTNU). Previously, she worked as a researcher fellow at the University of Maryland and Fraunhofer Center for Experimental Software Engineering-Maryland. Dr. Daniela Cruzes received her PhD in experimental software engineering from the University of Campinas - UNICAMP in Brazil in 2007. Her research interests are empirical software engineering, research methods and theory development, synthesis of SE studies, software security, software testing and agile and DevOps.

Michal Doležel is an Assistant Professor of Software Quality Management at the University of Economics, Prague, Czech Republic. He obtained his master's degrees in Electrical Engineering/Computer Science and Management, and a Ph.D. degree in Business Information Systems. Michal has over 10 years of industrial experience in IT management and software quality assurance acquired during his tenure with several large companies within the telecom, finance, and pharma industry domains. His main research interests are the software quality management techniques and philosophies, social dimension of software development, and healthcare IT systems.

Hector Duran-Limon is currently a full Professor at the Information Systems Department, University of Guadalajara, Mexico. He completed a PhD at Lancaster University, England in 2002. Following this, he was a post-doctoral researcher until December 2003. He obtained an IBM Faculty award in 2008. His research interests include Cloud Computing and High Performance Computing (HPC). He is also interested in Software Architectures, Software Product Lines and Component-based Development. In 2006, He was invited to create a PhD program in Information Technologies for the University of Guadalajara, becoming a member of the Academic-Council.

Nuno Ferreira is currently the head of research at i2S Insurance Knowledge, invited professor at ISEP of Porto's Polytechnique Institute and researcher at ALGORITMI research center of Minho's University in Portugal. He holds a PhD in Software Engineering. He has a strong background in software engineering, project management and process management. His research interests are requirements elicitation, process-to-product transitions, logical architectures derivation, and process maturity models.

Emanuel Dantas Filho received his degrees in Computer Science from the Federal University of Campina Grande, Paraiba, Brazil, in 2008. He is a professor at the Federal Institute of Paraiba since 2016. Further, he is a researcher in the Intelligent Software Engineering research group at VIRTUS which is a Research, Development, and Innovation Center in Information Technology. His current research interests are in Artificial Intelligence applied to Software Engineering to solve complex problems. In Software Engineering, the main topics of interest are software project management, agile software development, effort estimation and risk management.

Agnetha Flore, Dipl.-Kff., born 1977; part-time studies at the Fernuniversität Hagen, graduation as Diplom-Kauffrau. Since 1997 training as a bank clerk at the Bremer Landesbank in Oldenburg and from 1999 for the following 20 years continued to work there in various areas and positions. In the last few years of the career with a focus on project management. Certified Project Manager (GPM) (Level C) since 2017 and since 2019 owner of the additional certificate Hybrid + for agile project management. Since 2018 employed at the OFFIS Institute for Computer Science in Oldenburg as a researcher and sub-project manager, Energy Division in the group "Standardized Systems Engineering and Assessment". Since joining OFFIS, research has focused on maturity models in the energy sector and associated migration paths as well as their evaluation in various research projects. Furthermore, since October 2018 PhD student at the Carl-von-Ossietzky-University in Oldenburg in the department of information systems.

Heiko Gewald is Research Professor of Information Management at Neu-Ulm University of Applied Sciences in Germany. He received his PhD in Information Systems from Goethe University Frankfurt and holds a Master's degree in Business Administration from University of Bamberg and a European Master of Business Science from Heriot-Watt University, Edinburgh. His research focuses on the adoption and use of Information Systems in healthcare, Internet usage of the ageing society, outsourcing, IT strategy and project management. He frequently speaks at academic and practitioner-oriented conferences on these subjects. His work has been published in Health Systems, Information & Management, Journal of Economic Commerce Research, Information Technology and Management, International Journal of Electronic Finance and numerous other journals.

Alexandre Braga Gomes is PhD student in Computer Science, Federal University of Campina Grande- UFCG, Master of Science (2018), Interdisciplinary, Federal University of Vale do São Francisco- UNIVASF. Bachelor in Computer Science (2012), Postgraduate in Information Technology Management (2014) and in Software Engineering (2019), all three from the Faculty of Applied and Social Sciences of Petrolina - FACAPE. I have experience as: Junior System Support Technician at the Instituto de Medicina Integral Professor Fernando Figueira - IMIP; Systems Coordinator (SIA / SUS; SIH / SUS and SCNES), by the Municipal Health Department of the City of Petrolina. He has experience as a Substitute Teacher at the Faculty of Applied and Social Sciences in Petrolina, in the courses in Computer Science and Information Technology Management, with the disciplines of: Software Engineering; Software quality; CG; Database; Free and Algorithmic / Pascal Software. Further, he is a researcher in the Intelligent Software Engineering research group at VIRTUS which is a Research, Development, and Innovation Center in Information Technology. His current research interests are in Artificial Intelligence applied to Software Engineering to solve complex problems. In Software Engineering, the main topics of interest are software project management, agile software development, Personality and soft skills in theTeamwork Quality, and others.

Walter Guerra is a Software Developer and Engineer with more than 15 years working with embedded systems and mobile computing. Has Msc. in Electrical Engineering from the Federal University of Campina Grande, Brazil.

Everton Guimaraes is Assistant Professor of Software Engineering at Penn State University. Dr. Guimaraes' teaching involves algorithms and computer programming, software development and analysis, software architecture, and mobile software engineering. He has collaborated with many partners in industry and academia, both in Brazil and abroad, over the past 9 years. His main research interests are in software engineering and mobile computing. His most recent research investigates of problems related to software architecture and source code, and their impact on the overall software quality attributes (i.e. maintenance, evolution). He is also interested in research topics related to technical debt, architecture recovery techniques, pattern detection and mobile computing.

Espen A. Johansen is a board member and the Product Security Director of Visma. He has through his career held positions in both public and private sector, ranging from traditional military management to covert cyber operations in private sector. Espen has a focus on experimentation and implementation of innovative practical solutions in large scale. Espen`s interests are: Strategic Leadership, Human Aspects of Information Security, Organisation of Security Teams, TeamWork, Collection and analysis of Threat Intelligence, Prediction and prevention of Cyber Security Threats.

Helmut Krcmar was appointed in 2002 Professor of Information Systems, Department of Informatics, at the Technische Universität München (TUM) with a joint appointment to the School of Management. His work experience includes a Post-Doctoral Fellowship, IBM Los Angeles Scientific Center, and Assistant Professor of Information Systems, Leonard Stern School of Business, NYU, and Baruch College, CUNY. From 1987 to 2002 he was Chair for Information Systems, Hohenheim University, Stuttgart, where he served as Dean, Faculty of Business, Economics and Social Sciences. Helmut's research interests include information and knowledge management, engineering, piloting, and management of innovative IT-based services, computer support for collaboration in distributed and mobile work and learning processes. Helmut co-authored a plethora of research papers published in major IS journals including MISQ, JMIS, JIT, JSIS, ISJ, I&M, CAIS, TOCHI and BISE. In Germany, his "Information Management" is now in a 6th edition (2015). Interdisciplinary work incorporates areas such as accounting, mechanical engineering, and health care. Helmut collaborates in research with a wide range of leading global organizations. He is a Fellow of the Association of Information Systems (AIS) and member of acatech – National Academy of Science and Engineering.

Claude Y. Laporte is a Professor, since 2000, at the École de technologie supérieure, an 11,000-student engineering school, where he teaches software engineering. He is the lead editor of the ISO/IEC 29110 series of systems and software engineering standards and guides for Very Small Entities. He was awarded an Honorary Doctorate by the Universidad de San Martin de Porres. He is the co-author of two French books on software quality assurance published by the IEEE Press and John Wiley and Sons in 2018 and two French books on the same topic published by Hermes Science-Lavoisier in 2011. Dr. Laporte is a co-author of a French book, published in 2017, targeted at managers of small systems engineering organizations.

Ricardo J. Machado is a full professor of Information Systems Engineering and Technology in the Dept. of Information Systems at the University of Minho (UMinho), School of Engineering. Within the Information Systems Engineering domain, his primary research interests are in modelling and requirements for systems analysis and design and in process and project management life-cycles. He has supervised 50 completed PhD and MSc theses in these areas. He has published over 150 scientific publications and 4 industrial patents, and has acted as coordinator (PI) and senior researcher of over 50 R&D projects. Currently, at UMinho he is the vice-rector for institutional development, the director of the ALGORITMI Research Centre, the scientific coordinator of the EPMQ Laboratory at the CCG/ZGDV Institute, the director of the Doctoral Program in Advanced Engineering Systems for Industry, and member of the Board of the UM-Cities Platform.

Jorge Marx Gómez studied Computer Engineering and Industrial Engineering at the University of Applied Sciences Berlin (Technische Fachhochschule Berlin). He was a lecturer and researcher at the Otto-von-Guericke-Universität Magdeburg (Germany) where he also obtained a PhD degree in Business Information Systems with the work Computer-based Approaches to Forecast Returns of Scrapped Products to Recycling. From 2002 till 2003 he was a visiting professor for Business Informatics at the Technical University of Clausthal (TU Clausthal, Germany). In 2004 he received his habilitation for the work Automated Environmental Reporting through Material Flow Networks at the Otto-von-Guericke-Universität Magdeburg. In 2005 he became a full professor and chair of Business Information Systems at the Carl von Ossietzky University Oldenburg (Germany). His research interests include Very Large Business Applications, Business Information Systems, Federated ERP-Systems, Business Intelligence, Data Warehousing, Interoperability and Environmental Management Information Systems.

Jezreel Mejía is a Ph.D. in Computer Languages, Informatics Systems and Software Engineering from the Polytechnic University of Madrid. He is actually a Software Engineering researcher at CIMAT in México. He is a member of the National Researchers System of Mexico in Level I. He is a member of the scientific committee of several international conferences. He has participated in the Spanish Translation of CMMI-Dev model v1.2 and v1.3. His main research is focused on multi-model environments, project management, acquisition and outsourcing process, process and its assets definition in software and different domains, metrics definition and the implementation of both traditional and agile methodologies. His contribution will be given by collaborating in the definition of measure artifacts for test virtual environments, the definition of methods, approaches or methodologies, and the performance of systematic literature reviews.

Eduardo Miranda is an Associate Teaching Professor at Carnegie Mellon University where he teaches courses in project management and agile software development at the Master of Software Engineering Program. Dr. Miranda's areas of interest include project management, quality and process improvement. Before joining Carnegie Mellon Dr. Miranda worked for Ericsson where he was instrumental in implementing Project Management Offices (PMO) and improving project management and estimation practices. His work at Ericsson is reflected in the book "Running the Successful Hi-Tech Project Office" published by Artech House in March 2003. Dr. Miranda holds a PhD. in Software Engineering from the École de Technologie Supérieure, Montreal and Master degrees in Project Management and Engineering from the University of Linköping, Sweden, and Ottawa, Canada respectively and a Bachelor of Science from the University of Buenos Aires, Argentina. He has published over fifteen papers in software development methodologies, estimation and project management. Dr. Miranda is a certified Project Management Professional and a Senior Member of the IEEE.

Antonio Alexandre Moura Costa received his MSc and Ph.D. degrees in Computer Science from the Federal University of Campina Grande, Paraiba, Brazil, in 20124and 2019, respectively. He is a professor at the Federal Institute of Paraiba since 2020. Further, he is a researcher in the Intelligent Software Engineering research group at VIRTUS which is a Research, Development, and Innovation Center in Information Technology. His current research interests are in Artificial Intelligence applied to Software Engineering to solve complex problems. In the Software Engineering field, the main topics of interest are software project management, agile software development, resource allocation focused on team formation for software development, and others.

Mirna Muñoz has a Ph.D. in Computer Languages, Informatics Systems and Software Engineering from the Polytechnic University of Madrid. She has held a postdoctoral stay at the University of Carlos III of Madrid. She is working as a Software Engineering researcher at the Software Engineering Unit of CIMAT in México. She is a member of the Software Engineering research group at CIMAT. She is a member of the National Researchers System of Mexico in Level I. She has participated in the Spanish Translation of CMMI-Dev model v1.2 and v1.3. Her current research interest is on software process and its assets definition in software and different domains, project management, software process improvements focusing on the human factor, multi-model environments, the implementation of quality models and standards as well as methodologies, and the integration of highly effective teams. Her contribution will be given by collaborating in the identification of soft skills for engineers, the performance of systematic literature reviews and the use of gamification within teamwork. Besides, she is an expert in project management.

Mirko Perkusich is a Research Manager at Virtus, leading the Intelligent Software Engineering research group. His current research interests are in applying intelligent techniques, including recommender systems, to solve complex software engineering problems.

Felipe Barbosa Araújo Ramos received his MSc and Ph.D. degrees in Computer Science from the Federal University of Campina Grande, Paraiba, Brazil, in 2012 and 2019, respectively. He is currently a professor at the Federal Institute of Paraiba. Further, he is a member of the Intelligent Software Engineering research group at VIRTUS, which is a Research, Development, and Innovation Center in Information Technology. His current research interests are in Artificial Intelligence applied to Software Engineering to solve complex problems. The main topics of interest are in agile software development and requirement engineering focused on supporting the elicitation of non-functional requirements on scrum-based projects.

André Felipe Rodrigues holds a degree in Computer Science from Catholic University of Pernambuco (2005) and a Masters in Electrical Engineering from Federal University of Campina Grande (2008). He has experience in Software Engineering, Pervasive Computing, Artificial Intelligence, Digital Tv and Connected Health. Specialist in software development for embedded systems. He has worked in companies like C.E.S.A.R. and Itautec. Currently, he is shareholder of the company Signove Tecnologia.

Laura C. Rodriguez-Martinez is a full Professor at the Systems and Computing Department, Institute of Technology of Aguascalientes, Mexico. She holds a PhD in Computer Science at Universidad Autonomous University of Aguascalientes, Mexico in 2009. Her research interests include Software Systems Development Processes, Service-Oriented Software Engineering and Graphical-User Interfaces Development Processes.

Fayez Salma recieved MS in Management Information Systems (MIS) from the Arab Academy for Banking and Financial Sciences in 2011 and MS in software engineering from Damascus University in 2013. In 2016 he received an Erasmus scholarship to study for a doctorate at Carl von Ossietzky University of Oldenburg. He is currently researching and working on the web and its development processes to serve his PhD research.

Danilo F. S. Santos is a professor at the Electrical Engineering Department in the Federal University of Campina Grande. He has BSc (2005) and MSc in Electric Engineering (2008) and a PhD in Computer Science, all from the Federal University of Campina Grande - UFCG. Has experience in Computer Engineering, focusing on Pervasive and Embedded Systems, acting on the following subjects: wireless networks, mobile devices, m-Health, embedded systems, and software engineering.

Nuno Santos is currently a researcher at CCG - Centro de Computação Gráfica and at the ALGORITMI Center. He is currently pursuing a PhD in Technologies and Information Systems at University of Minho, where his thesis is called "An Agile Process for Modeling Logical Architectures: Demonstration Cases from Large-scale Software Projects". He also holds a Certified Competence in Business Analysis (CCBA) from the International Institute of Business Analysis (IIBA). He co-authored research papers, where 24 were published in conference proceedings and 5 were book chapters. His research interests focus on agile industrial process management, requirements analysis, interoperability, and software architectures.

Ashay Saxena holds a Doctorate in Information Systems from the Indian Institute of Management Bangalore. He has extensively pursued research on understanding management approaches adopted by software teams to succeed with agile methodologies in a globally distributed format. Ashay has conducted in-depth case studies at several global MNCs to analyse tenets of software project management. He has delivered talks as well as presented research on several international forums such as Australasian Conference on Information Systems, ACM Computers & People Research Conference, Agile Leadership Summit, India Agile Week and Software Product Management Summit.

Konstantinos Tsilionis earned a bachelor's degree in Physics from the Aristotle University of Thessaloniki, Greece. He also holds a Master's degree in International Business Economics and Management and a specialized Master of Business Administration (MBA) in Business Information Management from the Katholieke Universiteit Leuven, Belgium. He is currently a Ph.D. Researcher at the Research Centre for Information Systems Engineering (LIRIS) of the Katholieke Universiteit Leuven.

Dalton Valadares is an Assistant Professor at Federal Institute of Pernambuco (IFPE), currently finishing his Doctorate in Computer Science, at Federal University of Campina Grande (UFCG), studying data security/privacy in cloud/fog-based IoT applications. He is Master, Specialist and Bachelor in Computer Science, and MBA in Project Management. He has worked with IT for more than 15 years, with experience in many R&D projects, assuming different roles: systems analyst, embedded/web systems developer, quality/test analyst and project manager.

Shankar Venkatagiri is an Associate Professor of Information Systems at the Indian Institute of Management Bangalore. Prior to this, he worked as a consultant with Sapient Corporation, Cambridge and Reuters Consulting, Boston. Shankar's interests lie in machine learning, software development and healthcare. A technologist at heart, he is committed to the spread of digital learning in India. He holds a Ph.D. in Mathematics & M.S in Computer Science from Georgia Tech. Shankar has been developing management cases based on the IT scenario in India, some of which are listed on Harvard Business Press.

Fen Wang is a Full Professor in the Information Technology & Administrative Management Department at Central Washington University. She holds a B.S. in MIS, an M.S. and a Ph.D. in Information Systems from the University of Maryland Baltimore County. Dr. Wang has over fifteen years of professional and research experience in intelligent decision support technologies and business intelligence. These efforts have resulted in contributions to the applied literature on information technologies that have been well-received in the research community. Dr. Wang has published over fifty papers in internationally-circulated journals and book series, including the International Journal of Information Technology and Decision Making, Engineering Management Journal, Intelligent Decision Technologies, Information Technology for Development, International Journal of Business Information Systems, International Journal of E-Business Research, and International Journal of Decision Support System Technology. Dr. Wang has also consulted for a variety of public and private organizations on IT management and applications.

Yves Wautelet is professor in Information Systems at KU Leuven (campus Brussel) and invited professor at Université de Namur. He is also scientific collaborator at Université catholique de Louvain. He formerly has been an IT project manager and a postdoc fellow at the Université catholique de Louvain, Belgium. He completed a PhD thesis focusing on project and risk management issues in large enterprise software design. Dr. Wautelet also holds a bachelor and master in management sciences as well as a master in Information Systems. His research interests include aspects of software engineering such as requirements engineering, software project management and development life cycles, agile development, CASE-tools as well as IT Governance and information systems strategy.

Anna Wiedemann, M.Sc., completed her studies of Advanced Management with a focus on Information Management in 2014. Since September 2017 she is an external doctoral candidate at the Technical University of Munich and her research area covers the topics agile IT and DevOps teams. Her current research experiences and interests comprise exploratory studies as well as the use of Grounded Theory to gain new insights into these concepts and their applications. Anna Wiedemann has already published her research in the Communications of the ACM and a number of refereed conference proceedings, including but not limited to the International Conference on Information Systems, the European Conference on Information Systems, and the Hawaii International Conference on System Sciences.

Manuel Wiesche is Assistant Professor of Information Systems at TU Dortmund University. He graduated in Information Systems from Westfälische Wilhelms-Universität, Münster, Germany and holds a doctoral degree in Information Systems from Technische Universität München (TUM), Munich, Germany. His current research experiences and interests include project management, platform ecosystems, IT service innovation, and qualitative research methods. His research has been published in MIS Quarterly, JMAR, CACM, I&M, and MISQE.

Index

Ensure Quality Research is Introduced to the Academic Community

Become an IGI Global Reviewer for Authored Book Projects

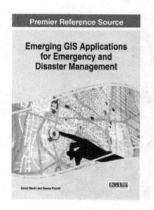

The overall success of an authored book project is dependent on quality and timely reviews.

In this competitive age of scholarly publishing, constructive and timely feedback significantly expedites the turnaround time of manuscripts from submission to acceptance, allowing the publication and discovery of forward-thinking research at a much more expeditious rate. Several IGI Global authored book projects are currently seeking highly-qualified experts in the field to fill vacancies on their respective editorial review boards:

Applications and Inquiries may be sent to:
development@igi-global.com

Applicants must have a doctorate (or an equivalent degree) as well as publishing and reviewing experience. Reviewers are asked to complete the open-ended evaluation questions with as much detail as possible in a timely, collegial, and constructive manner. All reviewers' tenures run for one-year terms on the editorial review boards and are expected to complete at least three reviews per term. Upon successful completion of this term, reviewers can be considered for an additional term.

If you have a colleague that may be interested in this opportunity, we encourage you to share this information with them.

IGI Global Proudly Partners With eContent Pro International

Receive a 25% Discount on all Editorial Services

Editorial Services

IGI Global expects all final manuscripts submitted for publication to be in their final form. This means they must be reviewed, revised, and professionally copy edited prior to their final submission. Not only does this support with accelerating the publication process, but it also ensures that the highest quality scholarly work can be disseminated.

English Language Copy Editing

Let eContent Pro International's expert copy editors perform edits on your manuscript to resolve spelling, punctuaion, grammar, syntax, flow, formatting issues and more.

Scientific and Scholarly Editing

Allow colleagues in your research area to examine the content of your manuscript and provide you with valuable feedback and suggestions before submission.

Figure, Table, Chart & Equation Conversions

Do you have poor quality figures? Do you need visual elements in your manuscript created or converted? A design expert can help!

Translation

Need your documjent translated into English? eContent Pro International's expert translators are fluent in English and more than 40 different languages.

Hear What Your Colleagues are Saying About Editorial Services Supported by IGI Global

"The service was very fast, very thorough, and very helpful in ensuring our chapter meets the criteria and requirements of the book's editors. I was quite impressed and happy with your service."

– Prof. Tom Brinthaupt,
Middle Tennessee State University, USA

"I found the work actually spectacular. The editing, formatting, and other checks were very thorough. The turnaround time was great as well. I will definitely use eContent Pro in the future."

– Nickanor Amwata, Lecturer,
University of Kurdistan Hawler, Iraq

"I was impressed that it was done timely, and wherever the content was not clear for the reader, the paper was improved with better readability for the audience."

– Prof. James Chilembwe,
Mzuzu University, Malawi

Email: customerservice@econtentpro.com   www.igi-global.com/editorial-service-partners

IGI Global
DISSEMINATOR OF KNOWLEDGE
www.igi-global.com

Publisher of Peer-Reviewed, Timely, and
Innovative Academic Research Since 1988

IGI Global's Transformative Open Access (OA) Model:
How to Turn Your University Library's Database Acquisitions Into a Source of OA Funding

In response to the OA movement and well in advance of Plan S, IGI Global, early last year, unveiled their OA Fee Waiver (Offset Model) Initiative.

Under this initiative, librarians who invest in IGI Global's InfoSci-Books (5,300+ reference books) and/or InfoSci-Journals (185+ scholarly journals) databases will be able to subsidize their patron's OA article processing charges (APC) when their work is submitted and accepted (after the peer review process) into an IGI Global journal.*

How Does it Work?

1. When a library subscribes or perpetually purchases IGI Global's InfoSci-Databases including InfoSci-Books (5,300+ e-books), InfoSci-Journals (185+ e-journals), and/or their discipline/subject-focused subsets, IGI Global will match the library's investment with a fund of equal value to go toward subsidizing the OA article processing charges (APCs) for their patrons.

   Researchers: Be sure to recommend the InfoSci-Books and InfoSci-Journals to take advantage of this initiative.

2. When a student, faculty, or staff member submits a paper and it is accepted (following the peer review) into one of IGI Global's 185+ scholarly journals, the author will have the option to have their paper published under a traditional publishing model or as OA.

3. When the author chooses to have their paper published under OA, IGI Global will notify them of the OA Fee Waiver (Offset Model) Initiative. If the author decides they would like to take advantage of this initiative, IGI Global will deduct the US$ 1,500 APC from the created fund.

4. This fund will be offered on an annual basis and will renew as the subscription is renewed for each year thereafter. IGI Global will manage the fund and award the APC waivers unless the librarian has a preference as to how the funds should be managed.

Hear From the Experts on This Initiative:

"I'm very happy to have been able to make one of my recent research contributions, 'Visualizing the Social Media Conversations of a National Information Technology Professional Association' featured in the *International Journal of Human Capital and Information Technology Professionals*, freely available along with having access to the valuable resources found within IGI Global's InfoSci-Journals database."

– **Prof. Stuart Palmer,**
Deakin University, Australia

For More Information, Visit: www.igi-global.com/publish/contributor-resources/open-access or contact IGI Global's Database Team at eresources@igi-global.com.

Printed in the United States
By Bookmasters